Course	Principles of Marketing Vol. 1
Course Number	**MK 351**
	Park University

http://create.mcgraw-hill.com

ISBN-10: 0390228451   ISBN-13: 9780390228451

Contents

Credits

Basic Marketing Is Designed to Satisfy Your Needs

This book is about marketing and marketing strategy planning. And, at its essence, marketing strategy planning is about figuring out how to do a superior job of satisfying customers. We take that point of view seriously and believe in practicing what we preach. So you can trust that this new edition of *Basic Marketing*—and all of the other teaching and learning materials that accompany it—will satisfy your needs. We're excited about this 17th edition of *Basic Marketing,* and we hope that you will be as well.

In developing this edition, we've made hundreds of big and small additions, changes, and improvements in the text and all of the supporting materials that accompany it. We'll highlight some of those changes in this preface, but first it's useful to put this newest edition in a longer-term perspective.

Building on Pioneering Strengths

Basic Marketing pioneered an innovative structure—using the "four Ps" with a managerial approach—for the introductory marketing course. It quickly became one of the most widely used business textbooks ever published because it organized the best ideas about marketing so that readers could both understand and apply them. The unifying focus of these ideas is on how to make the marketing decisions that a manager must make in deciding what customers to target and how best to meet their needs.

Over many editions of *Basic Marketing,* there have been constant changes in marketing management and the marketing environment. Some of the changes have been dramatic, and others have been subtle. As a result, we have made ongoing changes to the text to reflect marketing's best practices and ideas. Throughout all of these changes, *Basic Marketing* and the supporting materials that accompany it have been more widely used than any other teaching materials for introductory marketing. It is gratifying that the four Ps framework has proved to be an organizing structure that has worked well for millions of students and teachers.

What's Different about Basic Marketing?

The success of *Basic Marketing* is not the result of a single strength—or one long-lasting innovation. Other textbooks have adopted our four Ps framework, and we have continuously improved the book. And the text's four Ps framework, managerial orientation, and strategy planning focus have proved to be foundation pillars that are remarkably robust for supporting new developments in the field and innovations in the text and package. Thus, with each new edition of *Basic Marketing* we have continued to innovate to better meet the needs of students and faculty. In fact, we have made ongoing changes in how we develop the logic of the four Ps and the marketing strategy planning process. As always, though, our objective is to provide a flexible, high-quality text and choices from comprehensive and reliable support materials—so that instructors and students can accomplish their learning objectives. At least four characteristics of *Basic Marketing* distinguish it from other texts: (1) we focus on developing analytical abilities and how-to-do-it skills, (2) we integrate special topics, (3) we provide a flexible teaching and learning package that allows instructors to teach and students to learn marketing *their* way, and (4) we have an unmatched attention to detail. These combine to deliver a proven product for instructors and students. Let us show you what we mean—and why and how instructors and students benefit from the *Basic Marketing* teaching and learning package.

Marketing operates in dynamic markets—today more than ever. Fast-changing global markets, challenges to our environment and sustainability, and the blurring speed of advances in technology represent just a few of the dynamic trends confronting today's marketing manager. While some marketing texts attempt to describe this dynamic environment, *Basic Marketing* teaches students *analytical abilities and how-to-do-it skills* that prepare them for success. To move students in this direction, we deliberately include a variety of examples, explanations, frameworks, models, classification systems, cases, and how-to-do-it techniques that relate to our overall framework for marketing strategy planning. Similarly, the *Marketing Plan Coach* on the Student CD and the text website helps students see how to create marketing plans. Taken together, these items speed the development of "marketing sense" and enable the student to analyze marketing situations and develop marketing plans in a confident and meaningful way. They are practical and they work. And because they are interesting and understandable, they motivate students to see marketing as the challenging and rewarding area it is. In the end, the *Basic Marketing* teaching and learning package prepares students to analyze marketing situations and develop exceptional marketing strategies—not just recite endless sets of lists.

As opposed to many other marketing textbooks, we emphasize careful *integration of special topics*. Some textbooks treat "special" topics—like relationship marketing, international marketing, services marketing, marketing and the Internet, marketing for nonprofit organizations, marketing ethics, social issues, and business-to-business marketing—in separate chapters. We deliberately avoid doing that because we are convinced that treating such topics separately leads to an unfortunate compartmentalization of ideas. We think they are too important to be isolated in that way. For example, to simply tack on a new chapter on e-commerce or marketing applications on the Internet completely ignores the reality that these are not just isolated topics but rather must be considered broadly across the whole fabric of marketing decisions. Conversely, there is virtually no area of marketing decision making where it's safe to ignore the impact of e-commerce, the Internet, or information technology. The same is true with other topics. So they are interwoven and illustrated throughout the text to emphasize that marketing thinking is crucial in all aspects of our society and economy. Looking for the proof of how we integrate special topics across chapters? Check out the fold-out grid just inside the back cover.

The comprehensive package of materials gives you, the instructor, the *flexibility* to *teach marketing your way*—or you, the student, the ability to *learn marketing your way*. Marketing can be studied and used in many ways, and the *Basic Marketing* text material is only the central component of our Professional Learning Units System (P.L.U.S.) for students and teachers. Instructors and students can select from our units to develop their own personalized teaching and learning systems. Our objective is to offer you a P.L.U.S. "menu" so that you can conveniently select units you want—and disregard what you do not want. Many combinations of units are possible depending on course and learning objectives. Later

in this Preface we highlight each P.L.U.S. element—and the full details can be found in the discussion of the Instructor's Resource CD in the Instructor's Manual.

We take great pride in the *attention to detail* we put into revising each and every new edition of *Basic Marketing*. There are thousands of examples of this attention to detail throughout this edition of *Basic Marketing* and the rest of the learning package. In this edition of the book you will find we have extended, up-to-date case discussions of leading companies like Apple, Cirque du Soleil, Nintendo, and Under Armour—with which students can relate. The photos and advertisements provide real examples and complement and extend concepts in each chapter. The electronic presentation slides feature scripts, print advertisements, exciting graphics, interactive exercises, and video clips—all updated with this and every edition of the book. Unlike other marketing plan software, our *Marketing Plan Coach* was developed by the authors to work with this book. And because we understand the importance of fair tests in the introductory marketing course, we have personally developed, evaluated, and refined a test question database with thousands of objective test questions. Instructors and students who use *Basic Marketing* know and appreciate this attention to detail.

Students only take the introductory marketing course once—and for many students it is their only marketing class. They deserve the benefits of a highly innovative yet *proven* set of learning materials. Our teaching and learning materials—from the textbook to the iPod videos to the test question bank to the online materials—have been constantly updated yet are proven to work for generations of students. Do you want to use an unproven textbook with your students?

What's New in This Edition of *Basic Marketing*?

There are several big changes to this edition of *Basic Marketing* and hundreds of smaller ones. *Basic Marketing* is quick to recognize the many dramatic changes in the marketing environment and marketing strategy.

One of the big changes has been the attention we have given to *sustainability and its implications for marketers*. *Basic Marketing* has long included discussions of the impact of marketing on the environment. Recently society has grown increasingly concerned with sustainability—the idea that it's important to meet present needs without compromising the ability of future generations to meet their own needs. Marketing managers are responding to customer concerns—and almost every chapter in this edition of *Basic Marketing* now includes some discussion of sustainability. As with other special topics, we do more than just describe sustainability; we explain how marketing managers take these concerns into account in their analysis—and screen opportunities on this criterion. Strategy decisions that take sustainability into account are not straightforward—and the approach used throughout the book helps students understand and address this challenge.

We have continued our efforts at making *Basic Marketing* the most readable and interesting textbook on the market. The entire text has been critically revised, updated, and rewritten. We have carefully consolidated and reorganized, and sometimes made the difficult decision to cut topics to make the book shorter and even more readable. Thus, most chapters in this edition are shorter than in the previous edition and we've reduced the number of chapters to 21. You'll see that we discuss trends in the external market environment earlier in the text; further, we have moved the discussion of segmentation, targeting, and positioning so that it now leads directly into our discussion of customers in Chapters 5 through 7. All of the cases at the back of the book have also been updated, edited, revised, and/or replaced with new ones.

The aim of all this revising, refining, editing, and illustrating is to make the important concepts and points even clearer to students. We want to make sure that each student really does get a good feel for a market-directed system and how he or she can help it—and some company—run better. We believe marketing is important and interesting, and we want every student who reads *Basic Marketing* to share our enthusiasm. The result, we believe, is a book that is easier to read and more relevant for today's student.

There are hundreds of other changes spread throughout the book. Marketing is dynamic—the marketing environment and marketing practices are evolving quickly as technology, the economy, customers, and competition transform quickly in today's markets. Students want to read about the latest trends and marketing practices. Throughout every chapter, we have updated and added new discussions and examples of

- The evolution of advertising media including mobile advertising, blogs, social media like Facebook, and various forms of advertising on the Internet.
- The role and process of customers' search for information on the Internet—and its implications for marketing strategy.
- The influence of word-of-mouth and how it has changed in the era of the Internet and customer review sites.
- The needs of customers in emerging markets and developing countries—and how some organizations are meeting those customer needs.
- The use of innovation and idea generation for new products and marketing mix elements—and how they've become key sources of competitive advantage.
- The evolving nature of retailing on the Internet—as firms better understand what works and what doesn't—and successful strategies that have emerged.
- Lifetime customer value and customer equity.
- Best practices in marketing, and how to avoid the mistakes of death-wish marketing (including errors and omissions all too common among many failed dot-com operators).

- Effective e-commerce innovations and changes in marketing over the Internet.
- The costs and benefits of different approaches for customer acquisition and retention.
- Relationship building in marketing.
- Customer service and customer retention.
- Ethical issues and the social impacts of marketing and macro-marketing.
- The importance of providing superior customer value as the means to achieve customer satisfaction and competitive advantage.
- The growing uses of technology in organizational buying.
- Low-cost methods for conducting marketing research and the use of specialized search engines.
- The increasing emphasis on design in product development.
- The circumstances when using direct channels of distribution make sense—and how to manage channel conflict that might come about when direct and indirect channels are used in combination.
- Promotional campaigns that use viral communications to generate "buzz" among consumers.
- New and emerging applications of customer relationship management databases and tools.

Updates have extended beyond the book to our entire learning package, including

- PowerPoint presentations that have been completely updated and revised—including the addition of short video clips in each chapter—thereby reducing instructor preparation and increasing student interest.
- A completely updated test bank of more than 5,000 questions—with more than 1,000 completely new questions—all written and edited *by the authors*.
- Eight new full-length videos and video cases for use in your classes—to increase student involvement. These are in addition to the more than 150 video clips and 27 full-length videos.
- An updated software interface for the computer-aided problems—to make them even easier for students to use.
- An updated *Marketing Plan Coach* that has been converted to html and moved online—in addition to its home on the Student CD.

Twenty-One Chapters—with an Emphasis on Marketing Strategy Planning

The emphasis of *Basic Marketing* is on marketing strategy planning. Twenty-one chapters introduce the important concepts in marketing and help the student see marketing through the eyes of the manager. The organization of the chapters and topics is carefully planned. But we took special care in writing so that

- It is possible to rearrange and use the chapters in many different sequences—to fit different needs.
- All of the topics and chapters fit together into a clear, overall framework for the marketing strategy planning process.

Broadly speaking, the chapters fall into two groupings. The first eight chapters introduce marketing and a broad view of the marketing strategy planning process. They cover topics such as the marketing environment, segmentation, differentiation, and buyer behavior, as well as how marketing information systems and research provide information about these forces to improve marketing decisions. The second half of the text goes into the details of planning the four Ps, with specific attention to the key strategy decisions in each area. Then we conclude with an integrative review and coverage of overarching topics such as implementation and control, marketing's link with other functional areas, and an assessment of marketing's challenges and opportunities.

The first chapter deals with the important role of marketing—focusing not only on how a marketing orientation guides a business or nonprofit organization in the process of providing superior value to customers but also on the role of macro-marketing and how a market-directed economy shapes choices and quality of life for consumers. Chapter 2 builds on these ideas with a focus on the marketing strategy planning process and why it involves narrowing down to the selection of a specific target market and blending the four Ps into a marketing mix to meet the needs of those customers. With that foundation in place, the chapter introduces an integrative model of the marketing strategy planning process that serves as an organizing framework for the rest of the text.

Chapter 3 introduces students to the importance of evaluating opportunities in the external environments affecting marketing. This chapter also highlights the critical role of screening criteria for narrowing down from possible opportunities to those that the firm will pursue. Then, Chapter 4 shows how analysis of the market relates to segmentation and differentiation decisions as well as the criteria for narrowing down to a specific target market and marketing mix.

You have to understand customers to segment markets and satisfy target market needs. So the next three chapters take a closer look at *customers*. Chapter 5 introduces the demographic dimensions of the global consumer market and provides up-to-date coverage on important geodemographic trends. The next chapter studies the behavioral aspects of the final consumer market. Chapter 7 looks at how business and organizational customers—like manufacturers, channel members, and government purchasers—are similar to and different from final consumers.

Chapter 8 is a contemporary view of getting information—from marketing information systems and marketing research—for marketing planning. This chapter includes discussion of how information technology—ranging from intranets to speedy collection of market research data—is transforming the marketing job. This sets the stage for discussions in later chapters about how research and marketing information improve each area of marketing strategy planning.

The next group of chapters—Chapters 9 through 18—is concerned with developing a marketing mix out of the four Ps: Product, Place (involving channels of distribution, logistics, and distribution customer service), Promotion, and Price. These chapters are concerned with developing the "right" Product and making it available at the "right" Place with the "right" Promotion and the "right" Price—to satisfy target customers and still meet the objectives of the business. These chapters are presented in an integrated, analytical way—as part of the overall framework for the marketing strategy planning process—so students' thinking about planning marketing strategies develops logically.

Chapters 9 and 10 focus on product planning for goods and services as well as managing product quality, new-product development, and the different strategy decisions that are required at different stages of the product life cycle. We emphasize the value of an organized new-product development process for developing really new products that propel a firm to profitable growth. This chapter also details how quality management approaches can improve implementation, including implementation of better service quality.

Chapters 11 through 13 focus on Place. Chapter 11 introduces decisions a manager must make about using direct distribution (for example, selling from the firm's own website) or working with other firms in a channel of distribution. We put special emphasis on the need for channel members to cooperate and coordinate to better meet the needs of customers. Chapter 12 focuses on the fast-changing arena of logistics and the strides that firms are making in using e-commerce to reduce the costs of storing, transporting, and handling products while improving the distribution service they provide customers. Chapter 13 provides a clear picture of retailers, wholesalers, and their strategy planning, including exchanges taking place via the Internet. This composite chapter helps students see why the big changes taking place in retailing are reshaping the channel systems for many consumer products.

Chapters 14 through 16 deal with Promotion. These chapters build on the concepts of integrated marketing communications, direct-response promotion, and customer-initiated digital communication, which are introduced in Chapter 14. Chapter 15 deals with the roles of personal selling, customer service, and sales technology in the promotion blend. Chapter 16 covers advertising and sales promotion, including the ways that managers are taking advantage of the Internet and other highly targeted media to communicate more effectively and efficiently.

Chapters 17 and 18 deal with Price. Chapter 17 focuses on pricing objectives and policies, including use of information technology to implement flexible pricing, pricing in the channel, and the use of discounts, allowances, and other variations from a list price. Chapter 18 covers cost-oriented and demand-oriented pricing approaches and how they fit in today's competitive environments. The careful coverage of marketing costs helps equip students to deal with the renewed cost-consciousness of the firms they will join.

Chapter 19 offers completely updated coverage of how information technology is reshaping marketing implementation and control. Then, Chapter 20 deals with the links between marketing and other functional areas. The marketing concept says that people in an organization should work together to satisfy customers at a profit. No other text has a chapter that explains how to accomplish the "working together" part of that idea. Yet it's increasingly important in the business world today; so that's what this important chapter is designed to do.

The final chapter considers how efficient the marketing process is. Here we evaluate the effectiveness of both micro- and macro-marketing—and we consider the competitive, technological, ethical, and social challenges facing marketing managers now and in the future. Chapter 21 also reinforces the integrative nature of marketing management and reviews the marketing strategy planning process that leads to creative marketing plans.

Three appendices can be used to supplement the main text material. Appendix A provides some traditional economic analysis of supply and demand that can be a useful tool in analyzing markets. Appendix B reviews some quantitative tools—or marketing arithmetic—which helps marketing managers who want to use accounting data in analyzing marketing problems. Appendix B also reviews forecasting as a way to predict market potential and sales for a company's product. Finally, many students like to look at Appendix C—which is about career opportunities in marketing.

The following sections include 44 cases. Eight of these written cases supplement video cases available to instructors in their video package and online to students. Almost all of the 36 short written cases have been updated with new information to make sure they reflect the realities of the current marketplace. The focus of these cases is on problem solving. They encourage students to apply, and really get involved with, the concepts developed in the text. At the end of each chapter, we recommend particular cases that best relate to that chapter's content.

Teaching and Learning Your Way—Elements of P.L.U.S.

Basic Marketing can be studied and used in many ways—the *Basic Marketing* text material is only the central component of our *Professional Learning Units System* (*P.L.U.S.*) for students and teachers. Instructors (and students) can select from our units to develop their own personalized systems. Many combinations of units are possible, depending on course objectives. As a quick overview, in addition to the *Basic Marketing* text, the *P.L.U.S.* package include a variety of new and updated supplements.

Most of the instructor resources may be found on the *Instructor's Resource CD*. McGraw-Hill has found that many instructors rely on electronic versions of the instructor's materials so, in order to save trees, print versions of these supplements are only produced on-demand. If you prefer to have hard copies of the *Multimedia Lecture Support Guide* or any of the Instructor's Manuals, request them through your McGraw-Hill sales representative.

Beyond the *Basic Marketing* textbook, the key components of *P.L.U.S.* include

Electronic Presentation Slides. Our "best in the business" multimedia lecture support package includes a variety of materials. For each chapter there is a set of PowerPoint presentations for a complete lecture that includes television commercials and short video clip examples, plus a set of archive slides with a high-quality selection of ads and photos. Many chapters have engaging interactive exercises as well.

Multimedia Lecture Support Guide. This guide supports the presentation slides and includes detailed lecture scripts, outlines, and archives.

Videos and Video Cases. The video package has been updated with 8 new videos—to give you 27 full-length videos. In addition, we have more than 150 short (1 to 4 minutes) video clips—many integrated into the PowerPoint presentation slides. See the Video Instructor's Manual for more ideas about how to use the videos in class.

Instructor's Manual to Accompany *Basic Marketing*. This manual includes an overview of all the teaching/learning units, as well as suggested answers to all questions, exercises, and assignments.

Test Bank. Our test bank includes thousands of objective test questions—*developed by the authors* to ensure they work really well with the text. McGraw-Hill's EZ-Test program facilitates the creation of tests. We take great pride in having a test bank that works for students and instructors.

Online Learning Center: www.mhhe.com/fourps. The website for the book provides access to a variety of student and instructor resources.

Basic Marketing Cartridges for Blackboard and WebCT. Include *Basic Marketing* materials directly in your online course management program.

The Marketing Game! This simulation was designed to complement the strategy planning process in *Basic Marketing* and encourages students to compete and learn.

CPS (wireless Classroom Performance System) by eInstruction. Sometimes called "clicker" technology, this system allows for quick in-class online polls or quizzing. Ask your McGraw-Hill sales representative for more details.

Another set of resources is designed to be directly accessed by students. Optional book packages include the Student CD or access to the book's premium content website. These options allow motivated students to purchase access to additional resources that appeal to their learning style. Most of the student materials are available online, on a student CD, and/or in print. Look inside the back cover of this book for more details about how to obtain these learning resources. They include

Self-Test Quizzes and Bonus Quizzes. These help students prepare for tests and may be used with a computer or an iPod.

Applications in Basic Marketing. Links to current online articles, websites, podcasts, and videos are organized by content area and available at the book's website.

Marketing Plan Coach. This online software tool helps students build marketing plans using materials and concepts directly from the textbook. It was created by the authors specifically for use with *Basic Marketing*.

Computer-Aided Problems. This easy-to-use spreadsheet software program works with exercises at the end of each chapter in the text (and in the Learning Aid) to help develop analytical skills needed by today's managers.

Narrated Slide Shows. These provide overviews of key marketing concepts usually from a set of chapters. Eight in all, they are great to use before reading a new section in *Basic Marketing* or for help in studying for tests.

Learning with Ads. These are great for visual learners who can preview or study concepts from each chapter and examine applications in real print ads. About 10 to 15 ads per chapter. .

Video Cases. Clips from video cases in the book are available for viewing on computers or iPods.

Learning Aid for Use with Basic Marketing. This study aid gives students something extra from your marketing class. It includes chapter summaries, access to more than 1,225 additional practice test questions, and over 75 application exercises. Check out the textbook's website to download sample chapters.

Learning Objectives, Assurance of Learning, and Accreditation

Assurance of learning is an important element of many accreditation standards. We designed the components of *Basic Marketing*'s P.L.U.S. to support your teaching and learning objectives, so our P.L.U.S. provides excellent support for accreditation efforts. This topic is addressed in more detail in the *Instructor's Manual*. Briefly, however, each chapter in the book begins with a list of numbered learning objectives. Material related to these objectives is developed not only in the chapter but also in the exercises, questions, and problems for each chapter. Every test question is also classified by these objectives. In addition, questions are classified by level of difficulty, type of question (according to Bloom's Taxonomy), and skill areas specified by AACSB International, an accrediting group for business schools. EZ Test, McGraw-Hill's easy-to-use test bank software, can search the test bank by these and other categories, which helps with assurance of learning analysis and assessment.

Our publisher, the McGraw-Hill Companies is a proud corporate member of AACSB International. This text and the accompanying supplements explicitly recognize and support the AACSB curriculum standards for business accreditation. For example, our Computer-Aided Problems help to develop analysis skills and our case studies and *Marketing Plan Coach* encourage development of integrated thinking, problem solving, and communication skills. We should be clear, however, that AACSB does not provide some sort of evaluation or certification of texts or their supporting materials. Rather, AACSB leaves content coverage and assessment decisions to an individual school, depending on the mission of the school and objectives of its faculty. Thus, the flexible P.L.U.S. package can help both faculty and students tailor a learning experience that meets objectives not only for the marketing course but also for the curriculum and accreditation.

Responsibilities of Leadership

In closing, we return to a point raised at the beginning of this preface. *Basic Marketing* has been a leading textbook in marketing since its first edition. We take the responsibilities of that leadership seriously. We know that you want and deserve the very best teaching and learning materials possible. It is our commitment to bring you those materials—today with this edition and in the future with subsequent editions.

We recognize that fulfilling this commitment requires a process of continuous improvement. Revisions, updates, and development of new elements must be ongoing—because needs change. You are an important part of this evolution, of this leadership. We encourage your feedback. The most efficient way to get in touch with us is to send an e-mail message to Bill_Perreault@ unc.edu or Joe.Cannon@colostate.edu. If you prefer the traditional approach, send a letter to 2104 N. Lakeshore Dr., Chapel Hill, NC, 27514. Thoughtful criticisms and suggestions from students and teachers alike have helped to make *Basic Marketing* what it is. We hope that you will help make it what it will be in the future.

William D. Perreault, Jr.
Joseph P. Cannon
E. Jerome McCarthy

1

CHAPTER

Marketing's Value to Consumers, Firms, and Society

When it's time to roll out of bed in the morning, does the alarm ringtone on your Verizon cell phone wake you, or is it your Sony XM radio playing your favorite satellite station? Is the station playing hip-hop, classical, or country music—or perhaps a Red Cross ad asking you to contribute blood? Will you slip into your Levi's jeans, your shirt from Abercrombie and Fitch, and your Nikes, or does the day call for your Brooks Brothers interviewing suit? Will breakfast be Lender's Bagels with cream cheese or will you finish off that box of Kellogg's Frosted Mini-Wheats cereal made with whole grain wheat from America's heartland? Will you have some calcium-fortified Minute-Maid orange juice and brew a pot of Maxwell House coffee—or is this a day to meet a friend at the local Starbucks, where you'll pay someone else to fix you a Frappuccino while you use the Wi-Fi connection to log on to MSN.com to check your e-mail? Or perhaps if you're running late you can grab a ride to class in your friend's new Toyota Prius, swing by the McDonald's drive-thru for a McSkillet Burrito, a Vanilla Iced Coffee, and a smile from Ronald McDonald. What?

3

Your friend decided that the new hybrid was too pricey for someone with only a part-time job? Well then, maybe you'll just have to take the bus that the city bought from General Motors. At least as you ride along you can watch videos on your iPhone.

When you think about it, you can't get very far into a day without bumping into marketing—and what the whole marketing system does for you. It affects every aspect of our lives—often in ways we don't even consider.

In other parts of the world, people wake up each day to different kinds of experiences. A family in rural China may have little choice about what food they will eat or where their clothing will come from. A consumer in a large city like Tokyo may have many choices but not be familiar with names like Tony the Tiger, Lender's Bagels, or Brooks Brothers.

What's more, each element in the descriptions above could be viewed in more detail and through a different lens. Consider, for example, that visit to Starbucks. What exactly is it about Starbucks that makes so many customers so satisfied with the experience? Why do they come back time and time again when they could get a cup of coffee almost anywhere, at half the price? Do loyal customers use the Starbucks card because it lets them participate in sweepstakes and get e-mail notices of in-store promotions and new products? Or is it because the card makes it fast and easy to order and pay? Why does Starbucks' sell music CDs and offer Internet wireless hot spots at some locations—and, by the way, who dreamed up the idea of calling that tasty icy thing a Frappuccino? Twenty years ago, Starbucks was just another tiny company in Seattle; now it operates over 15,000 coffee bars in 43 countries, has expanded into distribution through supermarkets, and is one of the best-known brand names in the world (yes, even in Tokyo). Part of Starbucks' success comes from adapting its marketing strategy to changing market conditions—but not every change works. Starbucks brought out a line of breakfast sandwiches to compete with McDonald's, but withdrew them when customers complained that the smell of the warming sandwiches ruined the coffee aroma.

Over the years McDonald's has also introduced many new products to meet changing customer needs. For example, the McSalad Shaker was a salad in a cup for convenient eating on the go. Customers, however, were looking for a more premium salad, which led to the introduction of the Premium Salad line in 2003. On the other hand, the Snack Wrap satisfies McDonald's restaurant operations and its customers. The wrap can be quickly prepared using existing ingredients in McDonald's restaurants. And customers love that the wraps taste great, can be eaten on-the-go, and are a good value. Realizing the beverage category represented a multibillion-dollar industry. McDonald's believed that it was well-positioned—as a brand that offers everyday value and convenience—to capture a significant portion of the growing beverage category. In 2006, McDonald's dove into the high-end coffee market and introduced Premium Roast drip coffee. The new blend was a hit, bringing new customers into restaurants and boosting its coffee sales 40 percent in less than a year. Building on that success, McDonald's began to introduce Specialty Coffee in select restaurants nationwide, including Cappuccinos, Lattes, and Mochas—all at lower prices than Starbucks.

As Starbucks, McDonald's, and oh yeah Dunkin' Donuts and your local coffee shops and restaurants battle it out, customers are the big winners. With all this choice, these companies have to work hard to meet customer needs and earn their business.[1]

MARKETING—WHAT'S IT ALL ABOUT?

Marketing is more than selling or advertising

Many people think that marketing means "selling" or "advertising." It's true that these are parts of marketing. But *marketing is much more than selling and advertising.*

How did all those bicycles get here?

To illustrate some of the other important things that are included in marketing, think about all the bicycles being pedaled with varying degrees of energy by bike riders around the world. Most of us don't make our own bicycles. Instead, they are made by firms like Trek, Performance, Huffy, and Murray.

Most bikes do the same thing—get the rider from one place to another. But a bike rider can choose from a wide assortment of models. They are designed in different sizes and with or without gears. Off-road bikes have large knobby tires. Kids and older people may want more wheels—to make balancing easier. Some bikes need baskets or even trailers for cargo. You can buy a basic bike for less than $50. Or you can spend more than $2,500 for a custom frame.

This variety of styles and features complicates the production and sale of bicycles. The following list shows some of the things a manager should do before and after deciding to produce and sell a bike.

"Life Comes at You Fast." Nationwide's trademarked phrase and "buildingscape" ad really get attention and remind consumers that Nationwide can help when things go awry. Creative advertising like this is an important part of marketing, but modern marketing involves much more. For example, Nationwide conducts research to understand customers' needs and then develops new policies and services to satisfy those needs at a price that represents a good value.

1. Analyze the needs of people who might buy a bike and decide if they want more or different models.
2. Predict what types of bikes—handlebar styles and types of wheels, brakes, and materials—different customers will want and decide which of these people the firm will try to satisfy.
3. Estimate how many of these people will want to buy bicycles, and when.
4. Determine where in the world these bike riders are and how to get the firm's bikes to them.
5. Estimate what price they are willing to pay for their bikes and if the firm can make a profit selling at that price.
6. Decide which kinds of promotion should be used to tell potential customers about the firm's bikes.
7. Estimate how many competing companies will be making bikes, what kind, and at what prices.
8. Figure out how to provide customer service if a customer has a problem after buying a bike.

The above activities are not part of production—actually making goods or performing services. Rather, they are part of a larger process—called *marketing*—that provides needed direction for production and helps make sure that the right goods and services are produced and find their way to consumers.

You'll learn much more about marketing activities in Chapter 2. For now, it's enough to see that marketing plays an essential role in providing consumers with need-satisfying goods and services and, more generally, in creating customer satisfaction. Simply put, customer satisfaction is the extent to which a firm fulfills a customer's needs, desires, and expectations.

MARKETING IS IMPORTANT TO YOU

Marketing is important to every consumer

Marketing affects almost every aspect of your daily life. The choices you have among the goods and services you buy, the stores where you shop, and the radio and TV programs you tune in to are all possible because of marketing. In the process of providing all these choices, marketing drives organizations to focus on what it takes to

Edition

satisfy you, the customer. Most of the things you want or need are available conveniently *when* and *where* you want or need them.

Some courses are interesting when you take them but never relevant again once they're over. That's not so with marketing—you'll be a consumer dealing with marketing for the rest of your life regardless of what career you pursue. Moreover, as a consumer, you pay for the cost of marketing activities. In advanced economies, marketing costs about 50 cents of every consumer dollar. For some goods and services, the percentage is much higher. It makes sense to be an educated consumer and to understand what you get and don't get from all that spending.

Marketing will be important to your job

Another reason for studying marketing is that it offers many exciting and rewarding career opportunities. Throughout this book, you will find information about opportunities in different areas of marketing.

If you're aiming for a nonmarketing job, knowing about marketing will help you do your own job better. Throughout the book, we'll discuss ways that marketing relates to other functional areas—and Chapter 20 focuses on those issues. Further, marketing is important to the success of every organization. The same basic principles used to sell soap are also used to "sell" ideas, politicians, mass transportation, health care services, conservation, museums, and even colleges. Even your job résumé is part of a marketing campaign to sell yourself to some employer![2]

Marketing affects innovation and standard of living

An even more basic reason for studying marketing is that marketing plays a big part in economic growth and development. One key reason is that marketing encourages research and innovation—the development and spread of new ideas, goods, and services. As firms offer new and better ways of satisfying consumer needs, customers have more choices among products and this fosters competition for consumers' money. This competition drives down prices. Moreover, when firms develop products that really satisfy customers, fuller employment and higher incomes can result. The combination of these forces means that marketing has a big impact on consumers' standard of living—and it is important to the future of all nations.[3]

HOW SHOULD WE DEFINE MARKETING?

There are micro and macro views of marketing

In our bicycle example, we saw that a producer of bicycles has to perform many customer-related activities besides just making bikes. The same is true for an insurance company or an art museum. This supports the idea of marketing as a set of activities done by an individual organization to satisfy its customers.

On the other hand, people can't survive on bicycles and art museums alone! In advanced economies, it takes goods and services from thousands of organizations to satisfy the many needs of society. Further, a society needs some sort of marketing system to organize the efforts of all the producers, wholesalers, and retailers needed to satisfy the varied needs of all its citizens. So marketing is also an important social process.

We can view marketing in two ways: *from a micro view as a set of activities performed by organizations and also from a macro view as a social process.* Yet, in everyday use when people talk about marketing, they have the micro view in mind. So that is the way we will define marketing here. However, the broader macro view that looks at the whole production-distribution system is also important, so later we will provide a separate definition and discussion of macro-marketing.

Marketing defined

Marketing is the performance of activities that seek to accomplish an organization's objectives by anticipating customer or client needs and directing a flow of need-satisfying goods and services from producer to customer or client.

Let's look at this definition.[4]

Applies to profit and nonprofit organizations

Marketing applies to both profit and nonprofit organizations. Profit is the objective for most business firms. But other types of organizations may seek more members—or acceptance of an idea. Customers or clients may be individual consumers, business firms, nonprofit organizations, government agencies, or even foreign nations. While most customers and clients pay for the goods and services they receive, others may receive them free of charge or at a reduced cost through private or government support.

The aim of marketing is to identify customers' needs—and to meet those needs so well that the product almost sells itself.

More than just persuading customers

Marketing isn't just selling and advertising. Unfortunately, some executives still think of it that way. They feel that the job of marketing is to "get rid of" whatever the company happens to produce. In fact, the aim of marketing is to identify customers' needs and meet those needs so well that the product almost "sells itself." This is true whether the product is a physical good, a service, or even an idea. If the whole marketing job has been done well, customers don't need much persuading. They should be ready to buy. And after they buy, they'll be satisfied and ready to buy the same way the next time.

Begins with customer needs

Marketing should begin with potential customer needs—not with the production process. Marketing should try to anticipate needs. And then marketing, rather than production, should determine what goods and services are to be developed—including decisions about product design and packaging; prices or fees; credit and collection policies; transporting and storing policies; advertising and sales policies; and, after the sale, installation, customer service, warranty, and perhaps even disposal and recycling policies.

Does not do it alone

This does not mean that marketing should try to take over production, accounting, and financial activities. Rather, it means that marketing—by interpreting customers' needs—should provide direction for these activities and try to coordinate them.

Marketing involves exchanges

The idea that marketing involves a flow of need-satisfying offerings from a producer to a customer implies that there is an exchange of the need-satisfying offering for something else, such as the customer's money. Marketing focuses on facilitating exchanges. In fact, *marketing doesn't occur unless two or more parties are willing to exchange something for something else.* For example, in a pure subsistence economy—when each family unit produces everything it consumes—there is no need to exchange goods and services and no marketing is involved. (Although each producer-consumer unit is totally self-sufficient in such a situation, the standard of living is typically relatively low.)

Builds a relationship with the customer

Keep in mind that a marketing exchange is often part of an ongoing relationship, not just a single transaction. When marketing helps everyone in a firm really meet the needs of a customer before and after a purchase, the firm doesn't just get a single sale. Rather, it has a sale and an ongoing *relationship* with the customer. Then, in the future, when the customer has the same need again—or some other need that the firm can meet—other sales will follow. Often, the marketing *flow* of need-satisfying goods

Edition

and services is not just for a single transaction but rather is part of building a long-lasting relationship that benefits both the firm and the customer.

The focus of this text— management-oriented micro-marketing

Since you are probably preparing for a career in management, the main focus of this text will be on managerial marketing. We will see marketing through the eyes of the marketing manager.

The marketing ideas we will be discussing throughout this text apply to a wide variety of situations. They are important for new ventures started by one person as well as big corporations, in domestic and international markets, and regardless of whether the focus is on marketing physical goods, services, or an idea or cause. They are equally critical whether the relevant customers or clients are individual consumers, businesses, or some other type of organization. For editorial convenience, we will sometimes use the term *firm* as a shorthand way of referring to any type of organization, whether it is a political party, a religious organization, a government agency, or the like. However, to reinforce the point that the ideas apply to all types of organizations, throughout the book we will illustrate marketing concepts in a wide variety of situations.

Although marketing within individual firms is the primary focus of the text, marketing managers must remember that their organizations are just small parts of a larger macro-marketing system. Therefore, next we will briefly look at the macro view of marketing. Then, we will develop this idea more fully in later chapters.

MACRO-MARKETING

Macro-marketing is a social process that directs an economy's flow of goods and services from producers to consumers in a way that effectively matches supply and demand and accomplishes the objectives of society.[5]

Emphasis is on whole system

With macro-marketing we are still concerned with the flow of need-satisfying goods and services from producer to consumer. However, the emphasis with macro-marketing is not on the activities of individual organizations. Instead, the emphasis is on *how the whole marketing system works*. This includes looking at how marketing affects society and vice versa.

Every society needs a macro-marketing system to help match supply and demand. Different producers in a society have different objectives, resources, and skills.

Peruvian coffee farmers and their families provide coffee to Starbucks. But to overcome the spatial separation between growers and consumers, someone must first perform a variety of marketing functions, like standardizing and grading the coffee beans, transporting and storing them, and buying and selling them. When Starbucks sells consumers its branded coffee at one of its new "drive-thru" locations, it is providing the final activity of a process that began a continent away.

Likewise, not all consumers share the same needs, preferences, and wealth. In other words, within every society there are both heterogeneous (highly varied) supply capabilities and heterogeneous demands for goods and services. The role of a macro-marketing system is to effectively match this heterogeneous supply and demand *and* at the same time accomplish society's objectives.

An effective macro-marketing system delivers the goods and services that consumers want and need. It gets products to them at the right time, in the right place, and at a price they're willing to pay. It keeps consumers satisfied after the sale and brings them back to purchase again when they are ready. That's not an easy job—especially if you think about the variety of goods and services a highly developed economy can produce and the many kinds of goods and services consumers want.

Separation between producers and consumers

Effective marketing in an advanced economy is difficult because producers and consumers are often separated in several ways. As Exhibit 1-1 shows, exchange between producers and consumers is hampered by spatial separation, separation in time, separation of information and values, and separation of ownership. You may love your MP3 player, but you probably don't know when or where it was produced or how it got to you. The people in the factory that produced it don't know about you or how you live.

In addition, most firms specialize in producing and selling large amounts of a narrow assortment of goods and services. This allows them to take advantage of mass

Exhibit 1-1   Marketing Facilitates Production and Consumption

Production Sector
Specialization and division of labor result in heterogeneous supply capabilities

Discrepancies of Quantity. Producers prefer to produce and sell in large quantities. Consumers prefer to buy and consume in small quantities.

Discrepancies of Assortment. Producers specialize in producing a narrow assortment of goods and services. Consumers need a broad assortment.

Marketing needed to overcome discrepancies and separations

Spatial Separation. Producers tend to locate where it is economical to produce, while consumers are located in many scattered places.

Separation in Time. Consumers may not want to consume goods and services at the time producers would prefer to produce them, and time may be required to transport goods from producer to consumer.

Separation of Information. Producers do not know who needs what, where, when, and at what price. Consumers do not know what is available from whom, where, when, and at what price.

Separation in Values. Producers value goods and services in terms of costs and competitive prices. Consumers value them in terms of satisfying needs and their ability to pay.

Separation of Ownership. Producers hold title to goods and services that they themselves do not want to consume. Consumers want goods and services that they do not own.

Consumption Sector
Heterogeneous demand for different goods and services and when and where they need to be to satisfy needs and wants

Edition

production with its economies of scale—which means that as a company produces larger numbers of a particular product, the cost of each unit of the product goes down. Yet most consumers only want to buy a small quantity; they also want a wide assortment of different goods and services. These "discrepancies of quantity" and "discrepancies of assortment" further complicate exchange between producers and consumers (Exhibit 1-1). That is, each producer specializes in producing and selling large amounts of a narrow assortment of goods and services, but each consumer wants only small quantities of a wide assortment of goods and services.[6]

Marketing functions help narrow the gap

The purpose of a macro-marketing system is to overcome these separations and discrepancies. The "universal functions of marketing" help do this.

The universal functions of marketing are buying, selling, transporting, storing, standardization and grading, financing, risk taking, and market information. They must be performed in all macro-marketing systems. *How* these functions are performed—and *by whom*—may differ among nations and economic systems. But they are needed in any macro-marketing system. Let's take a closer look at them now.

Any kind of exchange usually involves buying and selling. The buying function means looking for and evaluating goods and services. The selling function involves promoting the product. It includes the use of personal selling, advertising, and other direct and mass selling methods. This is probably the most visible function of marketing.

The transporting function means the movement of goods from one place to another. The storing function involves holding goods until customers need them.

Standardization and grading involve sorting products according to size and quality. This makes buying and selling easier because it reduces the need for inspection and sampling. Financing provides the necessary cash and credit to produce, transport, store, promote, sell, and buy products. Risk taking involves bearing the uncertainties that are part of the marketing process. A firm can never be sure that customers will want to buy its products. Products can also be damaged, stolen, or outdated. The market information function involves the collection, analysis, and distribution of all the information needed to plan, carry out, and control marketing activities, whether in the firm's own neighborhood or in a market overseas.

Producers, consumers, and marketing specialists perform functions

Producers and consumers sometimes handle some of the marketing functions themselves. However, exchanges are often easier or less expensive when a marketing specialist performs some of the marketing functions. For example, both producers and consumers may benefit when an intermediary—someone who specializes in trade rather than production—plays a role in the exchange process. In Chapters 12 and 13 we'll cover the variety of marketing functions performed by the two basic types of intermediaries: retailers and wholesalers. Imagine what it would be like to shop at many different factories and farms for the wide variety of brands of packaged foods that you like rather than at a well-stocked local grocery store. While wholesalers and retailers must charge for services they provide, this charge is usually offset by the savings of time, effort, and expense that would be involved without them. So these intermediaries can help to make the whole macro-marketing system more efficient and effective.

A wide variety of other marketing specialists may also help smooth exchanges between producers, consumers, or intermediaries. These specialists are collaborators—firms that facilitate or provide one or more of the marketing functions other than buying or selling. These collaborators include advertising agencies, marketing research firms, independent product-testing laboratories, Internet service providers, public warehouses, transporting firms, communications companies, and financial institutions (including banks).

Internet EXERCISE

Go to the Target home page (www.target. com) and click on a tab for one of the product categories. How many different manufacturers' products are shown? Would consumers be better off if each manufacturer just sold directly from its own website?

Intermediaries and collaborators develop and offer specialized services that facilitate exchange between producers and customers.

Some marketing specialists perform all the functions. Others specialize in only one or two. Marketing research firms, for example, specialize only in the market information function. Further, technology may make a certain function easier to perform. For example, the buying process may require that a customer first identify relevant sellers and where they are. Even though that might be accomplished quickly and easily with an online search of the Internet, the function hasn't been cut out.

New specialists develop to fill market needs

As the Internet example suggests, new types of marketing specialists develop or evolve when new opportunities arise for someone to make exchanges between producers and consumers more efficient or effective. Such changes can come quickly, as is illustrated by the speed with which firms have adopted e-commerce. E-commerce refers to exchanges between individuals or organizations—and activities that facilitate these exchanges—based on applications of information technology. New types of Internet-based intermediaries—like Amazon.com and eBay.com—are helping to cut the costs of many marketing functions. Similarly, Google.com and MSN.com make it easier for many firms to satisfy their customers with Web-based information searches or transactions. Collectively, these developments have had a significant impact on the efficiency of our macro-marketing system. At the same time, many individual firms take advantage of these innovations to improve profitability and customer satisfaction.[7]

Through innovation, specialization, or economies of scale, marketing intermediaries and collaborators are often able to perform the marketing functions better—and at a lower cost—than producers or consumers can. This allows producers and consumers to spend more time on production, consumption, or other activities—including leisure.

Functions can be shifted and shared

From a macro-marketing viewpoint, all of the marketing functions must be performed by someone—an individual producer or consumer, an intermediary, a marketing collaborator, or, in some cases, even a nation's government. No function can be completely eliminated. *However, from a micro viewpoint, not every firm must perform all of the functions. Rather, responsibility for performing the marketing functions can be shifted and shared in a variety of ways. Further, not all goods and services require all the functions at every level of their production.* "Pure services"—like a plane ride—don't need storing,

Edition

for example. But storing is required in the production of the plane and while the plane is not in service.

Regardless of who performs the marketing functions, in general they must be performed effectively and efficiently or the performance of the whole macro-marketing system will suffer. With many different possible ways for marketing functions to be performed in a macro-marketing system, how can a society hope to arrive at a combination that best serves the needs of its citizens? To answer this question, we can look at the role of marketing in different types of economic systems.

THE ROLE OF MARKETING IN ECONOMIC SYSTEMS

All societies must provide for the needs of their members. Therefore, every society needs some sort of economic system—the way an economy organizes to use scarce resources to produce goods and services and distribute them for consumption by various people and groups in the society.

How an economic system operates depends on a society's objectives and the nature of its political institutions.[8] But regardless of what form these take, all economic systems must develop some method—along with appropriate economic institutions—to decide what and how much is to be produced and distributed by whom, when, to whom, and why.

There are two basic kinds of economic systems: command economies and market-directed economies. Actually, no economy is entirely command-oriented or market-directed. Most are a mixture of the two extremes.

Government officials may make the decisions

In a command economy, government officials decide what and how much is to be produced and distributed by whom, when, to whom, and why. These decisions are usually part of an overall government plan, so command economies are also called "planned" economies. It sounds good for a government to have a plan, but as a practical matter attempts by a government to dictate an economic plan often don't work out as intended.

Producers in a command economy generally have little choice about what goods and services to produce. Their main task is to meet the production quotas assigned in the plan. Prices are also set by government planners and tend to be very rigid—not changing according to supply and demand. Consumers usually have some freedom of

Artists and craftsmen in developing economies often do not have a local market for their products, but Ten Thousand Villages, which operates a website and retail stores in the U.S., helps them reach customers and earn a profit. Their earnings in turn improve their quality of life and what they spend prompts economic development in their local communities.

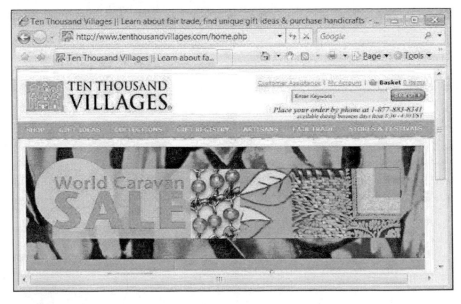

Marketing Helps India's Rural Poor

In recent decades India has experienced rapid economic growth. Many of its citizens have more income and enjoy a higher quality of life. That helps to explain why Unilever's Indian subsidiary, Hindustani Lever Limited (HLL), has worked hard to build a 40 percent share of the Indian market with its product lines that include soaps, toothpaste, and packaged foods.

Previously, HLL focused primarily on India's urban areas. Yet, almost three-fourths of India's one *billion* plus people still live in rural areas. Only half of these rural villagers have access to electricity—and less than half have basic sanitation. Many of them have an income less than $2 a day. Conventional wisdom suggests that these poor rural villagers have too little money to be an attractive market. Further, villages are far flung, so it's expensive to distribute products to them.

But now that is changing. HLL's marketing managers have decided that Indian villagers represent an opportunity for growth—and that villagers might benefit if they could purchase the soaps, toothpaste, and packaged food products that HLL is successfully selling in urban areas of India.

HLL has tailored a new marketing strategy to this target market. First, many products have been repackaged in "sachets"—small bags that contain a one- or two-day supply. HLL prices the small sachets so that villagers can afford them—and that in turn gives customers a chance to try quality products that were previously unavailable.

HLL has created its "Shakti Ammas" (women entrepreneurs) program to communicate the benefits of its products and distribute them in remote rural areas. The program sets rural women up as home-based distributors and sales agents. These women stock HLL products at their homes and go door-to-door to sell them. They also organize meetings in local schools and at village fairs to educate their fellow villagers on health and hygiene issues.

HLL will soon have more than 100,000 Shakti Ammas operating in 500,000 villages. These women have a new source of income and are learning about business. Another positive social impact is that they are teaching rural villagers about the benefits of improved hygiene. And, of course, HLL hopes to clean up with a new source of growth.[9]

choice—it's impossible to control every single detail! But the assortment of goods and services may be quite limited. Activities such as market research, branding, and advertising usually are neglected. Sometimes they aren't done at all.

Government planning in a command economy may work fairly well as long as an economy is simple and the variety of goods and services is small. It may even be necessary under certain conditions—during wartime, drought, or political instability, for example. However, as economies become more complex, government planning becomes more difficult and tends to break down. That's what happened to the economy in the former Soviet Union. Countries such as North Korea, Cuba, and Iran still rely on command-oriented economic systems. Even so, around the world there is a broad move toward market-directed economic systems—because they are more effective in meeting consumer needs.

A market-directed economy adjusts itself

In a **market-directed economy**, the individual decisions of the many producers and consumers make the macro-level decisions for the whole economy. In a pure market-directed economy, consumers make a society's production decisions when they make their choices in the marketplace. They decide what is to be produced and by whom—through their dollar "votes."

Price is a measure of value

Prices in the marketplace are a rough measure of how society values particular goods and services. If consumers are willing to pay the market prices, then apparently they feel they are getting at least their money's worth. Similarly, the cost of labor and materials is a rough measure of the value of the resources used in the production of goods and services to meet these needs. New consumer needs that can be served profitably—not just the needs of the majority—will probably be met by some profit-minded businesses.

Greatest freedom of choice

Consumers in a market-directed economy enjoy great freedom of choice. They are not forced to buy any goods or services, except those that must be provided for the good of society—things such as national defense, schools, police and fire protection, highway systems, and public-health services. These are provided by the community—and the citizens are taxed to pay for them.

Similarly, producers are free to do whatever they wish—provided that they stay within the rules of the game set by government *and* receive enough dollar "votes" from consumers. If they do their job well, they earn a profit and stay in business. But profit, survival, and growth are not guaranteed.

The role of government

The American economy and most other Western economies are mainly market-directed—but not completely. Society assigns supervision of the system to the government. For example, besides setting and enforcing the "rules of the game," government agencies control interest rates and the supply of money. They also set import and export rules that affect international competition, regulate radio and TV broadcasting, sometimes control wages and prices, and so on. Government also tries to be sure that property is protected, contracts are enforced, individuals are not exploited, no group unfairly monopolizes markets, and producers deliver the kinds and quality of goods and services they claim to be offering.[10]

Is a macro-marketing system effective and fair?

The effectiveness and fairness of a particular macro-marketing system must be evaluated in terms of that society's objectives. Obviously, all nations don't share the same objectives. For example, Swedish citizens receive many "free" services—like health care and retirement benefits. Goods and services are fairly evenly distributed among the Swedish population. By contrast, North Korea places little emphasis on producing goods and services for individual consumers—and more on military spending. In India the distribution of goods and services is very uneven—with a big gap between the have-nots and the elite haves. Whether each of these systems is judged "fair" or "effective" depends on the objectives of the society.

So far, we have described how a market-directed macro-marketing system adjusts to become more effective and efficient by responding to customer needs. See Exhibit 1-2.

As you read this book, you'll learn more about how marketing affects society and vice versa. You'll also learn more about specific marketing activities and be better informed when drawing conclusions about how fair and effective the macro-marketing system is. For now, however, we'll return to our

Exhibit 1-2
Model of a Market-Directed Macro-Marketing System

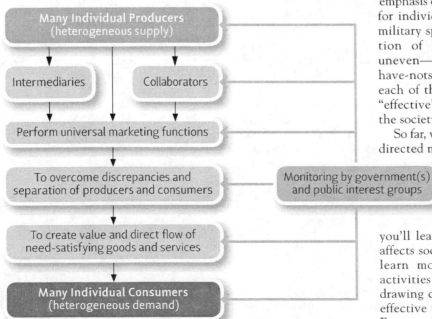

Edition

general emphasis on a managerial view of the role of marketing in individual organizations.

MARKETING'S ROLE HAS CHANGED A LOT OVER THE YEARS

It's clear that marketing decisions are very important to a firm's success. But marketing hasn't always been so complicated. In fact, understanding how marketing thinking has evolved makes the modern view clearer. So we will discuss five stages in marketing evolution: (1) the simple trade era, (2) the production era, (3) the sales era, (4) the marketing department era, and (5) the marketing company era. We'll talk about these eras as if they applied generally to all firms—but keep in mind that *some managers still have not made it to the final stages*. They are stuck in the past with old ways of thinking.

Specialization permitted trade—and distributors met the need

When societies first moved toward some specialization of production and away from a subsistence economy where each family raised and consumed everything it produced, traders played an important role. Early "producers for the market" made products that were needed by themselves and their neighbors. As bartering became more difficult, societies moved into the simple trade era—a time when families traded or sold their "surplus" output to local distributors. These specialists resold the goods to other consumers or other distributors. This was the early role of marketing—and it is still the focus of marketing in many of the less-developed areas of the world. In fact, even in the United States, the United Kingdom, and other more advanced economies, marketing didn't change much until the Industrial Revolution brought larger factories a little over a hundred years ago.

From the production to the sales era

From the Industrial Revolution until the 1920s, most companies were in the production era. The production era is a time when a company focuses on production of a few specific products—perhaps because few of these products are available in the market. "If we can make it, it will sell" is management thinking characteristic of the production era. Because of product shortages, many nations—including some of the

Most railroads try to meet customer needs with convenient routes and on-time service. To make traveling more enjoyable, this French railroad offers service that includes door-to-door delivery of the passenger's luggage. The ad says "your luggage is big enough to travel by itself. It's up to us to ensure you'd rather go by train."

Vos bagages sont assez grands pour voyager seuls.

SERVICE BAGAGES A DOMICILE
24H PORTE A PORTE
0 803 845 845*

À NOUS DE VOUS FAIRE PRÉFÉRER LE TRAIN.   SNCF

Edition

post-communist republics of Eastern Europe—continue to operate with production era approaches.

By about 1930, most companies in the industrialized Western nations had more production capability than ever before. Now the problem wasn't just to produce—but to beat the competition and win customers. This led many firms to enter the sales era. The sales era is a time when a company emphasizes selling because of increased competition.

To the marketing department era

For most firms in advanced economies, the sales era continued until at least 1950. By then, sales were growing rapidly in most areas of the economy. The problem was deciding where to put the company's effort. Someone was needed to tie together the efforts of research, purchasing, production, shipping, and sales. As this situation became more common, the sales era was replaced by the marketing department era. The marketing department era is a time when all marketing activities are brought under the control of one department to improve short-run policy planning and to try to integrate the firm's activities.

To the marketing company era

Since 1960, most firms have developed at least some managers with a marketing management outlook. Many of these firms have even graduated from the marketing department era into the marketing company era. The marketing company era is a time when, in addition to short-run marketing planning, marketing people develop long-range plans—sometimes five or more years ahead—and the whole company effort is guided by the marketing concept.

WHAT DOES THE MARKETING CONCEPT MEAN?

The marketing concept means that an organization aims *all* its efforts at satisfying its *customers*—at a *profit*. The marketing concept is a simple but very important idea. See Exhibit 1-3.

The marketing concept is not a new idea—it's been around for a long time. But some managers show little interest in customers' needs. These managers still have a production orientation—making whatever products are easy to produce and *then*

Exhibit 1-3
Organizations with a
Marketing Orientation
Carry Out the Marketing
Concept

Customer satisfaction

Total company effort

The Marketing Concept

Profit (or another measure of long-term success) as an objective

trying to sell them. They think of customers existing to buy the firm's output rather than of firms existing to serve customers and—more broadly—the needs of society.

Well-managed firms have replaced this production orientation with a marketing orientation. A marketing orientation means trying to carry out the marketing concept. Instead of just trying to get customers to buy what the firm has produced, a marketing-oriented firm tries to offer customers what they need.

Three basic ideas are included in the definition of the marketing concept: (1) customer satisfaction, (2) a total company effort, and (3) profit—not just sales—as an objective. These ideas deserve more discussion.

Customer satisfaction guides the whole system

"Give the customers what they need" seems so obvious that it may be hard for you to see why the marketing concept requires special attention. However, people don't always do the logical—especially when it means changing what they've done in the past. In a typical company 40 years ago, production managers thought mainly about getting out the product. Accountants were interested only in balancing the books. Financial people looked after the company's cash position. And salespeople were mainly concerned with getting orders for whatever product was in the warehouse. Each department thought of its own activity as the center of the business. Unfortunately, this is still true in many companies today.

Work together to do a better job

Ideally, all managers should work together as a team. Every department may directly or indirectly impact customer satisfaction. But some managers tend to build "fences" around their own departments. There may be meetings to try to get them to work together—but they come and go from the meetings worried only about protecting their own turf.

We use the term *production orientation* as a shorthand way to refer to this kind of narrow thinking—and lack of a central focus—in a business firm. But keep in mind that this problem may be seen in sales-oriented sales representatives, advertising-oriented agency people, finance-oriented finance people, directors of nonprofit organizations, and so on. It is not a criticism of people who manage production. They aren't necessarily any more guilty of narrow thinking than anyone else.

The fences come down in an organization that has accepted the marketing concept. There may still be departments because specialization often makes sense. But the total system's effort is guided by what customers want—instead of what each department would like to do.

In Chapter 20, we'll go into more detail on the relationship between marketing and other functions. Here, however, you should see that the marketing concept provides a guiding focus that *all* departments adopt. It should be a philosophy of the whole organization, not just an idea that applies to the marketing department.

Survival and success require a profit

Firms must satisfy customers. But keep in mind that it may cost more to satisfy some needs than any customers are willing to pay. Or it may be much more costly to try to attract new customers than it is to build a strong relationship with—and repeat purchases from—existing customers. So profit—the difference between a firm's revenue and its total costs—is the bottom-line measure of the firm's success and ability to survive. It is the balancing point that helps the firm determine what needs it will try to satisfy with its total (sometimes costly!) effort.

ADOPTION OF THE MARKETING CONCEPT HAS NOT BEEN EASY OR UNIVERSAL

The marketing concept was first accepted by consumer products companies such as General Electric and Procter & Gamble. Competition was intense in their markets—and trying to satisfy customers' needs more fully was a way to win in this competition. Widespread publicity about the success of the marketing concept at these companies helped spread the message to other firms.[11]

Edition

Producers of industrial commodities—steel, coal, paper, glass, and chemicals—have accepted the marketing concept slowly if at all. Similarly, many traditional retailers have been slow to accept the marketing concept.

Service industries are catching up

Service industries—including airlines, power and telephone companies, banks, investment firms, lawyers, physicians, accountants, and insurance companies—were slow to adopt the marketing concept, too. But in recent years this has changed dramatically. This is partly due to changes in government regulations that forced many of these businesses to be more competitive.

Banks used to be open for limited hours that were convenient for bankers—not customers. Many closed during lunch hour! But now banks stay open longer and also offer more services for their customers—automated teller machines, banking over the Internet, or a "personal banker" to give financial advice.[12]

It's easy to slip into a production orientation

The marketing concept may seem obvious, but it's very easy to slip into a production-oriented way of thinking. For example, a company might rush a new product to market—rather than first finding out if it will fill an unsatisfied need. Many firms in high-technology businesses fall into this trap. Consider the thousands of new dot-com firms that failed. They may have had a vision of what the technology could do, but they didn't stop to figure out all that it would take to satisfy customers or make a profit. Imagine how parents felt when eToys.com failed to deliver online purchases of Christmas toys on time. If you had that experience, would you ever shop there again? What would you tell others?

Take a look at Exhibit 1-4. It shows some differences in outlook between adopters of the marketing concept and typical production-oriented managers. As the exhibit

Exhibit 1-4   Some Differences in Outlook between Adopters of the Marketing Concept and the Typical Production-Oriented Managers

Topic	Marketing Orientation	Production Orientation
Attitudes toward customers	Customer needs determine company plans.	They should be glad we exist, trying to cut costs and bringing out better products.
An Internet website	A new way to serve customers.	If we have a website, customers will flock to us.
Product offering	Company makes what it can sell.	Company sells what it can make.
Role of marketing research	To determine customer needs and how well company is satisfying them.	To determine customer reaction, if used at all.
Interest in innovation	Focus is on locating new opportunities.	Focus is on technology and cost cutting.
Importance of profit	A critical objective.	A residual, what's left after all costs are covered.
Customer service	Satisfy customers after the sale and they'll come back again.	An activity required to reduce consumer complaints.
Inventory levels	Set with customer requirements and costs in mind.	Set to make production more convenient.
Focus of advertising	Need-satisfying benefits of goods and services.	Product features and how products are made.
Role of sales force	Help the customer to buy if the product fits customer's needs, while coordinating with rest of firm.	Sell the customer, don't worry about coordination with other promotion efforts or rest of firm.
Relationship with customer	Customer satisfaction before and after sale leads to a profitable long-run relationship.	Relationship ends when a sale is made.
Costs	Eliminate costs that do not give value to customer.	Keep costs as low as possible.

suggests, the marketing concept forces the company to think through what it is doing—and why. And it motivates the company to develop plans for accomplishing its objectives.

THE MARKETING CONCEPT AND CUSTOMER VALUE

Take the customer's point of view

A manager who adopts the marketing concept sees customer satisfaction as the path to profits. And to better understand what it takes to satisfy a customer, it's useful to take the customer's point of view.

A customer may look at a market offering from two views. One deals with the potential benefits of that offering; the other concerns what the customer has to give up to get those benefits. Consider a student who has just finished an exam and is thinking about getting a cup of mocha latte from Starbucks. Our coffee lover might see this as a great-tasting snack, a personal reward, a quick pick-me-up, and even as a way to get to know an attractive classmate. Clearly, different needs are associated with these different benefits. The cost of getting these benefits would include the price of the coffee and any tip, but there might be other nondollar costs. For example, how difficult it will be to park is a convenience cost. Slow service would be an aggravation. And you might worry about another kind of cost if the professor whose exam you have the next day sees you "wasting time" at Starbucks.

Customer value reflects benefits and costs

As this example suggests, both benefits and costs can take many different forms, perhaps ranging from economic to emotional. They also may vary depending on the situation. However, it is the customer's view of the various benefits and costs that is important. This leads us to the concept of customer value—the difference between the benefits a customer sees from a market offering and the costs of obtaining those benefits. A consumer is likely to be more satisfied when the customer value is higher—when benefits exceed costs by a larger margin. On the other hand, a consumer who sees the costs as greater than the benefits isn't likely to become a customer.

Some people think that low price and high customer value are the same thing. But that may not be the case at all. A good or service that doesn't meet a consumer's needs results in low customer value, even if the price is very low. Yet a high price may be more than acceptable when it obtains the desired benefits. Think again about our Starbucks example. You can get a cup of coffee for a much lower price, but Starbucks offers more than *just* a cup of coffee.

Customer may not think about it very much

It's useful for a manager to evaluate ways to improve the benefits, or reduce the costs, of what the firm offers customers. However, this doesn't mean that customers stop and compute some sort of customer value score before making each purchase. If they did, there wouldn't be much time in life for anything else. So a manager's objective and thorough analysis may not accurately reflect the customer's impressions. Yet it is the customer's view that matters—even when the customer has not thought about it.

Where does competition fit?

You can't afford to ignore competition. Consumers usually have choices about how they will meet their needs. So a firm that offers superior customer value is likely to win and keep customers. See Exhibit 1-5.

Often the best way to improve customer value, and beat the competition, is to be first to satisfy a need that others have not even considered.

The competition between Pepsi and Coke illustrates this. Coke and Pepsi were spending millions of dollars on promotion—fighting head-to-head for the same cola customers. They put so much emphasis on the cola competition that they missed other opportunities. That gave firms like Snapple the chance to enter the market and steal away customers. For these customers, the desired benefits—and the greatest customer value—came from the variety of a fruit-flavored drink, not from one more cola.

Edition

Exhibit 1-5
Customer Value and
Competition

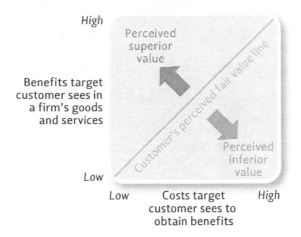

Build relationships with customer value

Firms that embrace the marketing concept seek ways to build a profitable long-term relationship with each customer. Even the most innovative firm faces competition sooner or later. And trying to get new customers by taking them away from a competitor is usually more costly than retaining current customers by really satisfying their needs. Satisfied customers buy again and again. This makes their buying job easier, and it also increases the selling firm's profits.

Building relationships with customers requires that everyone in a firm work together to provide customer value before *and after* each purchase. If there is a problem with a customer's bill, the accounting people can't just leave it to the salesperson to straighten it out or, even worse, act like it's "the customer's problem." The long-term relationship with the customer—and the lifetime value of the customer's future purchases—is threatened unless everyone works together to make things right for the customer. Similarly, the firm's advertising people can't just develop ads that try to convince a customer to buy once. If the firm doesn't deliver on the benefits promised in its ads, the customer is likely to go elsewhere the next time the need arises. And the same ideas apply whether the issue is meeting promised delivery dates, resolving

L.L. Bean has always focused on customer satisfaction and customer value as a way to build long-term relationships with customers.

Edition

Exhibit 1-6
Satisfying Customers
with Superior Customer
Value to Build Profitable
Relationships

warranty problems, giving a customer help on how to use a product, or even making it easy for the customer to return a purchase made in error.

In other words, any time the customer value is reduced—because the benefits to the customer decrease or the costs increase—the relationship is weakened.[13]

Exhibit 1-6 summarizes these ideas. In a firm that has adopted the marketing concept, everyone focuses on customer satisfaction. They look for ways to offer superior customer value. That helps attract customers in the first place—and keeps them satisfied after they buy. So when they are ready to make repeat purchases, the firm is able to keep them as customers. Sales may increase further because satisfied customers are likely to buy other products offered by the firm. In this way, the firm builds profitable relationships with its customers. In other words, when a firm adopts the marketing concept, it wins and so do its customers.

Curves' superior customer value satisfies customers

Curves fitness centers illustrate these ideas. They have been successful in building enduring relationships with their customers—women who are interested in a fast, regular workout. Research for Curves revealed that many women had simple fitness needs. They didn't want to work out with a lot of fancy training equipment; many didn't even want to shower at the workout center. Realizing this, Curves created smaller than normal fitness centers that fit in convenient strip malls. Smaller size and lower costs mean that Curves is able to open centers in small towns where larger fitness clubs could not survive. Its research also showed that many women preferred not to have men around when they exercise. Instead, they like the camaraderie of exercising with other women—which Curves enhances by arranging equipment in a circle. This arrangement is coupled with simple exercises so a customer doesn't waste time waiting on machines—and she can count on finishing in just 30 minutes. Compared to competitors, Curves' fee is also attractive—less than $50 per month. Curves' overall approach works well for its members, which explains why they keep coming back. And because it provides superior customer value for its members Curves now has grown to 10,000 fitness centers worldwide.[14]

Internet EXERCISE

What does Curves offer its customers at its website (www.curves.com)? How does this increase the value a customer receives from being a Curves member? What could Curves do with the website to further enhance its relationships with customers?

Edition

THE MARKETING CONCEPT APPLIES IN NONPROFIT ORGANIZATIONS

Newcomers to marketing thinking

The marketing concept is as important for nonprofit organizations as it is for business firms. In fact, marketing applies to all sorts of public and private nonprofit organizations—ranging from government agencies, health care organizations, educational institutions, and religious groups to charities, political parties, and fine arts organizations.

Support may not come from satisfied "customers"

As with any business firm, a nonprofit organization needs resources and support to survive and achieve its objectives. Yet support often does not come directly from those who receive the benefits the organization produces. For example, the World Wildlife Fund protects animals. If supporters of the World Wildlife Fund are not satisfied with its efforts—don't think the benefits are worth what it costs to provide them—they will put their time and money elsewhere.

Just as most firms face competition for customers, most nonprofits face competition for the resources and support they need. The Air Force faces a big problem if it can't attract new recruits. A shelter for the homeless may fail if supporters decide to focus on some other cause, such as AIDS education.

What is the "bottom line"?

As with a business, a nonprofit must take in as much money as it spends or it won't survive. However, a nonprofit organization does not measure "profit" in the same way as a firm. And its key measures of long-term success are also different. The YMCA, colleges, symphony orchestras, and the United Way, for example, all seek to achieve different objectives and need different measures of success. When everyone in an organization agrees to *some* measure(s) of long-run success, it helps the organization focus its efforts.

May not be organized for marketing

Some nonprofits face other challenges in organizing to adopt the marketing concept. Often no one has overall responsibility for marketing activities. Even when some leaders do the marketing thinking, they may have trouble getting unpaid volunteers with many different interests to all agree with the marketing strategy. Volunteers tend to do what they feel like doing![15]

Marketing is now widely accepted by many local, national, and international nonprofit organizations. For example, this World Wildlife Fund ad vividly conveys its environmental message that "a single tin of paint can pollute millions of litres of water."

Nonprofits achieve objectives by satisfying needs

A simple example shows how marketing thinking helped a small town reduce robberies. Initially the chief of police asked the town manager for a larger budget—for more officers and patrol cars. Instead of a bigger budget, the town manager suggested a different approach. She put two officers in charge of a community watch program. They helped neighbors to organize and notify the police of any suspicious situations. They also set up a program to engrave ID numbers on belongings. And new signs warned thieves that a community watch was in effect. Break-ins all but stopped—without increasing the police budget. What the town *really* needed was more effective crime prevention—not just more police officers.

Throughout this book, we'll be discussing the marketing concept and related ideas as they apply in many different settings. Often we'll simply say "in a firm" or "in a business"—but remember that most of the ideas can be applied in *any* type of organization.

THE MARKETING CONCEPT, SOCIAL RESPONSIBILITY, AND MARKETING ETHICS

Society's needs must be considered

The marketing concept is so logical that it's hard to argue with it. Yet when a firm focuses its efforts on satisfying some consumers—to achieve its objectives—there may be negative effects on society. For example, producers and consumers making free choices can cause conflicts and difficulties. This is called the micro-macro dilemma. What is "good" for some firms and consumers may not be good for society as a whole.

For instance, many people in New York City buy bottled water because they like the convenience of easy-to-carry disposable bottles with spill-proof caps. On the other hand, the city already provides citizens with good tasting, safe tap water at a fraction of the cost. Is this just a matter of free choice by consumers? It's certainly a popular choice! On the other hand, critics point out that it is an inefficient use of resources to waste oil making and transporting millions of plastic bottles that end up in landfills where they leach chemicals into the soil. That kind of thinking, about the good of society as a whole, explains why New York City has run ads that encourage consumers to "get your fill" of free city water. What do you think? Should future generations pay the environmental price for today's consumer conveniences?[16]

Questions like these are not easy to answer. The basic reason is that many different people may have a stake in the outcomes—and social consequences—of the choices made by individual managers *and* consumers in a market-directed system. This means that marketing managers should be concerned with social responsibility—a firm's obligation to improve its positive effects on society and reduce its negative effects. As you read this book and learn more about marketing, you will also learn

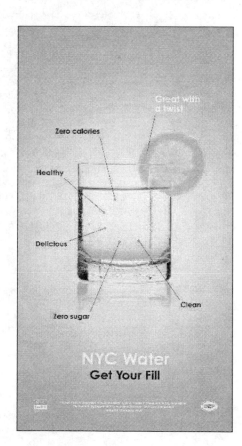

Zero calories
Great with a twist
Healthy
Delicious
Zero sugar
Clean
NYC Water
Get Your Fill

Nedbank has found creative ways for its marketing efforts to help the poor communities it serves in developing areas. Its solar-powered billboard converts the hot African sun to electricity that lights the ad and also powers the kitchen of the town's school, which feeds 1,100 children.

more about social responsibility in marketing—and why it must be taken seriously. You'll also see that being socially responsible sometimes requires difficult trade-offs.

Consider, for example, the environmental problems created by CFCs, chemicals that were used in hundreds of critical products, including fire extinguishers, cooling systems, and electronic circuit boards. When it was learned that CFCs deplete the earth's ozone layer, it was not possible to immediately stop producing and using all CFCs. For many products critical to society, there was no feasible short-term substitute. Du Pont and other producers of CFCs worked hard to balance these conflicting demands until substitute products could be found. Yet you can see that there are no easy answers for how such conflicts should be resolved.[17]

The issue of social responsibility in marketing also raises other important questions—for which there are no easy answers.

Should all consumer needs be satisfied?

Some consumers want products that may not be safe or good for them in the long run. Some critics argue that businesses should not offer high-heeled shoes, alcoholic beverages, or sugar-coated cereals because they aren't "good" for consumers in the long run.

Similarly, bicycles and roller blades are among the most dangerous products identified by the Consumer Product Safety Commission. Who should decide if these products will be offered to consumers?

What if it cuts into profits?

Being more socially conscious often seems to lead to positive customer response. For example, many consumers praise Wal-Mart as a "safe haven" for kids to shop because it does not carry CDs that are not suitable for children, lewd videos, plastic guns that look authentic, and video games judged to be too violent. Toyota and Honda have had very good response to hybrid cars that produce less pollution (even though the price is higher). And some consumers buy only from firms that certify that their overseas factories pay a "fair wage" and don't rely on child labor.[18]

Yet as the examples above show, there are times when being socially responsible conflicts with a firm's profit objective. Concerns about such conflicts have prompted critics to raise the basic question: Is the marketing concept really desirable?

Many socially conscious marketing managers are trying to resolve this problem. Their definition of customer satisfaction includes long-range effects—as well as immediate customer satisfaction. They try to balance consumer, company, *and* social interests.

The marketing concept guides marketing ethics

Certainly some concerns about social responsibility and marketing arise because some individual firm or manager was intentionally unethical and cheated the market. Of course, a manager cannot be truly consumer-oriented and at the same time intentionally unethical. However, at times, problems and criticism may arise because a manager did not fully consider the ethical implications of a decision. In either case, there is no excuse for sloppiness when it comes to marketing ethics—the moral standards that guide marketing decisions and actions. Each individual develops moral standards based on his or her own values. That helps explain why opinions about what is right or wrong often vary from one person to another, from one society to another, and among different groups within a society. It is sometimes difficult to say whose opinions are "correct." Even so, such opinions may have a very real influence on whether an individual's (or a firm's) marketing decisions and actions are accepted or rejected. So marketing ethics are not only a philosophical issue, they are also a pragmatic concern.

Problems may arise when some individual manager does not share the same marketing ethics as others in the organization. One person operating alone can damage a firm's reputation and even survival.

To be certain that standards for marketing ethics are as clear as possible, many organizations have developed their own written codes of ethics. These codes usually state—at least at a general level—the ethical standards that everyone in the firm should follow in dealing with customers and other people. Many professional societies also have such codes. For example, the American Marketing Association's code of ethics—see Exhibit 1-7—sets specific ethical standards for many aspects of marketing.[19]

Exhibit 1-7   Summary of American Marketing Association Statement of Ethics

The American Marketing Association has developed a Statement of Ethics to guide its members' behavior. We have reproduced the preamble and parts of key sections of this document. The full document can be found at the association's website (www.marketingpower.com).

Preamble

The American Marketing Association commits itself to promoting the highest standard of professional ethical norms and values for its members. Norms are established standards of conduct that are expected and maintained by society and/or professional organizations. Values represent the collective conception of what people find desirable, important, and morally proper. Values serve as the criteria for evaluating the actions of others. Marketing practitioners must recognize that they not only serve their enterprises but also act as stewards of society in creating, facilitating, and executing the efficient and effective transactions that are part of the greater economy. In this role, marketers should embrace the highest ethical norms of practicing professionals and the ethical values implied by their responsibility toward stakeholders (e.g., customers, employees, investors, channel members, regulators, and the host community).

General Norms

• Marketers must do no harm.

• Marketers must foster trust in the marketing system.

• Marketers must embrace, communicate, and practice the fundamental ethical values that will improve consumer confidence in the integrity of the marketing exchange system.

Ethical Values

• Honesty—to be truthful and forthright in our dealings with customers and stakeholders.

• Responsibility—to try to balance justly the needs of the buyer with the interests of the seller.

• Fairness—to try to balance the needs of the buyer with the interests of the seller.

• Respect—to acknowledge the basic human dignity of all stakeholders.

• Openness—to create transparency in our marketing operations.

• Citizenship—to fulfill the economic, legal, philanthropic, and societal responsibilities that serve stakeholders in a strategic manner.

Edition

Throughout the text, we will be discussing the types of ethical issues individual marketing managers face. But we won't be moralizing and trying to tell you how you should think on any given issue. Rather, by the end of the course we hope that *you* will have some firm personal opinions about what is and is not ethical in micro-marketing activities.[20]

Ethics QUESTION

A customer purchases a Sony digital camera that comes with a 90-day manufacturer's warranty on parts and labor. The salesperson suggests that the customer consider the store's three-year extended service to cover any problems with the camera. The customer replies, "I'm getting a Sony because it's a reputable brand—and at $98 the service agreement is one-third the cost of the camera." Four months later, the customer returns to the store and complains that the camera no longer takes pictures and that "the store needs to make it right." If you were the store manager, what would you say? Would your response be any different if you knew that the customer was going to post his complaint on a consumer website?

Fortunately, the prevailing practice of most businesspeople is to be fair and honest. However, not all criticisms of marketing focus on ethical issues.

Marketing has its critics

We must admit that marketing—as it exists in the United States and other developed societies—has many critics. Marketing activity is especially open to criticism because it is the part of business most visible to the public.

A number of typical complaints about marketing are summarized in Exhibit 1-8. Think about these criticisms and whether you agree with them or not. What complaints do you have that are not covered by one of the categories in Exhibit 1-8?

Such complaints should not be taken lightly. They show that many people are unhappy with some parts of the marketing system. Certainly, the strong public support for consumer protection laws proves that not all consumers feel they are being treated like royalty.

As you consider the various criticisms of marketing, keep in mind that not all of them deal with the marketing practices of specific firms. Some of the complaints about marketing really focus on the basic idea of a market-directed macro-marketing system—and these criticisms often occur because people don't understand what marketing is—or how it works.[21] As you go through this book, we'll discuss some of these criticisms. Then in our final chapter, we will return to a more complete appraisal of marketing in our consumer-oriented society.

Exhibit 1-8
Sample Criticisms of Marketing

- Advertising is everywhere, and it's often annoying, misleading, or wasteful.
- The quality of products is poor and often they are not even safe.
- There are too many unnecessary products.
- Packaging and labeling are often confusing and deceptive.
- Retailers add too much to the cost of distribution and just raise prices without providing anything in return.
- Marketing serves the rich and exploits the poor.
- Service stinks, and when a consumer has a problem nobody cares.
- Marketing creates interest in products that pollute the environment.
- Private information about consumers is collected and used to sell them things they don't want.
- Marketing makes people too materialistic and motivates them toward "things" instead of social needs.
- Easy consumer credit makes people buy things they don't need and can't afford.

CONCLUSION

The basic purpose of this chapter is to introduce you to marketing and highlight its value for consumers, firms, and society. In Chapter 2, we introduce a marketing strategy planning process that is the framework for ideas developed throughout the rest of the text—and that will guide your marketing thinking in the future. This chapter sets the stage for that by introducing basic principles that guide marketing thinking.

You've learned about two views of marketing, both of which are important. One takes a micro view and focuses on marketing activities by an individual business (or other type of organization). This is what most people (including most business managers) have in mind when they talk about marketing. But it's important to understand that marketing also plays a more macro role. Macro-marketing is concerned with the way the whole marketing system works in a society or economy. It operates to make exchanges and relationships between producers and their customers more effective.

We discussed the functions of marketing and who performs them. This includes not only producers and their customers but also marketing specialists who serve as intermediaries between producers and consumers and other specialists (like product-testing labs and advertising agencies) who are collaborators and facilitate marketing functions.

We explained how a market-directed economy works, through the macro-marketing system, to provide consumers with choices. We introduced macro-marketing in this chapter, and we'll consider macro-marketing issues throughout the text. But the major focus of this book is on marketing by individual organizations. Someone in an organization must plan and manage its activities to make certain that customer needs are satisfied.

That's why understanding the marketing concept is another objective. The marketing concept is the basic philosophy that provides direction to a marketing-oriented firm. It stresses that the company's efforts should focus on satisfying some target customers—at a profit. Production-oriented firms tend to forget this. The various departments within a production-oriented firm let their natural conflicts of interest get in the way of customer satisfaction.

We also introduced the customer value concept. It is marketing's responsibility to make certain that what the firm offers customers really provides them with value that is greater than they can obtain somewhere else. In today's competitive markets, a firm must offer superior customer value if it wants to attract customers, satisfy them, and build beneficial long-term relationships with them.

A final objective was for you to see how social responsibility and marketing ethics relate to the marketing concept. The chapter ends by considering criticisms of marketing— both of the way individual firms work and of the whole macro system. When you have finished reading this book, you will be better able to evaluate these criticisms.

By learning more about marketing-oriented decision making, you will be able to make more efficient and socially responsible decisions. This will help improve the performance of individual firms and organizations (your employers). And eventually it will help our macro-marketing system work better.

KEY TERMS

production, 5
customer satisfaction, 5
innovation, 6
marketing, 6
pure subsistence economy, 7
macro-marketing, 8
economies of scale, 10
universal functions of marketing, 10
buying function, 10
selling function, 10
transporting function, 10
storing function, 10

standardization and grading, 10
financing, 10
risk taking, 10
market information function, 10
intermediary, 10
collaborators, 10
e-commerce, 11
economic system, 12
command economy, 12
market-directed economy, 13
simple trade era, 15

production era, 15
sales era, 16
marketing department era, 16
marketing company era, 16
marketing concept, 16
production orientation, 16
marketing orientation, 17
customer value, 19
micro-macro dilemma, 23
social responsibility, 23
marketing ethics, 25

Edition

QUESTIONS AND PROBLEMS

1. List your activities for the first two hours after you woke up this morning. Briefly indicate how marketing affected your activities.

2. If a producer creates a really revolutionary new product and consumers can learn about it and purchase it at a website, is any additional marketing effort really necessary? Explain your thinking.

3. Distinguish between the micro and macro views of marketing. Then explain how they are interrelated, if they are.

4. Refer to Exhibit 1-1, and give an example of a purchase you made recently that involved separation of information and separation in time between you and the producer. Briefly explain how these separations were overcome.

5. Describe a recent purchase you made. Indicate why that particular product was available at a store and, in particular, at the store where you bought it.

6. Define the functions of marketing in your own words. Using an example, explain how they can be shifted and shared.

7. Online computer shopping at websites makes it possible for individual consumers to get direct information from hundreds of companies they would not otherwise know about. Consumers can place an order for a purchase that is then shipped to them directly. Will growth of these services ultimately eliminate the need for retailers and wholesalers? Explain your thinking, giving specific attention to what marketing functions are involved in these "electronic purchases" and who performs them.

8. Explain why a small producer might want a marketing research firm to take over some of its information-gathering activities.

9. Distinguish between how economic decisions are made in a command economy and how they are made in a market-directed economy.

10. Would the functions that must be provided and the development of wholesaling and retailing systems be any different in a command economy from those in a market-directed economy?

11. Explain why a market-directed macro-marketing system encourages innovation. Give an example.

12. Define the marketing concept in your own words, and then explain why the notion of profit is usually included in this definition.

13. Define the marketing concept in your own words, and then suggest how acceptance of this concept might affect the organization and operation of your college.

14. Distinguish between production orientation and marketing orientation, illustrating with local examples.

15. Explain why a firm should view its internal activities as part of a total system. Illustrate your answer for (a) a large grocery products producer, (b) a plumbing wholesaler, (c) a department store chain, and (d) a cell phone service.

16. Give examples of some of the benefits and costs that might contribute to the customer value of each of the following products: (a) a wristwatch, (b) a weight-loss diet supplement, (c) a cruise on a luxury liner, and (d) a checking account from a bank.

17. Give an example of a recent purchase you made where the purchase wasn't just a single transaction but rather part of an ongoing relationship with the seller. Discuss what the seller has done (or could do better) to strengthen the relationship and increase the odds of you being a loyal customer in the future.

18. Discuss how the micro-macro dilemma relates to each of the following products: high-powered engines in cars, nuclear power, bank credit cards, and pesticides that improve farm production.

SUGGESTED CASES

1. McDonald's "Seniors" Restaurant   2. Harvest Farm Foods, Inc.   18. Whisper Valley Volunteer Fire Department

COMPUTER-AIDED PROBLEM

1. REVENUE, COST, AND PROFIT RELATIONSHIPS

This problem introduces you to the computer-aided problem (CAP) software—which is on the CD that accompanies this text—and gets you started with the use of spreadsheet analysis for marketing decision making. This problem is simple. In fact, you could work it without the software. But by starting with a simple problem, you will learn how to use the program more quickly and see how it will help you with more complicated problems. Instructions for the software are available at the end of this text.

Sue Cline, the business manager at Magna University Student Bookstore, is developing plans for the next academic year. The bookstore is one of the university's nonprofit

activities, but any "surplus" (profit) it earns is used to support the student activities center.

Two popular products at the bookstore are the student academic calendar and notebooks with the school name. Sue Cline thinks that she can sell calendars to 90 percent of Magna's 3,000 students, so she has had 2,700 printed. The total cost, including artwork and printing, is $11,500. Last year the calendar sold for $5.00, but Sue is considering changing the price this year.

Sue thinks that the bookstore will be able to sell 6,000 notebooks if they are priced right. But she knows that many students will buy similar notebooks (without the school name) from stores in town if the bookstore price is too high.

Edition

Sue has entered the information about selling price, quantity, and costs for calendars and notebooks in the spreadsheet program so that it is easy to evaluate the effect of different decisions. The spreadsheet is also set up to calculate revenue and profit, based on

$$\text{Revenue} = (\text{Selling price}) \times (\text{Quantity sold})$$

$$\text{Profit} = (\text{Revenue}) - (\text{Total cost})$$

Use the program to answer the questions that follow. Record your answers on a separate sheet of paper.

a. From the Spreadsheet Screen, how much revenue does Sue expect from calendars? How much revenue from notebooks? How much profit will the store earn from calendars? From notebooks?

b. If Sue increases the price of her calendars to $6.00 and still sells the same quantity, what is the expected revenue? The expected profit? (Note: Change the price from $5.00 to $6.00 on the spreadsheet and the program will recompute revenue and profit.) On your sheet of paper, show the calculations that confirm that the program has given you the correct values.

c. Sue is interested in getting an overview of how a change in the price of notebooks would affect revenue and profit, assuming that she sells all 6,000 notebooks she is thinking of ordering. Prepare a table—on your sheet of paper—with column headings for three variables: selling price, revenue, and profit. Show the value for revenue and profit for different possible selling prices for a notebook—starting at a minimum price of $1.60 and adding 8 cents to the price until you reach a maximum of $2.40. At what price will selling 6,000 notebooks contribute $5,400.00 to profit? At what price would notebook sales contribute only $1,080.00? (Hint: Use the What If analysis feature to compute the new values. Start by selecting "selling price" for notebooks as the value to change, with a minimum value of $1.60 and a maximum value of $2.40. Select the revenue and profit for notebooks as the values to display.)

For additional questions related to this problem, see Exercise 1-5 in the *Learning Aid for Use with Basic Marketing*, 17th edition.

2

Marketing Strategy Planning

There was a time when it didn't seem to be an exaggeration for Barnum & Bailey's ads to tout the circus as "the greatest show on earth." For a hundred years, circuses had brought excitement and family entertainment to towns all over the country. Parents hardly noticed the hard benches that they sat on as they watched their kids cheer for the acrobats, clowns, and animal acts. But by the 1980s the popularity of traditional circuses was in decline; many simply went out of business.

You can imagine why this sad state of affairs would be a concern for Guy Laliberté—a stilt walker, accordion player, and fire eater—and others in his band of performers. But instead of bemoaning the demise of the circus, they saw an opportunity for a new kind of entertainment—and their idea gave birth to "Cirque du Soleil."

Their new style of circus still traveled to the audience and set up a "big top" tent, but costly and controversial animal acts were eliminated. Instead, the entertainment focused on an innovative combination of acrobatics, music, and theater. This more sophisticated offering appealed to adults. Importantly, adults were willing to pay more for tickets when the show was targeted at them and not just kids—especially when the traditional circus benches were replaced with more comfortable seats.

Cirque du Soleil quickly struck a chord with audiences and soon the producers were developing new shows and also expanding tours to reach new markets. For example, seven different Cirque du Soleil shows now travel across Europe, Asia, and North America. Each show performs in a host city for anywhere from two weeks to three months. In addition, six other Cirque du Soleil shows now have permanent homes and target tourists. Five are in Las Vegas and one is in Orlando, Florida. Each show is different and has a unique theme. For example, the theme of *KÀ* highlights the martial arts, *O* emphasizes fire and water while incorporating Polynesian folklore, and *LOVE* celebrates the music of The Beatles.

As all of this suggests, Cirque du Soleil's marketing managers constantly evaluate new opportunities. A few years ago the company even considered a plan to diversify into hotels and spas based on the circus theme. This idea was screened out—at least for now—and instead the focus has been on developing new products for current and new markets. Each idea for a new show is judged on its creativity, uniqueness, and likelihood of becoming a real blockbuster. New product development is very ambitious. New shows can take more than five years and $100 million to develop. But these development costs can be recouped over each show's anticipated 10-year run. For example, a program now in development will feature the music of Elvis Presley and other new Cirque du Soleil shows will have permanent facilities in the Chinese resort city of Macao; Japan's capital, Tokyo; and Dubai, United Arab Emirates.

Cirque du Soleil also now offers television specials and DVDs. This is another way for Cirque to reach new customers. These small screen shows not only generate additional revenue but they also give customers a taste of Cirque du Soleil and whet their appetite for a live show.

Once customers see a live Cirque du Soleil show, they want to see more. So Cirque's ad efforts focus on motivating customers to see that first show. For example, ads in airline magazines target travelers who are headed to cities with permanent shows and traveling shows are heavily advertised in local media. But publicity and word of mouth are also important. Local newspapers and TV shows are often interested in doing stories about touring productions that are coming to town. Cirque du Soleil's website helps reporters in this effort by providing photos, videos, and interviews for easy download. To encourage word of mouth, they also rely on exclusive "premiers" where influential people in the community are invited to a gala opening night. The troupe also offers free tickets and volunteers time to help build close relationships with local art and charitable organizations. After experiencing the troupe's magic, people often tell their friends and look forward to the next opportunity to see Cirque du Soleil in action.

These new fans are likely to visit Cirque du Soleil's website (www.cirquedusoleil.com), which gives information about all the shows. The site also encourages customers to join the hundreds of thousands who have already signed up for the free "Cirque Club." Members sign up for the specific news they want sent to their e-mail address. So those wanting information about the permanent shows in Orlando and traveling shows coming to Georgia get messages letting them know of changes at the Orlando show and advance ticket sales to the Atlanta show.

Cirque du Soleil has been very successful, but it must continue to focus on ways to improve its customers' experiences. Imitators, like Slava's Snowshow, the Canadian Cirque Éloize, and Le Rêve in Las Vegas now try to offer similar entertainment fare. The reputation of the powerful Cirque du Soleil brand name gives the troupe a competitive advantage when it introduces new shows. It also allows Cirque to charge a premium price for tickets, which range from $40 to over $200 for the exclusive *Tapis Rouge* (red carpet) tickets. Cirque du Soleil's carefully crafted marketing mix generates ticket sales that exceed half a billion dollars each year.[1]

LEARNING OBJECTIVES

Marketing managers at Cirque du Soleil make many decisions as they develop marketing strategies. Making good marketing strategy decisions is never easy, yet knowing what basic decision areas to consider helps you to plan a more successful strategy. This chapter will get you started by giving you a framework for thinking about marketing strategy planning—which is what the rest of this book is all about.

When you finish this chapter, you should be able to:

1 understand what a marketing manager does.

2 know what marketing strategy planning is—and why it is the focus of this book.

3 understand target marketing.

4 be familiar with the four Ps in a marketing mix.

5 know the difference between a marketing strategy, a marketing plan, and a marketing program.

6 understand what customer equity is and why marketing strategy planners seek to increase it.

7 be familiar with the text's framework for marketing strategy planning—and why it involves a process of narrowing down from broad opportunities to the most attractive marketing strategy.

8 know four broad types of marketing opportunities that help in identifying new strategies.

9 understand why strategies for opportunities in international markets should be considered.

10 understand the important new terms (shown in red).

THE MANAGEMENT JOB IN MARKETING

In Chapter 1 you learned about the marketing concept—a philosophy to guide the whole firm toward satisfying customers at a profit. From the Cirque du Soleil case, it's clear that marketing decisions are very important to a firm's success. So let's look more closely at the marketing management process.

The **marketing management process** is the process of (1) *planning* marketing activities, (2) directing the *implementation* of the plans, and (3) *controlling* these plans. Planning, implementation, and control are basic jobs of all managers—but here we will emphasize what they mean to marketing managers.

Exhibit 2-1 shows the relationships among the three jobs in the marketing management process. The jobs are all connected to show that the marketing management process is continuous. In the planning job, managers set guidelines for the implementing job and specify expected results. They use these expected results in the control job to determine if everything has worked out as planned. The link from the control job to the planning job is especially important. This feedback often leads to changes in the plans or to new plans.

Edition

Exhibit 2–1
The Marketing
Management Process

Whole-company strategic management planning
Match resources to market opportunities

Marketing planning
• Set objectives
• Evaluate opportunities
• Create marketing strategies
• Prepare marketing plans
• Develop marketing program

Adjust plans
as needed

Control marketing plan(s) and program
• Measure results
• Evaluate progress

Implement marketing plan(s) and program

Managers should seek
new opportunities

Smart managers are not satisfied just planning present activities. Markets are dynamic. Consumers' needs, competitors, and the environment keep changing. Consider Parker Brothers, a company that seemed to have a "Monopoly" in family games. While it continued selling board games, firms like Sega, Sony, and Nintendo zoomed in with video game competition. Of course, not every opportunity is good for every company. Really attractive opportunities are those that fit with what the whole company wants to do and is able to do well.

Strategic management
planning concerns the
whole firm

The job of planning strategies to guide a whole company is called strategic (management) planning—the managerial process of developing and maintaining a match between an organization's resources and its market opportunities. This is a top-management job. It includes planning not only for marketing but also for production, finance, human resources, and other areas. In Chapter 20, we'll look at links between marketing and these areas.

Although marketing strategies are not whole-company plans, company plans should be market-oriented. And the marketing plan often sets the tone and direction for the whole company. So we will use *strategy planning* and *marketing strategy planning* to mean the same thing.[2]

WHAT IS A MARKETING STRATEGY?

Marketing strategy planning means finding attractive opportunities and developing profitable marketing strategies. But what is a "marketing strategy"? We have used these words rather casually so far. Now let's see what they really mean.

What is a marketing strategy?

A marketing strategy specifies a target market and a related marketing mix. It is a big picture of what a firm will do in some market. Two interrelated parts are needed:

1. A target market—a fairly homogeneous (similar) group of customers to whom a company wishes to appeal.
2. A marketing mix—the controllable variables the company puts together to satisfy this target group.

Edition

Exhibit 2-2
A Marketing Strategy

The importance of target customers in this process can be seen in Exhibit 2-2, where the target customer—the "C"—is at the center of the diagram. The customer is surrounded by the controllable variables that we call the "marketing mix." A typical marketing mix includes some product, offered at a price, with some promotion to tell potential customers about the product, and a way to reach the customer's place.

The marketing strategy for The Learning Company's software aims at a specific group of target customers: young parents who have a computer at home and want their kids to learn while playing. The strategy calls for a variety of educational software products—like *Reader Rabbit* and *Where in the World Is Carmen Sandiego?* The firm's software is designed with entertaining graphics and sound, and it's tested on kids to be certain that it is easy to use. To make it convenient for target customers to buy the software, it can be ordered from the firm's own website (www.learningcompany.com) or from other retailers like Toys "R" Us. Promotion has helped build customer interest in the software. For example, when marketing managers released *Where in Time Is Carmen Sandiego?* they not only placed ads in family-oriented magazines but also sent direct-mail flyers or e-mail to registered customers of the firm's other products. Some firms sell less-expensive games for kids, but parents are loyal to The Learning Company brand because it caters to their needs and offers first-class customer service—including a 90-day, no-questions-asked guarantee that assures the buyer of good customer value.[3]

SELECTING A MARKET-ORIENTED STRATEGY IS TARGET MARKETING

Target marketing is not mass marketing

Note that a marketing strategy specifies some *particular* target customers. This approach is called "target marketing" to distinguish it from "mass marketing." Target marketing says that a marketing mix is tailored to fit some specific target customers. In contrast, mass marketing—the typical production-oriented approach—vaguely aims at "everyone" with the same marketing mix. Mass marketing assumes that everyone is the same—and it considers everyone to be a potential customer. It may help to think of target marketing as the "rifle approach" and mass marketing as the "shotgun approach." See Exhibit 2-3.

Mass marketers may do target marketing

Commonly used terms can be confusing here. The terms *mass marketing* and *mass marketers* do not mean the same thing. Far from it! *Mass marketing* means trying to

Exhibit 2-3
Production-Oriented and Marketing-Oriented Managers Have Different Views of the Market

Production-oriented manager sees everyone as basically similar and practices "mass marketing"

Marketing-oriented manager sees everyone as different and practices "target marketing"

sell to "everyone," as we explained above. *Mass marketers* like Kraft Foods and Wal-Mart are aiming at clearly defined target markets. The confusion with mass marketing occurs because their target markets usually are large and spread out.

Target marketing can mean big markets and profits

Target marketing is not limited to small market segments—only to fairly homogeneous ones. A very large market—even what is sometimes called the "mass market"—may be fairly homogeneous, and a target marketer will deliberately aim at it. For example, a very large group of parents of young children are homogeneous on many dimensions, including their attitudes about changing baby diapers. In the United States alone, this group spends about $5 billion a year on disposable diapers—so it should be no surprise that it is a major target market for companies like Kimberly-Clark (Huggies) and Procter & Gamble (Pampers). On the other hand, babies and their parents are not the only ones who need disposable diapers. Many elderly people, especially those who are in nursing homes and have mobility problems, use diapers. Needless to say, the marketing mix that's right for babies isn't right for elder care. It's not just the sizes that are different, but also the forms. The elderly don't like the idea of needing "diapers"—so instead they wear disposable "pull ups."

The basic reason to focus on some specific target customers is so that you can develop a marketing mix that satisfies those customers' *specific* needs better than they are satisfied by some other firm. For example, E*trade uses an Internet site (www.etrade.com) to target knowledgeable investors who want a convenient, low-cost way to buy and sell stocks online without a lot of advice (or pressure) from a salesperson.

When a firm carefully targets its marketing mix, it is less likely to face direct competitors. So superior customer value is achieved with the benefits provided by the whole marketing mix rather than just by relying on a lower price. Whole Foods Market (WFM) is a good example. Most grocery stores sell the same brands—so they compete on price and profits tend to be weak. In contrast, WFM makes attractive profits with a differentiated marketing mix that delights its target customers. WFM sees itself as a buying agent for its customers and not the selling agent for manufacturers—so it evaluates the ingredients, freshness, safety, taste, nutritive value, and appearance of all the products it carries. It hires people who love food. They don't just sell food—but rather help their customers appreciate the difference natural and organic products can make in the quality of their lives. Service is attentive, friendly, and offered with some flair, which helps make the store fun and inviting. Customers often socialize while they shop. And they know that when they check out, WFM expects them to provide their own reusable shopping bags to carry food home—since that's better for the environment than having millions of disposable WFM grocery bags end up in the trash. Not everyone wants the marketing mix that WFM offers; but its target customers love shopping there—and they spread the word to others.[4]

DEVELOPING MARKETING MIXES FOR TARGET MARKETS

There are many marketing mix decisions

There are many possible ways to satisfy the needs of target customers. A product might have many different features. Customer service levels before or after the sale can be adjusted. The package, brand name, and warranty can be changed. Various advertising media—newspapers, magazines, cable, the Internet—may be used. A company's own sales force or other sales specialists can be used. The price can be changed, discounts can be given, and so on. With so many possible variables, is there any way to help organize all these decisions and simplify the selection of marketing mixes? The answer is yes.

The "four Ps" make up a marketing mix

It is useful to reduce all the variables in the marketing mix to four basic ones:

Product.

Place.

Edition

Promotion.

Price.

It helps to think of the four major parts of a marketing mix as the "four Ps."

Customer is not part of the marketing mix

The customer is shown surrounded by the four Ps in Exhibit 2-4. Some students assume that the customer is part of the marketing mix—but this is not so. The customer should be the *target* of all marketing efforts. The customer is placed in the center of the diagram to show this. The C stands for some specific customers—the target market.

Exhibit 2-5 shows some of the strategy decision variables organized by the four Ps. These will be discussed in later chapters. For now, let's just describe each P briefly.

The Product area is concerned with developing the right "product" for the target market. This offering may involve a physical good, a service, or a blend of both. Keep in mind that Product is not limited to physical goods. For example, the Product of H & R Block is a completed tax form. The Product of a political party are the policies it works to achieve. The important thing to remember is that your good or service should satisfy some customers' needs.

Along with other Product-area decisions like branding, packaging, and warranties, we will talk about developing and managing new products, product quality, and whole product lines.

Place is concerned with all the decisions involved in getting the "right" product to the target market's Place. A product isn't much good to a customer if it isn't available when and where it's wanted.

A product reaches customers through a channel of distribution. A channel of distribution is any series of firms (or individuals) that participate in the flow of products from producer to final user or consumer.

Sometimes a channel of distribution is short and runs directly from a producer to a final user or consumer. This is common in business markets and in the marketing of

Exhibit 2-4
A Marketing Strategy—
Showing the Four Ps of
a Marketing Mix

Product—the good or
service for the target's
needs

Place—reaching the
target

Exhibit 2-5
Strategy Decision Areas
Organized by the
Four Ps

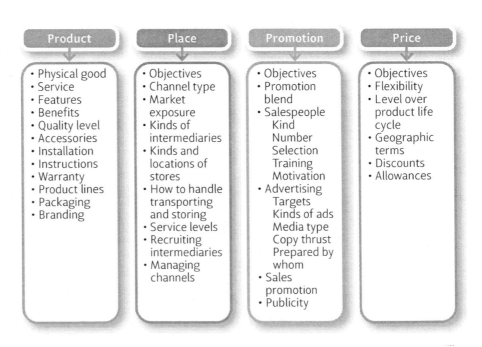

Product	Place	Promotion	Price
• Physical good	• Objectives	• Objectives	• Objectives
• Service	• Channel type	• Promotion	• Flexibility
• Features	• Market	blend	• Level over
• Benefits	exposure	• Salespeople	product life
• Quality level	• Kinds of	Kind	cycle
• Accessories	intermediaries	Number	• Geographic
• Installation	• Kinds and	Selection	terms
• Instructions	locations of	Training	• Discounts
• Warranty	stores	Motivation	• Allowances
• Product lines	• How to handle	• Advertising	
• Packaging	transporting	Targets	
• Branding	and storing	Kinds of ads	
	• Service levels	Media type	
	• Recruiting	Copy thrust	
	intermediaries	Prepared by	
	• Managing	whom	
	channels	• Sales	
		promotion	
		• Publicity	

A firm's product may involve a physical good or a service or a combination of both. British Airways provides a service, but the quality of its equipment, including the special sleeper seats on its planes, help the firm do a superior job in meeting the needs of international travelers.

services. For example, Geico sells its insurance directly to final consumers. However, as shown in Exhibit 2-6, channels are often more complex—as when Nestlé's food products are handled by wholesalers and retailers before reaching consumers. When a marketing manager has several different target markets, several different channels of distribution may be needed.

We will also see how physical distribution service levels and decisions concerning logistics (transporting, storing, and handling products) relate to the other Place decisions and the rest of the marketing mix.

Promotion—telling and selling the customer

The third P—Promotion—is concerned with telling the target market or others in the channel of distribution about the "right" product. Sometimes promotion is focused on acquiring new customers, and sometimes it's focused on retaining current customers. Promotion includes personal selling, mass selling, and sales promotion. It is the marketing manager's job to blend these methods of communication.

Personal selling involves direct spoken communication between sellers and potential customers. Personal selling may happen face-to-face, over the telephone or even via a videoconference over the Internet. Sometimes personal attention is required *after the sale*. Customer service—a personal communication between a seller and a

Exhibit 2-6   Four Examples of Basic Channels of Distribution for Consumer Products

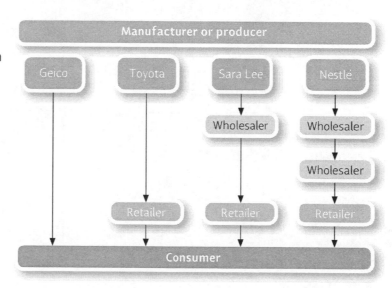

Edition

customer who wants the seller to resolve a problem with a purchase—is often a key to building repeat business. Individual attention comes at a price; personal selling and customer service can be very expensive. Often this personal effort has to be blended with mass selling and sales promotion.

Mass selling is communicating with large numbers of customers at the same time. The main form of mass selling is advertising—any *paid* form of nonpersonal presentation of ideas, goods, or services by an identified sponsor. Publicity—any *unpaid* form of nonpersonal presentation of ideas, goods, or services—is another important form of mass selling. Mass selling may involve a wide variety of media, ranging from newspapers and billboards to the Internet.

Sales promotion refers to those promotion activities—other than advertising, publicity, and personal selling—that stimulate interest, trial, or purchase by final customers or others in the channel. This can involve use of coupons, point-of-purchase materials, samples, signs, contests, events, catalogs, novelties, and circulars.

Price—making it right

In addition to developing the right Product, Place, and Promotion, marketing managers must also decide the right Price. Price setting must consider the kind of competition in the target market and the cost of the whole marketing mix. A manager must also try to estimate customer reaction to possible prices. Besides this, the manager must know current practices as to markups, discounts, and other terms of sale. And if customers won't accept the Price, all of the planning effort is wasted.

Each of the four Ps contributes to the whole

All four Ps are needed in a marketing mix. In fact, they should all be tied together. But is any one more important than the others? Generally speaking, the answer is no—all contribute to one whole. When a marketing mix is being developed, all (final) decisions about the Ps should be made at the same time. That's why the four Ps are arranged around the customer (C) in a circle—to show that they all are equally important.

Let's sum up our discussion of marketing mix planning thus far. We develop a *Product* to satisfy the target customers. We find a way to reach our target customers' *Place*. We use *Promotion* to tell the target customers (and others in the channel) about the product that has been designed for them. And we set *a Price* after estimating expected customer reaction to the total offering and the costs of getting it to them.

Toddler University's marketing strategy was successful because it developed a distinctive marketing mix that was precisely relevant to the needs of its target market.

Lifetime Value of Customers Can Be Very High—or Very Low

Investors lost millions when stock market values of dot-com firms collapsed after an initial, frenzied run up. But why did values get so high in the first place, especially when most dot-coms were not yet profitable? The stock went up because many investors expected that the firms would earn profits in the future as more consumers went online and the early dot-coms accumulated customers. These hopes were fueled by dot-coms that made optimistic predictions about the lifetime value of the customers they were acquiring. The lifetime value of the customer concept is not new. For decades General Motors has known that a consumer who buys a GM car and is satisfied is likely to buy another one the next time. If that happens again and again, over a lifetime the happy customer could spend $250,000 or more on GM cars. Of course, this only works if the firm's marketing mix attracts the target customers and the relationship keeps them satisfied before, during, and after every purchase. If you don't satisfy and retain customers, they don't have high lifetime value and don't generate sales. Of course, sales revenue alone does not guarantee profits. For example, a firm can't give away products—or spend so much on promotion to acquire new customers (or keep the ones it has)—that the future revenue will never be able to offset the costs. Unfortunately, that is what happened with many of the dot-coms. They saw how the financial arithmetic might work—*assuming* that new customers kept buying and costs came under control. But without a sensible marketing strategy, that assumption was not realistic.[5]

Strategy jobs must be done together

It is important to stress—it cannot be overemphasized—that selecting a target market *and* developing a marketing mix are interrelated. Both parts of a marketing strategy must be decided together. It is *strategies* that must be evaluated against the company's objectives—not alternative target markets or alternative marketing mixes.

Understanding target markets leads to good strategies

The needs of a target market often virtually determine the nature of an appropriate marketing mix. So marketers must analyze their potential target markets with great care. This book will explore ways of identifying attractive market opportunities and developing appropriate strategies.

These ideas can be seen more clearly with a classic example from the children's fashion market.

Market-oriented strategy planning at Toddler University

The case of Jeff Silverman and Toddler University (TU), Inc., a shoe company he started, illustrates the strategy planning process. During high school and college, Silverman worked as a salesperson at local shoe stores. He also gained valuable experience during a year working for Nike. From these jobs he learned a lot about customers' needs and interests. He also realized that some parents were not satisfied when it came to finding shoes for their preschool children.

Silverman thought that there was a large, but hard to describe, mass market for general-purpose baby shoes—perhaps 60 or 70 percent of the potential for all kinds of baby shoes. Silverman did not focus on this market because it didn't make sense for his small company to compete head on with many other firms where he had no particular advantage. However, he identified four other markets that were quite different. In the following description of these markets, note that useful marketing mixes come to mind immediately.

The *Traditionalists* seemed to be satisfied with a well-manufactured shoe that was available from "quality" stores where they could seek help in selecting the right size and fit. They didn't mind if the design was old-fashioned and didn't change. They wanted a well-known brand that had a reputation for quality, even if it was a bit more expensive.

Many of the *Economy Oriented* parents were in the lower income group. They wanted a basic shoe at a low price. They saw baby shoes as all pretty much the same—so a "name" brand didn't have much appeal. They were willing to shop around to see what was on sale at local discount, department, or shoe stores.

The *Fashion Conscious* were interested in dressing up baby in shoes that looked like smaller versions of the latest styles that they bought for themselves. Fit was important, but beyond that a colorful design is what got their attention. They were more likely to look for baby-size shoes at the shop where they bought their own athletic shoes.

The *Attentive Parents* wanted shoes that met a variety of needs. They wanted shoes to be fun and fashionable and functional. They didn't want just a good fit but also design and materials that were really right for baby play and learning to walk. These well-informed, upscale shoppers were likely to buy from a store that specialized in baby items. They were willing to pay a premium price if they found the right product.

Silverman thought that Stride Rite and Buster Brown were meeting the needs of the Traditionalists quite well. The Economy Oriented and Fashion Conscious customers were satisfied with shoes from a variety of other companies, including Nike. But Silverman saw a way to get a toe up on the competition by targeting the Attentive Parents with a marketing mix that combined, in his words, "fit and function with fun and fashion." He developed a detailed marketing plan that attracted financial backers, and at age 24 his company came to life.

TU didn't have its own production facilities, so Silverman contracted with a producer in Taiwan to make shoes with his brand name and to his specs. And his specs were different—they improved the product for his target market. Unlike most rigid high-topped infant shoes, he designed softer shoes with more comfortable rubber soles. The shoes lasted longer because they are stitched rather than glued. An extra-wide opening made fitting easier on squirming feet. He also patented a special insert so parents could adjust the width. This change also helped win support from retailers. Since there are 11 sizes of children's shoes—and five widths—retailers usually need to stock 55 pairs of each model. TU's adjustable width reduced this stocking problem and made it more profitable for retailers to sell the line. It also made it possible for TU to resupply soldout inventory faster than competitors. Silverman's Product and Place decisions worked together well to provide customer value and also to give him a competitive advantage.

For promotion, Silverman developed print ads with close-up photos of babies wearing his shoes and informative details about their special benefits. Creative packaging also helped promote the shoe and attract customers in the store. For example, he put one athletic-style shoe in a box that looked like a gray gym locker. Silverman also provided the stores with "shoe rides"—electric-powered rocking replicas of its shoes. The rides not only attracted kids to the shoe department, but since they were coin-operated, they paid for themselves in a year.

TU priced most of its shoes at $35 to $40 a pair. This is a premium price, but with today's smaller families, the Attentive Parents are willing to spend more on each child.

In just four years, TU's sales jumped from $100,000 to over $40 million. To keep growth going, Silverman expanded distribution to reach new markets in Europe. To take advantage of TU's relationship with its satisfied target customers, he also added shoes for older kids to the Toddler University product assortment. Then Silverman made his biggest sale of all: He sold his company to Genesco, one of the biggest firms in the footwear business.[6]

Internet EXERCISE

Jeffrey Silverman, the founder of Toddler University, recently started Preschoolians, which specializes in shoes for preschool kids. Go to the Preschoolians website (www.preschoolians.com) and review the site to learn about the company. Concisely describe its strategy.

THE MARKETING PLAN IS A GUIDE TO IMPLEMENTATION AND CONTROL

Marketing plan fills out marketing strategy

As the Toddler University case illustrates, a marketing strategy sets a target market and a marketing mix. It is a big picture of what a firm will do in some market. A marketing plan goes farther. A marketing plan is a written statement of a marketing strategy *and* the time-related details for carrying out the strategy. It should spell out the following in detail: (1) what marketing mix will be offered, to whom (that is, the target market), and for how long; (2) what company resources (shown as costs) will be needed at what rate (month by month perhaps); and (3) what results are expected (sales and profits perhaps monthly or quarterly, customer satisfaction levels, and the like). The plan should also include some control procedures—so that whoever is to carry out the plan will know if things are going wrong. This might be something as simple as comparing actual sales against expected sales—with a warning flag to be raised whenever total sales fall below a certain level.

The website for this text includes a feature called "Marketing Plan Coach." At the end of each chapter, there is a Marketing Plan Coach exercise that introduces you to aspects of a marketing plan that are related to the topics in that chapter. This gives you a step-by-step way to develop your plan-building skills as you progress through the text. In Chapter 21, we will review all of the elements in a marketing plan. At that point, you will have learned about all of the major strategy decision areas (Exhibit 2-5) and how to blend them into an innovative strategy.

Implementation puts plans into operation

After a marketing plan is developed, a marketing manager knows *what* needs to be done. Then the manager is concerned with implementation—putting marketing plans into operation. Strategies work out as planned only when they are effectively implemented. Many operational decisions—short-run decisions to help implement strategies—may be needed.

Managers should make operational decisions within the guidelines set down during strategy planning. They develop product policies, place policies, and so on as part of strategy planning. Then operational decisions within these policies probably will be necessary—while carrying out the basic strategy. Note, however, that as long as these operational decisions stay within the policy guidelines, managers are making no change in the basic strategy. If the controls show that operational decisions are not

Campbell's has developed different soups (and related marketing mixes) that are targeted to the specific needs of different target markets. The marketing plan for each type of soup fits into Campbell's overall marketing program.

producing the desired results, however, the managers may have to reevaluate the whole strategy—rather than just working harder at implementing it.

It's easier to see the difference between strategy decisions and operational decisions if we illustrate these ideas using our Toddler University example. Possible four Ps or basic strategy policies are shown in the left-hand column in Exhibit 2-7, and examples of operational decisions are shown in the right-hand column.

It should be clear that some operational decisions are made regularly—even daily—and such decisions should not be confused with planning strategy. Certainly, a great deal of effort can be involved in these operational decisions. They might take a good part of the sales or advertising manager's time. But they are not the strategy decisions that will be our primary concern.

Our focus in this text is on developing marketing strategies. But eventually marketing managers must control the marketing plans that they develop and implement.[7]

Control is analyzing and correcting what you've done

The control job provides the feedback that leads managers to modify their marketing strategies. To maintain control, a marketing manager uses a number of tools—like computer sales analysis, marketing research surveys, and accounting analysis of expenses and profits. Chapter 19 considers the important topic of controlling marketing plans and programs.

In addition, as we talk about each of the marketing decision areas, we will discuss some of the control problems. This will help you understand how control keeps the firm on course—or shows the need to plan a new course.

All marketing jobs require planning and control

At first, it might appear that only high-level management or large companies need be concerned with planning and control. This is not true. Every organization needs planning—and without control it's impossible to know if the plans are working.

Several plans make a whole marketing program

Most companies implement more than one marketing strategy—and related marketing plan—at the same time. Procter & Gamble targets users of laundry detergent with at least three different strategies. Some consumers want Tide's superior cleaning capabilities; others prefer the color protection of Cheer or the pleasant scents of Gain. Each detergent has a different formulation and a different approach for letting its target market know about its benefits. Yet P&G must implement each of these

Exhibit 2-7 Relation of Strategy Policies to Operational Decisions for Baby Shoe Company

Marketing Mix Decision Area	Strategy Policies	Likely Operational Decisions
■ Product	Carry as limited a line of colors, styles, and sizes as will satisfy the target market.	Add, change, or drop colors, styles, and/or sizes as customer tastes dictate.
■ Place	Distribute through selected "baby-products" retailers that will carry the full line and provide good in-store sales support and promotion.	In market areas where sales potential is not achieved, add new retail outlets and/or drop retailers whose performance is poor.
■ Promotion	Promote the benefits and value of the special design and how it meets customer needs.	When a retailer hires a new salesperson, send current training package with details on product line; increase use of local newspaper print ads during peak demand periods (before holidays, etc.).
■ Price	Maintain a "premium" price, but encourage retailers to make large-volume orders by offering discounts on quantity purchases.	Offer short-term introductory price "deals" to retailers when a new style is first introduced.

Exhibit 2-8   Elements of a Firm's Marketing Program

marketing strategies at the same time—along with strategies for Bounty, Olay, Charmin, and many other brands.

A marketing program blends all of the firm's marketing plans into one "big" plan. See Exhibit 2-8. This program, then, is the responsibility of the whole company. Typically, the whole *marketing program* is an integrated part of the whole-company strategic plan we discussed earlier.

THE MARKETING PROGRAM SHOULD BUILD CUSTOMER EQUITY

Expected profits depend on customer equity

We've highlighted the benefit for target customers when the firm does effective strategy planning and offers them superior customer value. Now it's time to expand this thinking and consider how the marketing program should also benefit the firm—by increasing customer equity. Customer equity is the expected earnings stream (profitability) of a firm's current and prospective customers over some period of time. Top management expects marketing strategy planners to help identify *opportunities that will lead to an increase in the firm's customer equity*. Let's consider the logic for and implications of this important idea.

Owners expect financial returns

A firm may be owned by management or by stockholders and other types of investors. The owners are better off the greater the earnings (profit) from the money they invest in the firm. So, the financial value of a firm—for example, the value of its stock or what the firm would be worth if it were sold—is based mainly on the earnings (profit) that can be expected from its current and future operations. Top executives are ultimately responsible to the owners for *increasing* the financial value of a firm. In turn, top executives expect marketing managers to develop strategies that consider current and future profitability.

Profit growth comes from customers

Profit is the difference between the firm's revenues (total dollar sales) and the total costs it runs up to make those sales. Customers are key; they are the source of the revenue. The revenue comes from the prices they are willing to pay for the quantity of purchases they make. There are also costs associated with attracting and serving customers. If those costs are too great, even high levels of revenue won't be profitable.

Obviously, a marketing manager doesn't control all of a firm's costs; for example, General Motors faces huge pension costs for retired workers regardless of its current marketing strategies. Even so, the marketing manager selects opportunities and creates marketing strategies—and should make choices where the revenues from target customers are greater than the costs of acquiring those customers, retaining their business, and (hopefully) increasing it. In other words, the best way to increase customer equity is to find cost-effective ways to increase earnings from current customers while bringing profitable new customers into the fold.

To make this idea more concrete, let's look at what happens to customer equity at a new bank that has just gone into business. The bank's initial strategy focuses on

Edition

acquiring *new* checking account customers. It offers personal attention and free checks—which are not available from the branches of big banks—and runs ads to tell potential customers about these benefits. Earnings increase as consumers sign on. At first, however, checking account earnings are a mere portion of what they could potentially be. That's because these customers will probably use more banking services if the bank meets their needs. For example, the bank might promote its helpful financial planning services to customers who have large checking account balances. Yet earnings, and customer equity, might grow even faster if the bank creates a strategy to attract *other* profitable customers. For example, it might encourage loan applications from owners of local businesses. Then, earnings from both consumers and business owners would contribute to growth and customer equity.

The parts of the marketing program must work as a whole

In Chapter 1 we introduced the idea that firms acquire new customers and retain the ones that they have by offering superior customer value. The customer equity idea shows how this translates to increased earnings over time—and why it determines the value of the firm and the return on investment it produces for the owners. So, a marketing manager needs to carefully consider what strategies will work well together—to produce an overall marketing program that increases customer equity—when seeking new opportunities.[8]

Planning for each strategy requires care

You can see that the success of the whole marketing program depends on the care that goes into planning individual strategies and how they will work together. Thus, in this text we will emphasize planning one marketing strategy at a time, rather than planning—or implementing—a whole marketing program. This is practical because it is important to plan each strategy carefully. Too many marketing managers fall into sloppy thinking. They try to develop too many strategies all at once—and don't develop any very carefully. However, when new strategies are evaluated, it makes sense to see how well they fit with the existing marketing program. So, throughout the book we'll discuss issues related to this fit as we cover the specific strategy decisions areas. In addition, in Chapter 20 we'll go into more detail on the relationship of financial issues and marketing strategy planning. Then, in Chapter 21 we'll summarize ideas about merging marketing plans into an overall marketing program.

Sony's high quality new products should help to increase its customer equity. For example, many customers who were pleased with their traditional Sony TVs are now trading up to one of the new Bravia large-screen, high definition LCD models. Similarly, many customers are attracted to the vivid video of Sony's Blu-ray disc players and Sony movies released on that media.

A marketing researcher conducts a study that reveals that a competing firm's brand-new marketing strategy is off to a very strong start in attracting new customers. He thinks that it will ultimately be so successful that it will increase the price of the competing firm's stock, so he decides to buy the stock before that happens. However, a friend suggests that the trade might not be ethical and perhaps could even be considered illegal insider trading. Does it seem unethical to you? Should it be illegal? Explain your thinking.

THE IMPORTANCE OF MARKETING STRATEGY PLANNING

We emphasize the planning part of the marketing manager's job for a good reason. The "onetime" strategy decisions—the decisions that decide what business the company is in and the strategies it will follow—usually determine success, or failure. An extremely good plan might be carried out badly and still be profitable, while a poor but well-implemented plan can lose money. The case history that follows shows the importance of planning and why we emphasize marketing strategy planning throughout this text.

Time for new strategies in the watch industry

The conventional watchmakers—both domestic and foreign—had always aimed at customers who thought of watches as high-priced, high-quality symbols to mark special events, like graduations or retirement. Advertising was concentrated around Christmas and graduation time and stressed a watch's symbolic appeal. Expensive jewelry stores were the main retail outlets.

This commonly accepted strategy of the major watch companies ignored people in the target market that just wanted to tell the time and were interested in a reliable, low-priced watch. So the U.S. Time Company developed a successful strategy around its Timex watches and became the world's largest watch company. Timex completely upset the watch industry—both foreign and domestic—not only by offering a good product (with a one-year repair or replace guarantee) at a lower price, but also by using new, lower-cost channels of distribution. Its watches were widely available in drugstores, discount houses, and nearly any other retail stores that would carry them.

Marketing managers at Timex soon faced a new challenge. Texas Instruments, a new competitor in the watch market, took the industry by storm with its low-cost but very accurate electronic watches—using the same channels Timex had originally developed. But other firms quickly developed a watch that used a more stylish liquid crystal display for the digital readout. Texas Instruments could not change quickly enough to keep up, and the other companies took away its customers. The

Timex has revised its strategy over the years and found new ways to meet consumer needs. Now it offers a watch in its Ironman line that makes it possible for runners and others who are music fans to wirelessly control their iPods.

Edition

competition became so intense that Texas Instruments stopped marketing watches altogether.

While Timex and others were focusing on lower-priced watches, Japan's Seiko captured a commanding share of the high-priced gift market for its stylish and accurate quartz watches by obtaining strong distribution. All of this forced many traditional watchmakers—like some of the once-famous Swiss brands—to close their factories.

Then Switzerland's Swatch launched its colorful, affordable plastic watches and changed what consumers see when they look at their watches. Swatch promoted its watches as fashion accessories and set them apart from those of other firms, whose ads squabbled about whose watches were most accurate and dependable. Swatch was also able to attract new retailers by focusing its distribution on upscale fashion and department stores. The total size of the watch market increased because many consumers bought several watches to match different fashions.

The economic downturn in the early 1990s brought more changes. Consumers were more cost conscious and less interested in expensive watches like those made by Rolex that were the "in" status symbol a few years earlier. The reemergence of value-seeking customers prompted Timex to return to its famous advertising tagline of the 1960s: "It takes a licking and keeps on ticking." Its position as the inexpensive-but-durable choice helped it strengthen its distribution and gave it a leg up in getting shelf space for new products, such as its Indiglo line of watches.

By the turn of the century, the total market for watches was growing at only about 5 percent a year. To spark higher sales of its lines, Timex pushed to introduce more watches that combine time-telling and other needs. For example, Timex watches include heart-rate monitors, GPS systems to compute a runner's distance and speed, personal digital assistant functions (including data links to a computer), and Internet messenger capabilities so a watch can receive short text messages, like an alert from the wearer's stockbroker that it's time to sell. Of course, all of the new features can make a watch more complicated, so Timex developed technologies to make its watches easier to use. For example, watches with Timex's iControl can wirelessly sync with an iPod and control it. Innovations like these appeal to many customers. Yet, Timex now faces a different kind of competition. Many people carry gadgets—like smart phones—that perform the same functions and also display the time. The constant changes in consumers and competitors mean that marketing strategies at Timex must be updated and revised often if it is to continue to succeed in the market.[9]

Internet EXERCISE

WatchReport.com provides information about new offerings from different companies that sell watches. Go to the site (www.watchreport.com) and identify a watch from one of Timex's competitors that you think offers attractive new features or benefits. Do you think that Timex should offer a similar watch? Why or why not?

CREATIVE STRATEGY PLANNING NEEDED FOR SURVIVAL

Dramatic shifts in strategy—like those described earlier—may surprise conventional, production-oriented managers. But such changes should be expected. Managers who embrace the marketing concept realize that they cannot just define their line of business in terms of the products they currently produce or sell. Rather, they have to think about the basic consumer needs they serve, how those needs may change in the future, and how they can improve the value they offer to customers. If they are too nearsighted, they may fail to see what's coming until too late.

Focus on "best practices" for improved results

The case studies and concepts in this chapter highlight effective marketing thinking. Throughout the text, we will continue with this thrust—focusing on marketing frameworks and concepts that produce good results. Some of these are new and innovative, and others are well established. What they have in common is that they all work well.

Sometimes we will warn you about marketing errors—so you can avoid them. But we won't just give you laundry lists of different approaches and then leave it to you to guess what might work. Rather, our focus will be on "best-practices" marketing.

Exhibit 2-9   Distribution of Different Firms Based on Their Marketing Performance

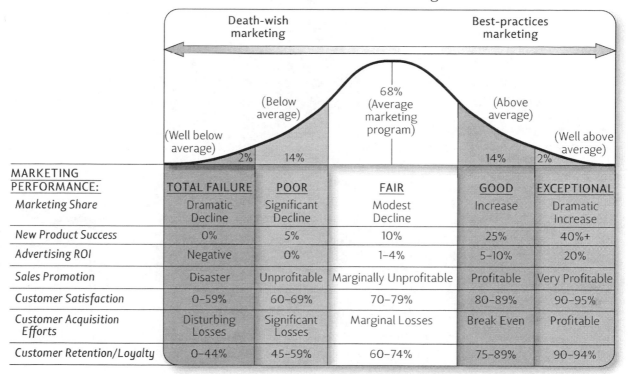

There is an important reason for this approach. In too many firms, managers do a poor job planning and implementing marketing strategies and programs. And, as shown in Exhibit 2-9, this type of "death-wish" marketing is both costly and ineffective. In fact, you can see that even the average marketing program isn't producing great results—and that accounts for the majority of firms!

Exhibit 2-9 was developed by experts at Copernicus, one of the premier marketing research and consulting firms in the world. As these experts indicate in the chart, some managers are creating marketing programs that produce exceptional results for their companies. This book will help you do exactly that.

WHAT ARE ATTRACTIVE OPPORTUNITIES?

Effective marketing strategy planning matches opportunities to the firm's resources (what it can do) and its objectives (what top management wants to do). Successful strategies get their start when a creative manager spots an attractive market opportunity. Yet an opportunity that is attractive for one firm may not be attractive for another. Attractive opportunities for a particular firm are those that the firm has some chance of doing something about—given its resources and objectives.

Breakthrough opportunities are best

Throughout this book, we will emphasize finding breakthrough opportunities—opportunities that help innovators develop hard-to-copy marketing strategies that will be very profitable for a long time. That's important because there are always imitators who want to "share" the innovator's profits—if they can. It's hard to continuously provide *superior* value to target customers if competitors can easily copy your marketing mix.

Edition

Attractive new opportunities are often fairly close to markets the firm already knows. Diet Coke is already famous for its great taste and low calories, but Diet Coke Plus adds vitamins and minerals. Similarly, Kleenex Moist Cloths are similar to Kleenex facial tissues but the big, strong cloth-like sheets are pre-moistened—and even better for sticky situations.

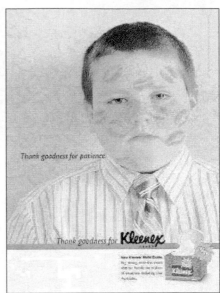

Competitive advantage is needed—at least

Even if a manager can't find a breakthrough opportunity, the firm should try to obtain a competitive advantage to increase its chances for profit or survival. **Competitive advantage** means that a firm has a marketing mix that the target market sees as better than a competitor's mix. A competitive advantage may result from efforts in different areas of the firm—cost cutting in production, innovative R&D, more effective purchasing of needed components, or financing for a new distribution facility. Similarly, a strong sales force, a well-known brand name, or good dealers may give it a competitive advantage in pursuing an opportunity. Whatever the source, an advantage only succeeds if it allows the firm to provide superior value and satisfy customers better than some competitor.[10]

Avoid hit-or-miss marketing with a logical process

You can see why a manager *should* seek attractive opportunities. But that doesn't mean that everyone does—or that everyone can turn an opportunity into a successful strategy. As Exhibit 2-9 shows, too many firms settle for the sort of death-wish marketing that doesn't satisfy customers or make a profit—to say nothing about achieving a breakthrough or providing superior value. It's all too easy for a well-intentioned manager to react in a piecemeal way to what appears to be an opportunity. Then by the time the problems are obvious, it's too late.

Developing a successful marketing strategy doesn't need to be a hit-or-miss proposition. And it won't be if you learn the marketing strategy planning process developed in this text. Exhibit 2-10 summarizes the marketing strategy planning process we'll be developing throughout the rest of the chapters.

MARKETING STRATEGY PLANNING PROCESS HIGHLIGHTS OPPORTUNITIES

We've emphasized that a marketing strategy requires decisions about the specific customers the firm will target and the marketing mix the firm will develop to appeal to that target market. We can organize the many marketing mix decisions (review Exhibit 2-5) in terms of the four Ps—Product, Place, Promotion, and Price. Thus, the "final" strategy decisions are represented by the target market surrounded by the four Ps. However, the idea isn't just to come up with *some* strategy. After all, there are

Exhibit 2-10
Overview of Marketing
Strategy Planning
Process

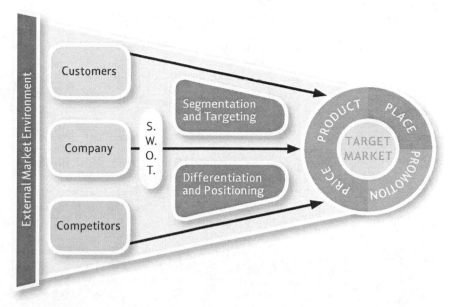

Note: Marketing manager narrows down from screening broad market opportunities to develop a focused marketing strategy.

hundreds or even thousands of combinations of marketing mix decisions and target markets (i.e., strategies) that a firm might try. Rather, the challenge is to zero in on the best strategy.

Process narrows down from broad opportunities to specific strategy

As Exhibit 2-10 suggests, it is useful to think of the marketing strategy planning process as a narrowing-down process. Later in this chapter and in Chapters 3 and 4 we will go into more detail about strategy decisions relevant to each of the terms in this figure. Then, throughout the rest of the book, we will present a variety of concepts and "how to" frameworks that will help you improve the way you make these strategy decisions. As a preview of what's coming, let's briefly overview the general logic of the process depicted in Exhibit 2-10.

The process starts with a broad look at a market—paying special attention to customer needs, the firm's objectives and resources, and competitors. This helps to identify new and unique opportunities that might be overlooked if the focus is narrowed too quickly.

Screening criteria make it clear why you select a strategy

There are usually more different opportunities—and strategy possibilities—than a firm can pursue. Each one has its own advantages and disadvantages. Trends in the external market environment may make a potential opportunity more or less attractive. These complications can make it difficult to zero in on the best target market and marketing mix. However, developing a set of specific qualitative and quantitative screening criteria can help a manager define what business and markets the firm wants to compete in. We will cover screening criteria in more detail in Chapter 3. For now, you should realize that the criteria you select in a specific situation grow out of an analysis of the company's objectives and resources.

Segmentation helps pinpoint the target

In the early stages of a search for opportunities we're looking for customers with needs that are not being satisfied as well as they might be. Of course, potential customers are not all alike. They don't all have the same needs—nor do they always want to meet needs in the same way. Part of the reason is that there are different possible types of customers with many different characteristics. In spite of the many possible differences, there often are subgroups (segments) of consumers who are similar and could be satisfied with the same marketing mix. Thus, we try to identify and

Edition

understand these different subgroups—with market segmentation. We will explain approaches for segmenting markets later in Chapter 4. Then, in Chapters 5 to 7, we delve into the many interesting aspects of customer behavior. For now, however, you should know that really understanding customers is at the heart of using market segmentation to narrow down to a specific target market. In other words, segmentation helps a manager decide to serve some segment(s)—subgroup(s) of customers—and not others.

Narrow down to a superior marketing mix

A marketing mix won't get a competitive advantage if it *just* meets needs in the same way as some other firm. So in evaluating possible strategies, the marketing manager should think about whether there is a way to differentiate the marketing mix. Differentiation means that the marketing mix is distinct from and better than what is available from a competitor. Sometimes the difference is based mainly on one important element of the marketing mix—say, an improved product or faster delivery. However, differentiation often requires that the firm fine-tune all of the elements of its marketing mix to the specific needs of a distinctive target market. Differentiation is also more obvious to target customers when there is a consistent theme integrated across the four Ps decision areas. That emphasizes the difference so target customers will think of the firm as being in a unique position to meet their needs. For example, in Norway many auto buyers are particularly concerned about safety in the snow. So Audi offers a permanent four-wheel-drive system, called quattro, that helps the car to hold the road. Audi ads emphasize this differentiation. Rather than show the car, however, the ads feature things that are very sticky (like bubblegum!) and the only text is the headline "sticks like quattro" and the Audi brand name. Of course, handling is not Audi's only strength, but it is an important one in helping to position Audi as better than competing brands with this target market.

In Chapter 4, we'll introduce concepts relevant to this sort of positioning. Then, in Chapters 9 to 18, we'll cover the many ways in which the four Ps of the marketing mix can be differentiated. For now you can see that the thrust is to narrow down from all possible marketing mixes to one that is differentiated to meet target customers' needs particularly well. Of course, finding the best differentiation requires that we understand competitors as well as customers.

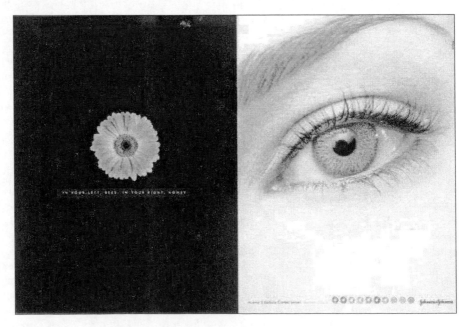

The natural colors available with Acuvue 2 Colours contact lenses help Johnson & Johnson differentiate its marketing mix as distinct from and better than what is available from its competitors.

S.W.O.T. analysis highlights advantages and disadvantages

A useful aid for identifying relevant screening criteria and for zeroing in on a feasible strategy is S.W.O.T. analysis—which identifies and lists the firm's strengths and weaknesses and its opportunities and threats. The name S.W.O.T. is simply an abbreviation for the first letters of the words strengths, weaknesses, opportunities, and threats. A good S.W.O.T. analysis helps the manager focus on a strategy that takes advantage of the firm's strengths and opportunities while avoiding its weaknesses and threats to its success.

The marketing strategy developed by Amilya Antonetti illustrates the basic ideas behind a S.W.O.T. analysis. Her son was allergic to the chemicals in standard detergents—and her research showed that many other children had the same problem. So she started SoapWorks and developed a line of hypoallergenic cleaning products to pursue this opportunity. Unlike the big firms, she didn't have relations with grocery chains or money for national TV ads. To get around these weaknesses, she used inexpensive radio ads in local markets and touted SoapWorks as a company created for moms by a mom who cared about kids. She had a credible claim that the big corporations couldn't make. Her ads also helped her get shelf space because they urged other mothers to ask for SoapWorks products and to tell friends about stores that carried them. This wasn't the fastest possible way to introduce a new product line, but her cash-strapped strategy played to her unique strengths with her specific target market.[11]

Exhibit 2-10 focuses on planning each strategy carefully. Of course, this same approach works well when several strategies are to be planned. Then, having an organized evaluation process is even more important. It forces everyone involved to think through how the various strategies fit together as part of an overall marketing program that increases customer equity.[12]

TYPES OF OPPORTUNITIES TO PURSUE

Many opportunities seem "obvious" only after someone else identifies them. So, early in the marketing strategy planning process it's useful for marketers to have a framework for thinking about the broad kinds of opportunities they may find. Exhibit 2-11 shows four broad possibilities: market penetration, market development, product development, and diversification. We will look at these separately to clarify the ideas. However, some firms pursue more than one type of opportunity at the same time.

Market penetration

Market penetration means trying to increase sales of a firm's present products in its present markets—probably through a more aggressive marketing mix. The firm may try to strengthen its relationship with customers to increase their rate of use or repeat purchases, or try to attract competitors' customers or current nonusers. Coleman got a 50 percent increase in sales of its outdoor equipment, like camping lanterns and coolers, by reaching its target market with special promotional displays at outdoor events like concerts, fishing tournaments, and NASCAR races. For example, about 250,000 auto racing fans camp on-site at NASCAR races each year—so a display at the campground is an effective way to reach customers when they have leisure time to browse through product displays and demos.[13]

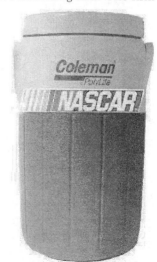

New promotion appeals alone may not be effective. A firm may need to make it easier for customers to place repeat orders on the Internet. Or it may need to add more stores in present areas for greater convenience. Short-term price cuts or coupon offers may help.

Edition

Exhibit 2-11
Four Basic Types of
Opportunities

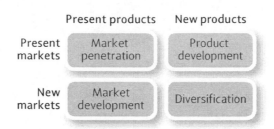

Many firms try to increase market penetration by developing closer relationships with customers so that they will be loyal. Frequent buyer clubs use this approach. Similarly, firms often analyze customer databases to identify "cross-selling" opportunities. For example, when a customer goes online to register Adobe's Acrobat Reader, the Web page promotes other related products, including its popular Photoshop software.

Market development

Market development means trying to increase sales by selling present products in new markets. This may involve searching for new uses for a product. E-Z-Go, a producer of golf carts, has done this. Its carts are now a quiet way for workers to get around malls, airports, and big factories. The large units are popular as utility vehicles on farms, at outdoor sports events, and at resorts. E-Z-Go even fits carts with ice compartments and cash drawers so they can be used for mobile food services.

Firms may also try advertising in different media to reach new target customers. Or they may add channels of distribution or new stores in new areas, including overseas. For example, to reach new customers, Dunkin' Donuts now sells its popular coffee at grocery stores and not just at its own outlets.[14]

Product development

Product development means offering new or improved products for present markets. By knowing the present market's needs, a firm may see new ways to satisfy customers. For example, in 2003 Campbell's came out with a line of soups with 25 percent less sodium than its regular product. That may seem like a minor change, but by 2008 it resulted in $650 million in sales because it was important to Campbell's health-conscious consumers. Ski resorts have developed trails for hiking and biking to bring their winter ski customers back in the summer. Nike moved beyond shoes and sportswear to offer its athletic target market a running watch, digital audio player, and even a portable heart-rate monitor. And of course Intel boosts sales by developing newer and faster chips.[15]

Diversification

Diversification means moving into totally different lines of business—perhaps entirely unfamiliar products, markets, or even levels in the production-marketing system. Products and customers that are very different from a firm's current base may look attractive to the optimists—but these opportunities are usually hard to evaluate. That's why diversification usually involves the biggest risk. McDonald's, for example, opened two hotels in Switzerland. The plan was to serve families on the weekend, but business travelers were the target during the week. Business travelers are not the group that McDonald's usually serves, and an upscale hotel is also very different from a fast-food restaurant. This helps to explain why operation of the Golden Arch hotels was taken over by a hospitality management company after two years. On the other hand, diversification can be successful—especially when the new strategy fits well with the firm's resources and marketing program.[16]

Which opportunities come first?

Usually firms find attractive opportunities fairly close to markets they already know. Most firms think first of greater market penetration. They want to increase profits and grow customer equity where they already have experience and strengths.

The Heinz ad is a clever visual reminder of the fresh taste of the tomatoes in Heinz Ketchup. The primary purpose of this type of promotion is to increase market penetration, which means increasing sales of a firm's present products in its present markets. The Crocs ad focuses on colorful new types of footwear it has added to its line as part of its product development efforts.

On the other hand, many firms are proving that market development—including the move into new international markets—is another profitable way to take advantage of current strengths.

INTERNATIONAL OPPORTUNITIES SHOULD BE CONSIDERED

It's easy for a marketing manager to fall into the trap of ignoring international markets, especially when the firm's domestic market is prosperous. Yet there are good reasons to go to the trouble of looking elsewhere for opportunities.

The world is getting smaller

International trade is increasing all around the world, and trade barriers are coming down. In addition, advances in e-commerce, transportation, and communications are making it easier and cheaper to reach international customers. With a website and e-mail, even the smallest firm can provide international customers with a great deal of information—and easy ways to order—at very little expense.

Develop a competitive advantage at home and abroad

If customers in other countries are interested in the products a firm offers—or could offer—serving them may improve economies of scale. Lower costs (and prices) may give a firm a competitive advantage both in its home markets *and* abroad. Black and Decker, for example, uses electric motors in many of its tools and appliances. By selling overseas as well as in the United States, it gets economies of scale and the cost per motor is very low.

Marketing managers who are only interested in the "convenient" customers in their own backyards may be rudely surprised to find that an aggressive, low-cost foreign producer is willing to pursue those customers. The owner of Purafil, a small firm in Atlanta that makes air purification equipment, puts it this way: "If I'm not [selling to an oil refinery] in Saudi Arabia, somebody else is going to solve their problem, then come attack me on my home turf."[17]

Get an early start in a new market

A company facing tough competition, thin profit margins, and slow sales growth at home may get a fresh start in another country where demand for its product is just beginning to grow. A marketing manager may be able to transfer marketing

Lipton is pursuing new customers and growth in over 100 countries. For example, its multilingual website in Belgium explains how to make exotic cocktails from Ice Tea, and in Asia it encourages consumer trial with free samples.

know-how—or some other competitive advantage—the firm has already developed. Consider JLG, a Pennsylvania-based producer of equipment used to lift workers and tools at construction sites. Faced with tough competition, JLG's profits all but evaporated. By cutting costs, the company improved its domestic sales. But it got an even bigger boost from expanding overseas. In the first five years, its international sales were greater than what its total sales had been before. Then, when JLG added distribution in China, international sales grew to be half of its business. Now JLG continues to enjoy growth, in spite of the home construction downturn in the United States, because JLG sales in Europe benefit from new safety rules that require workers to be on an aerial platform if they're working up high.[18]

Find better trends in variables

Unfavorable trends in the marketing environment at home—or favorable trends in other countries—may make international marketing particularly attractive. For example, population growth in the United States has slowed and income is leveling off. In other places in the world, population and income are increasing rapidly. Many U.S. firms can no longer rely on the constant market growth that once drove increased domestic sales. Growth—and perhaps even survival—will come only by aiming at more distant customers. It doesn't make sense to casually assume that all of the best opportunities exist "at home."[19]

Weigh the risks of going abroad

Marketing managers should consider international opportunities, but risks are often higher in foreign markets. Many firms fail because they don't know the foreign country's culture. Learning foreign regulations can be difficult and costly. Political or social unrest make it difficult to operate in some countries. Venezuela is a striking example. Current Venezuelan leaders have threatened to nationalize some international businesses that have located there. Careful planning can help reduce some of these risks, but ultimately managers must assess both the risks and opportunities that exist in each international market.

CONCLUSION

This chapter introduces you to the basic decision areas involved in marketing strategy planning and explains the logic for the marketing strategy planning process summarized in Exhibit 2-10. In the remainder of this book we'll rely on this exhibit as a way to highlight the organization of the topics we are discussing.

In this chapter, you learned that the marketing manager must constantly study the market environment—seeking attractive opportunities and planning new strategies. A marketing strategy specifies a target market and the marketing mix the firm will offer to provide that target market with superior customer value. A marketing mix has four major decision areas: the four Ps—Product, Place, Promotion, and Price.

There are usually more potential opportunities than a firm can pursue, so possible target markets must be matched with marketing mixes the firm can offer. This is a narrowing-down process. The most attractive strategies—really, marketing plans and whole marketing programs—are chosen for implementation.

A marketing program that is implemented well should increase the firm's customer equity. Customer equity refers to the expected earnings from a firm's current or prospective customers. This is a forward-looking idea and reinforces the need not only to acquire customers but to satisfy them with superior customer value so that, in the future, earnings from them will grow because of repeat business.

Controls are needed to be sure that the plans are carried out successfully. If anything goes wrong along the way, continual feedback should cause the process to be started over again—with the marketing manager planning more attractive marketing strategies. Thus, the job of marketing management is one of continuous planning, implementing, and control. Strategies are not permanent; changes should be expected as market conditions change.

Firms need effective strategy planning to survive in our increasingly competitive markets. The challenge isn't just to come up with some strategy, but to zero in on the strategy that is best for the firm given its objectives and resources—and taking into consideration its strengths and weaknesses and the opportunities and threats that it faces. To improve your ability in this area, this chapter introduces a framework for marketing strategy planning. The rest of this text is organized to deepen your understanding of this framework and how to use it to develop profitable marketing mixes for clearly defined target markets. After several chapters on analyzing target markets, we will discuss each of the four Ps in greater detail.

While market-oriented strategy planning is helpful to marketers, it is also needed by financial managers, accountants, production and personnel people, and all other specialists. A market-oriented plan lets everybody in the firm know what ballpark they are playing in and what they are trying to accomplish.

We will use the term *marketing manager* for editorial convenience, but really, when we talk about marketing strategy planning, we are talking about the planning that a market-oriented manager should do when developing a firm's strategic plans. This kind of thinking should be done—or at least understood—by everyone in the organization. And this includes even the entry-level salesperson, production supervisor, retail buyer, or human resources counselor.

KEY TERMS

marketing management process, 32	customer service, 37	customer equity, 43
strategic (management) planning, 33	mass selling, 38	breakthrough opportunities, 47
marketing strategy, 33	advertising, 38	competitive advantage, 48
target market, 33	publicity, 38	differentiation, 50
marketing mix, 33	sales promotion, 38	S.W.O.T. analysis, 51
target marketing, 34	marketing plan, 41	market penetration, 51
mass marketing, 34	implementation, 41	market development, 52
channel of distribution, 36	operational decisions, 41	product development, 52
personal selling, 37	marketing program, 43	diversification, 52

QUESTIONS AND PROBLEMS

1. Distinguish clearly between a marketing strategy and a marketing mix. Use an example.
2. Distinguish clearly between mass marketing and target marketing. Use an example.
3. Why is the target customer placed in the center of the four Ps in the text diagram of a marketing strategy (Exhibit 2-4)? Explain, using a specific example from your own experience.
4. If a company sells its products only from a website, which is accessible over the Internet to customers from all over the world, does it still need to worry about having a specific target market? Explain your thinking.

Edition

5. Explain, in your own words, what each of the four Ps involves.

6. Evaluate the text's statement, "A marketing strategy sets the details of implementation."

7. Distinguish between strategy decisions and operational decisions, illustrating for a local retailer.

8. In your own words, explain what customer equity means and why it is important.

9. Distinguish between a strategy, a marketing plan, and a marketing program, illustrating for a local retailer.

10. Outline a marketing strategy for each of the following new products: (*a*) a radically new design for a toothbrush, (*b*) a new fishing reel, (*c*) a new wonder drug, and (*d*) a new industrial stapling machine.

11. Provide a specific illustration of why marketing strategy planning is important for all businesspeople, not just for those in the marketing department.

12. Exhibit 2-9 shows that only about three out of every four customers are, on average, satisfied by a firm's marketing programs. Give an example of a purchase you made where you were not satisfied and what the firm could have changed to satisfy you. If customer satisfaction is so important to firms, why don't they score better in this area?

13. Distinguish between an attractive opportunity and a breakthrough opportunity. Give an example.

14. Explain how new opportunities may be seen by defining a firm's markets more precisely. Illustrate for a situation where you feel there is an opportunity—namely, an unsatisfied market segment—even if it is not very large.

15. In your own words, explain why the book suggests that you should think of marketing strategy planning as a narrowing-down process.

16. Explain the major differences among the four basic types of growth opportunities discussed in the text and cite examples for two of these types of opportunities.

17. Explain why a firm may want to pursue a market penetration opportunity before pursuing one involving product development or diversification.

18. In your own words, explain several reasons why a marketing manager should consider international markets when evaluating possible opportunities.

19. Give an example of a foreign-made product (other than an automobile) that you personally have purchased. Give some reasons why you purchased that product. Do you think that there was a good opportunity for a domestic firm to get your business? Explain why or why not.

CREATING MARKETING PLANS

The Marketing Plan Coach software on the Student CD and the text website includes a sample marketing plan for Hillside Veterinary Clinic. Skim through the different sections of the marketing plan. Look more closely at the "Marketing Strategy" section.

a.   What is the target market for this marketing plan?

b.   What is the strategy Hillside Veterinary Clinic intends to use?

c.   What are your initial reactions to this strategy? Do you think it will be successful? Why or why not?

SUGGESTED CASES

3. MANU Soccer Academy
4. Trusty Technology Services
5. PolyTech Products

12. DrRay.com
29. Specialized Castings, Inc.

COMPUTER-AIDED PROBLEM

2. TARGET MARKETING

Marko, Inc.'s managers are comparing the profitability of a target marketing strategy with a mass marketing "strategy." The spreadsheet gives information about both approaches.

The mass marketing strategy is aiming at a much bigger market. But a smaller percent of the consumers in the market will actually buy this product—because not everyone needs or can afford it. Moreover, because this marketing mix is not tailored to specific needs, Marko will get a smaller share of the business from those who do buy than it would with a more targeted marketing mix.

Just trying to reach the mass market will take more promotion and require more retail outlets in more locations—so

promotion costs and distribution costs are higher than with the target marketing strategy. On the other hand, the cost of producing each unit is higher with the target marketing strategy—to build in a more satisfying set of features. But because the more targeted marketing mix is trying to satisfy the needs of a specific target market, those customers will be willing to pay a higher price.

In the spreadsheet, "quantity sold" (by the firm) is equal to the number of people in the market who will actually buy one each of the product—multiplied by the share of those purchases won by the firm's marketing mix. Thus, a change in the size of the market, the percent of people who purchase, or the share captured by the firm will affect quantity sold. And a change in quantity sold will affect total revenue, total cost, and profit.

a. On a piece of paper, show the calculations that prove that the spreadsheet "total profit" value for the target marketing strategy is correct. (Hint: Remember to multiply unit production cost and unit distribution cost by the quantity sold.) Which approach seems better—target marketing or mass marketing? Why?

b. If the target marketer could find a way to reduce distribution cost per unit by $.25, how much would profit increase?

c. If Marko, Inc., decided to use the target marketing strategy and better marketing mix decisions increased its share of purchases from 50 to 60 percent—without increasing costs—what would happen to total profit? What does this analysis suggest about the importance of marketing managers knowing enough about their target markets to be effective target marketers?

For additional questions related to this problem, see Exercise 2-4 in the *Learning Aid for Use with Basic Marketing*, 17th edition.

3

CHAPTER

Evaluating Opportunities in the Changing Marketing Environment

Bank of America (BofA) is one of the best known brands in banking, so it's no surprise that when NationsBank acquired BofA it adopted that name. What is more surprising is how a small southern bank—North Carolina National Bank before it was renamed NationsBank—grew so quickly that it was ultimately able to acquire BofA, Fleet Bank, and other giant competitors. In fact, the innovative marketing strategy planning that originally fueled growth at NationsBank continues to make the new Bank of America unique.

BofA has offices in over 30 countries and serves clients from 175. It provides banking services for corporations, manages trusts for the wealthy, and offers investment services. But what differentiates BofA is that it has grown primarily by becoming a "local bank" that serves large numbers of final consumers and small businesses in communities across the land. Its banking centers are in 6,100 locations, and it has the largest network of ATMs—nearly 19,000 of them. It was also a pioneer in e-commerce and now, serving 24 million active customers online, is the world's largest online banker.

The bank's customers benefit from this strategy. For the first time, consumers can count on easy access to their hometown bank virtually anywhere they live, work, play, and travel. BofA is right there—in person, online, or via telephone or ATM. Along with that convenience, BofA has raised the stakes for service quality in banking.

How did managers at NationsBank know which opportunities to pursue and turn into strategies? Part of the explanation is that they evaluated not only customer needs and competitive rivals, but also trends in the external market environment. Even though the market environment is constantly changing, they spotted new trends and took advantage of them. An obvious example of this is the way the bank responded to shifts in the technological environment. The bank quickly built capabilities in information technology because that helped its growing number of branches. Then that competitive strength catapulted the bank ahead when the Internet opened the door to online services. Moreover, using online banking to expand the retail customer base fit with the marketing program the bank had been pursuing for years.

Consider, for example, how changes in the competitive and legal environments have shaped the bank's strategies for acquiring new customers. Regulations once governed how banks could operate, interstate banking was restricted, and many states limited the number and location of branch offices. As regulations began to ease, banking became more competitive and more market-oriented. For example, in college towns the bank targeted students with special accounts to build relationships that would last when they moved to new locations after graduation.

By the time interstate banking was allowed, the firm already had experience managing many branches—and the financial resources to acquire other banks and their customers. Initially they screened opportunities to focus on banks in Sun Belt states where population and income growth was rapid, regulations were more favorable, and consumers were less satisfied with available banks. NationsBank's customer base grew quickly—and it held on to new customers by improving the value they received from their banking relationship.

Although NationsBank was very profitable and growing rapidly, it did not have the international reputation of banks like Citicorp that were based in big financial centers. That was a weakness during a period when economies were becoming more global. However, the merger with BofA helped to offset that weakness.

Because the bank operated in many regions across the United States, managers were less provincial than managers of many other banks. They quickly saw and responded to cultural shifts that were taking place. For example, BofA's banking centers in Texas and Florida served many Hispanic customers and the Atlanta bank had a large proportion of African American customers. As society became more multicultural, the bank recruited associates (employees) from diverse ethnic backgrounds and made BofA a welcoming place for them to work and bank. Now BofA is one of the best companies in America for minority workers. Similarly, it offers flexible hours and other progressive benefits to help ease the pressure on dual-career families. Having a loyal group of associates has helped build a team culture where everyone tries to win in the market by providing excellent and efficient service. Catherine Bessant, a global marketing executive, put it this way, "Our strong brand is a significant competitive advantage, and in building it everything matters. The substance of our people, culture, process, and presence uniquely sets us apart."

BofA has enjoyed great successes, but it's not immune to problems caused by negative changes in the external environment. The downturn in the economy and serious problems in the mortgage market in 2008, for example, led to huge losses for many financial service firms, including BofA. However, this difficult external environment may ultimately lead to long-term opportunities. That's because Countrywide Financial Corporation, a competing home-mortgage firm, almost went belly up, and top management at BofA decided to acquire what was left. That made BofA the largest mortgage lender in the United States. Trying to predict how quickly the economy and mortgage market will improve is risky. Yet a mortgage is the foundation for relationships with many banking customers. So BofA's acquisition may open the door to even greater long-run successes and increases in customer equity.[1]

THE MARKETING ENVIRONMENT

The marketing strategy planning process (see Exhibit 2-10) requires narrowing down to the best opportunities and developing a strategy that gives the firm a competitive advantage and provides target customers with superior customer value. All of the decisions in this narrowing-down process should take into consideration the important elements of the marketing environment and how they are shifting.

A large number of forces shapes the marketing environment. To help organize your thinking, it's useful to classify the various forces as falling into either (1) the direct market environment or (2) the external market environment. The direct environment includes customers, the company, and competitors. The external market environment is broader and includes four major areas:

1. Economic environment.
2. Technological environment.
3. Political and legal environment.
4. Cultural and social environment.

Managers can't alter the variables of the marketing environment. That's why it's useful to think of them as uncontrollable variables. On the other hand, a manager should carefully analyze the environmental variables when making decisions that can be controlled. For example, a manager can select a strategy that leads the firm into a market where competition is not yet strong or where trends in the external environment are likely to support market growth. In this chapter, we'll look at the key marketing

Exhibit 3-1   Marketing Strategy Planning, Competitors, Company, and External Market Environment

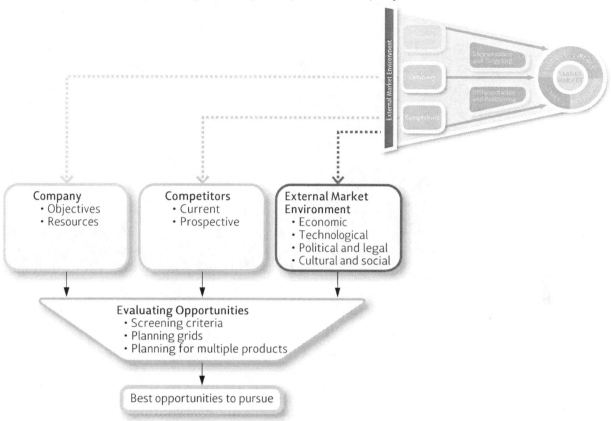

61

environment variables shown in Exhibit 3-1 in more detail. We'll see how they shape opportunities—limiting some possibilities but making others more attractive.

OBJECTIVES SHOULD SET FIRM'S COURSE

A company must decide where it's going, or it may fall into the trap expressed so well by the quotation: "Having lost sight of our objective, we redoubled our efforts." Company objectives should shape the direction and operation of the whole business.

It is difficult to set objectives that really guide the present and future development of a company. The marketing manager should be heard when the company is setting objectives. But setting whole-company objectives—within resource limits—is ultimately the responsibility of top management. Top management must look at the whole business, relate its present objectives and resources to the external environment, and then decide what the firm wants to accomplish in the future.

Three basic objectives provide guidelines

The following three objectives provide a useful starting point for setting a firm's objectives. They should be sought *together* because in the long run a failure in even one of the three areas can lead to total failure of the business. A business should

1. Engage in specific activities that will perform a socially and economically useful function.
2. Develop an organization to carry on the business and implement its strategies.
3. Earn enough profit to survive.[2]

Edition

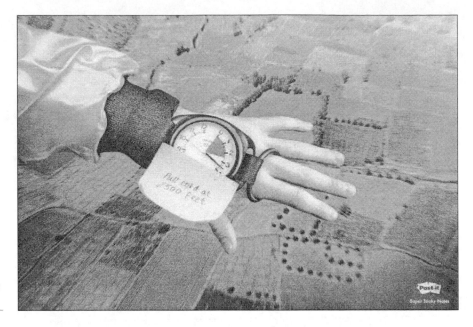

3M has introduced a super sticky version of its popular Post-It notes to stay ahead of competitors who try to imitate its original product.

Should be socially useful

The first objective isn't just a "do-gooder" objective. Businesses can't exist without the approval of consumers. If a firm's activities appear to be contrary to the consumer "good," the firm can be wiped out almost overnight by political or legal action—or consumers' own negative responses.[3]

Should earn some profit

A firm must make a profit to survive. But just saying that a firm should try to make a profit isn't enough. Management must specify the time period involved since many plans that maximize profit in the long run lose money during the first few years. Thousands of new firms go belly-up after a year or two of losses because they cannot cover their expenses in the short run.

On the other hand, seeking only short-term profits may steer the firm from opportunities that would offer larger long-run profits. For example, Fruit of the Loom struggled to maximize profits with its men's underwear and other clothing lines, but in those intensely competitive markets the maximum possible profit margins were so thin that it ultimately had to reorganize under the bankruptcy law. In a situation like this, it might be better to set a *target* rate of profit that will lead the firm into areas with more promising possibilities.

A mission statement helps set the course

Our three general objectives provide guidelines, but a firm should develop its own objectives. This is important, but top executives often don't state their objectives clearly. If objectives aren't clear from the start, different managers may hold unspoken and conflicting objectives.

Many firms try to avoid this problem by developing a mission statement, which sets out the organization's basic purpose for being. For example, the mission of the Fort Smith Public Library (www.fspl.lib.ar.us) is "to serve the minds of the citizens in our community by providing easy access to resources that meet their informational and recreational needs." A good mission statement should focus on a few key goals rather than embracing everything. It should also supply guidelines when managers face difficult decisions. For example, if an employee of the library is trying to decide whether or not to write a proposal for the funding of a Spanish language story time or new computers that provide Internet access, it should be clear that these services are within the scope of the library's stated mission. A mission statement may need to be revised as new market needs arise or as the marketing

63

environment changes. But this would be a fundamental change and not one that is made casually.[4]

The whole firm must work toward the same objectives

A mission statement is important, but it is not a substitute for more specific objectives that provide guidance in screening possible opportunities. For example, top management might set objectives such as "earn 25 percent annual return on investment" and "introduce at least three innovative and successful products in the next two years."

Of course, when there are a number of specific objectives stated by top management, it is critical that they be compatible. For example, the objective of introducing new products is reasonable. However, if the costs of developing and introducing the new products cannot be recouped within one year, the return on investment objective is impossible.[5]

Company objectives should lead to marketing objectives

To avoid such problems, the marketing manager should at least be involved in setting company objectives. Company objectives guide managers as they search for and evaluate opportunities—and later plan marketing strategies. Particular *marketing* objectives should be set within the framework of larger company objectives. As shown in Exhibit 3-2, firms need a hierarchy of objectives—moving from company objectives to marketing department objectives. For each marketing strategy, firms also need objectives for each of the four Ps—as well as more detailed objectives. For example, in the Promotion area, we need objectives for personal selling, mass selling, *and* sales promotion.

Toyota provides an example. One of its company objectives is to achieve high customer satisfaction. So the R&D people design vehicles to meet specific reliability objectives. Similarly, the production people work to cut manufacturing defects. The marketing department, in turn, sets specific customer satisfaction objectives for every product. That leads to specific promotion objectives to ensure that the sales and advertising people don't promise more than the company can deliver. Dealers and customer service people, in turn, work to quickly fix a problem the first time it's reported.

Both company objectives and marketing objectives should be realistic and achievable. Overly ambitious objectives are useless if the firm lacks the resources to achieve them.

Exhibit 3-2
A Hierarchy of Objectives

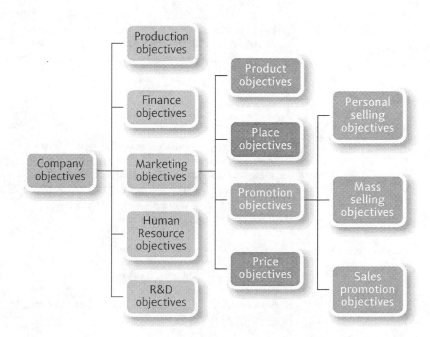

COMPANY RESOURCES MAY LIMIT SEARCH FOR OPPORTUNITIES

Every firm has some resources—hopefully some unique ones—that set it apart. Breakthrough opportunities—or at least some competitive advantage—come from making use of these strengths while avoiding direct competition with firms having similar strengths.

To find its strengths, a firm must evaluate its functional areas (production, research and engineering, marketing, general management, and finance) as well as its present products and markets. The knowledge of people at the firm can also be a unique resource. By analyzing successes or failures in relation to the firm's resources, management can discover why the firm was successful—or why it failed—in the past.

Financial strength

Some opportunities require large amounts of capital just to get started. Money may be required for R&D, production facilities, marketing research, or advertising before a firm makes its first sale. And even a really good opportunity may not be profitable for years. So lack of financial strength is often a barrier to entry into an otherwise attractive market.

Producing capability and flexibility

In many businesses, the cost of producing and selling each unit decreases as the quantity increases. Therefore, smaller firms can be at a great cost disadvantage if they try to win business from larger competitors.

On the other hand, new—or smaller—firms sometimes have the advantage of flexibility. They are not handicapped with large, special-purpose facilities that are obsolete or poorly located. Large steel producers once enjoyed economies of scale. But today they have trouble competing with producers using smaller, more flexible plants.

Many firms increase flexibility by not having any "in-house" manufacturing for their brands. Hanes is a good example. At one point, Hanes had U.S. factories for its underwear and t-shirts. But the factories were sold when most textile-related manufacturing moved to other countries with lower labor costs. Top managers for the brand said that they didn't have a competitive advantage in manufacturing anyway. Now, as Hanes' needs change, it has the flexibility to work with whatever suppliers around the world are best able to meet its specifications.

Marketing strengths

Our marketing strategy planning framework (Exhibit 2-10) helps in analyzing current marketing resources. In the product area, for example, a familiar brand can be a big strength. Starbucks is famous for its coffee beverages. When Starbucks introduced its Coffee Ice Cream, many people quickly tried it because they knew what Starbucks flavor meant.[6]

A new idea or process may be protected by a *patent*. A patent owner has a 20-year monopoly to develop and use its new product, process, or material. If one firm has a strong patent, competitors may be limited to second-rate offerings— and their efforts may be doomed to failure.[7]

Good relations with established wholesalers or retailers—or control of good locations—can be important resources. When marketing managers at Microsoft decided to introduce the Xbox game console, Microsoft software and computer accessories had already proved profitable for retailers like Best Buy and Wal-Mart that could reach the target market. So these retailers were willing to give the Xbox shelf space even if they were already carrying competing products from Nintendo or Sony.[8]

Similarly, existing computer systems that effectively share information in the channel, speed delivery of orders, and control inventory can be a big advantage. When P&G adds a new type of detergent, the systems to manage distribution are already in place.

Promotion and price resources must be considered too. Fidelity Investments already has a skilled sales force. Marketing managers know these sales reps can handle new

Campbell's soup has strengths that make it a very tough competitor in the consumer market. Knorr doesn't have as large a consumer advertising budget or as much shelf space in supermarkets. However, in the restaurant market, chefs often want ingredients that are different from what consumers have at home—and that's a strength for Knorr.

products and customers. And expertise to create an Internet website for online orders may enable a firm to expand its market and undercut competitors' prices.

Thorough understanding of a target market can give a company an edge. Many companies fail in new product-markets because they don't really understand the needs of the new customers or the new competitive environment.

ANALYZING COMPETITORS AND THE COMPETITIVE ENVIRONMENT

Choose opportunities that avoid head-on competition

The competitive environment affects the number and types of competitors the marketing manager must face and how they may behave. Although marketing managers usually can't control these factors, they can choose strategies that avoid head-on competition. And where competition is inevitable, they can plan for it.

Economists describe four basic kinds of market (competitive) situations: pure competition, oligopoly, monopolistic competition, and monopoly. Understanding the differences among these market situations is helpful in analyzing the competitive environment, and our discussion assumes some familiarity with these concepts. (For a review, see Exhibit A-11 and the related discussion in Appendix A, which follows Chapter 21.)

Most product-markets head toward pure competition—or oligopoly—over the long run. In these situations, competitors offer very similar products. Because customers see the different available products (marketing mixes) as close substitutes, managers just compete with lower and lower prices, and profit margins shrink. Sometimes managers cut prices much too quickly, without really thinking through the question of how to add more customer value. The marketing mix that offers the best customer value is not necessarily the one with the lowest price.

Avoiding pure competition is sensible and certainly fits with our emphasis on target marketing and the need to find a competitive advantage on which to differentiate the firm's marketing mix. This is why effective target marketing is fundamentally different from effective decision making in other areas of business. Accounting, production, and financial managers for competing firms can learn about and use the same standardized approaches—and they will work well in each case. By contrast, marketing managers can't just adopt the same "good" marketing strategy being used by other

Edition

Most consumers don't know the technical differences between various products for finishing wood, so Minwax ads emphasize that Minwax Polyshades saves them time by combining a stain and final finish in one product. Dirt Devil wants to convince customers that its Scorpion Hand Vac has more power than competitors so its ad gives the specific amp and watt rating. However, a consumer who does not know the ratings for other brands may not know that this is an advantage.

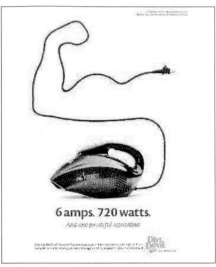

firms. That just leads to head-on competition and a downward spiral in prices and profits. So target marketers try to offer a marketing mix better suited to customers' needs than competitors' offerings.

Competitor-free environments are rare

Most marketing managers would like to have such a strong marketing mix that customers see it as uniquely able to meet their needs. This competitor-free ideal guides the search for breakthrough opportunities. Yet monopoly situations, in which one firm completely controls a broad product-market, are rare in market-directed economies. Further, governments commonly regulate monopolies. For example, in many parts of the world prices set by utility companies must be approved by a government agency. Although most marketing managers can't expect to operate with complete control in an unregulated monopoly, they can move away from head-on competition.

Monopolistic competition is typical—and a challenge

In monopolistic competition, a number of different firms offer marketing mixes that at least some customers see as different. Each competitor tries to get control (a monopoly) in its "own" target market. But competition still exists because some customers see the various alternatives as substitutes. Most marketing managers in developed economies face monopolistic competition.

In monopolistic competition, marketing managers sometimes try to differentiate very similar products by relying on other elements of the marketing mix. For example, Clorox Bleach uses the same basic chemicals as other bleaches. But marketing managers for Clorox may help to set it apart from other bleaches by offering an improved pouring spout, by producing ads that demonstrate its stain-killing power, or by getting it better shelf positions in supermarkets. Yet such approaches may not work, especially if competitors can easily imitate each new idea.

Analyze competitors to find a competitive advantage

The best way for a marketing manager to avoid head-on competition is to find new or better ways to satisfy customers' needs and provide value. The search for a break-through opportunity—or some sort of competitive advantage—requires an understanding not only of customers but also of competitors. That's why marketing managers turn to competitor analysis—an organized approach for evaluating the strengths and weaknesses of current or potential competitors' marketing strategies.

The basic approach to competitor analysis is simple. You compare the strengths and weaknesses of your current (or planned) target market and marketing mix with what competitors are currently doing or are likely to do in response to your strategy.

The initial step in competitor analysis is to identify potential competitors. It's useful to start broadly and from the viewpoint of target customers. Companies may

Many consumers think that toilet paper is a commodity—where one brand is about the same as any other. Cashmere's bathroom tissue is softer and its ad campaign encourages consumers to see how special it is. However, consumer attitudes may be difficult to change.

offer quite different products to meet the same needs, but they are competitors if customers see them as offering close substitutes. For example, disposable diapers, cloth diapers, and diaper rental services all compete in the same broad market concerned with baby care. Identifying a broad set of potential competitors helps marketing managers understand the different ways customers are currently meeting needs and sometimes points to new opportunities. For example, even parents who usually prefer the economy of cloth diapers may be interested in the convenience of disposables when they travel.

Usually, however, marketing managers quickly narrow the focus of their analysis to the set of competitive rivals—firms that will be the closest competitors. Rivals offering similar products are usually easy to identify. However, with a really new and different product concept, the closest competitor may be a firm that is currently serving similar needs with a different type of product. Although such firms may not appear to be close competitors, they are likely to fight back—perhaps with a directly competitive product—if another firm starts to take away customers.

Anticipate competition that will come

A successful strategy attracts copycats who jump in for a share of the profit. Sometimes a creative imitator figures out a way to provide customers with superior value. Then sales may disappear before the pioneer even knows what's happened.

Finding a sustainable competitive advantage requires special attention to competitor strengths and weaknesses. For example, it is very difficult to dislodge a firm that is already a market leader simply by attacking with a similar strategy. The leader can usually defend its position by quickly copying the best parts of what a new competitor is trying to do. On the other hand, a competitor may not be able to defend quickly if it is attacked where it is weak. For example, Netflix's online DVD rental business initially grew by taking customers away from Blockbuster. Blockbuster quickly fought back with its own online service, but with a twist. A customer who ordered a DVD from Blockbuster online could view it and then immediately trade it for another at a local Blockbuster store. Netflix doesn't have stores, so it couldn't copy Blockbuster's approach.[9]

Watch for competitive barriers

In a competitor analysis, you also consider competitive barriers—the conditions that may make it difficult, or even impossible, for a firm to compete in a market. Such barriers may limit your own plans or, alternatively, block competitors' responses to an innovative strategy.

Edition

Exhibit 3-3   Competitor Analysis (summary): Disposable Diaper Competition in Japan

	P&G's Current and Planned Strategy	Kao's Strengths (+) and Weaknesses (−)	Uni-Charm's Strengths (+) and Weaknesses (−)
Target Market(s)	Upscale, modern parents who can afford disposable diapers	Same as for P&G	Same as for P&G, but also budget-conscious segment that includes cloth diaper users (+)
Product	Improved fit and absorbency (+); brand name imagery weak in Japan (−)	Brand familiarity (+), but no longer the best performance (−)	Two brands—for different market segments—and more convenient package with handles (+)
Place	Distribution through independent wholesalers to both food stores and drugstores (+), but handled by fewer retailers (−)	Close relations with and control over wholesalers who carry only Kao products (+); computerized inventory reorder system (+)	Distribution through 80% of food stores in best locations (+); shelf space for two brands (+)
Promotion	Heaviest spending on daytime TV, heavy sales promotion, including free samples (+); small sales force (−)	Large efficient sales force (+); lowest advertising spending (−) and out-of-date ad claims (−)	Advertising spending high (+); effective ads that appeal to Japanese mothers (+)
Price	High retail price (−), but lower unit price for larger quantities (+)	Highest retail price (−), but also best margins for wholesalers and retailers (+)	Lowest available retail price (+); price of premium brand comparable to P&G (−)
(Potential) Competitive Barriers	Patent protection (+), limits in access to retail shelf space (−)	Inferior product (−), excellent logistics support system (+)	Economies of scale and lower costs (+); loyal customers (+)
Likely Response(s)	Improve wholesaler and retailer margins; faster deliveries in channel; change package to require less shelf space	Press retailers to increase in-store promotion; change advertising and/or improve product	Increase short-term sales promotions; but if P&G takes customers, cut price on premium brand

For example, Exhibit 3-3 summarizes a competitor analysis in the Japanese market for disposable diapers. P&G was about to replace its original Pampers, which were selling poorly, with a new version that offered improved fit and better absorbency. Kao and Uni-Charm, the two leading Japanese producers, both had better distribution networks. Kao also had a better computer system to handle reorders. Because most Japanese grocery stores and drugstores are very small, frequent restocking by wholesalers is critical. So getting cooperation in the channel was a potential competitive barrier for P&G. To overcome this problem, P&G changed its packaging to take up less space and offered wholesalers and retailers better markups.[10]

Seek information about competitors

A marketing manager should actively seek information about current or potential competitors. Although most firms try to keep the specifics of their plans secret, much public information may be available. Sources of competitor information include trade publications, alert sales reps, suppliers, and other industry experts. In business markets, customers may be quick to explain what competing suppliers are offering.

A firm that puts all of its marketing information on a public website for customers also makes it readily available to competitors. Similarly, it's easy to schedule a regular online search through thousands of publications and databases for any mention of a competitor.

Internet EXERCISE

If you were a new marketing manager at Rubbermaid, you might be interested in finding out more about Tupperware, an important competitor in some markets. What type of relevant information could you get by going to the Tupperware website (www.tupperware.com)?

Ethical issues may arise

The search for information about competitors sometimes raises ethical issues. For example, people who change jobs and move to competing firms may have a great deal of information about the competitor, but is it ethical for them to use it? Similarly, some firms have been criticized for going too far—like waiting at a landfill for competitors' trash to find copies of confidential company reports. And the high-tech version of that occurs when Internet "hackers" break into a competitor's computer network.

Beyond the moral issues, spying on competitors to obtain trade secrets is illegal. Damage awards can be huge. The courts ordered competing firms to pay Procter & Gamble about $125 million in damages for stealing secrets about its Duncan Hines soft cookies.[11]

> **Ethics QUESTION**
>
> You are a salesperson for a company that manufactures industrial lighting used in factories. During a recent sales call, an engineer at your customer firm complains about a new energy-saving lightbulb that his company is testing for a competing supplier. Your company was not aware of the competitor's new product—which you think may make one of your product lines obsolete. Should you pass this competitive intelligence to your sales manager? Should you question the engineer or others at the customer firm to learn more? If you gather more information, should you share that with your company?

Direct competition cannot always be avoided

A manager may desire to avoid highly competitive situations, but that may not be possible. Some firms are already in an industry before it becomes intensely competitive. For example, Rubbermaid was one of the first firms to introduce sturdy, low-cost plastic housewares. It is still a respected brand name but faces competition from hundreds of low-cost overseas producers. As competitors fail, new firms enter the market, possibly because they don't see more attractive alternatives. This is a common pattern with small retailers and wholesalers in less-developed economies. New entrants may not even know how competitive the market is—but they stick it out until they run out of money.

THE ECONOMIC ENVIRONMENT

The economic and technological environment affects the way firms—and the whole economy—use resources. We will treat the economic and technological environments separately to emphasize that the technological environment provides a *base* for the economic environment. Technical skills and equipment affect the way companies convert an economy's resources into output. The economic environment, on the other hand, is affected by the way all of the parts of a macro-economic system interact. This then affects such things as national income, economic growth, and inflation. The economic environment may vary from one country to another, but economies around the world are linked.

Economic conditions change rapidly

The economic environment can, and does, change quite rapidly. The effects can be far-reaching and require changes in marketing strategy.

Even a well-planned marketing strategy may fail if a country or region goes through a rapid business decline. You can see how quickly this can occur by considering what happened in the U.S. housing market in the past few years. Earlier in the decade the economy was growing, household incomes were increasing, and interest rates were low. As a result, the housing market was hot. Manufacturers of building materials, home contractors, real estate firms, and mortgage companies all enjoyed strong profits

Edition

as they scrambled to keep up with demand. However, by 2007 the economy was on the edge of recession and the housing market was in an abrupt collapse. Firms that had done so well a year earlier were suffering huge losses—and many went bankrupt. Worse, millions of people lost their homes when they could not afford rising payments for variable-rate mortgages. In a weak economy many consumers must really ratchet back on their spending—and do without products they would like to have. Many companies are not strong enough to survive such downturns.

Interest rates and inflation affect buying

Changes in the economy are often accompanied by changes in the interest rate—the charge for borrowing money. Interest rates directly affect the total price borrowers must pay for products. So the interest rate affects when, and if, they will buy. This is an especially important factor in some business markets. But it also affects consumer purchases of homes, cars, and other items usually bought on credit.

Interest rates usually increase during periods of inflation, and inflation is a fact of life in many economies. In some Latin American countries, inflation has exceeded 400 percent a year in recent years. In contrast, recent U.S. levels—3 to 20 percent—seem low. Still, inflation must be considered in strategy planning. When costs are rising rapidly and there are no more cost-cutting measures to take, a marketing manager may have to increase prices. For example, the series of big price increases by airlines and freight carriers in recent times is due to the spiraling cost of fuel.

The global economy is connected

The economies of the world are connected—and changes in one economy quickly affect others. One reason for this is that the amount of international trade is increasing—and it is affected by changes in and between economies. For example, International Harvester (IH) was very successful selling its earth-moving equipment in Asia when construction was booming. However, when an economic downturn spread across Asia, many customers could no longer make payments. IH faced big losses—and the cost of retrieving equipment that was 13,000 miles away!

Changes in the *exchange rate*—how much one country's money is worth in another country's money—have an important effect on international trade. When the dollar is strong, it's worth more in foreign countries. This sounds good—but it makes U.S. products more expensive overseas and foreign products cheaper in the United States. New domestic competition arises as foreign products gain a competitive edge with

The Smart car has been sold in Europe for a number of years. This European ad focuses on how easy it is to park. Now that the Smart car is being introduced in the U.S., the new market environment may require new promotion. For example, although the car is very small, advanced technology helps it meet tough U.S. safety regulations.

CHAPTER 3

71

Evaluating Opportunities in the Changing Marketing Environment

lower prices. A country's whole economic system can change as the balance of imports and exports shifts—affecting jobs, consumer income, and national productivity.

Marketing managers must watch the economic environment carefully. In contrast to the cultural and social environment, economic conditions can move rapidly and require immediate strategy changes.[12]

THE TECHNOLOGICAL ENVIRONMENT

Technology affects opportunities

Technology is the application of science to convert an economy's resources to output. Technology affects marketing in two basic ways: opportunities for new products and for new processes (ways of doing things). For example, advances in information technology make it possible for people in different parts of the world to communicate by satellite videoconferencing and to send complex design drawings over the Internet. Websites enable sophisticated e-commerce exchanges between remote firms. These process changes are accompanied by an exciting explosion of high-tech products—from genome-based medicines to cars that contact the police if they are stolen.

Technology transfer is rapid

New technologies have created important industries that didn't even exist a few years ago. Ten years ago Google didn't exist. Now it's one of the best known firms in the world. With such big opportunities at stake, you can also see why there is such rapid transfer of technology from one part of the world to another. But technology transfer is not automatic. Someone—perhaps you—has to see the opportunity.

Internet technologies are reshaping marketing

Many of the big advances in business have come from early recognition of new ways to do things. There is perhaps no better example of this than the World Wide Web and the Internet. The Internet is a system for linking computers around the world. The idea of linking computers in a network was not new. Even so, the Internet expanded the network concept to include any computer anywhere and the World Wide Web made the exchange of information easy. As a result, this technology has changed just about every aspect of marketing. We'll discuss these changes in more detail throughout the text, but for now we'll just illustrate the impact.

Consider the arena of promotion. The invention of TV changed marketing because it suddenly made it possible for a sponsor to broadcast a brief but vivid message to millions of people at the same time. Now, the Internet makes it possible for that sponsor to select any of millions of messages and to simultaneously narrowcast any of them to millions of different individuals. It is just as easy for customers to request the information in the first place, or to respond electronically once they have it. Thus, the Internet's capability changes our ideas about how firms communicate

New technology creates opportunities for new products but also new ways of handling marketing jobs. For example, Sirius wants advertisers to think about the advantages of satellite radio in reaching specific target markets. For instance, among its 110 varied satellite offerings are NBA Radio, the Catholic Channel, and Punk Function—all humorously illustrated by Sirius' Slam Dunking Punk Nun.

Edition

with customers, and vice versa. Similarly, the Internet has created totally different approaches to pricing. Airlines run online auctions of seats that might otherwise go unsold. If you sell every seat to the highest bidder, you are really pricing precisely to match supply and demand. To check out an online auction, go to www.ebay.com.

In hindsight, new approaches such as these seem obvious—given that the technology is available. But they are not obvious up front—unless you're really looking for them.[13]

Technology also poses challenges

Technological change opens up new opportunities, but it also poses challenges for marketers. For some firms, success hinges on how quickly new ideas can be brought to market. But it's easy for a firm to slip into a production orientation in the flush of excitement that comes from a new idea or R&D discovery. That makes it more important than ever for marketing thinking to guide the production process—starting at the beginning with decisions about what customers will really value and where development efforts should be focused.

Technology and ethical issues

Marketers often must help their firms decide what technological developments are ethically acceptable. For example, many firms track information about who "hits" the company Web page and what website they came from. The firm can then sell this information to whoever wants to use it to send promotional e-mail. Yet uninvited e-mail is just another form of invasion of privacy.

Some attractive technological developments may be rejected because of their long-run effects on the environment. Aseptic drink boxes, for example, are convenient but difficult to recycle. In a case like this, what's good for the firm and some customers may not be good for the cultural and social environment or acceptable in the political and legal environment. Being close to the market should give marketers a better feel for current trends and help firms avoid serious mistakes.[14]

THE POLITICAL ENVIRONMENT

The attitudes and reactions of people, social critics, and governments all affect the political environment. Consumers in the same country usually share a common political environment, but the political environment can also affect opportunities at a local or international level. Some business managers have become very successful by studying the political environment and developing strategies that take advantage of opportunities related to changing political dimensions.

Nationalism can be limiting in international markets

Strong sentiments of nationalism—an emphasis on a country's interests before everything else—affect how macro-marketing systems work. They can affect how marketing managers work as well. Nationalistic feelings can reduce sales—or even block all marketing activity—in some international markets. For many years, China has made it difficult for outside firms to do business there—in spite of the fact that the Chinese economy has experienced explosive growth as its factories have turned out larger and larger portions of the goods sold in the United States, Europe, and other parts of the world.

The "Buy American" policy in many government contracts and business purchases reflects this same attitude in the United States. There is broad consumer support for protecting U.S. producers—and jobs—from foreign competition. That's why GM promotes its trucks in TV commercials to strains of "This Is Our Country" (even though some of its most popular models are produced in Mexico).[15]

Nationalistic feelings can determine whether a firm can enter markets because businesses often must get permission to operate. In some political environments, this is only a routine formality. In others, a lot of red tape and personal influence are involved, and bribes are sometimes expected. This raises ethical issues for marketing managers—and legal issues too, since it's illegal for U.S. firms to offer such bribes.

オワリダ

THAT'S JAPANESE FOR "YOU'RE TOAST" IF YOUR WEBSITE CAN'T ACCOMMODATE OUR LANGUAGE AND CURRENCY.

adero›

Adero wants marketers to keep in mind that a website that can attract prospects from all over the world won't be successful in turning them into customers if it ignores nationalism and cultural differences.

Clearly, that can make it difficult for a U.S. firm to compete with a company from a country that doesn't have similar laws.

Regional groupings are becoming more important

Important dimensions of the political environment are likely to be similar among nations that have banded together to have common regional economic boundaries. The move toward the unification of Europe and free trade among the nations of North America are examples of this sort of regional grouping.

The unification of European markets

Twenty years ago, each country in Europe had its own unique trade rules and regulations. These differences made it difficult and expensive to move products from one country to the others. Now, the member countries of the European Union (EU) are reducing conflicting laws, taxes, and other obstacles to trade within Europe. This, in turn, is reducing costs and the prices European consumers pay and creating new jobs. Even bigger changes may come if Britain decides to join other countries that have moved to the euro, the unified money system for the EU. With the currencies of countries in the euro-zone phased out, transactions no longer involve the extra uncertainty and cost of converting payments from one currency to another.

Although Europe is becoming a large unified market, marketers will still encounter differences among European countries. What happened to Lands' End, the Wisconsin-based Internet and mail-order retailer, illustrates the issues. To better reach European consumers, Lands' End set up shop in England and Germany. As in the United States, its promotion and website touted the unconditional lifetime guarantee that is a key part of its strategy. However, German consumer protection rules prohibited promotion of the guarantee; the Germans argued that the promotion was a misleading gimmick (on the logic that the cost of the guarantee was "hidden" in higher prices that consumers would pay). German officials wanted this ban to apply even if the German consumer purchased the product from a Lands' End website in England. Quirky local rules like this could erode some of the benefits that should come from more European unification.[16]

NAFTA is building trade cooperation

The international competition fostered by the moves to unify Europe provided impetus for the United States, Mexico, and Canada to develop more cooperative trade agreements. The North American Free Trade Agreement (NAFTA) lays out

Edition

a plan to reshape the rules of trade among the United States, Canada, and Mexico. NAFTA basically enlarges the free-trade pact that had already knocked down most barriers to U.S.–Canada trade, and over a 15-year period it will eliminate most such barriers with Mexico. It also establishes a forum for resolving future trade disputes.

The long-term economic impact of NAFTA is yet to be seen. However, tariffs that have already dropped are having a significant impact on specific businesses. For example, Raychem Corp., a small producer of telecommunications equipment, no longer faces a 25 percent tariff on exports to Mexico. That is leveling its competitive playing field and creating new opportunities. On the other hand, many firms have moved production—and jobs—to Mexico where labor is cheaper. The backlash about this outflow of jobs may result in adjustments to NAFTA in the future.

Of course, removal of some economic and political barriers—whether across all of the Americas or Europe—will not eliminate the need to adjust strategies to reach submarkets of consumers. Centuries of cultural differences will not disappear overnight. Some may never disappear.[17]

Some dramatic changes in the political environment—like the fall of communism in Eastern Europe—happen fast and are hard to predict. Yet many important political changes—both within and across nations—evolve more gradually.

THE LEGAL ENVIRONMENT

Changes in the political environment often lead to changes in the legal environment and in the way existing laws are enforced. The legal environment sets the basic rules for how a business can operate in society. The legal environment may severely limit some choices, but changes in laws and how they are interpreted also create new opportunities. To illustrate the effects of the legal environment, we will discuss how it has evolved in the United States. However, laws often vary from one country to another.

Trying to encourage competition

American economic and legislative thinking is based on the idea that competition among many small firms helps the economy. Therefore, attempts by business to limit competition are considered contrary to the public interest.

Starting in 1890, Congress passed a series of antimonopoly laws. Exhibit 3-4 shows the names and dates of these laws. Although the specific focus of each law is different, in general they are all intended to encourage competition.

Antimonopoly law and marketing mix planning

In later chapters, we will specifically apply antimonopoly law to the four Ps. For now you should know what kind of proof the government must have to get a conviction under each of the major laws. You should also know which of the four Ps are most affected by each law. Exhibit 3-4 provides such a summary—with a phrase following each law to show what the government must prove to get a conviction.

Because of a change in regulations, some non-prescription drugs are no longer available on self-service retail shelves but rather are behind the pharmacy counter. With this change in the legal environment, marketers for Mucinex D want customers to know how to find the product in the store.

Edition

Exhibit 3-4   Focus (mostly prohibitions) of Federal Antimonopoly Laws on the Four Ps

Law	Product	Place	Promotion	Price
Sherman Act (1890) Monopoly or conspiracy in restraint of trade	Monopoly or conspiracy to control a product	Monopoly or conspiracy to control distribution channels		Monopoly or conspiracy to fix or control prices
Clayton Act (1914) Substantially lessens competition	Forcing sale of some products with others—tying contracts	Exclusive dealing contracts (limiting buyers' sources of supply)		Price discrimination by manufacturers
Federal Trade Commission Act (1914) Unfair methods of competition		Unfair policies	Deceptive ads or selling practices	Deceptive pricing
Robinson-Patman Act (1936) Tends to injure competition			Prohibits "fake" advertising allowances or discrimination in help offered	Prohibits price discrimination on goods of "like grade and quality" without cost justification, and limits quanitity discounts
Wheeler-Lea Amendment (1938) Unfair or deceptive practices	Deceptive packaging or branding		Deceptive ads or selling claims	Deceptive pricing
Antimerger Act (1950) Lessens competition	Buying competitors	Buying producers or distributors		
Magnuson-Moss Act (1975) Unreasonable practices	Product warranties			

Prosecution is serious—you can go to jail

Businesses and *individual managers* are subject to both criminal and civil laws. Penalties for breaking civil laws are limited to blocking or forcing certain actions—along with fines. Where criminal law applies, jail sentences can be imposed. For example, several managers at Beech-Nut Nutrition Company were fined $100,000 each and sent to jail. In spite of ads claiming that Beech-Nut's apple juice was 100 percent natural, they tried to bolster profits by secretly using low-cost artificial ingredients.[18]

Consumer protection laws are not new

Although antimonopoly laws focus on protecting competition, the wording of the laws in Exhibit 3-4 has, over time, moved toward protecting consumers. Some consumer protections are also built into the English and U.S. common law systems. A seller has to tell the truth (if asked a direct question), meet contracts, and stand behind the firm's product (to some reasonable extent). Beyond this, it is expected that vigorous competition in the marketplace will protect consumers—*so long as they are careful*.

Yet focusing only on competition didn't protect consumers very well in some areas. So the government found it necessary to pass other laws. For example, various laws regulate packaging and labels, credit practices, and environmental issues. Usually, however, the laws focus on specific types of products.

Edition

Foods and drugs are controlled

Consumer protection laws in the United States go back to 1906 when Congress passed the Pure Food and Drug Act. Unsanitary meat-packing practices in the Chicago stockyards stirred consumer support for this act. This was a major victory for consumer protection. Before the law, it was assumed that common law and the old warning "let the buyer beware" would take care of consumers.

Later acts corrected some loopholes in the law. The law now bans the shipment of unsanitary and poisonous products and requires much testing of drugs. The Food and Drug Administration (FDA) attempts to control manufacturers of these products. It can seize products that violate its rules—including regulations on branding and labeling.

Product safety is controlled

The Consumer Product Safety Act (of 1972), another important consumer protection law, set up the Consumer Product Safety Commission. This group has broad power to set safety standards and can impose penalties for failure to meet these standards. There is some question as to how much safety consumers really want—the commission found the bicycle the most hazardous product under its control!

Internet EXERCISE

The Consumer Product Safety Commission's (CPSC) mission is to protect the public from hazardous products. The government agency also provides safety information for consumers. Go to the website (www.cpsc.gov) and click on "CPSC Publications." Look through one of the safety publications that interests you. Did you find it useful? Would it make you change your behavior?

But given that the commission has the power to *force* a product off the market—or require expensive recalls to correct problems—it is obvious that safety must be considered in product design. And safety must be treated seriously by marketing managers. There is no more tragic example of this than the recalls of Firestone tires used as original equipment on Ford's Explorer SUV. Hundreds of consumers were killed or seriously injured in accidents.[19]

State and local laws vary

Besides federal legislation—which affects interstate commerce—marketers must be aware of state and local laws. There are state and city laws regulating minimum prices and the setting of prices, regulations for starting up a business (licenses, examinations, and even tax payments), and in some communities, regulations prohibiting certain activities—such as telephone selling or selling on Sundays or during evenings.

Know the laws— follow the courts and federal agencies

Often laws are vaguely phrased—to convey intent but not specific detail. Then it's up to the courts and government agencies to spell out the details. As a result, a law may be interpreted and enforced differently over time. For example, during the 1980s, many U.S. government agencies regulated businesses less zealously and instead focused more on encouraging competition. Attention to regulation was swinging the other way in the 1990s—in part to correct abuses such as those that occurred in the savings and loan industry.

It was in this sort of political environment that the U.S. Justice Department, and the attorneys general in a number of states, brought charges against Microsoft. Many government officials, competitors, and consumer interest groups felt that Microsoft violated the antimonopoly laws, and at one point a judge declared that Microsoft would be broken up into two or more competing companies. However, the court case dragged on for over five years, and the political climate changed toward less aggressive enforcement of the antimonopoly laws. In the end, Microsoft did not face serious penalties in the United States. However, Microsoft didn't get off as easily in Europe where the legal environment did not shift as quickly. The 2004 antitrust ruling against Microsoft by European regulators imposed a $613 million fine. In 2006 they added a $357 million fine for slow compliance, and in 2008 slammed the firm again on the same issue with a record $1.3 billion fine. "Talk is cheap," said a chief European regulator, but "flouting the rules is expensive." As Microsoft's very visible and important cases in the United States and Europe show, how the laws are interpreted and enforced can be even more important than the wording of the law when it was written.[20]

Because legislation must be interpreted by federal agencies and the courts, marketing managers need to study both legislative developments and the thinking of the courts and agencies.

Consumerists and the law say "let the seller beware"

The old rule about buyer–seller relations—*let the buyer beware*—has changed to *let the seller beware*. The shift to proconsumer laws and court decisions suggests that lawmakers are more interested in protecting consumers. This may upset production-oriented managers. But times have changed—and managers must adapt to this new political and legal environment.[21]

THE CULTURAL AND SOCIAL ENVIRONMENT

The cultural and social environment affects how and why people live and behave as they do—which affects customer buying behavior and eventually the economic, political, and legal environments. Many variables make up the cultural and social environment. Some examples are the languages people speak, the type of education they have, their religious beliefs, what type of food they eat, the style of clothing and housing they have, and how they view work, marriage, and family. Because the cultural and social environment has such broad effects, most people don't stop to think about it, or how it may be changing, or how it may differ for other people.

A marketing manager can't afford to take the cultural and social environment for granted. Although changes tend to come slowly, they can have far-reaching effects. A marketing manager who sees the changes early may be able to identify big opportunities. Further, within any broad society, different subgroups of people may be affected by the cultural and social environment in different ways. In most countries, the trend toward multiculturalism is making such differences even more important to marketers. They require special attention when segmenting markets. In fact, dealing with these differences is often one of the greatest challenges managers face when planning strategies, especially for international markets.

Since we will discuss details of how the cultural and social environment relates to buying behavior in Chapters 4 through 7, here we will just use an example to illustrate its impact on marketing strategy planning.

Changing women's roles

The shifting roles of women in society illustrate the importance of the cultural and social environment on marketing strategy planning. Fifty years ago, most people in the United States felt that a woman's role was in the home—first and foremost as a wife and mother. Women had less opportunity for higher education and were completely shut out of many of the most interesting jobs. Obviously, there have been big changes in that stereotyped thinking. With better job opportunities, more women are delaying marriage, and once married they are likely to stay in the workforce and have fewer children. For example, in 1950, only 24 percent of wives worked outside the home. Now that figure is over 60 percent. Among women in the 35–44 age group, the percentage is over 70.

The flood of women into the job market boosted economic growth and changed U.S. society in many other ways. Many in-home jobs that used to be done primarily by women—ranging from family shopping to preparing meals to doing volunteer work—still need to be done by someone. Husbands and children now do some of these jobs, a situation that has changed the target market for many products. Or a working woman may face a crushing "poverty of time" and look for help elsewhere, creating opportunities for producers of frozen meals, child care centers, dry cleaners, financial services, and the like.

Although there is still a big wage gap between men and women, the income working women generate gives them independence and purchasing power. For example, women

Edition

Citigroup is putting increased emphasis on financial services targeted at women. In the U.S., its Women & Co. division uses an ad for financial services that is a clever spoof on cosmetics ads. In Japan, its Unimat Ladys personal finance division targets women and is staffed entirely by women.

now purchase about half of all cars. Not long ago, many car dealers insulted a woman shopper by ignoring her or suggesting that she come back with her husband. Now car companies have realized that women are important customers. It's interesting that Japanese car dealers, especially Mazda and Toyota, were the first to really pay attention to women customers. In Japan, fewer women have jobs or buy cars—the Japanese society is still more male-oriented. Perhaps it was the contrast with Japanese society that prompted these firms to pay more attention to women buyers in the United States.[22]

Women's changing role has created opportunities for marketing but also complications. A marketing mix targeted at women, for example, may require a real balancing act. Advertising showing a woman at the office may attract some customers but alienate housewives who feel that their job doesn't command as much status as it should. Conversely, an ad that shows a woman doing housework might be criticized for encouraging stereotypes.

Changes come slowly

Most changes in basic cultural values and social attitudes come slowly. An individual firm can't hope to encourage big changes in the short run. Instead, it should identify current attitudes and work within these constraints—as it seeks new and better opportunities.[23]

USING SCREENING CRITERIA TO NARROW DOWN TO STRATEGIES

A progressive firm constantly looks for new opportunities. Once the opportunities are identified, the firm must screen and evaluate them. Usually, a firm can't pursue all available opportunities, so it must try to match its opportunities to its resources and objectives. First, management must quickly screen out obvious mismatches so other opportunities can be analyzed more carefully. Let's look at some approaches for screening and evaluating opportunities.

Developing and applying screening criteria

After you analyze the firm's resources (for strengths and weaknesses), the environmental trends the firm faces, and the objectives of top management, you merge them all into a set of product-market screening criteria. These criteria should include both quantitative and qualitative components. The quantitative components summarize the firm's objectives: sales, profit, and return on investment (ROI) targets. (Note: ROI analysis is discussed briefly in Appendix B, which comes after Chapter 21.) The

Toyota's ad says that "we believe in preserving the delicate balance between man and nature." In practice that means that Toyota is screening new opportunities by considering not just exhaust emissions and gas mileage but more broadly the environmental impact of every aspect of the vehicle's life cycle.

qualitative components summarize what kinds of businesses the firm wants to be in, what businesses it wants to exclude, what weaknesses it should avoid, and what resources (strengths) and trends it should build on.[24]

Developing screening criteria is difficult but worth the effort. They summarize in one place what the firm wants to accomplish—in quantitative terms—as well as roughly how and where it wants to accomplish it. When a manager can explain the specific criteria that are relevant to selecting (or screening out) an opportunity, others can understand the manager's logic. Thus, marketing decisions are not just made or accepted based on intuition and gut feel.

The criteria should be realistic—that is, they should be achievable. Opportunities that pass the screen should be able to be turned into strategies that the firm can implement with the resources it has.

Exhibit 3-5 illustrates some product-market screening criteria for a small retail and wholesale distributor. These criteria help the firm's managers eliminate unsuitable opportunities and find attractive ones to turn into strategies and plans.

Sometimes screening criteria can help bring focus to opportunities that fit well with trends in the external market environment. For example, GE operates many types of businesses, from jet aircraft engines and water treatment facilities to medical imaging and lightbulbs. Top management at GE believes that the really crucial needs of society relate to protecting the environment. They believe that efforts in this arena are so critical that they should be supported across all dimensions of the external environment. Thus, they want all GE managers to look for opportunities that fit what GE calls "ecomagination"—applying GE's creativity to solve problems related to ecology. GE is not alone in this kind of thinking. Many organizations now screen opportunities on sustainability—the idea that it's important to meet present needs without compromising the ability of future generations to meet their own needs. In many lines of business, that is a tall order. However, when managers begin to apply sustainability as a screening criteria, it leads them to better ways of meeting needs. At GE that means lightbulbs that use less energy, medical images with no toxic waste, jets that burn less fuel, and new ways to turn seawater into drinking water.[25]

Whole plans should be evaluated

You need to forecast the probable results of implementing a marketing strategy to apply the quantitative part of the screening criteria because only implemented plans

Edition

Exhibit 3-5   An Example of Product-Market Screening Criteria for a Small Retail and Wholesale Distributor ($10 million annual sales)

1. **Quantitative criteria**
   a. Increase sales by $1,500,000 per year for the next five years.
   b. Earn ROI of at least 25 percent before taxes on new ventures.
   c. Break even within one year on new ventures.
   d. Opportunity must be large enough to justify interest (to help meet objectives) but small enough so company can handle with the resources available.
   e. Several opportunities should be pursued to reach the objectives—to spread the risks.

2. **Qualitative criteria**
   a. Nature of business preferred.
      (1) Should take advantage of our Internet order system and website promotion.
      (2) New goods and services for present customers to strengthen relationships and customer equity.
      (3) "Quality" products that do not cannibalize sales of current products.
      (4) Competition should be weak and opportunity should be hard to copy for several years.
      (5) There should be strongly felt (even unsatisfied) needs—to reduce promotion costs and permit "high" prices.
   b. Constraints.
      (1) Nature of businesses to exclude.
         (a) Manufacturing.
         (b) Any requiring large fixed capital investments.
         (c) Any requiring many support people who must be "good" all the time and would require much supervision.
      (2) Geographic.
         (a) United States, Mexico, and Canada only.
      (3) General.
         (a) Make use of current strengths.
         (b) Attractiveness of market should be reinforced by more than one of the following basic trends: technological, demographic, social, economic, political.
         (c) Address environmental problems.

generate sales, profits, and return on investment. For a rough screening, you only need to estimate the likely results of implementing each opportunity over a logical planning period. If a product's life is likely to be three years, for example, a good strategy may not produce profitable results for 6 to 12 months. But evaluated over the projected three-year life, the product may look like a winner. When evaluating the potential of possible opportunities (product-market strategies), it is important to evaluate similar things—that is, *whole* plans.

Opportunities that pass the screening criteria should be evaluated in more detail before being accepted as *the* product-market strategic plans for implementation. Usually, a firm has more opportunities than resources and has to choose among them—to match its opportunities to its resources and objectives. The following approaches help firms select among possible plans.

Total profit approach can help evaluate possible plans

In the total profit approach, management forecasts potential sales and costs during the life of the plan to estimate likely profitability.

Managers may evaluate the prospects for each plan over a five-year planning period, using monthly and/or annual sales and cost estimates. This is shown graphically in Exhibit 3-6.

Marketing That Meets Earthly Needs

Twenty years ago, few managers worried about costs to the environment when evaluating market opportunities. And most consumers didn't see increased customer value in marketing strategies that were "planet friendly." Now that is changing. Problems like global warming and depletion of natural resources—even scarcity of drinking water for major urban areas—are receiving much attention. New federal and local laws push for conservation. The economics have changed as well; many firms are proving that it can be lucrative to solve ecological problems. There's also a cultural shift in consumers. Many seek "green" offerings and are even willing to pay a premium to get them.

Companies are finding a host of big and small ways to contribute solutions. In 2005, Unilever created a more concentrated version of its All liquid detergent and put it in a "small and mighty" bottle. In just two years, this simple change saved 1.3 million gallons of diesel fuel, 10 million pounds of plastic resin, and 80 million square feet of cardboard. Seeing results like that, P&G followed suit and converted all its liquid detergents to double concentration. Staples, the office supply retailer, has eco-modified 3,000 of its store-brand products—everything from sticky notes to cardboard boxes—to include 30 percent recycled paper. This isn't a choice that's left to Staples'

customers. The recycled product is the only version available. Competing firms are now copying this approach.

Marketers have usually focused on encouraging people to consume. But now more firms are looking for opportunities that relate to what happens to products when consumers are through with them. Sony, for example, has a new program to recycle all used Sony electronic products—from PlayStation game consoles and Trinitron TVs to Vaio laptops and Walkman tape players. Dell, HP, and others already have recycling programs in place, but Sony plans for its approach to earn profits. This type of thinking is prompting some firms to design new products for easy *disassembly*. Parts snap together without fasteners or glue, lead-based solder and other biohazards are avoided, and pieces that can't be recycled are biodegradable. Automobile companies are making headway in this area as well.

We are a long way from solving some of our most pressing environmental problems. However, creative marketers know that finding solutions to these problems can be good for their firms as well as their customers, not only in the short term but long into the future.[26]

Note that managers can evaluate different marketing plans at the same time. Exhibit 3-6 compares a much improved product and product concept (Product A) with a "me-too" product (Product B) for the same target market. In the short run, the me-too product will make a profit sooner and might look like the better choice—if managers consider only one year's results. The improved product, on the other hand, will take a good deal of pioneering—but over its five-year life will be much more profitable.

Return-on-investment (ROI) approach can help evaluate possible plans too

Besides evaluating the profit potential of possible plans, firms may also calculate the return on investment of resources needed to implement plans. ROI analyses can be useful for selecting among possible plans because equally profitable plans may require vastly different resources and offer different rates of return on investment.

Exhibit 3-6
Expected Sales and Cost Curves of Two Strategies over Five-Year Planning Periods

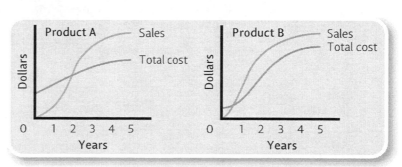

Edition

One plan may require a heavy investment in advertising and channel development, for example, while another relies primarily on lower price. Some firms are very concerned with ROI, especially those that borrow money for working capital. There is little point in borrowing to implement strategies that won't return enough to meet the cost of borrowing.

PLANNING GRIDS HELP EVALUATE A PORTFOLIO OF OPPORTUNITIES

When a firm has many possibilities to evaluate, it usually has to compare quite different ones. This problem is easier to handle with graphical approaches—such as the nine-box strategic planning grid developed by General Electric and used by many other companies. Such grids can help evaluate a firm's whole portfolio of strategic plans or businesses.

General Electric looks for green positions

General Electric's (GE) strategic planning grid—see Exhibit 3-7—forces company managers to make three-part judgments (high, medium, and low) about the business strengths and industry attractiveness of all proposed or existing product-market plans. As you can see from Exhibit 3-7, this approach helps a manager organize information about the company's marketing environments (discussed earlier in this chapter) along with information about its strategy and translate it into relevant screening criteria.

The industry attractiveness dimension helps managers answer the question: Does this product-market plan look like a good idea? To answer that question, managers have to judge such factors (screening criteria) as the size of the market and its growth rate, the nature of competition, the plan's potential environmental or social impact, and how laws might affect it. Note that an opportunity may be attractive for *some* company—but not well suited to the strengths (and weaknesses) of a particular firm. That is why the GE grid also considers the business strengths dimension.

The business strengths dimension focuses on the ability of the company to pursue a product-market plan effectively. To make judgments along this dimension, a manager evaluates whether the firm has people with the right talents and skills to implement the plan, whether the plan is consistent with the firm's image and profit objectives, and whether the firm could establish a profitable market share given its technical capability, costs, and size. Here again, these factors suggest screening criteria specific to this firm and market situation.

GE feels opportunities that fall into the green boxes in the upper left-hand corner of the grid are its best growth opportunities. Managers give these opportunities high marks on both industry attractiveness and business strengths. The red boxes in the lower right-hand corner of the grid, on the other hand, suggest a no-growth policy.

Exhibit 3-7
General Electric's Strategic Planning Grid

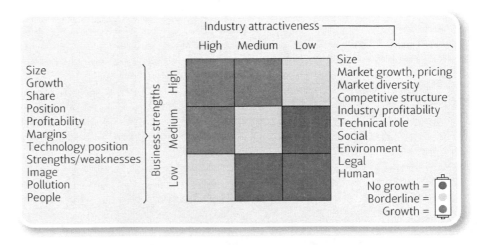

Existing red businesses may continue to generate earnings, but they no longer deserve much investment. Yellow businesses are borderline cases—they can go either way. GE may continue to support an existing yellow business but will probably reject a proposal for a new one. It simply wouldn't look good enough on the relevant screening criteria.

GE's "stoplight" evaluation method is a subjective, multiple-factor approach. It avoids the traps and possible errors of trying to use oversimplified, single-number criteria—like ROI or market share. Instead, top managers review detailed written summaries of many different screening criteria that help them make summary judgments. Then they can make a collective judgment. This approach helps everyone understand why the company supports some new opportunities and not others.[27]

General Electric considers factors that reflect its objectives. Another firm might modify the evaluation to emphasize other screening criteria—depending on its objectives and the type of product-market plans it is considering.

MULTIPRODUCT FIRMS HAVE A DIFFICULT STRATEGY-PLANNING JOB

Multiproduct firms, like General Electric, obviously have a more difficult strategic planning job than firms with only a few products or product lines aimed at the same target markets. Multiproduct firms have to develop strategic plans for very different businesses. And they have to balance plans and resources so the whole company reaches its objectives. This means they must approve plans that make sense for the whole company—even if it means getting needed resources by milking some businesses and eliminating others.

Details on how to manage a complicated multiproduct firm are beyond our scope. But you should be aware that the principles in this text are applicable—they just have to be extended. For example, some multiproduct firms form strategic business units (SBUs), and some use portfolio management.

Strategic business units may help

A strategic business unit (SBU) is an organizational unit (within a larger company) that focuses on some product-markets and is treated as a separate profit center. By forming SBUs, a company formally acknowledges its very different activities. One SBU of Sara Lee, for example, produces baked goods for consumers and restaurants; another produces and markets Kiwi brand shoe-care products.

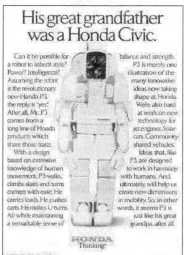

Large multiproduct firms, like Honda, evaluate and pursue a varied portfolio of strategic opportunities all around the world.

Edition

Some SBUs grow rapidly and require a great deal of attention and resources. Others produce only average profits and might be *milked*—that is, used to generate cash for the businesses with more potential. Product lines with poor market position, low profits, and slow growth should be dropped or sold.

Some firms use portfolio management

Some top managements handle strategic planning for a multiproduct firm with an approach called **portfolio management**—which treats alternative products, divisions, or strategic business units as though they were stock investments, to be bought and sold using financial criteria. Such managers make trade-offs among very different opportunities. They treat the various alternatives as investments that should be supported, milked, or sold off—depending on profitability and return on investment. In effect, they evaluate each alternative just like a stock market trader evaluates a stock.[28]

This approach makes some sense if alternatives are really quite different. Top managers feel they can't become very familiar with the prospects for all of their alternatives. So they fall back on the easy-to-compare quantitative criteria. And because the short run is much clearer than the long run, they place heavy emphasis on *current* profitability and return on investment. This puts great pressure on the operating managers to deliver *in the short run*—perhaps even neglecting the long run.

Neglecting the long run is risky—and this is the main weakness of the portfolio approach. This weakness can be overcome by enhancing the portfolio management approach with market-oriented strategic plans. They make it possible for managers to more accurately evaluate the alternatives' short-run and long-run prospects.

EVALUATING OPPORTUNITIES IN INTERNATIONAL MARKETS

Evaluate the risks

The approaches we've discussed so far apply to international markets just as they do to domestic ones. But in international markets it is often harder to fully understand the marketing environment variables. This may make it more difficult to see the risks involved in particular opportunities. Some countries are politically unstable; their governments and constitutions come and go. An investment safe under one government might become a takeover target under another.

Lamb Weston is successful in international markets because potatoes—in many different forms—are common in the diet of most cultures. Other products are much more sensitive to cultural differences.

Exhibit 3-8
Continuum of
Environmental
Sensitivity

Insensitive ← → Sensitive

| Industrial products | Basic commodity-type consumer products | Consumer products that arc linked to cultural variables |

To reduce the risk of missing some basic variable that may help screen out a risky opportunity, marketing managers sometimes need a detailed analysis of the market environment they are considering entering. Such an analysis can reveal facts about an unfamiliar market that a manager in a distant country might otherwise overlook. Further, a local citizen who knows the marketing environment may be able to identify an "obvious" problem ignored even in a careful analysis. Thus, it is very useful for the analysis to include inputs from locals—perhaps cooperative distributors.[29]

Risks vary with environmental sensitivity

The farther you go from familiar territory, the greater the risk of making big mistakes. But not all products, or marketing mixes, involve the same risk. Think of the risks as running along a "continuum of environmental sensitivity." See Exhibit 3-8.

Some products are relatively insensitive to the economic and cultural environment they're placed in. These products may be accepted as is—or they may require just a little adaptation to make them suitable for local use. Most industrial products are near the insensitive end of this continuum.

At the other end of the continuum, we find highly sensitive products that may be difficult or impossible to adapt to all international situations. Consumer products closely linked to other social or cultural variables are at this end. For example, some cultures view dieting as unhealthy; that explains why products like Diet Pepsi that are popular in the United States have done poorly there. "Faddy" type consumer products are also at this end of the continuum. It's sometimes difficult to understand why such products are well accepted in a home market. This, in turn, makes it even more difficult to predict how they might be received in a different environment.

This continuum helps explain why many of the early successes in international marketing were basic commodities such as gasoline, soap, transportation vehicles, mining equipment, and agricultural machinery. It also helps explain why some consumer products firms have been successful with basically the same promotion and products in different parts of the globe.

Yet some managers don't understand the reason for these successes. They think they can develop a global marketing mix for just about *any* product. They fail to see that firms producing and/or selling products near the sensitive end of the continuum should carefully analyze how their products will be seen and used in new environments—and plan their strategies accordingly.[30]

What if risks are still hard to judge?

If the risks of an international opportunity are hard to judge, it may be wise to look first for opportunities that involve exporting. This gives managers a chance to build experience, know-how, and confidence over time. Then the firm will be in a better position to judge the prospects and risks of taking further steps.

CONCLUSION

Businesses need innovative strategy planning to survive in our increasingly competitive markets. In this chapter, we discussed the variables that shape the broad environment of marketing strategy planning and how they may affect opportunities. First we looked at how the firm's own resources and objectives may help guide or limit the search for opportunities. Then we went on to look at the need to understand competition and how to do a competitive analysis. Next we shifted our focus to the external market environments. They are important because changes in these environments present new opportunities, as well as problems, that a marketing manager must deal with in marketing strategy planning.

The economic environment—including chances of recession or inflation—also affects the choice of strategies. And the marketer must try to anticipate, understand, and deal with these changes—as well as changes in the technology underlying the economic environment.

The marketing manager must also be aware of legal restrictions and be sensitive to changing political climates. The acceptance of consumerism has already forced many changes.

The cultural and social environment affects how people behave and what marketing strategies will be successful.

Developing good marketing strategies within all these environments isn't easy. You can see that marketing planning is a challenging job that requires integration of information from many disciplines.

Eventually, managers need procedures for screening and evaluating opportunities. We explained an approach for developing qualitative and quantitative screening criteria—from an analysis of the strengths and weaknesses of the company's resources, the environmental trends it faces, and top management's objectives. We also discussed ways for evaluating and managing quite different opportunities—using the GE strategic planning grid, SBUs, and portfolio management.

Now we can go on in the rest of the book to discuss how to turn opportunities into profitable marketing plans and programs.

KEY TERMS

mission statement, 62

competitive environment, 65

competitor analysis, 66

competitive rivals, 67

competitive barriers, 67

economic and technological environment, 69

technology, 71

Internet, 71

nationalism, 72

North American Free Trade Agreement (NAFTA), 73

cultural and social environment, 77

sustainability, 79

strategic business unit (SBU), 83

portfolio management, 84

QUESTIONS AND PROBLEMS

1. Do you think it makes sense for a firm to base its mission statement on the type of product it produces? For example, would it be good for a division that produces electric motors to have as its mission: "We want to make the best (from our customers' point of view) electric motors available anywhere in the world"?

2. Explain how a firm's objectives may affect its search for opportunities.

3. Specifically, how would various company objectives affect the development of a marketing mix for a new type of Internet browser software? If this company were just being formed by a former programmer with limited financial resources, list the objectives the programmer might have. Then discuss how they would affect the development of the programmer's marketing strategy.

4. Explain how a firm's resources may limit its search for opportunities. Cite a specific example for a specific resource.

5. Discuss how a company's financial strength may have a bearing on the kinds of products it produces. Will it have an impact on the other three Ps as well? If so, how? Use an example in your answer.

6. In your own words, explain how a marketing manager might use a competitor analysis to avoid situations that involve head-on competition.

7. The owner of a small hardware store—the only one in a medium-sized town in the mountains—has just learned that a large home improvement chain plans to open a new store nearby. How difficult will it be for the owner to plan for this new competitive threat? Explain your answer.

8. Discuss the probable impact on your hometown if a major breakthrough in air transportation allowed foreign producers to ship into any U.S. market for about the same transportation cost that domestic producers incur.

9. Will the elimination of trade barriers between countries in Europe eliminate the need to consider submarkets of European consumers? Why or why not?

10. Which way does the U.S. political and legal environment seem to be moving (with respect to business-related affairs)?

11. Why is it necessary to have so many laws regulating business? Why hasn't Congress just passed one set of laws to take care of business problems?

Edition

12. What and who is the U.S. government attempting to protect in its effort to preserve and regulate competition?

13. For each of the *major* laws discussed in the text, indicate whether in the long run the law will promote or restrict competition (see Exhibit 3-4). As a consumer without any financial interest in business, what is your reaction to each of these laws?

14. Explain the product-market screening criteria that can be used to evaluate opportunities.

15. Explain the differences between the total profit approach and the return-on-investment approach to evaluating alternative plans.

16. Explain General Electric's strategic planning grid approach to evaluating opportunities.

17. Distinguish between the operation of a strategic business unit and a firm that only pays lip service to adopting the marketing concept.

CREATING MARKETING PLANS

The Marketing Plan Coach software on the Student CD and the text website includes a sample marketing plan for Hillside Veterinary Clinic. The situation analysis section of the marketing plan includes sections labeled "Competitors" and "External Market Environment." Review those sections and answer the following questions.

a. In the Competitors section, what dimensions were used to analyze competitors? What other dimensions might have been examined?

b. How was competitor information gathered? How else could Hillside have gathered information about its competitors?

c. What aspects of the External Market Environment are included in the marketing plan? What do you think is the most important information in this section?

SUGGESTED CASES

2. Harvest Farm Foods, Inc.   6. Global Steel Company 33. Mulligan & Starling

COMPUTER-AIDED PROBLEM

3. COMPETITOR ANALYSIS

Mediquip, Inc., produces medical equipment and uses its own sales force to sell the equipment to hospitals. Recently, several hospitals have asked Mediquip to develop a laser-beam "scalpel" for eye surgery. Mediquip has the needed resources, and 200 hospitals will probably buy the equipment. But Mediquip managers have heard that Laser Technologies—another quality producer—is thinking of competing for the same business. Mediquip has other good opportunities it could pursue—so it wants to see if it would have a competitive advantage over Laser Tech.

Mediquip and Laser Tech are similar in many ways, but there are important differences. Laser Technologies already produces key parts that are needed for the new laser product—so its production costs would be lower. It would cost Mediquip more to design the product—and getting parts from outside suppliers would result in higher production costs.

On the other hand, Mediquip has marketing strengths. It already has a good reputation with hospitals—and its sales force calls on only hospitals. Mediquip thinks that each of its current sales reps could spend some time selling the new product and that it could adjust sales territories so only four more sales reps would be needed for good coverage in the market. In contrast, Laser Tech's sales reps call on only industrial customers, so it would have to add 14 reps to cover the hospitals.

Hospitals have budget pressures—so the supplier with the lowest price is likely to get a larger share of the business. But Mediquip knows that either supplier's price will be set high enough to cover the added costs of designing, producing, and selling the new product—and leave something for profit.

Mediquip gathers information about its own likely costs and can estimate Laser Tech's costs from industry studies and Laser Tech's annual report. Mediquip has set up a spreadsheet to evaluate the proposed new product.

a. The initial spreadsheet results are based on the assumption that Mediquip and Laser Tech will split the business 50/50. If Mediquip can win at least 50 percent of the market, does Mediquip have a competitive advantage over Laser Tech? Explain.

b. Because of economies of scale, both suppliers' average cost per machine will vary depending on the quantity sold. If Mediquip had only 45 percent of the market and Laser Tech 55 percent, how would their costs (average total cost per machine) compare? What if Mediquip had 55 percent of the market and Laser Tech only 45 percent? What conclusion do you draw from these analyses?

c. It is possible that Laser Tech may not enter the market. If Mediquip has 100 percent of the market, and quantity purchases from its suppliers will reduce the cost of producing one unit to $6,500, what price would cover all its costs and contribute $1,125 to profit for every machine sold? What does this suggest about the desirability of finding your own unsatisfied target markets? Explain.

For additional questions related to this problem, see Exercise 3-4 in the *Learning Aid for Use with Basic Marketing*, 17th edition.

4

CHAPTER

Focusing Marketing Strategy with Segmentation and Positioning

Back in the 1980s, Nintendo was a 100-year-old Japanese manufacturer of toys and playing cards. If Nintendo managers had continued to just think about the "toy market," the firm probably wouldn't even be around now. Instead, they realized there were profitable new opportunities to meet needs in the broader entertainment seekers market. In 1985, they released the Nintendo Entertainment System (NES) and interactive video games such as Super Mario Brothers and the Legend of Zelda. With nearly twice as many potential customers in the United States as in Japan, they saw that it made sense to fine-tune a marketing mix for each market. In those early days, video game consoles and software from different producers were quite similar. Even so, Nintendo's NES was a market leader because it stood out as offering better value. And Nintendo's profits took off because once a household owned an NES console it qualified as a prime target for new Nintendo games.

As the market evolved, Nintendo identified other types of products that met the needs of specific types of customers. Its very popular GameBoy, for instance, was a terrific way to deliver portable fun to kids. However, as the market grew, competition mainly focused on improving gaming consoles, like Nintendo's GameCube and Sony's PlayStation, with high-speed processors and better graphics quality. That seemed to be sensible because it was what hard-core gamers wanted. They were the first to buy new games and equipment and were also less price sensitive. Action, racing, and adventure games were most popular with this mainly male group, and those games required realistic video—which in turn was the key benefit of a powerful console.

Unfortunately, state-of-the-art power is pricey, and many budget-conscious buyers couldn't afford a high-end console. Another problem was that challenging games designed for hard-core gamers were hard for a novice player to learn. In addition, many people simply weren't interested in the type of action popular with gamers. In fact, critics argued that many action games—and ads for those games—were too violent for children. To address these concerns, Nintendo and other firms adopted a video game rating system and advertising code of ethics. Parents usually won't buy a game that is not rated as suitable for kids, and some retailers won't carry games that don't have a "family" rating.

Planners at Nintendo realized that the needs of the hard-core gamer segment were being served very well, but that other groups—like families, senior citizens, and even teenage females—were not. Moreover, in combination these subgroups had the potential to be a large target market of casual gamers. Research showed that this subgroup of potential customers was interested in interactive game entertainment, if it was affordable, easy to try and learn, and a fun social experience rather than a solo act.

89

To appeal to the casual gamers, Nintendo first developed a new handheld game player called the DS (for Dual Screen). The DS responds to an intuitive touch panel and spoken commands. Because there are no difficult rules or hard-to-learn controls, casual gamers can play with it immediately. Further, the DS's Wi-Fi connection makes it easy for people to play together. The games are also distinctive. Girls enjoy games like Nintendogs, in which they teach virtual pets to play fetch or do other tricks. Girls like the pink DS, but baby boomers prefer the clean look of the arctic white unit. Like the senior citizens, they find Brain Age engaging. It promises to "Train Your Brain in Minutes a Day" with a light mental workout of Sudoku puzzles and word quizzes. To spread this message, Nintendo put print ads in magazines for senior citizens. The ads showed gray-haired couples enjoying the Nintendo DS and promoted the idea that regular play aids memory. These efforts to attract first-time and casual gamers worked so well that the DS became the largest selling video game system of all time.

To build on its success with the casual gamers, Nintendo introduced the Wii (pronounced "we"). The Wii name emphasizes that the console is for everyone—and the $249 value price supports that position as well. The benefit of Wii's biggest innovation—its wireless, motion-sensitive controller—is that it makes video game play easy and

intuitive. The Wii's handheld controller guides on-screen actions when it is swung like a baseball bat, arced to simulate throwing a football, or tilted to steer a car or truck. Wii Sports, which comes packaged with the console, gets players off to a quick start with familiar games like tennis and bowling. Retirement communities even organize Wii bowling tournaments because they prompt senior citizens to socialize and exercise. As this suggests, Wii is not for couch potatoes. Many games—like Mario Galaxy and Dance Revolution—require players to get up and move. This is a positive with parents. And that's why much of Nintendo's promotion targets moms. For example, its Ambassadors program invited well-connected moms to luxury hotels where they sipped champagne, ate cookies, and played Wii. Many of these moms later threw their own parties and spread the word. Similarly, much of Wii's ad budget targeted women aged 25 to 49 on shows like "Dancing with the Stars."

Over the years, Nintendo has had successes by seeing new ways to meet customers' needs. That's why both DS and Wii have been smash hits. Now, Microsoft and Sony are developing similar offerings. Further, other innovators are coming on strong with different types of interactive entertainment, including multiplayer online games. Will Nintendo continue to compete with effective market segmentation? Stay tuned to find out. While you wait, Wii would like to play.[1]

SEARCH FOR OPPORTUNITIES CAN BEGIN BY UNDERSTANDING MARKETS

Strategy planning is a narrowing-down process

In Chapter 2 we provided a framework for a logical marketing strategy planning process. It involves careful evaluation of the market opportunities available before narrowing down to focus on the most attractive target market and marketing mix. In Chapter 3, we focused on approaches for analyzing how competitors and the external market environment shape the evaluation of opportunities. In this chapter we discuss concepts that can guide the selection of specific target customers. See Exhibit 4-1 for an overview.

In a broad sense, this chapter is about understanding and analyzing customers in a market. In Chapters 5, 6, and 7 we will look more closely at specific influences on the behavior of both final consumers and organizational customers. However, this chapter sets the stage for that by explaining how marketing managers combine different types of information about customers to guide targeting decisions.

Since this chapter is about bringing focus to the search for market opportunities, a good place to start is by discussing what we really mean when we use the term *market*.

What is a company's market?

Identifying a company's market is an important but sticky issue. In general, a market is a group of potential customers with similar needs who are willing to exchange something of value with sellers offering various goods or services—that is, ways of satisfying those needs. However, within a general market, marketing-oriented managers develop marketing mixes for *specific* target markets. Getting the firm to focus on specific target markets is vital.

Don't just focus on the product

Some production-oriented managers don't understand this narrowing-down process. They get into trouble because they ignore the tough part of defining markets. To make the narrowing-down process easier, they just describe their markets in terms of

Exhibit 4–1   Focusing Marketing Strategy with Segmentation and Positioning

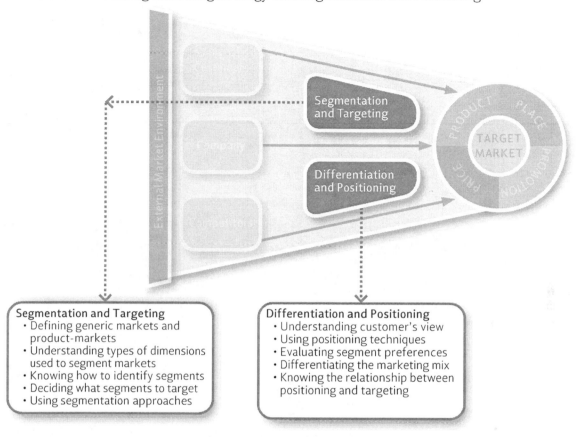

Segmentation and Targeting
- Defining generic markets and product-markets
- Understanding types of dimensions used to segment markets
- Knowing how to identify segments
- Deciding what segments to target
- Using segmentation approaches

Differentiation and Positioning
- Understanding customer's view
- Using positioning techniques
- Evaluating segment preferences
- Differentiating the marketing mix
- Knowing the relationship between positioning and targeting

products they sell. For example, producers and retailers of greeting cards might define their market as the "greeting card" market. But this production-oriented approach ignores customers—and customers make a market! This also leads to missed opportunities. Hallmark isn't missing these opportunities. Instead, Hallmark aims at the "personal-expression" market. Hallmark stores offer all kinds of products that can be sent as "memory makers"—to express one person's feelings toward another. And as opportunities related to these needs change, Hallmark changes too. For example, at the Hallmark website (www.hallmark.com) it is easy to get shopping suggestions from an online "gift assistant," to order flowers, or to personalize an electronic greeting card to send online.[2]

From generic markets to product-markets

To understand the narrowing-down process, it's useful to think of two basic types of markets. A generic market is a market with *broadly* similar needs—and sellers offering various, *often diverse*, ways of satisfying those needs. In contrast, a product-market is a market with *very* similar needs and sellers offering various *close substitute* ways of satisfying those needs.[3]

A generic market description looks at markets broadly and from a customer's viewpoint. Entertainment-seekers, for example, have several very different ways to satisfy their needs. An entertainment-seeker might buy a Blu-ray disc player and a high-definition TV (HDTV), sign up for a cruise on the Carnival Line, or reserve season tickets for the symphony. Any one of these *very different* products may satisfy this entertainment need. Sellers in this generic entertainment-seeker market have to focus

Flam is an eat-on-the-go French snack "in a wrap" that contains pieces of pork and onions in a thick sauce made with soft white cheese. It is not a sandwich, but if it were available in this country it might compete in the same generic market with Blimpie's Panini. The products are different, but they both serve the need for a convenient and tasty luncheon treat.

on the need(s) the customers want satisfied—not on how one seller's product (HDTV system, vacation, or live music) is better than that of another producer.

It is sometimes hard to understand and define generic markets because *quite different product types may compete with each other*. For example, a person on a business trip to Italy might want a convenient way to record memories of the trip. Minolta's digital camera, Sony's video camcorder, and even postcards from local shops may all compete to serve our traveler's needs. If customers see all these products as substitutes—as competitors in the same generic market—then marketers must deal with this complication.

Suppose, however, that our traveler decides to satisfy this need with a digital camera. Then—in this product-market—Minolta, Kodak, Panasonic, Nikon, and many other brands may compete with each other for the customer's dollars. In this *product-*market concerned with digital cameras *and* needs to conveniently record memories, consumers compare similar products to satisfy their image needs.

Broaden market definitions to find opportunities

Broader market definitions—including both generic market definitions and product-market definitions—can help firms find opportunities. But deciding *how* broad to go isn't easy. Too narrow a definition limits a firm's opportunities—but too broad a definition makes the company's efforts and resources seem insignificant. Consider, for example, the mighty Coca-Cola Company. It has great success and a huge market share in the U.S. cola-drinkers' market. On the other hand, its share of all beverage drinking worldwide is very small.

Here we try to match opportunities to a firm's resources and objectives. So the *relevant market for finding opportunities* should be bigger than the firm's present product-market—but not so big that the firm couldn't expand and be an important competitor. A small manufacturer of screwdrivers in Mexico, for example, shouldn't define its market as broadly as "the worldwide tool users market" or as narrowly as "our present screwdriver customers." But it may have the capabilities to consider "the handyman's hand-tool market in North America." Carefully naming your product-market can help you see possible opportunities.

Nestlé targets customers in many different geographic markets around the world, but often the product-markets in one country are different than in another. For example, Nestlé created banana-flavored milk ice on a stick to fit the local tastes and preferences of Chinese consumers. The same product would probably not have a following in other places.

NAMING PRODUCT-MARKETS AND GENERIC MARKETS

Some managers think about markets just in terms of the product they already produce and sell. But this approach can lead to missed opportunities. For example, think about all of the minivans and SUVs that you see and how many cars they've replaced on the road. If Chrysler had been thinking only about the "car" market, the minivan opportunity might have been missed altogether. Similarly, photographic film is being replaced with digital pictures, digital video recorders (DVRs) are replacing VCRs, and MP3 players have replaced portable CD players.

As this suggests, when evaluating opportunities, product-related terms do not—by themselves—adequately describe a market. A complete product-market definition includes a four-part description.

What:	1. **Product type (type of good and type of service)**
To meet what:	2. **Customer (user) needs**
For whom:	3. **Customer types**
Where:	4. **Geographic area**

We refer to these four-part descriptions as product-market "names" because most managers label their markets when they think, write, or talk about them. Such a four-part definition can be clumsy, however, so we often use a nickname. And the nickname should refer to people—not products—because, as we emphasize, people make markets!

Product type should meet customer needs

Product type describes the goods and/or services that customers want. Sometimes the product type is strictly a physical good or strictly a service. But marketing managers who ignore the possibility that *both* are important can miss opportunities.

Customer (user) needs refer to the needs the product type satisfies for the customer. At a very basic level, product types usually provide functional benefits such as nourishing, protecting, warming, cooling, transporting, cleaning, holding, and saving time. Although we need to identify such "basic" needs first, in advanced economies, we usually go on to emotional needs—such as needs for fun, excitement, pleasing appearance, or status. Correctly defining the need(s) relevant to a market is crucial and requires a good understanding of customers. We discuss these topics more fully in Chapters 6 and 7. As a brief example, however, a buyer might want a small van to

Edition

handle various cargo- and people-moving needs. The marketer would need to consider related needs such as economy in use, flexibility and convenience in changing the seat arrangement, comfort for the driver and passengers, and perhaps the image the driver wants to project.

Customer type refers to the final consumer or user of a product type. Here we want to choose a name that describes all present (possible) types of customers. To define customer type, marketers should identify the final consumer or user of the product type, rather than the buyer—if they are different. For instance, producers should avoid treating intermediaries as a customer type—unless intermediaries actually use the product in their own business.

The *geographic area* is where a firm competes, or plans to compete, for customers. Naming the geographic area may seem trivial, but understanding the geographic boundaries of a market can suggest new opportunities. A firm aiming only at the domestic market, for example, may want to expand to other countries.

Product-market boundaries provide focus

This idea of making a decision about the boundaries of a market applies not just to geographic areas served but also to decisions about customer needs and product and customer types. Thus, naming the market is not simply an exercise in assigning labels. Rather, the manager's market definition sets the limits of the market(s) in which the firm will compete. For example, both final consumers and business customers have a variety of "fastening" needs that might be met with products ranging from screws and glues to tapes and welding. However, if a marketing manager decides that the firm should focus on business customers and not on individual consumers, then that should be explicit in the market definition. That decision limits the scope of the market and, at the same time, sharpens the focus.

No product type in generic market names

A generic market description *doesn't include any product-type terms*. It consists of only three parts of the product-market definition—without the product type. This emphasizes that any product type that satisfies the customer's needs can compete in a generic market. Exhibit 4-2 shows the relationship between generic market and product-market definitions.

Later we'll study the many possible dimensions for segmenting markets. But for now you should see that defining markets only in terms of current products is not the best way to find new opportunities. Instead, the most effective way to find opportunities is to use market segmentation.

Exhibit 4-2
Relationship between Generic and Product-Market Definitions

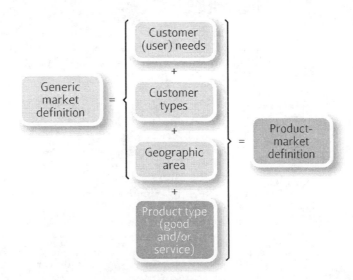

Edition

MARKET SEGMENTATION DEFINES POSSIBLE TARGET MARKETS

Market segmentation is a two-step process

Market segmentation is a two-step process of (1) *naming* broad product-markets and (2) *segmenting* these broad product-markets in order to select target markets and develop suitable marketing mixes.

This two-step process isn't well understood. First-time market segmentation efforts often fail because beginners start with the whole mass market and try to find one or two demographic characteristics to divide up (segment) this market. Customer behavior is usually too complex to be explained in terms of just one or two demographic characteristics. For example, not all elderly men buy the same products or brands. Other dimensions usually must be considered—starting with customer needs.

Naming broad product-markets is disaggregating

The first step in effective market segmentation involves naming a broad product-market of interest to the firm. Marketers must break apart—disaggregate—all possible needs into some generic markets and broad product-markets in which the firm may be able to operate profitably. See Exhibit 4-3. No one firm can satisfy everyone's needs. So the naming—disaggregating—step involves brainstorming about very different solutions to various generic needs and selecting some broad areas—broad product-markets—where the firm has some resources and experience. This means that a car manufacturer would probably ignore all the possible opportunities in food and clothing markets and focus on the generic market, "transporting people in the world," and probably on the broad product-market, "cars, trucks, and utility vehicles for transporting people in the world."

Disaggregating, a practical rough-and-ready approach, tries to narrow down the marketing focus to product-market areas where the firm is more likely to have a competitive advantage or even to find breakthrough opportunities.

Market grid is a visual aid to market segmentation

Assuming that any broad product-market (or generic market) may consist of submarkets, picture a market as a rectangle with boxes that represent the smaller, more homogeneous product-markets.

Exhibit 4-4, for example, represents the broad product-market of bicycle riders. The boxes show different submarkets. One submarket might focus on people who

Exhibit 4-3
Narrowing Down to Target Markets

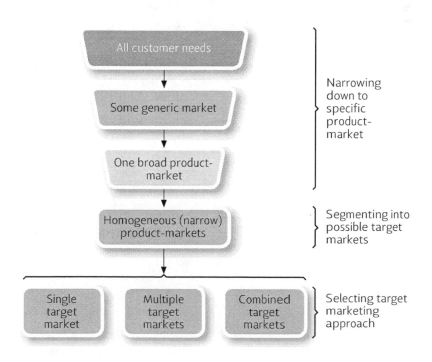

All customer needs

⬇

Some generic market

⬇

One broad product-market

⬇

Homogeneous (narrow) product-markets

⬇

Single target market   Multiple target markets   Combined target markets

Narrowing down to specific product-market

Segmenting into possible target markets

Selecting target marketing approach

Edition

Initially the Clorox brand name became well known as laundry bleach, but now the brand is used with other products related to the broader product-market for household cleaning needs.

want basic transportation, another on people who want exercise, and so on. Alternatively, in the generic "transporting market" discussed earlier, we might see different product-markets of customers for bicycles, motorcycles, cars, airplanes, ships, buses, and "others."

Segmenting is an aggregating process

Marketing-oriented managers think of segmenting as an aggregating process—clustering people with similar needs into a "market segment." A market segment is a (relatively) homogeneous group of customers who will respond to a marketing mix in a similar way.

This part of the market segmentation process takes a different approach from the naming part. Here we look for similarities rather than basic differences in needs. Segmenters start with the idea that each person is one of a kind but that it may be possible to aggregate some similar people into a product-market.

Segmenters see each of these one-of-a-kind people as having a unique set of dimensions. Consider a product-market in which customers' needs differ on two important segmenting dimensions: need for status and need for dependability. In Exhibit 4-5A, each dot shows a person's position on the two dimensions. While each person's position is unique, many of these people are similar in terms of how much status and dependability they want. So a segmenter may aggregate them into three (an arbitrary number) relatively homogeneous submarkets—A, B, and C. Group A might be called

Exhibit 4-4
A Market Grid Diagram with Submarkets

Broad product-market (or generic market) name goes here
(The bicycle-riders product-market)

Submarket 1 (Exercisers)	Submarket 3 (Transportation riders)	Submarket 4 (Socializers)
Submarket 2 (Off-road adventurers)	Submarket 5 (Environmentalists)	

Edition

Exhibit 4-5
Every Individual Has His or Her Own Unique Position in a Market—Those with Similar Positions Can Be Aggregated into Potential Target Markets

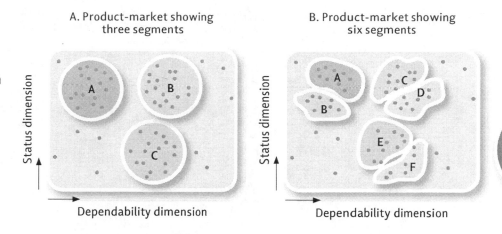

A. Product-market showing three segments

B. Product-market showing six segments

"status-oriented" and Group C "dependability-oriented." Members of Group B want both and might be called the "demanders."

How far should the aggregating go?

The segmenter wants to aggregate individual customers into some workable number of relatively homogeneous target markets and then treat each target market differently.

Look again at Exhibit 4-5A. Remember we talked about three segments. But this was an arbitrary number. As Exhibit 4-5B shows, there may really be six segments. What do you think—does this broad product-market consist of three segments or six?

Another difficulty with segmenting is that some potential customers just don't fit neatly into market segments. For example, not everyone in Exhibit 4-5B was put into one of the groups. Forcing them into one of the groups would have made these segments more heterogeneous and harder to please. Further, forming additional segments for them probably wouldn't be profitable. They are too few and not very similar in terms of the two dimensions. These people are simply too unique to be catered to and may have to be ignored—unless they are willing to pay a high price for special treatment.

The number of segments that should be formed depends more on judgment than on some scientific rule. But the following guidelines can help.

Criteria for segmenting a broad product-market

Ideally, "good" market segments meet the following criteria:

1. *Homogeneous (similar) within*—the customers in a market segment should be as similar as possible with respect to their likely responses to marketing mix variables *and* their segmenting dimensions.
2. *Heterogeneous (different) between*—the customers in different segments should be as different as possible with respect to their likely responses to marketing mix variables *and* their segmenting dimensions.
3. *Substantial*—the segment should be big enough to be profitable.
4. *Operational*—the segmenting dimensions should be useful for identifying customers and deciding on marketing mix variables.

It is especially important that segments be *operational*. This leads marketers to include demographic dimensions such as age, sex, income, location, and family size. In fact, it is difficult to make some Place and Promotion decisions without such information.

Avoid segmenting dimensions that have no practical operational use. For example, you may find a personality trait such as moodiness among the traits of heavy buyers of a product, but how could you use this fact? Salespeople can't give a personality test to each buyer. Similarly, advertising couldn't make much use of this information. So although moodiness might be related in some way to previous purchases, it would not be a useful dimension for segmenting.

Edition

Firms that compete in the oral health care market have developed a variety of products that appeal to the needs of different customer segments. Sensodyne targets consumers who have sensitive teeth. Crest Pro-Health targets consumers, especially adults, who have a combined set of oral care concerns. Orajel targets parents of toddlers with a gentle, nonabrasive toothpaste and fun flavors that toddlers will love.

Target marketers aim at specific targets

Once you accept the idea that broad product-markets may have submarkets, you can see that target marketers usually have a choice among many possible target markets.

There are three basic ways to develop market-oriented strategies in a broad product-market.

1. The single target market approach—segmenting the market and picking one of the homogeneous segments as the firm's target market.
2. The multiple target market approach—segmenting the market and choosing two or more segments, and then treating each as a separate target market needing a different marketing mix.
3. The combined target market approach—combining two or more submarkets into one larger target market as a basis for one strategy.

Note that all three approaches involve target marketing. They all aim at specific, clearly defined target markets. See Exhibit 4-6. For convenience, we call people who follow the first two approaches the "segmenters" and people who use the third approach the "combiners."

Combiners try to satisfy "pretty well"

Combiners try to increase the size of their target markets by combining two or more segments. Combiners look at various submarkets for similarities rather than differences. Then they try to extend or modify their basic offering to appeal to these "combined" customers with just one marketing mix. For example, a combiner who faces the broad bicycle-riders product-market shown in Exhibit 4-4 might try to develop a marketing mix that would do a pretty good job of appealing to both the *Exercisers* and the *Off-road adventurers*. The combined market would be bigger than either segment by itself. However, there are some distinct differences between the two submarkets. Thus, our combiner will have to make compromises in developing the marketing mix. The combiner doesn't try to fine-tune each element of the marketing mix to appeal to each of the smaller submarkets. Rather, the marketing mix is selected to work "fairly well" with each segment.

A combined target market approach may help achieve some economies of scale. It may also require less investment than developing different marketing mixes for different segments—making it especially attractive for firms with limited resources.

Exhibit 4–6
Segmenters and Combiners Aim at Specific Target Markets

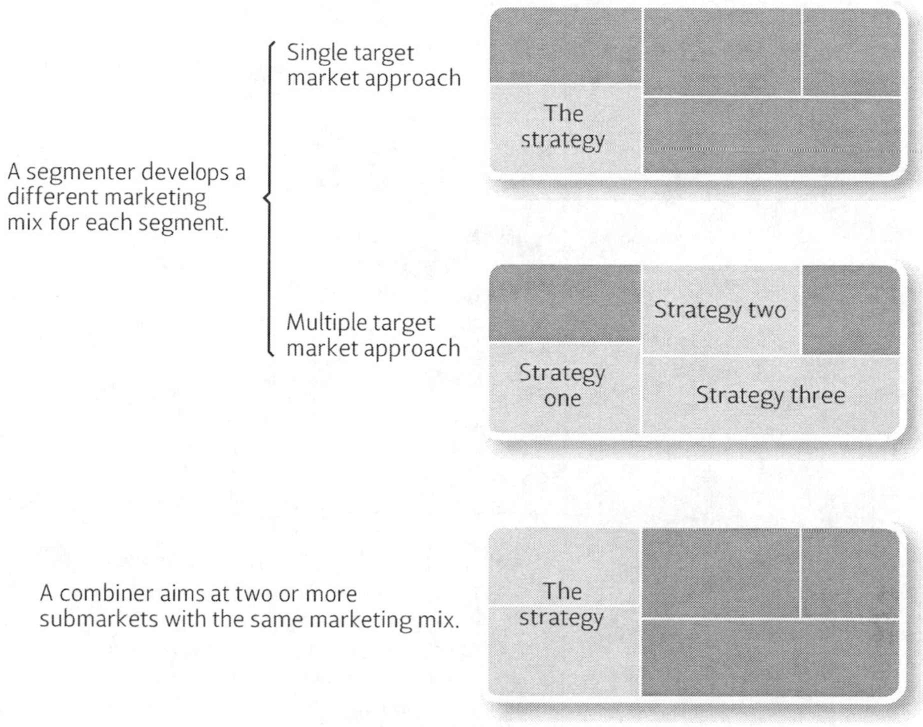

A segmenter develops a different marketing mix for each segment.

Single target market approach

The strategy

Multiple target market approach

Strategy two

Strategy one

Strategy three

A combiner aims at two or more submarkets with the same marketing mix.

The strategy

Too much combining is risky

It is tempting to aim at larger combined markets instead of using different marketing mixes for smaller segmented markets. But combiners must be careful not to aggregate too far. As they enlarge the target market, individual differences within each submarket may begin to outweigh the similarities. This makes it harder to develop marketing mixes that can satisfy potential customers.

A combiner faces the continual risk of innovative segmenters chipping away at the various segments of the combined target market—by offering more attractive marketing mixes to more homogeneous submarkets. ATI Technologies saw this happen. It produced high-quality graphics chips with features desired by a wide variety of computer users. But then ATI lost business to more specialized competitors like Nvidia Corp. Nvidia focused on the needs of video-game lovers who don't want to compromise when it comes to realistic special effects. Nvidia developed chips that did fewer things, but by doing those specialized things really well it captured much of the video-game lovers' business—until ATI did more segmenting and was ultimately acquired by AMD.[4]

Segmenters try to satisfy "very well"

Segmenters aim at one or more homogeneous segments and try to develop a different marketing mix for each segment. Segmenters usually fine-tune their marketing mixes for each target market—perhaps making basic changes in the product itself—because they want to satisfy each segment very well.

Instead of assuming that the whole market consists of a fairly similar set of customers (like the mass marketer does) or merging various submarkets together (like the combiner), segmenters believe that aiming at one, or some, of these smaller markets makes it possible to provide superior value and satisfy them better. This then provides greater profit potential for the firm.

Segmenting may produce bigger sales

Note that segmenters are not settling for a smaller sales potential or lower profits. Instead, they hope to increase sales by getting a much larger share of the business in the market(s) they target. A segmenter that really satisfies the target market can often build such a close relationship with customers that it faces no real competition. A segmenter that offers a marketing mix precisely matched to the needs of the target market can

Edition

often charge a higher price that produces higher profits. Customers are willing to pay a higher price because the whole marketing mix provides better customer value.

Consider the success of the Aeron desk chair developed by Herman Miller (HM), an 80-year-old company that makes office furniture. Most firms that sell office furniture offered similar lines of executive desk chairs that were padded for comfort and conveyed the look of success. Marketing managers at HM realized that some customers felt that these traditional chairs were boring. Further, in an e-commerce world, even top executives sit at computers and want a chair that provides both good support and good looks. So to satisfy this upscale segment, HM designed a new type of chair from scratch. There's no fabric or padding, but everything about it adjusts to your body. It's so comfortable that HM positions it as "the chair you can wear." With a price tag close to $1,000, the Aeron chair became a status symbol for high-tech managers and has been as profitable as it is popular.[5]

Should you segment or combine?

Which approach should a firm use? This depends on the firm's resources, the nature of competition, and—most important—the similarity of customer needs, attitudes, and buying behavior.

In general, it's usually safer to be a segmenter—that is, to try to satisfy some customers *very* well instead of many just *fairly* well. That's why many firms use the single or multiple target market approach instead of the combined target market approach. Procter & Gamble, for example, offers many products that seem to compete directly with each other (e.g., Tide versus Cheer or Crest versus Gleem). However, P&G offers tailor-made marketing mixes to each submarket large and profitable enough to deserve a separate marketing mix. Though extremely effective, this approach may not be possible for a smaller firm with more limited resources. A smaller firm may have to use the single target market approach—focusing all its efforts at the one submarket niche where it sees the best opportunity.[6]

Kaepa, Inc., is a good example. Sales of its all-purpose sneakers plummeted as larger firms like Nike and Reebok stole customers with a multiple target market approach. They developed innovative products and aimed their promotion at specific needs—like jogging, aerobics, cross-training, and walking. Kaepa turned things around by catering to the needs of cheerleaders. Cheerleading squads can order Kaepa shoes with custom team logos and colors. The soles of the shoes feature finger grooves that make it easier for cheerleaders to build human pyramids. Kaepa also carefully targets its market research and promotion. Kaepa salespeople attend the cheerleading camps that each summer draw 40,000 enthusiasts. Kaepa even arranges for the cheering teams it sponsors to do demos at retail stores. This generates publicity and pulls in buyers, so retailers put more emphasis on the Kaepa line.[7]

Profit is the balancing point

In practice, cost considerations probably encourage more aggregating—to obtain economies of scale—while demand (and revenue) considerations suggest less aggregating—to satisfy needs more exactly.

Profit is the balancing point. It determines how unique a marketing mix the firm can afford to offer to a particular group.

WHAT DIMENSIONS ARE USED TO SEGMENT MARKETS?

Segmenting dimensions guide marketing mix planning

Market segmentation forces a marketing manager to decide which product-market dimensions might be useful for planning marketing strategies. The dimensions should help guide marketing mix planning. Exhibit 4-7 shows the basic kinds of dimensions

Exhibit 4-7   Relation of Potential Target Market Dimensions to Marketing Strategy Decision Areas

Potential Target Market Dimensions	Effects on Strategy Decision Areas
1. Behavioral needs, attitudes, and how present and potential goods and services fit into customers' consumption patterns.	Affects *Product* (features, packaging, product line assortment, branding) and *Promotion* (what potential customers need and want to know about the firm's offering, and what appeals should be used).
2. Urgency to get need satisfied and desire and willingness to seek information, compare, and shop.	Affects *Place* (how directly products are distributed from producer to customer, how extensively they are made available, and the level of service needed) and *Price* (how much potential customers are willing to pay).
3. Geographic location and other demographic characteristics of potential customers.	Affects size of *Target Markets* (economic potential), *Place* (where products should be made available), and *Promotion* (where and to whom to target advertising and personal selling).

we'll be talking about in Chapters 5 and 6—and their probable effect on the four Ps. Ideally, we want to describe any potential product-market in terms of all three types of customer-related dimensions—plus a product type description—because these dimensions help us develop better marketing mixes.

Many segmenting dimensions may be considered

Customers can be described by many specific dimensions. Exhibit 4-8 shows some dimensions useful for segmenting consumer markets. A few are behavioral dimensions; others are geographic and demographic. We discuss these final consumer segmenting dimensions in Chapters 5 and 6. Exhibit 4-9 shows some additional dimensions for segmenting markets when the customers are businesses, government agencies, or other types of organizations. These dimensions for segmenting organizational customers are covered in Chapter 7. Regardless of whether customers are final consumers or organizations, segmenting a broad product-market *usually* requires using several different dimensions at the same time.[8]

People who are out in the sun should protect their skin. This safety need is a qualifying dimension of consumers in the marketing for sunblock products. However, parents may buy Banana Boat Baby and Kids Sunblock Lotion and Baby Sprays because they are easy on kids' eyes and don't cause tearing. For these parents this is a determining need. There are a variety of ways that Coffee-Mate is different from cream, but this ad focuses on the idea that it does not need to be refrigerated. For some consumers, that determines what they will buy.

Edition

Exhibit 4-8   Possible Segmenting Dimensions and Typical Breakdowns for Consumer Markets

Behavioral	
Needs	Economic, functional, physiological, psychological, social, and more detailed needs.
Benefits sought	Situation specific, but to satisfy specific or general needs.
Thoughts	Favorable or unfavorable attitudes, interests, opinions, beliefs.
Rate of use	Heavy, medium, light, nonusers.
Purchase relationship	Positive and ongoing, intermittent, no relationship, bad relationship.
Brand familiarity	Insistence, preference, recognition, nonrecognition, rejection.
Kind of shopping	Convenience, comparison shopping, specialty, none (unsought product).
Type of problem solving	Routinized response, limited, extensive.
Information required	Low, medium, high.
Geographic	
Region of world, country	North America (United States, Canada), Europe (France, Italy, Germany), and so on.
Region in country	(Examples in United States): Pacific, Mountain, West North Central, West South Central, East North Central, East South Central, South Atlantic, Middle Atlantic, New England.
Size of city	No city; population under 5,000; 5,000–19,999; 20,000–49,999; 50,000–99,999; 100,000–249,999; 250,000–499,999; 500,000–999,999; 1,000,000–3,999,999; 4,000,000 or over.
Demographic	
Income	Under $5,000; $5,000–9,999; $10,000–14,999; $15,000–19,999; $20,000–29,999; $30,000–39,999; $40,000–59,999; $60,000 and over.
Sex	Male, female.
Age	Infant; under 6; 6–11; 12–17; 18–24; 25–34; 35–49; 50–64; 65 or over.
Family size	1, 2, 3–4, 5 or more.
Family life cycle	Young, single; young, married, no children; young, married, youngest child under 6; young, married, youngest child over 6; older, married, with children; older, married, no children under 18; older, single; other variations for single parents, divorced, etc.
Occupation	Professional and technical; managers, officials, and proprietors; clerical sales; craftspeople; foremen; operatives; farmers; retired; students; housewives; unemployed.
Education	Grade school or less; some high school; high school graduate; some college; college graduate.
Ethnicity	Asian, Black, Hispanic, Native American, White, multiracial.
Social class	Lower-lower, upper-lower, lower-middle, upper-middle, lower-upper, upper-upper.

Note: Terms used in this table are explained in detail later in the text.

What are the qualifying and determining dimensions?

To select the important segmenting dimensions, think about two different types of dimensions. Qualifying dimensions are those relevant to including a customer type in a product-market. Determining dimensions are those that actually affect the customer's purchase of a specific product or brand in a product-market.

A prospective car buyer, for example, has to have enough money—or credit—to buy a car and insure it. Our buyer also needs a driver's license. This still doesn't guarantee a purchase. He or she must have a real need—like a job that requires "wheels" or kids who have to be carpooled. This need may motivate the purchase of *some* car. But these qualifying dimensions don't determine what specific brand or model car the person might buy. That depends on more specific interests—such as the kind of safety, performance, or appearance the customer wants. Determining dimensions related to these needs affect the specific car the customer purchases. If safety is a determining

Exhibit 4–9
Possible Segmenting
Dimensions for
Business/Organizational
Markets

Kind of relationship	Weak loyalty → strong loyalty to vendor Single source → multiple vendors "Arm's length" dealings → close partnership
Type of customer	Manufacturer, service producer, government agency, military, nonprofit, wholesaler or retailer (when end user), and so on.
Demographics	Geographic location (region of world, country, region within country, urban → rural); Size (number of employees, sales volume); Primary business or industry (North American Industry Classification System); Number of facilities
How customer will use product	Installations, components, accessories, raw materials, supplies, professional services
Type of buying situation	Decentralized → centralized Buyer → multiple buying influence Straight rebuy → modified rebuy → new-task buying
Purchasing methods	Vendor analysis, purchasing specifications, Internet bids, negotiated contracts, long-term contracts, e-commerce websites

Note: Terms used in this table are explained in detail later in the text.

dimension for a customer, a Volvo wagon that offers side impact protection, air bags, and all-wheel drive might be the customer's first choice.

Determining dimensions may be very specific

How specific the determining dimensions are depends on whether you are concerned with a general product type or a specific brand. See Exhibit 4-10. The more specific you want to be, the more particular the determining dimensions may be. In a particular case, the determining dimensions may seem minor. But they are important because they *are* the determining dimensions.

Marketers at General Mills know this. Lots of people try to check e-mail or drive a car while eating breakfast or lunch. General Mills has figured out that for many of these target customers the real determining dimension in picking a snack is whether it can be eaten "one-handed."

Exhibit 4–10   Finding the Relevant Segmenting Dimensions

Segmenting dimensions become more specific to reasons why the target segment chooses to buy a particular brand of the product

All potential dimensions	Qualifying dimensions	Determining dimensions (product type)	Determining dimensions (brand specific)
Dimensions generally relevant to purchasing behavior	Dimensions relevant to including a customer type in the product-market	Dimensions that affect the customer's purchase of a specific type of product	Dimensions that affect the customer's choice of a specific brand

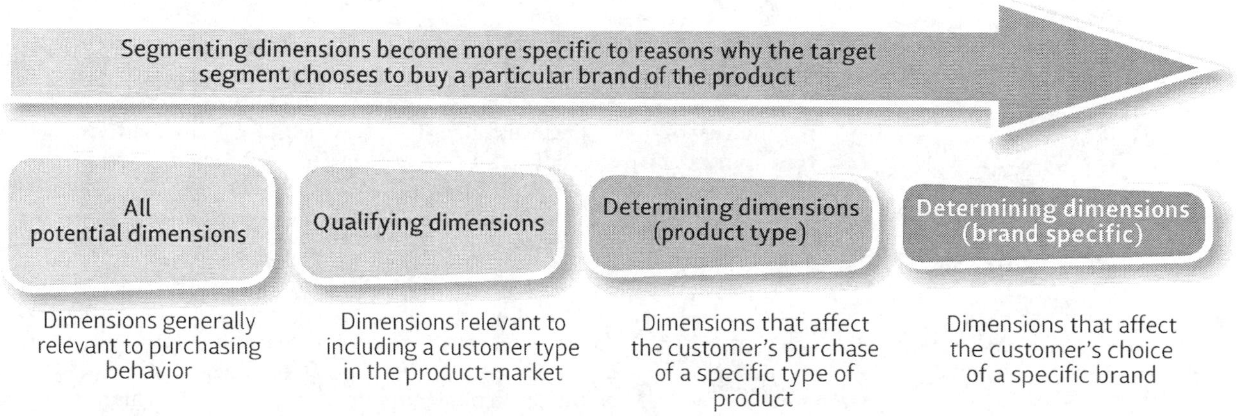

Edition

Qualifying dimensions are important too

The qualifying dimensions help identify the "core benefits" that must be offered to everyone in a product-market. For example, people won't choose General Mills' one-handed snacks unless they qualify as being tasty. Qualifying and determining dimensions work together in marketing strategy planning.

Different dimensions needed for different submarkets

Note that each different submarket within a broad product-market may be motivated by a different set of dimensions. In the snack food market, for example, health food enthusiasts are interested in nutrition, dieters worry about calories, and economical shoppers with lots of kids may want volume to "fill them up."

Ethical issues in selecting segmenting dimensions

Marketing managers sometimes face ethical decisions when selecting segmenting dimensions. Problems may arise if a firm targets customers who are somehow at a disadvantage in dealing with the firm or who are unlikely to see the negative effects of their own choices. For example, some people criticize shoe companies for targeting poor, inner-city kids who see expensive athletic shoes as an important status symbol. Many firms, including producers of infant formula, have been criticized for targeting consumers in less-developed nations. Some nutritionists criticize firms that market soft drinks, candy, and snack foods to children.

> **Ethics QUESTION**
>
> A consumer group has criticized an encyclopedia publisher for targeting low-income parents. They respond well to sales appeals that focus on the low cost-per-day of encyclopedias that help kids enjoy learning. The critics say that the parents can't afford the books and don't understand the publisher's credit plan. In reply, the publisher cites a teacher group that touts the books as an excellent value. What do you think about this issue? If you were the marketing manager for the encyclopedia company, would you change its strategy?

Sometimes a marketing manager must decide whether a firm should serve customers it really doesn't want to serve. For example, banks sometimes offer marketing mixes that are attractive to wealthy customers but that basically drive off low-income consumers.

People often disagree about what segmenting dimensions are ethical in a given situation. A marketing manager needs to consider not only his or her own view but also the views of other groups in society. Even when there is no clear "right" answer, negative publicity may be very damaging. This is what Amazon.com encountered when it was revealed that it was charging some regular customers higher prices than new customers at its site.[9]

International marketing requires even more segmenting

Success in international marketing requires even more attention to segmenting. There are over 192 nations with their own unique cultures! And they differ greatly in language, customs (including business ethics), beliefs, religions, race, and income distribution patterns. (We'll discuss some of these differences in Chapters 5 and 6.) These additional differences can complicate the segmenting process. Even worse, critical data is often less available—and less dependable—as firms move into international markets. This is one reason why some firms insist that local operations and decisions be handled by natives. They, at least, have a feel for their markets.

There are more dimensions—but there is a way

Segmenting international markets may require more dimensions. But one practical method adds just one step to the approach discussed earlier. First, marketers segment by country or region—looking at demographic, cultural, and other characteristics, including stage of economic development. This may help them find regional or national submarkets that are fairly similar. Then—depending on whether the firm is aiming at final consumers or business markets—they apply the same basic approaches presented before.

A BEST PRACTICE APPROACH TO SEGMENTING PRODUCT-MARKETS

Most marketing managers embrace the idea of using market segmentation to narrow down from a broad set of opportunities to a specific target market and marketing strategy (review Exhibit 2-10). There are also hundreds of books and articles about different approaches and tools for market segmentation that a manager might consider. Yet many managers don't do a good job with market segmentation. One reason is that they are often unclear where to start or how to fit the ideas together. So that *you* don't have this knowledge gap, here we introduce a logical seven-step approach to market segmentation. Later in Chapter 8 you'll learn more about how marketing research can help to fine-tune some of the decisions made with this approach. But even without additional research, *this approach works*—and it has led to successful strategies. It is especially useful for finding the determining dimensions for product types. However, when you want to find dimensions for specific brands—especially when there are several competing brands—you may need more sophisticated techniques.

Exhibit 4-11 provides an overview of the seven-step approach, which ties together the concepts we have been discussing. To be sure you understand this approach, we will review each step separately and use an ongoing example to show how each step works. The example concerns people who need a place to stay—in particular, the market for motel guests in a big urban area.

1: Select the broad product-market

First, decide what broad product-market the firm wants to be in. This may be stated in the firm's objectives. Or if the firm is already successful in some product-market, its current position might be a good starting point. Try to build on the firm's strengths and avoid its weaknesses and competitors' strengths. Available resources, both human and financial, will limit the possibilities—especially if the firm is just getting started.

Example

A firm has been building small motels around the edges of a large city and renting rooms to travelers. A narrow view—considering only the firm's current products and markets—might lead the firm to think only of more small motels. A bigger view might see such motels as only a small part of the larger "overnight lodging needs" market in the firm's geographic area. Taking an even bigger view, the firm could consider expanding to other geographic areas—or moving into other kinds of products (like

Exhibit 4-11   A Best Practice Approach for Segmenting Product-Markets

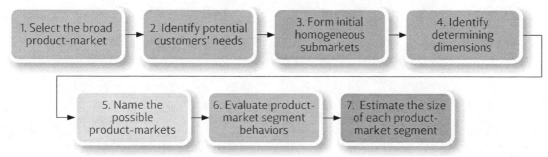

Edition

apartment buildings, retirement centers, or even parks for people who travel in their own recreational vehicles).

There has to be some balance between naming the product-market too narrowly (same old product, same old market) and naming it too broadly (the whole world and all its needs). Here the firm decides on the whole market of motel users in one city—because this is a city where the number of visitors is growing and where the firm has some experience.

2: Identify potential customers' needs

Identify and write down as many relevant needs as you can—considering all of the potential customers in the broad product-market. This is a brainstorming step. The list doesn't have to be complete yet, but it should provide enough input to help stimulate your thinking in the next steps. To see possible needs, think about *why* some people buy the present offerings in this broad product-market. At this point, focus on the basic needs—but begin to consider what a company could offer to meet those needs.

Example

In the broad motel guest market, you can easily list some possible needs: privacy (including a private room and furnishings), safety and security (security guards, lighted parking lots with video coverage), comfort (a good bed and nice furnishings), space for activities (exercise, work, socializing), entertainment (TV, radio, video games), convenience (registration, check-out, reservations, access to highways), economy (costs), communicating (phone, messages, fax, voice mail, wireless Internet), and the like.

3: Form homogeneous submarkets—narrow product-markets

Assuming that some people have (or emphasize) different needs than others, form different submarkets based on each submarket's specific needs. Start by forming one submarket around some typical type of customer (perhaps even yourself), and then aggregate similar people into this segment as long as they can be satisfied by the same marketing mix. Write down the important need dimensions and customer-related characteristics (including demographic characteristics) of each submarket to help you decide whether each new customer type should be included in the first segment. This will also help later—when you name the submarkets.

For example, if the people in one market are young families looking for a good place to stay on vacation, this will help you understand what they want and why—and will help you name the market (perhaps as "family vacationers").

It is better for promotion to focus on what customer needs are satisfied by products rather than on the product characteristics themselves.

Put people who are not homogeneous—who don't fit in the first segment—in a new submarket. List their different need dimensions on another line. Continue this classifying until three or more submarkets emerge.

Example

A young family on a vacation probably wants a motel to provide a clean room large enough for adults and children, convenient parking, a location near tourist attractions, a pool for recreation with a lifeguard for safety, entertainment in the room (a TV, video games, and movies on demand), and perhaps a refrigerator or vending machine for snacks. A traveling executive, on the other hand, has quite different interests—a room with a desk, but *also* a nice restaurant, fast transportation to and from an airport, more services (room service, dry cleaning, a way to send and receive a fax, and fast check-in)—without distracting noise from children. See Exhibit 4-12.

4: Identify the determining dimensions

Review the list of need dimensions for each possible segment and identify the determining dimensions (perhaps by putting an asterisk beside them). Although the qualifying dimensions are important—perhaps reflecting "core needs" that should be satisfied—they are not the *determining* dimensions we are seeking now.

To help identify the determining dimensions, think carefully about the needs and attitudes of the people in each possible segment. They may not seem very different from market to market, but if they are determining to those people then they *are* determining!

Exhibit 4-12   Segmenting the Broad Product-Market for Motel Guests in a Large Urban Area

Nickname of Product-Market	Need Dimensions (benefits sought)	Customer-Related Characteristics
1 Family vacationers	Comfort, security, privacy, *family fun, recreation (playground, pool), entertainment (video games, movies), child care, and snacks*	Couples and single parents with children who want a fun family experience: young, active, and energetic.
2 Upscale executives	Comfort, security, privacy, *distinctive furnishings, attentive staff, prestige status, easy access to airport and business meetings, express check-in and check-out, quality dining, business services (copying, fax, Wi-Fi Internet)*	Senior business executives with a big expense account who want to be pampered with "very important person" service and accommodations; often repeat guests.
3 Budget-oriented travelers	Comfort, security, privacy, *economy, (no extras that increase cost), convenience (to low-cost restaurants, highways), free parking*	Young people, retirees, and salespeople who travel by car, pay their own expenses, and want a simple place for one night—before moving on.
4 Long-stay guests	Comfort, security, privacy, *homelike amenities (kitchenette, separate living room), laundry and exercise facilities, pleasant grounds, entertainment, staying "connected" (e-mail, etc.)*	Businesspeople, out-of-town visitors, and others who stay in the same motel for a week or more; want many of the comforts they have at home.
5 Event-centered visitors	Comfort, security, privacy, *socializing (lounges and public areas), conference facilities (including catering of group meals), message and transportation services*	Individuals who are attending events scheduled at the motel (a business meeting or conference, family reunion, wedding, etc.) often for several days.
6 Resort seekers	Comfort, security, privacy, *relaxation (golf, whirlpool bath), pleasure (fine dining, nice views), fun, variety information (arrangements for theater, activities)*	Sophisticated couples with leisure time to relax and have "adult" fun; they want to show their individuality and have discretionary income to spend.

Note: Comfort, security, and privacy are core qualifying needs. Determining dimensions for each segment are in italic.

Edition

Example

With our motel customers, basic comfort needs (heating and cooling, a good bed, a clean bathroom), a telephone for communicating, and safety and security are probably not determining. Everyone has these qualifying needs. Looking beyond these common needs helps you see the determining dimensions—such as different needs with respect to recreation, restaurant facilities, services, and so on. See the needs highlighted in italic in Exhibit 4-12.

5: Name (nickname) the possible product-markets

Review the determining dimensions—market by market—and name (nickname) each one based on the relative importance of the determining dimensions (and aided by your description of the customer types). A market grid is a good way to help visualize this broad product-market and its narrow product-markets.

Draw the market grid as a rectangle with boxes inside representing smaller, more homogeneous segments. See Exhibit 4-12. Think of the whole grid as representing the broad product-market and each of the rows as a different (narrower) product-market. Since the markets within a broad product-market usually require very different segmenting dimensions, don't try to use the same dimensions to name every submarket. Then label each segment with its nickname.

Example

Exhibit 4-12 identifies the following overnight guest submarkets: (1) family vacationers, (2) upscale executives, (3) budget-oriented travelers, (4) long-stay guests, (5) event-centered visitors, and (6) resort seekers. Note that each segment has a different set of determining dimensions (benefits sought) that follow directly from customer type and needs.

6: Evaluate why product-market segments behave as they do

After naming the markets as we did in step 5, think about what else you know about each segment to see how and why these markets behave the way they do. Different segments may have similar, but slightly different, needs. This may explain why some competitive offerings are more successful than others. It can also mean you have to split and rename some segments.

Example

The resort seekers might have been treated as family vacationers in step 5 because the "family" characteristic did not seem important. But with more thought, we see that while some of the resort seekers are interested in the same sort of fun and recreation as the family vacationers, resort seekers focus on adult fun—not activities with children. For them, getting away from the family vacationer's children may be part of the escape they want. Further, although the resort seekers are a higher-income group who are similar to the upscale executives, they have different needs than the executives and probably should be treated as a separate market. The point is that you might discover these market differences only in step 6. At this step you would name the "resort seekers" market—and create a related row in the grid to describe the new segment.

7: Make a rough estimate of the size of each product-market segment

Remember, we are looking for profitable opportunities. So now we must try to tie our product-markets to demographic data—or other customer-related characteristics—to make it easier to estimate the size of these markets. We aren't trying to estimate our likely sales yet. Sales depend on the competition as well as the particulars of the marketing mix. Now we only want to provide a basis for later forecasting and marketing mix planning. The more we know about possible target markets, the easier those jobs are.

Fortunately, we can obtain a lot of data on the size of markets—especially demographic data. And bringing in demographics adds a note of economic reality. Some possible product-markets may have almost no market potential. Without hard facts, we risk aiming at such markets.

To refine the market grid, you might want to change the height of the rows so that they give a better idea of the size of the various segments. This will help highlight the larger, and perhaps more attractive, opportunities. Remember, the relative sizes of the markets might vary depending on what geographic areas you consider. The market sizes might vary from city to city or from one country to another.

Example

We can tie the family vacationers to demographic data. Most of them are between 21 and 45. The U.S. Census Bureau publishes detailed data by age, family size, and related information. Moreover, a state tourist bureau or city Chamber of Commerce might be able to provide estimates of how many families vacation in a specific city during a year and how long they stay. Given this information, it's easy to estimate the total number of nights family vacationers will need motel rooms in a certain city.

Market dimensions suggest a good mix

Once we follow all seven steps, we should be able to outline the kinds of marketing mixes that would appeal to the various markets. For example, based on the determining dimensions (benefits sought) in Exhibit 4-12, a motel designed to appeal to the upscale executives might offer rooms with quality furniture (including a desk and chair for reading and an extra comfortable bed with special luxury sheets and pillows), a high-quality restaurant with all-hours room service, special business services (copying, fax, wireless Internet) on an extra-cost basis, limousine pickup at the airport, someone to help with travel problems, and precleared check-in and check-out. The motel might also provide a quiet bar and exercise room and extras such as thick bath towels and a valet service for free shoe shines. It might also offer a business library for after-hours reading and a free copy of *The Wall Street Journal* delivered every morning. Of course, the price could be high to pay for this special treatment. It's also useful to think about what the executives would *not* want: noisy facilities shared by families with young children!

While the discussion above focuses on the upscale executives, profitable marketing mixes can be developed for the other segments as well. For example, Super 8 has done very well by targeting budget-oriented travelers. Similarly, Residence Inns cater to the needs of long-stay guests with kitchens and grocery shopping services, fireplaces, and convenient recreation areas. Courtyard by Marriott has been successful with facilities designed for event-centered visitors. During the week, many of its customers are there for business conferences, but on the weekend the focus often shifts to family events—such as meals and receptions related to a wedding or family reunion.[10]

Improve the marketing mix for current customers

Our motel example highlights an approach to identify new target market and marketing mix opportunities. However, the same approaches provide a basis for identifying new ways to serve existing customers and strengthen the relationship with them. Too often, firms let their strategies get stagnant. For example, special business services related to the determining needs of upscale executives (like voice mail) might initially help a motel win this business with superior customer value. However, the motel loses its competitive edge if other motels start to offer the same benefits. Or the benefit might disappear if customer needs change; executives who carry a cell phone don't need voice mail at the motel. Then the determining dimensions change. To retain the base of customers it has built or attract new ones, the motel needs to find new and better ways to meet the executives' needs. Reevaluating the need dimensions and customer-related characteristics, perhaps in greater detail, may point to new opportunities. For example, our motel might equip rooms with a wireless access point to a high-speed Internet connection.

MORE SOPHISTICATED TECHNIQUES MAY HELP IN SEGMENTING

Marketing researchers and managers often turn to computer-aided methods for help with the segmenting job. A detailed review of the possibilities is beyond the scope of this book. But a brief discussion will give you a flavor of how computer-aided methods work. In addition, the computer-aided problem for this chapter (4, Segmenting

Edition

Amazon.com sends e-mails to customers with recommendations based on their past purchases. Many customers find these messages, which inform them of new books, music, or movies that actually match their interests, useful.

Customers) on the Student CD that accompanies the text gives you a hands-on feel for how managers use them.

Clustering usually requires a computer

Clustering techniques try to find similar patterns within sets of data. Clustering groups customers who are similar on their segmenting dimensions into homogeneous segments. Clustering approaches use computers to do what previously was done with much intuition and judgment.

The data to be clustered might include such dimensions as demographic characteristics, the importance of different needs, attitudes toward the product, and past buying behavior. The computer searches all the data for homogeneous groups of people. When it finds them, marketers study the dimensions of the people in the groups to see why the computer clustered them together. The results sometimes suggest new, or at least better, marketing strategies.[11]

A cluster analysis of the toothpaste market, for example, might show that some people buy toothpaste because it tastes good (the sensory segment), while others are concerned with the effect of clean teeth and fresh breath on their social image (the sociables). Still others worry about decay or gum disease (the worriers), and some are just interested in the best value for their money (the value seekers). Each of these market segments calls for a different marketing mix—although some of the four Ps may be similar.

Customer database can focus the effort

A variation of the clustering approach is based on customer relationship management methods. With **customer relationship management (CRM)**, the seller fine-tunes the marketing effort with information from a detailed customer database. This

Internet EXERCISE

Visit the website for onContact Software (www.oncontact.com), and from the demo link at the top of the page select "screenshot tour" (*note:* the interactive tour requires that you register). Select the links to review the different examples of the firm's customer relationship management software. Give several examples of how this software could help a salesperson be more effective in working with customers.

CDW Targets the Small Business Segment with Uncommon Service

Sellers in business markets often rely on customer size as a key segmentation dimension. When potential profit from serving a big customer is high, the selling firm may even treat that customer as a "segment of one"—and develop a unique marketing mix targeted to win and keep its business. Even if a unique marketing mix isn't justified, big customers in these segments often get volume discounts, extra services, and personalized attention. By contrast, smaller customers are often left to get information and handle orders themselves—at a seller's website. This can be efficient, reduce costs for both the seller and customer, and serve the need. But that is not always the case.

CDW is a wholesaler that sells all sorts of computer gear produced by many manufacturers. There's a reason that *Fortune* magazine recognized it as one of "America's Most Admired Companies" in 2008. Most of its 360,000 business customers are too small to command much attention from equipment manufacturers. Yet they also have smaller IT departments and know less about buying IT equipment. CDW has enjoyed rapid growth because it offers a marketing mix that is atypical for these customers. Even the smallest customer gets a dedicated account manager

(AM). These salespeople don't just take orders; they go through months of CDW training so that they really understand a customer's needs and can help the buyer make the right purchases. The AM is a single point-of-contact with the account over time and is encouraged to act almost as an extension of the client's IT department. This relationship helps the AM anticipate client needs; the AM is also supported with customer relationship management databases that help predict when an upgrade is needed—rather than wait for the customer to ask. This is especially helpful to small customers who don't have backup systems in place to tide them over if something goes wrong. This is also why CDW fills orders fast—usually on the same day they are received. To provide that level of service with over 35,000 boxes shipped each day, CDW operates a 450,000-square-foot distribution center and keeps over $150 million in inventory on hand. CDW's "high-touch" strategy is costly, but high volume keeps its prices competitive. And CDW's sales volume is high because CDW delivers superior customer value that wins a large share of its target customers' business.[12]

usually includes data on a customer's past purchases as well as other segmenting information. For example, an auto-repair garage that keeps a database of customer oil changes can send a reminder postcard when it's time for the next oil change. Similarly, a florist that keeps a database of customers who have ordered flowers for Mother's Day or Valentine's Day can call them in advance with a special offer. Firms that operate over the Internet may have a special advantage with these database-focused approaches. They are able to communicate with customers via a website or e-mail, which means that the whole effort is not only targeted but also very inexpensive. Further, it's fast and easy for a customer to reply.[13]

Amazon.com takes this idea further. When a customer orders a book, the Amazon CRM system at the website recommends related books that have been purchased by other customers who bought that book.

DIFFERENTIATION AND POSITIONING TAKE THE CUSTOMER POINT OF VIEW

Differentiate the marketing mix—to serve customers better

As we've emphasized throughout, the reason for focusing on a specific target market— by using marketing segmentation approaches or tools such as cluster analysis or CRM— is so that you can fine-tune the whole marketing mix to provide some group

Edition

When VW introduced the first Coupé-Cabriolet with a panoramic sunroof, this ad helped to position the car as uniquely able to offer a wide-open feel by showing what someone inside the car would see if a cat was on the sunroof.

of potential customers with superior value. By *differentiating* the marketing mix to do a better job meeting customers' needs, the firm builds a competitive advantage. When this happens, target customers view the firm's position in the market as uniquely suited to their preferences and needs. Further, because everyone in the firm is clear about what position it wants to achieve with customers, the Product, Promotion, and other marketing mix decisions can be blended better to achieve the desired objectives.

Although the marketing manager may want customers to see the firm's offering as unique, that is not always possible. Me-too imitators may come along and copy the firm's strategy. Further, even if a firm's marketing mix is different, consumers may not know or care. They're busy and, simply put, the firm's product may not be that important in their lives. Even so, in looking for opportunities it's important for the marketing manager to know how customers *do* view the firm's offering. It's also important for the marketing manager to have a clear idea about how he or she would like for customers to view the firm's offering. This is where another important concept, *positioning*, comes in.

Positioning is based on customers' views

Positioning refers to how customers think about proposed or present brands in a market. A marketing manager needs a realistic view of how customers think about offerings in the market. Without that, it's hard to differentiate. At the same time, the manager should know how he or she *wants* target customers to think about the firm's marketing mix. Positioning issues are especially important when competitors in a market appear to be very similar. For example, many people think that there isn't much difference between one provider of home owner's insurance and another. But State Farm Insurance uses advertising to emphasize the value of the service and personal attention from its agents, who live right in the customer's neighborhood. Low-price insurers who sell from websites or toll-free numbers can't make that claim.

Once you know what customers think, then you can decide whether to leave the product (and marketing mix) alone or reposition it. This may mean *physical changes in*

Edition

Exhibit 4–13
"Product Space"
Representing
Consumers' Perceptions
for Different Brands of
Bar Soap

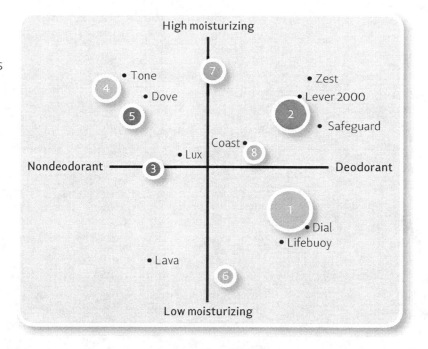

the product or simply *image changes based on promotion*. For example, most cola drinkers can't pick out their favorite brand in a blind test—so physical changes might not be necessary (and might not even work) to reposition a cola.

Figuring out what customers really think about competing products isn't easy, but there are approaches that help. Most of them require some formal marketing research. The results are usually plotted on graphs to help show how consumers view the competing products. Usually, the products' positions are related to two or three product features that are important to the target customers.

Managers make the graphs for positioning decisions by asking consumers to make judgments about different brands—including their "ideal" brand—and then use computer programs to summarize the ratings and plot the results. The details of positioning techniques—sometimes called *perceptual mapping*—are beyond the scope of this text. But Exhibit 4-13 shows the possibilities.[14]

Exhibit 4-13 shows the "product space" for different brands of bar soap using two dimensions—the extent to which consumers think the soaps moisturize and deodorize their skin. For example, consumers see Dove as quite high on moisturizing but low on deodorizing. Dove and Tone are close together—implying that consumers think of them as similar on these characteristics. Dial is viewed as different and is further away on the graph. Remember that positioning maps are based on *customers' perceptions*—the actual characteristics of the products (as determined by a chemical test) might be different!

Each segment may have its own preferences

The circles in Exhibit 4-13 show different sets (submarkets) of consumers clustered near their ideal soap preferences. Groups of respondents with a similar ideal product are circled to show apparent customer concentrations. In this graph, the size of the circles suggests the size of the segments for the different ideals.

Ideal clusters 1 and 2 are the largest and are close to two popular brands—Dial and Lever 2000. It appears that customers in cluster 1 want more moisturizing than they see in Dial. However, exactly what this brand should do about this isn't clear. Perhaps Dial should leave its physical product alone—but emphasize moisturizing more in its promotion to make a stronger appeal to those who want moisturizers. A marketing manager talking about this approach might simply refer to it as "positioning

Edition

the brand as a good moisturizer." Of course, whether the effort is successful depends on whether the whole marketing mix delivers on the promise of the positioning communication.

Note that ideal cluster 7 is not near any of the present brands. This may suggest an opportunity for introducing a new product—a strong moisturizer with some deodorizers. A firm that chooses to follow this approach would be making a segmenting effort.

Combining versus segmenting

Positioning analysis may lead a firm to combining—rather than segmenting—if managers think they can make several general appeals to different parts of a "combined" market. For example, by varying its promotion, Coast might try to appeal to segments 8, 1, and 2 with one product. These segments are all quite similar (close together) in what they want in an ideal brand. On the other hand, there may be clearly defined submarkets—and some parts of the market may be "owned" by one product or brand. In this case, segmenting efforts may be practical—moving the firm's own product into another segment of the general market area where competition is weaker.

Positioning as part of broader analysis

A positioning analysis helps managers understand how customers see their market. It is a visual aid to understanding a product-market. The first time such an analysis is done, managers may be shocked to see how much customers' perceptions of a market differ from their own. For this reason alone, positioning analysis may be crucial. But a positioning analysis usually focuses on specific product features and brands that are close competitors in the product-market. Thus, it is a product-oriented approach. Important *customer*-related dimensions—including needs and attitudes—may be overlooked.

Premature emphasis on product features is dangerous in other ways as well. As our bar soap example shows, starting with a product-oriented definition of a market and how bar soaps compete against other bar soaps can make a firm miss more basic shifts in markets. For example, bars have lost popularity to liquid soaps. Other products, like bath oils or body shampoos for use in the shower, are now part of the relevant competition also. Managers wouldn't see these shifts if they looked only at alternative bar soap brands—the focus is just too narrow.

It's also important to realize that the way consumers look at a product isn't just a matter of chance. Let's return to our bar soap example. While many consumers do think about soap in terms of moisturizing and deodorizing, other needs shouldn't be overlooked. For example, some consumers are especially concerned about wiping out germs. Marketers for Dial soap recognized this need and developed ads that positioned Dial as "the choice" for these target customers. This helped Dial win new customers, including those who switched from Lifebuoy—which was otherwise similar to Dial (see Exhibit 4-13). In fact, what happened to Lifebuoy highlights what happens if managers don't update their marketing strategy as customer needs and competition change. Lifebuoy was the first deodorant soap on the market; it was a leading brand for over 100 years. But it gradually lost sales to competitors with stronger marketing mixes (clearer differentiation, better positioning, and superior customer value) until 2002, when Lever stopped selling it.

As we emphasize throughout the text, you must understand potential needs and attitudes when planning marketing strategies. If customers treat different products as substitutes, then a firm has to position itself against those products too. Customers won't always be conscious of all of the detailed ways that a firm's marketing mix might be different, but careful positioning can help highlight a unifying theme or benefits that relate to the determining dimensions of the target market. Thus, it's useful to think of positioning as part of the broader strategy planning process—because the purpose is to ensure that the whole marketing mix is positioned for competitive advantage.

CONCLUSION

Chapters 2 and 3 introduced a framework for strategy planning that starts with analysis of the broad market and then narrows down to a specific target market and marketing mix. The basic purpose of this chapter is to show how marketing managers use market segmentation and positioning to guide that narrowing-down process.

Now that you've read this chapter you should understand how to carefully define generic markets and product-markets and how that can help in identifying and evaluating opportunities. We stressed the shortcomings of a too narrow, product-oriented view of markets and explained why it's better to take a broader view that also includes consideration of customer needs, the product type, the customer type, and the geographic area.

We also discussed approaches for market segmentation—the process of naming and then segmenting broad product-markets to find potentially attractive target markets. Some people try to segment markets by starting with the mass market and then dividing it into smaller submarkets based on a few demographic characteristics. But this can lead to poor results. Instead, market segmentation should first focus on a broad product-market and then group similar customers into homogeneous submarkets. The more similar the potential customers are, the larger the submarkets can be. Four criteria for evaluating possible product-market segments were presented.

Once a broad product-market is segmented, marketing managers can use one of three approaches to market-oriented strategy planning: (1) the single target market approach, (2) the multiple target market approach, or (3) the combined target market approach. In general, we encourage marketers to be segmenters rather than combiners.

We also offer a logical seven-step approach for segmentation that will help you better understand and apply concepts from this chapter. Then we cover computer-aided approaches such as clustering techniques, CRM, and positioning. We emphasize the role of positioning in providing a focus or theme to the various elements of a differentiated marketing mix that fits the preferences of target customers.

In summary, good marketers should be experts on markets and likely segmenting dimensions. By creatively segmenting markets, they may spot opportunities— even breakthrough opportunities— and help their firms succeed against aggressive competitors offering similar products. Segmenting is basic to target marketing. And the more you practice segmenting, the more meaningful market segments you will see. In Chapters 5 through 7 you'll learn more about the buying behavior of final consumers and organizational customers. As you enrich your understanding of customers and how they behave, you will develop command of a broader set of dimensions that are important for segmentation and positioning.

KEY TERMS

market, 90

generic market, 91

product-market, 91

market segmentation, 95

segmenting, 96

market segment, 96

single target market approach, 98

multiple target market approach, 98

combined target market approach, 98

combiners, 98

segmenters, 99

qualifying dimensions, 102

determining dimensions, 102

clustering techniques, 110

customer relationship management (CRM), 110

positioning, 112

QUESTIONS AND PROBLEMS

1. Distinguish between a generic market and a product-market. Illustrate your answer.
2. Explain what market segmentation is.
3. List the types of potential segmenting dimensions, and explain which you would try to apply first, second, and

third in a particular situation. If the nature of the situation would affect your answer, explain how.
4. Explain why segmentation efforts based on attempts to divide the mass market using a few demographic dimensions may be very disappointing.

Edition

5. Illustrate the concept that segmenting is an aggregating process by referring to the admissions policies of your own college and a nearby college or university.

6. Review the types of segmenting dimensions listed in Exhibits 4-8 and 4-9, and select the ones you think should be combined to fully explain the market segment you personally would be in if you were planning to buy a new watch today. List several dimensions and try to develop a shorthand name, like "fashion-oriented," to describe your own personal market segment. Then try to estimate what proportion of the total watch market would be in your market segment. Next, explain if there are any offerings that come close to meeting the needs of your market. If not, what sort of a marketing mix is needed? Would it be economically attractive for anyone to try to satisfy your market segment? Why or why not?

7. Identify the determining dimension or dimensions that explain why you bought the specific brand you did in your most recent purchase of a (*a*) soft drink, (*b*) shampoo, (*c*) shirt or blouse, and (*d*) larger, more expensive item, such as a bicycle, camera, or boat. Try to express the determining dimension(s) in terms of your own personal characteristics rather than the product's characteristics. Estimate what share of the market would probably be motivated by the same determining dimension(s).

8. Consider the market for off-campus apartments in your city. Identify some submarkets that have different needs and determining dimensions. Then evaluate how well the needs in these market segments are being met in your geographic area. Is there an obvious breakthrough opportunity waiting for someone?

9. Explain how positioning analysis can help a marketing manager identify target market opportunities.

CREATING MARKETING PLANS

The Marketing Plan Coach software on the Student CD and the text website includes a sample marketing plan for Hillside Veterinary Clinic. Look through the "Customers" section.

a. How does the marketing plan segment the market?

b. Can you think of other segmentation dimensions that could be used?

c. What do you think of the approach Hillside used to determine target markets? Are they using a single target market, multiple target market, or combined target market approach?

d. How does Hillside plan to differentiate and position its offering?

SUGGESTED CASES

3. MANU Soccer Academy   7. Waituiwa Lodge   10. Taffe's Ice Land
30. Eden Prairie Mills, Ltd.

COMPUTER-AIDED PROBLEM

4. SEGMENTING CUSTOMERS

The marketing manager for Audiotronics Software Company is seeking new market opportunities. He is focusing on the voice recognition market and has narrowed down to three segments: the Fearful Typists, the Power Users, and the Professional Specialists. The Fearful Typists don't know much about computers—they just want a fast way to create e-mail messages, letters, and simple reports without errors. They don't need a lot of special features. They want simple instructions and a program that's easy to learn. The Power Users know a lot about computers, use them often, and want a voice recognition program with many special features. All computer programs seem easy to them—so they aren't worried about learning to use the various features. The Professional Specialists have jobs that require a lot of writing. They don't know much about computers but are willing to learn. They want special features needed for their work—but only if they aren't too hard to learn and use.

The marketing manager prepared a table summarizing the importance of each of three key needs in the three segments (see table that follows).

Edition

Market Segment	Importance of Need (1 = not important; 10 = very important)		
	Features	Easy to Use	Easy to Learn
Fearful typists	3	8	9
Power users	9	2	2
Professional specialists	7	5	6

Audiotronics' sales staff conducted interviews with seven potential customers who were asked to rate how important each of these three needs were in their work. The manager prepared a spreadsheet to help him cluster (aggregate) each person into one of the segments—along with other similar people. Each person's ratings are entered in the spreadsheet, and the clustering procedure computes a similarity score that indicates how similar (a low score) or dissimilar (a high score) the person is to the typical person in each of the segments. The manager can then "aggregate" potential customers into the segment that is most similar (that is, the one with the *lowest* similarity score).

a. The ratings for a potential customer appear on the first spreadsheet. Into which segment would you aggregate this person?

b. The responses for seven potential customers who were interviewed are listed in the following table. Enter the ratings for a customer in the spreadsheet and then write down

the similarity score for each segment. Repeat the process for each customer. Based on your analysis, indicate the segment into which you would aggregate each customer. Indicate the size (number of customers) of each segment.

c. In the interview, each potential customer was also asked what type of computer he or she would be using. The responses are shown in the table along with the ratings. Group the responses based on the customer's segment. If you were targeting the Fearful Typists segment, what type of computer would you focus on when developing your software?

d. Based on your analysis, which customer would you say is least like any of the segments? Briefly explain the reason for your choice.

For additional questions related to this problem, see Exercise 4-4 in the *Learning Aid for Use with Basic Marketing*, 17th edition.

Potential Customer	Importance of Need (1 = not important; 10 = very important)			
	Features	Easy to Use	Easy to Learn	Type of Computer
A.	8	1	2	Dell laptop
B.	6	6	5	HP desktop
C.	4	9	8	Apple
D.	2	6	7	Apple
E.	5	6	5	HP desktop
F.	8	3	1	Dell laptop
G.	4	6	8	Apple

5

CHAPTER

Demographic Dimensions of Global Consumer Markets

By spring of 2008, economists debated whether or not the economy was in recession. Nowhere was the economic pain clearer than in the U.S. housing market. As interest rates increased, many consumers didn't have enough income to handle higher mortgage payments—and they lost their homes. New homes were not selling, and the inventory of unsold homes grew to record levels, in spite of builders' desperate price cuts of 25 percent or more. Lower prices often didn't result in sales because mortgage credit was so tight. Even dual-income couples with bright prospects had trouble borrowing. In this environment, many home builders went bust. Pulte Homes was not immune to these problems; its revenue dropped by 30 percent and it faced losses. However, previous plans that Pulte had put in place during the good times helped to insulate it from the full impact of the downturn. And its successes put cash in the bank—to help weather the storm. So, let's take a look at the marketing strategies that have given Pulte an advantage over its competitors.

Bill Pulte built his first house in 1950 and sold it for $10,000. Since then, his company, Pulte Homes, has built more than 450,000 homes in 27 states. Pulte Homes has become the largest home builder in the United States, and one reason for that success is that it consistently receives more J. D. Power customer satisfaction awards than any other home builder.

Another reason for Pulte's success is that managers at the company carefully analyze needs related to housing—and adjust what Pulte offers to serve specific markets in different locations. To help in this effort, Pulte marketers pay attention to changes in consumer demographics. For example, at the national level, Pulte focuses on geographic areas where population is growing and demand for new housing is greatest. At a local level, Pulte analyzes income patterns and other demographics, such as age and family life cycle stage in the market area. By combining such data with information about consumer housing preferences, the company has identified the needs of 11 key consumer segments. Then it focuses on building the type of homes for which demand exceeds the available supply.

For example, in one area of Michigan, Pulte focused on the specific needs of singles and young couples without children. Many of these first-time buyers wanted affordable starter homes that were close to work and play—and that didn't involve maintenance hassles. Rather than build separate houses, Pulte responded by building new communities of town homes and condominiums. Many featured swimming pools to enhance socializing and fun.

Pulte knows that the segment of first-time buyers who are "moving up" after they have a child has different needs. These customers often stretch to buy as much house as they can afford, but it must be situated in the best school district available. They want to be near other young families who will provide plenty of playmates for their children. They also want playgrounds as well as community facilities for indoor recreation. Pulte further splits this market based on income because buyers with higher incomes are more style conscious, while those with lower incomes are more value oriented. Pulte uses this knowledge about its target segments to design homes and communities that meet the needs of each type of family.

Pulte's Del Webb division targets the fast-growing market of active consumers who are over 55. Many of these baby-boomer consumers want to downsize and retire to a low-maintenance home, but they want amenities that support their active lifestyles. So Pulte creates whole neighborhoods with golf courses, walking paths, tennis courts, and health clubs that are close to restaurants and supermarkets. For many years Del Webb focused on building communities, like Sun City in Arizona, to appeal to people in this group who wanted to retire to Sun Belt states. But now that more retirees want to stay close to friends and family, Pulte is having new success building similar communities in northern climates near large cities like Chicago. In recent years, more than one-third of Pulte's revenues were derived from the over-55 segment.

Of course, what worked best yesterday may not be best tomorrow. So Pulte works to stay ahead of the competition by spotting and responding to changes in demographic trends. For example, its bilingual website is designed to appeal to recent Hispanic immigrants, who are a fast-growing ethnic group with increasing purchasing power.

Regardless of what type of home customers buy, Pulte knows that many will ultimately move again as their needs change. Yet, because Pulte has a customer-oriented focus, 45 percent of its business comes from satisfied customers who are moving from one Pulte home to another. In the highly competitive construction business, retaining customers at that rate is certainly a recipe for more growth in the future, even if growth isn't possible while the economy is down.

In the meantime, Pulte has developed some strategies to help address the problems of the bad economic environment. For example, some of the baby-boomer prospects for its Sun City development are unable to buy a new house because they can't sell the one they currently own. Pulte knows that sooner or later they'll sell and be able to move, so in the meantime Pulte encourages them to rent a Sun City "vacation villa" for a few nights and get to know the community's benefits. At $33 a night for rent, the customer gets a bargain. And Pulte wins too because half of the people who rent a villa later buy a Pulte home.[1]

119

TARGET MARKETERS FOCUS ON THE CUSTOMER

Target marketers believe that customers should be the focus of all business and marketing activity. Their goal is to develop unique marketing strategies that find unsatisfied customers to whom they can then offer superior value through more attractive marketing mixes. They want to work in less-competitive markets with more inelastic demand curves. Finding opportunities in these areas takes real knowledge of potential customers and what they want or need.

Marketers need to answer three important questions about any potential market:

1. What are its relevant segmenting dimensions?
2. How big is it?
3. Where is it?

The first question draws on an understanding of the differences between groups of customers. Management judgment—perhaps aided by analysis of existing data and new findings from marketing research—is needed to pick just the right dimensions. We discuss how to do this in Chapter 4.

To help build your judgment regarding buying behavior, this chapter and the next two discuss what we know about various kinds of customers and their buying behavior. In this chapter we focus on the demographic dimensions that provide marketing managers with critical information about the size, location, and characteristics of target markets. Marketing managers must pay special attention to trends and patterns in demographic data. These can provide early indicators about new opportunities—or the need to adjust existing marketing mixes. In this chapter we present data and a process of analyzing that data that will help you learn more about U.S. and global consumer markets. Then, Chapter 6 takes a closer look at what influences individual consumers to buy as they do. In Chapter 7 we'll expand our scope and look at organizational customers. See Exhibit 5-1.

Edition

Exhibit 5-1   Marketing Strategy Planning and Demographic Dimensions of Final Consumers

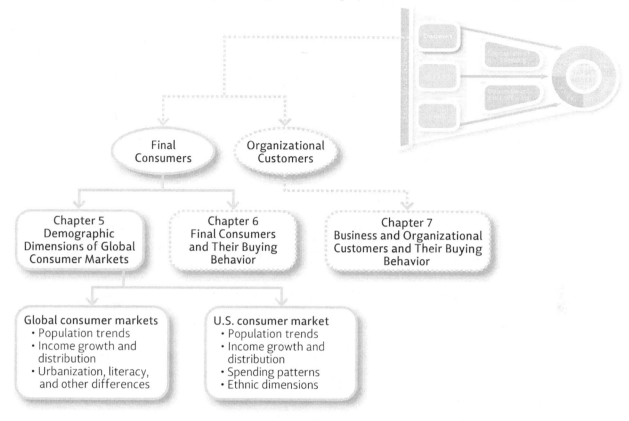

As you read, keep in mind that it's not our intention to make generalizations about average customers or how the mass market behaves. Rather, the focus is on how some people in some markets behave. You should expect to find differences in behavior.

Get the facts straight—for good marketing decisions

Everybody "knows" that there are vast and fast-growing markets in India and China and that many people in Somalia live in desperate poverty. It's also clear that demographic dimensions vary within countries: Lots of retired people live in Florida, many Californians speak Spanish, and the population in the Sun Belt states is growing fast. Generalities like these may be partly true—but "partly true" isn't good enough when it comes to making marketing strategy decisions.

Fortunately, much useful information is available on the demographic dimensions of consumer markets around the world. Most of it is free because it has been collected by government agencies. With valid data available, managers have no excuse for basing their decisions on guesses. Look at the data in the next few chapters in terms of selecting relevant market dimensions—and estimating the potential in different market segments. Also, check your own assumptions against these data. Now is a good time to get your facts straight!

PEOPLE WITH MONEY MAKE MARKETS

Markets consist of people with money to spend. So it makes sense to start with a broad view of how population, income, and other key demographic dimensions vary for different countries around the world. This will help you to see why so many firms pursue opportunities in international markets. And our examples will illustrate why

Edition

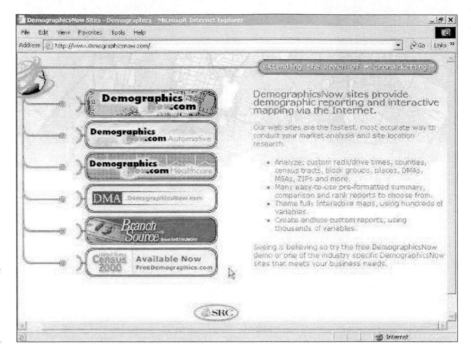

Information about demographic characteristics of consumer markets is readily available and can help marketing managers plan more successful strategies.

companies can't depend on half-truths in increasingly competitive international markets.

Marketers search for growing markets

Some marketing managers never consider opportunities outside of their own country. That may make sense in some cases, but it may also lead to missed opportunities. For example, crowded cities in the United States may seem to offer great potential, but the U.S. population makes up less than 5 percent of the total world population, which is now over 6.6 billion.

Although a country's current population is important, it provides only a snapshot of the market. The population trend is also important.

Between 1950 and 2000, world population doubled. Early in that period, global population growth was over 2 percent per year. Now it's down to about 1.2 percent. However, that's still an additional 82 million people a year and less-developed countries account for 99 percent of that growth. Much long-term world population growth will come from countries in the Middle and Far East. India (with a population of almost 1.2 billion) and China (with a population of over 1.3 billion) are getting even larger. You can see why so many firms from all over the world want to reach consumers in these countries now that trade barriers are relaxing and their economies are growing.

Over the long term population growth is expected in most countries. But how rapidly? And will output and income increase faster than population? These are important questions for marketers. The answers affect how quickly a country moves to higher stages of development and becomes a new market for different kinds of products.

Population, income, and other demographic dimensions help to answer these questions. Exhibit 5-2 summarizes current data for representative countries in different regions around the world. From country to country, population growth varies dramatically but, in general, less-developed countries experience the fastest rates. Haiti, Madagascar, Nigeria, Somalia, and Uganda, for example, are projected to increase their populations by more than 40 percent between 2010 and 2025. The U.S. population, on the other hand, will grow about 13 percent. During the same time frame, the growth of China's large population is expected to be less than 8 percent while Japan, Russia, and many European countries are projecting population declines.[2]

For firms interested in pursuing international markets, the growing concentration of population and income in major cities often simplifies Place and Promotion strategy decisions.

Population is becoming more concentrated

The population in some countries is spread over a very large area. Population density is important to marketers. If the population is very spread out, as it is in many of the African countries, it is difficult and expensive for marketers to adjust time and place discrepancies between producers and consumers. This is especially a problem in countries without efficient highway and rail systems. Similarly, a widely spread population may make promotion more difficult, especially if there are language differences or communication systems are poor. Of course, even in countries with low population density, major cities may be packed with people.

The extent to which a country's population is clustered around urban areas varies a lot. In the United Kingdom, Kuwait, Australia, Israel, and Singapore, for example, more than 90 percent of people live in urban areas. (See Exhibit 5-2.) By contrast, in Ethiopia, Nepal, and Uganda less than 16 percent of the people live in major urban areas.

People everywhere are moving off the farm and into industrial and urban areas. Shifts in population—combined with already dense populations—have led to extreme crowding in some parts of the world. And the crowding is likely to get worse.

The worldwide trend toward urbanization has prompted increased interest in international markets. For many firms, the concentration of people in major cities simplifies Place and Promotion decisions, especially for major cities in the wealthiest nations. Affluent, big-city consumers often have similar lifestyles and needs. Thus, many of the products successful in Toronto, New York, or Paris are likely to be successful in Caracas and Tokyo. The spread of the Internet, satellite TV, and other communication technologies will accelerate this trend.

However, keep in mind that many of the world's consumers—whether crowded in cities or widely spread in rural areas—live in deplorable conditions. These people have little hope of escaping the crush of poverty. They certainly have needs—but they don't have the income to do anything about their needs.

There's no market when there's no income

Profitable markets require income—as well as people. The amount of money people can spend affects the products they are likely to buy. When considering international markets, income is often one of the most important demographic dimensions.

There are a variety of different measures of national income. One widely used measure is gross domestic product (GDP)—the total market value of all goods and services provided in a country's economy in a year by both residents and nonresidents of that

Edition

Exhibit 5-2   Demographic Dimensions for Representative Countries

Country	2010 Projected Population (000s)	2025 Projected Population (000s)	2010–2025 Projected Population Change (%)	2006 Population Density (per square mile)	2006 Percent of Population in Urban Areas	2006 GNI Per Capita ($U.S.)	2006 GDP (billions of $U.S.)	Estimated Literacy Percent
Algeria	34,555	40,255	16.5	36	58	3,030	114.7	69.9
Argentina	41,405	45,757	10.5	38	89	5,150	214.1	97.2
Australia	20,925	23,023	10.0	7	91	35,990	768.2	99.0
Bangladesh	159,765	204,539	28.0	2,850	23	480	62.0	43.1
Brazil	195,580	217,822	11.4	58	81	4,730	1,068.0	88.6
Cameroon	19,294	25,522	32.3	97	53	1,080	18.3	67.9
Canada	34,253	38,165	11.4	9	81	36,170	1,251.5	99.0
Chile	16,720	18,521	10.8	56	88	6,980	145.8	95.7
China	1,347,563	1,453,000	7.8	365	44	2,010	2,668.1	90.9
Colombia	46,271	55,271	19.5	109	72	2,740	135.8	92.8
Croatia	4,487	4,374	−2.5	206	56	9,330	42.7	98.1
Cuba	11,477	11,650	1.5	265	76	—	—	99.8
Ecuador	14,245	17,099	20.0	127	62	2,840	40.8	91.0
Egypt	84,440	103,573	22.7	205	43	1,350	107.5	71.4
Ethiopia	81,754	107,804	31.9	173	16	180	13.3	42.7
Finland	5,255	5,251	−0.1	45	62	40,650	209.4	100.0
France	64,806	68,522	5.7	256	77	36,550	2,230.7	99.0
Germany	82,283	80,637	−2.0	611	75	36,620	2,906.7	99.0
Ghana	24,279	30,536	25.8	252	44	520	12.9	57.9
Greece	10,750	10,671	−0.7	212	59	21,690	245.0	96.0
Haiti	9,386	13,254	41.2	799	36	480	5.0	52.9
Hungary	9,880	9,438	−4.5	280	65	10,950	112.9	99.4
Iceland	309	338	9.4	8	93	50,580	15.9	99.0
India	1,184,090	1,449,000	22.4	968	28	820	906.3	61.0
Indonesia	242,968	278,503	14.6	329	42	1,420	364.5	90.4
Iran	67,038	76,779	14.5	103	67	3,000	222.9	77.0
Iraq	29,672	40,418	36.2	161	67	—	—	74.1
Ireland	4,250	4,842	13.9	153	60	45,580	222.6	99.0
Israel	6,645	7,612	14.6	809	92	18,580	123.4	97.1
Italy	58,091	56,234	−3.2	512	68	32,020	1,844.7	98.4
Jamaica	2,843	3,128	10.0	660	49	3,480	10.5	87.9
Japan	126,804	117,816	−7.1	881	79	38,410	4,340.1	99.0
Kenya	40,047	51,261	28.0	163	19	580	21.2	85.1
Kuwait	2,788	4,175	49.7	352	98	30,630	80.8	93.3
Libya	6,447	8,323	29.1	9	85	7,380	50.3	82.6
Madagascar	21,282	32,431	52.4	84	26	280	5.5	68.9
Malaysia	26,144	33,065	26.5	192	62	5,490	148.9	88.7

Edition

Country	2010 Projected Population (000s)	2025 Projected Population (000s)	2010–2025 Projected Population Change (%)	2006 Population Density (per square mile)	2006 Percent of Population in Urban Areas	2006 GNI Per Capita ($U.S.)	2006 GDP (billions of $U.S.)	Estimated Literacy Percent
Mexico	112,469	130,199	15.8	145	75	7,870	839.2	91.0
Morocco	35,301	42,553	20.5	193	55	1,900	57.3	52.3
Mozambique	22,061	28,893	31.0	68	35	340	7.6	47.8
Nepal	30,758	39,918	29.8	512	14	290	8.1	48.6
Netherlands	16,783	17,540	4.5	1,261	65	42,670	657.6	99.0
Nicaragua	5,990	7,510	25.4	120	59	1,000	5.4	67.5
Nigeria	145,032	206,166	42.2	375	44	640	114.7	68.0
North Korea	23,802	25,755	8.2	497	60	—	—	99.0
Norway	4,676	4,917	5.2	39	78	66,530	311.0	100.0
Pakistan	173,814	218,496	25.7	538	34	770	128.8	49.9
Panama	3,393	4,110	21.1	109	64	4,890	17.1	91.9
Peru	29,758	34,476	15.9	57	73	2,920	93.3	87.7
Philippines	95,868	118,686	23.8	777	48	1,420	116.9	92.6
Poland	38,464	37,350	−2.9	328	62	8,190	338.7	99.8
Romania	22,181	21,260	−4.2	251	55	4,850	121.6	97.3
Russia	139,390	128,180	−8.0	22	73	5,780	986.9	99.4
Saudi Arabia	29,222	35,669	22.1	33	81	12,510	309.8	78.8
Singapore	4,701	5,101	8.5	17,060	100	29,320	132.2	92.5
Somalia	9,922	14,862	49.8	37	34	—	—	37.8
South Africa	43,333	39,906	−7.9	94	53	5,390	255.0	86.4
South Korea	49,568	50,561	2.0	1,288	82	17,690	888.0	97.9
Spain	40,549	39,578	−2.4	209	77	27,570	1,244.0	97.9
Sri Lanka	21,514	23,707	10.2	829	15	1,300	27.0	90.7
Sudan	41,980	57,462	36.9	42	41	810	37.6	61.1
Sweden	9,074	9,316	2.7	57	84	43,580	384.9	99.0
Switzerland	7,623	7,774	2.0	490	68	57,230	379.8	99.0
Syria	20,606	26,548	28.8	266	50	1,570	34.9	79.6
Tanzania	41,893	53,428	27.5	113	23	350	12.8	69.4
Thailand	66,303	70,524	6.4	327	33	2,990	206.2	92.6
Turkey	73,322	82,205	12.1	237	66	5,400	402.7	87.4
Uganda	33,399	56,745	69.9	379	12	300	9.3	66.8
Ukraine	45,416	41,038	−9.6	200	68	1,950	106.1	99.4
U.K.	61,285	63,819	4.1	650	90	40,180	2,345.0	99.0
U.S.	309,163	349,666	13.1	84	79	44,970	13,201.8	99.0
Venezuela	27,223	33,189	21.9	75	88	6,070	181.9	93.0
Vietnam	87,814	99,978	13.9	672	27	690	60.9	90.3
Zimbabwe	12,516	12,915	3.2	82	36	340	5.0	90.7

Edition

Marketing managers for eBay have found many opportunities for new growth in international markets.

country. *Gross national income (GNI)* is a measure that is similar to GDP, but GNI does not include income earned by foreigners who own resources in that nation. By contrast, GDP does include foreign income. (Note: Until recently, GNI was called gross national product or GNP, so many government documents still include that label.)

When you compare countries with different patterns of international investment, the income measure you use can make a difference. For example, Ford has a factory in Thailand. The GDP measure for Thailand would include the profits from that factory because they were earned in that country. However, Ford is not a Thai firm and most of its profit will ultimately flow out of Thailand. Thus, the Thai GNI would not include those profits. You should see that using GDP income measures can give the impression that people in less-developed countries have more income than they really do. In addition, in a country with a large population the income of the whole nation must be spread over more people. So *GNI per capita* (per person) is a useful figure because it gives some idea of the income level of people in the country.

Developed economies have most of the income

Exhibit 5-2 gives an estimate of GNI per capita and GDP for each country listed. You can see that the more developed industrial nations—including the United States, Japan, and Germany—account for the biggest share of the world's GDP. In these countries the GNI per capita is also quite high. This explains why so much trade takes place between these countries—and why many firms see them as the more important markets. In general, markets like these offer the best potential for products that are targeted at consumers with higher income levels. As a point of comparison, the GNI per capita in the United States is $44,970.[3]

Many managers, however, see great potential—and less competition—where GNI per capita is low. For example, Mars is making a big push to promote its candy in the countries of Eastern Europe. As with many other firms, it hopes to establish a relationship with consumers now, and then turn strong brand loyalty into profitable growth as consumer incomes increase.

A business and a human opportunity

The large number of countries with low GNI per capita is a stark reminder that much of the world's population lives in extreme poverty. You see some sign of this even among some countries with large overall GDP. For example, GNI per capita in China is only about $2,010 per year (in U.S. dollars) and in India it is less than half that at $820.

Many countries are in the early stages of economic development. Most of their people work on farms and live barely within the money economy. At the extreme, in Ethiopia GNI per capita per year is only about $180.

These people, however, have needs, and many are eager to improve themselves. But they may not be able to raise their living standards without outside help. This presents a challenge and an opportunity to the developed nations—and to their business firms. Some companies are trying to help the people of less-developed countries. Corporations such as Pillsbury, Monsanto, and Coca-Cola have developed nutritious foods that can be sold cheaply, but still profitably, in poorer countries.[4]

What do Third World consumers really need?

Marketing managers from developed nations sometimes face an ethical dilemma about whether their products help or hurt consumers in less-developed nations. For example, a United Nations report criticized Coke and Pepsi for expanding their soft-drink sales in the Philippines. The study concluded that consumers had shifted to soft drinks from local beverages—such as a mixture of lime juice and coconut water—that provided needed vitamins.

In another much publicized case, producers of infant formula were criticized for giving free samples to hospitals. Nestlé and other big suppliers in this market say that they only gave the free samples to children who were in need—and at the request of hospitals. But critics argued that the practice encouraged new mothers to give up breast feeding. Away from the hospital, mothers would rely on unsanitary water supplies. Such improper use of the formula could lead to malnutrition and other illnesses. So

Most people would agree that a motorcycle is not a good way for a family of six to get around. But, most people in India don't have the money to afford cars that are common in the United States. That's why Tata Motors in India plans to produce a very basic "People's Car" that will sell for about $2,500.

Nestlé and the others pledged to stop giving away free samples. Although that step stopped some misuse, now the formula is not available to many people who really need it. For example, over a million babies have been infected with AIDS from breast feeding. To help fight this staggering epidemic, Nestlé said it was willing to donate formula, but not unless the World Health Organization agreed that it was not a violation of its pledge.

In cases like these, a marketing manager may need to weigh the benefits and risks of trying to serve third-world markets. For example, in the United States, Quicksilver Enterprises sold its 250-pound aluminum and fiberglass "ultralight" airplanes—which look like go-carts with wings—to wealthy hobbyists. However, Quicksilver found a growing market for ultralights in developing nations, where farmers use them for crop dusting. They help farmers increase production of much needed foods. So what's the problem? In the United States the government bans ultralights as not being safe enough for crop dusting. Some critics argue that a firm shouldn't sell its products in foreign markets if they are illegal in the United States. But ultimately, the marketing manager often must decide what to do.[5]

Edition

Reading, writing, and marketing problems

The ability of a country's people to read and write has a direct influence on the development of its economy—and on marketing strategy planning. The degree of literacy affects the way information is delivered, which in marketing means promotion. Data on illiteracy rates is inexact because different countries use different measures. But the U.S. Census Bureau estimates that 18 percent of adults (age 15 or older) in the world cannot read and write. Two-thirds of them are women. You may be surprised by the low literacy rates for some of the countries in Exhibit 5-2.

Illiteracy sometimes causes difficulties with product labels and instructions, for which we normally use words. This was one issue in the infant formula conflict. In an even more extreme case, some producers of baby food found that consumers misinterpreted a baby's picture on their packages. Illiterate natives believed that the product was just that—a ground-up baby! Many companies meet this lack of literacy with instructions that use pictures instead of words. Singer used this approach with its sewing machines.

Even in Latin America—which has generally higher literacy rates than Africa or Asia—a large number of people cannot read and write. Marketers have to use symbols, colors, and radio advertising to communicate to the masses.[6]

Much segmenting may be required

Marketers can learn a great deal about possible opportunities in different countries by studying available demographic data and trends. The examples we considered here give you a feel, but much more useful data is available. For example, *The World Factbook* is prepared by the Central Intelligence Agency (CIA) for the use of U.S. government officials, but it is available to everyone. It gives facts and statistics on each country in the world. This book can be accessed at the CIA's website (www.odci.gov/cia/publications/factbook). The World Bank publishes *The World Development Indicators*, another excellent source for statistics on individual countries. It is available at the World Bank's website (www.worldbank.org/data/wdi). The International Programs Center of the U.S. Census Bureau also publishes an analysis on world population and related topics called *World Population Profile*. You can also access useful statistics for individual countries at the Census Bureau's website (www.census.gov/ipc/www/idb).

After finding some countries or regions of possible interest (and eliminating unattractive ones), much more segmenting may be required. To illustrate how useful demographic dimensions can be in this effort, we will consider specific characteristics of the U.S. market in some detail. For additional data on the U.S. market, you can go to the Census Bureau's website (www.census.gov). Similar ideas apply to other markets around the world.

Michigan State University's Center for International Business Education and Research (CIBER) created globalEDGE—a website with information and tools for learning about global markets. At the home page for the globalEDGE website (http://globaledge.msu.edu) select "Resource Desk>Country Insights> All Countries." Scroll down and select "Italy>Statistics." Examine the statistics listed under the headings "Economy" and "People." Now check the same statistics for Brazil. How are these countries similar? How are they different? What marketing opportunities might be available in each country?

Internet EXERCISE

POPULATION TRENDS IN THE U.S. CONSUMER MARKET

CHAPTER 5

129

Demographic Dimensions of Global Consumer Markets

U.S. population
is shifting

We've said that the U.S. population is not growing as quickly as in some other countries, but Exhibit 5-3 shows that current population and population growth vary a lot in different regions of the country. Note that California is the most populated state, with Texas a distant second. New York is in third place, and Florida is fourth.

As is the case in many countries, the most populated U.S. areas developed near inexpensive water transportation—on ocean harbors (East and West Coasts), along major rivers (like the Mississippi), or in the Great Lakes region. Obviously, these markets are attractive to many marketers. But this can also mean tough competition, as in the big urban East and West Coast markets.

Marketers anxious to avoid the extremely competitive East and West Coast markets often view the midwestern and southern states as unique target markets. Note, too, the few people in the plains and mountain states, which explains why some national marketers pay less attention to these areas.

Population figures for a single year don't show the dynamic aspects of markets. The estimated U.S. population for 2010 is over 309 million. By 2025, the U.S. population could rise to almost 350 million. But it is important to remember that the population will grow at different rates in different places. Marketers always look for fast-growing markets. They want to know where growth has occurred recently—and where growth is likely to occur in the future.

Exhibit 5-3 shows the projected percent growth in population for each state from 2000 to 2010. The states shaded blue and green are growing at the fastest rate. Note that the greatest growth is in western states like Nevada, Arizona, Idaho, and Utah. Growth will continue in the Sun Belt states as well. With growth over 20 percent, Florida leads the way. But Texas, Georgia, North Carolina, and Virginia are also growing rapidly.

Exhibit 5-3 2006 Population (in thousands) and Percent Change by State, 2000–2010

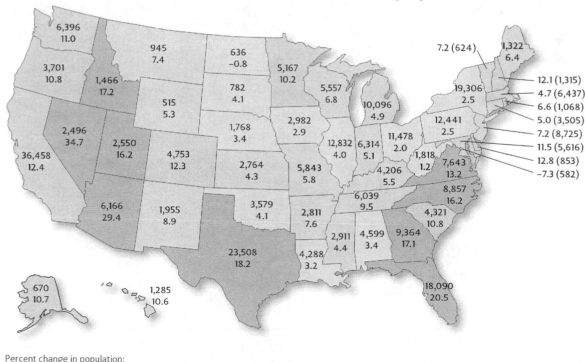

Percent change in population:
☐ Decreasing–4.2   ☐ 4.3–9.9   ☐ 10.0–12.9   ☐ 13.0 or higher

Edition

Notice that some of the most populated areas shown in Exhibit 5-3 aren't the ones growing the fastest. Between 2000 and 2010 the population of New York is estimated to grow only 2.5 percent. In fact, combined population growth in all of the northeastern states will only be about 2.4 percent, while growth in the West will average around 7.8 percent.

These different rates of growth are important to marketers. Sudden growth in one area may create a demand for many new shopping centers—while retailers in declining areas face tougher competition for a smaller number of customers. In growing areas, demand may increase so rapidly that profits may be good even in poorly planned facilities.

The map summarizes state-level data to give the big picture. However, much more detailed population data is available. You can obtain detailed census data—or updated estimates—for very small geographic areas. Just as we mapped population changes at the state level, a local marketer can divide a big metropolitan area into many smaller areas to see where the action is. Census data may become outdated before a new census is conducted—but by then local and state government planning groups may be able to provide updates. This type of data can help a local restaurant decide where to send a direct mail promotion—or show Kinko's the best location for a new store.

Population will keep growing, but . . .

Despite the large increases, the *rate* of population growth in the United States has slowed dramatically—to less than 1 percent a year during the last decade. In fact, many U.S. marketers who enjoyed rapid and profitable growth until the 1990s know that the domestic picnic is now over. Some turned to international markets where population—and sales revenues—continue to grow.

In the United States most of our future growth is expected to come from immigration. In fact, even now the total U.S. population would start to decline if immigration stopped. Let's look at some of these trends and what they mean to marketing managers.[7]

Birthrate—boom or bust?

The U.S. birthrate—the number of babies born per 1,000 people—fluctuated greatly in the last 60 years. Exhibit 5-4 shows a clear pattern. A post–World War II baby boom began as returning soldiers started families, and it lasted about 15 years

Exhibit 5-4   Changes in the U.S. Birthrate, 1935–2006

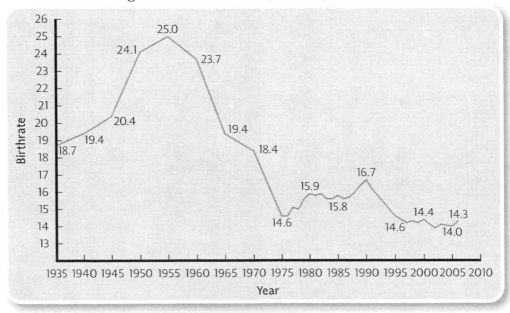

into the early 1960s. In the 1970s, the situation changed to a "baby bust" as more women stayed in the workforce and couples waited longer to have children. When you see the dip in the birthrate—and think about the declining market for baby products—you can understand why Johnson & Johnson promotes its baby shampoo to adults who want a gentle product. You can also understand why Johnson & Johnson looks for opportunities in Asia and Latin America where the birthrate is higher.

The U.S. birthrate hit a low in 1975 and 1976 and then rose again—but only slightly. From 1977 to 1995 the birthrate was between 15 and 17, but then slowly started to drop again—with an estimated birthrate of about 14 during this decade. These shifts are easy to explain. As the baby-boomer generation entered its child-bearing years, there were more women to have babies. However, as the boomers aged this baby "boomlet" passed and turned to what some have called a "baby bust." In addition, American couples are having fewer children. There will be more demand for small apartments, in-home entertainment, travel, and smaller food packages.

With fewer children, parents can spend more money on each child. For example, expensive bikes, video game consoles, MP3 players, and designer clothes for children have all sold well in recent years because parents can indulge one or two children more easily than a houseful.[8]

The graying of America

In 1980, the median age of the U.S. population was 30—but by 2010 the median age will be about 37. The median age is growing because the percentage of population in older age groups has increased.

Exhibit 5-5 shows the number of people in different age groups in 2000—and the expected sizes for 2010 and 2020. Note the big increases under way in the 45 to 64 and 65 and older groups. From 2000 to 2010, the 45 to 64 group grows by 30.8 percent, but then growth in that age group slows to a 3.3 percent increase in the next decade. The over-65 age group is also increasing during this decade by 15.0 percent. However, from 2010 to 2020, a whopping increase of 35.8 percent is expected!

The major reason for the changing distribution is that the post–World War II baby boom produced over one-fourth of the U.S. population. This large group crowded into schools in the 1950s and 1960s—and then into the job market in the 1970s. In the 1980s and 1990s, they swelled the middle-aged group. And early in the 21st century, they are now beginning to reach retirement—still a dominant group in the total population.

Some of the effects of this big market are very apparent. For example, recording industry sales exploded—to the beat of rock-and-roll music and the Beatles—as the

Highly targeted advertising media are proving especially effective at targeting messages to specific demographic groups. For example, CNBC targets high-income consumers whom it says have an average net worth over $2.7 million.

Edition

Exhibit 5–5   Population Distribution (and Percent Growth Rate) by Age Groups for Different 10-Year Periods

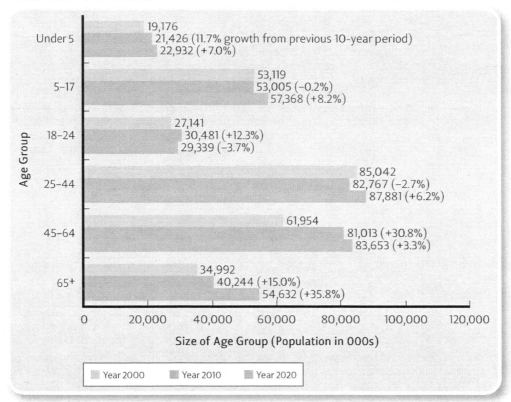

baby-boomer group moved into their record-buying teens. Soon after, colleges added facilities and faculty to handle the surge, but then had to cope with excess capacity and loss of revenue when the student-age population dwindled. To relieve financial strain, many colleges now add special-interest courses to attract the aging baby boomers, some of whom are beginning to retire. This ongoing growth creates new opportunities for such industries as tourism, health care, and financial services—all of which are important to the middle-aged and retired.[9]

Household composition is changing

Many people incorrectly think of the "typical" American household as a married couple with two children—living in the suburbs. This never was true and is even less true now. Only 22.7 percent of households consist of a husband, wife, and children under 18. Another 28.1 percent of households involve married couples, but ones without children living at home. Moreover, kids don't always have a mom and dad at home. Today, 36.8 percent of the babies in the United States are born to a single parent.

Although about 85 percent of all Americans marry, they are marrying later, delaying child bearing, and having fewer children. And couples don't stay together as long as they used to. The United States has the highest divorce rate in the world— about 50 percent of marriages end in divorce. That helps to explain why 12 percent of U.S. households are now families headed by a single woman. Yet divorce does not seem to deter people from marrying again. Over 80 percent of divorced people remarry in what is described as "the triumph of hope over experience." Still, even with all this shifting around, at any given time only about 60 percent of all adults are married.

Aging of Japan Motivates New Products at Toyota

The population of Japan is getting old. Currently half of all Japanese people are older than 43 (the median age). Further, by 2025, the median age is expected to jump to 50. Many developed countries are experiencing growth in the older age groups, but Japan provides a dramatic preview of the coming effects of this global shift. Change in the age distribution hit Japan early because its people tend to live long lives, it is a country with a low birthrate, and it has resisted immigration.

To better meet the needs of aging customers in Japan, Toyota has introduced models that offer Welcab options, like swivel seats and wheelchair ramps. Welcab options are designed to appeal to the elderly as well as the disabled. In the past, Toyota sold hospitals and nursing homes expensive customized vehicles that were retrofitted with these features. Now, with the larger market (and production-line economies of scale), Toyota is offering standard Welcab options at lower prices. For example, Toyota's Ractis, an attractively priced four-seat minivan with Welcab features, is gaining in popularity with older drivers. Toyota dealers, seeing the growth opportunity, are aggressively advertising these "elder-cars." And at home health care conventions—sandwiched between booths selling walkers and adult diapers—Toyota holds seminars to promote the advantages of the Ractis.

Toyota has also expanded its research to better understand the needs of the elderly. For example, it is difficult for many older drivers to twist and look over their shoulder or to hear high-pitched sounds—like the beeping signal when a truck backs up. By researching such issues Toyota hopes to design vehicles that will be safer for everyone. For example, it is adding back-up cameras to some cars.

Toyota's help for aging Japanese consumers doesn't just stop at the end of the road. Shoichiro Toyoda, a former Toyota CEO who had firsthand experience caring for an elderly family member, called for a greater focus on innovations to meet the needs of elderly consumers. The Toyota Group and its suppliers responded with a variety of products. These include a computerized wheelchair that delivers its passenger to a programmed location, kitchen cabinets that lower to wheelchair height at the touch of a switch, and electronic house keys that do not need to be removed from the homeowner's pocket.

Catering to the needs of older Japanese consumers will ultimately give Toyota and its suppliers a head start in serving this market in other countries. Globally, there are over 450 million people aged 65 and over—and this market is expected to grow to over 800 million by 2025.[10]

Nonfamily households are increasing

Many households are not families in the traditional sense. There are now about 6 million unmarried couples who live together. Some of these arrangements are temporary—as in college towns or in large cities where recent graduates go for their first "real" job. But the majority are older couples who choose not to get married. The number of these nontraditional households is still relatively small. But marketers pay special attention to them because they are growing at a much higher rate than the traditional family households. And they have different needs and attitudes than the stereotypical American family. To reach this market, some banks changed their policies about loans to unmarried couples for homes, cars, and other major purchases. And some insurance companies designed coverage for unmarried couples.

Single-adult households are also on the rise, and they account for almost 27 percent of all households—over 30 million people! These include young adults who leave home when they finish school, as well as separated, divorced, or widowed people who live alone. In some big cities, the percentage of single-person households is even higher—over 40 percent in New York and Washington, D.C. These people need

Edition

The number of "mature" consumers is increasing rapidly, so established brands like Pond's are seeking opportunities for growth with new health and beauty products developed to meet the special needs of this market.

smaller apartments, smaller cars, smaller food packages, and, in some cases, less-expensive household furnishings because many singles don't have much money. Other singles have ample discretionary income and are attractive markets for top-of-the-line clothing, expensive electronic gadgets, status cars, travel, nice restaurants, and trendy bars.[11]

The shift to urban and suburban areas

Migration from rural to urban areas has been continuous in the United States since 1800. In 1920, about half the population lived in rural areas. By 1950, the number living on farms dropped to 15 percent—and now it is less than 2 percent. We have become an urban and suburban society.[12]

Since World War II, there has been a continuous flight to the suburbs by middle-income consumers. By 1970, more people lived in the suburbs than in the central cities. Retailers moved too—following their customers. Lower-income consumers—often with varied ethnic backgrounds—moved in, changing the nature of markets in the center of the city.

Industries too have been fleeing the cities, moving many jobs closer to the suburbs. Today's urban economic system is not as dependent on central cities. A growing population must go somewhere—and the suburbs can combine pleasant neighborhoods with easy transportation to higher-paying jobs nearby or in the city.

Purchase patterns are different in the suburbs. For example, a big city resident may not need or own a car. But with no mass transportation, living carless in the suburbs is difficult. And in some areas, it almost seems that an SUV or a minivan—to carpool kids and haul lawn supplies or pets—is a necessity.

Local political boundaries don't define market areas

These continuing shifts—to and from urban and suburban areas—mean that the usual practice of reporting population by city and county boundaries can result in misleading descriptions of markets. Marketers are more interested in the size of homogeneous *marketing* areas than in the number of people within political boundaries. To meet this need, the U.S. Census Bureau also reports data by Metropolitan Statistical Area (MSA) which is an integrated economic and social unit with a large population nucleus. Generally, an MSA centers on one city or urbanized area of 50,000 or more inhabitants and includes bordering urban areas.

The largest MSAs—basically those with a population of more than a million—are called Consolidated Metropolitan Statistical Areas. About 38 percent of all Americans live in the 20 largest CMSAs. More detailed data is available for areas within these sprawling, giant urban areas.

Big targets are attractive—but very competitive

Some national marketers sell only in these metro areas because of their large, concentrated populations. They know that having so many customers packed into a small area can simplify the marketing effort. They can use fewer intermediaries and still offer products conveniently. One or two local advertising media—a city newspaper or cable TV channel—can reach most residents. If a sales force is needed, it will incur less travel time and expense because people are closer together.

Metro areas are also attractive markets because they offer greater sales potential than their large population alone suggests. Consumers in these areas have more money to spend because wages tend to be higher. In addition, professionals—with higher salaries—are concentrated there. But remember that competition for consumer dollars is usually stiff in an MSA.[13]

The mobile ones are an attractive market

Of course, none of these population shifts is necessarily permanent. People move, stay awhile, and then move again. In fact, about 13 percent of Americans move each year. Although almost 7 out of 10 moves are within the same county, both the local and long-distance mobiles are important market segments.

People who move are an attractive market—they tend to be ready to spend. They must find new sources of food, clothing, medical and dental care, and household products. Once they make these basic buying decisions, they may not change for a long time. Alert marketers try to locate these potential customers early—to inform them of offerings before they make their purchase decisions. Retail chains, "national" brands, and franchised services available in different areas have a competitive advantage with mobiles. The customer who moves to a new town may find a familiar Walgreens or Blockbuster sign down the street and never even try their local competitors.[14]

INCOME DIMENSIONS OF THE U.S. MARKET

So far, we have been concerned mainly with the *number* of different types of people—and *where* they live.

More people are in middle and upper income levels

Earlier in this chapter you saw how GNI figures can be helpful in analyzing markets. But GNI figures are more meaningful to marketing managers when converted to family or household income and its distribution. Family incomes in the United States generally increased with GNI. But even more important to marketers, the *distribution* of income changed drastically over time.

Fifty years ago, the U.S. income distribution looked something like a pyramid. Most families were bunched together at the low end of the income scale—just over a subsistence level—to form the base of the income pyramid. There were many fewer families in the middle range, and a relative handful formed an elite market at the top. This pattern still exists in many nations.

Edition

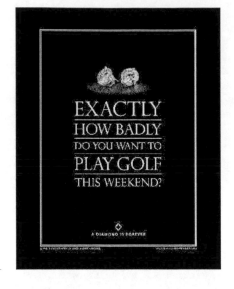

Marketers for diamonds are very aware that spending varies with income and other demographic dimensions.

By the 1970s, real income (buying power) in the United States had risen so much that most families—even those near the bottom of the income distribution—could afford a comfortable standard of living. And the proportion of people with middle incomes was much larger. Such middle-income people enjoyed real choices in the marketplace.

This revolution broadened markets and drastically changed the U.S. marketing system. Products viewed as luxuries in most parts of the world sell to "mass" markets in the United States. And these large markets lead to economies of scale, which boost our standard of living even more. Similar situations exist in Canada, many Western European countries, Australia, New Zealand, and Japan.

Real income growth has slowed—but for how long?

The long-run trend in family income since the 1960s reflects this general upward shift in distribution—and the increased number of families with larger amounts of disposable income. See Exhibit 5-6. While the overall trend has been upward, growth in income slowed during the inflation-ridden 1970s and, more recently, there's been no growth at all.

Note that the increases in income we've been discussing are not just the increases that are sometimes prompted by inflation—the general increase in the cost of goods and services over time. Therefore, to make it easier to compare income levels across time, Exhibit 5-6 shows estimates of real income—income that is adjusted to take out the effects of inflation on purchasing power.

Exhibit 5-6   Median Family Income over Time (in 2005 dollars)

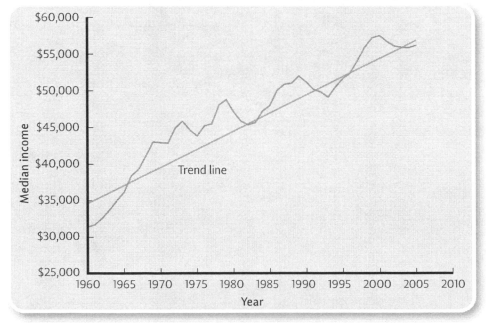

CHAPTER 5

137

Demographic Dimensions of Global Consumer Markets

Given the recent slowdown in real income, there is heated debate about what will happen to consumer incomes—and income distribution—in the future. Some business analysts feel that the lack of significant income growth signals worse things to come. They think that a decline in the manufacturing sector of the economy threatens America's middle-class standard of living. These analysts argue that in industries with traditionally high wages, firms are replacing workers with technology—to be able to compete with low-cost foreign producers. At the same time, new jobs are coming from growth of the lower-paying service industries. But other analysts are not so pessimistic. They agree that the percentage of the workforce earning middle-income wages has declined recently—but they think this is a temporary shift, not a long-term trend, and that over time the efficiencies that come from new information technologies will "lift" the whole economy.

What happens to income levels will be critical to you and to American consumers in general. It is easy for both consumers and marketing managers to be lulled by the promise of a constantly increasing standard of living. Both consumer thinking and marketing strategy will have to adjust if growth does not resume.

The higher-income groups receive a big share

Higher-income groups in the United States receive a very large share of total income, as you can see in Exhibit 5-7, which divides all families into five equal-sized groups—from lowest income to highest. Note that although the median income of U.S. families in 2005 was about $56,194, the top 20 percent of the families—those with incomes over $103,100—received over 48 percent of the total income. This gave them extra buying power, especially for luxury items like memberships in country clubs and yachts. Well-to-do families with incomes over $184,500—the top 5 percent nationally—got over 21 percent of the total income.

At the lower end of the scale, almost 15.5 million families had less than $25,616 income. They account for 20 percent of all families but receive only 4.0 percent of total income. Even this low-income group is an attractive market for some basic commodities, especially food and clothing—even though almost half of them live below the poverty level of $19,971 for a family of four. These consumers may receive food stamps, medicare, and public housing, which increases their buying power. Some marketers target this group, usually with a lower-price marketing mix.

Exhibit 5-7
Percent of Total Income Going to Different Income Groups in 2005

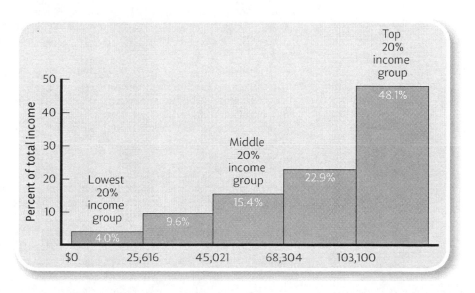

Edition

How much income is "enough?"

We can't stress the importance of income distribution too much. Many managers make serious marketing strategy errors by overestimating the amount of income in various target markets. Marketers can easily make such errors because of the natural tendency for people to associate with others like themselves and to assume that almost everyone lives like they do. A marketing manager who earns $135,000 a year may have no clue what life is like for a family that lives on $25,000 a year.

The 2005 median family income of about $56,194 is a useful reference point because some college graduates start near this level. And a young working couple together can easily go way over this figure. This may seem like a lot of money at first—but it is surprising how soon needs and expenses rise and adjust to available income. America's middle-income consumers have been hit hard by the spiraling costs of health care, housing, energy, cars, taxes, and tuition bills. More than ever, these consumers look for purchases that offer good value for the money spent. Some high-living marketers may not understand that these consumers *need* to pinch their pennies, but that practical reality now explains much of the buying behavior of lower and middle-income markets in the United States.[15]

Can low-income consumers protect themselves?

In considering statistics such as these, it is important for all of us to think about the enormous problems of poverty that low-income consumers face. There are 37 million people in the United States who live in poverty, and their lives are frequently hard. They often can't afford enough to eat, to obtain insurance or proper medical care, clothing for their children, or even a safe place to live. In market-directed economies, consumers are free to make choices in the marketplace. But with little income, education, or opportunity to become informed, many consumers in the lowest income groups have few real choices. Some marketing managers struggle over whether to serve these markets. A credit company, for example, may find customers willing to pay a high finance charge to borrow money. And the high rate may be needed to cover the risk of unpaid loans. But is it exploitation to charge a higher rate to those who can least afford it and who really have no other choice?[16]

SPENDING VARIES WITH INCOME AND OTHER DEMOGRAPHIC DIMENSIONS

We've been using the term *family income* because consumer budget studies show that many consumers spend their incomes as part of family or household units. They usually pool their incomes when planning major expenditures. So most of our discussion will concern how families or households spend their income.

Disposable income is what you get to spend

Families don't get to spend all of their income. Disposable income is what is left after taxes. Out of this disposable income—together with gifts, pensions, cash savings, or other assets—the family makes its expenditures. Some families don't spend all their disposable income—they save part of it. Therefore, when trying to estimate potential sales in target markets, we should distinguish among income, disposable income, and what consumers actually spend.

Discretionary income is elusive

Most families spend a good portion of their income on such "necessities" as food, rent or house payments, car and home furnishings payments, and insurance. A family's purchase of "luxuries" comes from discretionary income—what is left of disposable income after paying for necessities.

Discretionary income is an elusive concept because the definition of necessities varies from family to family and over time. It depends on what they think is necessary for their lifestyle. A cable TV service might be purchased out of discretionary income by a lower-income family but be considered a necessity by a higher-income family. But if many people in a lower-income neighborhood subscribe to cable TV, it might

Schwan's uses catalogs and a website (www.schwans.com) to promote food products and complete meals which it delivers directly to a consumer's home. A service like this is especially valuable to dual-career families and professionals who face a poverty of time.

RESEARCH SHOWS *that* **95% OF HOUSEWIVES COULD USE A HOUSEWIFE.**

Prepared to serve.

139

become a "necessity" for the others—and severely reduce the discretionary income available for other purchases.

The majority of U.S. families do not have enough discretionary income to afford the lifestyles they see on TV and in other mass media. On the other hand, some young adults and older people without family responsibilities have a lot of discretionary income. They may be especially attractive markets for electronic gear, digital cameras, new cars, foreign travel, designer fashions, and various kinds of recreation—tennis, skiing, boating, concerts, and fine restaurants.[17]

Spending varies over the family life cycle

Income has a direct bearing on spending patterns, but many other demographic dimensions are also useful in understanding consumer buying. Marital status, age, and the age of any children in the family have an especially important effect on how people spend their income. Put together, these dimensions tell us about the life-cycle stage of a family. Exhibit 5-8 shows a summary of stages in the family life cycle. In our

Exhibit 5-8   Stages in Modern Family Life Cycles

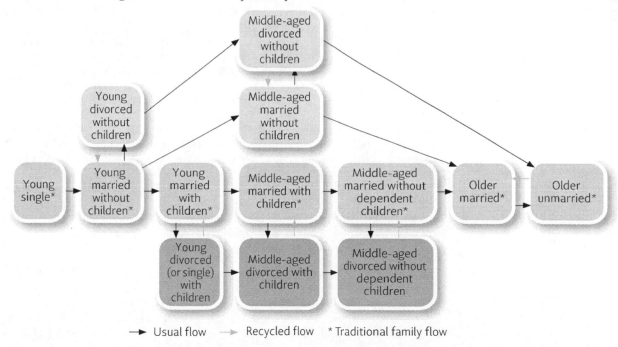

→ Usual flow   ⇢ Recycled flow   * Traditional family flow

Edition

discussion, we will focus on the traditional flow from one stage to the next—as shown in the middle of the diagram. However, as shown at the top and bottom of the exhibit, divorce does interrupt the flow for many people; after a divorce, they may recycle through earlier stages.[18]

Young people and families accept new ideas

Singles and young couples seem to be more willing to try new products and brands—and they are careful, price-conscious shoppers. Younger people often earn less than older consumers, but they spend a greater proportion of their income on discretionary items because they don't have the major expenses of home ownership, education, and family rearing. Although many young people are waiting longer to marry, most do tie the knot eventually. These younger families—especially those with no children—are still accumulating durable goods, such as automobiles and home furnishings. They spend less on food. Only as children arrive and grow does family spending shift to soft goods and services, such as education, medical, and personal care. This usually happens when the family head reaches the 35–49 age group. To meet expenses, people in this age group often make more purchases on credit, and they save less of their income.

Divorce—increasingly a fact of American life—disrupts the family life-cycle pattern. Divorced parents don't spend like other singles. The mother usually has custody of the children, and the father may pay child support. The mother and children typically have much less income than two-parent families. Such families spend a larger percent of their income on housing, child care, and other necessities—with little left for discretionary purchases. If a single parent remarries, the family life cycle may start over again.[19]

Reallocation for teenagers

Once children become teenagers, further shifts in spending occur. Teenagers eat more, want to wear expensive clothes, and develop recreation and education needs that are hard on the family budget. The parents—or increasingly, the single parent—may be forced to reallocate expenditures to cover these expenses—spending less on durable goods, such as appliances, automobiles, household goods, and housing. The fast-rising expense of sending a son or daughter to college can create a major financial crisis.

For many firms, teens are an important and attractive market. The amount of money involved may surprise you. America's teens currently spend over $170 billion a year and spending is growing. Further, in today's families with a single parent or with two wage earners, teens play an increasingly important role in shopping and shaping family purchases. With teens spending more money, they are a target for many firms. MasterCard is targeting teens with its credit card promotions, and Bausch & Lomb's contact-lens sales hit record levels when the firm refocused its marketing efforts on teens.[20]

Selling to the empty nesters

Another important category is the empty nesters—people whose children are grown and who are now able to spend their money in other ways. Usually these people are in the 50–64 age group. But this is a varied group because some people marry later and are still raising a family at this age. And in recent years lots of empty nesters have been surprised when adult singles move back in to avoid the big costs of housing.

Empty nesters are an attractive market for many items. Often they have paid for their homes, and the big expenses of raising a family are behind them. They are more interested in travel, sports cars, and other things they couldn't afford before. Much depends on their income, of course. But this is a high-income period for many workers, especially white-collar workers.[21]

Senior citizens are a big market

Finally, marketers should not neglect the senior citizens—people over 65. The number of people over 65 is increasing rapidly because of modern medicine, improved sanitary conditions, and better nutrition. This group now makes up 13 percent of the population.

Our senior citizens are more prosperous than ever before. Their income is often lower than in their peak earning years, but most do have money to spend. They don't

Empty nesters and senior citizens are often an attractive market for leisure travel and other discretionary purchases.

just squeak by on Social Security. Such prosperity is a dramatic change. In 1960, about a third of all senior citizens had incomes below the poverty level. Now, only 9.8 percent are considered "poor"—lower than the 12.5 percent figure for all adults.

Older people also have very different needs. Many firms already cater to senior citizens—and more will be serving this market. For example, some companies have developed housing and "life care" centers designed to appeal to older people. Casio makes a calculator with large, easy-to-read numbers. Publix Super Markets, a big Florida chain, trains employees to cater to older customers. Checkout clerks, for example, give older customers two light bags instead of one heavier one. Some travel agents find that senior citizens are an eager market for expensive tours and cruises. Other companies offer diet supplements and drug products, often in special easy-to-open packages. And senior citizen discounts at drugstores are more than just a courtesy—the elderly make up the biggest market for medicines.

Keep in mind, however, that older people are not all the same. With a group this large, generalities and stereotypes can be dangerous. Different senior citizen target markets have different needs and require different marketing strategies.[22]

ETHNIC DIMENSIONS OF THE U.S. MARKET

Do ethnic groups buy differently?

America may be called the melting pot, but ethnic groups deserve special attention when analyzing markets. One basic reason is that people from different ethnic groups may be influenced by very different cultural variables. They may have quite varied needs and their own ways of thinking. Moreover, Americans value diversity and the United States is becoming a multicultural market. As a result, rather than disappearing in a melting pot, some important cultural and ethnic dimensions are being preserved and highlighted. This creates both opportunities and challenges for marketers.

Some important ethnic differences are obvious. For example, about 1 out of 5 families in the United States speaks a language other than English at home. Some areas have a much higher rate. In Miami and San Antonio, for example, about 1 out of 3 families speaks Spanish. This

Internet EXERCISE Visit the website for EthnicGrocer (www. ethnicgrocer.com). From the home page, click "Shop by Product>Edible Wrappings." Examine a few products to learn more about each of them. Do you think any of these products have a chance to become popular in the United States? Why or why not?

Edition

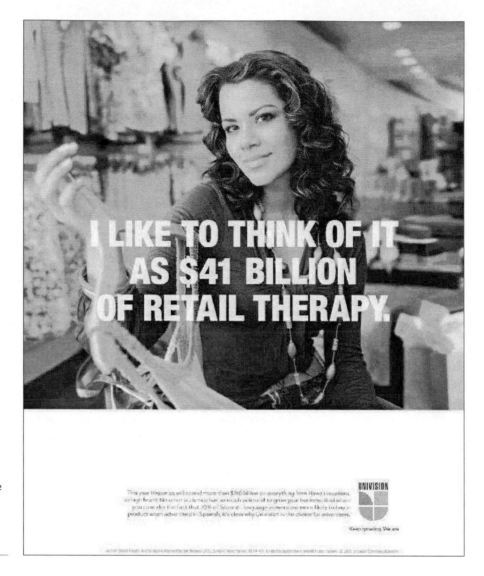

I LIKE TO THINK OF IT AS $41 BILLION OF RETAIL THERAPY.

UNIVISION

Many firms are developing strategies to appeal to fast-growing ethnic markets in the United States. For example, Univision's ad promotes the accelerated buying power of the Hispanic market.

obviously affects promotion planning. Similarly, brand preferences vary for some ethnic groups. For example, cosmetic companies offer products tailored to different skin tones. But ethnic groups don't just differ in the color of their skin. Differences in attitudes, experiences, and values, as well as where they shop and what advertising appeals they attend to, come together to shape differences in buying behavior.

Stereotypes are common—and misleading

A marketer needs to study ethnic dimensions very carefully because they can be subtle and fast-changing. This is also an area where stereotyped thinking is the most common—and misleading. Many firms make the mistake of treating all consumers in a particular ethnic group as homogeneous. For example, some marketing managers treat all 40.5 million African American consumers as "the black market," ignoring the great variability among African American households on other segmenting dimensions. Income variability is a good example. The median income of black families ($35,464) is still lower than for the whole population, but that is changing. Today, over 64 percent of black families have an income of at least $50,000—and over 10 percent have an income of $100,000 or more. These affluent consumers are also a relatively youthful market and a larger percentage (compared with white consumers) are in earlier stages of the life cycle and therefore a better market for certain products—especially durable goods like cars, furniture, home appliances, and electronic equipment.

Ethnic markets are becoming more important

More marketers pay attention to ethnic groups now because the number of ethnic consumers is growing at a much faster rate than the overall society. Much of this growth results from immigration. In addition, however, the median age of Asian Americans, African Americans, and Hispanics is much lower than that of whites—and the birthrate is higher. In combination, these factors have a dramatic effect.

Hispanic market is growing

Let's take a closer look at Hispanic Americans—now the largest and fastest-growing ethnic group in the United States—with a median family income of 37,867. Recently, their numbers have increased at the rate of about 1 million per year. In 2010, the Hispanic population will be about 48 million and make up 15.5 percent of the total population. To put this in perspective, the Hispanic population in the United States will be almost 20 percent greater than the population of Spain and almost 40 percent greater than the population of Canada. Hispanics also provide marketing opportunities for the future because they tend to be younger than the U.S. population as a whole.

Many companies are responding to this trend. For example, many Wells Fargo branches in the Southwest have added Latin-style decor, bicultural tellers, and Spanish-language promotion, including free coloring books for Hispanic kids. Efforts such as these have significantly increased Wells Fargo's business. Similarly, P&G found that Hispanic consumers spend twice as much as other customers on some household cleaning products. So P&G adapted some brands to appeal to Hispanic preferences. When research revealed that many Hispanics are particular about the scent of their laundry, marketers at P&G changed the scent of Gain detergent and promoted the change on Spanish TV and radio stations. Gain's market share with Hispanics is now 80 percent higher than with other segments.

Asian American market grows fast too

While there are fewer Asian Americans (about 14.2 million in 2010 and 4.2 percent of the population) the number has more than tripled since 1980. Asian Americans have the highest median family income ($68,957) of the major ethnic groups. Because of this growth and income, companies as varied as Kraft, Wal-Mart, and Allstate are targeting these consumers, especially in local markets where the Asian American population is concentrated.

Income and population create ethnic market buying power

The buying power of ethnic submarkets is also increasing rapidly. Estimates indicate that by the end of the decade Hispanics and African Americans will each spend nearly $1 trillion a year and Asian Americans over $500 billion a year. It's also important to marketers that much of this buying power is often concentrated in certain cities and states, which makes targeted promotion and distribution more efficient. For example, over 20 percent of San Francisco residents are Asians.

Strategy changes may be needed

These ethnic shifts are changing the face of the American market. Already more than 36 percent of American children are African American, Hispanic, or Asian. Longer term, whites are expected to become a minority by 2050. Many companies will need separate strategies for these ethnically or racially defined markets. Some may only require changes in Place and Promotion. But many companies have had difficulty developing strategies and segmenting ethnic submarkets. For example, Asian Americans emigrated from China, Japan, the Philippines, India, Korea, Vietnam, Laos, and Cambodia. Many come from very different backgrounds with no common language, religion, or culture. That adds to the marketing challenge; it means marketers must really understand the basic needs that motivate specific target markets to think and act as they do. This is important with any consumer market, regardless of people's ethnic or racial background or where in the world they live. We'll deal with that important issue in more detail in Chapter 6.[23]

CONCLUSION

In this chapter, we studied population, income, and other demographic dimensions of final consumer markets. Our first two learning objectives addressed the need to understand key demographic differences and trends in global markets. Getting the facts straight on how over 6.6 billion people are spread over the world is important to marketing managers. Understanding the growth of urban areas around the world helps marketers provide more efficient promotion and distribution. This chapter also provides a more in-depth look at population trends in the United States.

But we must also understand income and spending patterns to adequately assess the potential of markets. So our third learning objective addressed the importance of knowing about the distribution of income in the United States. We highlighted the fact that it has gradually changed—leaving more people in upper and lower income categories. We also saw that real income has leveled off in the United States. Income is important because it is closely tied to spending.

Understanding the family life cycle is this chapter's fourth learning objective. It is important because

how much people buy—and what they buy—changes in relatively predictable patterns as they move through different stages of the family life cycle.

People continue to move around the world, and marketers need to understand international migration. We examine this influence in the United States, where immigration has created large and important ethnic communities. The Hispanic community is large and has been growing rapidly—creating new opportunities. But African American and Asian American populations also offer significant opportunities in the U.S. market. Increasingly, we are a multicultural society.

The kind of demographic data discussed in this chapter can be very useful for estimating the market potential within possible target markets. But unfortunately, it is not very helpful in explaining specific consumer behavior—why people buy *specific* products and *specific* brands. Marketing managers need to understand the behavioral dimensions of the final consumer market to explain how specific individuals will react to a marketing mix. So, this important subject is the focus of Chapter 6.

KEY TERMS

gross domestic product (GDP), 123

birthrate, 130

Metropolitan Statistical Area (MSA), 134

real income, 136

disposable income, 138

discretionary income, 138

empty nesters, 140

senior citizens, 140

QUESTIONS AND PROBLEMS

1. Drawing on data in Exhibit 5-2, do you think that Romania would be an attractive market for a firm that produces home appliances? What about Finland? Discuss your reasons.

2. Discuss the value of gross domestic product and gross national income per capita as measures of market potential in international consumer markets. Refer to specific data in your answer.

3. Discuss how the worldwide trend toward urbanization is affecting opportunities for international marketing.

4. Discuss how slower population growth will affect businesses in your local community.

5. Discuss the impact of changes in the size of the 18–24 age group on marketing strategy planning in the United States.

6. Name three specific examples of firms that developed a marketing mix to appeal to senior citizens. Name three examples of firms that developed a marketing mix to appeal to teenagers.

7. Some demographic characteristics are more important than others in determining market potential. For each of the following characteristics, identify two products for which this characteristic is *most* important: (a) size of geographic area, (b) population, (c) income, (d) stage of life cycle.

8. Name three specific examples (specific products or brands—not just product categories) and explain how demand in the United States will differ by geographic location *and* urban–rural location.

9. Explain how the continuing mobility of U.S. consumers—as well as the development of big metropolitan areas—should affect marketing strategy planning in the future. Be sure to consider the impact on the four Ps.

10. Explain why the concept of the Metropolitan Statistical Area was developed. Is it the most useful breakdown for retailers?

11. Explain why mobile consumers can be an attractive market.

12. Why are marketing managers paying more attention to ethnic dimensions of consumer markets in the United States?

13. Name three categories of products marketed in the United States that are influenced by Hispanic culture.

14. A large bank plans to open offices in a state where it did not previously have locations. The managers know where other banks in the state are located. What kind of demographic data would be useful in helping them to decide where to establish the bank's new locations?

CREATING MARKETING PLANS

The Marketing Plan Coach software on the Student CD and the text website includes a sample marketing plan for Hillside Veterinary Clinic. Look through the "Customers" section and consider the following questions.

a. What demographic data is included in this marketing plan?

b. What demographic data could be added to the plan?

c. Go to the U.S. Census Bureau's website (www.census.gov). Explore the site. What data do you find that might be helpful?

d. The American Veterinary Medicine Association (www.avma.org) publishes the *U.S. Pet Ownership & Demographics Sourcebook*. Search the Internet or the AVMA site and find information about this book. Review the table of contents. What information might be useful for a veterinary clinic?

145

SUGGESTED CASES

8. Lombardi's Italian Grill   10. Taffe's Ice Land   22. Bright Light Innovations   30. Eden Prairie Mills, Ltd.

COMPUTER-AIDED PROBLEM

5. DEMOGRAPHIC ANALYSIS

Stylco, Inc., is a producer of specialty clothing. To differentiate its designs and appeal to its African American target market, Stylco uses authentic African prints. Originally, it just focused on designs targeted at adults in the 35–44 age range. However, sales to these middle-aged adults started to level off, so Stylco added a more conservative line of clothes for older consumers. Most buyers of the conservative styles are in the 45–59 age group.

Stylco has focused on distributing its products through select fashion boutiques in metropolitan market areas with the highest concentrations of African American consumers. This approach has reduced Stylco's personal selling expense; as a result, however, only a percentage of the total black population is served by current Stylco retailers. For example, about half of the consumers in the 35–44 age group are in the market areas served by Stylco retailers.

Naomi Davis, Stylco's marketing manager, read an article about the "graying of America." This left her wondering how shifts in the age distribution might affect her market and sales.

To get a long-run view of these trends, she looked at census data on black consumers by age group. She also looked up estimates of the expected percent rate of change in the size of each group through the year 2010. By multiplying these rates by the size her target markets were in 2005, she can estimate how large they are likely to be in the year 2010. Further, from analysis of past sales data, she knows that the number of units the firm sells is directly proportional to the size of each age group. Specifically, the ratio of units sold to target market size has been about 5 units per 1,000 people (that is, a ratio of .005). Finally, she determined the firm's average unit profit for each of the lines. To see how changes in population are likely to affect Stylco units sold and future profits from each line, Davis programmed all of the data, and the relationships discussed earlier, into a spreadsheet.

a. Briefly compare the profit data for 2005 and estimated profit for 2010 as it appears on the initial spreadsheet. What is the basic reason for the expected shift? What are the implications of this and other data in the spreadsheet for Stylco's marketing strategy planning?

b. The rate of growth or decline for different age groups tends to vary from one geographic region to another. Davis thinks that in the market areas that Stylco serves the size of the 35–44 age group may decrease by as much as 10 to 12 percent by 2010. However, the Census Bureau estimates that the decline of the black 35–44 age group for the whole country will only be about −1.7 percent. If the decline in the target market size for Davis' market areas turns out to be −1.7 percent rather than the −10.1 she has assumed, what is the potential effect on profits from the young adult line? On overall profits?

c. Because more firms are paying attention to fast-growing ethnic markets, Davis thinks competition may increase in lines targeted at affluent African Americans in the 45–59 age group. Because of price competition, the line targeted at this group already earns a lower average profit per unit. Further, as more firms compete for this business, she thinks that her "ratio of units sold to market size" may decrease. Use the what-if analysis to prepare a table showing how percent of profit from this group, as well as total profit, might change as the ratio of units sold to market size varies between a minimum of .001 and a maximum of .010. Explain the implications to the firm.

For additional questions related to this problem, see Exercise 5-4 in the *Learning Aid for Use with Basic Marketing*, 17th edition.

6

CHAPTER

Final Consumers and Their Buying Behavior

When Sony introduced its Walkman in the late 1970s, it quickly became a popular way for on-the-go music lovers to play tapes of their favorite music—anywhere they went. Competing players quickly emerged, but Sony kept its lead by improving its Walkman and then offering models for CDs and digital audiotapes when those media came on the market.

In the late 1990s, the new MP3 format offered quality music from a small digital file that played on a computer or portable player. Diamond Multimedia's Rio was the first MP3 player. The Rio was innovative, but users had to download music from virus-ridden websites like Napster—or use special software to "rip" CDs to MP3 format. Many music buffs liked the idea of having songs at their fingertips but believed that getting the digital files was just too complicated. Further, lawsuits by music companies charged that sharing downloaded MP3 music files was illegal. All of this slowed down the initial adoption of MP3 players.

Attitudes quickly changed when Apple offered an innovative marketing mix that addressed the needs of these target customers. Its online iTunes.com store offered legal downloads of songs at a reasonable price and without the risk of viruses. Apple's free iTunes software made it easy to organize digital music on a computer and transfer it to Apple's iPod. The iPod was designed to be stylish and very easy to use in spite of its ability to play a huge number of songs. And Apple's ads made consumers aware of its new concept and motivated them with the promise of "a thousand songs in your pocket." Even skeptics who ignored the ads couldn't help but notice the distinctive white iPod cords dangling from the ears of a friend who was "in" on this cool new product. That prompted a lot of product conversations and persuasive on-the-spot iPod demos. Testimonials on blogs, website postings, and e-mails also helped spread the word.

Although most iPod owners were satisfied with their purchases, competitors like Dell, Sony, and Creative Labs raised expectations in the market by promoting benefits like longer battery life, capacity for more songs, and lower prices. For some consumers, all of this choice required a more careful purchase decision. For example, some would search for information and reviews on the Internet or talk with salespeople in stores to figure out which model was best. Of course, some iPod fanatics didn't bother with that extra effort; they just upgraded to whatever improved models Apple brought to market.

147

In just a few years, consumers around the world bought more than 150 million iPods. iPods were so common that some snooty trendsetters thought that they were no longer cool. To counter that thinking, Apple used creative television, print, and outdoor advertising that showed silhouettes of people dancing while listening to their iPods. Apple also encouraged other companies to develop iPod accessories—like new cases, car kits, and portable speakers—so consumers could individualize their players. All of this also appealed to retailers who liked the high profit margins and the large number of customers who returned for accessories.

Apple also began promoting iPod versions to appeal to different market segments. For example, a Harry Potter iPod, complete with the Hogwarts crest, appealed to kids and a black and red U2 model targeted their parents. In the former Yugoslav republics, a special edition silver iPod Nano featured the popular band Cubismo. And Apple offered the Shuffle for music lovers who wanted a small, bargain-priced player. To increase the benefits of owning an iPod, Apple also promoted podcasting—the creation of online audio or video programs that consumers can download and play on an iPod. Podcasts of sports, news, and specialty talk shows that are available at iTunes often appeal to people who don't shop there for online music.

Innovative iPods provided consumers with fresh styles, more songs, smaller sizes, and more media, including videos. But the iPhone was the most exciting addition to the product line. Other cell phones that could play music were already on the market, but consumers didn't see their benefits. The iPhone changed that. Its colorful touch-screen display, web-surfing, and cool handling of multimedia downloads wowed consumers. Apple's most loyal customers even waited in lines to be the first to own an iPhone. But, after a few months, the $600 price took its toll; sales were slower than expected. So, Apple slashed

$200 off of the price and sales exploded again. However, many early adopters of iPhone felt betrayed. They complained on message boards and in e-mails to Steve Jobs, Apple's CEO, that they had paid more. To try to appease this vocal group, Apple offered $100 store credits.

Initially, the iPhone was available only for use with AT&T's cellular service. To attract other customers, Apple introduced the iPod Touch, which has most of the iPhone's features but can't make calls.

Apple's strategies have been very successful. Yet, in technology markets consumer attitudes and preferences can change quickly. So, to build on its successes, Apple will need to continue to identify new and better ways to meet consumer needs.[1]

LEARNING OBJECTIVES

Many variables influence consumer buying behavior. As the Apple case highlights, successful marketing strategy planning requires a clear understanding of how target consumers buy—and what factors affect their decisions. The learning objectives for this chapter will help you develop that understanding.

When you finish this chapter, you should be able to:

1 describe how economic needs influence the buyer decision process.

2 understand how psychological variables affect an individual's buying behavior.

3 understand how social influences affect an individual's buying behavior.

4 explain how characteristics of the purchase situation influence consumer behavior.

5 explain the process by which consumers make buying decisions.

6 understand important new terms (shown in red)

CONSUMER BEHAVIOR: WHY DO THEY BUY WHAT THEY BUY?

In Chapter 5, we discussed basic data on population, income, and other demographic dimensions of the final consumer market. Such data are especially helpful for estimating the size of markets and for understanding broad buying patterns. Unfortunately, when many firms sell similar products, demographic analysis isn't much help in predicting which specific products and brands consumers will purchase—and why.

So, in this chapter we take a deeper look at influences on final consumers and their buying behavior. The topics that we'll discuss are overviewed in Exhibit 6-1, which includes a simplified model of consumer behavior. In the first part of the chapter we'll focus on how economic needs, psychological variables, social influences, and the purchase situation all affect a person's buying behavior. Then we'll expand the model and cover the purchase decision process in more detail.

Specific consumer behaviors vary a great deal between purchases and from one target market to the next, so it's impractical to try to catalog all the possibilities for every situation. For example, how and why a given consumer buys a specific brand of soft drink may be different from how that same consumer buys an iPod Touch. Likewise, customers in different countries may react differently to the marketing of either product. Even so, there are general behavioral principles—frameworks—that marketing managers can apply to better understand their specific target markets. Our approach focuses on developing your skill in working with these frameworks.

Edition

Exhibit 6-1 Consumer Behavior for Marketing Strategy Planning

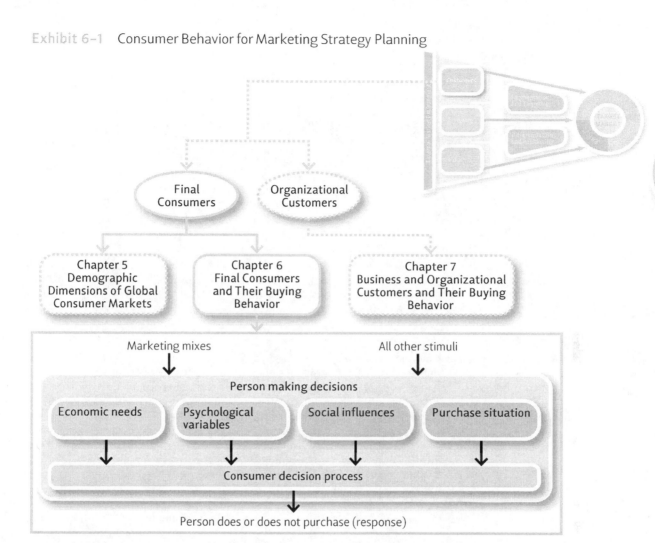

ECONOMIC NEEDS AFFECT MOST BUYING DECISIONS

Economic value
influences consumer
buying

Most economists assume that consumers are economic buyers—people who know all the facts and logically compare choices to get the greatest satisfaction from spending their time and money. The economic-buyer theory assumes that economic needs guide most consumer behavior. Economic needs are concerned with making the best use of a consumer's time and money—as the consumer judges it. Some consumers look for the lowest price. Others will pay extra for convenience. And others may weigh price and quality for the best value. Some economic needs are

1. Economy of purchase or use.
2. Efficiency in operation or use.
3. Dependability in use.
4. Improvement of earnings.
5. Convenience.

Marketing managers must be alert to new ways to appeal to economic needs. Most consumers appreciate firms that offer them improved economic value for the money they spend. But improved value does not just mean offering lower and lower prices.

Edition

Exhibit 6-2   A Model of Influences on Consumer Behavior

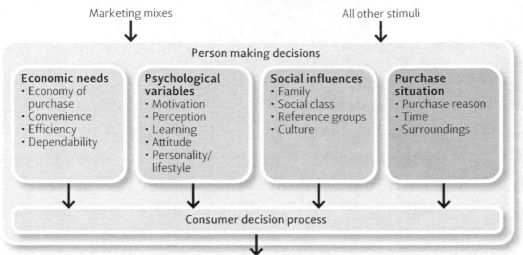

For example, products can be designed to work better, require less service, or last longer. Promotion can inform consumers about product benefits in terms of measurable factors like operating costs, the length of the guarantee, or the time a product will save. Carefully planned Place decisions can make it easier and faster for customers who face a poverty of time to make a purchase.

Many firms adjust their marketing mixes for target markets that place a high value on convenience. Whole Foods Market sells more takeout food than most restaurants. Tide-to-Go is an instant stain remover that fits easily in a purse or briefcase and requires no water. A growing number of consumers like the convenience of online shopping at Amazon.com.

Economic value is an important factor in many purchase decisions. But most marketing managers think that buyer behavior is not as simple as the economic-buyer model suggests. A product that one person sees as a good value—and is eager to buy— is of no interest to someone else. So we can't expect to understand buying behavior without taking a broader view. See Exhibit 6-2.

PSYCHOLOGICAL INFLUENCES WITHIN AN INDIVIDUAL

Needs motivate consumers

Everybody is motivated by needs and wants. Needs are the basic forces that motivate a person to do something. Some needs involve a person's physical well-being, others the individual's self-view and relationship with others. Needs are more basic than wants. Wants are "needs" that are learned during a person's life. For example, everyone needs water or some kind of liquid, but some people also have learned to want Clearly Canadian's raspberry-flavored sparkling water on the rocks.

When a need is not satisfied, it may lead to a drive. The need for liquid, for example, leads to a thirst drive. A drive is a strong stimulus that encourages action to reduce a need. Drives are internal—they are the reasons behind certain behavior patterns. In marketing, a product purchase results from a drive to satisfy some need.

Some critics imply that marketers can somehow manipulate consumers to buy products against their will. But trying to get consumers to act against their will is a waste of time. Instead, a good marketing manager studies what consumer drives, needs, and wants already exist and how they can be satisfied better.

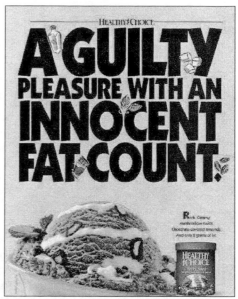

Economic needs affect many buying decisions, but for some purchases the behavioral influences on a consumer are more important.

Consumers seek benefits to meet needs

We're all a bundle of needs and wants. Exhibit 6-3 lists some important needs that might motivate a person to some action. This list, of course, is not complete. But thinking about such needs can help you see what *benefits* consumers might seek from a marketing mix.

When a marketing manager defines a product-market, the needs may be quite specific. For example, the food need might be as specific as wanting a Domino's thick-crust pepperoni pizza—delivered to your door hot and ready to eat.

Several needs at the same time

Consumer psychologists often argue that a person may have several reasons for buying—at the same time. Maslow is well known for his five-level hierarchy of needs.

Exhibit 6-3 Possible Needs Motivating a Person to Some Action

Types of Needs	Specific Examples			
Physiological needs	Food Sex Rest	Liquid Body elimination	Activity Self-preservation	Sleep Warmth/coolness
Psychological needs	Aggression Family preservation Nurturing Playing-relaxing Self-identification	Curiosity Imitation Order Power Tenderness	Being responsible Independence Personal fulfillment Pride	Dominance Love Playing-competition Self-expression
Desire for . . .	Acceptance Affiliation Comfort Esteem Knowledge Respect Status	Achievement Appreciation Leisure Fame Prestige Retaliation Sympathy	Acquisition Beauty Distance—"space" Happiness Pleasure Self-satisfaction Variety	Affection Companionship Distinctiveness Identification Recognition Sociability Fun
Freedom from . . .	Fear Pain Harm	Depression Stress Ridicule	Discomfort Loss Sadness	Anxiety Illness Pressure

Edition

Exhibit 6-4   The PSSP Hierarchy of Needs

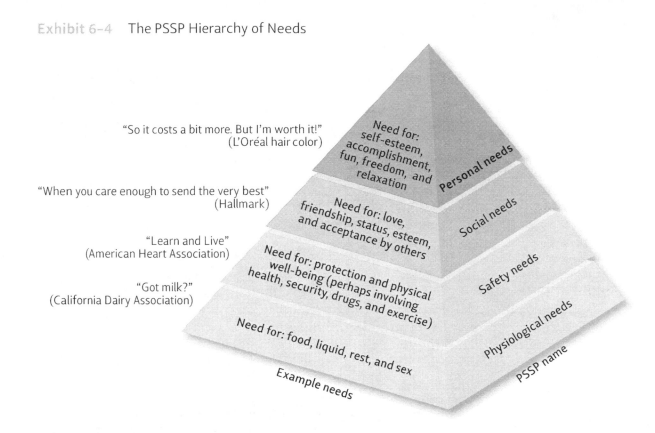

"So it costs a bit more. But I'm worth it!"
(L'Oréal hair color)

"When you care enough to send the very best"
(Hallmark)

"Learn and Live"
(American Heart Association)

"Got milk?"
(California Dairy Association)

We will discuss a similar four-level hierarchy that is easier to apply to consumer behavior. Exhibit 6-4 illustrates the four levels along with an advertising slogan showing how a company has tried to appeal to each need. The lowest-level needs are physiological. Then come safety, social, and personal needs.[2]

Physiological needs are concerned with biological needs—food, liquid, rest, and sex. Safety needs are concerned with protection and physical well-being (perhaps involving health, security, medicine, and exercise). Social needs are concerned with love, friendship, status, and esteem—things that involve a person's interaction with others. Personal needs, on the other hand, are concerned with an individual's need for personal satisfaction—unrelated to what others think or do. Examples include self-esteem, accomplishment, fun, freedom, and relaxation.

Motivation theory suggests that we never reach a state of complete satisfaction. As soon as we get our lower-level needs reasonably satisfied, those at higher levels become more dominant. This explains why marketing efforts targeted at affluent consumers in advanced economies often focus on higher-level needs. It also explains why these approaches may be useless in parts of the world where consumers' basic needs are not being met.

It is important to see, however, that a particular product may satisfy more than one need at the same time. In fact, most consumers try to fill a *set* of needs rather than just one need or another in sequence.

Obviously marketers should try to satisfy different needs. Yet discovering these specific consumer needs may require careful analysis. Consider, for example, the lowly vegetable peeler. Marketing managers for OXO International realized that many people, especially young children and senior citizens, have trouble gripping the handle of a typical peeler. OXO redesigned the peeler with a bigger handle that addressed this physical need. OXO also coated the handle with dishwasher-safe rubber. This makes

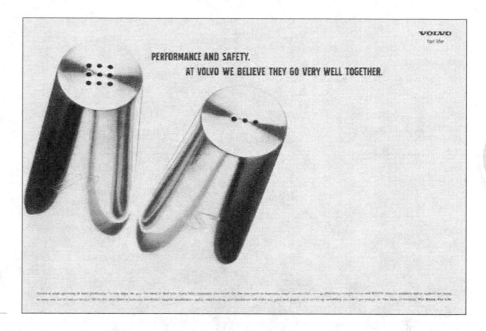

Most products must fill more than one need at the same time.

cleanup more convenient—and the sharp peeler is safer to use when the grip is wet. The attractively designed grip also appeals to consumers who get personal satisfaction from cooking and who want to impress their guests. Even though OXO priced the peeler much higher than most kitchen utensils, it has sold very well because it appeals to people with a variety of needs. Since that initial success, OXO has redesigned hundreds of everyday utensils, including its new Good Grip Convertible Colander. The colander's nonslip legs spring out and hold it securely in place over the sink for easy draining, but the legs fold down for use on a countertop.[3]

Perception determines what consumers see and feel

Consumers select varying ways to meet their needs sometimes because of differences in perception—how we gather and interpret information from the world around us.

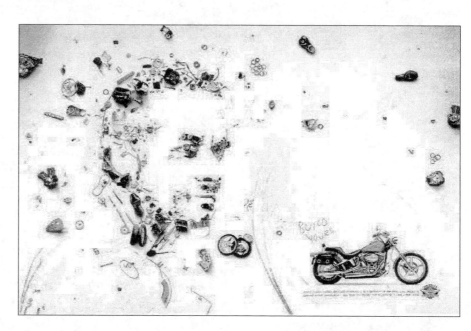

How consumers perceive a product or marketing communication may depend on consumer interest and the urgency of the need. When people first view this ad for Harley-Davidson, some just see the assorted parts that go with the "Build Yours" appeal. Other people focus on the face that is formed by the parts.

Edition

We are constantly bombarded by stimuli—ads, products, stores—yet we may not hear or see anything. This is because we apply the following selective processes:

1. Selective exposure—our eyes and minds seek out and notice only information that interests us. How often have you closed a pop-up ad at a website without even noticing what it was for?
2. Selective perception—we screen out or modify ideas, messages, and information that conflict with previously learned attitudes and beliefs.
3. Selective retention—we remember only what we want to remember.

These selective processes help explain why some people are not affected by some advertising—even offensive advertising. They just don't see or remember it! Even if they do, they may dismiss it immediately. Some consumers are skeptical about any advertising message.

These selective processes are stronger than many people realize. For example, to make their positioning efforts memorable, many companies use a common slogan ("tag line") on all of their ads. However, when researchers showed consumers the tag lines for 22 of the biggest advertisers (each spending over $100 million a year), 16 were recognized by less than 10 percent of the consumers. At the extreme, no one in the sample recognized Circuit City's "We're with you" slogan that had been running in ads for two years.[4]

Our needs affect these selective processes. And current needs receive more attention. For example, Goodyear tire retailers advertise some sale in the newspaper almost weekly. Most of the time we don't even notice these ads. Only when we need new tires do we tune in to Goodyear's ads.

Marketers are interested in these selective processes because they affect how target consumers get and retain information. This is also why marketers are interested in how consumers *learn*.

Learning determines what response is likely

Learning is a change in a person's thought processes caused by prior experience. Learning is often based on direct experience: A little girl tastes her first cone of Ben & Jerry's Cherry Garcia flavor ice cream, and learning occurs! Learning may also be based on indirect experience or associations. If you watch an ad that shows other people enjoying Ben & Jerry's Chocolate Fudge Brownie low-fat frozen yogurt, you might conclude that you'd like it too.

Consumer learning may result from things that marketers do, or it may result from stimuli that have nothing to do with marketing. Either way, almost all consumer behavior is learned.[5]

Experts describe a number of steps in the learning process. We've already discussed the idea of a drive as a strong stimulus that encourages action. Depending on the cues—products, signs, ads, and other stimuli in the environment—an individual chooses some specific response. A response is an effort to satisfy a drive. The specific response chosen depends on the cues and the person's past experience.

Reinforcement of the learning process occurs when the response is followed by satisfaction—that is, reduction in the drive. Reinforcement strengthens the relationship between the cue and the response. And it may lead to a similar response the next time the drive occurs. Repeated reinforcement leads to development of a habit—making the individual's decision process routine. Exhibit 6-5 shows the relationships of the important variables in the learning process.

Exhibit 6-5
The Learning Process

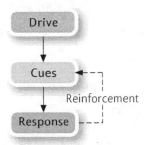

The learning process can be illustrated by a thirsty person. The thirst *drive* could be satisfied in a variety of ways. But if the person happened to walk past a vending machine and saw a Mountain Dew sign—a *cue*—then he might satisfy the drive with a *response*—buying a Mountain Dew. If the experience is satisfactory, positive *reinforcement* occurs, and our friend may be quicker to satisfy this drive in the same way in the future. This emphasizes the importance of developing good products that live up to the promises of the firm's advertising. People can learn to like or dislike Mountain Dew—reinforcement and learning work both ways. Unless marketers satisfy their customers, they must constantly try to attract new ones to replace the dissatisfied ones who don't come back.

Most consumers don't know what Apple Beer is, but as this ad suggests they may still form an attitude based on the name.

Positive cues help a marketing mix

Sometimes marketers try to identify cues or images that have positive associations from some other situation and relate them to their marketing mix. Many people associate the smell of lemons with a fresh, natural cleanliness. So companies often add lemon scent to household cleaning products—Clorox bleach and Pledge furniture polish, for example—because it has these associations. Similarly, firms like Calvin Klein use ads suggesting that people who use their products have more appeal to the opposite sex. Simple cues may even be important for a big purchase. Luxury-car makers try for a "new car smell" with an aroma of leather and wood, even though the car would really smell more like metal and adhesives as it comes off the production line in a factory.[6]

Many needs are culturally learned

Many needs are culturally (or socially) learned. The need for food, for instance, may lead to many specific food wants. Many Japanese enjoy sushi (raw fish), and their children learn to like it. Fewer Americans, however, have learned to enjoy it.

Some critics argue that marketing efforts encourage people to spend money on learned wants totally unrelated to any basic need. For example, Germans are less concerned about perspiration, and many don't buy or use antiperspirants. Yet Americans spend millions of dollars on such products. Advertising says that using Ban deodorant "takes the worry out of being close." But is marketing activity the cause of the difference in the two cultures? Most research says that advertising can't convince buyers of something contrary to their basic attitudes.

Attitudes relate to buying

An **attitude** is a person's point of view toward something. The "something" may be a product, an advertisement, a salesperson, a firm, or an idea. Attitudes are an important topic for marketers because attitudes affect the selective processes, learning, and eventually the buying decisions people make.

Because attitudes are usually thought of as involving liking or disliking, they have some action implications. Beliefs are not so action-oriented. A **belief** is a person's opinion about something. Beliefs may help shape a consumer's attitudes but don't necessarily involve any liking or disliking. It is possible to have a belief—say, that Listerine PocketPak strips have a medicinal taste—without really caring what they taste like. On the other hand, beliefs about a product may have a positive or negative effect in shaping consumers' attitudes. For example, promotion for Splenda, a no-cal sweetener in a yellow packet, informs consumers that it's "made from sugar so it tastes

Edition

Consumer beliefs, whether correct or incorrect, often influence consumer attitudes and choices.

like sugar." A dieter who believes that Splenda will taste better because it is made from sugar might try it instead of just routinely rebuying another brand, like Equal. On the other hand, a person with diabetes might believe that he should avoid Splenda—like he avoids other products made from sugar—even though Splenda is actually suitable for people with diabetes.[7]

In an attempt to relate attitude more closely to purchase behavior, some marketers stretch the attitude concept to include consumer "preferences" or "intention to buy." Managers who must forecast how much of their brand customers will buy are particularly interested in the intention to buy. Forecasts would be easier if attitudes were good predictors of intentions to buy. Unfortunately, the relationships usually are not that simple. A person may have positive attitudes toward GPS navigation systems for cars, but no intention of buying one.

"Green" attitudes and beliefs change marketing mixes

A growing number of consumers believe that they can have a positive effect on the environment if they buy from companies that can help them make "greener" choices. Marketing managers have responded by developing marketing mixes to address these ecological interests. Subway sandwich shops have added recycling bins. Both UPS and Enterprise Rent-A-Car have fleets of alternative fuel vehicles. General Mills changed Hamburger Helper from curly to straight noodles; that helped shrink package sizes by 20 percent and resulted in 500 fewer distribution trucks on the road each year. And Nike makes its Trash Talk basketball shoes from manufacturing waste—literally turning garbage into shoes. It is unclear how these changes will affect consumer attitudes. Some experts think that too many "green" claims will confuse customers or even prompt a backlash of negative attitudes.[8]

Internet EXERCISE

Climate Counts provides information to help consumers make choices that have a positive impact on the planet. Go to the Climate Counts website (www.climatecounts.org), click on the Scorecard link, choose a market sector, and compare the different companies. Select one company and view its efforts. How do you think this information might affect how *consumers* behave? Do you think the information will affect how *companies* behave?

Changing negative attitudes may be necessary

Negative attitudes about a product or company can be strongly held and difficult to change. Consider something as unemotional as a cup of tea. The British have a strong belief about how you drink tea—a cup of hot tea is a tradition, a special moment with

Salud! For Better Health, Spaniards Drink Bacteria for Breakfast

During the 1990s, many European consumers began to change their relaxed approach to meals. A bustling economy led to busier lifestyles, which prompted more interest in eat-on-the-go foods. This was even true of breakfast, which for many Europeans traditionally had meant a leisurely cup of coffee and croissant. And, with more consumers entering the older age groups, there was also increased attention to healthy eating.

Marketing managers for France's Danone spotted these trends and thought the firm's Actimel yogurt might address some of these needs. Indeed, scientists had already shown that consumers who regularly drink Actimel were healthier. Yet, there were challenges. Actimel is healthy because each serving contains over 10 billion live bacteria, like the "friendly" ones in the human body, that aid digestion. Yet, most consumers didn't understand that—and drinking bacteria doesn't sound like an appealing idea. To make things worse, marketing research revealed that consumers thought that yogurts were either tasty *or* healthy—but not both! They believed that healthy yogurts had an undesirable medicinal taste.

To help change this perception, Danone developed new Actimel flavors that would delight consumers once they tried the product. Even so, some consumers lost interest when they learned that the cost of Actimel was double that of regular yogurts. On the other hand, Actimel's higher price helped to pay for heavy introductory advertising to inform more consumers about its valuable health benefits. Actimel's attention-getting ads used appeals such as "Fight the cold. Practice self-defense." Still, many doubters remained unconvinced that Actimel could either improve their health or taste good. Danone was finally able to gain more trial and change attitudes with the "Actimel Challenge." With this challenge Danone promised to give consumers their money back if they didn't like Actimel and feel better after drinking it for two weeks.

Selling Actimel at health food stores might have reinforced its premium health positioning and provided more initial sales support. But Danone wanted customers to be able to find and buy Actimel easily. So distribution focused on placing four packs in regular supermarkets and single-serve packages in convenience stores.

Over time, favorable consumer experience with this marketing mix has grown Actimel into a brand that many Europeans routinely purchase. In Spain it even outsells Coca-Cola. It has also sold well in other parts of the world, including Asia. Danone has had trouble selling its bacteria-based products in the United States. But it keeps trying. Actimel was recently launched across the United States with the name DanActive. Danone's marketers hope American culture is now ready to accept the idea of drinking "bugs" as a tasty way to be healthy.[9]

friends or co-workers. But few British consumers ever drink iced tea—most have a negative attitude about it. Consumers there associate iced tea with the dregs in the bottom of the teapot after it has cooled off. It's not an appealing image. While Lipton, Nestea, and other iced-tea makers would like to change that, it isn't likely to happen fast, if it happens at all. Changing negative attitudes is probably the most difficult job marketers face.[10]

Ethical issues may arise

Part of the marketing job is to inform and persuade consumers about a firm's offering. An ethical issue sometimes arises, however, if consumers have *inaccurate* beliefs. For example, promotion of a "children's cold formula" may play off parents' fears that adult medicines are too strong—even though the basic ingredients in the children's formula are the same and only the dosage is different. And when Tiger Woods' winning smile appears in a Buick ad, it's easy to forget that he's paid for his endorsement.

Edition

Marketers must also be careful about promotion that might encourage false beliefs, even if the advertising is not explicitly misleading. For example, ads for Ultra Slim-Fast low-fat beverage don't claim that anyone who buys the product will lose all the weight they want or look like the slim models who appear in the ads—but some critics argue that the advertising gives that impression.

Ethics QUESTION

You are a marketing assistant for a large firm that recently ran a test market for Tastee DeeLites, a new brand of cookies that have less fat than your company's regular cookies. Tastee DeeLites were developed to comply with government rules for what could be called "low fat," so the ads and package used in the test market highlighted that benefit. Test-market sales were very promising. However, now a consumer activist group is sending out a chain e-mail that denounces Tastee DeeLites and your company for encouraging obesity. The e-mail complains that high calories make Tastee DeeLites even more fattening than regular cookies and that the product's name and "low fat" claim are misleading. Your boss has asked you to recommend how the firm should handle this situation. Drawing on what you've learned about consumer behavior, do you think consumers would be misled? Does your company have any responsibility to respond to these charges? Should changes be made to the product, package, or promotion?

Meeting expectations is important

Attitudes and beliefs sometimes combine to form an expectation—an outcome or event that a person anticipates or looks forward to. Consumer expectations often focus on the benefits or value that the consumer expects from a firm's marketing mix. This is an important issue for marketers because a consumer is likely to be dissatisfied if his or her expectations are not met. Promotion that overpromises what the rest of the marketing mix can really deliver leads to problems in this area. Finding the right balance, however, can be difficult. Consider the challenge faced by marketing managers for Van Heusen when Van Heusen came up with a new way to treat its wash-and-wear shirts so that they look better when they come out of the wash. Van Heusen promoted these shirts as "wrinkle-free." The new shirt is an improvement, but consumers who expect it to look as if it had been ironed are disappointed. For them, the improvement is not enough.[11]

Personality affects how people see things

Many researchers study how personality affects people's behavior, but the results have generally been disappointing to marketers. A trait like neatness can be associated with users of certain types of products—like cleaning materials. But marketing managers have not found a way to use personality in marketing strategy planning.[12] As a result, they've stopped focusing on personality measures borrowed from psychologists and instead developed lifestyle analysis.

Psychographics focus on activities, interests, and opinions

Psychographics or lifestyle analysis is the analysis of a person's day-to-day pattern of living as expressed in that person's Activities, Interests, and Opinions—sometimes referred to as AIOs. Exhibit 6-6 shows a number of variables for each of the AIO dimensions—along with some demographics used to add detail to the lifestyle profile of a target market.

Understanding the lifestyle of target customers has been especially helpful in providing ideas for advertising themes. Let's see how it adds to a typical demographic description. It may not help Toyota marketing managers much to know that an average member of the target market for a Highlander SUV is 34.8 years old, married, lives in a three-bedroom home, and has 2.3 children. Lifestyles help marketers paint a more human portrait of the target market. For example, lifestyle analysis might show

Exhibit 6-6
Lifestyle Dimensions
(and some related
demographic
dimensions)

Dimension	Examples		
Activities	Work	Vacation	Surfing Web
	Hobbies	Entertainment	Shopping
	Social events	Club membership	Sports
Interests	Family	Community	Food
	Home	Recreation	Media
	Job	Fashion	Achievements
Opinions	Themselves	Business	Products
	Social issues	Economics	Future
	Politics	Education	Culture
Demographics	Income	Geographic area	Occupation
	Age	Ethnicity	Family size
	Family life cycle	Dwelling	Education

159

that the 34.8-year-old is also a community-oriented consumer with traditional values who especially enjoys spectator sports and spends much time in other family activities. An ad might show the Highlander being used by a happy family at a ball game so the target market could really identify with the ad. And the ad might be placed on an ESPN show whose viewers match the target lifestyle profile.[13]

Marketing managers for consumer products firms who are interested in learning more about the lifestyle of a target market sometimes turn to outside specialists for help. For example, SRI Consulting Business Intelligence (SRIC-BI), a research firm, offers a service called geo-VALS (VALS is an abbreviation for values, attitudes, and lifestyles). GeoVALS uses psychographics to show where customers live and why they behave as they do; it is especially useful for targeting direct-mail ad campaigns.[14]

Internet EXERCISE

Go to the SRIC-BI Internet site (www.sric-bi.com), click on VALS survey, and then click on "Take the Survey" to review the VALS questionnaire. If you wish, complete the short questionnaire online.

Most people love homemade cake, but some think that baking and frosting a cake is a time-consuming hassle. Betty Crocker's new pourable frosting is fast and easy, but promotion such as this ad gives consumers a way to learn that it's available.

Edition

SOCIAL INFLUENCES AFFECT CONSUMER BEHAVIOR

We've been discussing some of the ways needs, attitudes, and other psychological variables influence the buying process. Now we'll look at how the individual interacts with family, social class, and other groups who may have influence.

Who is the real decision maker in family purchases?

Relationships with other family members influence many aspects of consumer behavior. We saw specific examples of this in Chapter 5 when we considered the effects of the family life cycle on family spending patterns. Family members may also share many attitudes and values, consider each other's opinions, and divide various buying tasks. In years past, most marketers in the United States targeted the wife as the family purchasing agent. Now, with sex-role stereotypes changed and with night and weekend shopping more popular, men and older children take more responsibility for shopping and decision making. Family roles vary from one culture to another.

Although only one family member may go to the store and make a specific purchase, when planning marketing strategy it's important to know who else may be involved. Other family members may have influenced the decision or really decided what to buy. Still others may use the product.

You don't have to watch much Saturday morning TV to see cartoon characters like Tony the Tiger tell kids about the goodies found in certain cereal packages and urge them to remind Dad or Mom to pick up that brand at the store. Similarly, a lot of kids just have to have a Burger King hamburger because the Burger King crown giveaway is what they really want. Surveys also show that kids often have a big say in a family's choice of products such as apparel, cars, vacations, electronics, and health and beauty aids.

Family considerations may overwhelm personal ones

A husband and wife may jointly agree on many important purchases, but sometimes they may have strong personal preferences. However, such individual preferences may change if the other spouse has different priorities. One might want to take a family vacation to Disneyland—when the other wants a new Toshiba large-screen HDTV. The actual outcome in such a situation is unpredictable. Buying responsibility and influence vary greatly depending on the product and the family. A marketer trying to plan a strategy will find it helpful to research the specific target market. Remember, many buying decisions are made jointly, and thinking only about who actually buys the product can misdirect the marketing strategy.[15]

Social class affects attitudes, values, and buying

Up to now, we've been concerned with individuals and their family relationships. Now let's consider how society looks at an individual and perhaps the family—in terms of social class. A social class is a group of people who have approximately equal social position as viewed by others in the society.

Almost every society has some social class structure. In most countries, social class is closely related to a person's occupation, but it may also be influenced by education, community participation, where a person lives, income, possessions, social skills, and other factors—including what family a person is born into.

In most countries—including the United States—there is *some* general relationship between income level and social class. But the income level of people within the same social class can vary greatly, and people with the same income level may be in different social classes. So income by itself is usually not a good measure of social class. And people in different social classes may spend, save, and borrow money in very different ways. For example, spending for clothing, housing, home furnishings, and leisure activities, as well as choices of where and how to shop, often vary with social class.

The U.S. class system is far less rigid than those in most countries. Children start out in the same social class as their parents—but they can move to a different social class depending on their education and job. By contrast, India's social structure is much more rigid, and individuals can't easily move up in the class system.

Marketers want to know what buyers in various social classes are like. In the United States, simple approaches for measuring social class groupings are based on a person's *occupation, education,* and *type and location of housing.* By using marketing research surveys or available census data, marketers can get a feel for the social class of a target market.

What do these classes mean?

Many people think of America as a middle-class society. In fact, when asked to classify themselves, most people just say that they're middle class or working class. But social class studies suggest that in many marketing situations the social class groups are more distinct than that suggests. Various classes shop at different stores. They prefer different treatment from salespeople. They buy different brands of products—even though prices are about the same. And they have different spending–saving attitudes, even when they have the same income level.

Reference groups are relevant too

A reference group is the people to whom an individual looks when forming attitudes about a particular topic. People normally have several reference groups for different topics. Some they meet face-to-face. Others they just wish to imitate. In either case, they may take values from these reference groups and make buying decisions based on what the group might accept.

We're always making comparisons between ourselves and others. So reference groups are more important when others will be able to "see" which product or brand we're using. Influence is stronger for products that relate to status in the group. For one group, owning an expensive fur coat may be a sign of "having arrived." A group of animal lovers might view it as a sign of bad judgment. In either case, a consumer's decision to buy or not buy a fur coat might depend on the opinions of others in that consumer's reference group.[16]

Reaching the opinion leaders who are buyers

An opinion leader is a person who influences others. Opinion leaders aren't necessarily wealthier or better educated. And opinion leaders on one subject aren't necessarily opinion leaders on another. For example, you may have a friend who is ahead of

Reference group influence is usually more important when others will be able to see which product a consumer is using, but Jockey wants young people to view its underwear more like a fashion accessory and encourages them to "Let 'em know you're Jockey."

Edition

Many consumers enjoy the social nature of shopping. Websites like Kaboodle provide a way to shop and interact online. Members of Kaboodle build shopping lists, find others with similar interests, and share recommendations. Similarly, Amazon provides online customer reviews so consumers considering a purchase can gather additional information. For example, there are 398 customer reviews of the camera shown here.

the curve in knowing about videogames, but you might not want that friend's opinion about new clothing styles and cosmetics. On the other hand, sometimes a leader in one area earns respect in another.

Some marketing mixes aim especially at opinion leaders since their opinions affect others and research shows that they are involved in many product-related discussions with "followers." Favorable word-of-mouth publicity from opinion leaders can really help a marketing mix. But the opposite is also true. If opinion leaders aren't satisfied, they're likely to spread the word and negatively influence others.[17]

Culture surrounds the other influences

Culture is the whole set of beliefs, attitudes, and ways of doing things of a reasonably homogeneous set of people. In Chapters 3 and 5, we looked at the broad impact of culture.

We can think of the American culture, the French culture, or the Latin American culture. People within these cultural groupings tend to be more similar in outlook and behavior. But often it is useful to think of subcultures within such groupings. For example, within the American culture, there are various religious, ethnic, and regional subcultures.

Failure to consider cultural differences, even subtle ones, can result in problems. To promote their product and get people to try it, marketers for Pepto-Bismol often provide free samples at festivals and street fairs. Their idea is that people tend to overindulge at such events. However, when they distributed sample packets at a festival in San Francisco's Chinatown, they insulted many of the people they wanted to influence. Booths with Chinese delicacies lined the streets, and many of the participants interpreted the sample packets (which featured the word "Nauseous" in large letters) as suggesting that Chinese delicacies were nauseating. The possibility of this misinterpretation may seem obvious in hindsight, but if it had been that obvious in advance the whole promotion would have been handled differently.[18]

Culture varies in international markets

Planning strategies that consider cultural differences in international markets can be even harder—and such cultures usually vary more. Each foreign market may need to be treated as a separate market with its own submarkets. Ignoring cultural differences—or assuming that they are not important—almost guarantees failure in international markets.

Consider the situation faced by marketers as they introduced Swiffer, the fast-selling wet mop, in Italy. Research showed that Italian women wash their floors four times more often than Americans. Based on that, you might predict a big success for Swiffer in Italy. Yet, many new cleaning products flop there. Fortunately, the research suggested a reason. Many Italians have negative attitudes about ad claims that a product makes cleaning *easier*. This is a popular appeal in the United States, but many Italian women doubt that something that works easily will meet their standards for cleanliness. So, for the Italian market Swiffer was modified and beeswax was added to polish floors after they have been mopped. The strategy for Cif, a popular cleaner, had a similar twist. Rather than tout the convenience of Cif as an all-purpose spray cleaner, different versions were tailored for specific cleaning tasks and the ads were changed to promote the cleaner's strength. Now both Swiffer and Cif are top sellers in Italy.[19]

INDIVIDUALS ARE AFFECTED BY THE PURCHASE SITUATION

Purchase reason can vary

Why a consumer makes a purchase can affect buying behavior. For example, a student buying a pen to take notes might pick up an inexpensive Bic. But the same student might choose a Cross pen as a gift for a friend. And a gadget-lover with some free time on his hands might buy a digital pen that transfers handwritten notes to a tablet computer—just for the fun of trying it.

Time affects what happens

Time influences a purchase situation. *When* consumers make a purchase—and the time they have available for shopping—will influence their behavior. A leisurely

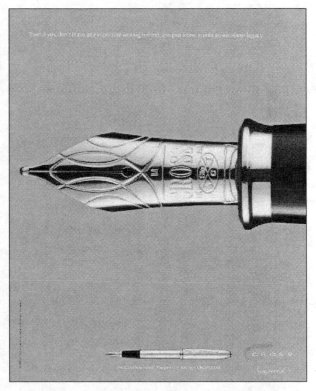

Consumer behavior varies in different situations. As the Expedia ad suggests, some people who are frugal most of the time think differently—and spend freely—while on vacation. As reflected in the ad for the Cross pen, consumers who are shopping for a gift often make different choices than they would for an everyday pen.

Edition

dinner or socializing with friends at a Starbucks induces different behavior than grabbing a quick cup of 7-Eleven coffee on the way to work.

The urgency of the need is another time-related factor. A sports buff who needs a digital video recorder with an "instant replay" feature in time for the Super Bowl—that evening—might spend an hour driving across town in heavy traffic to get the right unit. In a different circumstance, the same person might order a unit online from a website and figure that the extra time for it to be shipped is well worth the money saved.

On the other hand, how long something takes may be relative. Our online shopper might be frustrated by a Web page that takes two minutes to load and abandon his virtual shopping cart after the digital video recorder is already selected. This happens all of the time online. On the other hand, you don't often see a consumer walk away from a shopping cart because of a two-minute wait in a checkout line at a store.

Surroundings affect buying too

Surroundings can affect buying behavior. The excitement at an on-site auction may stimulate impulse buying. Checking out an auction online might lead to a different response.

Surroundings may discourage buying too. For example, some people don't like to stand in a checkout line where others can see what they're buying—even if the other shoppers are complete strangers.[20]

Needs, benefits sought, attitudes, motivation, and even how a consumer selects certain products all vary depending on the purchase situation. So different purchase situations may require different marketing mixes—even when the same target market is involved.

THE CONSUMER DECISION PROCESS

The model in Exhibit 6-2 organizes the many different influences on consumer behavior. It helps explain *why* consumers make the decisions they make. Now, we'll expand that model with a closer look at the steps in the consumer decision process and a focus on *how* consumers make decisions.[21] See Exhibit 6-7.

Exhibit 6-7   An Expanded Model of Consumer Behavior

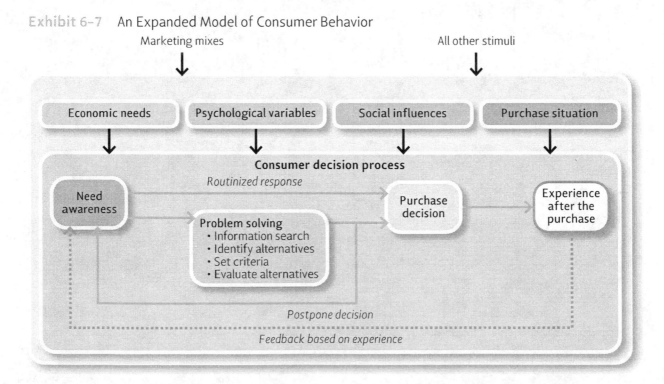

In Saudi Arabia, McDonald's modifies its marketing mix to adapt to the local culture. For example, the McDonald's in Riyadh is segregated by sex with a separate section for women and children.

Sometimes an understanding of local cultural influences points to new ways to blend the four Ps. For example, Nestlé knew that free samples would be a good way to kick start the adoption process when it wanted to introduce a new line of food flavorings in Brazil. In the United States, it's common to distribute samples at stores. But local Nestlé managers knew a more effective approach. In Brazil, cooks rely on stoves that run on gas rather than electricity, so local deliverymen regularly bring canisters of gas into consumers' kitchens. Nestlé paid the deliverymen to offer their customers samples of the flavoring and explain how to use them. Consumers showed more interest in the samples when they were offered by someone they knew and trusted—and the conversation usually took place right by the stove where the flavorings would be used.[27]

Watch out for stereotypes, and change

Consumers in a foreign culture may be bound by some similar cultural forces, but that doesn't mean that they are all the same. So it's important to watch out for over-simplifying stereotypes. Further, changes in the underlying social forces may make outdated views irrelevant.

Developing a marketing mix that really satisfies the needs of a target market takes a real understanding of consumer behavior and the varied forces that shape it. So when planning strategies for international markets, it's best to involve locals who have a better chance of understanding the experiences, attitudes, and interests of your customers.

Recognizing a need creates a problem for the consumer

The consumer decision process begins when a consumer becomes aware of an unmet need. The consumer's problem-solving process then focuses on how best to meet that need. Problem recognition often happens quickly. A student on the way to class, for example, may realize that she's thirsty and wants something to drink. Or problem recognition may take shape over time. For example, a recent grad with a new apartment might want a comfortable place to sit while watching TV in the evening. These situations present problems that may be solved with a purchase. But what purchase should it be?

Three levels of problem solving are useful

How a consumer solves the problem depends on the situation. Exhibit 6-8 highlights the basic problem-solving steps a consumer may go through to satisfy a need. A consumer may search for information, identify alternatives and decide what factors (criteria) are important, and then evaluate one or more alternative products that might meet the need. How long this process takes or how much conscious thought a consumer gives to each step varies from product to product. It is helpful, therefore, to recognize three levels of problem solving that consumers may use for any kind of product. See Exhibit 6-9.

Exhibit 6-8
Consumer Problem Solving

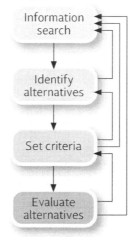

Consumers use extensive problem solving when they put much effort into deciding how to satisfy a need—as is likely for a completely new purchase or to satisfy an important need. For example, an avid computer "gamer" may put a great deal of effort into buying a new gaming computer. Our gamer might solicit friends' opinions about the graphics speed and audio quality for different models before going online to compare options and prices and read technical reviews. Then, the gamer might visit a local store for a hands-on demo of a favorite game on a few computers. To narrow down to a final choice, the gamer could evaluate customer-service support and warranties. This is certainly not an impulse purchase! The decision to buy—and what to buy—comes only after an extensive effort.

Limited problem solving is used by consumers when some effort is required in deciding the best way to satisfy a need. This is typical when the consumer has some previous experience with a product but isn't quite sure which choice to make at the moment. A seasoned computer gamer, for instance, may already know that he likes sports games and what store has the newest releases. At the store he might get the salesperson's advice and check out the video quality on a few games before deciding which to buy. This is a deliberate purchase, but only a limited amount of effort is expended before making the decision.

A consumer uses routinized response behavior when he or she regularly selects a particular way of satisfying a need when it occurs. Routinized response is typical when a consumer has considerable experience in how to meet a specific need and requires no new information. For example, our gamer might automatically buy the latest version of "Madden NFL" as soon as EA Sports makes it available.

Routine response behavior is also typical for low-involvement purchases—purchases that have little importance or relevance for the customer. Let's face it, buying a box of salt is probably not one of the burning issues in your life.[22]

Buying isn't always rational

The idea of a decision process does *not* imply that consumers always apply *rational* processes in their buying decisions. To the contrary, consumers don't always seek accurate information or make smart choices that provide the best economic value.

Exhibit 6-9   Problem-Solving Continuum

Low involvement
Frequently purchased
Inexpensive
Little risk
Little information needed

 Routinized response behavior
 Limited problem solving
 Extensive problem solving

High involvement
Infrequently purchased
Expensive
High risk
Much information desired

This is often because of the influences on consumer behavior that we discussed earlier in the chapter. For example, most sport utility vehicles never leave the paved road, but buyers like the image of driving an SUV and *knowing* they can get off the paved road if they want to. When a tourist spends 1,000 euros on a Loewe leather purse, it may simply be that she loves the style, can afford it, and "has to have it." Needs are operating in such a purchase, but they are higher-level needs and not some sort of functional "requirement."

Problem solving may not lead to a purchase

The consumer problem-solving process doesn't always lead to a purchase. A consumer may delay a purchase or not make it at all. Consumers delay choices when the options they identify are not satisfactory or when the problem-solving process changes how they view their needs. Have you ever found a sweater you love, but then been disappointed that it isn't your size or cost more than you could afford?

Consumers can have second thoughts after a purchase

After making a purchase, buyers often have second thoughts and wonder if they made the right choice. The resulting tension is called **dissonance**—a feeling of uncertainty about whether the correct decision was made. This may lead a customer to seek additional information to confirm the wisdom of the purchase and thus reduce the tension. Marketing managers can reduce this tension by reassuring customers with marketing communications after the purchase. For example, a customer is likely to feel better when a customer service representative responds to a customer's concerns quickly and effectively. Some companies even send e-mails to remind customers of the benefits of their purchase.

Post-purchase regret is a bigger problem

Sometimes uncertainty isn't the issue. Rather the consumer is certain about being unhappy with a purchase. The disappointment of a new pair of shoes that don't fit quite right can be experienced for a long time. A consumer may regret making a purchase for a variety of reasons that the consumer didn't anticipate when making the purchase. But, whatever the reason, regret is not likely to lead to the same decision in the future.

Some consumers spread the word after they buy

Many consumers talk about their purchases and share opinions about their good and bad experiences. Recommendations from friends can have a big influence on whether we try a new restaurant, buy a hybrid car, or choose a different dentist. Consumers are even more likely to share stories about being dissatisfied than satisfied.

The Internet gives people a forum to share their opinions with a large audience. Many people rely on such information in making purchase choices. For example, online audiobook retailer Audible.com's customers often use reviews by other listeners to help make selections. A recent study revealed that more than a fourth of Google search results on the top 20 brands link to consumer opinions. However, sometimes information posted by consumers isn't accurate—and that can be a real headache for marketers.[23]

New concepts require an adoption process

When consumers face a really new concept, their previous experience may not be relevant. These situations involve the **adoption process**—the steps individuals go through on the way to accepting or rejecting a new idea. Although the adoption process is similar to the decision-making process, learning plays a clearer role and promotion's contribution to a marketing mix is more visible.

In the adoption process, an individual moves through some fairly definite steps:

1. *Awareness*—the potential customer comes to know about the product but lacks details. The consumer may not even know how it works or what it will do.
2. *Interest*—if the consumer becomes interested, he or she will gather general information and facts about the product.

3. *Evaluation*—a consumer begins to give the product a mental trial, applying it to his or her personal situation.
4. *Trial*—the consumer may buy the product to experiment with it in use. A product that is either too expensive to try or isn't available for trial may never be adopted.
5. *Decision*—the consumer decides on either adoption or rejection. A satisfactory evaluation and trial may lead to adoption of the product and regular use. According to psychological learning theory, reinforcement leads to adoption.
6. *Confirmation*—the adopter continues to rethink the decision and searches for support for the decision—that is, further reinforcement.[24]

A new pomegranate and blueberry juice is probably a less familiar product for most people, so Minute Maid offers a free trial to speed the adoption process.

PepsiCo had to work with the adoption process when it introduced Pepsi One, a low-calorie cola. Many consumers are interested in staying trim, but diet sodas have an image of bad taste. In light of that, Pepsi's initial ads didn't directly say that Pepsi One was a diet drink. Rather, they used the slogan "True Cola Taste. One Calorie." But that confused a lot of consumers who couldn't tell what made it different from Diet Pepsi. As a result, consumer interest was not as great as Pepsi had expected. Because awareness and interest were low among consumers, retailers didn't devote much shelf space to Pepsi One, so it often wasn't even there for a consumer to consider. Even after a year on the market, trial was low. To help more consumers through the adoption process, Pepsi made changes. To build awareness and interest, new ads explained that Pepsi One was using a new sweetener, recently approved by the government, which tasted better than the sweetener used in other diet drinks. The ads showed consumers drinking Pepsi One and not being able to taste the difference from a regular cola; they used the tagline "Too good to be one calorie, but it is." Pepsi also changed the packaging graphics to put more emphasis on the sweetener at the point of purchase. To generate more trial, Pepsi pushed to get Pepsi One promoted on special end-aisle displays and stepped up its sampling program with taste-testing booths on campuses, in office cafeterias, and at movie theaters. Of course, consumers who tried Pepsi One would seek it out again only if they were satisfied with the taste.[25]

CONSUMER BEHAVIOR IN INTERNATIONAL MARKETS

All the influences interact—often in subtle ways

You're a consumer, so you probably have very good intuition about the many influences on consumer behavior that we've been discussing. That's good, but it's also a potential trap—especially when developing marketing mixes for consumers in international markets. The less a marketing manager knows about the *specific* social and intrapersonal variables that shape the behavior of target customers, the more likely it is that relying on intuition or personal experience will be misleading. Many specific influences do not generalize from one culture to another.

Cadbury's effort to develop a Japanese market for its Dairy Milk Chocolate candy bar illustrates the point. In marketing research, Japanese consumers said that they didn't like the high milk-fat content of Cadbury's bar. But Cadbury's managers reasoned that this reaction must be from lack of opportunity to become accustomed the candy. After all, in most other countries it's the rich taste of the candy that turns consumers into "chocoholics." When Cadbury introduced the bar in Japan was a real flop. Taste preferences in other countries simply didn't generalize Japan.[26]

CONCLUSION

In this chapter, we analyzed the individual consumer as a problem solver who is influenced by economic needs, psychological variables, social influences, and the purchase situation. We showed how these variables influence the consumer decision process, what the steps in that process are, and why it is important to consider these steps when planning a marketing strategy. For example, we discussed three levels of problem solving that you can use to evaluate how consumers approach different types of purchase decisions. We also discussed how the consumer's experience after the purchase impacts what that consumer will do in the future.

From a broader perspective, this chapter makes it clear that each consumer and purchase decision is somewhat unique. So, it isn't possible to catalog all of the individual possibilities. Rather, the overall focus of this chapter is to provide you with general frameworks that you can use to analyze consumers regardless of what the particular product or decision may be. This also helps you to identify the dimensions of consumer behavior that are most important for segmenting the market and developing a targeted marketing mix.

By now it should be clear that expensive marketing errors can be made when you assume that other consumers will behave in the same manner as you or your family and friends. That's why we rely on the social and behavior sciences for insight about consumer behavior in general and why marketing research is so important to marketing managers when they are developing a marketing strategy for a particular target market. When managers understand how and why consumers behave the way they do, they are better able to develop effective marketing mixes that really meet the needs of their target market.

KEY TERMS

economic buyers, 149

economic needs, 149

needs, 150

wants, 150

drive, 150

physiological needs, 152

safety needs, 152

social needs, 152

personal needs, 152

perception, 153

selective exposure, 154

selective perception, 154

selective retention, 154

learning, 154

cues, 154

response, 154

reinforcement, 154

attitude, 155

belief, 155

expectation, 158

psychographics, 158

lifestyle analysis, 158

social class, 160

reference group, 161

opinion leader, 161

culture, 162

extensive problem solving, 165

limited problem solving, 165

routinized response behavior, 165

low-involvement purchases, 165

dissonance, 166

adoption process, 166

QUESTIONS AND PROBLEMS

1. In your own words, explain economic needs and how they relate to the economic-buyer model of consumer behavior. Give an example of a purchase you recently made that is consistent with the economic-buyer model. Give another that is not explained by the economic-buyer model. Explain your thinking.

2. Explain what is meant by a hierarchy of needs and provide examples of one or more products that enable you to satisfy each of the four levels of need.

3. Cut out or photocopy two recent advertisements: one full-page color ad from a magazine and one large display from a newspaper. In each case, indicate which needs the ads are appealing to.

4. Explain how an understanding of consumers' learning processes might affect marketing strategy planning. Give an example.

5. Briefly describe your own *beliefs* about the potential value of low-energy compact fluorescent lightbulbs, your *attitude* toward them, and your *intention* about buying one the next time you need to replace a bulb.

6. Give an example of a recent purchase experience in which you were dissatisfied because a firm's marketing mix did not meet your expectations. Indicate how the purchase fell short of your expectations—and also explain whether your expectations were formed based on the firm's promotion or on something else.

Edition

7. Explain psychographics and lifestyle analysis. Explain how they might be useful for planning marketing strategies to reach college students, as opposed to average consumers.

8. A supermarket chain is planning to open a number of new stores to appeal to Hispanics in southern California. Give some examples that indicate how the four Ps might be adjusted to appeal to the Hispanic subculture.

9. How should social class influences affect the planning of a new restaurant in a large city? How might the four Ps be adjusted?

10. Illustrate how the reference group concept may apply in practice by explaining how you personally are influenced by some reference group for some product. What are the implications of such behavior for marketing managers?

11. Give two examples of recent purchases where the specific purchase situation influenced your purchase decision. Briefly explain how your decision was affected.

12. Give an example of a recent purchase in which you used extensive problem solving. What sources of information did you use in making the decision?

13. On the basis of the data and analysis presented in Chapters 5 and 6, what kind of buying behavior would you expect to find for the following products: (a) a haircut, (b) a shampoo, (c) a digital camera, (d) a tennis racket, (e) a dress belt, (f) a cell phone, (g) life insurance, (h) an ice cream cone, and (i) a new checking account? Set up a chart for your answer with products along the left-hand margin as the row headings and the following factors as headings for the columns: (a) how consumers would shop for these products, (b) how far they would travel to buy the product, (c) whether they would buy by brand, (d) whether they would compare with other products, and (e) any other factors they should consider. Insert short answers—words or phrases are satisfactory—in the various boxes. Be prepared to discuss how the answers you put in the chart would affect each product's marketing mix.

14. Review the model in Exhibit 6-2 and then reread the Apple case at the beginning of this chapter. List and briefly describe specific points in the case that illustrate the model.

15. Interview a friend or family member about two recent purchase decisions. One decision should be an important purchase, perhaps the choice of an automobile, a place to live, or a college. The second purchase should be more routine, such as a meal from a fast-food restaurant or a regularly purchased grocery item. For each purchase, ask your friend questions that will help you understand how the decision was made. Use the model in Exhibit 6-7 to guide your questions. Describe the similarities and differences between the two purchase decisions.

CREATING MARKETING PLANS

The Marketing Plan Coach software on the Student CD and the text website includes a sample marketing plan for Hillside Veterinary Clinic. Look through the "Customers" section and consider the following questions.

a. Based on the marketing plan, what do we know about the consumer behavior of the target market?

b. What additional information do you think would be helpful before developing a marketing strategy for Hillside?

SUGGESTED CASES

1. McDonald's "Seniors" Restaurant   3. MANU Soccer Academy   9. Sweetest Dreams Inn   11. The Next Step

COMPUTER-AIDED PROBLEM

6. SELECTIVE PROCESSES

Submag, Inc., uses direct-mail promotion to sell magazine subscriptions. Magazine publishers pay Submag $3.12 for each new subscription. Submag's costs include the expenses of printing, addressing, and mailing each direct-mail advertisement plus the cost of using a mailing list. There are many suppliers of mailing lists, and the cost and quality of different lists vary.

Submag's marketing manager, Shandra Debose, is trying to choose between two possible mailing lists. One list has been generated from phone directories. It is less expensive than the other list, but the supplier acknowledges that about 10 percent of the names are out-of-date (addresses where people have moved away.) A competing supplier offers a list of active members of professional associations. This list costs 4 cents per name more than the phone list, but only 8 percent of the addresses are out-of-date.

In addition to concerns about out-of-date names, not every consumer who receives a mailing buys a subscription. For example, *selective exposure* is a problem. Some target customers never see the offer—they just toss out junk mail without even opening the envelope. Industry studies show that this wastes about 10 percent of each mailing—although the precise percentage varies from one mailing list to another.

Selective perception influences some consumers who do open the mailing. Some are simply not interested. Others don't want to deal with a subscription service. Although the price is good, these consumers worry that they'll never get the magazines. Submag's previous experience is that selective perception causes more than half of those who read the offer to reject it.

Of those who perceive the message as intended, many are interested. But *selective retention* can be a problem. Some people set the information aside and then forget to send in the subscription order.

Submag can mail about 25,000 pieces per week. Shandra Debose has set up a spreadsheet to help her study effects of the various relationships discussed earlier and to choose between the two mailing lists.

a. If you were Debose, which of the two lists would you buy based on the initial spreadsheet? Why?

b. For the most profitable list, what is the minimum number of items that Submag will have to mail to earn a profit of at least $3,500?

c. For an additional cost of $.01 per mailing, Submag can include a reply card that will reduce the percent of consumers who forget to send in an order (Percent Lost—Selective Retention) to 45 percent. If Submag mails 25,000 items, is it worth the additional cost to include the reply card? Explain your logic.

For additional questions related to this problem, see Exercise 6-3 in the *Learning Aid for Use with Basic Marketing*, 17th edition.

7

CHAPTER

Business and Organizational Customers and Their Buying Behavior

MetoKote Corp. specializes in protective coating applications, like powder-coat and liquid paint, that other manufacturers need for the parts and equipment they make. For example, when you see John Deere agricultural, construction, or lawn and grounds-care equipment, many of the components have likely been coated (painted) in a MetoKote facility. In fact, Deere & Company and MetoKote have a close buyer–seller relationship. While Deere uses a variety of methods to identify suppliers and get competitive bids for many items it needs, it's different with MetoKote. Deere isn't going to switch to some other supplier just because other options provide cheaper coatings. MetoKote not only provides protective coatings for many John Deere products, it has built facilities right next to some Deere plants. When it's time for a component to be coated, a conveyer belt moves the part out of the John Deere plant and into the MetoKote facility. A short time later it's back—and it's green or yellow.

Deere favors this type of arrangement. It lets MetoKote's experts keep up with all of the environmental regulations and new technologies for coatings.

For a manufacturer, this type of relationship allows its facilities to be smaller and less costly to build and maintain, as the space isn't required for large spray booths. With MetoKote's facilities located nearby, newly coated parts for Deere do not have to be shipped, resulting in fewer scratches and dents—which results in higher-quality parts with less rework required.

Many people were involved in the decision to purchase coating services in this way. The responsibility for choosing vendors didn't just rest with the purchasing department but involved input from people in finance, quality control, and in some cases even the production employees.

John Deere needs high-quality protective finishes because its customers want durable, long-lasting equipment. Like John Deere, they want good value. Upholding Deere & Company's long reputation for quality service is equally as important as the company's reputation for a quality product.

For example, if a huge commercial farm in Brazil needs a repair part, workers can contact the local John Deere dealer or at any hour visit the company's website (www.deere.com) to access its online service that allows customers to learn which dealers have a needed part in inventory, check the price, and place an order for fast delivery. But helping John Deere customers and dealers earn better profits doesn't stop there.

For example, some John Deere farm equipment includes a global positioning device that tracks exactly where the equipment goes when it is plowing, seeding, or cutting. The company's GreenStar system, which can easily be moved from machine to machine, uses advanced technology to measure average farm and field yields and to facilitate documentation

173

of tillage practices, planting, spraying, weather, and more. For example, Deere's new cotton harvester inserts a radio frequency ID (RFID) tag as it spools a 4,750 pound bale of cotton fiber and then automatically wraps it in a plastic film. The RFID chip, combined with global positioning system (GPS) data, lets cotton processors trace the precise origin of each bale. They know, for instance, if the cotton was grown without pesticides and qualifies to be sold as organic. The plastic film eliminates the 20 percent drop in the quality of the cotton fiber that can result from water damage. Deere innovations like these can help a farmer make better management decisions, increase productivity, and provide better value to the entire operation.

To give farmers and other equipment customers better service, Deere is streamlining distribution. It is dropping dealers who don't measure up to its goals on measures such as customer satisfaction—and encouraging the dealers that remain to consolidate so that they will have economies of scale in purchasing, be able to afford more specialists in important areas like e-commerce, and be able to share inventory among multiple locations. Of course, this changes Deere's relationship with its dealers. Now Deere views them as members of a high-performance team rather than as members of the Deere family.

John Deere recognizes that different customers have different needs. For example, golf courses buy Deere equipment to maintain their fairways, roughs, greens, and sand traps. Golf course managers value the reliability and durability of Deere equipment. However, they also need a variety of operating supplies—ranging from grass seed and irrigation equipment to ball washers and chemicals. Golf course managers have many responsibilities besides purchasing, and it's time-consuming for them to have to work with many different suppliers. So, John Deere introduced its One Source service which provides golf course managers with a "one-stop shop" for the things they need—all backed by the trusted Deere name. One Source strengthens Deere's relationships with both its dealers and their golf course customers. Of course, it creates new challenges for John Deere's purchasing department. It must identify, evaluate, monitor, and recommend the suppliers for the products that golf courses need. Deere's dealers and golf course customers rely on Deere's purchasing specialists to make the right decisions, and that's part of the customer value that Deere provides. Innovative approaches to delivering customer value, such as One Source for golf courses, make Deere the supplier of choice for many business customers.[1]

BUSINESS AND ORGANIZATIONAL CUSTOMERS—A BIG OPPORTUNITY

Most people think about an individual final consumer when they hear the term *customer*. But many marketing managers aim at customers who are not final consumers. In fact, more purchases are made by businesses and other organizations than by final consumers.

Business and organizational customers are any buyers who buy for resale or to produce other goods and services. There are many different types of organizational customers, including

- *Producers of goods and services*—including manufacturers, farmers, real estate developers, hotels, banks, even doctors and lawyers.
- *Intermediaries*—wholesalers and retailers.
- *Government units*—federal agencies in the United States and other countries as well as state and local governments.
- *Nonprofit organizations*—national organizations like the Red Cross and Girl Scouts as well as local organizations like museums and churches.

As this suggests, not all organizational customers are business firms. Even so, they are sometimes loosely referred to as *business buyers, intermediate buyers,* or *industrial buyers*—and marketing managers often refer to organizational customers collectively as the "business-to-business" market, or simply, the *B2B market*.

In this chapter, we'll focus on organizational customers and their buying behavior. See Exhibit 7-1. In Chapters 5 and 6 we focused on buying by final consumers, so here we'll start by covering important ways that organizational buying tends to be different from buying by final consumers. Then, later in the chapter, we'll focus on some key differences among the specific types of organizational customers.

Edition

Exhibit 7-1   Understanding Business and Organizational Customers for Marketing Strategy Planning

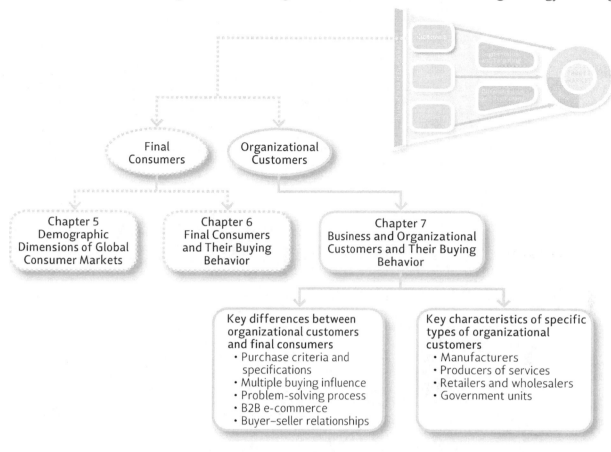

So, keep in mind that, for many firms, marketing strategy planning is about meeting the needs of organizational customers, not final consumers. A firm can target both final consumers and organizations, but different marketing mixes may be needed. As you learn about the buying behavior of organizations, think about how a firm's marketing mix may need to be different and how it may be adjusted.

ORGANIZATIONAL CUSTOMERS ARE DIFFERENT

Organizations buy for a basic purpose

Like final consumers, organizations make purchases to satisfy needs. But it's often easier to understand an organization's needs because most organizations make purchases for the same basic reason. They buy goods and services that will help them meet the demand for the goods and services that they in turn supply to their markets. In other words, their basic need is to satisfy their own customers and clients. A producer buys because it wants to earn a profit by making and selling goods or services. A wholesaler or retailer buys products it can profitably resell to its customers. A town government wants to meet its legal and social obligations to citizens.

Basic purchasing needs are economic

Organizations typically focus on economic factors when they make purchase decisions and are usually less emotional in their buying than final consumers.

Buyers try to consider the total cost of selecting a supplier and its particular marketing mix, not just the initial price of the product. For example, a hospital that needs

Edition

Promotion to organizational buyers often focuses on economic factors. Kyocera's ad, targeted at office and information technology managers, promotes the long life and lower operating costs of its business printers. Michelin's ad, from a trade magazine for commercial trucking firms, focuses on the fuel and weight savings of its X One wide single tire.

a new type of digital X-ray equipment might look at both the original cost and ongoing costs, how it would affect doctor productivity, and, of course, the quality of the images it produces. The hospital might also consider the seller's reliability and its ability to provide speedy maintenance and repair.

The matter of dependability deserves further emphasis. An organization may not be able to function if purchases don't arrive when they're expected. For example, there's nothing worse to a manufacturer than shutting down a production line because sellers haven't delivered the goods. Dependable product quality is important too. For example, a bug in e-commerce software purchased by a firm might cause the firm's online order system to shut down. The costs of finding and correcting the problem—to say nothing about the cost of the lost business—could be much greater than the original cost of the software.

Even small differences are important

Understanding how the buying behavior of a particular organization differs from others can be very important. Even seemingly trivial differences in buying behavior may be important because success often hinges on fine-tuning the marketing mix.

Sellers often approach each organizational customer directly, usually through a sales representative. This gives the seller more chance to adjust the marketing mix for each individual customer. A seller may even develop a unique strategy for each individual customer. This approach carries target marketing to its extreme. But sellers often need unique strategies to compete for large-volume purchases.

In such situations, the individual sales rep takes much responsibility for strategy planning and coordinates the whole buyer–seller relationship. That may involve working with many people—including top management—in both firms. This is relevant to your career planning since these interesting jobs are very challenging, and they pay well too.

Serving customers in international markets

Many marketers discover that there are good opportunities to serve business customers in different countries around the world. Specific business customs do vary from one country to another—and the differences can be important. For example, a salesperson working in Japan must know how to handle a customer's business card with respect. Japanese businesspeople consider it rude to write notes on the back of a card or put it in a wallet while the person who presented it is still in the room.

The basic approaches marketers use to deal with business customers in different parts of the world are much less varied than those required to reach individual consumers. This is probably why the shift to a global economy has been so rapid for many firms. Their business customers in different countries tend to buy in similar ways and can usually be reached with similar marketing mixes. Moreover, business customers are often willing to work with distant suppliers who have developed superior marketing mixes.

Specifications describe the need

Organizational buyers often buy on the basis of a set of purchasing specifications—a written (or electronic) description of what the firm wants to buy. When quality is highly standardized, as is often the case with manufactured items, the specification may simply consist of a brand name or part number. Often, however, the purchase requirements are more complicated; then the specifications may set out detailed information about the performance standards the product must meet. Purchase specifications for services tend to be detailed because services are less standardized and usually are not performed until after they're purchased.

In business-to-business markets, information technology, including the Internet, is making it faster, easier, and less expensive for firms to connect with suppliers and customers. IBM is an important supplier in this area. For example, with its systems banks can open a new account in minutes rather than the hours or even days it took in the past.

Customers may expect quality certification

Organizational customers considering a new supplier or one from overseas may be concerned about product quality. However, this is becoming less of an obstacle because of ISO 9000. ISO 9000 is a way for a supplier to document its quality procedures according to internationally recognized standards.

ISO 9000 assures a customer that the supplier has effective quality checks in place, without the customer having to conduct its own costly and time-consuming audit. Some customers won't buy from any supplier who doesn't have it. To get ISO 9000 certified, a company basically must prove to outside auditors that it documents in detail how the company operates and who is responsible for quality every step of the way.[2]

MANY DIFFERENT PEOPLE MAY INFLUENCE A DECISION

Purchasing managers are specialists

Many organizations rely on specialists to ensure that purchases are handled sensibly. These specialists have different titles in different firms (such as procurement officer, supply manager, purchasing agent, or buyer), but basically they are all purchasing managers—buying specialists for their employers. In large organizations, they usually specialize by product area and are real experts.

Some people think purchasing is handled by clerks who sit in cubicles and do the paperwork to place orders. That view is out-of-date. Today, most firms look to their procurement departments to help cut costs and provide competitive advantage. In this environment, purchasing people have a lot of clout. And there are good job opportunities in purchasing for capable business graduates.

Salespeople often have to see a purchasing manager first—before they contact any other employee. These buyers hold important positions and take a dim view of sales reps who try to go around them. Rather than being "sold," these buyers want

Edition

salespeople to provide accurate information that will help them buy wisely. They like information on new goods and services, and tips on potential price changes, supply shortages, and other changes in market conditions. Sometimes all it takes for a sales rep to keep a buyer up-to-date is to send an occasional e-mail. But a buyer can tell when a sales rep has the customer firm's interest at heart.

Although purchasing managers usually coordinate relationships with suppliers, other people may also play important roles in influencing the purchase decision.[3]

Multiple buying influence in a buying center

Multiple buying influence means that several people—perhaps even top management—play a part in making a purchase decision. Possible buying influences include

1. *Users*—perhaps production line workers or their supervisors.
2. *Influencers*—perhaps engineering or R&D people who help write specifications or supply information for evaluating alternatives.
3. *Buyers*—the purchasing managers who have the responsibility for working with suppliers and arranging the terms of the sale.
4. *Deciders*—the people in the organization who have the power to select or approve the supplier—often a purchasing manager but perhaps top management for larger purchases.
5. *Gatekeepers*—people who control the flow of information within the organization—perhaps a purchasing manager who shields users or other deciders. Gatekeepers can also include receptionists, secretaries, research assistants, and others who influence the flow of information about potential purchases.

An example shows how the different buying influences work. Suppose Electrolux, the Swedish firm that produces vacuum cleaners, wants to buy a machine to stamp out the various metal parts it needs. An assistant to the purchasing manager does an Internet search to identify possible vendors. However, the list that the assistant (a gatekeeper) prepares for the manager excludes a few vendors on the basis of an initial evaluation of information from their websites. The manager e-mails a description of the problem to vendors on the list. It turns out that each of them is eager to get the business and submits a proposal. Several people (influencers) at Electrolux help to evaluate the vendors' proposals. A finance manager worries about

A person who works on a utility firm's high-power wires needs safe, durable climbing gear. A number of different people may influence the decision about which gear the firm should buy.

Exhibit 7-2
Multiple Influence and
Roles in the Buying
Center

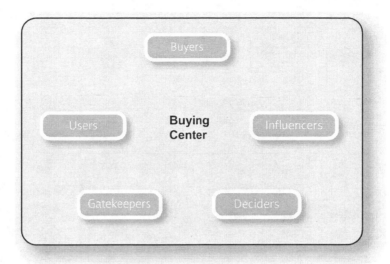

the high cost and suggests leasing the machine. The quality control people want a machine that will do a more accurate job—although it's more expensive. The production manager is interested in speed of operation. The production line workers want the machine that is easiest to use so workers can continue to rotate jobs.

The company president (the decider) asks the purchasing department to assemble all the information but retains the power to select and approve the supplier. The purchasing manager's assistant schedules visits for salespeople. After all these buying influences are considered, one of the purchasing agents for the firm (the buyer) will be responsible for making recommendations and arranging the terms of the sale.

It is helpful to think of a buying center as all the people who participate in or influence a purchase. Because different people may make up a buying center from one decision to the next, the salesperson must study each case carefully. Just learning who to talk with may be hard, but thinking about the various roles in the buying center can help. See Exhibit 7-2.

The salesperson may have to talk to every member of the buying center—stressing different topics for each. This not only complicates the promotion job but also lengthens it. Approval of a routine order may take anywhere from a day to several months. On very important purchases—a new building, major equipment, or a new information system—the selling period may take a year or more.[4]

Vendor analysis considers all of the influences

Considering all of the factors relevant to a purchase decision can be very complex. A supplier or product that is best in one way may not be best in others. To try to deal with these situations, many firms use vendor analysis—a formal rating of suppliers on all relevant areas of performance. The purpose isn't just to get a low price from the supplier on a given part or service. Rather, the goal is to lower the *total costs* associated with purchases. Analysis might show that the best vendor is the one that helps the customer reduce costs of excess inventory, retooling of equipment, or defective parts.[5]

Behavioral needs are relevant too

Vendor analysis tries to focus on economic factors, but purchasing in organizations may also involve many of the same behavioral dimensions we discussed in Chapter 6. Purchasing managers and others involved in buying decisions are human, and they want friendly relationships with suppliers.

The purchasing people in some firms are eager to imitate progressive competitors or even to be the first to try new products. Such "innovators" deserve special attention when new products are being introduced.

The different people involved in purchase decisions are also human with respect to protecting their own interests and their own position in the company. That's one

Edition

A seller's marketing mix may need to consider both the needs of the customer company as well as the needs of individuals who influence the purchase decision.

reason people from different departments may have different priorities in trying to influence what is purchased. Similarly, purchasing managers may want to avoid taking risks that might reflect badly on their decisions. If a new source delivers late or quality is poor, you can guess who will be blamed. Marketers who can help the buyer avoid risk have a definite appeal. In fact, this may make the difference between a successful and unsuccessful marketing mix.

A seller's marketing mix should satisfy *both* the needs of the customer company as well as the needs of individuals who influence the purchase. Therefore, sellers need to find an overlapping area where both can be satisfied. See Exhibit 7-3 for a summary of this idea.

Ethical conflicts may arise

Although organizational buyers are influenced by their own needs, most are serious professionals who are careful to avoid a conflict between their own self-interest and company outcomes. Marketers must be careful here. A salesperson who offers one of his company pens to a prospect may view the giveaway as part of the promotion effort—but the customer firm may have a policy against any employee accepting *any* gift from a supplier. For example, General Motors developed an ethics policy that forbids employees from accepting anything of value from a vendor. It specifically includes entertainment—like a golf outing, a steak dinner, or tickets to a sporting event.

Exhibit 7-3
Overlapping Needs of Individual Influencers and the Customer Organization

Most organizational buyers do their work ethically and expect marketers to do the same. Yet there have been highly publicized abuses. For example, the telephone company that serves New York found out that some of its buyers were giving contracts to suppliers who offered them vacation trips and other personal favors. Abuses of this sort have prompted many organizations to set up policies that prohibit a buyer or other employees from accepting anything from a potential supplier.

Marketers need to take concerns about conflict of interest very seriously. Part of the promotion job is to persuade different individuals who may influence an organization's purchase. Yet the whole marketing effort may be tainted if it even *appears* that a marketer has encouraged a person who influences a decision to put personal gain ahead of company interest.[6]

Ethics QUESTION

Assume that you are a salesperson in a small company. For months you've been trying to get a big order from a large firm. A purchasing manager at the firm casually mentions that she is trying to help two friends find tickets for a big hockey game. Your boss has season tickets for entertaining customers, but you know that the purchasing manager's company strictly prohibits any gift to employees. When you ask your boss what to do, the reply is, "Well, the tickets would be used by the friends and not the customer firm's employee, so you can offer them if you think you should." What should you do? What are the pros and cons of your decision?

Purchasing may be centralized

If a large organization has facilities at many locations, much of the purchasing work may be done at a central location. With centralized buying, a sales rep may be able to sell to facilities all over a country—or even across several countries—without leaving a base city. Wal-Mart handles most of the purchase decisions for stores in its retail chain from its headquarters in Arkansas. Many purchasing decisions for agencies of the U.S. government are handled in Washington, D.C.

Many firms also have centralized controls on who can make purchases. A person who needs to purchase something usually completes a requisition—a request to buy something. This is frequently handled online to cut time and paper shuffling. Even so, there may be delays before a supervisor authorizes the requisition and a purchasing manager can select the "best" seller and turn the authorization into a purchase order. The process may take a few hours for a simple purchase—but it may turn into months for a complex purchase.

Many firms give employees some freedom when it comes to making smaller purchases. Administrative costs of purchase requisitions can be $50 or more—and delays can cause hassles. So some companies give credit cards to select employees for smaller purchases.[7]

Spend management systems control purchasing

Some firms use "spend management" systems to track every single purchase. In large firms this helps the purchasing department analyze the details of who is buying what and how. Sometimes this leads to cost-cutting opportunities or better purchasing policies. Computer purchases by a college illustrate the idea. Colleges buy hundreds of computers each year, but often they're purchased one at a time by different departments. If the college documents the total spending, it can contract for better terms from preferred vendors. The college might also change its policies so that any department can quickly order a standard computer from these vendors without approval from a purchasing manager.

The buying firm's values affect purchasing practices

A firm's own strategy and values often influence how suppliers are evaluated and who is selected. For example, Ben and Jerry's corporate values include helping the environment and reducing the effects of poverty. Its buyers spend more than half their purchasing budget with suppliers who share those priorities.[8]

Edition

Eastman Chemical Co. developed Eastman Tritan, an innovative copolyester (plastic-like) material. Tritan is durable, heat resistant, and offers design flexibility and ease of processing. For example, it is ideal for the molded parts needed by kitchen appliance manufacturers. Yet, Eastman still faces a challenge. A customer firm that is making straight rebuys from a supplier it has worked with in the past may not be seeking new materials or suppliers.

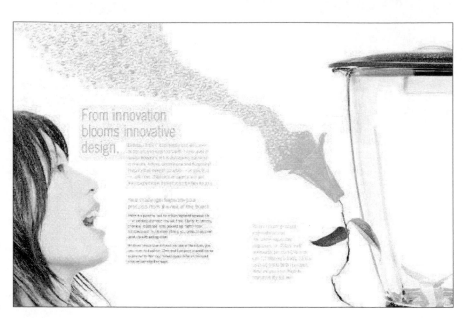

ORGANIZATIONAL BUYERS ARE PROBLEM SOLVERS

Three kinds of buying processes are useful

In Chapter 6, we discussed problem solving by consumers and how it might vary from extensive problem solving to routine buying. In organizational markets, we can adapt these concepts slightly and work with three similar buying processes: a new-task buying process, a modified rebuy process, or a straight rebuy.[9] See Exhibit 7-4.

New-task buying occurs when a customer organization has a new need and wants a great deal of information. New-task buying can involve setting product specifications, evaluating sources of supply, and establishing an order routine that can be followed in the future if results are satisfactory. Multiple buying influence is typical in new-task buying.

A straight rebuy is a routine repurchase that may have been made many times before. Buyers probably don't bother looking for new information or new sources of supply. Most of a company's small or recurring purchases are of this type—but they take only a small part of an organized buyer's time. Important purchases may be made this way too—but only after the firm has decided what procedure will be "routine."

The modified rebuy is the in-between process where some review of the buying situation is done—though not as much as in new-task buying. Sometimes a competitor will get lazy enjoying a straight rebuy situation. An alert marketer can turn these situations into opportunities by providing more information or a better marketing mix.

Exhibit 7-4
Organizational Buying Processes

Characteristics	Type of Process		
	New-Task Buying	Modified Rebuy	Straight Rebuy
Time Required	Much	Medium	Little
Multiple Influence	Much	Some	Little
Review of Suppliers	Much	Some	None
Information Needed	Much	Some	Little

Warming Up to Sustainable Purchasing

With increased attention on global warming and the environment, managers in many organizations are wondering what their responsibility should be. It's true that the first focus of most organizational buying decisions is on green—dollars, that is. However, when purchasing managers focus on sustainability—in combination with their detailed approaches for looking at the total cost of different purchases or vendors—green choices often prove to be winners even in the short term.

A focus on sustainability often identifies ways to save that previously were not obvious. Sometimes all that is involved is a simple change from what's routine. For example, when Falconbridge Limited's aluminum smelter changed to more efficient (but more expensive) lightbulbs, it saved almost $100,000 per year in energy bills. When the Fairmont Hotel in Vancouver searched for alternative chemicals to use in its pool, it found new ones that were healthier for guests and cut costs by $2,000. Hotels everywhere cleaned up when they stopped rewashing all of their linens every day. All it took was a card in the bath that says, "If you'd like us to replace a towel with a clean one, put it on the floor." The cards cost pennies, whereas the hot water, detergent, labor, and wear on linens cost millions.

Retailers and wholesalers must be guided by what customers want; putting green products on their shelves will just rack up losses unless there's customer demand. But firms like Wal-Mart and Home Depot are advertising their sustainable choices because many consumers do want them. Wal-Mart took note when in one year its customers bought 100 million eco-friendly fluorescent lightbulbs. Home Depot has identified more that 3,000 Eco Option products that promote energy conservation, sustainability, and clean water. Both retailers are building more energy-efficient stores and prodding their suppliers to think green by using less packaging. Cynics question their motives—because there's a benefit for retailers when packages take up less shelf space.

In California, some city governments are cooperating with energy firms to develop generators powered by ocean waves. Across the Atlantic, the mayor of London requires city agencies to buy recycled goods whenever possible. And federal agencies in the United States must buy energy-efficient PCs and monitors made without toxins that could later pollute landfills.

Sometimes ecology and cost cutting collide. For example, construction firms that use GM's big Yukon trucks for hauling will save gas with the new hybrid model, but it will take 5 years to make up for the higher initial price. Even so, as competition to provide ecological choices increases, those choices will become more economical. Of course, some progressive firms are not waiting. New Belgium Brewing Company puts sustainable values in its mission statement; that means its purchasing people select more energy efficient (but higher-priced) brew kettles, use wind-powered electricity, and build facilities that are more costly but use the latest green ideas. Many nonprofit organizations take this altruistic approach. It's hard to imagine the Sierra Club not having sustainability as a value when it's time to make purchases.[10]

Straight rebuys often use e-commerce order systems

E-commerce computer systems *automatically* handle a large portion of straight rebuys. Buyers program decision rules that tell the computer how to order and leave the details of following through to the computer. For example, when an order comes in that requires certain materials or parts, the computer information system automatically orders them from the appropriate suppliers, sets the delivery date, and schedules production.

If economic conditions change, buyers modify the computer instructions. When nothing unusual happens, however, the computer system continues to routinely rebuy as needs develop—electronically sending purchase orders to the regular supplier.

Edition

Exhibit 7-5
Major Sources of
Information Used by
Organizational Buyers

	Marketing sources	Nonmarketing sources
Personal sources	• Salespeople • Others from supplier firms • Trade shows	• Buying center members • Outside business associates • Consultants and outside experts
Impersonal sources	• Advertising in trade publications • Sales literature • Sales catalogs • Web page	• Rating services • Trade associations • News publications • Product directories • Internet

Obviously, it's a big deal to be selected as the major supplier that routinely receives all of a customer's electronic orders for the products you sell. Often this type of customer will be more impressed by an attractive marketing mix for a whole line of products than just a lower price for a particular order. Further, it may be too expensive and too much trouble to change the whole buying system just because somebody is offering a lower price on a particular day.

New-task buying requires information

Customers in a new-task buying situation are likely to seek information from a variety of sources. See Exhibit 7-5. Many of the impersonal sources are readily available in online digital formats. How much information a customer collects depends on the importance of the purchase and the level of uncertainty about what choice might be best. The time and expense of searching for information may not be justified for a minor purchase. But a major purchase often involves real detective work by the buyer.

New-task buying situations provide a good opportunity for a new supplier to make inroads with a customer. With a buyer actively searching for information, the seller's promotion has a much greater chance of being noticed and having an impact. Advertising, trade show exhibits, sales brochures, and salespeople can all help build the buyer's attention, but an informative website may be essential for getting attention in the first place.[11]

Internet EXERCISE

Go to the BuyerZone website (www.buyerzone.com). What types of products could be purchased by requesting a free quote on this site? From the home page click "Buying Advice> Furniture> Chairs> Chair Buyer's Guide," then look through this Buyer's Guide. Look at the Buyer's Guides for other products as well. What can be learned about buying different products from BuyerZone.com? For a marketing manager targeting smaller businesses, how could this site be helpful?

Search engines—a first step to gathering information

Most purchasing managers start with an Internet search when they need to identify new suppliers, better ways to meet needs, or information to improve decisions. Buyers often rely on highly specialized search engines—like one that finds all types of steel that meet certain technical specifications and then compares delivered prices. But buyers also use general-purpose search engines like Google. A search across the whole Web can often locate off-the-shelf products that eliminate the need to buy expensive, custom-made items. For example, a firm in Saudi Arabia ordered $1,000 worth of tiny rubber grommets from Allstates Rubber & Tool, a small firm in the suburbs of Chicago. If the buyer's search hadn't located the Allstates website, the only alternative would have been to pay much more for custom-made grommets—and Allstates wouldn't have picked up a new customer.[12]

Marketing managers know that it is critical to have a website that buyers can find. That's why suppliers often pay for a sponsored link (an ad) that appears when certain keywords are included in a search. A supplier might also change its website so that it is more likely to appear high on a list of searches.

Once a buyer arrives at the supplier's website, the site should make it fast and easy for the buyer to get information—or the buyer will simply click away to another site. Recognizing this, Staples did research to identify seven segments of office-supply customers and then fine-tuned its website to their preferences. For example, one segment plans routine orders in advance and wants to place orders as quickly as possible. For this group, Staples improved speed with fewer ordering steps. For another segment that doesn't plan ahead and likes help deciding on a particular product, Staples added "Learn More About" and "Help Me Decide" tools.[13]

Online marketplaces connect buyers and sellers in particular industries

Online marketplace websites are another source of information that are usually specific to particular industries. At VertMarkets (www.vertmarkets.com), there are links to 68 distinct online marketplaces that cover businesses ranging from semiconductor manufacturing to food service. Online marketplaces provide some organizational buyers with "one-stop shopping"; they can keep up with industry news, identify suppliers, gather information relevant to purchases, and place orders. For sellers, marketplaces are a good way to generate new sales leads.

Buyers ask for competitive bids to compare offerings

When buyers in B2B markets have identified potential suppliers, they sometimes ask them to submit a competitive bid—the terms of sale offered by the supplier in response to the purchase specifications posted by a buyer. If different suppliers' quality, dependability, and delivery schedules all meet the specs, the buyer will select the low-price bid. But a creative marketer needs to look carefully at the buyer's specs—and the need—to see if other elements of the marketing mix could provide a competitive advantage.

Rather than search for suppliers, buyers sometimes post their requirements and invite qualified suppliers to submit a bid. Some firms set up or participate in a procurement website that directs suppliers to companies (or divisions of a company) that need to make purchases. These sites make it easy for suppliers to find out about the purchase needs of the organizations that sponsor the sites. This helps increase the number of suppliers competing for the business and that can drive down prices or provide more beneficial terms of sale. For example, when the California Department of Transportation was planning $4 billion in new construction projects, it established a procurement site so that potential suppliers knew each project's requirements for submitting a competitive bid.

Reverse auctions foster price competition among suppliers

Competitive bidding has been around for a long time. However, before the Internet it was slow and inconvenient. Now, a buyer can go though multiple rounds of bidding very quickly with an online reverse auction. First, suppliers are invited to place a bid for specific goods or services. Usually the bidding focuses on price, but sometimes other terms of sale (like warranty or delivery time) are considered as well. Typically, each bid, and the supplier who made it, will be visible to all potential bidders on the auction website. An auction takes place over a period of several hours—making it fast, cost effective, and convenient for buyers looking for the lowest price. Reverse auctions work best for undifferentiated products, including products such as plastic resin, personal computers, or transportation services. Reverse auctions are less effective when the value provided to the customer comes from a complete marketing mix, not just a low price.

While reverse auctions can help buyers get lower prices, suppliers have to carefully decide how to respond. A seller who gets caught up in trying to "win" a reverse auction may bid at a price that loses money. This is what happened with stationery supplier Gartner Studios. Its competitive strength was product design, but when many of its regular customers switched to reverse auctions, suppliers with lower bid prices were getting the business. Gartner was faced with losing customers or losing money to keep them. To win with low bids and still make profits, Gartner worked to cut its own supply costs and switched production to Asia. Now, when planning a bid, Gartner has

Edition

lower costs but also knows how low a bid is still profitable for the company. Gartner also pays attention to whom else is bidding. That impacts how low Gartner's bid needs to be. Many of its customers won't choose the lowest bidder if it is a supplier that has a reputation for poor quality or late delivery.[14]

What buying procedure becomes routine is critical

From the discussion above, you can see that buyers make important decisions about how to deal with one or more suppliers. At one extreme, a buyer might want to rely on competition among all available vendors to get the best price on each and every order it places. At the other extreme, it might just routinely buy from one vendor with whom it already has a good relationship. In practice, there are many important and common variations between these extremes. To better understand the variations, let's take a closer look at the benefits and limitations of different types of buyer–seller relationships.

BUYER–SELLER RELATIONSHIPS IN BUSINESS MARKETS

Close relationships may produce mutual benefits

There are often significant benefits of a close working relationship between a supplier and a customer firm. And such relationships are becoming common. Many firms are reducing the number of suppliers with whom they work—expecting more in return from the suppliers that remain. The best relationships involve real partnerships where there's mutual trust and a long-term outlook. Closely tied firms often share tasks at lower total cost than would be possible working at arm's length.

The partnership between AlliedSignal and Betz Laboratories, for example, shows the benefits of a good relationship. A while back, Betz was just one of several suppliers that sold Allied chemicals to keep the water in its plants from gunking up pipes and rusting machinery. But Betz didn't stop at selling commodity powders. Teams of Betz experts and Allied engineers studied each plant to find places where water was being wasted. In less than a year, a team in one plant found $2.5 million in potential cost reductions. For example, by adding a few valves to recycle the water in a cooling tower, Betz was able to save 300 gallons of water a minute, which resulted in savings of over $100,000 a year and reduced environmental impact. Because of ideas like this, Allied's overall use of water treatment chemicals decreased. However, Betz sales to Allied doubled because it became Allied's sole supplier.[15]

In today's business markets, suppliers of both goods and services are working to build closer relationships with their business customers—to meet needs better and create a competitive advantage. Similarly, some customers are rewarding their best vendors by making them the "single source" of supply.

Relationships may not make sense

Although close relationships can produce benefits, they are not always best. A long-term commitment to a partner may reduce flexibility. When competition drives down prices and spurs innovation, the customer may be better off letting suppliers compete for the business. It may not be worth the customer's investment to build a relationship for purchases that are not particularly important or made that frequently.

It may at first appear that a seller would *always* prefer to have a closer relationship with a customer, but that is not so. Some customers may place orders that are too small or require so much special attention that the relationship would never be profitable for the seller. Also, in situations where a customer doesn't want a relationship, trying to build one may cost more than it's worth. Further, many small suppliers have made the mistake of relying too heavily on relationships with too few customers. One failed relationship may bankrupt the business.[16]

Relationships have many dimensions

Relationships are not "all or nothing" arrangements. Many firms may have a close relationship in some ways and not in others. Thus, it's useful to think about five key dimensions that help characterize most buyer–seller relationships: cooperation, information sharing, operational linkages, legal bonds, and relationship-specific adaptations. Purchasing managers for the buying firm and salespeople for the supplier usually coordinate the different dimensions of a relationship. However, as shown in Exhibit 7-6, close relationships often involve direct contacts between a number of people from other areas in both firms.[17]

Cooperation treats problems as joint responsibilities

In cooperative relationships, the buyer and seller work together to achieve both mutual and individual objectives. The two firms treat problems that arise as a joint responsibility. National Semiconductor (NS) and Siltec, a supplier of silicon wafers, found clever ways to cooperate and cut costs. Workers at the NS plant used to throw away the expensive plastic cassettes that Siltec uses to ship the silicon wafers. Now Siltec and NS cooperate to recycle the cassettes. This helps the environment and also saves more than $300,000 a year. Siltec passes along most of that to NS as lower prices.[18]

In some situations, cooperation is informal. For example, collaboration hubs are websites designed to help people in different firms work together. The cooperative effort might involve design, manufacturing, or distribution. Many of these sites focus on the needs of smaller firms in a specific industry. For example, at CTSpace (www.ctspace.com), construction contractors and architects can collaborate on projects by sharing blueprints, working through building permit requirements, and purchasing building materials.[19]

Exhibit 7-6
Key Dimensions of Relationships in Business Markets

Edition

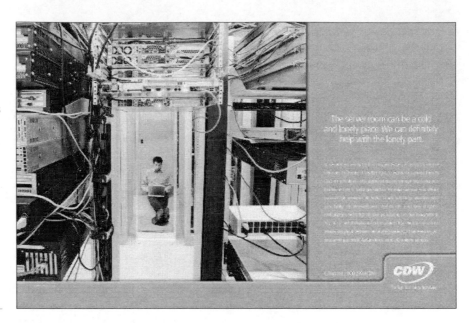

CDW is a wholesaler that offers its business customers a full array of computing and technology products. CDW has an ongoing, cooperative relationship with many of its customers, but its relationship with most customers is not structured with a long-term legal bond. Rather, CDW earns the customer's trust and business by sharing information and helping the customer solve problems.

Shared information is useful but may be risky

Some relationships involve open sharing of information. This might include the exchange of proprietary cost data, discussion of demand forecasts, and joint work on new product designs. Information might be shared through information systems or over the Internet. This is often a key facet of relationships that involve e-commerce.

Many firms provide relationship partners with access to password-protected websites. One big advantage of this approach is that it is fast and easy to update the information. It also saves time. A customer can check detailed product specs or the status of a job on the production line without having to wait for someone to respond.

National Semiconductor's website, for example, creates easy links between its customers, products, and distributors. Large customers get special services, like access to a secure website that shows specific purchase histories and production or shipping status of their orders. Smaller customers can get all the product information they need and then link directly to the order page for the distributor that serves them.[20]

Information sharing can lead to better decisions, reduced uncertainty about the future, and better planning. However, firms don't want to share information if there's a risk that a partner might misuse it. For example, some suppliers claim that a former General Motors' purchasing chief showed blueprints of their secret technology to competing suppliers. Violations of trust in a relationship are an ethical matter and should be taken seriously.

Marketers who ask for feedback from customers can learn how to improve and increase the value of the relationship. Good buying organizations provide regular feedback to their suppliers without being asked—and smart suppliers listen closely and respond to them. Honda, for example, provides a monthly report card that details the supplier's performance in five areas: quality, delivery, quantity delivered, performance history, and any special incidents. The report fosters an ongoing dialogue between Honda and its suppliers and makes sure both parties know how things are going.[21]

Operational linkages share functions between firms

Operational linkages are direct ties between the internal operations of the buyer and seller firms. These linkages usually involve ongoing coordination of activities between the firms. Shared activities are especially important when neither firm, working on its own, can perform a function as well as the two firms can working together.

Business customers often require operational linkages to reduce total inventory costs, maintain adequate inventory levels, and keep production lines moving. On the other hand, keeping too much inventory is expensive. Providing a customer with inventory when it's needed may require that a supplier be able to provide just-in-time delivery—reliably getting products there *just* before the customer needs them. We'll discuss just-in-time systems in more detail in Chapter 12. For now, it's enough to know that closer relationships between buyers and sellers involve operational linkages that lower costs and increase efficiency. Vertex Fasteners, for example, makes corrosion-resistant fasteners that are used by manufacturers in many different industries. Vertex creates value for its cost-conscious customers by working closely with a network of expert distributors. Distributors know each customer's specific needs so they can carefully label and pack orders for Vertex products in a way that saves the customer time and money when a truck is unloaded and shelves are stocked at the customer's factory.[22]

Operational linkages may also involve the routine activities of individuals who almost become part of the customer's operations. Design engineers, salespeople, and service representatives may participate in developing solutions to ongoing problems, conduct regular maintenance checks on equipment, or monitor inventory and coordinate orders. Consider the relationship between Jeep and Johnson Controls, the firm that supplies instrument panels for Jeep's Liberty SUV. When the Liberty was still in the planning stages, teams of people from both firms worked together to develop a special system of racks to move the instrument panels from JC's plant to the Jeep production line. Similar equipment was installed at the instrument panel plant and at the receiving dock for Jeep's assembly line. When the instrument panels get to the end of their own assembly line, the equipment automatically rolls them onto the racks in a waiting truck. The truck hauls the panels to the Jeep plant, and they are automatically unloaded, in sequence to match the next Liberty on the production line.[23]

Contracts spell out obligations

Many purchases in business markets are simple transactions. The seller's responsibility is to transfer title to goods or perform services, and the buyer's responsibility is to pay the agreed price. However, more complex relationships may be spelled out in detailed legal contracts. An agreement may apply only for a short period, but long-term contracts are also common.

For example, a customer might ask a supplier to guarantee a 6 percent price reduction for a particular part for each of the next three years and pledge to virtually eliminate defects. In return, the customer might offer to double its orders and help the supplier boost productivity.

Sometimes the buyer and seller know roughly what is needed but can't fix all the details in advance. For example, specifications or total requirements may change over time. Then the relationship may involve negotiated contract buying, which means agreeing to contracts that allow for changes in the purchase arrangements. In such cases, the general project and basic price is described but with provision for changes and price adjustments up or down.

Some managers figure that even a detailed contract isn't a good substitute for regular, good-faith reviews to make sure that neither party gets hurt by changing business conditions. Harley-Davidson used this approach when it moved toward closer relationships with a smaller number of suppliers. Purchasing executives tossed out detailed contracts and replaced them with a short statement of principles to guide relationships between Harley and its suppliers. This "handshake" approach is typical of relationships with Japanese firms.

Specific adaptations invest in the relationship

Relationship-specific adaptations involve changes in a firm's product or procedures that are unique to the needs or capabilities of a relationship partner. Industrial suppliers often custom design a new product for just one customer; this may require investments in R&D or new manufacturing technologies. MetoKote, in its relationship with John Deere described at the beginning of this chapter, made a specific adaptation by building its coating plant right next door to Deere's factory.

Buying firms may also adapt to a particular supplier; Lenovo designed its ultramobile IdeaPad notebook to work with Intel's new Atom N270 processor. However, buyers are often hesitant about making big investments that increase dependence on a specific supplier. Typically, they do it only when there isn't a good alternative—perhaps because only one or a few suppliers are available to meet a need—or if the benefits of the investment are clear before it's made.

Specific adaptations are usually made when the buying organization chooses to outsource—contract with an outside firm to produce goods or services rather than to produce them internally. Many firms have turned to outsourcing to cut costs—and that's why much outsourcing is handled by suppliers in countries where labor costs are lower. For example, many American companies are outsourcing production to firms in China.[24]

Powerful customer may control the relationship

Although a marketing manager may want to work in a cooperative partnership, that may be impossible with large customers who have the power to dictate how the relationship will work. For example, Duall/Wind was a supplier of small plastic parts for Polaroid. But when Duall/Wind wanted to raise its prices to cover increasing costs, Polaroid balked. Polaroid's purchasing manager demanded that Duall/Wind show a breakdown of all its costs, from materials to labor to profit. As Duall/Wind's president said, "I had a tough time getting through my head that Polaroid wanted to come right in here and have us divulge all that." But Polaroid is a big account—and it got the information it wanted. Polaroid buyers agreed to a price increase only after they were confident that Duall/Wind was doing everything possible to control costs.[25]

Buyers may still use several sources to spread their risk

Even if a marketing manager develops the best marketing mix possible and cultivates a close relationship with the customer, the customer may not give *all* of its business to one supplier. Buyers often look for several dependable sources of supply to protect themselves from unpredictable events such as strikes, fires, or floods in one of their suppliers' plants. A good marketing mix is still likely to win a larger share of the total business—which can prove to be very important. From a buyer's point of view, it may not seem like a big deal to give a particular supplier a 30 percent share of the orders rather than a 20 percent share. But for the seller that's a 50 percent increase in sales![26]

Variations in buying by customer type

We've been discussing aspects of relationships and buying approaches that generally apply with different types of customer organizations—in both the United States and internationally. However, it's also useful to have more detail about specific types of customers.

MANUFACTURERS ARE IMPORTANT CUSTOMERS

There are not many big ones

One of the most striking facts about manufacturers is how few there are compared to final consumers. This is true in every country. In the United States, for example, there are about 339,100 factories. Exhibit 7-7 shows that the majority of these are quite small—over half have less than 10 workers. But output from these small firms accounts for less than 3 percent of manufacturing value. In small plants, the owners often do the buying. And they buy less formally than buyers in the relatively few large manufacturing plants—which employ most of the workers and produce a large share of the value added by manufacturing. For example, only about 3 percent of all plants have 250 or more employees, yet they employ nearly half of the production workers and produce about 60 percent of the value added by manufacturers.

In other countries, the size distribution of manufacturers varies. But across different countries, the same general conclusion holds: Marketers often segment industrial markets on the basis of customer size because large firms do so much of the buying.

Customers cluster in geographic areas

In addition to concentration by company size, industrial markets are concentrated in certain geographic areas. Internationally, industrial customers are concentrated in countries that are at the more advanced stages of economic development. From all the talk in the news about the United States shifting from an industrial economy to a

Exhibit 7-7   Size Distribution of Manufacturing Establishments

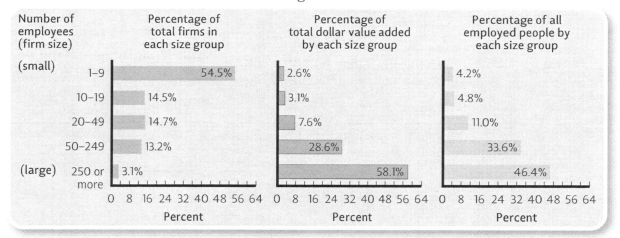

Number of employees (firm size)	Percentage of total firms in each size group	Percentage of total dollar value added by each size group	Percentage of all employed people by each size group
(small) 1–9	54.5%	2.6%	4.2%
10–19	14.5%	3.1%	4.8%
20–49	14.7%	7.6%	11.0%
50–249	13.2%	28.6%	33.6%
(large) 250 or more	3.1%	58.1%	46.4%

service and information economy, you might conclude that the United States is an exception—that the industrial market in this country is shrinking. It is true that the number of people employed in manufacturing has been shrinking, but U.S. manufacturing output is higher than at any other time in the nation's history. The rate of growth, however, is fastest in countries where labor is cheap.[27]

Within a country, there is often further concentration of manufacturing in specific areas. In the United States, many factories are concentrated in big metropolitan areas—especially in New York, Pennsylvania, Ohio, Illinois, Texas, and California. There is also concentration by industry. In Germany, for example, the steel industry is concentrated in the Ruhr Valley. Similarly, U.S. manufacturers of high-tech electronics are concentrated in California's famous Silicon Valley near San Francisco and also along Boston's Route 128.

Business data often classifies industries

The products an industrial customer needs to buy depend on the business it is in. Because of this, sales of a product are often concentrated among customers in similar businesses. For example, apparel manufacturers are the main customers for zippers.

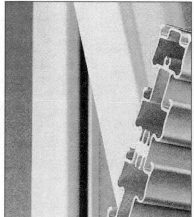

A firm like Alcoa Aluminum is likely to find that the majority of its customers are concentrated within a few industries that it can identify by North American Industry Classification System code number.

Edition

Exhibit 7–8   Illustrative NAICS Code Breakdown for Apparel Manufacturers

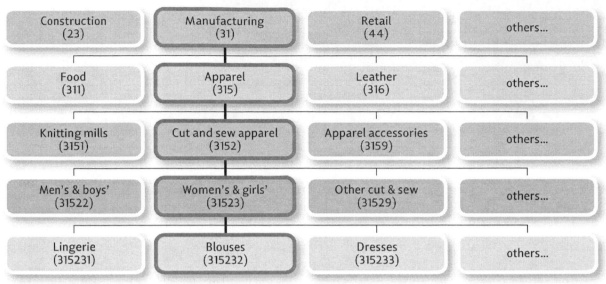

Marketing managers must focus their marketing mixes on prospective customers who exhibit characteristics similar to their current customers.

Detailed information is often available to help a marketing manager learn more about customers in different lines of business. The U.S. government collects and publishes data by the North American Industry Classification System (NAICS) codes—groups of firms in similar lines of business. (NAICS is pronounced like "nakes.") The number of establishments, sales volumes, and number of employees—broken down by geographic areas—are given for each NAICS code. A number of other countries collect similar data, and some of them try to coordinate their efforts with an international variation of the NAICS system. However, in many countries data on business customers is incomplete or inaccurate.

So let's take a closer look at how the NAICS codes work. The NAICS code breakdowns start with broad industry categories such as construction (23), manufacturing (31), retail trade (44), finance and insurance (52), and so on. See Exhibit 7-8. Within each two-digit industry breakdown, much more detailed data may be available for three-digit industries (that is, subindustries of the two-digit industries). For example, within the two-digit manufacturing industry (code 31) there are manufacturers of food (311), leather (316), and others, including apparel manufacturers (315). Then each three-digit group of firms is further subdivided into more detailed four-, five-, and six-digit classifications. For instance, within the three-digit (315) apparel manufacturers there are four-digit subgroups for knitting mills (3151), cut and sew firms (3152), and producers of apparel accessories (3159). Exhibit 7-8 illustrates that breakdowns are more detailed as you move to codes with more digits. However, detailed data (say, broken down at the four-digit level) isn't available for all industries in every geographic area. The government does not provide detail when only one or two plants are located in an area.

Many firms find their *current* customers' NAICS codes and then look at NAICS-coded lists for similar companies that may need the same goods and services. Other companies look at which NAICS categories are growing or declining to discover new opportunities.[28]

Internet EXERCISE

Comprehensive information about NAICS codes is available online (www.naics.com). At the website select "NAICS Code Search" and when the search page appears submit a query for the keyword "welding." If your firm was interested in selling its lasers to manufacturers of laser welding equipment, what is the NAICS code of the industry for which you would want to get a list of manufacturers?

Edition

PRODUCERS OF SERVICES—SMALLER AND MORE SPREAD OUT

The service side of the U.S. economy is large and has been growing fast. Service operations are also growing in some other countries. There are many good opportunities to provide these service companies with the products they need to support their operations. But there are also challenges.

The United States has about 4.6 million service firms—over 13 times as many as it has manufacturers. Some of these are big companies with international operations. Examples include AT&T, Hilton Hotels, Prudential Insurance, CitiGroup, and EDS (Electronic Data Systems). These firms have purchasing departments that are like those in large manufacturing organizations. But as you might guess given the large number of service firms, most of them are small. They're also more spread out around the country than manufacturing concerns. Factories often locate where transportation facilities are good, raw materials are available, and it is less costly to produce goods in quantity. Service operations, in contrast, often have to be close to their customers.

Buying may not be as formal

Purchases by small service firms are often handled by whoever is in charge. This may be a doctor, lawyer, owner of a local insurance agency, or manager of a hotel. Suppliers who usually deal with purchasing specialists in large organizations may have trouble adjusting to this market. Personal selling is still an important part of promotion, but reaching these customers in the first place often requires more advertising. And small service firms may need much more help in buying than a large corporation.

Small service customers like Internet buying

Small service companies that don't attract much personal attention from salespeople often rely on e-commerce for many of their purchases. Purchases by small customers can add up—so for many suppliers these customers are an important target market. Increasingly suppliers cater to the needs of these customers with specially designed websites. A well-designed website can be efficient for both customers and suppliers. Customers can get information, place orders, or follow up with a call or e-mail for personal attention from a salesperson or customer service rep when it's needed.

In a smaller service organization, purchases may be made by the person who is in charge rather than a person with full-time responsibility for purchasing.

Edition

RETAILERS AND WHOLESALERS BUY FOR THEIR CUSTOMERS

Most retail and wholesale buyers see themselves as purchasing agents for their target customers—remembering the old saying that "Goods well bought are half sold." Typically, retailers do *not* see themselves as sales agents for particular manufacturers. They buy what they think they can profitably sell. For example, the buying specialist at Walgreens Drugstores who handles products targeted at ethnic consumers is a real expert. He knows what ethnic customers want and won't be persuaded by a sales rep for a manufacturer who can't provide it. Of course, there is a place for collaboration, as when the Walgreens buyer works with people at Soft Sheen Products to develop a new product for the African American target market. That's profitable for both firms.

Committee buying is impersonal

Space in retail stores is limited, and buyers for retail chains simply are not interested in carrying every product that some salesperson wants them to sell. In an average week, 150 to 250 new items are offered to the buying offices of a large chain like Safeway. If the chain accepted all of them, it would add 10,000 new items during a single year! Obviously, these firms need a way to deal with this overload.

The entrepreneurs who started PenAgain, for example, had to have more than a unique product to get shelf space at Wal-Mart. Their presentation to Wal-Mart had to include hard data that showed their marketing mix was already working well in other retail stores and evidence of their ability to supply the large quantities a retailer the size of Wal-Mart would need.[29]

Decisions to add or drop lines or change buying policies may be handled by a *buying committee*. The seller still calls on and gives a pitch to a buyer—but the buyer does not have final responsibility. Instead, the buyer prepares forms summarizing proposals for new products and passes them on to the committee for evaluation. The seller may not get to present her story to the buying committee in person. This rational, almost cold-blooded approach certainly reduces the impact of a persuasive salesperson. On the other hand, it may favor a firm that has hard data on how its whole marketing mix will help the retailer to attract and keep customers.

Buyers watch computer output closely

Most larger firms use sophisticated computerized inventory replenishment systems. Scanners at retail checkout counters keep track of what goes out the door—and computers use this data to update the records. Even small retailers and wholesalers use automated control systems that create daily reports showing sales of every product. Buyers with this kind of information know, in detail, the profitability of the different competing products. If a product isn't moving, the retailer isn't likely to be impressed by a salesperson's request for more in-store attention or added shelf space.

Reorders are straight rebuys

Retailers and wholesalers usually carry a large number of products. A drug wholesaler, for example, may carry up to 125,000 products. Because they deal with so many products, most intermediaries buy their products on a routine, automatic reorder basis—straight rebuys—once they make the initial decision to stock specific items. Automatic computer ordering is a natural

Firms that partner with retailers to reach final consumers often must work with retail buying specialists. These specialists buy what they think the retailer can profitably resell to its customers.

outgrowth of computerized checkout systems. Sellers to these markets must understand the size of the buyer's job and have something useful to say and do when they call.

Some are not "open to buy"

Retail buyers are sometimes controlled by a miniature profit and loss statement for each department or merchandise line. In an effort to make a profit, the buyer tries to forecast sales, merchandise costs, and expenses. The figure for "cost of merchandise" is the amount buyers have budgeted to spend over the budget period. If the money has not yet been spent, buyers are open to buy—that is, the buyers have budgeted funds that can be spent during the current period. However, if the budget has been spent, they are no longer in the market and no amount of special promotion or price-cutting is likely to induce them to buy.

Resident buyers may help a firm's buyers

Resident buyers are independent buying agents who work in central markets (New York City, Paris, Rome, Hong Kong, Chicago, Los Angeles) for several retailer or wholesaler customers based in outlying areas or other countries. They buy new styles and fashions and fill-in items as their customers run out of stock during the year.

Resident buying organizations fill a need. They help small channel members (producers and intermediaries) reach each other inexpensively. Resident buyers usually are paid an annual fee based on their purchases.

THE GOVERNMENT MARKET

Size and diversity

Some marketers ignore the government market because they think that government red tape is more trouble than it's worth. They probably don't realize how big the government market really is. Government is the largest customer group in many countries—including the United States. About 30 percent of the U.S. gross domestic product is spent by various government units; the figure is much higher in some economies. Different government units in the United States buy almost every kind of product. They run not only schools, police departments, and military organizations, but also supermarkets, public utilities, research laboratories, offices, hospitals, and even liquor stores. These huge government expenditures cannot be ignored by an aggressive marketing manager.

Competitive bids may be required

Government buyers in the United States are expected to spend money wisely—in the public interest—so their purchases are usually subject to much public review. To avoid charges of favoritism, most government customers buy by specification using a mandatory bidding procedure. Often the government buyer must accept the lowest bid that meets the specifications. You can see how important it is for the buyer to write precise and complete specifications. Otherwise, sellers may submit a bid that fits the specs but doesn't really match what is needed. By law, a government unit might have to accept the lowest bid—even for an unwanted product.

Writing specifications is not easy—and buyers usually appreciate the help of well-informed salespeople. Salespeople *want* to have input on the specifications so their product can be considered or even have an advantage. A contract can be landed without the lowest bid when lower bids don't meet minimum or requested specifications.

Rigged specs are an ethical concern

At the extreme, a government customer who wants a specific brand or supplier may try to write the description so that no other supplier can meet all the specs. The buyer may have good reasons for such preferences—a more reliable product, prompt delivery, or better service after the sale. This kind of loyalty sounds great, but marketers must be sensitive to the ethical issues involved. Laws that require government customers to get bids are intended to increase competition among suppliers, not reduce it. Specs that are written primarily to defeat the purpose of these laws may be viewed as illegal bid rigging.

Edition

 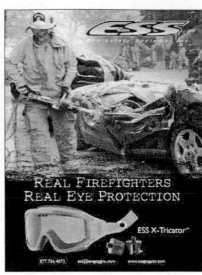

Government agencies are important customers for a wide variety of products.

The approved supplier list

Specification and bidding difficulties aren't problems in all government orders. Items that are bought frequently—or for which there are widely accepted standards— are purchased routinely. The government unit simply places an order at a previously approved price. To share in this business, a supplier must be on the list of approved suppliers and agree on a price that will stay the same for a specific period—perhaps a year.

Negotiated contracts are common too

Negotiation is often necessary when there are many intangible factors. Unfortunately, this is exactly where favoritism and influence can slip in. And such influence is not unknown—especially in city and state government. Nevertheless, negotiation is an important buying method in government sales—so a marketing mix should emphasize more than just low price.[30]

Learning what government wants

In the United States, there are more than 87,575 local government units (school districts, cities, counties, and states) as well as many federal agencies that make purchases. Keeping on top of all of them is nearly impossible. Potential suppliers should focus on the government units they want to cater to and learn the bidding methods of those units. Then it's easier to stay informed since most government contracts are advertised. Target marketing can make a big contribution here—making sure the marketing mixes are well matched with the different bid procedures.

A marketer can learn a lot about potential government target markets from various government publications and by using the Internet. For example, the General Services Administration handles vendor contracts for off-the-shelf goods and services; information for vendors is available at www.gsa.gov. There is an online resource center for government contracting at www.govcon.com. The Small Business Administration (www.sba.gov) offers many resources, including the *U.S. Purchasing, Specifications, and Sales Directory*. It explains government procedures to encourage competition for such business. Various state and local governments also offer guidance, as do government units in many other countries.

Dealing with foreign governments

Selling to government units in foreign countries can be a real challenge. In many cases, a firm must get permission from the government in its own country to sell to a foreign government. Moreover, most government contracts favor domestic suppliers if they are available. Even if such favoritism is not explicit, public sentiment may make it very difficult for a foreign competitor to get a contract. Or the government bureaucracy may simply bury a foreign supplier in so much red tape that there's no way to win.

Edition

Is it unethical to "buy help"?   In some countries, government officials expect small payments (grease money) just to speed up processing of routine paperwork, inspections, or decisions from the local bureaucracy. Outright influence peddling—where government officials or their friends request bribe money to sway a purchase decision—is common in some markets. In the past, marketers from some countries have looked at such bribes as a cost of doing business. However, the Foreign Corrupt Practices Act, passed by the U.S. Congress in 1977, prohibits U.S. firms from paying bribes to foreign officials. A person who pays bribes, or authorizes an agent to pay them, can face stiff penalties. However, the law was amended in 1988 to allow small grease money payments if they are customary in a local culture. Further, a manager isn't held responsible if an agent in the foreign country secretly pays bribes.[31]

CONCLUSION

In this chapter, we examined organizational buying and how it differs from final consumer buying. We saw that organizational buyers rely heavily on economic factors and cost–benefit analysis to make purchase decisions. The chapter showed how multiple influences are important in buying decisions—and how marketing managers must recognize and attend to the needs of all members of the buying center.

Buying behavior—and marketing opportunities—may change when there's a close relationship between a supplier and a customer. However, close relationships are not all or nothing. There are different ways that a supplier can build close relationships with its customers. We identified key dimensions of relationships and their benefits and limitations.

This chapter also showed how buying differs with the buying situation. The problem-solving modes used by final consumers and discussed in Chapter 6 also apply here—with some modification.

E-commerce plays a key role in organizational buying and B2B marketing. We discussed some of the different ways that these technologies are being used.

We saw that organizational buyers buy for resale or to produce other goods and services—and include manufacturers, farms, distributors, retailers, government agencies, and nonprofit organizations. There are many similarities in how these organizations buy—but also differences. The chapter concludes by providing insights about buying practices particular to manufacturers, service firms, and governments.

Understanding how organizations buy can help marketing managers identify logical dimensions for segmenting markets and developing marketing mixes. But the nature of products being offered may require further adjustments in the mix. Different product classes are discussed in Chapter 9. Variations by product may provide additional segmenting dimensions to help a marketing manager fine-tune a marketing strategy.

KEY TERMS

business and organizational customers, 174
purchasing specifications, 177
ISO 9000, 177
purchasing managers, 177
multiple buying influence, 178
buying center, 179

vendor analysis, 179
requisition, 181
new-task buying, 182
straight rebuy, 182
modified rebuy, 182
competitive bid, 185
just-in-time delivery, 189

negotiated contract buying, 189
outsource, 190
North American Industry Classification System (NAICS) codes, 192
open to buy, 195
resident buyers, 195
Foreign Corrupt Practices Act, 197

QUESTIONS AND PROBLEMS

1. In your own words, explain how buying behavior of business customers in different countries may have been a factor in speeding the spread of international marketing.

2. Compare and contrast the buying behavior of final consumers and organizational buyers. In what ways are they most similar and in what ways are they most different?

3. Briefly discuss why a marketing manager should think about who is likely to be involved in the buying center for a particular purchase. Is the buying center idea useful in consumer buying? Explain your answer.

4. If a nonprofit hospital were planning to buy expensive MRI scanning equipment (to detect tumors), who might be involved in the buying center? Explain your answer and describe the types of influence that different people might have.

5. Describe the situations that would lead to the use of the three different buying processes for a particular product—lightweight bumpers for a pickup truck.

6. Why would an organizational buyer want to get competitive bids? What are some of the situations when competitive bidding can't be used?

7. How likely would each of the following be to use competitive bids? (a) a small town that needed a road resurfaced, (b) a scouting organization that needed a printer to print its scouting handbook, (c) a hardware retailer that wants to add a new lawn mower line, (d) a grocery store chain that wants to install new checkout scanners, and (e) a sorority that wants to buy a computer to keep track of member dues. Explain your answers.

8. Discuss the advantages and disadvantages of just-in-time supply relationships from an organizational buyer's point of view. Are the advantages and disadvantages merely reversed from the seller's point of view?

9. Explain why a customer might be willing to work more cooperatively with a small number of suppliers rather than pitting suppliers in a competition against each other. Give an example that illustrates your points.

10. Would a tool manufacturer need a different marketing strategy for a big retail chain like Home Depot than for a single hardware store run by its owner? Discuss your answer.

11. How do you think a furniture manufacturer's buying habits and practices would be affected by the specific type of product to be purchased? Consider fabric for upholstered furniture, a lathe for the production line, cardboard for shipping cartons, and lubricants for production machinery.

12. Discuss the importance of target marketing when analyzing organizational markets. How easy is it to isolate homogeneous market segments in these markets?

13. Explain how NAICS codes might be helpful in evaluating and understanding business markets. Give an example.

14. Considering the nature of retail buying, outline the basic ingredients of promotion to retail buyers. Does it make any difference what kinds of products are involved? Are any other factors relevant?

15. The government market is obviously an extremely large one, yet it is often slighted or even ignored by many firms. Red tape is certainly one reason, but there are others. Discuss the situation and be sure to include the possibility of segmenting in your analysis.

16. Some critics argue that the Foreign Corrupt Practices Act puts U.S. businesses at a disadvantage when competing in foreign markets with suppliers from other countries that do not have similar laws. Do you think that this is a reasonable criticism? Explain your answer.

CREATING MARKETING PLANS

The Marketing Plan Coach software on the Student CD and the text website includes a sample marketing plan for Hillside Veterinary Clinic. Hillside decided to focus on final consumers and their pets rather than include organizational customers that might need veterinary care for animals. Such customers might range from dog breeders and farmers to animal protection shelters and law enforcement agencies that work with dogs. Would it be easy or hard for Hillside to expand its focus to serve customers who are not final consumers? Explain your thinking.

SUGGESTED CASES   5. PolyTech Products   6. Global Steel Company

COMPUTER-AIDED PROBLEM

7. VENDOR ANALYSIS

CompuTech, Inc., makes circuit boards for microcomputers. It is evaluating two possible suppliers of electronic memory chips.

The chips do the same job. Although manufacturing quality has been improving, some chips are always defective. Both suppliers will replace defective chips. But the only practical way to test for a defective chip is to assemble a circuit board and "burn it in"—run it and see if it works. When one chip on a

board is defective at that point, it costs $2.00 for the extra labor time to replace it. Supplier 1 guarantees a chip failure rate of not more than 1 per 100 (that is, a defect rate of 1 percent). The second supplier's 2 percent defective rate is higher, but its price is lower.

Supplier 1 has been able to improve its quality because it uses a heavier plastic case to hold the chip. The only disadvantage of the heavier case is that it requires CompuTech to use a connector that is somewhat more expensive.

Transportation costs are added to the price quoted by either supplier, but Supplier 2 is further away so transportation costs are higher. And because of the distance, delays in supplies reaching CompuTech are sometimes a problem. To ensure that a sufficient supply is on hand to keep production going, CompuTech must maintain a backup inventory—and this increases inventory costs. CompuTech figures inventory costs—the expenses of finance and storage—as a percentage of the total order cost.

To make its vendor analysis easier, CompuTech's purchasing agent has entered data about the two suppliers on a spreadsheet. He based his estimates on the quantity he thinks he will need over a full year.

a. Based on the results shown in the initial spreadsheet, which supplier do you think CompuTech should select? Why?

b. CompuTech estimates it will need 100,000 chips a year if sales go as expected. But if sales are slow, fewer chips will be needed. This isn't an issue with Supplier 2; its price is the same at any quantity. However, Supplier 1's price per chip will be $1.95 if CompuTech buys less than 90,000 during the year. If CompuTech only needs 84,500 chips, which supplier would be more economical? Why?

c. If the actual purchase quantity will be 84,500 and Supplier 1's price is $1.95, what is the highest price at which Supplier 2 will still be the lower-cost vendor for CompuTech? (Hint: You can enter various prices for Supplier 2 in the spreadsheet—or use the analysis feature to vary Supplier 2's price and display the total costs for both vendors.)

For additional questions related to this problem, see Exercise 7-3 in the *Learning Aid for Use with Basic Marketing*, 17th edition.

8

Improving Decisions with Marketing Information

When you see the array of products—strips, gels, swabs, and more—on drugstore shelves to make your smile whiter and brighter, it's easy to forget that just a few years ago this category of products—for a combination of oral care and beauty needs—didn't exist. Movie stars would pay Hollywood dentists thousands of dollars for special whitening treatments, but the rest of us would just envy their pearly smiles.

That changed after research convinced marketing managers for Crest oral care products that this unmet need was a big opportunity. A variety of marketing research firms, including National Opinion Research and Semaphore, helped with the research. For example, focus group interviews suggested that consumers would be excited about a do-it-yourself whitening treatment that was effective, simple to use, and affordable. Responses by representative samples of consumers to survey questionnaires confirmed that this was a large market. Online product concept tests revealed that there would be demand even at a price around $50, which would cover development and introductory promotion costs. On the other hand, research also revealed that dentists, who are influential in recommending oral care products, were concerned that the product might eat into their business.

When the R&D people came up with the idea of using a clear, tape-like strip that works by sticking to the teeth, product effectiveness tests confirmed that consumers could see a difference in whiteness. Research also showed that 30 minutes was the consumer limit for wearing the strips. Research even helped in selecting a brand name, Crest Whitestrips, and in focusing the positioning with advertising copy on "easy to use" and "superior whitening versus toothpaste" benefits.

Rather than work with traditional test markets in retail stores, marketing managers used infomercials and ads in consumer magazines to explain the product and direct consumers to a website (www.whitestrips.com) where they could buy Whitestrips. That approach not only produced sales quickly but also showed retailers that there was strong demand, even at a $44 retail price. Moreover, by doing studies on the Internet, researchers were able to deliver consumer test market input to marketing managers within days. For example, when researchers found that 80 percent of customers were female rather than the 50/50 split of men and women that was expected, the ad agency refined the focus of the advertising media.

When Whitestrips went into national distribution, the new product launch was one of the most successful in 20 years. Within a year, sales of Whitestrips surpassed $200 million and the product became the category leader. A professional version of Whitestrips for dentists to sell contributed to this success. Some dentists reported that the strips even helped increase interest in other types of cosmetic dentistry.

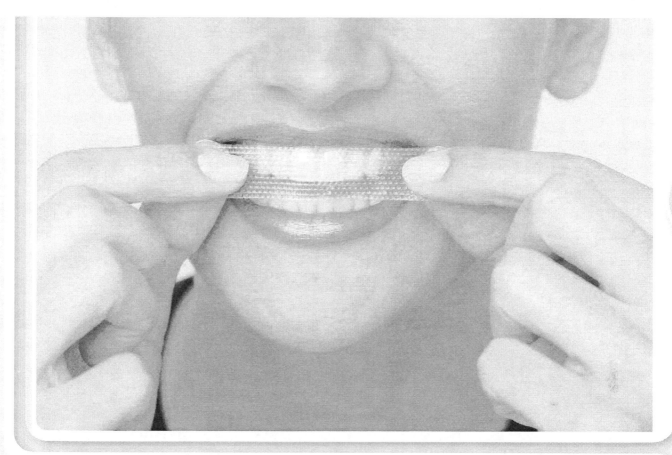

Crest soon faced competition from entries such as Mentadent's Tooth Whitening System and Colgate's Simply White, which was half the price of Whitestrips. Although more consumers were buying whiteners, data from Information Resources, Inc., showed that Whitestrips' market share was slipping. Consumer research also showed that customers wanted more convenience, so Crest fought back with new products. One was a premium version of Whitestrips that works in half the time. Another was Crest Night Effects—a lower-price product that is dabbed on the teeth and worn while sleeping. Many retailers took shelf space away from Mentadent to stock all three of Crest's whitening products. They could see in their routine sales analysis reports that Mentadent was losing sales to both Colgate and Crest.

Crest also switched its promotion to attract new customers. Although early adopters had wanted scientific evidence of the effectiveness of whiteners, research revealed that consumers adopting the product later were more focused on what other people thought. So Crest developed advertising that urged consumers to try Whitestrips for special social occasions, like a wedding or college reunion.

Efforts such as these were successful in generating sales growth for Crest—and competitors had successes of their own. But, when the marketing information system showed that sales of Whitestrips were falling again—as were sales of competing whitening products—marketing managers knew that it was time to work on a different problem—how to attract different segments of customers than those who had been the first to adopt whiteners. Research on different segments of the oral care market identified one segment of busy customers who liked the idea of whiter teeth, but didn't want to spend the 30 minutes needed to use the product. For these customers Crest developed Whitestrips Daily Multicare. It only takes a single five-minute a day application. Research also uncovered a segment of women who were not persuaded by previous Whitestrips promotion that used a vanity appeal. These women were interested as much in health benefits as appearance benefits. For this segment Crest created Whitestrips Daily Whitening Plus Tartar Protection and emphasized both benefits in its promotion to this target group. These new strategies reinvigorated Whitestrips sales in the U.S. market—and sales are again growing at more than 10 percent per year. Crest has even greater hopes for Whitestrips in the fast-growing Chinese market, where it already has a 25 percent share of toothpaste sales.[1]

EFFECTIVE MARKETING REQUIRES GOOD INFORMATION

Information is a bridge to the market

To make good marketing decisions, managers need accurate information about what is happening in the market. They usually can't get all of the information that they'd like, but part of their job is to find cost-effective ways to get the information that they really must have.

In this chapter, we'll focus on the two key sources that marketing managers turn to for information to make better decisions. One source is marketing research—procedures that develop and analyze new information about a market. Marketing research may involve use of questionnaires, interviews with customers, experiments, and many other approaches. But most marketing managers have some information needs that would take too long, or cost too much, to address with one-at-a-time marketing research projects. So, in many companies, marketing managers also routinely get help from a marketing information system (MIS)—which is an organized way of continually gathering, accessing, and analyzing information that marketing managers need to make ongoing decisions.

Marketing managers may need marketing research, an MIS, or a combination of both to get the information they need to make decisions during any step in the marketing strategy planning process—or to improve implementation and control. See Exhibit 8-1. In this chapter, we'll discuss ways to make marketing research and an MIS more useful, and the key issues that marketing managers face in using them.

Success requires cooperation with specialists

Most large companies have a separate marketing research department to plan and manage research projects. People in these departments usually rely on outside specialists—like interviewing and tabulating services—to carry out the work on particular projects. Further, they may call in specialized marketing consultants and marketing research organizations to take charge of a whole project.

Smaller companies usually don't have separate marketing research departments. They often depend on their salespeople or managers to conduct what research they do.

Exhibit 8-1 Marketing Information Inputs to Marketing Strategy Planning Decisions

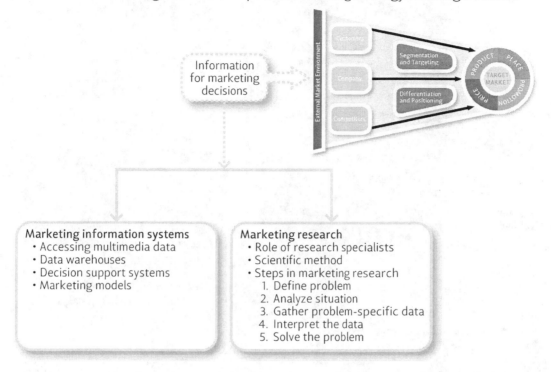

Marketing information systems
- Accessing multimedia data
- Data warehouses
- Decision support systems
- Marketing models

Marketing research
- Role of research specialists
- Scientific method
- Steps in marketing research
  1. Define problem
  2. Analyze situation
  3. Gather problem-specific data
  4. Interpret the data
  5. Solve the problem

Some nonprofit organizations have begun to use marketing research—usually with the help of outside specialists. For example, there are research firms that specialize in conducting marketing research for colleges, museums, and politicians.

Most companies also have a separate department with information technology specialists to help set up and maintain an MIS. Even small firms may have a person who handles all of the technical work on its computer systems. Increasingly, both small and large firms are turning to outside consultants and service providers for help with information systems. As we will discuss, collaboration and good communication between the marketing manager and these internal and external technical specialists is sometimes a challenge.

CHANGES ARE UNDERWAY IN MARKETING INFORMATION SYSTEMS

Marketing managers for some companies make decisions based almost totally on their own judgment—with very little hard data. The manager may not even know that he or she is about to make the same mistake that the previous person in that job already made! When it's time to make a decision, they may wish they had more information. But by then it's too late, so they do without.

MIS makes information available and accessible

Many firms realize that it doesn't pay to wait until you have important questions you can't answer. They anticipate the information they will need. They work to develop a *continual flow of information* that is available and quickly accessible from an MIS when it's needed.

We won't cover all of the technical details of planning for an MIS. But you should understand what an MIS is so you know some of the possibilities. We'll be discussing the elements of a complete MIS as shown in Exhibit 8-2. As part of that review, we'll highlight how technology is changing MIS use.

Edition

Development of powerful computer networks, software, and information technology makes it easier and less expensive for companies to gather and analyze marketing information.

Get more information—faster and easier

Advances in information technology have ushered in *radical* improvements in marketing information systems. Now it's easy to set up and use an MIS and exchange data among remote computers. Managers have access to much more information. It's instantly available, and often just a mouse click away.

The *type* of information available is also changing dramatically. Until recently, marketing managers relied on computers mainly for number crunching. The multimedia revolution in computing lifted that limitation. Now it doesn't matter whether marketing information takes the form of a report, spreadsheet, database, presentation, photo, graphic, video, or table of statistics. It is all being created on computer. So it can be easily stored and accessed by computer. When we talk about a "database" of marketing information, it may include all types of information, not just numbers.

Exhibit 8-2   Elements of a Complete Marketing Information System

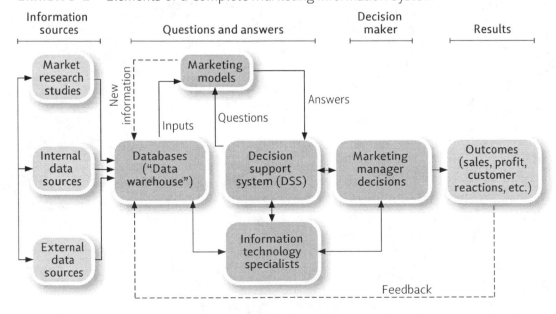

An intranet is easy to update

Many firms, even very small ones, have their own intranet—a system for linking computers within a company. An intranet works like the Internet. However, to maintain security, access to websites or data on an intranet is usually limited to employees. Even so, information is available on demand. Further, it's a simple matter to "publish" new information to a website as soon as it becomes available.

You seldom have all the information you need. Both customers and competitors can be unpredictable. Getting the precise information you want may cost too much or take too long. For example, data on international markets is often incomplete, outdated, or difficult to obtain. So a manager often must decide what information is really critical and how to get it.

Marketing managers must help develop an MIS

In some companies, an MIS is set up by a person or group that provides *all* departments in the firm with information technology support. Or it may be set up by marketing specialists.

These specialists are important, but the marketing manager should play an important role, too. Marketing managers know what data they've routinely used or needed in the past. They can also foresee what types of data might be useful. They should communicate these needs to the specialists so the information will be there when they want it and in the form they want it.

Decision support systems put managers online

An MIS system organizes incoming information into a data warehouse—a place where databases are stored so that they are available when needed. You can think of a data warehouse as an electronic library, where all of the information is indexed extremely well. Firms with an MIS often have information technology specialists who help managers get specialized reports and output from the warehouse. However, to get better decisions, most MIS systems now provide marketing managers with a decision support system. A decision support system (DSS) is a computer program that makes it easy for a marketing manager to get and use information *as he or she is making decisions*.

A decision support system usually involves some sort of search engine—a computer program that helps a marketing manager find information that is needed. For example, a manager who wants sales data for the previous week or day might search for any database or computer file that references the term *unit sales* as well as the relevant data. The search engine would identify any files where that term appeared. If there were many, the manager could narrow the search further (say by specifying the product of interest).

When the search is focused on numerical data, simply finding the information may not go far enough. Thus, a DSS typically helps change raw data—like product sales for the previous day—into more *useful information*. For example, it may draw graphs to show relationships in data—perhaps comparing yesterday's sales to the sales on the same day in the last four weeks.

At Verizon Communications, marketing managers' computers display a "marketing dashboard." Like the speedometer and fuel gauge on a car, a marketing dashboard displays up-to-the-minute marketing data in an easy-to-read format. A marketing dashboard is usually customized to a manager's areas of responsibility. A Verizon dashboard might show the percentage of customer calls dropped by cell towers, the number and location of repair trucks in the field, or the number of callers "on hold" waiting for customer service help. With early warning about potential problems, the manager can quickly make corrections. For example, a manager might call in extra customer service help if too many customers are "on hold."

Some decision support systems go even further. They allow a manager to see how answers to questions might change in various situations. For example, a manager at Home Depot may want to decide whether to use radio advertising or newspaper inserts to stimulate paint sales in a particular store or market area. The Home Depot MIS has data on sales by product and store over time, as well as data on spending for different types of promotion by market. Drawing on data about how a promotion had worked

Edition

If marketing managers don't plan ahead, they often don't have the information they need to make good decisions. Even with advance planning, it takes collaboration and good communication between the research specialist and the marketing manager to be certain that information is cost effective and on target.

in the past (in this market and in other markets), the DSS will make sale estimates using a marketing model. A marketing model is a statement of relationships among marketing variables. The manager can look at the sales (and costs) expected with different types of promotion and select the marketing mix that is best for that target market.[2]

In short, the decision support system puts managers online so they can study available data and make better marketing decisions—faster.[3]

Information for planning, implementation, and control

Once marketing managers use an MIS—and perhaps a DSS—they are eager for more information. They realize that they can improve all aspects of their planning—blending individual Ps, combining the four Ps into mixes, and developing and selecting plans. Further, they can monitor the implementation of current plans, comparing results against plans and making necessary changes more quickly. For example, LensCrafters is the sales leader in optical retailing. Each of its 890 North American stores carries a very large selection of frame styles, lenses, and sunglasses tailored not only to the age, gender, and ethnic makeup of the local market but also to what is selling at that particular store. Shifts in eyewear fashions can come fast. So managers at Lens-Crafters routinely analyze sales data available in the firm's marketing information system. By breaking down sales by product, store, and time period, they can spot buying trends early and plan for them. Sales analysis is helping in a different way in China. Since 2006 LensCrafters has opened 166 stores—and used different types of promotion to attract customers. LensCrafters analyzed the sales levels achieved with each type of promotion, so now when it opens a new store it can concentrate on what works best. For example, scratch-off cards that give various levels of discounts are popular with price-sensitive Chinese families.[4] (*Note:* The sales and cost analysis techniques discussed in Chapter 18 are often used in an MIS.)

Many firms are not there yet

Of course, not every firm has a complete MIS system. And in some firms that do, managers don't know how to use what's there. A major problem is that many managers are used to doing it the old way—and they don't think through what information they need.

One sales manager thought he was progressive when he asked his assistant for a report listing each sales rep's sales for the previous month and the current month. The assistant quickly found the relevant information on the firm's intranet, put it into an Excel spreadsheet, and printed out the report. Later, however, she was surprised to see the sales manager working on the list with a calculator. He was figuring the percentage change in sales for the month and ranking the reps from largest increase in sales to smallest. The spreadsheet software could have done all of that—instantly—but the sales manager got what he *asked for*, not what he really needed. An MIS can provide information—but only the marketing manager knows what problem needs solving. It's the job of the manager—not the computer or the MIS specialist—to ask for the right information in the right form.[5]

THE SCIENTIFIC METHOD AND MARKETING RESEARCH

Marketing research—combined with the strategy planning framework we discussed in Chapter 2—can also help marketing managers make better decisions.

Marketing research is guided by the scientific method, a decision-making approach that focuses on being objective and orderly in *testing* ideas before accepting them. With the scientific method, managers don't just *assume* that their intuition is correct. Instead, they use their intuition and observations to develop hypotheses—educated guesses about the relationships between things or about what will happen in the future. Then they test their hypotheses before making final decisions.

A manager who relies only on intuition might introduce a new product without testing consumer response. But a manager who uses the scientific method might say, "I think (hypothesize) that consumers currently using the most popular brand will prefer our new product. Let's run some consumer tests. If at least 60 percent of the consumers prefer our product, we can introduce it in a regional test market. If it doesn't pass the consumer test there, we can make some changes and try again." With this approach, decisions are based on evidence, not just hunches.

The scientific method forces an orderly research process. Some managers don't carefully specify what information they need. They blindly move ahead—hoping that research will provide "the answer." Other managers may have a clearly defined problem or question but lose their way after that. These hit-or-miss approaches waste both time and money.

Online surveys provide fast feedback and often at a lower cost than the old-fashioned way. Of course, the manager needs to be certain that the online sample is representative. If it is not, the result may be misleading.

Edition

FIVE-STEP APPROACH TO MARKETING RESEARCH

The **marketing research process** is a five-step application of the scientific method that includes:

1. Defining the problem.
2. Analyzing the situation.
3. Getting problem-specific data.
4. Interpreting the data.
5. Solving the problem.

Exhibit 8-3 shows the five steps in the process. Note that the process may lead to a solution before all of the steps are completed. Or as the feedback arrows show, researchers may return to an earlier step if needed. For example, the interpreting step may point to a new question—or reveal the need for additional information—before a final decision can be made.

Effective research usually requires cooperation

Good marketing research requires cooperation between researchers and marketing managers. Researchers must be sure their research focuses on real problems.

Marketing managers must be able to explain what their problems are and what kinds of information they need. They should be able to communicate with specialists in the specialists' language. Marketing managers may only be "consumers" of research. But they should be informed consumers—able to explain exactly what they want from the research. They should also know about some of the basic decisions made during the research process so they know the limitations of the findings.

For this reason, our discussion of marketing research won't emphasize mechanics but rather how to plan and evaluate the work of marketing researchers.[6]

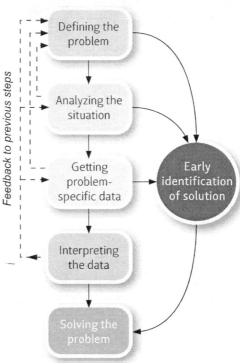

Exhibit 8-3   Five-Step Scientific Approach to Marketing Research Process

DEFINING THE PROBLEM—STEP 1

Defining the problem is often the most difficult step in the marketing research process. But it's important for the objectives of the research to be clearly defined. The best research job on the wrong problem is wasted effort.

Finding the right problem level almost solves the problem

Our strategy planning framework is useful for guiding the problem definition step. It can help the researcher identify the real problem area and what information is needed. Do we really know enough about our target markets to work out all of the four Ps? Before deciding how to position our product, do we understand our competitor's strengths and weaknesses? Do we know enough to decide what celebrity to use in an ad or how to handle the price war in New York City or Tokyo? If not, we may want to do research rather than rely on intuition.

Don't confuse problems with symptoms

The problem definition step sounds simple—and that's the danger. It's easy to confuse problems with symptoms. Marketers for Kiwi shoe polish encountered this situation. Kiwi's palm-size tin, embossed with the image of a Kiwi bird, is already the market leader in many countries. So, to get more growth, Kiwi managers did a number of consumer studies focused on the problem of how to improve the polish. Yet, none of the new product ideas clicked with consumers. Things changed when a new CEO realized that the lack of interest in new polish products was just a symptom of the fact that today's footwear is made less from leather and more from synthetic materials. Further, Kiwi had traditionally targeted men rather than women, who tend to toss out worn shoes rather than work to keep them in good condition. So the CEO changed the focus of research to another problem—figuring out what feet and footwear related needs were not currently being met. That research showed that having comfortable, fresh-smelling shoes was the top priority for women. Further research focusing on how to solve that problem led to the development of several new products, including Kiwi Fresh'ins, which are lightly scented disposable and ultrathin shoe inserts that keep feet feeling fresh and comfortable all day.[7]

Setting research objectives may require more understanding

Sometimes the research objectives are very clear. A manager wants to know if the targeted households have tried a new product and what percent of them bought it a second time. But research objectives aren't always so simple. The manager might also want to know *why* some didn't buy or whether they had even heard of the product. Companies rarely have enough time and money to study everything. A manager must narrow the research objectives. One good way is to develop a list of research questions that includes all the possible problem areas. Then the manager can consider the items on the list more completely—in the situation analysis step—before narrowing down to final research objectives.

ANALYZING THE SITUATION—STEP 2

What information do we already have?

When the marketing manager thinks the real problem has begun to surface, a situation analysis is useful. A situation analysis is an informal study of what information is already available in the problem area. It can help define the problem and specify what additional information, if any, is needed.

The situation analysis may begin with quick research—perhaps an Internet search; a closer look at information in an MIS; and phone calls or informal talks with people familiar with the industry, problem, or situation.

Let's consider a situation where the MIS shows declining sales in the Chicago region. The marketing manager might begin a situation analysis by digging deeper into the MIS. She might discover that the decline is due to a drop in sales by just one wholesaler. A next step might involve an e-mail inquiry to the salesperson who calls on this account. She might even phone the wholesaler to ask about the sales decline. In the process, she might discover that the wholesaler switched to a new product from a competitor. Or, she might learn that the wholesaler became fed up with slow delivery of orders. Depending on the result of this initial situation analysis, the marketing manager may redefine the problem and start a more focused situation analysis—or identify a solution and put it in place.

Situation analysis helps educate a researcher

The situation analysis is especially important if the marketing manager is dealing with unfamiliar areas or if the researcher is a specialist who doesn't know much about the management decisions to be made. They *both* must be sure they understand the problem area—including the nature of the target market, the marketing mix, competition, and other external factors. Otherwise, the researcher may rush ahead and make costly mistakes or simply discover facts that management already knows. The following case illustrates this danger.

A marketing manager at the home office of a large retail chain hired a research firm to do in-store interviews to learn what customers liked most, and least, about some of its stores in other cities. Interviewers diligently filled out their questionnaires. When the results came in, it was apparent that neither the marketing manager nor the researcher

Edition

Exhibit 8-4   Sources of Secondary and Primary Data

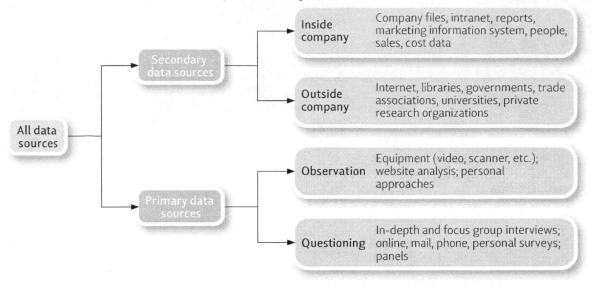

had done their homework. No one had even talked with the local store managers! Several of the stores were in the middle of some messy remodeling—so all the customers' responses concerned the noise and dust from the construction. The research was a waste of money.

Secondary data may provide the answers— or some background

The situation analysis should also find relevant secondary data—information that has been collected or published already. Later, in Step 3, we will cover primary data—information specifically collected to solve a current problem. Too often researchers rush to gather primary data when much relevant secondary information is already available—at little or no cost! See Exhibit 8-4.

Much secondary data is available

Ideally, much secondary data is already available from the firm's MIS. Data that has not been organized in an MIS may be available from the company's files and reports. Secondary data also is available from libraries, trade associations, government agencies, and private research organizations; increasingly, these organizations put their information online. So one of the first places a researcher should look for secondary data is on the Internet.

Search the Internet for information

Marketing managers can find a treasure trove of useful information on the Internet. It's all readily accessible from a computer (or even by wireless smart phone). But available is not the same as reliable. Anyone can post anything on the Internet. So, as with any other research source, you should carefully evaluate the accuracy of Internet sources.

The key to the Internet is finding what's needed. Internet subject directories that categorize websites by topic are a good place to start. Yahoo.com has a popular directory, but libraries and other organizations have created many more. Two good directory resources are the Librarians' Index to the Internet (www.lii.org) and INFOMINE (http://infomine.ucr.edu). Powerful Internet search engines, like the ones at Google.com and Ask.com, provide lists of links to websites that include words or phrases specified by the researcher. A problem is that searches often identify too many irrelevant sources.

Search engines miss important databases

Many managers don't realize that much of the information stored on the Internet is in database formats that standard website search engines can't find. To search for

Edition

CHAPTER 8

211

Improving Decisions with Marketing Information

Targeting Change
with **Behavior-Based Marketing**.

CATALINA MARKETING
Targeting Change

A firm's own data on customers' past purchases, if properly analyzed, can be an important source of information for evaluating new opportunities.

information in those databases you must first locate the website with the relevant database and then use software at the site to search inside the database. Directories that describe database sites help with the first step. The directory at the website www. completeplanet.com, for example, provides an organized listing of more than 70,000 searchable databases.

Special-interest groups on the Web

Many marketing managers join discussion groups or newsgroups that share information on topics of specific interest. Belonging to these groups is like subscribing to an electronic newsletter. Similarly, some websites provide automatic e-mail notifications when information is updated. This service can be valuable for information you need to come to you automatically—before you even know it's available. Indeed, it may be available at the website of a competing firm. A competitor's press releases or job listings sometimes provide important information about future plans. Microsoft, for example, was alerted to a competitor's plans by looking at its online job postings.

Some marketing managers take a more hands-on approach. They log in to blogs or online discussion groups to "eavesdrop" or ask questions as customers chat about companies or brands of interest. Specialized search engines like Blogdex and Google Groups locate this type of site.[8]

Government data is inexpensive

Federal and state governments publish data on many subjects. Government data is often useful in estimating the size of markets. In Chapter 5 we gave a number of examples of the different types of data that are available and suggested some websites. Almost all government data is available in inexpensive print and digital publications, on websites, and in downloads ready for further analysis.

Edition

Internet EXERCISE

Blogs provide a place for people to write about what interests them and post it on the Internet for all to read. One way to learn more about trends in Internet word-of-mouth is to track the frequency with which certain words are used in blogs. BlogPulse automates this process. Go to www.blogpulse.com and click on "Tools" and then "Trend Search." You'll compare three digital camera brands: type the names "Canon," "Kodak," and "Nikon" in the trend search terms edit box. Choose 6 months for the date range and then click "Get Trend." Which brand name appears most frequently in blogs? What causes the sudden spikes in the charts? How could this information be helpful to a marketing manager at Canon?

Sometimes it's more practical to use summary publications for leads to more detailed reports. For the U.S. market, one of the most useful summary references is the *Statistical Abstract of the United States*. Like an almanac, it is issued in print form each year and gives 1,500 summary tables from more than 200 published sources. Detailed footnotes guide readers to more specific information on a topic. The abstract and much of the source material on which it is based are available online at www.census.gov. Similarly, the *United Nations Statistical Yearbook* is one of the best summaries of worldwide data; like many other international statistical references, it is available on CD-ROM and online (www.un.org/depts/unsd).

Secondary data is very limited on some international markets. However, most countries with advanced economies have government agencies that help researchers get the data they need. For example, Statistics Canada (www.statcan.ca) compiles a great deal of information on the Canadian market. Eurostat (europa.eu.int/comm/eurostat), the statistical office for the European Union countries, and the Organization for Economic Cooperation (in Paris) offer many publications packed with data on Europe. In the United States, the Department of Commerce (www.doc.gov) distributes statistics compiled by all other federal departments. Some city and state governments have similar agencies for local data. The Yahoo website (www.yahoo.com) provides an index to a large amount of information about different governments.

Private sources are useful, too

Many private research organizations—as well as advertising agencies, newspapers, and magazines—regularly compile and publish data. A good business library is valuable for sources such as *Sales & Marketing Management*, *Advertising Age*, *Journal of Marketing*, and the publications of the National Industrial Conference Board.

The *Encyclopedia of Associations* lists 75,000 U.S. and international trade and professional associations that can be a good source of information. For example, the American Marketing Association (www.ama.org) has an information center with many marketing publications.

Situation analysis yields a lot—for very little

The virtue of a good situation analysis is that it can be very informative but takes little time. And it's inexpensive compared with more formal research efforts—like a large-scale survey. A phone, access to the Internet, and time might be all a marketing manager needs to gather a lot of insight. Situation analysis can help focus further research or even eliminate the need for it entirely. The situation analyst is really trying to determine the exact nature of the situation and the problem.

Determine what else is needed

At the end of the situation analysis, you can see which research questions—from the list developed during the problem definition step—remain unanswered. Then you have to decide exactly what information you need to answer those questions and how to get it. This may require discussion between technical experts and the marketing manager. Often companies use a written research proposal—a plan that specifies what information will be obtained and how—to be sure no misunderstandings occur later. The research plan may include information about costs, what data will be collected, how it will be collected, who will analyze it and how, and how long the process will take.

GETTING PROBLEM-SPECIFIC DATA—STEP 3

Gathering primary data

There are different methods for collecting primary data. Which approach to use depends on the nature of the problem and how much time and money are available.

In most primary data collection, the researcher tries to learn what customers think about some topic or how they behave under some conditions. There are two basic methods for obtaining information about customers: *questioning* and *observing*. Questioning can range from qualitative to quantitative research. And many kinds of observing are possible.

Qualitative questioning— open-ended with a hidden purpose

Qualitative research seeks in-depth, open-ended responses, not yes or no answers. The researcher tries to get people to share their thoughts on a topic—without giving them many directions or guidelines about what to say.

A researcher might ask different consumers, "What do you think about when you decide where to shop for food?" One person may talk about convenient location, another about service, and others about the quality of the fresh produce. The real advantage of this approach is *depth*. Each person can be asked follow-up questions so the researcher really understands what *that* respondent is thinking. The depth of the qualitative approach gets at the details—even if the researcher needs a lot of judgment to summarize it all.

Focus groups stimulate discussion

The most widely used form of qualitative questioning in marketing research is the focus group interview, which involves interviewing 6 to 10 people in an informal group setting. The focus group also uses open-ended questions, but here the interviewer wants to get group interaction—to stimulate thinking and get immediate reactions.

A skilled focus group leader can learn a lot from this approach. A typical session may last an hour, so participants can cover a lot of ground. Sessions are often recorded (or broadcast over the Internet or by satellite) so different managers can form their own impressions of what happened. Some research firms create electronic focus groups in which participants log onto a specified website and with others participate in a chat session; each person types in comments that are shared on the computer screen of each of the other participants. What they type is the record of the session.[9]

MOD-PAC, a large printing company, faced a problem: Business from its traditional large customers was drying up. MOD-PAC managers wanted to know if there were niche markets willing to buy printing services over the Internet. So, they conducted *online* focus groups, each with prospects from a different target market. The focus groups helped MOD-PAC managers see that each group had different needs and used different terms to discuss its problems. Each focus group also indicated that there was interest in buying printing services online. In response, MOD-PAC developed its "Print Lizard" website; the home page uses tabs to route customers from different segments to the part of the site that caters to their specific needs.[10]

Online focus groups can offset some of the limitations of traditional focus groups. Participants who meet online feel freer to express their honest thoughts—and an aggressive individual is less likely to dominate the group. For example, AOL found that men were often embarrassed to admit to others in a traditional focus group that they had trouble controlling spam on their computers. In online groups, they revealed their real concerns. The online groups' inputs helped in AOL's revamp of its spam blocker system and its ads to explain the benefits of using AOL.[11]

Regardless of how a focus group is conducted, conclusions reached from a session usually vary depending on who watches it. A typical problem—and serious limitation—with qualitative research is that it's hard to measure the results objectively. The results seem to depend largely on the viewpoint of the researcher. In addition, people willing to participate in a focus group—especially those who talk the most—may not be representative of the broader target market.

Focus groups can be conducted quickly and at relatively low cost—an average of about $4,000 each. This is part of their appeal. But focus groups are probably being

Edition

Focus groups are popular, and well-run groups can provide useful information. Similarly, online interview sessions can be conducted quickly and affordably. As with any type of marketing research, a marketing manager should be aware of both the advantages and limitations of the specific approach used when drawing conclusions and making decisions.

overused. It's easy to fall into the trap of treating an idea arising from a focus group as a "fact" that applies to a broad target market.

To avoid this trap, some researchers use qualitative research to prepare for quantitative research. For example, the Jacksonville Symphony Orchestra wanted to broaden its base of support and increase ticket sales. It hired a marketing research firm to conduct focus group interviews. These interviews helped the marketing managers refine their ideas about what these target "customers" liked and did not like about the orchestra. The ideas were then tested with a larger, more representative sample. When the managers planned their promotion and the orchestra's program on the basis of the research, ticket sales nearly doubled.[12]

Qualitative research can provide good ideas—hypotheses. But we need other approaches—perhaps based on more representative samples and objective measures—to *test* the hypotheses.

Structured questioning gives more objective results

When researchers use identical questions and response alternatives, they can summarize the information quantitatively. Samples can be larger and more representative, and various statistics can be used to draw conclusions. For these reasons, most survey research is quantitative research—which seeks structured responses that can be summarized in numbers, like percentages, averages, or other statistics. For example, a marketing researcher might calculate what percentage of respondents have tried a new product and then figure an average score for how satisfied they were.

CHAPTER 8

215

Improving Decisions with Marketing Information

Fixed responses speed answering and analysis

Survey questionnaires usually provide fixed responses to questions to simplify analysis of the replies. This multiple-choice approach also makes it easier and faster for respondents to reply. Simple fill-in-a-number questions are also widely used in quantitative research. Fixed responses are also more convenient for computer analysis, which is how most surveys are analyzed.

Surveys come in many forms

Decisions about what specific questions to ask and how to ask them usually depend on how respondents will be contacted—by mail (or electronic mail), via a website, on the phone, or in person. What question and response approach is used may also affect the survey. There are many possibilities. For example, whether the survey is self-administered or handled by an interviewer, the questionnaire may be on paper or in an interactive computer format (perhaps distributed on a CD or disk or displayed on a website). The computer can be programmed to skip certain questions, depending on answers given. Computerized questionnaires also allow the research to show pictures or play audio/video clips (for example, to get reactions to an advertising jingle). In an automated telephone interview, questions may be prerecorded on an audio tape or computer and the subject responds by pushing touch-tone buttons on the phone.

Mail and online surveys are common and convenient

A questionnaire distributed by mail, e-mail, or online is useful when extensive questioning is necessary. Respondents can complete the questions at their convenience. They may be more willing to provide personal information—since a questionnaire can be completed anonymously. But the questions must be simple and easy to follow since no interviewer is there to help. If the respondent is likely to be a computer user, a questionnaire on a website can include a help feature with additional directions for people who need them.

A big problem with questionnaires is that many people don't complete them. The response rate—the percentage of people contacted who complete the questionnaire—is often low and respondents may not be representative. Mail, e-mail, and online surveys are economical if a large number of people respond. But they may be quite expensive if the response rate is low. Worse, the results may be misleading if the respondents are not representative. For example, people who complete online questionnaires tend to be younger, better educated, or different in other ways that impact how they answer.

Southwest uses surveys and other types of research to "listen" to customer inputs, but it also has a blog at www.blogsouthwest.com where it encourages customers and employees to share their opinions.

Edition

Internet EXERCISE

Assume that your boss has asked you to do a customer satisfaction survey. As part of a situation analysis, you want to get ideas about what others have done in this area. Go to the website for the Google search engine (www. google.com). In the dialogue box type 'customer satisfaction survey' (include the single quote marks) and click on Google search. Look at some of the websites identified. How helpful is this? How could it be improved?

Distributing questionnaires by e-mail, or at a website, is popular. It is quick, and the responses come back in computer form. Surveys sent by regular mail usually take a lot longer.

Regardless of how quickly a questionnaire is distributed, it often takes a month or more to get the data back. That is too slow for some decisions. Moreover, it is difficult to get respondents to expand on particular points. In markets where illiteracy is a problem, it may not be possible to get any response. In spite of these limitations, the convenience and economy of self-administered surveys makes them popular.

Telephone surveys—fast and effective

Telephone interviews are also popular. They are effective for getting quick answers to simple questions. Telephone interviews allow the interviewer to probe and really learn what the respondent is thinking. In addition, with computer-aided telephone interviewing, answers are immediately recorded on a computer, resulting in fast data analysis. On the other hand, many consumers find calls intrusive—and about a third refuse to answer any questions. Moreover, respondents can't be certain who is calling or how personal information might be used.

Personal interview surveys—can be in-depth

A personal interview survey is usually much more expensive per interview than e-mail, mail, or telephone surveys. But it's easier to get and keep the respondent's attention when the interviewer is right there. The interviewer can also help explain complicated directions and perhaps get better responses. For these reasons, personal interviews are commonly used for research on business customers. To reduce the cost of locating consumer respondents, interviews are sometimes done at a store or shopping mall. This is called a mall intercept interview because the interviewer stops a shopper and asks for responses to the survey.

Researchers have to be careful that having an interviewer involved doesn't affect the respondent's answers. Sometimes people won't give an answer they consider embarrassing. Or they may try to impress or please the interviewer. Further, in some cultures people don't want to give any information. For example, many people in Africa, Latin America, and Eastern Europe are reluctant to be interviewed. This is also a problem in many low-income, inner-city areas in the United States; even Census Bureau interviewers have trouble getting cooperation.[13]

Sometimes questioning has limitations. Then observing may be more accurate or economical.

Observing—what you see is what you get

Observing—as a method of collecting data—focuses on a well-defined problem. Here we are not talking about the casual observations that may stimulate ideas in the early steps of a research project. With the observation method, researchers try to see or record what the subject does naturally. They don't want the observing to *influence* the subject's behavior.

A museum director wanted to know which of the many exhibits was most popular. A survey didn't help. Visitors seemed to want to please the interviewer and usually said that all of the exhibits were interesting. Putting observers near exhibits—to record how long visitors spent at each one—didn't help either. The curious visitors stood around to see what the observer was recording, and that messed up the measures. Finally, the museum floors were waxed to a glossy shine. Several weeks later, the floors around the exhibits were inspected. It was easy to tell which exhibits were most popular—based on how much wax had worn off the floor!

In some situations, consumers are recorded on video. This may be in a store, at home, or out with friends. Later, researchers can study the tape by running the film at very slow speed or actually analyzing each frame. Researchers use this technique to study the routes consumers follow through a store or how they select products. A dog food manufacturer put video cameras on the pet food aisle in supermarkets to learn more about how people choose dog food and treats. The videos showed that kids often picked the treats, but that the kids' parents chose the food. The videos also revealed that kids couldn't reach treats when they were on higher shelves. Sales immediately increased when the treats were moved to lower shelves.[14]

Many franchise companies use the observation method to check how well a franchisee is performing. Krispy Kreme hires people to go to its stores and act like normal customers. Then these "secret shoppers" report back to Krispy Kreme on the quality of the food, how they were treated, and the cleanliness of the store. The report may include digital pictures or videos that are instantly sent over the Internet from a laptop computer.

Marketers sometimes can find ways to improve products by observing customers as they use them. For example, product developers at Microsoft watch customers try new software products so that they can change features that are confusing or hard to learn. This sort of usability testing is a good idea when changes are made to a website. In fact, firms that have online shopping sites often use software to "watch" how consumers use the website, how much time they spend at each display, and the like.[15]

Observing is common in advertising research

Observation methods are common in advertising research. For example, Nielsen Media Research (www.nielsenmedia.com) uses a device called the "people meter" that adapts the observation method to television audience research. This device is attached to the TV set in the homes of selected families. It records when the set is on and what station is tuned in. Similarly, Arbitron developed its Portable People Meter (PPM) to automatically measure radio listening habits.

Observing website visitors

Website analysis software allows marketing managers to observe customer behavior at a firm's website. For example, there are tools that help marketing managers understand how a customer came to a website—was it the keyword used in a Google search, a response to an e-mail promotion, or a link from an online review site? Reports show the series of clicks made by visitors and how long they stayed on each page. This information can help marketing managers make changes to the site so that it attracts the right customers and offers useful information so they stay and make purchases.

Online retailer Shipwreck Beads wanted to promote a summer sale of fire-polished beads, so it e-mailed 76,000 customers and placed banner ads on the websites for *BeadStyle* and *Bead and Button* magazines. Web analysis tools showed which promotions and which keywords generated the most leads. Because the answers were available very quickly, the firm revised the advertising copy to include more instances of the phrase "fire-polished beads." This simple change improved placement on search pages and, within a month, hits to its website increased fourfold.[16]

Checkout scanners see a lot

Computerized scanners at retail checkout counters help researchers collect very specific, and useful, information. Often this type of data feeds directly into a firm's MIS. Managers of a large chain of stores can see exactly what products have sold each day and how much money each department in each store has earned. But the scanner also has wider applications for marketing research.

Information Resources, Inc. (www.infores.com), and ACNielsen (www.acnielsen. com) use consumer panels—a group of consumers who provide information on a continuing basis. Whenever a panel member shops for groceries, he or she gives an ID card to the clerk, who scans the number. Then the scanner records every purchase—including

Edition

brands, sizes, prices, and any coupons used. In a variation of this approach, consumers use a handheld scanner to record purchases once they get home. Sometimes members of a panel answer questions and the answers are merged with the scanner data.

Analysis of panel data revealed that Ocean Spray was seeing sales slip to competitors. Households with kids are the heaviest purchasers of juice; yet they were purchasing

Ocean Spray on a less frequent basis. Further research with these panel members revealed this was due to its "too tart" taste and tendency to stain. To combat this, the company focused its energies on developing White Cranberry Juice Drinks by harvesting the berries before they develop their traditional red color and pungent taste. An ad for the new product depicted a mom and her small son enjoying the taste of the new White Cranberry juice. When the boy accidentally spills it on the floor, it's also clear that it doesn't stain. Now that the "no stain" message has sunk in, Ocean Spray's ads put more emphasis on the idea that kids love the taste.[17]

Data captured by electronic scanners is equally important to e-commerce in business-to-business markets. Increasingly, firms mark their shipping cartons and packages with computer-readable bar codes that make it fast and easy to track inventory, shipments, orders, and the like. As information about product sales or shipments becomes available, it is instantly included in the MIS and accessible over the Internet.[18]

Experimental method controls conditions

A marketing manager can get a different kind of information—with either questioning or observing—using the experimental method. With the **experimental method**, researchers compare the responses of two (or more) groups that are similar except on the characteristic being tested. Researchers want to learn if the specific characteristic—which varies among groups—*causes* differences in some response among the groups. For example, a researcher might be interested in comparing responses of consumers who had seen an ad for a new product with consumers who had not seen the ad. The "response" might be an observed behavior—like the purchase of a product—or the answer to a specific question—like "How interested are you in this new product?" See Exhibit 8-5.

Exhibit 8-5   Illustration of Experimental Method in Comparing Effectiveness of Two Ads

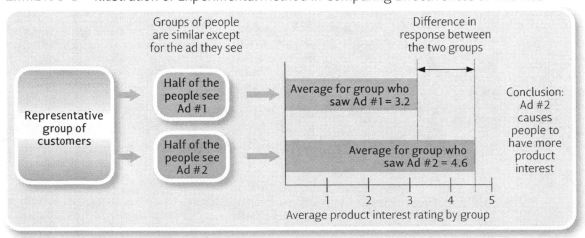

Low-Cost Research

When millions are at stake, Kraft General Foods doesn't blink at spending $100,000 or more for a single market research project. Managers in small companies can only dream of having the research budgets to do that. But, ironically, not having good information may pose an even greater risk for small companies. While a big firm with deeper pockets can survive a marketing misstep or two, a mistake in an important marketing strategy decision can put a small firm out of business.

With a little creativity a good marketing manager can generate a lot of information using relatively little cash. For example, if you were thinking about starting a soccer training academy for kids, you might start by asking a lot of questions. Ask your friends for ideas about what to do and where to advertise. Go out to local soccer fields and question parents. Are they interested? When would they want the training to be available? How much are they willing to pay? Talk to kids, too. What could make soccer camp more fun?

If a firm's target market is accessible via the Internet, online surveys can be an economical way for running ideas and questions past a larger group. Greenfield Online (www.greenfieldonline.com), for instance, recruits people to respond to the online surveys it hosts for clients. For about $6,000, Greenfield can get responses to a 12-question survey from a representative sample of 150 people—and do it within a week. Look for other, do-it-yourself approaches. For example, Waterpik offers new customers a $5 coupon to encourage them to fill out its online survey.

Managers at small companies can learn a lot by studying competitors' promotion material, monitoring their websites, and shopping in their stores. Get on competitors' e-mail lists and study their advertising, products, and pricing on a regular basis. Firms that compete in business markets can also check each other out at trade shows. And trade magazines have articles, ads, and even letters to the editor that can alert you to new developments.

Make everyone in your company a researcher. Let them know you want them to be aware of important information that they see and to share useful ideas that they hear from a customer, similar business in a different market, or the like. Above all, keep an eye on your current customers. Be sincere and regular about asking them, "Is there anything we can do better?" Be sure to listen when they answer. Set up internal monitoring systems that alert you to the loss of a customer—and then be conscientious about calling to find out what happened. What you learn may help you prevent another customer from defecting—and it may even get the old customer back.

Finally, don't be unnecessarily frugal. Marketing managers should remember the scientific method and be wary of shortcuts that can result in misleading information and bad decisions. For example, don't skip the step of pretesting a questionnaire; that may save some money or a few hours of work, but waste the total amount spent on a real study with a "bad" questionnaire. Samples should still represent the target market, and that includes focus groups. A focus group with a group of employees may be convenient, but it isn't the same as using real customers.[19]

Marketing managers for Mars—the company that makes Snickers candy bars—used the experimental method to help solve a problem. They wanted to know if making their candy bar bigger would increase sales enough to offset the higher cost. To decide, they conducted a marketing experiment in which the company carefully varied the size of candy bars sold in *different* markets. Otherwise, the marketing mix stayed the same. Then researchers tracked sales in each market area to see the effect of the different sizes. They saw a big difference immediately: The added sales more than offset the cost of a bigger candy bar.

Test-marketing of new products is another type of marketing experiment. In a typical approach, a company tries variations on its planned marketing mix in a few geographic market areas. The results of the tests help to identify problems or refine the marketing mix—before the decision is made to go to broader distribution. However,

Edition

alert competitors may disrupt such tests—perhaps by increasing promotion or offering retailers extra discounts.[20]

Syndicated research shares data collection costs

Some private research firms specialize in collecting data and then sell it to managers in many different client firms. Often the marketing manager subscribes to the research service and gets regular updates. About 40 percent of marketing research spending is for syndicated research, and this helps explain why it can be an economical approach when marketing managers from many different firms need the same type of data. For example, many different auto producers use J. D. Power's (www.jdpa.com) surveys of customer satisfaction—often as the basis for advertising claims. Subscription data services are available for many different industries—ranging from food services to prescription drugs to micro electronic devices.[21]

A combination of research methods may be needed

Using one research method to solve an initial problem may identify new questions that are best answered with different research methods. Consider WD-40, a popular all-purpose lubricant sold in a blue-and-yellow spray can. To find potential new uses of WD-40, researchers visited mechanics and watched them as they worked. These observers realized that even small cans of WD-40 were difficult for mechanics to handle in tight spaces. In addition, the spray created drips and messes because it was difficult to control the amount being applied.

To address these problems, the new-product team developed a prototype for the No Mess Pen, a small marker that delivers a precise amount of the lubricant. Then, researchers held focus groups to get reactions from mechanics. They weren't encouraging. Mechanics didn't think that the small unit would handle their large application needs. Yet, many thought their spouses might like the pen for small household lubrication jobs. To follow up on this idea, WD-40 conducted online surveys. More than two-thirds of the women respondents said they would buy the product. To fine-tune targeting and promotion, WD-40 then conducted more than 40 in-home studies to learn how families actually used the No Mess Pen. This research confirmed that women were the primary target market, but that men used the pens as well. Moreover, the pen didn't replace the can of WD-40 already found in most households; rather, pens were stored in desk drawers, cars, and toolboxes so they'd be handy. WD-40 used different research methods to address different problems, but in combination they contributed to making the No Mess Pen a great success.[22]

Understand the costs and benefits of research

Whether collecting secondary data for a situation analysis or primary data from a focus group or survey, marketing research takes time and money. A good marketing manager knows that the value of additional information lies in the ability to design more effective marketing strategies. Similarly, different research methods provide different insights—and come at different costs. There are also benefits to getting information quickly—particularly in some markets. Small companies with limited budgets often must be creative in identifying low-cost ways to get the information they need.

INTERPRETING THE DATA—STEP 4

What does it really mean?

After someone collects the data, it has to be analyzed to decide what it all means. In quantitative research, this step usually involves statistics. Statistical packages—easy-to-use computer programs that analyze data—have made this step easier. As we noted earlier, some firms provide *decision support systems* so managers can use a statistical package to interpret data themselves. More often, however, technical specialists are involved at the interpretation step.

Cross-tabulation is one of the most frequently used approaches for analyzing and interpreting marketing research data. It shows the relationship of answers to two

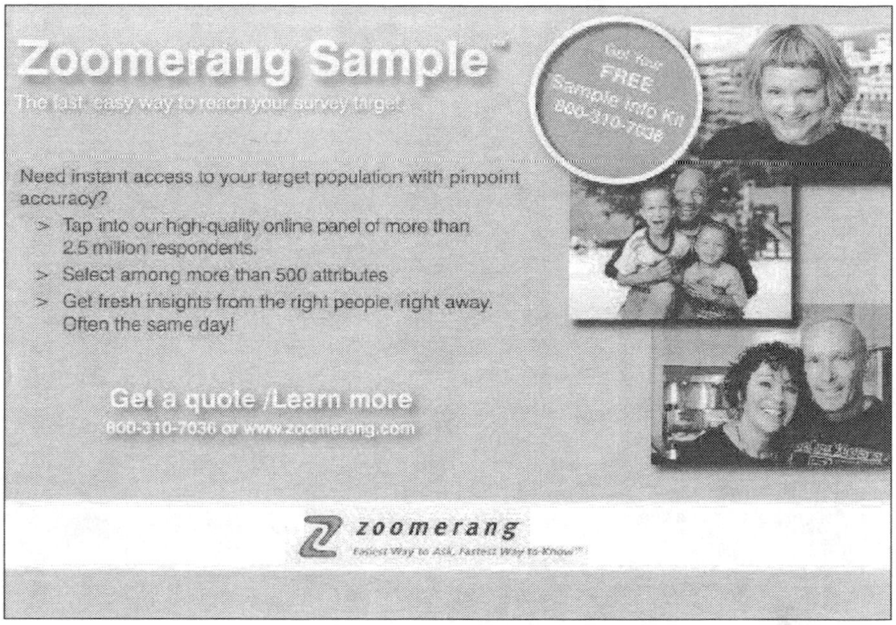

Zoomerang makes it fast and easy for a researcher to create an online questionnaire and to recruit respondents from its online panel of 2.5 million people.

different questions. Exhibit 8-6 is an example. The cross-tab analysis shows that households with higher incomes are much more likely to have broadband Internet service.

There are many other approaches for statistical analysis—the best one depends on the situation. The details of statistical analysis are beyond the scope of this book. But a good manager should know enough to understand what a research project can and can't do.[23]

Is your sample really representative?

It's usually impossible for marketing managers to collect all the information they want about everyone in a population—the total group they are interested in. Marketing researchers typically study only a sample, a part of the relevant population. How well a sample *represents* the total population affects the results. Results from a sample that is not representative may not give a true picture.

The manager of a retail store might want a phone survey to learn what consumers think about the store's hours. If interviewers make all of the calls during the day, consumers who work outside the home during the day won't be represented. Those interviewed might say the limited store hours are "satisfactory." Yet it would be a mistake to assume that *all* consumers are satisfied.

Exhibit 8-6   Cross-Tabulation Breakdown of Responses to an Internet Service Provider Consumer Survey

		What is your household income?				
		Less than $30,000	$30,000 to 50,000	$50,000 to $75,000	More than $75,000	Total Sample
Does your home have broadband Internet service?	Yes	23.7%	46.2%	52.3%	72.4%	47.1%
	No	76.3	53.8	47.7	27.6	52.9
	Total	100.0%	100.0%	100.0%	100.0%	100.0%

Interpretation: In the survey 47.1 percent of people said that they had broadband Internet service in their homes. However, the adoption of broadband Internet service was higher at higher income levels. For example, 72.4 percent of households with over $75,000 income have broadband but only 23.7 percent have it among homes with income less than $30,000.

Edition

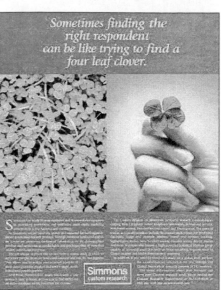

Survey Sampling Inc., and Simmons Custom Research help marketing researchers develop samples that are really representative of the target market.

Research results are not exact

An estimate from a sample, even a representative one, usually varies somewhat from the true value for a total population. Managers sometimes forget this. They assume that survey results are exact. Instead, when interpreting sample estimates, managers should think of them as *suggesting* the approximate value.

If random selection is used to develop the sample, researchers can use various methods to help determine the likely accuracy of the sample value. This is done in terms of confidence intervals—the range on either side of an estimate that is likely to contain the true value for the whole population. Some managers are surprised to learn how wide that range can be.

Consider a wholesaler who has 2,000 retail customers and wants to learn how many of these retailers carry a product from a competing supplier. If the wholesaler randomly samples 100 retailers and 20 say yes, then the sample estimate is 20 percent. But with that information the wholesaler can only be 95 percent confident that the percentage of all retailers is in the confidence interval between 12 and 28 percent. The larger the sample size, the greater the accuracy of estimates from a random sample. With a larger sample, a few unusual responses are less likely to make a big difference.[24]

Validity problems can destroy research

Even if the sampling is carefully planned, it is also important to evaluate the quality of the research data itself.

Managers and researchers should be sure that research data really measures what it is supposed to measure. Many of the variables marketing managers are interested in are difficult to measure accurately. Questionnaires may let us assign numbers to consumer responses, but that still doesn't mean that the result is precise. An interviewer might ask, "How much did you spend on soft drinks last week?" A respondent may be perfectly willing to cooperate—and be part of the representative sample—but just not be able to remember.

Validity concerns the extent to which data measures what it is intended to measure. Validity problems are important in marketing research because many people will try to answer even when they don't know what they're talking about. Further, a poorly worded question can mean different things to different people and invalidate the results. Often, pretests of a research project are required to evaluate the quality of the questions and measures and to ensure that potential problems have been identified.

CHAPTER 8

223

Improving Decisions with Marketing Information

Poor interpretation can destroy research

Besides sampling and validity problems, a marketing manager must consider whether the analysis of the data supports the *conclusions* drawn in the interpretation step. Sometimes technical specialists pick the right statistical procedure—their calculations are exact—but they misinterpret the data because they don't understand the management problem. In one survey, car buyers were asked to rank five cars in order from "most preferred" to "least preferred." One car was ranked first by slightly more respondents than any other car, so the researcher reported it as the "most liked car." That interpretation, however, ignored the fact that 70 percent of the respondents ranked the car *last!*

Interpretation problems like this can be subtle but crucial. Some people draw misleading conclusions on purpose to get the results they want. Marketing managers must decide whether *all* of the results support the interpretation and are relevant to their problem.

Marketing manager and researcher should work together

Marketing research involves many technical details. But the marketing researcher and the marketing manager must work together to be sure that they really do solve the problem facing the firm. If the whole research process has been a joint effort, then the interpretation step can move quickly to solving the problem.

Ethics involved in interpreting and presenting results

Marketing managers want information they can trust when they make marketing decisions. But research often involves many hidden details. A person who wants to misuse research to pursue a personal agenda can often do so.

Perhaps the most common ethical issues concern decisions to withhold certain information about the research. For example, a manager might selectively share only those results that support his or her viewpoint. Others involved in a decision might never know that they are getting only partial truths. [25]

> **Ethics QUESTION**
>
> You're the new marketing manager for a small firm that offers computer repair services. The company's owner approves your proposal for a telephone survey to learn more about the needs of firms that are not current customers. You identify local firms for the sample and hire a researcher to call them. The interviewer tells respondents that their answers will be anonymous and used only for research purposes. About halfway through the data collection, the interviewer tells you that respondents are confused by one of the questions and that their answers to that question are probably useless. The question concerns the issue that is most important to your new boss. Do you admit the problem to others in your company? If the sales manager asks for the completed questionnaires, including all the names and responses, what would you say?

SOLVING THE PROBLEM—STEP 5

The last step is solving the problem

In the problem solution step, managers use the research results to make marketing decisions.

Some researchers, and some managers, are fascinated by the interesting tidbits of information that come from the research process. They are excited if the research reveals something they didn't know before. But if research doesn't have action implications, it has little value and suggests poor planning by the researcher and the manager.

When the research process is finished, the marketing manager should be able to apply the findings in marketing strategy planning—the choice of a target market or the mix of the four Ps. If the research doesn't provide information to help guide these decisions, the company has wasted research time and money.

We emphasize this step because it is the reason for and logical conclusion to the whole research process. This final step must be anticipated at each of the earlier steps.

Edition

INTERNATIONAL MARKETING RESEARCH

Research contributes to international success

Marketing research on overseas markets is often a major contributor toward international marketing success. Conversely, export failures are often due to a lack of home office expertise concerning customer interests, needs, and other segmenting dimensions as well as environmental factors such as competitors' prices and products. Effective marketing research can help to overcome these problems.

Accurate data may be hard to find

In many countries, it is difficult—especially for a foreigner—to gather accurate information. Let's look at the challenge in China. Because the economy is growing so rapidly, secondary data that is out of date may be much more inaccurate than would be the case in a country with slow growth. Some important secondary data (such as the *China Statistical Yearbook*) is now available in an English language version, but that is often not the case. There are other problems, such as no explanation of the methods used to collect the data. That's important because the Chinese market is both large and complicated. Imagine how you would try to do a competitor analysis when there are over 1,000 Chinese firms that brew beer! Collecting primary data is difficult too. Western researchers feel that Chinese managers and consumers are not very receptive to direct questioning. Those who agree to cooperate may be hesitant to say anything negative about their own companies or anything favorable about competitors. So, it takes experienced interviewers to carefully interpret responses.[26]

Avoid mistakes with local researchers

Whether a firm is small and entering overseas markets for the first time or already large and well established internationally, there are often advantages to working with local marketing research firms. They know the local situation and are less likely to make mistakes based on misunderstanding the customs, language, or circumstances of the customers they study.

Nestlé's success with its Kit Kat candy bar in Japan is a good example. Nestlé partnered with a Tokyo-based ad agency and a marketing research firm that specializes in customer management relationship to design a new CRM center. When Nestlé marketers turned greater attention to analyzing calls to the customer hotline at the center, they learned that most calls were not complaints—but rather inquiries about

There are a large number of international marketing research firms that offer specialized services to marketing managers.

products. For example, analysis of the calls revealed that many were from teens asking about the Kit Kat name because it sounds like "kitto katsu," a Japanese phrase for "sure winner." Follow-up research suggested an opportunity to build Kit Kat's image as a sort of "lucky charm," through a sampling program targeted at Japanese youth when they go to college campuses to take entrance exams. As a result, Kit Kat has become very popular in Japan and sales have increased, but the opportunity would have been missed were it not for help from researchers who knew the local market.[27]

Many large research firms have a network of local offices around the world to help with such efforts. Similarly, multinational or local advertising agencies and intermediaries can often provide leads on identifying the best research suppliers.

Some coordination and standardization makes sense

When a firm is doing similar research projects in different markets around the world, it makes sense for the marketing manager to coordinate the efforts. If the manager doesn't establish some basic guidelines at the outset, the different research projects may all vary so much that the results can't be compared from one market area to another. Such comparisons give a home office manager a better chance of understanding how the markets are similar and how they differ.

Companies with operations in various countries often attempt to centralize some market research functions. One reason is to reduce costs or achieve research economies of scale. The centralized approach also improves the firm's ability to transfer experience and know-how from one market area or project to another. For example, one of Eastman Kodak's International Divisions appointed a market research specialist in each subsidiary company throughout the Asian region. The specialists report to local marketing managers but also receive research direction from expert research managers in the head office in the United States.

There is even greater opportunity and need to standardize and coordinate elements of a marketing information system in an international marketing operation. Computer databases and information systems are most useful when they are designed to include the same variables organized consistently over time. Without this, it is impossible for the manager to go into much depth in comparing and contrasting data from different markets.[28]

CONCLUSION

Marketing managers face difficult decisions in selecting target markets and managing marketing mixes, but they rarely have all the information they would like to have before making those decisions. Even less information may be available in international markets. This doesn't mean that managers have to rely solely on intuition; they can usually obtain some good information that will improve the quality of their decisions. Both large and small firms can take advantage of Internet and intranet capabilities to develop marketing information systems (MIS) that help to ensure routinely needed data is available and quickly accessible.

Some questions can only be answered with marketing research. Marketing research should be guided by the scientific method. This approach to solving marketing problems involves five steps: (1) defining the problem, (2) analyzing the situation, (3) obtaining data, (4) interpreting data, and (5) developing and implementing a solution. This objective and organized approach helps to keep problem solving on task. It reduces the risk of doing costly and unnecessary research that doesn't achieve the desired end—solving the marketing problem.

Our strategy planning framework can be very helpful in evaluating marketing research. By finding and focusing on real problems, researchers and marketing managers may be able to move more quickly to a useful solution during the situation analysis stage—without the costs and risks of gathering primary data. With imagination, they may even be able to find answers in their MIS or in readily available secondary data. However, primary data from questioning, observing, or conducting experiments may be needed. Qualitative data often provides initial insights or hypotheses—which might be tested with more representative samples and quantitative approaches.

Edition

KEY TERMS

QUESTIONS AND PROBLEMS

1. Discuss the concept of a marketing information system and why it is important for marketing managers to be involved in planning the system.

2. In your own words, explain why a decision support system (DSS) can add to the value of a marketing information system. Give an example of how a decision support system might help.

3. If a firm's intranet and marketing decision support system do not include a search engine, would they still be useful to a marketing manager? Why?

4. Discuss how output from a marketing information system (MIS) might differ from the output of a typical marketing research department.

5. Discuss some of the likely problems facing the marketing manager in a small firm who plans to search the Internet for information on competitors' marketing plans.

6. Explain the key characteristics of the scientific method and show why these are important to managers concerned with research.

7. How is the situation analysis different from the data collection step? Can both these steps be done at the same time to obtain answers sooner? Is this wise?

8. Distinguish between primary data and secondary data and illustrate your answer.

9. With so much secondary information now available free or at low cost over the Internet, why would a firm ever want to spend the money to do primary research?

10. If a firm were interested in estimating the distribution of income in the state of California, how could it proceed? Be specific.

11. If a firm were interested in estimating sand and clay production in Georgia, how could it proceed? Be specific.

12. Go to the library (or get on the Internet) and find (in some government publication or website) three marketing-oriented "facts" on international markets that you did not know existed or were available. Record on one page and show sources.

13. Explain why a company might want to do focus group interviews rather than individual interviews with the same people.

14. Distinguish between qualitative and quantitative approaches to research—and give some of the key advantages and limitations of each approach.

15. Define response rate and discuss why a marketing manager might be concerned about the response rate achieved in a particular survey. Give an example.

16. Prepare a table that summarizes some of the key advantages and limitations of mail, e-mail, telephone, and personal interview approaches for administering questionnaires.

17. Would a firm want to subscribe to a shared cost data service if the same data were going to be available to competitors? Discuss your reasoning.

18. Explain how you might use different types of research (focus groups, observation, survey, and experiment) to forecast market reaction to a new kind of disposable baby diaper, which is to receive no promotion other than what the retailer will give it. Further, assume that the new diaper's name will not be associated with other known products. The product will be offered at competitive prices.

19. Marketing research involves expense—sometimes considerable expense. Why does the text recommend the use of marketing research even though a highly experienced marketing executive is available?

20. A marketing manager is considering opportunities to export her firm's current consumer products to several different countries. She is interested in getting secondary data that will help her narrow down choices to countries that offer the best potential. The manager then plans to do more detailed primary research with consumers in those markets. What suggestions would you give her about how to proceed?

21. Discuss the concept that some information may be too expensive to obtain in relation to its value. Illustrate.

CREATING MARKETING PLANS

The Marketing Plan Coach software on the Student CD and the text website includes a sample marketing plan for Hillside Veterinary Clinic. Look through the "Customers" and "Competitors" sections in the Situation Analysis and consider the following questions.

a.   What different types of marketing research were conducted to fill out these sections of the marketing plan?

b.   What are the strengths of the research conducted? What are the weaknesses?

c.   Keeping in mind probable cost and time to complete, what additional research would you recommend?

SUGGESTED CASES   3. MANU Soccer Academy   8. Lombardi's Italian Grill   9. Sweetest Dreams Inn

COMPUTER-AIDED PROBLEM

8. MARKETING RESEARCH

Texmac, Inc., has an idea for a new type of weaving machine that could replace the machines now used by many textile manufacturers. Texmac has done a telephone survey to estimate how many of the old-style machines are now in use. Respondents using the present machines were also asked if they would buy the improved machine at a price of $10,000.

Texmac researchers identified a population of about 5,000 textile factories as potential customers. A sample of these were surveyed, and Texmac received 500 responses. Researchers think the total potential market is about 10 times larger than the sample of respondents. Two hundred twenty of the respondents indicated that their firms used old machines like the one the new machine was intended to replace. Forty percent of those firms said that they would be interested in buying the new Texmac machine.

Texmac thinks the sample respondents are representative of the total population, but the marketing manager realizes that estimates based on a sample may not be exact when applied to the whole population. He wants to see how sampling error would affect profit estimates. Data for this problem appears in the spreadsheet. Quantity estimates for the whole market are computed from the sample estimates. These quantity estimates are used in computing likely sales, costs, and profit contribution.

a.   An article in a trade magazine reports that there are about 5,200 textile factories that use the old-style machine. If the total market is really 5,200 customers—not 5,000 as Texmac originally thought—how does that affect the total quantity estimate and profit contribution?

b.   Some of the people who responded to the survey didn't know much about different types of machines. If the actual number of old machines in the market is really 200 per 500 firms—not 220 as estimated from survey responses—how much would this affect the expected profit contribution (for 5,200 factories)?

c.   The marketing manager knows that the percentage of textile factories that would actually buy the new machine might be different from the 40 percent who said they would in the survey. He estimates that the proportion that will replace the old machine might be as low as 36 and as high as 44 percent—depending on business conditions. Use the analysis feature to prepare a table that shows how expected quantity and profit contribution change when the sample percent varies between a minimum of 36 and a maximum of 44 percent. What does this analysis suggest about the use of estimates from marketing research samples? (*Note:* Use 5,200 for the number of potential customers and use 220 as the estimate of the number of old machines in the sample.)

For additional questions related to this problem, see Exercise 8-3 in the *Learning Aid for Use with Basic Marketing*, 17th edition.

9

CHAPTER

Elements of Product Planning for Goods and Services

The founders of iRobot didn't know that their company would become the world leader in home robots. However, from the start they didn't intend to just imitate other firms' products. Instead they wanted to create totally new product concepts that would change society. That is where they're headed, with products like Packbot and ConnectR. The Packbot is a business and military product. This nimble but rugged computer-controlled equipment shoots audio and video in places that are too dangerous for humans. It helps soldiers clear roadside bombs in Iraq and searches caves in Afghanistan. It can even work underwater or climb stairs in a factory.

The just-released ConnectR is also a mobile videocam of sorts, but it's a consumer product with a $500 price—about 1 percent of what a Packbot costs. iRobot calls the ConnectR a "virtual visiting robot" that is a fun way to "stay close to those you love no matter where you are." A parent who is on a business trip can use the Internet and "drive" the wireless ConnectR around the house, see what the dog is doing, read the kids a bedtime story, and even check what the baby sitter is watching on TV.

The ConnectR looks like and moves around like the Roomba, the robotic vacuum cleaner that iRobot introduced in 2002. Roomba grew quickly and now is a well-known brand with more than 2 million units sold. Roomba's design seems perfect for its target market—the large group of people who hate to vacuum. It's a slick-looking, 15-inch disk and is less than 4 inches tall—not the odd-shaped clunker that our grandparents owned. It's a robot but it requires no programming. You simply place it on the floor, press a button to turn it on, and Roomba automatically wanders around the room doing its job. It can scoot under the sofa, scurry around the furniture, and return to the battery charger when the job is done.

Design engineers are undoubtedly impressed with Roomba's features. It has counterrotating brushes, a technology to prevent rugs from tangling, an algorithm for gently bouncing off furniture without leaving marks, and an infrared system for signals from a "virtual wall" that keep it where it's supposed to be.

However, what has made the Roomba a success is that the new-product developers—including some brilliant scientists—knew they needed to look at the Roomba from the customer's perspective. And most customers didn't care about all the technical details. In fact, consumers worried that it might be too complicated for them to use. Instead, they wanted it to be simple but do a superior job cleaning floors without a lot of hassle.

To keep focused on these consumer concerns, the executive in charge of new-product development added people to the team who had experience in developing toys. These people understood the idea of keeping it simple and helped keep everyone on track. For example, at one point when design engineers were talking abut how best to train customers to use

229

the Roomba, the team realized that was backwards. Instead of training customers, they decided to change all of Roomba's software so that it figured out what to do when the customer pushed the start button. The owner's manual is available in many languages, but because the Roomba is simple to use it is only a few pages long and most people won't need it.

The original idea was for Roomba to just have sweeper brushes. However, in focus groups consumers said that the Roomba also needed a vacuum. Responding to this consumer input added extra expense late in the project, but iRobot was ready because it had already learned valuable lessons from working with Hasbro to develop new robotic toys. In spite of some clever ideas for toys, the projects with Hasbro were disappointing because iRobot had not paid enough attention to cost control—which is essential with consumer products. With Roomba, they had controlled every penny from the outset, and so they were able to add the vacuum and value that consumers wanted. Business customers like NASA had not been so price sensitive when they asked iRobot for a custom product.

To offset consumer concerns, the introductory promotion described the Roomba as an intelligent vacuum cleaner, not a robot. For the first three years, the word robot didn't even appear on the package

(except in the iRobot company name). iRobot planners didn't want consumers to worry about Roomba's reliability. So, the Roomba went through a number of prototypes and thousands of hours of quality testing before it was commercialized. The Roomba was even subjected to drop tests to make sure it would hold up if it were mishandled. Further, to assure consumers that such quality is built in, Roomba was given a limited one-year parts-and-labor warranty.

By controlling costs, iRobot was able to offer Roomba at $200. A higher price might have been acceptable to some customers, but that low price helped fend off potential competitors, including Electrolux. It had hopes for its own $1,500 robotic vacuum.

Roomba was launched in time for Christmas season shopping through Sharper Image, Hammacher Schlemmer, and Brookstone. These retailers appeal to upscale gift buyers and were willing to train their salespeople to actively promote Roomba at their stores. The extra promotion push was important because initially customers didn't know the brand name and were not looking for this sort of product. However, iRobot was able to quickly generate publicity for the Roomba—with everything from appearances on the "Today" show and videos on mySpace. com to reviews in magazines, newspapers, and CNET. com. All of this media attention—and some traditional ads—propelled sales and quickly made Roomba a familiar brand. After production caught up with demand, iRobot expanded distribution to include Bed Bath and Beyond and Linens 'n' Things. By spring Target was also carrying Roomba—and the phone was ringing off the wall with calls from other retailers who wanted to carry iRobot's hot new brand.

The next-generation Scooba robot, introduced in 2005, washes sealed hardwood and tile floors and appeals to the same market. When it came out, many people who already loved their Roombas were willing to search far and wide to find a Scooba. In addition, both repeat and new customers are buying the improved models of Roomba as well as other new additions to iRobot's consumer product line. This lineup has expanded quickly to include products that sweep workshops (Dirt Dog), clean pools (Verro), and clear out roofing gutters (Looj).

iRobot's creative product development, along with the strategies that it developed to reach its target markets, resulted in remarkable growth—with sales increasing from $54 million in 2003 to $249 million in 2007. Keeping that growth going will be tough as more competitors enter the market. However, iRobot has shown that it has the technical skills to create innovative and reliable new products while being guided by the voices of its customers. iRobot may encounter some more bumps along the way—few firms can completely avoid problems with new products. Even so, iRobot is likely to enjoy more success as the product-market it has pioneered experiences rapid growth in the next decade.[1]

LEARNING OBJECTIVES

Developing a marketing mix that provides superior customer value for target customers is ultimately the focus of the marketing strategy planning process. To develop a successful marketing mix requires that each of the four Ps is carefully planned and works well with all the others. Many important strategy decisions are required. This chapter focuses on key ideas related to strategy planning for Product.

When you finish this chapter you should be able to:

1 understand what "Product" really means.

2 know the key differences between goods and services.

3 understand what branding is and how to use it in strategy planning.

4 understand the importance of packaging in strategy planning.

5 understand the role of warranties in strategy planning.

6 know the differences among various consumer and business product classes.

7 understand how product classes can help a marketing manager plan marketing strategies.

8 understand important new terms (shown in red).

THE PRODUCT AREA INVOLVES MANY STRATEGY DECISIONS

The iRobot case highlights some of the important topics and strategy decision areas that we'll discuss in this chapter and Chapter 10. As shown in Exhibit 9-1, there are many strategy decisions in the Product area. They're the focus of this chapter. Then, in Chapter 10, we'll take a "how to" look at developing new products and also explain how strategy usually changes as products move through their life in the market.

We'll start here by looking at Product through the eyes of the customer. This focuses attention on the total benefits provided by the Product—regardless of whether it is a physical good, a service, or both. Then we'll review strategy decisions for three important Product areas: branding, packaging, and warranties. We'll conclude by considering product classes, which are based on how customers think about and shop for products. They help show how strategy decisions for Product relate to decisions for Place, Promotion, and Price.

Exhibit 9-1   Product Decisions for Marketing Strategy Planning

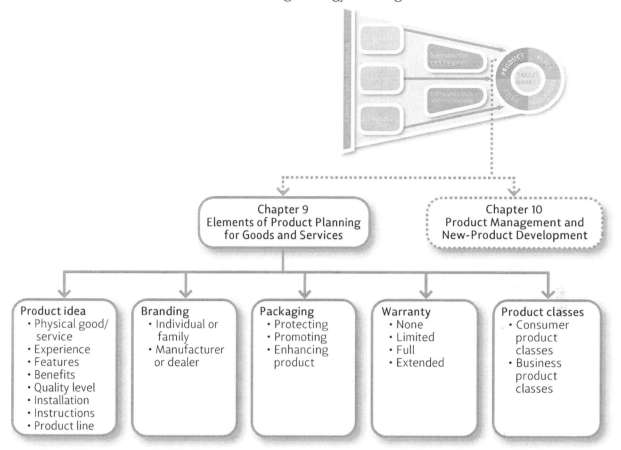

Chapter 9	Chapter 10
Elements of Product Planning for Goods and Services	Product Management and New-Product Development

Product idea
- Physical good/ service
- Experience
- Features
- Benefits
- Quality level
- Installation
- Instructions
- Product line

Branding
- Individual or family
- Manufacturer or dealer

Packaging
- Protecting
- Promoting
- Enhancing product

Warranty
- None
- Limited
- Full
- Extended

Product classes
- Consumer product classes
- Business product classes

WHAT IS A PRODUCT?

Customers buy satisfaction, not parts

When Kodak sells an EasyShare digital camera, is it just selling a certain number of switches and buttons, a plastic case, a lens, and megapixels of memory?

When Air Jamaica sells a ticket for a flight to the Caribbean, is it just selling so much wear and tear on an airplane and so much pilot fatigue?

The answer to these questions is *no*. Instead, what these companies are really selling is the satisfaction, use, or benefit the customer wants.

Consumers care that their EasyShare camera makes it easy to take great pictures *and* share them. They care that with the EasyShare's software they can organize or e-mail their photos, or send them to the EasyShare website when they want prints. Retailers who sell cameras add their own needs. They would like for customers to come into the store asking for the camera by name—so that it's easy to sell. And they want an attractive package that calls attention to all of these benefits.

Similarly, Air Jamaica's customers want a safe, comfortable flight—but they also want quick and accurate reservations, smooth check-in at the airport, and luggage that arrives undamaged and on time. In other words, marketing managers deliver the highest level of satisfaction when the customer's *entire experience* with the product meets the customer's needs.

Product means the need-satisfying offering of a firm. The idea of "Product" as potential customer satisfaction or benefits is very important. Many business managers

Edition

Product means the need-satisfying offering of a firm. Many firms promote the features of a product, but it's usually better to focus on the needs those features satisfy. For example, this ad for the MotoRokr Z6 highlights a woman bursting free from a tangle of wires—because the unit downloads music wirelessly.

get wrapped up in the technical details involved in producing a product. But most customers think about a product in terms of the total satisfaction it provides. That satisfaction may require a "total" product offering that is really a combination of excellent service, a physical good with the right features, useful instructions, a convenient package, a trustworthy warranty, and perhaps even a familiar name that has satisfied the consumer in the past.

Product quality and customer needs

Product quality should also be determined by how customers view the product. From a marketing perspective, quality means a product's ability to satisfy a customer's needs or requirements. This definition focuses on the customer—and how the customer thinks a product will fit some purpose. For example, the "best" satellite TV service may not be the one with the highest number of channels but the one that includes a local channel that a consumer wants to watch. Similarly, the best-quality clothing for casual wear on campus may be a pair of jeans, not a pair of dress slacks made of a higher-grade fabric.

Among different types of jeans, the one with the most durable fabric might be thought of as having the highest grade or *relative quality* for its product type. Marketing managers often focus on relative quality when comparing their products to competitors' offerings. However, a product with better features is not a higher-quality product if the features aren't what the target market wants.

In Chapter 10, we'll look at ways to manage product quality. For now, however, it is important to see that quality and satisfaction depend on the total product offering. If potato chips get stale on the shelf because of poor packaging, the consumer will be dissatisfied. A broken button on a shirt will disappoint the customer—even if the laundry did a nice job cleaning and pressing the collar.[2]

Ethics QUESTION

Your construction firm was the low price bidder on a plan to build three new runways at an airport. After winning the contract, you assured the airport commissioner that your work would far exceed the minimum quality specs in the contract. However, a test of the batch of concrete for the second runway shows that it's not as strong as the concrete you've been using. It does exceed the specs in the contract, but barely. Throwing the concrete away would eat up most of the profit expected from the job and also delay the airport in using the runway. There are various options. You could proceed with the project and be quiet about it, or perhaps call the commissioner and ask for quick approval. Alternatively, you could proceed but later admit what happened. With or without approval, you could offer a special warranty. Explain what you would do. What, if anything, would you say to your employees about your decision?[3]

Exhibit 9-2   Examples of Possible Blends of Physical Goods and Services in a Product

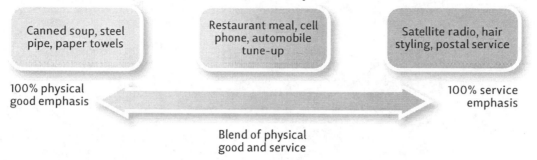

Goods and/or services are the product

A product may be a physical *good* or a *service*, or a *blend of both.* Exhibit 9-2 shows that a product can range from a 100 percent emphasis on a physical good—for a commodity like steel pipe—to a 100 percent emphasis on service—for a product like satellite radio from Sirius. Many products include a combination of goods and services. When you eat out, you are buying food (a physical good) that is prepared and served by a restaurant's staff (a service).

When competitors focus only on physical goods, a firm can sometimes differentiate its offering by blending in a service that the target market values. Many companies make high-quality HDTVs, but Panasonic's research revealed that many consumers worry about how to set up a new unit. So Panasonic added Plasma Concierge service to support its HDTV customers with well-trained advisors and priority in-home service. This idea also works when the emphasis is on services. Luxury hotels compete to take care of their guests with excellent service, but sometimes differentiate by also offering the softest linens or an extra-comfy bed.

Regardless of the blend of goods and services involved, the marketing manager must consider most of the same elements in planning products and marketing mixes. Given this, we usually won't make a distinction between goods and services but will call all of them *Products.* However, understanding key differences in goods and services can help fine-tune marketing strategy planning. So, let's look at some of these differences next.

DIFFERENCES IN GOODS AND SERVICES

How tangible is the product?

Because a good is a physical thing, it can be seen and touched. You can try on a pair of Timberland shoes, smell Starbucks beans as they roast, and page through the latest issue of *People* magazine. A good is a *tangible* item. It's usually easy to know exactly what you will get before you decide to buy it. And once you've bought it, you own it.

In contrast, services are not physical—they are *intangible.* When you provide a customer with a service, the customer can't keep it. Rather, a service is experienced, used, or consumed. You go to a DreamWorks Pictures movie, but afterward all you have is a memory. You can buy a pass to ski at Vail and enjoy the experience, but you don't own the ski lift. Sometimes it's a challenge that customers can't see, feel, or smell a service before they buy it. For example, a person who wants advice from an accountant doesn't know in advance how good the advice will be.

To reduce this uncertainty, service customers often seek referrals from friends or advice from online reviews. They may also look for cues to help them judge the quality of a service before they buy. That's why some service providers emphasize physical evidence of quality. A lawyer is likely to have diplomas on the wall, shelves loaded with books, and furnishings that suggest success.

Edition

Where the product is produced

Goods are typically mass-produced in a factory far away from the customer. A service is usually produced in person—where the customer is located—*after* the customer has committed to buy. It is often difficult to achieve economies of scale with personal services. One reason is that service suppliers often need duplicate equipment and staff at places where the service is actually provided. Merrill Lynch sells investment advice along with financial products worldwide. That advice could, perhaps, be produced more economically in a single building in New York City and made available only on its website. But Merrill Lynch has offices all over the world because many customers want a personal touch from their stockbroker.

Quality consistency

A worker in a factory that makes Whirlpool appliances can be in a bad mood and customers will never know. Even if there are production problems, quality controls are likely to catch defective goods before they leave the factory. Service quality often isn't that consistent; one reason is that it's hard to separate the service experience from the person who provides it. A rude teller in a bank can drive customers away. Service providers also vary in their ability, and problems with the service they deliver are usually obvious to customers. In addition, when many people must all work well together—as in a hospital or on a cruise ship—it's even more of a challenge to deliver consistent service quality.

Satisfaction of customers and whether they recommend a service to their friends is often influenced by interactions with the service firm's employees. Marketing managers in service firms must pay special attention that the right kinds of people are hired and that they receive training that matches the marketing objectives.

Services cannot be stored

Services are perishable. They can't be produced and then stored to sell at some future time when more customers want to buy. This makes it difficult to balance supply and demand, especially if demand varies a lot. At Thanksgiving, Southwest Airlines has to turn away customers because most of its flights are fully booked; other airlines may get that business. Perhaps Southwest could buy more planes and hire more pilots, but most of the time that would result in costly excess capacity—planes flying with empty seats. The revenue that could have come from any empty seats is lost forever.

Because of problems like this, airlines, doctors, hotels, and other service firms sometimes charge fees to clients who don't show up when they say they will. Service organizations also use a variety of approaches to shift customer demand to less busy times. Movie

A consumer can't hold a service and look at it before purchasing, so service firms often use messages and images in their promotion that help make the benefits of the service experience more vivid.

The Tostitos product line includes several types of chips as well as dips. The HON Company offers a full-line of office furniture, including chairs, storage, panel systems, tables, and desks.

tickets are cheaper for afternoon shows, restaurants offer early-bird specials, and hotels that cater to business travelers promote weekend getaways. Firms also try to reduce the dissatisfaction that customers may feel if they must wait for service. Golf courses provide practice greens, and some doctors' offices provide comfortable seating and magazines.[4]

WHOLE PRODUCT LINES MUST BE DEVELOPED TOO

A product assortment is the set of all product lines and individual products that a firm sells. A product line is a set of individual products that are closely related. The seller may see the products in a line as related because they're produced or operate in a similar way, sold to the same target market, sold through the same types of outlets, or priced at about the same level. Sara Lee, for example, has many product lines in its product assortment—including beverages, luncheon meats, desserts, insecticides, body care, air care, and shoe care. But Enterprise has one product line—different types of vehicles to rent. An individual product is a particular product within a product line. It usually is differentiated by brand, level of service offered, price, or some other characteristic. For example, each size and flavor of a brand of soap is an individual product. Intermediaries usually think of each separate product as a stock-keeping unit (SKU) and assign it a unique SKU number.

Each individual product and target market may require a separate strategy. For example, Sara Lee's strategy for selling its Café Pilão coffee in Brazil is different from its strategy for selling Endust cleaning spray in the United States. We'll focus mainly on developing one marketing strategy at a time. But remember that a marketing manager may have to plan *several* strategies to develop an effective marketing program for a whole company.

BRANDING IS A STRATEGY DECISION

There are so many brands—and we're so used to seeing them—that we take them for granted. But branding is an important decision area, so we will treat it in some detail.

What is branding?

Branding means the use of a name, term, symbol, or design—or a combination of these—to identify a product. It includes the use of brand names, trademarks, and practically all other means of product identification.

Edition

Exhibit 9-3   Recognized Trademarks and Symbols Help in Promotion

Brand name has a narrower meaning. A brand name is a word, letter, or a group of words or letters. Examples include America Online (AOL), WD-40, 3M Post-its, and PT Cruiser.

Trademark is a legal term. A trademark includes only those words, symbols, or marks that are legally registered for use by a single company. A service mark is the same as a trademark except that it refers to a service offering.

The word *FedEx* can be used to explain these differences. The FedEx overnight delivery service is branded under the brand name FedEx (whether it's spoken or printed in any manner). When "FedEx" is printed in a certain kind of script, however, it becomes a trademark. A trademark need not be attached to the product. It need not even be a word—it can be a symbol. Exhibit 9-3 shows some common trademarks.

These differences may seem technical. But they are very important to business firms that spend a lot of money to protect and promote their brands. Sometimes a firm's brand name is the only element in its marketing mix that a competitor can't copy.

Brands meet needs

Well-recognized brands make shopping easier. Think of trying to buy groceries, for example, if you had to evaluate each of 25,000 items every time you went to a supermarket. Many customers are willing to buy new things—but having gambled and won, they like to buy a sure thing the next time. Brand names connect a product with the benefits a customer can expect. The connection may be learned from past consumer experience, from the firm's promotion, or in other ways. *Certified Angus Beef* stands for "tender, high-quality meat," and *Jiffy Lube* means "fast and convenient oil change." Consumers know what they will get when they buy these branded products.

Brand promotion has advantages for branders as well as customers. A good brand reduces the marketer's selling time and effort. Good brands can also improve the company's image—speeding acceptance of new products marketed under the same name. For example, many consumers quickly tried Listerine PocketPaks breath fresheners when they appeared because they already knew they trusted Listerine mouthwash.[5]

CONDITIONS FAVORABLE TO BRANDING

Can you recall a brand name for file folders, bed frames, electric extension cords, or nails? As these examples suggest, it's not always easy to establish a respected brand.

The following conditions are favorable to successful branding:

1. The product is easy to label and identify by brand or trademark.
2. The product quality is easy to maintain and the best value for the price.

3. Dependable and widespread availability is possible. When customers start using a brand, they want to be able to continue using it.
4. Demand is strong enough that the market price can be high enough to make the branding effort profitable.
5. There are economies of scale. If the branding is really successful, costs should drop and profits should increase.
6. Favorable shelf locations or display space in stores will help. This is something retailers can control when they brand their own products.

In general, these conditions are less common in less-developed economies, and that may explain why efforts to build brands in less-developed nations often fail.

ACHIEVING BRAND FAMILIARITY IS NOT EASY

Today, familiar brands exist for most product categories, ranging from crayons (Crayola) to real estate services (RE/MAX). However, what brand is familiar often varies from one country to another.

Brand acceptance must be earned with a good product and regular promotion. Brand familiarity means how well customers recognize and accept a company's brand. The degree of brand familiarity affects the planning for the rest of the marketing mix—especially where the product should be offered and what promotion is needed.

Five levels of brand familiarity

Five levels of brand familiarity are useful for strategy planning: (1) rejection, (2) non-recognition, (3) recognition, (4) preference, and (5) insistence.

Some brands have been tried and found wanting. Brand rejection means that potential customers won't buy a brand unless its image is changed. Rejection may suggest a change in the product or perhaps only a shift to target customers who have a better image of the brand. Overcoming a negative image is difficult and can be very expensive.

Brand rejection is a big concern for service-oriented businesses because it's hard to control the quality of service. A business traveler who gets a dirty room in a Hilton Hotel in Caracas, Venezuela, might not return to a Hilton anywhere. Yet it's difficult for Hilton to ensure that every maid does a good job every time.

It takes time and money to build brand awareness. The benefits of that investment can sometimes be extended to new products, even ones in related product categories. Dove has introduced moisturizing shampoos and conditioners. While a well-known brand name is an advantage, a firm must protect its brand if it falls into use as a general name for a product category. That's why Dow reminds people that Styrofoam is its registered brand name for insulating board—and not a general name for foam cups.

Edition

Exhibit 9-4
Characteristics of a
Good Brand Name

• Short and simple	• Suggestive of product benefits
• Easy to spell and read	• Adaptable to packaging/labeling needs
• Easy to recognize and remember	• No undesirable imagery
• Easy to pronounce	• Always timely (does not go out-of-date)
• Can be pronounced in only one way	• Adaptable to any advertising medium
• Can be pronounced in all languages (for international markets)	• Legally available for use (not in use by another firm)

Some products are seen as basically the same. Brand nonrecognition means final consumers don't recognize a brand at all—even though intermediaries may use the brand name for identification and inventory control. Examples include school supplies, inexpensive dinnerware, many of the items that you'd find in a hardware store, and thousands of dot-coms on the Internet.

Brand recognition means that customers remember the brand. This may not seem like much, but it can be a big advantage if there are many "nothing" brands on the market. Even if consumers can't recall the brand without help, they may be reminded when they see it in a store among other less familiar brands.

Most branders would like to win brand preference—which means that target customers usually choose the brand over other brands, perhaps because of habit or favorable past experience. Brand insistence means customers insist on a firm's branded product and are willing to search for it.

A brand is likely to have target market customers at each level of brand familiarity. The ideal is to move more customers to the brand preference and insistence levels over time. However, it doesn't always work that way. A few decades ago, some Americans thought that a Cadillac was the ultimate sign of success; these car buyers insisted on Cadillac when it was time to trade—and Cadillac dealers thought they had customers for life. But the size of that group declined rapidly as new generations of luxury-car buyers were attracted to the status and reliability of imports like Lexus and BMW. It didn't help that many young people barely recognized the brand; ads had completely ignored this segment. In addition, there had always been some who completely rejected the brand; they just saw it as a symbol of conspicuous consumption. Recently, Cadillac's brand familiarity has taken an upturn, especially among baby boomers. Ads with classic-rock anthems draw their attention to and win preference for the performance and style of models like the Escalade and CTS.

The right brand name can help

A good brand name can help build brand familiarity. It can help tell something important about the company or its product. Exhibit 9-4 lists some characteristics of a good brand name.

Companies that compete in international markets face a special problem in selecting brand names. A name that conveys a positive image in one language may be meaningless in another. Or, worse, it may have unintended meanings. GM's Nova car is a classic example. GM stuck with the Nova name when it introduced the car in South America. It seemed like a sensible decision because *nova* is the Spanish word for star. However, Nova also sounds the same as the Spanish words for "no go." Consumers weren't interested in a no-go car, and sales didn't pick up until GM changed the name.[6]

A respected name builds brand equity

Because it's costly to build brand recognition, some firms prefer to acquire established brands rather than try to build their own. The value of a brand to its current owner or to a firm that wants to buy it is sometimes called brand equity—the value

Differentiation by Design

Today, many companies are finding that they can get a competitive advantage by having designers involved in basic decisions about product features and functions—rather than just having them there to finalize the look. Designers now help with decisions about what benefits a product will offer, including the right look and feel to achieve ease of use.

Office equipment and furniture manufacturer Herman Miller has redesigned many common products to appeal to customers who value sustainability. Its design for the Leaf personal desk lamp uses light-emitting diodes (LEDs) that allow the user to choose the color and intensity of the light. The LEDs last for 60,000 hours—much longer than the traditional fluorescent lightbulbs they replace—yet use only 40 percent as much electricity. Leaf also contains 37 percent recycled materials. The sustainable features, combined with an artistic and functional design, differentiate the lamp and help it sell well, even at a price of almost $500.

Kaiser Permanente, the health care giant, did research that revealed that its facilities were alienating many patients. Most patients already had health concerns when they arrived, so the stark waiting rooms made them anxious, the poor signage was confusing, and small exam rooms were lonely. Kaiser turned to designers for help. They expanded the exam rooms, added privacy curtains, and invited patients to have a friend wait with them. After the redesign, Kaiser's patients reported more satisfaction with the health care they received. The health care was actually the same, but the facilities were improved.

In Europe, the circulation of newspapers steadily declined for years. Young adults with fast-paced lifestyles had little time and weren't reading them. However, Metro attracted many new customers from this demographic group after changing the morning newspaper experience. Switching to a tabloid design and short-article format did the trick.

A decade ago, discount retailer Target relied on TV and magazine ads to try to build a cool image. But the products it carried were mostly the same stuff sold by rival Wal-Mart. To differentiate itself, Target put more emphasis on products with affordable, attractive, and functional designs. Target recruited designers like Michael Graves to create new lines of housewares, office supplies, furniture, toys, and games—all of which helped to reposition Target's image. Today, Target's design-centered differentiation helps it reduce direct price competition.

Trends in design change frequently because they depend on what look is in fashion as well as what functions well. So, it may be costly if it requires frequent product updates. In recent years, Apple has been able to balance design, costs, and premium prices. By comparison, other companies, including Sony, have had a harder time keeping their design edge.[7]

of a brand's overall strength in the market. For example, brand equity is likely to be higher if many satisfied customers insist on buying the brand and if retailers are eager to stock it. That almost guarantees ongoing profits.

The financial value of the Yahoo! brand name illustrates the brand equity idea. In 1994, Yahoo! was just a tiny start-up trying to make it with a directory site on the Internet. Most people had never heard the name, and few even knew what the Internet was or why you'd need a directory site. As interest in the Internet grew, Yahoo! promoted its brand name with quirky TV and magazine ads. At a time when many people were just getting to know the Web, Yahoo! came across as an approachable and fun place to go on the Internet. Within a few years, Yahoo! attracted more than 100 million unique customer visits. Yahoo! wants its brand to become just as well known in places like Taiwan, China, and France. Because Yahoo! charges fees to advertisers eager to reach these users, the familiarity of its brand translates directly into ad revenues.[8]

Edition

As these trade ads suggest, both Chiquita and Del Monte want retailers to remember that many consumers already know and trust their brand names. Establishing successful brand names in the produce section is no easy feat.

PROTECTING BRAND NAMES AND TRADEMARKS

U.S. common law and civil law protect the rights of trademark and brand name owners. The Lanham Act (of 1946) spells out what kinds of marks (including brand names) can be protected and the exact method of protecting them. The law applies to goods shipped in interstate or foreign commerce.

The Lanham Act does not force registration. But registering under the Lanham Act is often a first step toward protecting a trademark to be used in international markets. That's because some nations require that a trademark be registered in its home country before they will register or protect it.

You must protect your own

A brand can be a real asset to a company. Each firm should try to see that its brand doesn't become a common descriptive term for its kind of product. When this happens, the brand name or trademark becomes public property—and the owner loses all rights to it. This happened with the names cellophane, aspirin, shredded wheat, and kerosene.[9]

Counterfeiting is accepted in some cultures

Even when products are properly registered, counterfeiters may make unauthorized copies. Counterfeit products cause a brand to lose sales and jeopardize its reputation. Many well-known brands—ranging from Levi's jeans to Rolex watches to Zantax medicine—face this problem. International trade in counterfeit and pirated goods may exceed $500 billion annually. Counterfeiting continues to grow and is especially common in developing countries. In China for example, many DVDs, CDs, and software programs are bootleg copies. And counterfeiters are increasingly brazen. In Azerbaijan and Bulgaria, BP discovered counterfeit BP service stations—with low-quality fuel. Weak regulation in many developing countries makes it difficult for companies to protect their brands from counterfeits. There are also differences in cultural values. In South Korea, for example, many people don't see counterfeiting as unethical.[10]

WHAT KIND OF BRAND TO USE?

Keep it in the family

Branders of more than one product must decide whether they are going to use a family brand—the same brand name for several products—or individual brands for

General Mills owns the Cascadian Farm brand name, but uses the separate name to reinforce the positioning of its organic line of cereals. Both General Mills cereals and Cascadian Farm cereals may have to compete for shelf space—and consumer attention—against similar store (dealer) brands of cereal which often sell at lower prices.

each product. Examples of family brands are Keebler snack food products and Sears' Kenmore appliances.

The use of the same brand for many products makes sense if all are similar in type and quality. The main benefit is that the goodwill attached to one or two products may help the others. Money spent to promote the brand name benefits more than one product, which cuts promotion costs for each product.

A special kind of family brand is a licensed brand—a well-known brand that sellers pay a fee to use. For example, the familiar Sunkist brand name has been licensed to many companies for use on more than 400 products in 30 countries.[11]

Individual brands for outside and inside competition

A company uses individual brands—separate brand names for each product—when it's important for the products to each have a separate identity, as when products vary in quality or type.

If the products are really different, such as Elmer's glue and Borden's ice cream, individual brands can avoid confusion. Some firms use individual brands with similar products to make segmentation and positioning efforts easier. For example, when General Mills introduced a line of organic cereals, it used the Cascadian Farm name and the Big G logo was not on the box. The rationale was that consumers who try to avoid additives might not trust a big corporate brand.[12]

> **Internet EXERCISE**
>
> Go to the Procter & Gamble website (www.pg.com) and, under "U.S. Product Information," choose the category "Hair Care." Look at the brand names of the different shampoos that P&G makes. How are the different brands positioned, and what target markets do they appeal to?

Generic "brands"

Products that some consumers see as commodities may be difficult or expensive to brand. Some manufacturers and intermediaries have responded to this problem with generic products—products that have no brand at all other than identification of their contents and the manufacturer or intermediary. Generic products are usually offered in plain packages at lower prices. They are quite common in less-developed nations.[13]

WHO SHOULD DO THE BRANDING?

Manufacturer brands versus dealer brands

Manufacturer brands are brands created by producers. These are sometimes called *national brands* because the brand is promoted all across the country or in large regions. Note, however, that many manufacturer brands are now distributed globally. Such brands include Nabisco, Campbell's, Whirlpool, Ford, and IBM. Many creators of service-oriented firms—like McDonald's, Orkin Pest Control, and Bank of America—promote their brands this way too.

Edition

The elegant bottle used in the packaging of Lancome's Hypnôse fragrance is typical of expensive perfumes and reinforces Lancome's image and positioning. In contrast, the package for Grillero beef looks different from the way most beef is packaged and also provides a way to tell French consumers that the product is organic.

Dealer brands, also called private brands, are brands created by intermediaries. Examples of dealer brands include the brands of Kroger, Ace Hardware, Radio Shack, Wal-Mart, and Sears. Some of these are advertised and distributed more widely than many national brands. For example, national TV ads helped Original Arizona Jeans (by JCPenney) and Canyon River Blues (by Sears) compete with Levi's and Wrangler.

From the intermediary's perspective, the major advantage of selling a popular manufacturer brand is that the product is already presold to some target customers. The major disadvantage is that manufacturers normally offer lower gross margins than the intermediary might be able to earn with a dealer brand. In addition, the manufacturer maintains control of the brand and may withdraw it from an intermediary at any time. Customers, loyal to the brand rather than to the retailer or wholesaler, may go elsewhere if the brand is not available.

Dealer branders take on more responsibility and must promote their own product. They must be able to arrange a dependable source of supply and usually have to buy in fairly large quantities. This increases their risk and cost of carrying inventory. However, these problems are easier to overcome if the intermediary deals in a large sales volume, as is the case with many large retail chains.

Who's winning the battle of the brands?

The battle of the brands, the competition between dealer brands and manufacturer brands, is just a question of whose brands will be more popular and who will be in control.

At one time, manufacturer brands were much more popular than dealer brands. Now sales of both kinds of brands are about equal—but sales of dealer brands are expected to continue growing. Intermediaries have some advantages in this battle. With the number of large retail chains growing, they are better able to arrange reliable sources of supply at low cost. They can also give the dealer brand special shelf position or promotion.

Consumers benefit from the battle. Competition has already narrowed price differences between manufacturer brands and well-known dealer brands. And big retailers are constantly pushing manufacturers to lower prices—because national brands at low prices bring in even more customers than store brands.[14]

THE STRATEGIC IMPORTANCE OF PACKAGING

Packaging involves promoting, protecting, and enhancing the product. Packaging can be important to both sellers and customers. See Exhibit 9-5. It can make a product more convenient to use or store. It can prevent spoiling or damage. Good packaging makes products easier to identify and promotes the brand at the point of purchase and even in use.

Exhibit 9-5   Some Ways Packaging Benefits Consumers and Marketers

Opportunity to Add Value	Some Decision Factors	Examples
Promoting	Link product to promotion	The bunny on the Energizer battery package is a reminder that it "keeps going and going."
	Branding at point of purchase or consumption	Coke's logo greets almost everyone each time the refrigerator is opened.
	Product information	Nabisco's nutrition label helps consumers decide which cookie to buy, and a UPC code reduces checkout time and errors.
Protecting	For shipping and storing	Sony's MP3 player is kept safe by Styrofoam inserts.
	From tampering	Tylenol's safety seal prevents tampering.
	From shoplifting	Cardboard hang-tag on Gillette razor blades is too large to hide in hand.
	From spoiling	Kraft's shredded cheese has a resealable zipper package to keep it fresh.
Enhancing product	The environment	Tide detergent bottle can be recycled.
	Convenience in use	Squeezable tube of Yoplait Go-Gurt is easy to eat on the go and in new situations.
	Added product functions	Plastic tub is useful for refrigerator leftovers after the Cool Whip is gone.

Packaging can enhance the product

A new package can make *the* important difference in a new marketing strategy—by meeting customers' needs better. Sometimes a new package makes the product easier or safer to use. For example, most drug and food products now have special seals to prevent product tampering. And clever packaging is an important part of a new effort by Campbell's Soup to pump new life into an old product—soup. Campbell's developed its Soup at Hand with a package that doesn't require a can opener or a stirring pot and instead is microwavable. Soup at Hand is just right for today's on-the-go consumers who want a portable meal solution, so it also helps Campbell's get distribution in convenience stores and vending machines. Consumers value convenience, so the Soup at Hand price of $1.49 (versus $0.79 for a traditional can of soup) also produces attractive profits.[15]

Packaging sends a message

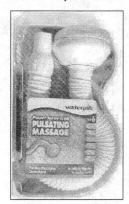

Packaging can tie the product to the rest of the marketing strategy. Packaging for Energizer batteries features the pink bunny seen in attention-getting TV ads and reminds consumers that the batteries are durable. A good package sometimes gives a firm more promotional effect than it could get with advertising. Customers see the package in stores, when they're actually buying. A consumer who needs a new showerhead is likely to pick the brand and style by comparing alternatives at a retail store. Waterpik's package makes it easy for the consumer to see and evaluate the product and the curved design helps to focus attention on the flexible hose.

Packaging may lower distribution costs

Better protective packaging is very important to manufacturers and wholesalers. They sometimes have to pay the cost of goods damaged in shipment. Retailers need protective packaging too. It can reduce storing costs by cutting breakage, spoilage, and theft. Good packages also save space and weight so they are easier to transport, handle, and display.[16]

Edition

Universal product codes speed handling

To speed handling of fast-selling products, government and industry representatives have developed a universal product code (UPC) that identifies each product with marks readable by electronic scanners. A computer then matches each code to the product and its price. These codes speed the checkout process and reduce the need to mark the price on every item. They also reduce errors by cashiers and make it easy to control inventory and track sales of specific products.[17]

WHAT IS SOCIALLY RESPONSIBLE PACKAGING?

Customers benefit from many of the advances that have been made in packaging. However, packaging is an area where managers face issues of social responsibility, including concerns about the role of packaging in pollution, global warming, and resource use.

Packaging excesses can hurt the environment

There have been several times when a crisis has brought attention to the environmental impact of packaging. For example, when scientists revealed that chemicals used in spray cans (for hairspray, deodorant, and other products) were damaging the earth's atmosphere, firms scrambled to find alternatives. However, it turns out that what we view as "normal" is actually a bigger problem. U.S. shoppers generate much more trash per person than anywhere else on earth. Much of what is tossed out is packaging. It overloads landfills, litters our streets, and pollutes the environment. For years plastic seemed to be the perfect packaging material because it is clean, light, and durable; now the consequence is that discarded plastic is everywhere and lasts forever. Even colorful package graphics are troublesome. The ink to print them often has toxins that later creep into the soil and water. Firms should try to give consumers what they want, but in applying that logic to packaging many people have been short-sighted. And both managers and consumers have often acted as if there was nothing an *individual* could do to reduce environment problems. Now that attitude is changing.

Many firms are taking steps to preserve the environment. Timberland makes its shoe boxes with 100 percent recycled materials, soy-based inks, and water-based glues. Music groups like Pearl Jam have eliminated plastic jewel cases from their CDs; of course, downloads from iTunes don't use CDs or packages. Whole Foods Market uses salad-bar containers made from sugar-cane waste; they safely turn into compost within about 90 days. It makes sense for firms to publicize such efforts to attract like-minded consumers. Publicity also calls attention to the idea that even small changes can add up to big improvements, especially when many people are involved. The recycling

Stonyfield Farm wants its customers to know that it is sensitive to the environment. It communicates how it is trying to improve the environmental performance of its packaging with messages on the lids of its yogurt containers and at the company's website.

programs that thrive in many communities illustrate this point. The total cost of the programs are often covered by selling mounds of cans, bottles, and other package materials that would otherwise be in dumps.

Can consumers evaluate eco impacts?

The benefits of recycling now seem obvious. However, consumers often don't know if a particular product and package is an eco-friendly choice. Some firms are beginning to provide such information. Tesco, the largest retail chain in Britain, posts a "carbon rating" on all 70,000 products it carries. These ratings remind consumers that what they buy impacts global warming. With ratings displayed at the point of purchase, producers have an incentive to improve. Clearly, producers are trying to appeal to green consumers in a variety of ways. For example, Canon created its Generation Green brand of printer cartridges that can be recycled and that come in a biodegradable package.

Efforts like these also highlight challenges. Some critics think that the environmental claims that firms make will be misleading or confusing if they are not standardized and regulated. It's hard to know, for example, how the environmental impact of Generation Green print cartridges compares to competitors' products. Similarly, Tesco's carbon rating plan is innovative, but measuring carbon usage is imprecise and many consumers don't know how to use the ratings.

Despite such difficulties, more effort to protect the environment is needed. Of course, some things are already regulated by laws. For example, many states require consumers to pay a deposit on bottles and cans until they're returned. These laws challenge managers to rethink channels of distribution, which are usually set up to distribute products, not return empty packages.[18]

Laws reduce confusion

The Federal Fair Packaging and Labeling Act (of 1966) requires that consumer goods be clearly labeled in easy-to-understand terms to give consumers more information. The law also calls on industry to try to reduce the confusing number of package sizes and make labels more useful. Since then, there have been further guidelines. The most far-reaching are based on the Nutrition Labeling and Education Act of 1990. It requires food manufacturers to use a uniform format that allows consumers to compare the nutritional value of different products. Recently there have been more changes, including requirements to clearly show the fat content of food and ingredients that trigger common food allergies.[19]

Ethical decisions remain

Although various laws provide guidance on many packaging issues, many areas still require marketing managers to make ethical choices. For example, some firms have been criticized for designing packages that conceal a downsized product, giving consumers less for their money. Similarly, some retailers design packages and labels for their private-label products that look just like, and are easily confused with, manufacturer brands. Are efforts such as these unethical, or are they simply an attempt to make packaging a more effective part of a marketing mix? Different people will answer differently.

Many critics think that labeling information is too often incomplete or misleading. For example, what does it really mean if a label says a food product is "organic" or "low fat"? But how far should a marketing manager go in

Edition

putting potentially negative information on a package? For example, should Häagen-Dazs affix a label that says "this product will clog your arteries"? That sounds extreme, but what type of information *is* appropriate?

Many consumers like the convenience that accompanies the myriad product and packaging choices available. Is it unethical for a marketing manager to give consumers with different preferences a choice? Some critics argue that it is. Others praise firms that give consumers choices.[20]

WARRANTY POLICIES ARE A PART OF STRATEGY PLANNING

Warranty puts promises in writing

A warranty explains what the seller promises about its product. A marketing manager should decide whether to offer a specific warranty, and if so what the warranty will cover and how it will be communicated to target customers. This is an area where the legal environment—as well as customer needs and competitive offerings—must be considered.

U.S. common law says that producers must stand behind their products—even if they don't offer a specific warranty. A written warranty provided by the seller may promise more than the common law provides. However, it may actually *reduce* the responsibility a producer would have under common law.

The federal Magnuson-Moss Act (of 1975) says that producers must provide a clearly written warranty if they choose to offer any warranty. The warranty does not have to be strong. However, Federal Trade Commission (FTC) guidelines try to ensure that warranties are clear and definite and not deceptive or unfair. A warranty must also be available for inspection before the purchase.

A company has to make it clear whether it's offering a full or limited warranty—and the law defines what *full* means. Most firms offer a limited warranty if they offer one at all. In recent years, many firms have reduced the period of warranty coverage. Apple's popular iPod music player, for example, only has a 90-day warranty.

Warranty may improve the marketing mix

Some firms use warranties to improve the appeal of their marketing mix. They design more quality into their goods or services and offer refunds or replacement, not just repair, if there is a problem. A strong warranty sends consumers a signal about brand quality. A few years ago, Hyundai, the South Korean car maker, pushed to

In a competitive market, a product's warranty or guarantee can be the critical difference in a firm's marketing mix.

improve quality. Yet among consumers its old reputation lingered. That changed after Hyundai put a 10-year warranty on its cars and used TV ads to tout it as "America's best warranty."

Service guarantees

Service guarantees are becoming more common as a way to attract, and keep, customers. Some Pizza Hut locations guarantee a luncheon pizza in five minutes or it's free. General Motors set up a fast-oil-change guarantee to compete with fast-lube specialists who were taking customers away from dealers. If the dealer doesn't get the job done in 29 minutes or less, the next oil change is free.

There's more risk in offering a service guarantee than a warranty on a physical product. A lazy employee or a service breakdown can create a big expense. However, without the guarantee, dissatisfied customers may just go away mad without ever complaining.

Warranty support can be costly

The cost of warranty support ultimately must be covered by the price that consumers pay. This has led some firms to offer warranty choices. The basic price for a product may include a warranty that covers a short time period or that covers parts but not labor. Consumers who want more or better protection pay extra for an extended warranty or a service contract.[21]

PRODUCT CLASSES HELP PLAN MARKETING STRATEGIES

So far in this chapter, we've focused on key strategy decisions for Product (see Exhibit 9-1). Managers usually try to blend those decisions in a unique way to differentiate the firm's offering and create superior customer value. However, you don't have to treat *every* product as unique when planning strategies. Rather, some classes of products require similar marketing mixes. So, now we'll introduce these product classes and show why they are a useful starting point for developing marketing mixes for new products and for evaluating present mixes.

Product classes start with type of customer

All products fit into one of two broad groups—based on the type of customer that will use them. Consumer products are products meant for the final consumer. Business products are products meant for use in producing other products.

The same product—like Bertolli Olive Oil—*might* be both a consumer product and a business product. Consumers buy it to use in their own kitchens, but food processing companies and restaurants buy it in large quantities as an ingredient in the products they sell. Selling the same product to both final consumers and business customers requires (at least) two different strategies.

There are product classes within each group. Consumer product classes are based on *how consumers think about and shop for products*. Business product classes are based on *how buyers think about products and how they'll be used*.

CONSUMER PRODUCT CLASSES

Consumer product classes divide into four groups: (1) convenience, (2) shopping, (3) specialty, and (4) unsought. *Each class is based on the way people buy products.* See Exhibit 9-6 for a summary of how these product classes relate to marketing mixes.[22]

Convenience products—purchased quickly with little effort

Convenience products are products a consumer needs but isn't willing to spend much time or effort shopping for. These products are bought often, require little service or selling, don't cost much, and may even be bought by habit. A convenience product may be a staple, impulse product, or emergency product.

Staples are products that are bought often, routinely, and without much thought—like breakfast cereal, canned soup, and most other packaged foods used almost every day in almost every household.

Edition

Exhibit 9-6   Consumer Product Classes and Marketing Mix Planning

Consumer Product Class	Marketing Mix Considerations	Consumer Behavior
Convenience products		
Staples	Maximum exposure with widespread, low-cost distribution; mass selling by producer; usually low price; branding is important.	Routinized (habitual), low effort, frequent purchases; low involvement.
Impulse	Widespread distribution with display at point of purchase.	Unplanned purchases bought quickly.
Emergency	Need widespread distribution near probable point of need; price sensitivity low.	Purchase made with time pressure when a need is great.
Shopping products		
Homogeneous	Need enough exposure to facilitate price comparison; price sensitivity high.	Customers see little difference among alternatives, seek lowest price.
Heterogeneous	Need distribution near similar products; promotion (including personal selling) to highlight product advantages; less price sensitivity.	Extensive problem solving; consumer may need help in making a decision (salesperson, website, etc.).
Specialty products	Price sensitivity is likely to be low; limited distribution may be acceptable, but should be treated as a convenience or shopping product (in whichever category product would typically be included) to reach persons not yet sold on its specialty product status.	Willing to expend effort to get specific product, even if not necessary; strong preferences make it an important purchase; Internet becoming important information source.
Unsought products		
New unsought	Must be available in places where similar (or related) products are sought; needs attention-getting promotion.	Need for product not strongly felt; unaware of benefits or not yet gone through adoption process.
Regularly unsought	Requires very aggressive promotion, usually personal selling.	Aware of product but not interested; attitude toward product may even be negative.

Impulse products are products that are bought quickly—as *unplanned* purchases—because of a strongly felt need. True impulse products are items that the customer hadn't planned to buy, decides to buy on sight, may have bought the same way many times before, and wants right now. If the buyer doesn't see an impulse product at the right time, the sale may be lost.[23]

Emergency products are products that are purchased immediately when the need is great. The customer doesn't have time to shop around when a traffic accident occurs, a thunderstorm begins, or an impromptu party starts. The price of the ambulance service, raincoat, or ice cubes won't be important.

Shopping products—
are compared

Shopping products are products that a customer feels are worth the time and effort to compare with competing products. Shopping products can be divided into two types, depending on what customers are comparing: (1) homogeneous or (2) heterogeneous shopping products.

Homogeneous shopping products are shopping products the customer sees as basically the same and wants at the lowest price. Some consumers feel that certain sizes and types of computers, television sets, washing machines, and even cars are very similar. So they shop for the best price. For some products, the Internet has become the fast way to do that.

CHAPTER 9

249

Elements of Product Planning for Goods and Services

Firms may try to emphasize and promote their product differences to avoid head-to-head price competition. For example, Rustoleum says that its spray paint goes on smoother and does a better job of preventing rust. But if consumers don't think the differences are real or important in terms of the value they seek, they'll just look at price.

Heterogeneous shopping products are shopping products the customer sees as different and wants to inspect for quality and suitability. Furniture, clothing, and membership in a spa are good examples. Often the consumer expects help from a knowledgeable salesperson. Quality and style matter more than price. In fact, once the customer finds the right product, price may not matter as long as it's reasonable. For example, you may have asked a friend to recommend a good dentist without even asking what the dentist charges.

Branding may be less important for heterogeneous shopping products. The more carefully consumers compare price and quality, the less they rely on brand names or labels. Some retailers carry competing brands so consumers won't go to a competitor to compare items.

Specialty products— no substitutes please!

Specialty products are consumer products that the customer really wants and makes a special effort to find. Shopping for a specialty product doesn't mean comparing—the buyer wants that special product and is willing to search for it. It's the customer's *willingness to search*—not the extent of searching—that makes it a specialty product.

Any branded product that consumers insist on by name is a specialty product. Marketing managers want customers to see their products as specialty products and ask for them over and over again. Building that kind of relationship isn't easy. It means satisfying the customer every time. However, that's easier and a lot less costly than trying to win back dissatisfied customers or attract new customers who are not seeking the product at all.

Unsought products— need promotion

Unsought products are products that potential customers don't yet want or know they can buy. So they don't search for them at all. In fact, consumers probably won't buy these products if they see them—unless promotion can show their value.

There are two types of unsought products. New unsought products are products offering really new ideas that potential customers don't know about yet. Informative

For consumers who have never heard of Joint Juice, it is a new unsought product. Effective promotion, and its catchy brand name, will help to end its unsought status, especially among target consumers who want healthy joints. In contrast, most people hate to wash dishes and know the benefits of having a dishwasher. Still, many consumers see dishwashers as homogeneous products and shop by price. But Bosch wants its target customers to see its distinctively quiet dishwashers as heterogeneous shopping products, or perhaps even specialty items.

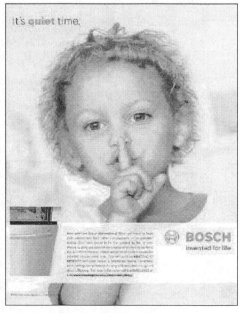

Edition

Many items in Bush's Best line of food products sell as both consumer and business products, and different marketing mixes are required to reach the different target markets.

promotion can help convince customers to accept the product, ending its unsought status. Dannon's yogurt, Litton's microwave ovens, and AOL's Netscape browser are all popular items now, but initially they were new unsought products.

Regularly unsought products are products—like gravestones, life insurance, and encyclopedias—that stay unsought but not unbought forever. There may be a need, but potential customers aren't motivated to satisfy it. For this kind of product, personal selling is *very* important.

Many nonprofit organizations try to "sell" their unsought products. For example, the Red Cross regularly holds blood drives to remind prospective donors of how important it is to give blood.

One product may be seen in several ways

The same product might be seen in different ways by different target markets at the same time. For example, a product viewed as a staple by most consumers in the United States, Canada, or some similar affluent country might be seen as a heterogeneous shopping product by consumers in another country. The price might be much higher when considered as a proportion of the consumer's budget, and the available choices might be very different. Similarly, for some people salsa is seen as a staple; for others—who, for example, think it is worth tracking down W. B. Williams Georgia Style Peach Salsa on the Internet—it is a specialty product.

BUSINESS PRODUCTS ARE DIFFERENT

Business product classes are different from the consumer product classes—because they relate to how and why business firms make purchases. Thus, knowing the specific classes of business products helps in strategy planning. First, however, it's useful to note some important ways that the market for business products is different from the market for consumer products.

One demand derived from another

The big difference between the consumer products market and the business products market is derived demand—the demand for business products derives from the demand for final consumer products. For example, car manufacturers buy about one-fifth of all steel products. But if demand for cars drops, they'll buy less steel. Then even the steel supplier with the best marketing mix is likely to lose sales.[24]

Edition

Price increases might not reduce quantity purchased

Total *industry* demand for business products is fairly inelastic. Business firms must buy what they need to produce their own products. Even if the cost of basic silicon doubles, for example, Intel needs it to make computer chips. However, sharp business buyers try to buy as economically as possible. So the demand facing *individual sellers* may be extremely elastic—if similar products are available at a lower price.

Tax treatment affects buying too

How a firm's accountants—and the tax laws—treat a purchase is also important to business customers. An expense item is a product whose total cost is treated as a business expense in the year it's purchased. A capital item is a long-lasting product that can be used and depreciated for many years. Often it's very expensive. Customers pay for the capital item when they buy it, but for tax purposes the cost is spread over a number of years. This may reduce the cash available for other purchases.

BUSINESS PRODUCT CLASSES—HOW THEY ARE DEFINED

Business product classes are based on how buyers think about products and how the products will be used. The classes of business products are (1) installations, (2) accessories, (3) raw materials, (4) components, (5) supplies, and (6) professional services. Exhibit 9-7 relates these product classes to marketing mix planning.

Exhibit 9-7   Business Product Classes and Marketing Mix Planning

Business Product Classes	Marketing Mix Considerations	Buying Behavior
Installations	Usually requires skillful personal selling by producer, including technical contacts, or understanding of applications; leasing and specialized support services may be required.	Multiple buying influence (including top management) and new-task buying are common; infrequent purchase, long decision period, and boom-or-bust demand are typical.
Accessory equipment	Need fairly widespread distribution and numerous contacts by experienced and sometimes technically trained personnel; price competition is often intense, but quality is important.	Purchasing and operating personnel typically make decisions; shorter decision period than for installations; Internet sourcing.
Raw materials	Grading is important, and transportation and storing can be crucial because of seasonal production and/or perishable products; markets tend to be very competitive.	Long-term contract may be required to ensure supply; online auctions.
Component parts and materials	Product quality and delivery reliability are usually extremely important; negotiation and technical selling typical on less-standardized items; replacement after market may require different strategies.	Multiple buying influence is common; online competitive bids used to encourage competitive pricing.
Maintenance, repair, and operating (MRO) supplies	Typically require widespread distribution or fast delivery (repair items); arrangements with appropriate intermediaries may be crucial.	Often handled as straight rebuys, except important operating supplies may be treated much more seriously and involve multiple buying influence.
Professional services	Services customized to buyer's need; personal selling very important; inelastic demand often supports high prices.	Customer may compare outside service with what internal people could provide; needs may be very specialized.

Edition

Installations—a boom-or-bust business

Installations—such as buildings, land rights, and major equipment—are important capital items. One-of-a-kind installations—like office buildings and custom-made machines—generally require special negotiations for each sale. Negotiations often involve top management and can stretch over months or even years. Standardized major equipment is treated more routinely.

Installations are a boom-or-bust business. During growth periods, firms may buy installations to increase capacity. But during a downswing, sales fall off sharply.[25]

Specialized services are needed as part of the product

Suppliers sometimes include special services with an installation at no extra cost. A firm that sells (or leases) equipment to dentists, for example, may install it and help the dentist learn to use it.

Accessories— important but short-lived capital items

Accessories are short-lived capital items—tools and equipment used in production or office activities—like Canon's small copy machines, Rockwell's portable drills, and Steelcase's filing cabinets. Accessories are more standardized than installations and they're usually needed by more customers.

Since these products cost less and last a shorter time than installations, multiple buying influence is less important. Operating people and purchasing agents, rather than top managers, may make the purchase decision. As with installations, some customers may wish to lease or rent—to expense the cost.

Raw materials become part of a physical good

Raw materials are unprocessed expense items—such as logs, iron ore, and wheat—that are moved to the next production process with little handling. Unlike installations and accessories, *raw materials become part of a physical good and are expense items.*

There are two types of raw materials: (1) farm products and (2) natural products. Farm products are grown by farmers—examples are oranges, sugar cane, and cattle. Natural products are products that occur in nature—such as timber, iron ore, oil, and coal.

The need for grading is one of the important differences between raw materials and other business products. Nature produces what it will—and someone must sort and grade raw materials to satisfy various market segments.

Most buyers of raw materials want ample supplies in the right grades for specific uses—fresh vegetables for Green Giant's production lines or logs for Weyerhaeuser's paper mills. To ensure steady quantities, raw materials customers often sign long-term contracts, sometimes at guaranteed prices.

Component parts and materials must meet specifications

Components are processed expense items that become part of a finished product. Component *parts* are finished (or nearly finished) items that are ready for assembly into the final product. Intel's microprocessors included in personal computers and TRW's air bags in cars are examples. Component *materials* are items such as wire, plastic, or textiles. They have already been processed but must be processed further before becoming part of the final product. Quality is important with components because they become part of the firm's own product.

Some components are custom-made. Then teamwork between the buyer and seller may be needed to arrive at the right specifications. So a buyer may develop a close partnership with a dependable supplier. In contrast, standardized component materials are more likely to be purchased online using a competitive bidding system.

Since component parts go into finished products, a replacement market often develops. Car tires are components originally sold in the OEM (*original equipment market*) that become consumer products in the *after market.*[26]

Supplies for maintenance, repair, and operations

Supplies are expense items that do not become part of a finished product. Supplies can be divided into three types: (1) maintenance, (2) repair, and (3) operating supplies—giving them their common name: MRO supplies.

PerkinElmer produces component parts used by aircraft engine original equipment manufacturers (OEMs). It also sells airplane owners the maintenance, repair, and operating (MRO) supplies they need. The marketing mix for the two target markets is different, but the firm wants MRO customers to know that they are dealing with the same team of experts who sold the original equipment. Grant Thornton, by contrast, sells professional services, where competitors differentiate themselves by level of client service. The premise of its ad is that clients will receive better service from people who love what they do.

Maintenance and small operating supplies are like convenience products. The item will be ordered because it is needed—but buyers won't spend much time on it. For such "nuisance" purchases branding is important, and so are breadth of assortment and the seller's dependability. Intermediaries usually handle the many supply items. They are often purchased via online catalog sites.[27]

Important operating supplies, like coal and fuel oil, receive special treatment. Usually there are several sources for such commodity products—and large volumes may be purchased at global exchanges on the Internet.

Professional services— pay to get it done

Professional services are specialized services that support a firm's operations. They are usually expense items. Management consulting services can improve the company's efficiency. Information technology services can maintain a company's networks and websites. Advertising agencies can help promote the firm's products. And food services can improve morale.

Managers compare the cost of buying professional services outside the firm (*outsourcing*) to the cost of having company people do them. Work that was previously done by an employee is now often purchased from an independent specialist. Clearly, the number of service specialists is growing in our complex economy.

CONCLUSION

In this chapter, we looked at Product broadly—which is the right vantage point for marketing strategy planning. We saw that a product may be a good or a service, or some combination of both. And we saw that a firm's Product is what it offers to *satisfy the needs of its target market*—which may include the customer's experience both before and after the purchase. We also described some key marketing differences between goods and services.

We reviewed the Product area strategy decisions required for branding and packaging—and saw how the right decisions can add value for customers and give a product a competitive edge. Customers view a brand as a guarantee of quality, which leads to repeat purchases, lower promotion costs, higher sales figures, and greater customer equity. Packaging offers promotional opportunities and informs customers.

Variations in packaging can also help a product appeal to different segments of the market. And packaging can help protect the product anywhere in the channel of distribution. We also saw how warranties can play an important role in strategy planning—by reducing buying risk. Customers see warranties as a signal of quality.

The brand familiarity a product earns is a measure of the marketing manager's ability to carve out a separate market. Therefore, ultimately, brand familiarity affects place, price, and promotion decisions. Strategy planning for the marketing mix will vary across product classes. We introduced both consumer product classes (based on *how consumers think about and shop for products*) and business product classes (based on *how buyers think about products and how they'll be used*). In addition, we showed how the product classes affect planning marketing mixes.

KEY TERMS

product, 231

quality, 232

product assortment, 235

product line, 235

individual product, 235

branding, 235

brand name, 236

trademark, 236

service mark, 236

brand familiarity, 237

brand rejection, 237

brand nonrecognition, 238

brand recognition, 238

brand preference, 238

brand insistence, 238

brand equity, 238

Lanham Act, 240

family brand, 240

licensed brand, 241

individual brands, 241

generic products, 241

manufacturer brands, 241

dealer brands, 242

private brands, 242

battle of the brands, 242

packaging, 242

universal product code (UPC), 244

Federal Fair Packaging and Labeling Act, 245

warranty, 246

Magnuson-Moss Act, 246

consumer products, 247

business products, 247

convenience products, 247

staples, 247

impulse products, 248

emergency products, 248

shopping products, 248

homogeneous shopping products, 248

heterogeneous shopping products, 249

specialty products, 249

unsought products, 249

new unsought products, 249

regularly unsought products, 250

derived demand, 250

expense item, 251

capital item, 251

installations, 252

accessories, 252

raw materials, 252

farm products, 252

natural products, 252

components, 252

supplies, 252

professional services, 253

QUESTIONS AND PROBLEMS

1. Define, in your own words, what a Product is.

2. Discuss several ways in which physical goods are different from pure services. Give an example of a good and then an example of a service that illustrates each of the differences.

3. What products are being offered by a shop that specializes in bicycles? By a travel agent? By a supermarket? By a new car dealer?

4. Consumer services tend to be intangible, and goods tend to be tangible. Use an example to explain how the lack of

a physical good in a pure service might affect efforts to promote the service.

5. Explain some of the different aspects of the customer experience that could be managed to improve customer satisfaction if you were the marketing manager for: (*a*) an airport branch of a rental car agency, (*b*) a fast-food restaurant, (*c*) an online firm selling software directly to consumers from a website, and (*d*) a hardware store selling lawn mowers.

6. Is there any difference between a brand name and a trademark? If so, why is this difference important?

7. Is a well-known brand valuable only to the owner of the brand?

8. Suggest an example of a product and a competitive situation where it would not be profitable for a firm to spend large sums of money to establish a brand.

9. List five brand names and indicate what product is associated with the brand name. Evaluate the strengths and weaknesses of the brand name.

10. Explain family brands. Should Best Buy carry its own dealer brands to compete with some of the popular manufacturer brands it carries? Explain your reasons.

11. In the past, Sears emphasized its own dealer brands. Now it is carrying more well-known manufacturer brands. What are the benefits to Sears of carrying more manufacturer brands?

12. What does the degree of brand familiarity imply about previous and future promotion efforts? How does the degree of brand familiarity affect the Place and Price variables?

13. You operate a small hardware store with emphasis on manufacturer brands and have barely been breaking even. Evaluate the proposal of a large wholesaler who offers a full line of dealer-branded hardware items at substantially lower prices. Specify any assumptions necessary to obtain a definite answer.

14. Give an example where packaging costs probably (*a*) lower total distribution costs and (*b*) raise total distribution costs.

15. Is it more difficult to support a warranty for a service than for a physical good? Explain your reasons.

16. How would the marketing mix for a staple convenience product differ from the one for a homogeneous shopping product? How would the mix for a specialty product differ from the mix for a heterogeneous shopping product? Use examples.

17. Give an example of a product that is a *new* unsought product for most people. Briefly explain why it is an unsought product.

18. In what types of stores would you expect to find (*a*) convenience products, (*b*) shopping products, (*c*) specialty products, and (*d*) unsought products?

19. What kinds of consumer products are the following: (*a*) watches, (*b*) automobiles, and (*c*) toothpastes? Explain your reasoning.

20. Cite two examples of business products that require a substantial amount of service in order to be useful.

21. Explain why a new law office might want to lease furniture rather than buy it.

22. Would you expect to find any wholesalers selling the various types of business products? Are retail stores required (or something like retail stores)?

23. What kinds of business products are the following: (*a*) lubricating oil, (*b*) electric motors, and (*c*) a firm that provides landscaping and grass mowing for an apartment complex? Explain your reasoning.

24. How do raw materials differ from other business products? Do the differences have any impact on their marketing mixes? If so, what specifically?

25. For the kinds of business products described in this chapter, complete the following table (use one or a few well-chosen words).

    1. *Kind of distribution facility(ies) needed and functions they will provide.*

    2. *Caliber of salespeople required.*

    3. *Kind of advertising required.*

Products	1	2	3
Installations			
Buildings and land rights			
Major equipment			
Standard			
Custom-made			
Accessories			
Raw materials			
Farm products			
Natural products			
Components			
Supplies			
Maintenance and small operating supplies			
Important operating supplies			
Professional services			

CREATING MARKETING PLANS

The Marketing Plan Coach software on the Student CD and the text website includes a sample marketing plan for Hillside Veterinary Clinic. Look through the "Marketing Strategy" section.

a.   What goods does Hillside Veterinary Clinic sell?

b.   What services does Hillside Veterinary Clinic sell?

c.   What consumer product classes are offered by Hillside Veterinary Clinic?

d.   The discussion of product classes in this chapter indicates what marketing mix is typical for different classes of products. Does the marketing strategy recommended in the marketing plan fit with those considerations? Why or why not?

SUGGESTED CASES

1. McDonald's "Seniors" Restaurant
3. MANU Soccer Academy

13. File-It Supplies, Inc.
31. At-Home Health Services, Inc.

COMPUTER-AIDED PROBLEM

9. BRANDING DECISION

Wholesteen Dairy, Inc., produces and sells Wholesteen brand condensed milk to grocery retailers. The overall market for condensed milk is fairly flat, and there's sharp competition among dairies for retailers' business. Wholesteen's regular price to retailers is $8.88 a case (24 cans). FoodWorld—a fast-growing supermarket chain and Wholesteen's largest customer—buys 20,000 cases of Wholesteen's condensed milk a year. That's 20 percent of Wholesteen's total sales volume of 100,000 cases per year.

FoodWorld is proposing that Wholesteen produce private-label condensed milk to be sold with the FoodWorld brand name. FoodWorld proposes to buy the same total quantity as it does now, but it wants half (10,000 cases) with the Wholesteen brand and half with the FoodWorld brand. FoodWorld wants Wholesteen to reduce costs by using a lower-quality can for the FoodWorld brand. That change will cost Wholesteen $.01 less per can than it costs for the cans that Wholesteen uses for its own brand. FoodWorld will also provide preprinted labels with its brand name—which will save Wholesteen an additional $.02 a can.

Wholesteen spends $70,000 a year on promotion to increase familiarity with the Wholesteen brand. In addition, Wholesteen gives retailers an allowance of $.25 per case for their local advertising, which features the Wholesteen brand. FoodWorld has agreed to give up the advertising allowance for its own brand, but it is only willing to pay $7.40 a case for the milk that will be sold with the FoodWorld brand name. It will continue under the old terms for the rest of its purchases.

Sue Glick, Wholesteen's marketing manager, is considering the FoodWorld proposal. She has entered cost and revenue data on a spreadsheet—so she can see more clearly how the proposal might affect revenue and profits.

a.   Based on the data in the initial spreadsheet, how will Wholesteen profits be affected if Glick accepts the Food-World proposal?

b.   Glick is worried that FoodWorld will find another producer for the FoodWorld private label milk if Wholesteen rejects the proposal. This would immediately reduce Wholesteen's annual sales by 10,000 cases. FoodWorld might even stop buying from Wholesteen altogether. What would happen to profits in these two situations?

c.   FoodWorld is rapidly opening new stores and sells milk in every store. The FoodWorld buyer says that next year's purchases could be up to 25,000 cases of Wholesteen's condensed milk. But Sue Glick knows that FoodWorld may stop buying the Wholesteen brand and want all 25,000 cases to carry the FoodWorld private label brand. How will this affect profit? (Hint: enter the new quantities in the "proposal" column of the spreadsheet.)

d.   What should Wholesteen do? Why?

For additional questions related to this problem, see Exercise 9-5 in the *Learning Aid for Use with Basic Marketing*, 17th edition.

10

Product Management and New-Product Development

Kevin Plank was a business major and football player at the University of Maryland when he spotted an opportunity. He and his teammates wore cotton T-shirts under their football pads, but the T-shirts quickly became sweat-soaked, heavy, and uncomfortable during practices and games. When Plank began looking for a product that would perform better than a T-shirt, he learned about new types of fabrics and performance clothing for bicyclists and hikers. But he realized a shirt that would meet the needs of football players was a really new idea, not just a minor variation on existing clothing.

In New York City's garment district, Plank learned about a polyester-Lycra blend fabric that didn't trap moisture. He worked with a tailor to develop several prototype shirts and then asked friends who were players in the National Football League, like Vernon Davis of the San Francisco 49ers, to try them. The players really liked the skintight, compression shirts. They fit comfortably under football gear and wicked away sweat—keeping the players cooler, drier, and lighter. When Plank's friends clamored for more shirts, he knew he had a good start. However, he couldn't afford a big ad campaign to tout the benefits of his product, and he didn't have relationships with retailers who could help build demand with final consumers. So Plank moved to commercialization with a focus on a target market he knew: college football teams.

Plank went back to New York and ordered 500 shirts, the first products with the Under Armour brand name and the start of what became the HeatGear warm weather product line. Then he loaded his shirts in his SUV and traveled to colleges across the Southeast. He tried to persuade coaches, players, and equipment managers about the benefits of his unique shirts. Many were not initially convinced of the value—especially since the price was 3 to 5 times the price of a T-shirt. But its advantage was clear after a player would try one for a football practice—and praise for the product spread quickly.

Success with college and professional athletes helped the company build credibility. It also led to relationships with specialty-sports retailers who could reach the larger and more profitable consumer market. Sports retailers provided attractive displays and promoted the brand because they liked having a profitable new offering that was not available at lower prices in local discount or department stores.

As the market for sports-performance clothes grew, Nike, Adidas, and other firms came out with competing products. To fight back, Under Armour put more emphasis on creative promotion to build customer preference for the Under Armour brand. For example, Under Armour got a prominent product placement in the football movie *Any Given Sunday*. Similarly,

Under Armour ran TV and print ads featuring professional athletes, like Dallas Cowboys football player (and former Plank teammate) Eric Ogbogu. When the muscular Ogbogu barked the firm's tag line, "Protect This House," it instantly became a part of popular sports culture. It was the rallying cry of players, fans, and banners in football stadiums across the country.

Of course, the firm continued to look for growth through new product ideas. One successful idea came from a coach who wanted a cold weather version of the shirt that would keep players warm as well as dry. Under Armour responded with the first products in its ColdGear line. New products for a variety of other athletic markets have followed, including leggings that are popular with skiers and polo shirts that are a hit with golfers.

It's tough to quickly steal away a large share of the customers in a mature product-market, but that is just what Under Armour accomplished with its new design for football cleats. The new-product development team researched playing surfaces, player movements, and body types to design cleats that were more durable, lighter, and more breathable. Player feedback led to even more refinements. Of course, it also took an innovative ad campaign and point-of-purchase promotion for the cleats to capture a 20 percent share of sales in this highly competitive market.

Even the best firms sometimes experience problems with new products, and Under Armour is no exception. Its initial line for women failed to meet expectations because of concerns about fit and quality. To fix the problems, Under Armour brought in more female designers and developed a clearer understanding of the needs of female athletes. The new line was expanded and included redesigned shorts, sleeveless tops, sports bras, and socks. The brand manager supported the improved line with ads featuring soccer star Heather Mitts. Now the women's line accounts for more than one-fifth of the company's sales.

In just 10 years, Under Armour has grown from a start-up into a firm with over $430 million in annual sales. Of course, growth in the performance clothing market is now slowing and competition from big-name firms like Nike is increasing. But Kevin Plank is used to taking on bigger competitors. Once during his college football days, the 5-foot 11-inch, 229-pound Plank was assigned to block his 6-foot 4-inch, 269-pound buddy Ogbogu, and the bigger man ended up on his back with a concussion. Watch out Nike![1]

INNOVATION AND MARKET CHANGES CREATE OPPORTUNITIES

Successful new products, like those in the Under Armour case, are critical in driving profitable growth for both new and established companies. Under Armour pioneered a fast-growing new product-market—and "performance clothing" is meeting customer needs in new ways. Similarly, in Chapter 6, we looked at how the iPod and other innovations in digital media are changing personal entertainment. In fact, all around us there is a constant life-and-death struggle where old products are replaced by new products. Digital video recorders are quickly making videotapes obsolete, just as cell phones have replaced shortwave radios and phone booths and made it possible for people to communicate from places where it was previously impossible. Really new product ideas disrupt the old ways of doing things—not only for marketers, but also for consumers.

These innovations show that products, customer behavior, and competition change over time. These changes create opportunities for marketing managers and pose challenges as well. Developing new products and managing existing products to meet changing conditions is important to the success of every firm. In Chapter 9 we looked at important strategy planning decisions that need to be made for new products and sometimes changed for existing products. In this chapter, we'll look at how successful new products are developed in the first place—and what marketing managers need to know and do to manage their growth. We'll start by explaining the cycle of growth and decline that new product innovations go through. When you understand the stages in this cycle, you can see *why* it is so critical for a firm to have an effective new-product development process—and why the challenges of managing a product change as it matures. See Exhibit 10-1.

Exhibit 10-1   The Role of Product Management and New-Product Development in Marketing Strategy

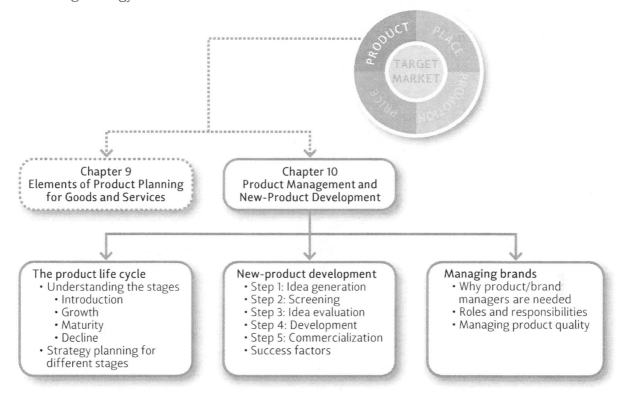

MANAGING PRODUCTS OVER THEIR LIFE CYCLES

Revolutionary products create new product-markets. But competitors are always developing and copying new ideas and products—making existing products out-of-date more quickly than ever. Products, like consumers, go through life cycles.

Product life cycle has four major stages

The **product life cycle** describes the stages a really new product idea goes through from beginning to end. The product life cycle is divided into four major stages: (1) market introduction, (2) market growth, (3) market maturity, and (4) sales decline. The product life cycle is concerned with new types (or categories) of products in the market, not just what happens to an individual brand.

A particular firm's marketing mix usually must change during the product life cycle. There are several reasons why customers' attitudes and needs may change over the product life cycle. The product may be aimed at entirely different target markets at different stages. And the nature of competition moves toward pure competition or oligopoly.

Further, total sales of the product—by all competitors in the industry—vary in each of its four stages. They move from very low in the market introduction stage to high at market maturity and then back to low in the sales decline stage. More important, the profit picture changes too. These general relationships can be seen in Exhibit 10-2. Note that sales and profits do not move together over time. *Industry profits decline while industry sales are still rising.*[2]

Market introduction— investing in the future

In the **market introduction** stage, sales are low as a new idea is first introduced to a market. Customers aren't looking for the product. Even if the product offers superior value, customers don't even know about it. Informative promotion is needed to tell potential customers about the advantages and uses of the new product concept.

Edition

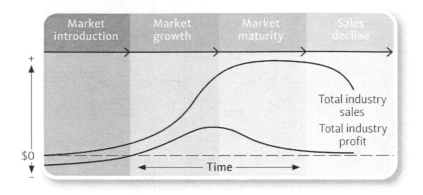

Exhibit 10-2
Typical Life Cycle of a
New Product Concept

Even though a firm promotes its new product, it takes time for customers to learn that the product is available. Most companies experience losses during the introduction stage because they spend so much money for Product, Place, and Promotion development. Of course, they invest the money in the hope of future profits.

Market growth—
profits go up and down

In the market growth stage, industry sales grow fast—but industry profits rise and then start falling. The innovator begins to make big profits as more and more customers buy. But competitors see the opportunity and enter the market. Some just copy the most successful product or try to improve it to compete better. Others try to refine their offerings to do a better job of appealing to some target markets. The new entries result in much product variety. So monopolistic competition—with down-sloping demand curves—is typical of the market growth stage.

This is the time of biggest profits *for the industry*. It is also a time of rapid sales and earnings growth for companies with effective strategies. *But it is toward the end of this stage when industry profits begin to decline* as competition and consumer price sensitivity increase. See Exhibit 10-2.

Some firms make big strategy planning mistakes at this stage by not understanding the product life cycle. They see the big sales and profit opportunities of the early market growth stage but ignore the competition that will soon follow. When they realize their mistake, it may be too late. This happened with many dot-coms during the late 1990s. Marketing managers who understand the cycle and pay attention to competitor analysis are less likely to encounter this problem.

Now that GPS devices are in the market growth stage of the product life cycle, competition is intense between a number of firms who offer a variety of models with different features. To stay ahead, Magellan continues to innovate. For example, its Maestro targets people who want a thin, portable unit with advanced features like voice command and live traffic reporting.

Market maturity—sales level off, profits continue down

The market maturity stage occurs when industry sales level off and competition gets tougher. Many aggressive competitors have entered the race for profits—except in oligopoly situations. Industry profits go down throughout the market maturity stage because promotion costs rise and some competitors cut prices to attract business. Less efficient firms can't compete with this pressure—and they drop out of the market. There is a long-run downward pressure on prices.

New firms may still enter the market at this stage—increasing competition even more. Note that late entries skip the early life-cycle stages, including the profitable market growth stage. And they must try to take a share of the saturated market from established firms, which is difficult and expensive. The market leaders have a lot at stake, so they fight hard to defend their share. Customers who are happy with their current relationship won't switch to a new brand. So late entrants usually have a tough battle.

Persuasive promotion becomes even more important during the market maturity stage. Products may differ only slightly. Most competitors have discovered effective appeals or just copied the leaders. As the various products become almost the same in the minds of potential consumers, price sensitivity is a real factor.[3]

The video game market vividly illustrates these competitive forces. By the time Microsoft introduced its Xbox game console, Nintendo's GameCube and Sony's PlayStation were already established leaders in the maturing market. Microsoft hoped to grab market share with a superior product designed to sell at a competitive price. To tout the advantages of the Xbox, it spent heavily on promotion. The others fought back with costly promotions of their own. Then Sony took advantage of its economies of scale and slashed the PlayStation II price by a third soon after Xbox hit the market. Nintendo followed with its own cuts. Experts estimate that, after matching the lower prices, Microsoft *lost* about $100 on each unit it sold. All the low prices did prompt renewed growth in unit sales. As the market leader, the added volume helped Sony make up for revenue lost from its price cut. However, for Microsoft, the expanded volume resulted in even greater total costs of coming into the market late. Time will tell if Microsoft's strengths will help it recoup profits by capturing share in video game software, a market that is still growing.[4]

In the United States, the markets for most cars, boats, and many household appliances are in market maturity. This stage may continue for many years—until a basically new product idea comes along—even though individual brands or models come and go. For example, high-definition digital TV (HDTV) is coming on now, so it is making obsolete not only the old-style TVs but also the broadcast systems on which they rely.

Sales decline—a time of replacement

During the sales decline stage, new products replace the old. Price competition from dying products becomes more vigorous—but firms with strong brands may make profits until the end because they have successfully differentiated their products.

As the new products go through their introduction stage, the old ones may keep some sales by appealing to their most loyal customers or those who are slow to try new ideas. These conservative buyers might switch later—smoothing the sales decline.

PRODUCT LIFE CYCLES SHOULD BE RELATED TO SPECIFIC MARKETS

Remember that product life cycles describe industry sales and profits for a *product idea* within a particular product-market. The sales and profits of an individual brand may not, and often do not, follow the life-cycle pattern. They may vary up and down throughout the life cycle—sometimes moving in the opposite direction of industry sales and profits. Further, a product idea may be in a different life-cycle stage in different markets.

Individual brands may not follow the pattern

A given firm may introduce or drop a specific product during *any* stage of the product life cycle. A "me-too" brand introduced during the market growth stage, for example, may never get sales at all and suffer a quick death. For instance, Wal-Mart tried to rent DVDs by mail—but the innovator, Netflix, was already established as the market

Edition

In the market maturity stage of the product life cycle, product improvements usually don't result in big increases in the size of the overall market but rather help the improved brand take a larger market share. For example, Colgate's new brush for sensitive teeth may win a larger share of business from segments with that need. Similarly, Dawn may become even more popular with an air freshener built into the base.

leader. When customers did not see Wal-Mart's marketing mix as better, it failed to attract enough customers and closed operations.

Strategy planners who naively expect sales of an individual product to follow the general product life-cycle pattern are likely to be rudely surprised. In fact, it might be more sensible to think in terms of "product-market life cycles" rather than product life cycles—but we will use the term *product life cycle* because it is commonly accepted and widely used.

Each market should be carefully defined

How we see product life cycles depends on how broadly we define a product-market. For example, milk is a mature product in the United States. U.S. consumers drink about 18 times more milk than consumers in Asia. Milk is a good source of calcium in diets, so higher milk consumption there could help reduce Asia's high level of osteoporosis, a bone disease related to low calcium levels. To get sales growth in Asia, milk producers promote this benefit—but they've also added ginger and honey flavors to appeal to Asian palates.[5] As this example suggests, a firm with a mature product can sometimes find new growth in international markets.

How broadly we define the needs of customers in a product-market also affects how we view product life cycles—and who the competitors are. Consider the needs related to storing and preparing foods. Wax paper sales in the United States started to decline when Dow introduced Saran Wrap. Then sales of Saran Wrap (and other similar products) fell sharply when small plastic storage bags became popular. However, sales picked up again later when microwave cooking became popular. Then resealable bags like those from Ziploc took over because they can be used in both the freezer and the microwave.

If a market is defined broadly, there may be many competitors—and the market may appear to be in market maturity. On the other hand, if we focus on a narrow submarket—and a particular way of satisfying specific needs—then we may see much shorter product life cycles as improved product ideas come along to replace the old.

PRODUCT LIFE CYCLES VARY IN LENGTH

How long a whole product life cycle takes—and the length of each stage—varies a lot across products. The cycle may vary from 90 days—in the case of toys like the *Incredibles* movie line—to possibly 100 years for gas-powered cars.

IF AN EAR
THERMOMETER
SOUNDS PECULIAR,
IMAGINE THE
REACTION TO THE
FIRST RECTAL
THERMOMETER.

THERMOSCAN

New products that do a better job of meeting the needs of specific target customers are more likely to move quickly and successfully through the introductory stage of the product life cycle.

The product life-cycle concept does not tell a manager precisely *how long* the cycle will last. But a manager can often make a good guess based on the life cycle for similar products. Sometimes marketing research can help too. However, it is more important to expect and plan for the different stages than to know the precise length of each cycle.

Some products move fast

A new-product idea will move through the early stages of the life cycle more quickly when it has certain characteristics. For example, the greater the *comparative advantage* of a new product over those already on the market, the more rapidly its sales will grow. Sales growth is also faster when the product is *easy to use* and if its advantages are *easy to communicate*. If the product *can be tried* on a limited basis—without a lot of risk to the customer—it can usually be introduced more quickly. Finally, if the product is *compatible* with the values and experiences of target customers, they are likely to buy it more quickly.

The fast adoption of DVD players is a good example. The idea of renting or buying movies to view at home was already compatible with consumer lifestyles, but many consumers hesitated before buying a DVD player. They wanted to see if DVD movies would be readily available. As movies appeared, DVD player sales took off because they had advantages over VHS tape players. Consumers could tell that the picture and audio quality were better from a store demo—without buying anything. Further, ads highlighted DVD extras such as deleted scenes and interviews with directors. DVD players also worked with music CDs. Now that the price of DVD recorders (and digital video recorders) have fallen, they have driven VHS recorders into the market decline stage of the product life cycle. Note, however, that DVD player adoption has not been as fast in less-developed countries where TV penetration is still low, movies are not available, and the costs are higher relative to consumer income.[6]

> **Internet EXERCISE**
>
> A number of software, hardware, and programming firms are working on products that deliver Internet information via TV. Explore the MSN TV website (www.msntv.com) to find out about one aspect of this idea and try the demos. How does MSN TV stack up when you consider the characteristics that help a new product move through the life cycle more quickly?

Product life cycles are getting shorter

Although the life of different products varies, in general product life cycles are getting shorter. This is partly due to rapidly changing technology. One new invention may make possible many new products that replace old ones. Tiny electronic microchips led to thousands of new products—from Texas Instruments calculators in the early days to microchip-controlled heart valves now.

The XO Laptop is another interesting case. It is a stripped-down unit with a sunlight-friendly screen that was developed by a professor at MIT. He created it as a way to help kids in the developing world, and he hoped a low $150 price would

Edition

encourage governments to buy in bulk. Some people thought he was just an idealist, but the XO created such a stir that it prodded Microsoft and Intel to figure out what they should do for this market.[7]

Although life cycles keep moving in the developed economies, many advances bypass most consumers in less-developed economies. These consumers struggle at the subsistence level, without an effective macro-marketing system to stimulate innovation. However, some of the innovations and economies of scale made possible in the advanced societies do trickle down to benefit these consumers. Inexpensive antibiotics and drought-resistant plants, for example, are making a life-or-death difference.

The early bird usually makes the profits

The product life cycle means that firms must be developing new products all the time. Further, they must try to use marketing mixes that will make the most of the market growth stage—when profits are highest.

During the growth stage, competitors are likely to rapidly introduce product improvements. Fast changes in marketing strategy may be required here because profits don't necessarily go to the innovator. Sometimes fast copiers of the basic idea win in the market growth stage. General Motors' electric car, the EV1, was the first zero-emission vehicle on the market when it was first sold in California. However, Toyota and Honda leapfrogged past GM when they introduced hybrid vehicles powered by a combination of gas engine and electric motor. Their hybrids did not eliminate all emissions, but they met other needs better. They have more power and are less expensive. The market for low-emission hybrids is growing rapidly, yet GM is still playing catch-up. Marketers need to be innovative, but at the same time they must be flexible in adapting to the needs and attitudes of their target markets.[8]

The short happy life of fashions and fads

The sales of some products are influenced by fashion—the currently accepted or popular style. Fashion-related products tend to have short life cycles. What is currently popular can shift rapidly. A certain color or style of clothing—baggy jeans, miniskirts, or four-inch-wide ties—may be in fashion one season and outdated the next. Marketing managers who work with fashions often have to make really fast product changes.

How fast is fast enough? Zara, a women's fashion retailer based in Spain, takes only about two weeks to go from a new fashion concept to having items on the racks of its stores. At headquarters, sales managers sit at computers monitoring sales at every store around the world. When a garment is hot, more is produced and shipped. Otherwise, it's dropped. And then Zara's market-watching designers, who are sitting nearby, get the order to whip up fresh designs. The designers get a constant flow of new fashion ideas from music videos, fashion shows, and magazines. Zara quickly produces just enough of a design to test the waters and then sends it out for overnight delivery to some of its stores around the world. Stores are stocked with new designs, not just new orders, about twice a week. Shipping labels identify the newest collections so they can be rushed to the sales floor on their plastic shipping hangers, and only later are they switched to Zara's normal wood hangers. Zara regulars know to search out the black plastic hangers for the latest looks. Store managers use handheld computers that show how garments rank by sales, so clerks can reorder best-sellers in less than an hour. These orders arrive, together with new pieces, two days later. With this system, items are rarely on the shelves of Zara stores for more than a few weeks, but that helps to convey an air of exclusivity.[9]

Spring Summer 08 / Woman & Man

A certain color or style may be in fashion one season and outdated the next. Zara, a fashion retailer, puts its catalog on its website (www.zara.com) so it can be updated quickly each season.

A **fad** is an idea that is fashionable only to certain groups who are enthusiastic about it. But these groups are so fickle that a fad is even more short lived than a regular fashion. Low-carbohydrate diets were very popular for a while, for example. Many toys—whether it's a Hasbro *Lord of the Rings* plastic figure or a Toymax Paintball pack—are fads but do well during a short-lived cycle.[10]

PLANNING FOR DIFFERENT STAGES OF THE PRODUCT LIFE CYCLE

Length of cycle affects strategy planning

Where a product is in its life cycle—and how fast it's moving to the next stage—should affect marketing strategy planning. Marketing managers must make realistic plans for the later stages. Exhibit 10-3 shows the relationship of the product life cycle to the marketing mix variables. The technical terms in this figure are discussed later in the book.

Introducing new products

Exhibit 10-3 shows that a marketing manager has to do a lot of strategy planning to introduce a really new product. Money must be spent developing the new product. Even if the product is unique, this doesn't mean that everyone will immediately come running to the producer's door. The firm will have to build channels of distribution—perhaps offering special incentives to win cooperation. Promotion is needed to build demand *for the whole idea* not just to sell a specific brand. Because all this is expensive, it may lead the marketing manager to try to "skim" the market—charging a relatively high price to help pay for the introductory costs.

The correct strategy, however, depends on how quickly the new idea will be accepted by customers—and how quickly competitors will follow with their own versions of the product. When the early stages of the cycle will be fast, a low initial (penetration) price may make sense to help develop loyal customers early and keep competitors out.

Pioneer may need help from competitors

Sometimes it's not in the best interest of the market pioneer for competitors to stay out of the market. Building customer interest in a really new product idea—and obtaining distribution to make the product available—can be too big a job for a

Edition

Exhibit 10-3
Typical Changes in
Marketing Variables
over the Product Life
Cycle

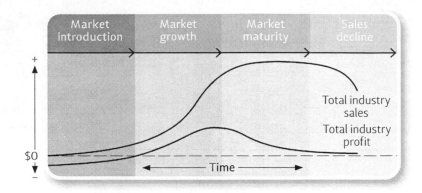

	Market introduction	Market growth	Market maturity	Sales decline
Product	One or few	Variety—try to find best product Build brand familiarity	All "same" Battle of brands	Some drop out
Place	Build channels Maybe selective distribution	} Move toward more intensive distribution ➝		
Promotion	Build primary demand Pioneering-informing	Build selective demand ————————➝ Informing/Persuading ⟶ Persuading/Reminding (frantically competitive)		
Price	Skimming or penetration	Meet competition (especially in oligopoly) ————➝ or Price dealing and price cutting ——————————➝		
Competitive situation	Monopoly or monopolistic competition	Monopolistic competition or oligopoly	Monopolistic competition or oligopoly heading toward pure competition }	➝

single company. Two or more companies investing in promotion to build demand may help to stimulate the growth of the whole product-market. Similarly, a new product may languish if it is not compatible with other products that customers rely on. This is what happened with Digital Video Express (Divx) video disks. When Divx came out, many consumer-electronics firms were launching DVD format products. Divx had advantages over DVD, but it was not compatible with many of the ordinary DVD players that were already on the market. Video stores didn't want to stock movies in both formats, so Divx fizzled. Clearly, the long-term stakes can be huge in this sort of battle. That's why the same sort of fight occurred again recently between a "team" of firms who supported Blu-ray video discs and another team that supported HD-DVD. Each side invested hundreds of millions of dollars in promotion before Blu-ray won out.[11]

New product sales may not take off

Not all new-product ideas catch on. Customers or intermediaries may not be satisfied with the marketing mix, or other new products may meet the same need better. But the success that eludes a firm with its initial strategy can sometimes be

CHAPTER 10

269

Product Management and New-Product Development

achieved by modifying the strategy. David Mintz invented a soy-based frozen dessert and started Tofutti Brands, Inc., to sell it. Tofutti was especially appealing to people who could not eat dairy products. Mintz's strategy was to offer a limited number of flavors and partner with a big company that already had national distribution in supermarkets. Häagen-Dazs agreed to the plan but wanted exclusive distribution rights. Sales grew quickly at first but then plummeted when conflicts between Mintz and Häagen-Dazs ended the relationship. To keep consumers interested in Tofutti while he slowly rebuilt distribution through a dozen specialized wholesalers, Mintz had to constantly offer new flavors.[12]

Managing maturing products

It's important for a firm to have some competitive advantage as it moves into market maturity. Even a small advantage can make a big difference—and some firms do very well by carefully managing their maturing products. They are able to capitalize on a slightly better product or perhaps lower production or marketing costs. Or they are simply more successful at promotion—allowing them to differentiate their more or less homogeneous product from competitors. For example, graham crackers were competing in a mature market and sales were flat. Nabisco used the same ingredients to create bite-sized Teddy Grahams and then promoted them heavily. These changes captured new sales and profits for Nabisco.[13]

Industry profits are declining in market maturity. Top managers must see this, or they will expect the attractive profits that are no longer possible. If top managers don't understand the situation, they may place impossible burdens on the marketing department—causing marketing managers to think about deceptive advertising or some other desperate attempt to reach impossible objectives.

Product life cycles keep moving. But that doesn't mean a firm should just sit by as its sales decline. There are other choices. A firm can improve its product or develop an innovative new product for the same market. Or it can develop a strategy for its product (perhaps with modifications) targeted at a new market. For example, it might try to serve a new need or find a market in a country where the life cycle is not so far along. That approach is working for InSinkErator. It has an 80 percent share of all garbage disposals, but in the mature U.S. market, disposals are already in half of all homes. In contrast, garbage disposals are in only about 10 percent of homes in many areas of Europe and Asia. Many households there can afford a disposal, but in congested cities they have often been prohibited because the ground-up food puts an extra load on water treatment facilities. However, these restrictions are easing in some areas because of new treatment facilities that recycle the food sludge and convert it to

Some companies continue to do well in market maturity by improving their products or by finding new uses and applications. As shown in this ad, DuPont International's Lycra has expanded from personal apparel to furniture upholstery.

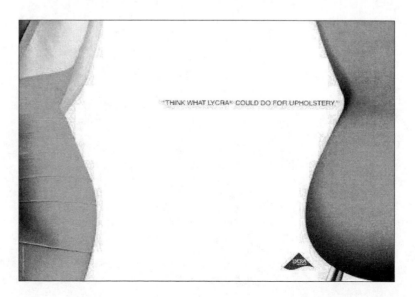

"THINK WHAT LYCRA® COULD DO FOR UPHOLSTERY."

Edition

Tide detergent has been improved many times over the years, and currently there are 37 different versions of Tide, including the new 2X Ultra Tide. However, some innovations, like Tide's convenient Rapid Action Tablets, that were introduced in the market maturity stage of the product life cycle are no longer on the market. On the other hand, the handy Tide to Go stain remover extends the brand name to a new product category.

methane gas energy. These changes are giving InSinkErator new growth in overseas markets.[14]

Improve the product or develop a new one

When a firm's product has won loyal customers, it can be successful for a long time—even in a mature or declining market. However, continued improvements may be needed as customers' needs shift. An outstanding example is Procter & Gamble's Tide. Introduced in 1947, Tide led to a whole new generation of powdered laundry products that cleaned better with fewer suds. But Tide continues to change because of new washing machines and fabrics. The Tide sold today has had at least 55 modifications.

Do product modifications—like those made with powdered Tide—create a wholly new product that should have its own product life cycle? Or are they technical adjustments of the original product idea? We will take the latter position—focusing on the product idea rather than changes in features. This means that some of these Tide changes were made in the market maturity stage. But this type of product improvement can help to extend the product life cycle.

On the other hand, a firm that develops an innovative new product may move to a new product life cycle. For example, by 1985 new liquid detergents like Wisk were moving into the growth stage, and sales of powdered detergents were declining. To share in the growth-stage profits for liquid detergents and to offset the loss of customers from powdered Tide, Procter & Gamble introduced Liquid Tide.

Even though regular powdered detergents are in the decline stage, traditional powdered Tide continues to sell well because it still does the job for some consumers. But sales growth is likely to come from liquid detergents and the newer low-suds detergents.[15]

Develop new strategies for different markets

In a mature market, a firm may be fighting to keep or increase its market share. But if the firm finds a new use for the product, it may stimulate overall demand. DuPont's Teflon fluorocarbon resin is a good example. It was developed more than 50 years ago and has enjoyed sales growth as a nonstick coating for cookware and as a lining for chemically resistant equipment. But marketing managers for Teflon are not waiting to be stuck with declining profits in those mature markets. They are constantly developing strategies for new markets. For example, Teflon is now selling well as a special coating for the wires used in high-speed communications between computers and as a lightweight film that offers greater output power for photovoltaic solar panels.[16]

Phasing out dying products

Not all strategies are exciting growth strategies. If prospects are poor in a product-market, a phase-out strategy may be needed. The need for phasing out becomes more obvious as the sales decline stage arrives. But even in market maturity, it may be clear that a particular product is not going to be profitable enough to reach the company's objectives. In any case, it is wise to remember that marketing plans are implemented as ongoing strategies. Salespeople make calls, inventory moves in the channel, advertising is scheduled for several months into the future, and so on. So the firm usually experiences losses if managers end a plan too abruptly. Because of this, it's sometimes better to phase out the product gradually.

Phasing out a product may involve some difficult implementation problems. But phase-out is also a *strategy*—and it must be market-oriented to cut losses. In fact, it is possible to milk a dying product for some time if competitors move out more quickly and there is ongoing (though declining) demand. Some customers are willing to pay attractive prices to get their old favorite.

NEW-PRODUCT PLANNING

In most markets, progress marches on. So it is essential for a firm to develop new products or modify its current products to meet changing customer needs and competitors' actions. Not having an active new-product development process means that consciously, or subconsciously, the firm has decided to milk its current products and go out of business. New-product planning is not an optional matter. It has to be done just to survive in today's dynamic markets. Consider something as basic as a Bic lighter. It's always been a reliable product and a good value. For years, most of them were used to light cigarettes. But in response to changes in the cultural environment, Bic is coming out with new products for other needs. The Luminere lighter, for example, has a long stem that can move into several positions that make it ideal for lighting candles in hard-to-reach places.

What is a new product?

In discussing the introductory stage of product life cycles, we focused on the types of really new product innovations that tend to disrupt old ways of doing things. However, each year firms introduce many products that are basically refinements of existing products. So a **new product** is one that is new *in any way* for the company concerned.

A product can become "new" in many ways. A fresh idea can be turned into a new product and start a new product life cycle. For example, Alza Corporation's time-release skin patches are replacing pills and injections for some medications.

Variations on an existing product idea can also make a product new. For example, Logitech has improved the lowly computer mouse by making it wireless and Gatorade has made its bottle easier to grip. Even small changes in an existing product can make it new.[17]

FTC says product is "new" only six months

A firm can call its product new for only a limited time. Six months is the limit according to the Federal Trade Commission (FTC)—the federal government agency that polices antimonopoly laws. To be called new, says the FTC, a product must be entirely new or changed in a "functionally significant or substantial respect."[18]

Ethical issues in new-product planning

New-product decisions—and decisions to abandon old products—often involve ethical considerations. For example, some firms (including firms that develop drugs) have been criticized for holding back important new-product innovations until patents run out, or sales slow down, on their existing products.

Edition

At the same time, others have been criticized for "planned obsolescence"—releasing new products that the company plans to soon replace with improved new versions. Similarly, wholesalers and retailers complain that producers too often keep their new-product introduction plans a secret and leave intermediaries with dated inventory that they can sell only at a loss.

Companies also face ethical dilemmas when they decide to stop supplying a product or the service and replacement parts to keep it useful. An old model of a Cuisinart food processor, for example, might be in perfect shape except for a crack in the plastic mixing bowl. It's sensible for the company to improve the design if the crack is a frequent problem, but if consumers can't get a replacement part for the model they already own, they're left holding the bag.

Criticisms are also leveled at firms that constantly release minor variations of products that already saturate markets. Consider what happened with disposable diapers. Marketing managers thought that they were serving some customers' needs better when they offered diapers in boys' and girls' versions and in a variety of sizes, shapes, and colors. But many retailers felt that the new products were simply a ploy to get more shelf space. Further, some consumers complained that the bewildering array of choices made shopping difficult. Some people would level the same criticism at Huggies Little Swimmers Disposable Swimpants. But unlike other disposables, this product doesn't swell in the water. They have been a success because they seem to fill a different need.

Different marketing managers might have very different reactions to such criticisms. However, product management decisions often have a significant effect on customers and intermediaries. A too-casual decision may lead to a negative backlash that affects the firm's strategy or reputation.[19]

AN ORGANIZED NEW-PRODUCT DEVELOPMENT PROCESS IS CRITICAL

Identifying and developing new-product ideas—and effective strategies to go with them—is often the key to a firm's success and survival. But the costs of new-product development and the risks of failure are high. Experts estimate that consumer packaged-goods companies spend more than $20 million to introduce a new brand—and 80 to 95 percent of those new brands flop. That's a big expense—and a waste. In the service sector, the front-end cost of a failed effort may not be as high, but it can have a devastating long-term effect if dissatisfied consumers turn elsewhere for help.[20]

A new product may fail for many reasons. Most often, companies fail to offer a unique benefit or underestimate the competition. Sometimes the idea is good but the company has design problems—or the product costs much more to produce than was expected. Some companies rush to get a product on the market without developing a complete marketing plan.[21]

Internet EXERCISE

Marketing Intelligence Service, Ltd., is a U.S.-based firm that tracks new consumer packaged-goods—both successes and failures. Enter its website (www.productscan.com) and click on the *What's New* button; then review its selections for new-product innovations of the year. Do you think that these products offer customers superior value, or are they just me-too imitations?

But moving too slowly can be a problem too. With the fast pace of change for many products, speedy entry into the market can be a key to competitive advantage. Marketing managers at Xerox learned this the hard way. Japanese competitors were taking market share with innovative new models of copiers. It turned out that the competitors were developing new models twice as fast as Xerox and at half the cost. For Xerox to compete, it had to slash its five-year product development cycle.[22]

The longer new-product development takes, the more likely it is that customer needs will be different when the product is actually introduced. Back in 2005, consumer interest in trucks and SUVs was high. General Motors expected that popularity to continue when planning new models. But, by the time those vehicles were on the market in 2008, gasoline prices had skyrocketed—and consumer preferences were

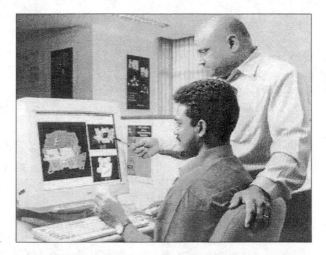

GE developed a software system so that its design engineers in different parts of the world could collaborate over the Internet in real time—which helps GE develop new products more quickly and effectively.

switching to smaller cars. In contrast, Toyota's new-product planning had focused on more fuel efficiency, and its new 2008 hybrid models were in hot demand.

To move quickly and also avoid expensive new-product failures, companies should follow an organized new-product development process. The following pages describe such a process, which moves logically through five steps: (1) idea generation, (2) screening, (3) idea evaluation, (4) development (of product and marketing mix), and (5) commercialization.[23] See Exhibit 10-4.

The general process is similar for both consumer and business markets—and for both goods and services. There are some significant differences, but we will emphasize the similarities in the following discussion.

Process tries to kill new ideas—economically

An important element in the new-product development process is continued evaluation of a new idea's likely profitability and return on investment. The hypothesis tested is that the new idea will *not* be profitable. This puts the burden on the new idea—to prove itself or be rejected. Such a process may seem harsh, but experience shows that most new ideas have some flaw. Marketers try to discover those flaws early, and either find a remedy or reject the idea completely. Applying this process requires much analysis of the idea *before* the company spends money to develop and market a product. This is a major departure from the usual production-oriented approach—in which a company develops a product first and then asks sales to "get rid of it."

Step 1: Idea generation

Finding new-product ideas can't be left to chance. Instead, firms need a formal procedure to generate a continuous flow of ideas. New ideas can come from a company's own sales or production staff, wholesalers or retailers, competitors, consumer surveys, or other sources such as trade associations, advertising agencies, or government agencies. By analyzing new and different views of the company's markets and studying

Exhibit 10-4 New-Product Development Process

Idea generation	Screening	Idea evaluation	Development	Commercialization
Ideas from: Customers and users Marketing research Competitors Other markets Company people Intermediaries, etc.	Strengths and weaknesses Fit with objectives Market trends Rough ROI estimate	Concept testing Reactions from customers Rough estimates of costs, sales, and profits	R&D Develop model or service prototype Test marketing mix Revise plans as needed ROI estimate	Finalize product and marketing plan Start production and marketing "Roll out" in select markets Final ROI estimate

present consumer behavior, a marketing manager can spot opportunities that have not yet occurred to competitors or even to potential customers. For example, ideas for new service concepts may come directly from analysis of consumer complaints.

No one firm can always be first with the best new ideas. So companies should pay attention to what competitors are doing. Some firms use what's called *reverse engineering*. For example, new-product specialists at Ford Motor Company buy other firms' cars as soon as they're available. Then they take the cars apart to look for new ideas or improvements. British Airways talks to travel agents to learn about new services offered by competitors.[24]

Other firms "shop" in international markets for new ideas. For instance, food companies in Europe are experimenting with an innovation from Japan—a clear, odorless, natural film for wrapping food. Consumers don't have to unwrap it; when they put the product in boiling water or a microwave, the wrapper vanishes.[25]

Step 2: Screening

Screening involves evaluating the new ideas with the type of S.W.O.T analysis described in Chapter 2 and the product-market screening criteria described in Chapter 3. Recall that these criteria include the combined output of a resources (strengths and weaknesses) analysis, a long-run trends analysis, and a thorough understanding of the company's objectives. See Exhibit 2-10 and Exhibit 3-5. A "good" new idea should eventually lead to a product (and marketing mix) that will give the firm a competitive advantage—hopefully, a lasting one.

The life-cycle stage at which a firm's new product enters the market has a direct bearing on its prospects for growth. So screening should consider how the strategy for a new product will hold up over the whole product life cycle.

Thinking about the strengths and weaknesses of a new-product idea from both a short- and long-term perspective can be a challenge. However, decisions about how the firm brings a new product to market often shape future market opportunities (and threats). A classic example is IBM's decision to license the operating system for the IBM PC when it was introduced. At that time, designing a PC to use an existing operating system (like the one then available from Microsoft) was a fast and low-cost way to get to market. However, the operating system ultimately produced more profit for Microsoft than the hardware did for IBM.

Some companies screen based on consumer welfare

Screening should also consider how a new product will affect consumers over time. Ideally, the product should increase consumer welfare, not just satisfy a whim. Exhibit 10-5 shows different kinds of new-product opportunities. Obviously, a socially responsible firm tries to find desirable opportunities rather than deficient ones. This may not be as easy as it sounds, however. Some consumers want pleasing products and give little thought to their own long-term welfare.

A consumer in the United States may conclude that a new product with a low price is a good value and purchase it. If the product's low price was possible because it was produced in China—where there are fewer costly pollution controls—the real value may not be what it seems. Even if the product itself is satisfactory right now, unchecked pollution from Chinese factories is contributing to global climate change. Over time that will reduce the welfare of the product's customers—and all other

Exhibit 10–5
Types of New-Product Opportunities

		Immediate satisfaction	
		High	Low
Long-run consumer welfare	High	Desirable products	Salutary products
	Low	Pleasing products	Deficient products

Great New-Product Ideas May Be Ready to Bloom

To generate better new-product ideas, marketing managers need to ask the right questions of the right people, and often that's customers. Jim McCann, CEO of online gift shop 1-800-Flowers.com, always asks for new-product ideas when he's making a presentation. One customer answered his question by sending him a photo of a flower arrangement in an oversized martini glass. Soon afterwards, the "Happy Hour Bouquet" became the company's biggest new-product introduction ever.

When asking customers for new-product ideas, marketing managers have to be careful what they ask. Customers usually think about such questions in terms of what they have already experienced—so they typically suggest minor improvements to products they already know rather than something bigger or more different. Consider Kawasaki's experience. The inventor of the original Jet Ski asked customers for ideas on how to improve the Jet Ski ride. Customers suggested extra padding on the sides to make the standing position more comfortable, and Kawasaki added this feature. But competitors asked a different question: "What can we do to give you a better experience riding your personal watercraft?" When customers said they wanted a more comfortable ride, competitors responded with *seated* models, which soon outsold Kawasaki's *stand-up* Jet Ski.

Marketing managers should also seek out the advice of people in the firm who work in other departments, such as sales, research and development, and customer service. Focused questions are often best for getting the juices flowing. For example, a focused question like, "What much-loved children's product could we re-create in an extreme form for adults?" might have inspired highly successful new products like Jelly Belly gourmet beans, Rollerblades, and Spider Man movies. Or, a marketing manager might ask, "What is the biggest hassle about buying our product that customers tolerate without really knowing it?" CarMax asked this question, and the answers changed the way used cars are bought and sold—with CarMax's warranties, comfortable showrooms, and no-haggle prices. The mountain bike moved beyond a small group of enthusiasts when someone asked, "Who is using our product in ways we did not expect?"

Some managers have learned that when they want big ideas they need to pose big questions! In the late 1980s, if a computer company had asked, "How can I reduce costs?" answers might have suggested that the company switch from costly salespeople to less expensive newspaper ads, or perhaps carry less inventory. But if a computer company had instead asked, "What part of our business would we have to eliminate to cut costs by 50 percent?" it might have beaten Michael Dell to his build-to-order distribution model.

So, managers who are looking for more—and better—new-product ideas need to ask the right questions and listen carefully to the answers. They need to ask customers about their needs and wants, and not just solicit their ideas. And they should aim to focus and inspire fellow employees with specific questions.[26]

people. This story isn't about some fictional shopper or product. Rather, many of us can't judge the impact on consumer welfare of the products we buy. However, thinking through such issues is part of the challenge that managers face in trying to develop socially responsible new products. [27]

Safety must be considered

Real acceptance of the marketing concept prompts managers to screen new products on the basis of how safe they are. Safety is not a casual matter. The U.S. Consumer Product Safety Act (of 1972) set up the Consumer Product Safety Commission to encourage safety in product design and better quality control. The commission has a great deal of power. It can set safety standards for products. It can order costly repairs or return of unsafe products. And it can back up its orders with fines and jail sentences. The Food and Drug Administration has similar powers for foods and drugs.

Edition

Product safety complicates strategy planning because not all customers—even those who want better safety features—are willing to pay more for safer products. Some features cost a lot to add and increase prices considerably. These safety concerns must be considered at the screening step because a firm can later be held liable for unsafe products.

Products can turn to liabilities

Product liability means the legal obligation of sellers to pay damages to individuals who are injured by defective or unsafe products. Product liability is a serious matter. Liability settlements may exceed not only a company's insurance coverage but its total assets!

Relative to most other countries, U.S. courts enforce a very strict product liability standard. Sellers may be held responsible for injuries related to their products no matter how the items are used or how well they're designed. In one widely publicized judgment, McDonald's paid a huge settlement to a woman who was burned when her coffee spilled. The court concluded that there was not enough warning about how hot the coffee was.

Product liability is a serious ethical and legal matter. Many countries are attempting to change their laws so that they will be fair to both firms and consumers. But until product liability questions are resolved, marketing managers must be even more sensitive when screening new-product ideas.[28]

ROI is a crucial screening criterion

Getting by the initial screening criteria doesn't guarantee success for the new idea. But it does show that at least the new idea is in the right ballpark *for this firm*. If many ideas pass the screening criteria, a firm must set priorities to determine which ones go on to the next step in the process. This can be done by comparing the ROI (return on investment) for each idea—assuming the firm is ROI-oriented. The most attractive alternatives are pursued first.

Step 3: Idea evaluation

When an idea moves past the screening step, it is evaluated more carefully. Note that an actual product has not yet been developed—and this can handicap the firm in getting feedback from customers. For help in idea evaluation, firms use concept testing—getting reactions from customers about how well a new-product idea fits their needs. Concept testing uses market research—ranging from informal focus groups to formal surveys of potential customers.

Companies can often estimate likely costs, revenue, and profitability at this stage. And marketing research can help identify the size of potential markets. Even informal focus groups are useful—especially if they show that potential users are not excited about the new idea. If results are discouraging, it may be best to kill the idea at this stage. Remember, in this hypothesis-testing process, we're looking for any evidence that an idea is *not* a good opportunity for this firm and should be rejected.

Product planners must think about wholesaler and retailer customers as well as final consumers. Intermediaries may have special concerns about handling a proposed product. A Utah ice-cream maker was considering a new line of ice-cream novelty products—and he had visions of a hot market in California. But he had to drop his idea when he learned that grocery store chains wanted payments of $20,000 each just to stock his frozen novelties in their freezers. [29]

Idea evaluation is often more precise in business markets. Potential customers are more informed—and their needs focus on the economic reasons for buying rather than emotional factors. Further, given the derived nature of demand in business markets, most needs are already being satisfied in some way. So new products just substitute for existing ones. This means that product planners can compare the cost advantages and limitations of a new product with those currently being used. And by interviewing well-informed people, they can determine the range of product requirements and decide whether there is an opportunity.

Whatever research methods are used, the idea evaluation step should gather enough information to help decide whether there is an opportunity, whether it fits with the firm's resources, *and* whether there is a basis for developing a competitive advantage. With such information, the firm can estimate likely ROI in the various market segments and decide whether to continue the new-product development process.[30]

Step 4: Development

Product ideas that survive the screening and idea evaluation steps must now be analyzed further. Usually, this involves some research and development (R&D) and engineering to design and develop the physical part of the product. In the case of a new service offering, the firm will work out the details of what training, equipment, staff, and so on will be needed to deliver on the idea. Input from a firm's earlier efforts helps guide this technical work.

With computer-aided design (CAD) systems, designers can develop lifelike 3-D color drawings of packages and products. Changes can be made almost instantly. They can be sent by e-mail to managers all over the world for immediate review. They can even be put on a website for marketing research with remote customers. Then once the designs are finalized, they feed directly into computer-controlled manufacturing systems. Companies like Motorola and Timex have found that these systems cut their new-product development time in half—giving them a leg up on many competitors.

Even so, it is still useful to test models and early versions of the product in the market. This process may have several cycles. A manufacturer may build a model of a physical product or produce limited quantities; a service firm may try to train a small group of service providers. Product tests with customers may lead to revisions—*before* the firm commits to full-scale efforts.

With actual goods or services, potential customers can react to how well the product meets their needs. Focus groups, panels, and larger surveys can react to specific features and to the whole product idea. Sometimes that reaction kills the idea. For example, Coca-Cola Foods believed it had a great idea with Minute Maid Squeeze-Fresh, frozen orange juice concentrate in a squeeze bottle. In tests, however,

Microsoft Office Live Meeting makes it easy for managers to collaborate and share information without leaving their desks even if they are in different locations. Capabilities such as this are helping to make new-product development efforts faster and easier.

Edition

Squeeze-Fresh bombed. Consumers loved the idea but hated the product. It was messy to use, and no one knew how much concentrate to squeeze in the glass.[31]

Firms often use full-scale market testing to get reactions in real-market conditions or to test variations in the marketing mix. For example, a firm may test alternative brands, prices, or advertising copy in different test cities. Note that the firm is testing the whole marketing mix, not just the product. For example, a hotel chain might test a new service offering at one location to see how it goes over.

Running market tests is costly, but *not* testing is risky. Frito-Lay was so sure it understood consumers' snack preferences that it introduced a three-item cracker line without market testing. Even with network TV ad support, MaxSnax met with overwhelming consumer indifference. By the time Frito-Lay pulled the product from store shelves, it had lost $52 million.[32]

When Schick developed its new Quattro shaving system, it also developed a marketing plan that included a special end-of-aisle display (like this one created by Weyerhaeuser) that showcases the new razor, blades, and packaging.

Step 5: Commercialization

A product idea that survives this far can finally be placed on the market. Putting a product on the market is expensive, and success usually requires cooperation of the whole company. Manufacturing or service facilities have to be set up. Goods have to be produced to fill the channels of distribution, or people must be hired and trained to provide services. Further, introductory promotion is costly—especially if the company is entering a very competitive market.

Because of the size of the job, some firms introduce their products city by city or region by region—in a gradual "rollout"—until they have complete market coverage. Rollouts also permit more market testing, but the main purpose is to do a good job implementing the marketing plan. Marketing managers also need to pay close attention to control—to ensure that the implementation effort is working and that the strategy is on target.

Ethics QUESTION

You are the marketing manager for a company that creates video games. A big competitor has just released an action game that appeals to kids who own your best-selling game. Your competitor's release is a better game because it takes advantage of features available in a hot new video game box. Your firm's updated release won't be available for at least four months. One of your game developers suggests that you preannounce your game will be ready in two months—which is about as long as gamers are likely to wait. Should you announce that your new version is coming or just wait until you know more? If a reporter for a popular gaming magazine calls and asks for a statement about when your firm's release will be on the market, should you say two months, four months, or "we don't know yet"? If your product is preannounced but then not ready by that date, what should your firm communicate to customers? Explain your thinking.

NEW-PRODUCT DEVELOPMENT: A TOTAL COMPANY EFFORT

We've been discussing the steps in a logical, new-product development process. However, as shown in Exhibit 10-6, many factors can impact the success of the effort.

Exhibit 10-6   New-Product Development Success Factors

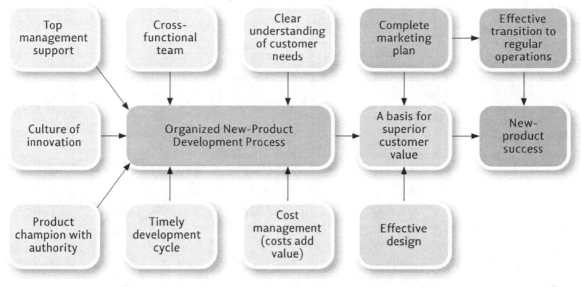

Top-level support is vital

Companies that are particularly successful at developing new goods and services seem to have one key trait in common: enthusiastic top-management support for new-product development. New products tend to upset old routines that managers of established products often try in subtle but effective ways to maintain. So someone with top-level support, and authority to get things done, needs to be responsible for new-product development.[33]

A culture of innovation

A culture that supports innovation can generate more ideas. For example, Google allows its employees the freedom to spend 20 percent of their time working on new ideas, even if the ideas are unrelated to their job description. When people don't see the incentive to push for new ideas, they are likely to get distracted by other priorities that seem more pressing. For many years 3M has had an objective that 30 percent of sales should come from products that didn't exist four years earlier. Consistent with that goal, 3M's innovative culture produced breakthrough products like Scotch Stretchy Tape, Post-it Note Cards, Scotch Brite Tub & Tile Scrubber, and Vikuiti brand films for video screens. However, when the company moved toward more emphasis on cost cutting, the new-product pipeline began to dry up. To regain its innovative edge, 3M is going back to a better balance of efficiency *and* innovation.

In a culture that supports innovation people know that it's okay to take risks. Otherwise, the fear of failure may make managers too cautious. Marketing managers at Coca-Cola had this problem after the flop of New Coke. Instead of pushing for big new ideas, most Coke managers were content with minor variations of existing products.[34]

Put someone in charge

Rather than leaving new-product development to someone in engineering, R&D, or sales who happens to be interested in taking the initiative, successful companies *put* someone in charge. It may be a person, department, or team. But it's not a casual thing. It's a major responsibility of the job.

A new-product development team with people from different departments helps ensure that new ideas are carefully evaluated and profitable ones are quickly brought to market. It's important to choose the right people for the job. Overly conservative managers may kill too many, or even all, new ideas. Or committees may create bureaucratic delays that make the difference between a product's success or failure.

Edition

Market needs guide R&D effort

From the idea generation stage to the commercialization stage, the R&D specialists, the operations people, and the marketing people must work together to evaluate the feasibility of new ideas. They may meet in person, or communicate with e-mail or intranet sites, or perhaps via teleconferencing or some other technology. There are many ways to share ideas. So it isn't sensible for a marketing manager to develop elaborate marketing plans for goods or services that the firm simply can't produce—or produce profitably. It also doesn't make sense for R&D people to develop a technology or product that does not have potential for the firm and its markets. Clearly, a balancing act is involved here. But the critical point is the basic one we've been emphasizing throughout the whole book: Marketing-oriented firms seek to satisfy customer needs at a profit with an integrated, whole company effort.

Steps should not be skipped

Because speed can be important, it's always tempting to skip needed steps when some part of the process seems to indicate that the company has a "really good idea." But the process moves in steps—gathering different kinds of information along the way. By skipping steps, a firm may miss an important aspect that could make a whole strategy less profitable or actually cause it to fail.

NEED FOR PRODUCT MANAGERS

Product variety leads to product managers

When a firm has only one or a few related products, everyone is interested in them. But when a firm has products in several different product categories, management may decide to put someone in charge of each category, or each brand, to be sure that attention to these products is not lost in the rush of everyday business. Product managers or brand managers manage specific products—often taking over the jobs formerly handled by an advertising manager. That gives a clue to what is often their major responsibility—Promotion—since the products have already been developed by the new-product people. However, some brand managers start at the new-product development stage and carry on from there.

Product managers are especially common in large companies that produce many kinds of products. Several product managers may serve under a marketing manager. Sometimes these product managers are responsible for the profitable operation of a particular product's whole marketing effort. Then they have to coordinate their efforts with others, including the sales manager, advertising agencies, production and research people, and even channel members. This is likely to lead to difficulties if product managers have no control over the marketing strategy for other related brands or authority over other functional areas whose efforts they are expected to direct and coordinate.

To avoid these problems, in some companies the product manager serves mainly as a "product champion"—concerned with planning and getting the promotion effort implemented. A higher-level marketing manager with more authority coordinates the efforts and integrates the marketing strategies for different products into an overall plan.

Consumer packaged-goods companies, like Nabisco, usually assign brand managers who are responsible for individual products. However, when there are a number of products in the same product category, there is often a higher-level manager who ensures that the marketing program for the whole category is effective.

The activities of product managers vary a lot depending on their experience and aggressiveness and the company's organizational philosophy. Today, companies are emphasizing marketing *experience*—because this important job takes more than academic training and enthusiasm. But it is clear that someone must be responsible for developing and implementing product-related plans, especially when a company has many products.[35]

CHAPTER 10

281

Product Management and New-Product Development

MANAGING PRODUCT QUALITY

Total quality management meets customer requirements

In Chapter 9 we explained that product quality means the ability of a product to satisfy a customer's needs or requirements. Now we'll expand that idea and discuss some ways a manager can improve the quality of a firm's goods and services. We'll develop these ideas from the perspective of total quality management (TQM), the philosophy that everyone in the organization is concerned about quality, throughout all of the firm's activities, to better serve customer needs.

The cost of poor quality is lost customers

Most of the early attention in quality management focused on reducing defects in goods produced in factories. At one time most firms assumed defects were an inevitable part of mass production. They saw the cost of replacing defective parts or goods as just a cost of doing business—an insignificant one compared to the advantages of mass production. However, many firms were forced to rethink this assumption when Japanese producers of cars, electronics, and cameras showed that defects weren't inevitable. Much to the surprise of some production-oriented managers, the Japanese experience showed that it is less expensive to do something right the first time than it is to pay to do it poorly and *then* pay again to fix problems. And their success in taking customers away from established competitors made it clear that the cost of defects wasn't just the cost of replacement!

From the customer's point of view, getting a defective product and having to complain about it is a big headache. The customer can't use the defective product and suffers the inconvenience of waiting for someone to fix the problem—if *someone* gets around to it. It certainly doesn't deliver superior value. Rather, it erodes goodwill and leaves customers dissatisfied. The big cost of poor quality is the cost of lost customers.

Firms that adopted TQM methods to reduce manufacturing defects soon used the same approaches to overcome many other problems. Their success brought attention to what is possible with TQM—whether the problem concerns poor customer service, flimsy packaging, or salespeople who can't answer customers' questions.

Getting a handle on doing things right the first time

The idea of identifying customer needs and doing things right the first time seems obvious, but it's easier said than done. Problems always come up, and it's not always clear what isn't being done as well as it could be. People tend to ignore problems that don't pose an immediate crisis. But firms that adopt TQM always look for ways to improve implementation with continuous improvement—a

A firm that understands the needs of its target customers can focus on the aspects of quality that are most important for developing superior customer value in its goods or services.

Edition

commitment to constantly make things better one step at a time. Once you accept the idea that there *may* be a better way to do something and you look for it, you may just find it! The place to start is to clearly define "defects" from the customer's point of view.

Things gone right and things gone wrong

Managers who use the TQM approach think of quality improvement as a sorting process—a sorting out of things gone right and things gone wrong. The sorting process calls for detailed measurements related to a problem. Then managers use a set of statistical tools to analyze the measurements and identify the problem areas that are the best candidates for fixing. The statistical details are beyond our focus here, but it's useful to get a feel for how managers use the tools.

Starting with customer needs

Let's consider the case of a restaurant that does well during the evening hours but wants to improve its lunch business. The restaurant develops a strategy that targets local businesspeople with an attractive luncheon buffet. The restaurant decides on a buffet because research shows that target customers want a choice of good healthy food and are willing to pay reasonable prices for it—as long as they can eat quickly and get back to work on time.

As the restaurant implements its new strategy, the manager wants a measure of how things are going. So she encourages customers to fill out comment cards that ask "How did we do today?" After several months of operation, things seem to be going reasonably well—although business is not as brisk as it was at first. The manager reads the comment cards and divides the ones with complaints into categories—to count up different reasons why customers weren't satisfied.

Slay the dragons first

Then the manager creates a graph (see Exhibit 10–7) showing a frequency distribution for the different types of complaints. Quality people call this a Pareto chart—a graph that shows the number of times a problem cause occurs, with problem causes ordered from most frequent to least frequent. The manager's Pareto chart reveals that customers complain most frequently that they have to wait for a seat. There were other common complaints—the buffet was not well organized, the table was not clean, and so on. However, the first complaint is much more common than the next most frequent one.

This is typical. The worst problems often occur over and over again. This focuses the manager's attention on which quality problem to fix first. A rule of quality management is to slay the dragons first—which simply means start with the biggest problem. After removing that problem, the battle moves on to the next most frequent

Exhibit 10–7
Pareto Chart Showing Frequency of Different Complaints

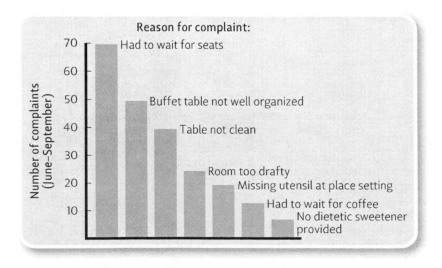

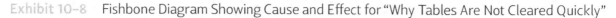

Exhibit 10-8   Fishbone Diagram Showing Cause and Effect for "Why Tables Are Not Cleared Quickly"

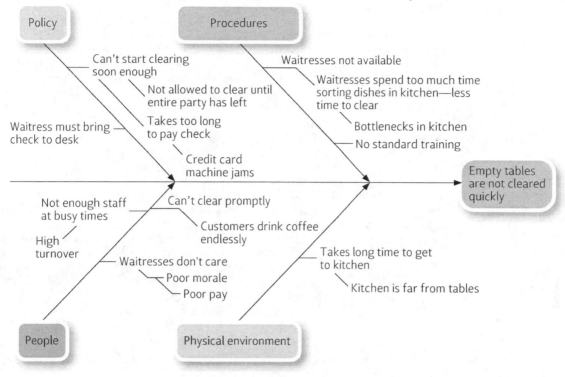

problem. If you do this *continuously*, you solve a lot of problems—and you don't just satisfy customers, you delight them.

Figure out why things go wrong

So far, our manager has only identified the problem. To solve it, she creates a **fishbone diagram**—a visual aid that helps organize cause-and-effect relationships for "things gone wrong." See Exhibit 10–8. With this diagram, our restaurant manager discovers that customers wait to be seated because tables aren't cleared soon enough. In fact, the Pareto chart (Exhibit 10–7) shows that customers also complain frequently about tables not being clean. So the two implementation problems may be related.

The manager's fishbone diagram also summarizes other causes for tables not being cleaned quickly. There are different basic categories of causes—restaurant policy, procedures, people problems, and the physical environment. With this overview of different ways the service operation is going wrong, the manager can decide what to fix. She establishes different formal measures. For example, she counts how frequently different causes delay customers from being seated. She finds that the cashier's faulty credit card scanning machine holds up check processing. About half the time the cashier has to stop and enter the credit card information by hand. The fishbone diagram shows that restaurant policy is to clear the table after the entire party leaves. But customers have to wait at their tables while the staff deals with the faulty credit card machine, and cleaning is delayed. With the credit card machine replaced, the staff can clear the tables sooner—and because they're not so hurried they do a better cleaning job. Two dragons are on the way to being slayed!

Our case shows that people in different areas of the restaurant affect customer satisfaction. The waitperson couldn't do what was needed to satisfy customers because the cashier had trouble with the credit card machine. The TQM approach helps

Edition

everyone see and understand how their job affects what others do and the customer's satisfaction.[36]

Building quality into services

The restaurant case illustrates how a firm can improve product quality with TQM approaches. We used a service example because providing customer service is often a difficult area, regardless of whether a firm's product is primarily a service, primarily a physical good, or a blend of both. For example, a manufacturer of ball bearings isn't just providing wholesalers or producers with round pieces of steel. Customers need information about deliveries, they need orders filled properly, and they may have questions to ask the firm's accountant or engineers. Because almost every firm must manage the service it provides customers, let's focus on some of the special concerns of managing service quality.

Train people and empower them to serve

It's difficult to maintain consistent quality in services because the server is inseparable from the service. A person doing a specific service job may perform one specific task correctly but still annoy the customer in a host of other ways. So two keys to improving service quality are: (1) training and (2) empowerment.

All employees who have any contact with customers need training—many firms see 40 hours a year of training as a minimum. Good training usually includes role-playing on handling different types of customer requests and problems. A rental car attendant who is rude when a customer is trying to turn in a car may leave the customer dissatisfied—even if the rental car was perfect.

Companies can't afford an army of managers to inspect how each employee implements a strategy—and such a system usually doesn't work anyway. Quality cannot be "inspected in." It must come from the people who do the service jobs. So firms that commit to service quality empower employees to satisfy customers' needs. Empowerment means giving employees the authority to correct a problem without first checking with management. At a hotel, for instance, an empowered room-service employee knows it's OK to run across the street to buy the specific brand of bottled water a guest requests.

Managers lead the quality effort

Managers must show that they are committed to doing things right to satisfy customers and that quality is everyone's job. Without top-level support, some people won't get beyond their business-as-usual attitude—and TQM won't work.

Specify jobs and benchmark performance

Managers who develop successful quality programs clearly specify and write out exactly what tasks need to be done, how, and by whom. This may seem unnecessary. After all, most people know, in general, what they're supposed to do. However, if the tasks are clearly specified, it's easier to see what criteria should be used to measure performance.

Once criteria are established, there needs to be some basis on which to evaluate the job being done. In our restaurant example, one part of the job specification for the cashier is to process credit card payments. In that case, relevant criteria might include the amount of time that it takes and the number of people waiting in line to pay. If the restaurant manager had seen a record of how long it was taking to process credit cards, she would have known that for many customers it was taking too long. Without the measure, the precise nature of the problem was hidden.

That takes us to the issue of benchmarking—picking a basis of comparison for evaluating how well a job is being done. For example, consider a case in which an airline asks customers to rate their satisfaction with a flight. Then the company might benchmark each route against the others on average customer satisfaction. But if the service of all the airline's flights is poor, that isn't a sensible approach. The ones that stink the least would look good on a relative basis. Therefore, many firms try to benchmark against some external standard. For example, an airline might want to benchmark against a competitor. Or better, the manager might identify other travel firms that earn superlative customer satisfaction ratings and benchmark against them.

CHAPTER 10

285

Product Management and New-Product Development

www.mhhe.com/fourps

Getting a return on quality is important

While the cost of poor quality is lost customers, the type of quality efforts we've been discussing also result in costs. It's easy to fall into the trap of running up *unnecessary costs* trying to improve some facet of quality that really isn't that important to customer satisfaction or customer retention. When that happens, customers may still be satisfied, but the firm can't make a profit because of the extra costs. In other words, there isn't a financial return on the money spent to improve quality. A manager should focus on quality efforts that really provide the customer with superior value—quality that costs no more to provide than customers will ultimately be willing to pay.[37]

CONCLUSION

This chapter introduced the product life-cycle concept and showed how life cycles affect marketing strategy planning. The product life-cycle concept shows why new products are so important to growth in markets and also helps to explain why different strategies—including strategies for new improved products—need to be developed over time. Innovators—or fast copiers—that successfully bring new products to market are usually the ones who achieve the greatest growth in customer equity.

In today's highly competitive marketplace it is no longer profitable to simply sell "me-too" products. Markets, competition, and product life cycles are changing at a fast pace. New products help a company appeal to new target markets by appealing to unmet needs. New products can also encourage current customers to purchase more. In addition, they can help retain customers by adapting to changing customer needs.

Just because a product is new to a company doesn't mean that it is a really new innovation and starts a new-product life cycle. However, from a marketing manager's perspective, a product is new to the firm if it is new in any way or to any target market. Firms don't just develop and introduce new products; they do so within the context of the whole marketing strategy.

Many new products fail. But we presented an organized new-product development process that helps to prevent that fate. The process makes it clear that new-product success isn't just the responsibility of people from R&D or marketing but rather requires a total company effort.

We also described product and brand management. To help a product or brand grow, managers in these positions usually recommend ways to adjust all of the elements of the marketing mix, but the emphasis is often on Promotion.

Poor product quality results in dissatisfied customers. So alert marketers look for ways to design better quality into new products and to improve the quality of ones they already have. Approaches developed in the total quality management (TQM) movement can be a big help in this regard. Ultimately, the challenge is for the manager to focus on aspects of quality that really matter to the target customer. Otherwise, the cost of the quality offered may be higher than what target customers are willing to pay.

In combination, this chapter and Chapter 9 introduce strategy decision areas for Product and important frameworks that help you see how Product fits within an overall strategy. These chapters also start you down the path to a deeper understanding of the 4Ps. In Chapter 11, we expand on that base by focusing on the role of Place in the marketing mix.

KEY TERMS

product life cycle, 261
market introduction, 261
market growth, 262
market maturity, 263
sales decline, 263
fashion, 266
fad, 267

new product, 271
Federal Trade Commission (FTC), 271
Consumer Product Safety Act, 275
product liability, 276
concept testing, 276
product managers, 280
brand managers, 280

total quality management (TQM), 281
continuous improvement, 281
Pareto chart, 282
fishbone diagram, 283
empowerment, 284
benchmarking, 284

Edition

QUESTIONS AND PROBLEMS

1. Explain how industry sales and industry profits behave over the product life cycle.

2. Cite two examples of products that you think are currently in each of the product life-cycle stages. Consider services as well as physical goods.

3. Explain how you might reach different conclusions about the correct product life-cycle stage(s) in the worldwide automobile market.

4. Explain why individual brands may not follow the product life-cycle pattern. Give an example of a new brand that is not entering the life cycle at the market introduction stage.

5. Discuss the life cycle of a product in terms of its probable impact on a manufacturer's marketing mix. Illustrate using personal computers.

6. What characteristics of a new product will help it to move through the early stages of the product life cycle more quickly? Briefly discuss each characteristic—illustrating with a product of your choice. Indicate how each characteristic might be viewed in some other country.

7. What is a new product? Illustrate your answer.

8. Explain the importance of an organized new-product development process and illustrate how it might be used for (a) a new hair care product, (b) a new children's toy, and (c) a new subscribers-only cable television channel.

9. Discuss how you might use the new-product development process if you were thinking about offering some kind of summer service to residents in a beach resort town.

10. Explain the role of product or brand managers. When would it make sense for one of a company's current brand managers to be in charge of the new-product development process? Explain your thinking.

11. If a firm offers one of its brands in a number of different countries, would it make sense for one brand manager to be in charge, or would each country require its own brand manager? Explain your thinking.

12. Discuss the social value of new-product development activities that seem to encourage people to discard products that are not all worn out. Is this an economic waste? How worn out is all worn out? Must a shirt have holes in it? How big?

13. What are the major advantages of total quality management as an approach for improving the quality of goods and services? What limitations can you think of?

CREATING MARKETING PLANS

The Marketing Plan Coach software on the Student CD and the text website includes a sample marketing plan for Hillside Veterinary Clinic. Look through the "Marketing Strategy" section.

a. Hillside offers many different products. Identify several of these products and indicate where you think each of them is in its product life cycle.

b. Exhibit 10-3 summarizes some marketing mix characteristics based on where a product fits in the product life cycle. Is Hillside's marketing plan consistent with what this exhibit suggests. Why or why not?

SUGGESTED CASES

6. Global Steel Company   20. Recreation Supplies Unlimited
22. Bright Light Innovations

COMPUTER-AIDED PROBLEM

10. GROWTH STAGE COMPETITION

AgriChem, Inc., has introduced an innovative new product—a combination fertilizer, weed killer, and insecticide that makes it much easier for soybean farmers to produce a profitable crop. The product introduction was quite successful, with 1 million units sold in the year of introduction. And AgriChem's profits are increasing. Total market demand is expected to grow at a rate of 200,000 units a year for the next five years. Even so, AgriChem's marketing managers are concerned about what will happen to sales and profits during this period.

Based on past experience with similar situations, they expect one new competitor to enter the market during each of the next five years. They think this competitive pressure will drive prices down about 6 percent a year. Further, although the total market is growing, they know that new competitors will chip away at AgriChem's market share—even with the 10 percent a year increase planned for the promotion budget. In spite of the competitive pressure, the marketing managers are sure that familiarity with AgriChem's brand will help it hold a large share of the total market and give AgriChem greater economies of scale than competitors. In fact, they

Edition

expect that the ratio of profit to dollar sales for AgriChem should be about 10 percent higher than for competitors.

AgriChem's marketing managers have decided the best way to get a handle on the situation is to organize the data in a spreadsheet. They have set up the spreadsheet so they can change the "years in the future" value and see what is likely to happen to AgriChem and the rest of the industry. The starting spreadsheet shows the current situation with data from the first full year of production.

a. Compare AgriChem's market share and profit for this year with what is expected next year—given the marketing managers' current assumptions. What are they expecting? (Hint: Set number of years in the future to 1.)

b. Prepare a table showing AgriChem's expected profit, and the expected industry revenue and profit, for the current year and the next five years. Briefly explain what happens to industry sales and profits and why. (Hint: Do an analysis to vary the number of years in the future value in the spreadsheet from a minimum of 0—the current year—to a maximum of 5. Display the three values requested.)

c. If market demand grows faster than expected—say, at 280,000 units a year—what will happen to AgriChem's profits and the expected industry revenues and profits over the next five years? What are the implications of this analysis?

For additional questions related to this problem, see Exercise 10-4 in the *Learning Aid for Use with Basic Marketing*, 17th edition.

11

CHAPTER

Place and Development of Channel Systems

In the 1970s, the early "microcomputers" were very hard to set up and difficult to use—so there were not many people who wanted them. That also explains why there were no computer stores. Altair, one of the first brands, was initially sold mainly at "electronics fairs." Most of these gatherings were in California; often buyers and sellers would just meet in an open market on Saturday mornings. By the time Heath's more powerful H89 was introduced, ordering from the Heath mail-order catalog was a simpler proposition; however, the H89 came as a kit and the customer had to assemble it. Heath did add value with good telephone technical support—which was already in place for Heath's other electronics kits. Soon after that, when Xerox introduced its 820 model, it had a competitive advantage in distribution because its business customers were able to buy a computer from the same wholesalers who regularly handled Xerox copiers.

By 1980, Radio Shack's easy-to-use TRS-80 was the best-selling computer. The key to its success was that the retail chain already had stores in many cities—so individual consumers could get buying help and tech support from specialists at their local store. Apple saw Radio Shack's success and opened more stores of its own.

As you read this, it is probably occurring to you that most of the firms mentioned are no longer selling computers. Although distribution was expanding, these early firms couldn't adjust quickly enough when IBM introduced its first personal computer (PC). The pull of the IBM brand gave customers the confidence to buy—so sales of PCs surged as IBM quickly established a chain of its own retail stores and also worked closely with select dealers who promised to pay special attention to the IBM brand. Big-business customers bought in quantity directly from IBM's aggressive sales force.

Because IBM's design became an industry standard, firms like Compaq, HP, Toshiba, Samsung, and Dell quickly jumped in with PC models of their own. Many new independent computer dealers popped up to sell these name-brand computers and accessories and share in the profit growth. Before long, large chains like Best Buy, CompUSA, and Office Depot joined the fray. They offered low prices and made it easy for customers to go to one place and compare different brands. Then, as the product life cycle marched along—more customers just wanted a low price and left it to Wal-Mart to offer it. With all of this tough price competition, most independent computer dealers disappeared.

So, after 25 years of change in PCs distribution, no one was surprised in November of 2007 to find computers for sale in a Staples store. Yet, that was the very first time that Staples had ever handled Dell computers, and it was one of the first times that Dell had moved away from its direct-sales model to sell through an independent retailer. Dell's decision

to change its Place arrangement was not made lightly. To see the significance of this strategy change, it's helpful to look back at how Dell's strategy evolved.

As a freshman in college, Michael Dell started buying and reselling computers from his dorm room. At that time, the typical marketing mix for PCs emphasized distribution through specialized computer stores that sold to business users and some final consumers. Often the dealers' service quality didn't justify the high prices they charged, the features of the PCs they had in stock didn't match what customers wanted, and repairs were a hassle.

Dell decided there was a target market of price-conscious customers who would respond to a different marketing mix. He used direct-response advertising in computer magazines—and customers called a toll-free number to order a computer with the exact features they wanted. Dell built computers to match the specific orders that came in and used UPS to quickly ship orders directly to the customer. Prices were low, too, because the direct channel meant there was no retailer markup and the build-to-order approach reduced inventory costs. This approach also kept Dell in constant contact with customers. Problems could be identified quickly and corrected. Dell also implemented the plan well—with constant

improvements—to make good on his promise of reliable machines and superior customer service. For example, Dell also set up ongoing programs to train all employees to work together to please customers. It would have been tough to centralize all of this if he had been working with thousands of retailers.

As sales grew, Dell's firm put more money into advertising. The company's ad agency crafted ads to position Dell in consumers' minds as an aggressive, value-oriented source of computers. At the same time, Dell added a direct-sales force to call on big government and corporate buyers—because they expected in-person selling and a relationship, not just a telephone contact. And when these important customers said they wanted Dell to offer high-power servers to run their corporate networks, Dell put money into R&D to create what they needed.

Dell also saw the prospect for international growth. Many computer firms had moved into Europe by exporting. But Dell made direct investments in the company's own operations there. Dell knew it would be tough to win over skeptical European buyers. They had never bought such big-ticket items as PCs over the phone. On the other hand, there were fewer big retail chains with low prices there, which gave Dell an even better price advantage. So, in less than five years, sales in Europe grew to 40 percent of Dell's total revenue, and Dell pushed into Asian markets for more growth. That also posed challenges, so Dell's advertising manager worked closely with major ad agencies to get better results from Dell's $80 million global advertising campaign.

By the mid-1990s, IBM and other firms were trying to imitate Dell's direct-order approach. However, the retailers who were already selling the bulk of IBM's PCs were not happy about facing price competition from their own supplier! This resulted in real conflict for IBM, and soon it was apparent that it simply couldn't copy Dell's strategy without losing the distribution it already had.

All of the competition to sell PCs pushed down prices—and many firms were worried about how to cope with slim profits. But with the growth of the Internet, Dell saw an opportunity to extend the direct model to a website (www.dell.com). Online selling helped reduce costs, which proved to be especially important when the economy softened and demand for PCs fell off. Dell cut prices in what many competitors saw as an "irrational" price war. But the design of Dell's website and sales system allowed it to charge different prices to different segments to match demand with supply. For example, high-margin laptops were priced lower to educational customers—to stimulate demand—than to government buyers who were less price sensitive. Similarly, if the supply of new 30-inch flat-screen monitors fell short, Dell could use an online promotion for 19-inch monitors and shift demand. To earn more profit from existing customers, Dell also put more emphasis on selling extended-care service agreements.

In spite of the success of Dell's direct approach,

growth in the overall market was not what it had been. IBM, for example, sold its PC business to Lenovo and moved on to other opportunities. To increase sales, Dell started to add small kiosks in retail malls to reach customers who want to shop "in person." It also expanded its product-development efforts with new lines of printers, handheld devices, MP3 players, and TVs. But, these efforts to expand the product line were not that successful, so Dell has had to search for new ways to reach computer customers. One way is to get a share of the business of customers who wouldn't consider shopping online and instead want to purchase from a local retail store. Sony and Apple were already using this approach, and Dell needed to be able to compete with them. So, now when you walk into a Staples or a Wal-Mart you are likely to see Dell's displays.

In its mature market, Dell will need to continue to adjust its marketing program if it is to succeed against tough competitors. And it is likely that an important part of the competitive environment will relate to how Dell and other firms handle strategy decisions for Place.[1]

LEARNING OBJECTIVES

This case shows that offering customers a good product at a reasonable price is not the whole story. Marketing managers must make decisions about how they will make goods and services available to a target customer's Place when the customer wants them. This chapter's learning objectives will help you understand the role of Place in marketing strategy.

When you finish this chapter you should be able to:

1 understand what product classes suggest about Place objectives.
2 understand why some firms use direct channel systems while others work with intermediaries and indirect systems.
3 understand how and why marketing specialists develop to make channel systems more effective.
4 understand how to develop cooperative relationships and avoid conflict in channel systems.
5 know how channel members in vertical marketing systems shift and share functions to meet customer needs.
6 understand the differences between intensive, selective, and exclusive distribution.
7 know the main approaches firms use to reach customers in international markets.
8 understand important new terms (shown in red).

Exhibit 11–1 Marketing Strategy Planning Decisions for Place

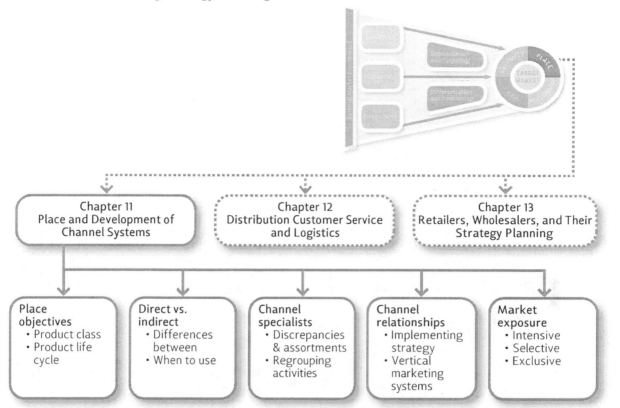

Chapter 11 Place and Development of Channel Systems	Chapter 12 Distribution Customer Service and Logistics	Chapter 13 Retailers, Wholesalers, and Their Strategy Planning

Place objectives	Direct vs. indirect	Channel specialists	Channel relationships	Market exposure
• Product class • Product life cycle	• Differences between • When to use	• Discrepancies & assortments • Regrouping activities	• Implementing strategy • Vertical marketing systems	• Intensive • Selective • Exclusive

MARKETING STRATEGY PLANNING DECISIONS FOR PLACE

Managers must think about Place—making goods and services available in the right quantities and locations, when customers want them. And when different target markets have different needs, a number of Place variations may be required. Our opening case makes it clear that new Place arrangements can dramatically change the competition in a product-market. This is especially important in business today because information technology, including websites and e-commerce, makes it easier for firms to work together more efficiently and also to reach customers directly.

In this chapter and the two that follow, we'll deal with the many important marketing strategy decisions that a marketing manager must make concerning Place. Exhibit 11-1 gives an overview. We'll start here with a discussion of Place objectives and how they relate to product classes and the product life cycle—ideas introduced in the Product chapters (9 and 10). We'll then discuss the type of channel that's needed to meet customers' needs. We'll show why specialists are often involved and how they come together to form a channel of distribution—any series of firms or individuals who participate in the flow of products from producer to final user or consumer. We'll also consider how to manage relations among channel members to reduce conflict and improve cooperation. This chapter concludes by considering the desired level of market exposure (and how many channel outlets are needed) as well as approaches for reaching customers in international markets.

In Chapter 12, we'll expand the Place discussion to decisions that a marketing manager makes about physical distribution, including customer service level, transporting, and storing. Then, in Chapter 13, we'll take a closer look at the many different types of retailing and wholesaling firms. We'll consider their role in channels as well as the strategy decisions they make to satisfy their own customers.

Edition

PLACE DECISIONS ARE GUIDED BY "IDEAL" PLACE OBJECTIVES

All marketing managers want to be sure that their goods and services are available in the right quantities and locations—when customers want them. But customers may have different needs in these areas as they make different purchases.

Product classes suggest Place objectives

In Chapter 9 we introduced the product classes, which summarize consumers' urgency to have needs satisfied and willingness to seek information, shop, and compare. Now you should be able to use the product classes to handle Place decisions.

Exhibit 9-6 shows the relationship between consumer product classes and ideal Place objectives. Similarly, Exhibit 9-7 shows the business product classes and how they relate to customer needs. Study these exhibits carefully. They set the framework for making Place decisions. In particular, the product classes help us decide how much market exposure we'll need in each geographic area.

Place system is not automatic

Several different product classes may be involved if different market segments view a product in different ways. Thus, marketing managers may need to develop several strategies, each with its own Place arrangements. There may not be one Place arrangement that is best.

For example, many consumers view Tide laundry detergent as a staple for doing laundry at home. To meet their needs, it is widely distributed in grocery and discount stores. Customers who run out of detergent while doing wash at a Laundromat see Tide

When the market for premium pet foods grew, Procter & Gamble acquired the Iams brand. To increase sales, P&G moved to more intensive distribution in supermarkets, pet superstores, mass-merchandisers, and other outlets. By contrast, Science Diet brand focused on selective distribution through veterinary offices and pet stores to reach consumers in the United States, Japan, France, and Italy. Because Science Diet developed cooperative relationships with members of its channel, they often gave Science Diet products special promotion support at the point of purchase. However, as overall demand has increased, Science Diet has expanded to other types of outlets.

as an emergency product and want small boxes available in a vending machine. And some hotels look at Tide as an operating supply that the housekeeping department needs to provide guests with clean sheets and towels. For these hotels, Tide comes in large drums that are sold and delivered by wholesalers of housekeeping supplies.

Place decisions have long-run effects

The marketing manager must also consider Place objectives in relation to the product life cycle; see Exhibit 10-3. Place decisions often have long-run effects. They're usually harder to change than Product, Promotion, and Price decisions. Many firms that thought they could quickly establish effective websites for direct online sales, for example, found that it took several years and millions of dollars to work out the kinks. It can take even longer and cost more to develop effective working relationships with others in the channel. Legal contracts with channel partners may limit changes. And it's hard to move retail stores and wholesale facilities once they are set up. Yet as products mature, they typically need broader distribution to reach different target customers.

The distribution of premium pet foods followed this pattern. A decade ago, supermarkets wouldn't carry specialized pet foods because there wasn't much demand. So marketing managers for Science Diet products concentrated on getting distribution through pet shops and veterinary offices. Science Diet's sales in this channel grew rapidly. What's more, profit margins on the specialty foods were much higher than on traditional fare. Seeing this growth, Purina, Kal Kan, and other producers developed new products and worked with their supermarket channels to set up special "nutrition centers" on the pet food aisle. As market growth continued, P&G bought Iams and pushed for distribution in pet superstores, at mass-merchandisers, and online.[2]

CHANNEL SYSTEM MAY BE DIRECT OR INDIRECT

One of the most basic Place decisions producers must make is whether to handle the whole distribution job themselves—perhaps by relying on direct-to-customer e-commerce selling—or use wholesalers, retailers, and other specialists (see Exhibit 11-1). Intermediaries, in turn, must select the producers they'll work with.

Oakley wants its sunglasses to be conveniently available when customers want them, so it works with retailers who will carry a good selection. The Oakley website also has a dealer locator that lists retailers in the consumer's area and provides maps so the stores are easy to find.

Edition

In the United States and many other developed nations, Unilever relies primarily on indirect distribution through a variety of wholesalers and retailers. However, in Spain it delivers frozen foods directly to consumer homes, and in Vietnam a mobile store brings products to local consumers. And now some products are sold direct to consumers from an Internet website.

Why a firm might want to use direct distribution

Many firms prefer to distribute directly to the final customer or consumer because they want to control the whole marketing job. They may think that they can serve target customers at a lower cost or do the work more effectively than intermediaries. Since wholesalers and retailers often carry products of several competing producers, they might not give any one item the special emphasis its producer wants.

The Internet makes direct distribution easier

Website-based e-commerce systems give many firms direct access to customers whom it would have been impossible to reach in the past. Even small, specialized firms may be able to establish a web page and draw customers from all over the world.

Direct contact with customers

If a firm is in direct contact with its customers, it is more aware of changes in customer attitudes. It is in a better position to adjust its marketing mix quickly because there is no need to convince other channel members to help. If a product needs an aggressive selling effort or special technical service, the marketing manager can ensure that salespeople receive the necessary training and motivation.

Suitable intermediaries are not available

A firm may have to go direct if suitable intermediaries are not available or will not cooperate. For example, when Glacéau began selling its now popular Vitaminwater, wholesale distributors had no interest in carrying it. So the owner of the company delivered the bottled water directly to small retailers in New York City. Once he proved his product would sell, distributor interest grew. On the other hand, to enter the California market, Glacéau gave distribution rights to just one distributor. As a result, it was in this distributor's interest to work closely with Glacéau to build the market. Eventually Coca-Cola purchased Glacéau; at that point Coke added many of its own distributors. Glacéau became a success by slowly building support from retailers and wholesalers, but many new products fail because the producer can't find willing channel partners and doesn't have the resources to handle direct distribution.[3]

In the United States, the Census Bureau publishes detailed data concerning wholesalers and retailers, including breakdowns by kind of business, product line, and geographic territory. Similar information is available for many other countries. It can be very valuable in strategy planning—especially to learn whether potential channel members are serving a target market. You can also learn what sales volume current intermediaries are achieving.

Common with business customers and services

Many business products are sold direct-to-customer. Alcan sells aluminum to General Motors direct. And Honda sells its motors direct to lawn mower producers. This is understandable since in business markets there are fewer transactions, orders

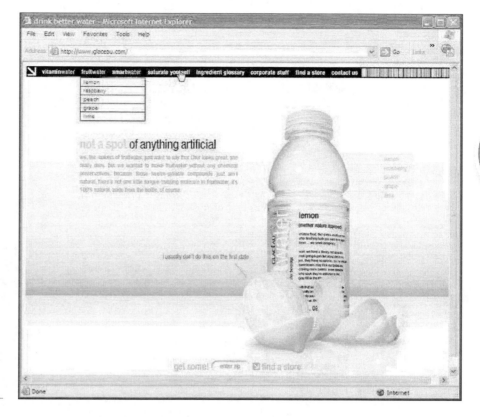

As a small company trying to obtain distribution, Glacéau focused on putting freestanding coolers for its Vitaminwater in stores, like Bed Bath & Beyond, that had not carried beverages in the past. Thus, Glacéau didn't just compete for the same shelf space but rather expanded the distribution outlets available for beverages.

are larger, and customers may be concentrated in one geographic area. Further, once relationships are established, e-commerce systems can efficiently handle orders.

Service firms often use direct channels. If the service must be produced in the presence of customers, there may be little need for intermediaries. An accounting firm like PricewaterhouseCoopers, for example, must deal directly with its customers.

However, many firms that produce physical goods turn to channel specialists to help provide the services customers expect. GE may hope that its authorized appliance dealers don't get many repair calls, but the service is available when customers need it. Here the intermediary produces the service.[4]

Some consumer products are sold direct

Many companies that produce consumer products have websites where a consumer can place a direct order. But for most consumer products this is still a small part of total sales. Most consumer products are sold through intermediaries.

Of course, some consumer products are sold direct to consumers where they live or work. Mary Kay and Avon cosmetics, Electrolux vacuum cleaners, Quixtar-Amway household products, and Tupperware are examples. These firms and many others are finding that this is a good way to crack open international markets ranging from India and China to Brazil and the U.K. Most of these firms rely on direct selling, which involves personal sales contact between a representative of the company and an individual consumer. However, most of these "salespeople" are *not* company employees. Rather, they usually work independently and the companies that they sell for refer to them as *dealers*, *distributors*, *agents*, or some similar term. So in a strict technical sense, this is not really direct producer-to-consumer distribution.[5]

Internet EXERCISE

Gateway is a computer company that uses direct distribution to its customers in the United States. Go to the Gateway website (www.gateway.com) and think about how it is organized. Is the website organized well to help Gateway reach different segments of customers in the United States?

Edition

Don't be confused by the term *direct marketing*

Even though most consumer products are sold through intermediaries, an increasing number of firms rely on **direct marketing**—direct communication between a seller and an individual customer using a promotion method other than face-to-face personal selling. Sometimes direct marketing promotion is coupled with direct distribution from a producer to consumers. Park Seed Company, for example, sells the seeds it grows directly to consumers with a mail catalog and website. However, many firms that use direct marketing promotion distribute their products through intermediaries. So the term *direct marketing* is primarily concerned with the Promotion area, not Place decisions. We'll talk about direct marketing promotion in more detail in Chapter 14.[6]

When indirect channels are best

Even if a producer wants to handle the whole distribution job, sometimes it's simply not possible. Customers often have established buying patterns. For example, Square D, a producer of electrical supplies, might want to sell directly to electrical contractors. It can certainly set up a website for online orders or even open sales offices in key markets. But if contractors like to make all of their purchases in one convenient stop—at a local electrical wholesaler— the only practical way to reach them is through a wholesaler.

Similarly, consumers are spread throughout many geographic areas and often prefer to shop for certain products at specific places. Some consumers, for instance, see Sears as *the* place to shop for tires, so they'll only buy the brands that Sears carries. This is one reason most firms that produce consumer products rely so heavily on indirect channels (see Exhibit 2-6).[7]

Direct distribution usually requires a significant investment in facilities, people, and information technology. A company that has limited financial resources or that wants to retain flexibility may want to avoid that investment by working with established intermediaries.

For many years, Levi Strauss did not distribute its jeans through Wal-Mart. Rather, it worked with fashion shops to project a more selective image. However, as Wal-Mart and other mass-merchandisers attracted a larger and larger share of jeans shoppers, Levi Strauss created its Signature line to reach this segment. Signature jeans feature lighter-weight denim and less detailing, and they are now available at Wal-Mart, Target, and Kmart.

Intermediaries may further reduce a producer's need for working capital by buying the producer's output and carrying it in inventory until it's sold. If customers want a good "right now," there must be inventory available to make the sale. And if customers are spread over a large area, it will probably be necessary to have widespread distribution.

Some wholesalers play a critical role by providing credit to customers at the end of the channel. A wholesaler who knows local customers can help reduce credit risks. As sales via the Internet grow, sellers are looking for faster and better ways to check the credit ratings of distant customers. It's an unhappy day when the marketing manager learns that a customer who was shipped goods based on an online order can't pay the invoice.

The most important reason for using an indirect channel of distribution is that an intermediary can often help producers serve customer needs better and at lower cost. Remember that we discussed this briefly in Chapter 1. Now we'll go into more detail.

Edition

CHANNEL SPECIALISTS MAY REDUCE DISCREPANCIES AND SEPARATIONS

The assortment and quantity of products customers want may be different from the assortment and quantity of products companies produce. Producers are often located far from their customers and may not know how best to reach them. Customers in turn may not know about their choices. Specialists develop to adjust these discrepancies and separations.[8]

Intermediaries may supply needed information

Specialists often help provide information to bring buyers and sellers together. For example, most consumers don't know much about the wide variety of home and auto insurance policies available. A local independent insurance agent may help them decide which policy, and which insurance company, best fits their needs.

Intermediaries who are close to their customers are often able to anticipate customer needs and forecast demand more accurately. This information can help reduce inventory costs in the whole channel—and it may help the producer smooth out production.

Most producers seek help from specialists when they first enter international markets. Specialists can provide crucial information about customer needs and insights into differences in the marketing environment.

Discrepancies of quantity and assortment

Discrepancy of quantity means the difference between the quantity of products it is economical for a producer to make and the quantity final users or consumers normally want. For example, most manufacturers of golf balls produce large quantities—perhaps 200,000 to 500,000 in a given time period. The average golfer, however, wants only a few balls at a time. Adjusting for this discrepancy usually requires intermediaries—wholesalers and retailers.

Producers typically specialize by product—and therefore another discrepancy develops. **Discrepancy of assortment** means the difference between the lines a typical producer makes and the assortment final consumers or users want. Most golfers, for example, need more than golf balls. They want golf shoes, gloves, clubs, a bag, and, of course, a golf course to play on. And they usually don't want to shop for each item separately. So, again, there is a need for wholesalers and retailers to adjust these discrepancies.

Amazon, the large online retailer, helps to match supply and demand when it fills Internet orders from its warehouse in Nevada. It accumulates large quantities of the most popular books from thousands of publishers, and then breaks bulk when it takes orders and ships them— often a single book at a time— to millions of individual consumers.

Edition

Regrouping activities adjust the quantities or assortments of products handled at each level in a channel of distribution.

There are four regrouping activities: accumulating, bulk-breaking, sorting, and assorting. When one or more of these activities is needed, a marketing specialist may develop to fill this need.

Adjusting quantity discrepancies by accumulating and bulk-breaking

Accumulating involves collecting products from many small producers. Much of the coffee that comes from Colombia is grown on small farms in the mountains. Accumulating the small crops into larger quantities is a way of getting the lowest transporting rate and making it more convenient for distant food processing companies to buy and handle it. Accumulating is especially important in less-developed countries and in other situations, like agricultural markets, where there are many small producers.

Accumulating is also important with professional services because they often involve the combined work of a number of individuals, each of whom is a specialized producer. A hospital makes it easier for patients by accumulating the services of a number of health care specialists, many of whom may not actually work for the hospital.

Many wholesalers and retailers who operate from Internet websites focus on accumulating. Specialized sites for everything from Chinese art to Dutch flower bulbs bring together the output of many producers.

Bulk-breaking involves dividing larger quantities into smaller quantities as products get closer to the final market. The bulk-breaking may involve several levels in the channel. Wholesalers may sell smaller quantities to other wholesalers or directly to retailers. Retailers continue breaking bulk as they sell individual items to their customers.

Adjusting assortment discrepancies by sorting and assorting

Different types of specialists adjust assortment discrepancies. They perform two types of regrouping activities: sorting and assorting.

Sorting means separating products into grades and qualities desired by different target markets. For example, an investment firm might offer its customers shares in a mutual fund made up only of stocks for companies that pay regular dividends. Similarly, a wholesaler that specializes in serving convenience stores may focus on smaller packages of frequently used products.

Assorting means putting together a variety of products to give a target market what it wants. This usually is done by those closest to the final consumer or user—retailers or wholesalers who try to supply a wide assortment of products for the convenience of their customers. Thus, a wholesaler selling Yazoo tractors and mowers to golf courses might also carry Pennington grass seed and Scott fertilizer.

Specialists should develop to adjust discrepancies *if they must be adjusted*. But there is no point in having intermediaries just because that's the way it's been done in the past. Sometimes a breakthrough opportunity can come from finding a better way to reduce discrepancies. Some manufacturers of business products can now reach more customers in distant markets with an Internet website than it was previously possible for them to reach with independent manufacturers' reps who sold on commission (but otherwise left distribution to the firm). The website cost advantage can translate to lower prices and a marketing mix that is a better value for some target segments.[9]

CHANNEL RELATIONSHIP MUST BE MANAGED

Intermediary specialists can help make a channel more efficient. But there may be problems getting the different firms in a channel to work together well. How well they work together depends on the type of relationship they have. This should be carefully considered since marketing managers usually have choices about what type of channel system to join or develop.

Acting as channel captains in their respective channels, both Peterson and Electrolux are able to get cooperation from many independent wholesalers and retailers (as well as big chains like Lowe's) because they develop marketing strategies that help the whole channel compete more effectively and that also help everyone in the channel do a better job of meeting the needs of target customers at the end of the channel.

The whole channel should have a product-market commitment

Ideally, all of the members of a channel system should have a shared *product-market commitment*—with all members focusing on the same target market at the end of the channel and sharing the various marketing functions in appropriate ways. When members of a channel do this, they are better able to compete effectively for the customer's business. Unfortunately, many marketing managers overlook this idea because it's not the way their firms have traditionally handled channel relationships.

Traditional channel systems involve weak relationships

In traditional channel systems, the various channel members make little or no effort to cooperate with each other. They buy and sell from each other—and that's the extent of their relationship. Each channel member does only what it considers to be in its own best interest. It doesn't worry about other members of the channel. This is shortsighted, but it's easy to see how it can happen. The objectives of the various channel members may be different. For example, Cooper Industries wants a wholesaler of electrical building supplies to sell Cooper products. But a wholesaler who works with different producers may not care whose products get sold. The wholesaler just wants happy customers and a good profit margin.[10]

Conflict gets in the way

Specialization can make a channel more efficient—but not if the specialists are so independent that the channel doesn't work smoothly. Because members of traditional channel systems often have different objectives—and different ideas about how things should be done—conflict is common.

Edition

There are two basic types of conflict in channels of distribution. *Vertical conflicts* occur between firms at different levels in the channel of distribution. A vertical conflict may occur if a producer and a retailer disagree about how much shelf space or promotion effort the retailer should give the producer's product. For example, when Wherehouse Entertainment (a large retail music chain) started to sell used CDs—at about half the price of new ones—several recording companies said that they would halt cooperative advertising payments to any retailer that sold used CDs. The recording companies felt that the used CDs hurt their sales.[11]

Horizontal conflicts occur between firms at the same level in the channel of distribution. For example, a furniture store that keeps a complete line of furniture on display isn't happy to find out that a discount chain store down the street offers customers lower prices on special orders of the same items. The discounter gets a free ride from the competing store's investment in inventory. And nothing gets an independent retailer more charged up than finding out that a chain store sells some product for less than the wholesale price the independent pays.

Adding new channels creates conflict

Conflict often results when a manufacturer opens a new distribution channel that competes with existing intermediaries. In these situations, jilted channel members may fight back. For example, when Estée Lauder set up a website to sell its Bobbi Brown and Clinique brands direct to consumers, Dayton Hudson department stores cut back the space devoted to the Lauder brands. Lauder is certainly not the only firm that has made retailers unhappy by setting up a website. However, many conflicts are old-fashioned turf battles.[12]

Managing conflict in channels

Some level of conflict may be inevitable—or even useful if that is what it takes for customers at the end of the channel to receive better value. However, most marketing managers try to avoid conflicts that harm relationships with channel partners. For example, a new channel is less likely to prompt conflict if it focuses on segments not already served by a current channel. For example, customers looking to make a quick purchase of a soft drink will consider a 7-Eleven convenience store, but probably not Costco. So having the same product at both stores probably does not create competition between the two, especially if the package sizes are different.

Some firms minimize conflict by offering different products through each channel. Gibson stopped selling guitars on its website after getting complaints from its traditional retailers and distributors. On the other hand, Gibson continued to sell accessories on its website. Dealers didn't want to carry inventory for all the variations of accessories, especially given that selling a few accessories wasn't very profitable.

Another option is to provide some compensation to members of the older channel—particularly when they still play an important role in the strategy. When Allstate decided to sell insurance on the Internet, it worked out an arrangement with its 15,600 local agents. The agents receive 2 percent commission when they provide face-to-face service with customers who receive quotes on the Internet. This is lower than the usual 10 percent commission, but agents provide less selling effort and customers get personal service when they need it.

Treating channel partners fairly—even when one partner is more powerful—tends to build trust and reduce conflict. When channel members trust each other, they can work together in a cooperative relationship focused on a basic objective—satisfying target customers at the end of the channel. This leads us away from traditional channels to cooperative channel relationships and the channel captain concept.[13]

Channel captain can guide channel relationships

Each channel system should act as a unit, where each member of the channel collaborates to serve customers at the end of the channel. In this view, cooperation is everyone's responsibility. However, some firms are in a better position to take the lead in the relationship and in coordinating the whole channel effort. This situation calls for a channel captain—a manager who helps direct the activities of a whole channel and tries to avoid or solve channel conflicts.

For example, when Harley-Davidson wanted to expand sales of fashion accessories, it was difficult for motorcycle dealers to devote enough space to all of the different styles. Harley considered selling the items directly from its own website, but that would take sales away from dealers who were working hard to help Harley sell both cycles and fashions. So Harley's president asked a group of dealers and Harley managers to work together to come up with a plan they all liked. The result was a website that sells Harley products through the dealer that is closest to the customer.[14]

The concept of a single channel captain is logical. But most traditional channels don't have a recognized captain. The various firms don't act as a coordinated system. Yet firms are interrelated, even if poorly, by their policies. So it makes sense to try to avoid channel conflicts by planning for channel relations. The channel captain arranges for the necessary functions to be performed in the most effective way.[15]

Some producers lead their channels

In the United States, producers frequently take the lead in channel relations. Intermediaries often wait to see what the producer intends to do and wants them to do. Then they decide whether their roles will be profitable and whether they want to join in the channel effort.

Exhibit 11-2A shows this type of producer-led channel system. Here the producer has selected the target market and developed the Product, set the Price structure, done some consumer and channel Promotion, and developed the Place setup. Intermediaries are then expected to finish the Promotion job in their respective places. Of

Exhibit 11-2 How Channel Functions May Be Shifted and Shared in Different Channel Systems

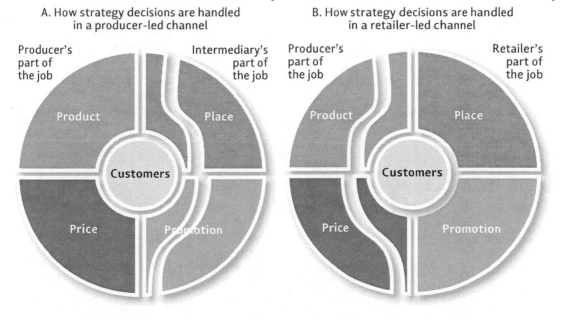

A. How strategy decisions are handled in a producer-led channel

Producer's part of the job — Product, Price

Intermediary's part of the job — Place, Promotion

Customers

B. How strategy decisions are handled in a retailer-led channel

Producer's part of the job — Product, Price

Retailer's part of the job — Place, Promotion

Customers

Edition

course, in a retailer-dominated channel system, the marketing jobs would be handled in a different way.

Some intermediaries are channel captains

Sometimes wholesalers or retailers do take the lead. They are closer to the final user or consumer and are in an ideal position to assume the channel captain role. These firms analyze their customers' needs and then seek out producers who can provide these products at reasonable prices. With the growth of powerful chains, like Wal-Mart and Toys "R" Us, retailers now dominate the channel systems for many products in the United States. In Japan, very large wholesalers (trading companies) are often the channel captains.

Retailers like Sears and wholesalers like Ace Hardware who develop their own dealer brands in effect act like producers. They specify the whole marketing mix for a product and merely delegate production to a factory. Exhibit 11-2B shows how marketing strategy might be handled in this sort of retailer-led channel system.[16]

VERTICAL MARKETING SYSTEMS FOCUS ON FINAL CUSTOMERS

Many marketing managers accept the view that a coordinated channel system can help everyone in the channel. These managers are moving their firms away from traditional channel systems and instead developing or joining vertical marketing systems. Vertical marketing systems are channel systems in which the whole channel focuses on the same target market at the end of the channel. Such systems make sense, and are growing, because if the final customer doesn't buy the product, the whole channel suffers. There are three types of vertical marketing systems—corporate, administered, and contractual. Exhibit 11-3 summarizes some characteristics of these systems and compares them with traditional systems.

Inspired by the success of self-serve ticketing kiosks at airports, Apple is supplementing its own retail stores and distribution through other retailers with special vending machines that sell iPods in airports and high-traffic areas.

Exhibit 11-3   Characteristics of Traditional and Vertical Marketing Systems

		Type of Channel		
		Vertical Marketing Systems		
Characteristics	Traditional	Administered	Contractual	Corporate
Amount of cooperation	Little or none	Some to good	Fairly good to good	Complete
Control maintained by	None	Economic power and leadership	Contracts	Ownership by one company
Examples	Typical channel of "independents"	General Electric, Miller Beer, Scotts Miracle Grow	McDonald's, Holiday Inn, Ace Hardware, Super Valu, Coca-Cola, Chevrolet	Florsheim Shoes, Sherwin-Williams, Mothers Work

Can I Download Some Popcorn with That Movie?

The market for entertainment is changing rapidly—and Hollywood has responded with new channels of distribution. For a long time, movie studios carefully managed how their films proceeded through tightly controlled channels. Movies took years to trickle down from theaters to premium cable TV channels like HBO and eventually to network television. This approach maximized the studios' revenue from each channel—and kept channel conflict at a minimum. But those days are gone and movie studios are scrambling to get revenue faster from more channels of distribution.

Each new outlet for movies has provided more convenience or a different consumer experience. In the late 1970s, the first video stores started renting movies for $10 a day. Studios also began selling movies. Disney's animated classics were especially popular at first because kids would watch the same movie many times. However, sales did not really take off until prices dropped below $25. As sales grew, distribution became more intense and retailers like Wal-Mart and Kmart were added to the mix. Blockbuster and other big rental chains also took off.

Now, if you don't feel like driving to pick up a flick, your cable channel or satellite television provider probably offers pay-per-view. Or, if you prefer, Netflix offers movie downloads or mails DVDs to your home and you can return them whenever you want. Illegal channels have developed, too. Pirates often post movies on the Internet before they're even available in theaters, and some consumers copy DVDs on home computers and pass them around. However, new movie download services that are legal are also coming online, and smaller digital file formats make movies portable with a video cell phone or iPod. You may not care about portability if you've got your own comfy home theater setup. And bricks-and-mortar theaters, the traditional channel, are fighting to get customers back with stadium seating, bar and table service, and giant IMAX screens.

Concerns about movie piracy eroding sales have prompted movie studios to speed up the timing of movie distribution across channels. This has increased competition and conflict across channels. Some studios are releasing movies to theaters and on DVD at the same time—or skipping the theater channel altogether.

So where will you watch your next movie? At an IMAX theater, in your home theater, or on your cell phone in a seat on a train—you can decide. These changes give you the power to choose—and movie studios hope all these channels get more people watching more movies.[17]

Corporate channel systems shorten channels

Some corporations develop their own vertical marketing systems by internal expansion or by buying other firms, or both. With corporate channel systems—corporate ownership all along the channel—we might say the firm is going "direct." But actually the firm may be handling manufacturing, wholesaling, *and* retailing—so it's more accurate to think of the firm as a vertical marketing system.

Corporate channel systems may develop by vertical integration—acquiring firms at different levels of channel activity. For example, in England, most of the quaint local pubs are now actually owned and operated by the large beer breweries.

Vertical integration has potential advantages—stable sources of supplies, better control of distribution and quality, greater buying power, and lower executive overhead. Provided that the discrepancies of quantity and assortment are not too great at each level in a channel, vertical integration can be profitable. However, many managers have found that it's hard to be really good at running manufacturing, wholesaling, and retailing businesses that are very different from each other. Instead, they try to be more efficient at what they do best and focus on ways to get cooperation in the channel for the other activities.[18]

Administered and contractual systems may work well

Firms can often gain the advantages of vertical integration without building a costly corporate channel. A manager can develop administered or contractual channel systems instead. In administered channel systems, the channel members

Edition

Mothers Work is a good example of a corporate channel system started by a retailer. It began as a mail-order catalog specializing in maternity clothes. Now it sells more than a third of all maternity clothes in the United States. Vertical integration has been a key factor in its ability to give its customers what they want. It has over 700 company-run stores, its own designers, fabric-cutting operations, warehouses, and information systems to tie them all together.

informally agree to cooperate with each other. They can agree to routinize ordering, share inventory and sales information over computer networks, standardize accounting, and coordinate promotion efforts. In contractual channel systems, the channel members agree by contract to cooperate with each other. With both of these systems, the members retain some of the flexibility of a traditional channel system.

The opportunities to reduce costs and provide customers with superior value are growing in these systems because of help from information technology. For example, like many retailers, Costco has a system that it calls "vendor managed inventory" in which key suppliers take over responsibility for managing a set of products, often a whole product category. Costco uses this approach with Kimberly-Clark (KC), the firm that makes Huggies. Every day, an analyst at KC's headquarters reviews Costco's online data that details Huggies' sales and inventory at every Costco store. If inventory is getting low, a new order is placed and shipping is scheduled. This system reduces buying and selling costs, inventory management, lost sales from inventory stock-outs, and consumer frustration when products aren't available. Because KC does this job well, it makes more money and so does Costco.[19]

Vertical marketing systems—dominant force in the marketplace

Vertical systems in the consumer products area have a healthy majority of retail sales and should continue to increase their share in the future. Vertical marketing systems are becoming the major competitive units in the U.S. distribution system—and they are growing rapidly in other parts of the world as well.[20]

THE BEST CHANNEL SYSTEM SHOULD ACHIEVE IDEAL MARKET EXPOSURE

You may think that all marketing managers want their products to have maximum exposure to potential customers. This isn't true. Some product classes require much less market exposure than others. Ideal market exposure makes a product available

Edition

Stihl sells its high-quality chain saws through 8,000 independent Stihl dealers nationwide. They give product demonstrations, good advice, and expert on-site service. These dealers know that the Stihl brand is not available at home-improvement warehouses that put more emphasis on price competition and less on service.

widely enough to satisfy target customers' needs but not exceed them. Too much exposure only increases the total cost of marketing.

Ideal exposure may be intensive, selective, or exclusive

Intensive distribution is selling a product through all responsible and suitable wholesalers or retailers who will stock or sell the product. Selective distribution is selling through only those intermediaries who will give the product special attention. Exclusive distribution is selling through only one intermediary in a particular geographic area. As we move from intensive to exclusive distribution, we give up exposure in return for some other advantage—including, but not limited to, lower cost.

Intensive distribution—sell it where they buy it

Intensive distribution is commonly needed for convenience products and business supplies—such as laser printer cartridges, ring binders, and copier paper—used by all offices. Customers want such products nearby. For example, Rayovac batteries were not selling well even though their performance was very similar to other batteries. Part of that was due to heavier advertising for Duracell and Energizer. But consumers usually don't go shopping for batteries. They're purchased on impulse 83 percent of the time. To get a larger share of purchases, Rayovac had to be in more stores. It offered retailers a marketing mix with less advertising and a lower price. In three years, the brand moved from being available in 36,000 stores to 82,000 stores—and that increase gave sales a big charge.[21]

Selective distribution—sell it where it sells best

Selective distribution covers the broad area of market exposure between intensive and exclusive distribution. It may be suitable for all categories of products. Only the better intermediaries are used here. Companies commonly use selective distribution to gain some of the advantages of exclusive distribution—while still achieving fairly widespread market coverage.

Reduce costs and get better partners

A selective policy might be used to avoid selling to wholesalers or retailers that (1) place orders that are too small to justify making calls, (2) make too many returns or request too much service, (3) have a poor credit rating, or (4) are not in a position to do a satisfactory job.

Selective distribution is becoming more popular than intensive distribution as firms see that they don't need 100 percent coverage of a market to support national advertising. Often the majority of sales come from relatively few customers—and the others buy too little compared to the cost of working with them. This is called the

Edition

ROC uses selective distribution and sells its skin care products in drugstores, but not in grocery stores or mass-merchandisers. Altoids seeks intensive distribution for its fresh-breath products in a wide variety of retail outlets—ranging from drugstores and grocery stores to convenience stores and office supply retailers.

80/20 rule—80 percent of a company's sales often come from only 20 percent of its customers *until it becomes more selective in choosing customers*.

Esprit—a producer of women's clothing—was selling through about 4,000 department stores and specialty shops in the United States. But Esprit's sales analysis showed that sales in Esprit's own stores were about four times better than sales in other outlets. Profits increased when Esprit cut back to about half as many outlets and opened more of its own stores and a website. When competition from retailers like The Gap and Abercrombie & Fitch increased in the United States, Esprit focused on building profitability in its shops in Europe and Asia.[22]

Get special effort from channel members

Selective distribution can produce greater profits not only for the producer but for all channel members. Wholesalers and retailers are more willing to promote products aggressively if they know they're going to obtain the majority of sales through their own efforts. They may carry wider lines, do more promotion, and provide more service—all of which lead to more sales.

Selective often moves to intensive as market grows

In the early part of the life cycle of a new unsought good, a producer may have to use selective distribution. Well-known wholesalers and retailers may have the power to get such a product introduced, but sometimes on their own terms. That often means limiting the number of competing wholesalers and retailers. The producer may be happy with such an arrangement at first but dislike it later when more retailers want to carry the product.

Exclusive distribution sometimes makes sense

Exclusive distribution is just an extreme case of selective distribution—the firm selects only one wholesaler or retailer in each geographic area. Besides the various advantages of selective distribution, producers may want to use exclusive distribution to help control prices and the service offered in a channel.

Retailers of shopping products and specialty products often try to get exclusive distribution rights in their territories. Fast-food franchises often have exclusive distribution—and that's one reason they're popular. Owners of McDonald's franchises pay a share of sales and follow McDonald's strategy to keep their exclusive right to a market.

Unlike selective distribution, exclusive distribution usually involves a verbal or written agreement stating that channel members will buy all or most of a given product from the seller. In return, these retailers are granted the exclusive rights to that product in their territories.

Edition

Is limiting market exposure legal?

Exclusive distribution is an area considered under U.S. antimonopoly laws. Courts currently focus on whether an exclusive distribution arrangement hurts competition.

Horizontal arrangements among competitors are illegal

Horizontal arrangements—among *competing* retailers, wholesalers, or producers— to limit sales by customer or territory have consistently been ruled illegal by the U.S. Supreme Court. Courts consider such arrangements obvious collusion that reduces competition and harms customers.

Vertical arrangements may or may not be legal

The legality of vertical arrangements—between producers and intermediaries—is not as clear-cut. A 1977 Supreme Court decision (involving Sylvania and the distribution of TV sets) reversed an earlier ruling that it was always illegal to set up vertical relationships limiting territories or customers. Now courts can weigh the possible good effects against the possible restrictions on competition. They look at competition between whole channels rather than just focusing on competition at one level of distribution.

The Sylvania decision does not mean that all vertical arrangements are legal. Rather, it says that a firm has to be able to legally justify any exclusive arrangements.

Thus, firms should be extremely cautious about entering into *any* exclusive distribution arrangement. The courts can force a change in relationships that were expensive to develop. And even worse, the courts can award triple damages if they rule that competition has been hurt.

The same cautions apply to selective distribution. Here, however, less formal arrangements are typical—and the possible impact on competition is more remote. It is now more acceptable to carefully select channel members when building a channel system. Refusing to sell to some intermediaries, however, should be part of a logical plan with long-term benefits to consumers.[23]

CHANNEL SYSTEMS CAN BE COMPLEX

Trying to achieve the desired degree of market exposure can lead to complex channels of distribution. Firms may need different channels to reach different segments of a broad product-market or to be sure they reach each segment. Sometimes this results in competition between different channels.

Consider the different channels used by a company that publishes computer books. See Exhibit 11-4. This publisher sells through a general book wholesaler who in turn sells to Internet book retailers and independent book retailers. The publisher may have some direct sales of its best-selling books to a large chain or even to consumers who order directly from its website. However, it might also sell through a computer supplies wholesaler that serves electronics superstores like Best Buy. This can cause problems because different wholesalers and retailers want different markups. It also increases competition, including price competition. And the competition among different intermediaries may lead to conflicts between the intermediaries and the publisher.

Multichannel distribution systems may be needed

Multichannel distribution occurs when a producer uses several competing channels to reach the same target market—perhaps using several intermediaries in addition to selling directly. Multichannel distribution is becoming more common. For instance, big retail chains want large quantities and low prices. A producer may sell directly to retail chains and rely on wholesalers to sell to smaller accounts. Some established intermediaries resent this because they don't appreciate *any* competition— especially price competition set up by their own suppliers.

Other times, producers are forced to use multichannel distribution because their present channels are doing a poor job or aren't reaching some potential customers. For example, Reebok International had been relying on local sporting goods stores to sell its shoes to high school and college athletic teams. But Reebok wasn't getting much of the business. When it set up its own team-sales department to sell directly to the schools, it got a 30,000-unit increase in sales.[24]

Edition

Exhibit 11–4   An Example of Multichannel Distribution by a Publisher of Computer Books

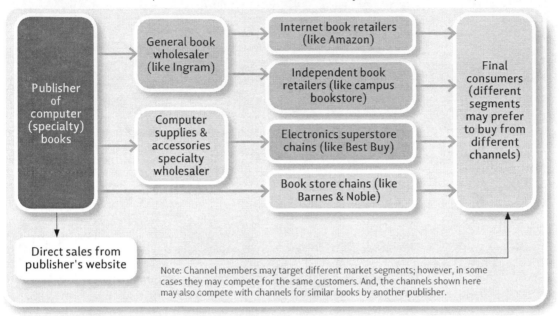

Note: Channel members may target different market segments; however, in some cases they may compete for the same customers. And, the channels shown here may also compete with channels for similar books by another publisher.

Ethical decisions may be required

If competition changes or customers' Place requirements shift, the current channel system may not be effective. The changes required to serve customer needs may hurt one or more members of the channel. Ethical dilemmas in the channels area arise in situations like this—because not everyone in the channel can win.

For example, wholesalers and the independent retailers that they serve in a channel of distribution may trust a producer channel-captain to develop marketing strategies that will work for the whole channel. However, the producer may decide that consumers, and its own business, are best served by a change (say, dropping current wholesalers and selling directly to big retail chains). A move of this sort, if implemented immediately, may not give current wholesaler-partners a chance to make adjustments of their own. The more dependent they are on the producer, the more severe the impact is likely to be. It's not easy to determine the best or most ethical solution in these situations. However, marketing managers must think carefully about the consequences of Place strategy changes for other channel members. In channels, as in any business dealing, relationships of trust must be treated with care.[25]

Ethics QUESTION

Assume you are the sales manager for a small producer of hip-hop fashions. As you arrive at a trade show to promote your firm's new line, your assistant pulls you aside to warn you that some of the owners of shops that usually carry your line are looking for you—and several are hopping mad. They've heard rumors that a big retail chain will be carrying your new line in all of its stores. In the past, your firm has distributed its fashions only through these small, "independent" retail shops, and they see the big chains as threats. Although you have had some negotiations with a buyer for the big retail chain, no deal has been reached yet. What will you say to the owners of the small shops, many of whom helped your firm get started and have always supported your marketing plans? If you are certain that most of these small retailers will *not* place any orders if they think the big chain will be carrying the same line, will you respond differently? Explain your thinking.

CHAPTER 11

309

Place and Development of Channel Systems

Reverse channels are important too

Most firms focus on getting products to their customers. But some marketing managers must also plan for reverse channels—channels used to retrieve products that customers no longer want. The need for reverse channels may arise in a variety of different situations. Toy companies, automobile firms, drug companies, and others sometimes have to recall products because of safety problems. A firm that makes an error in completing an order may have to take returns. If a Viewsonic computer monitor breaks while it's still under warranty, someone needs to get it to the repair center. Soft-drink companies may need to recycle empty bottles. And, of course, consumers sometimes buy something in error and want to return it. This is common with online purchases where consumers can't see, touch, or try the product before purchasing it.[26]

Reverse channels can support sustainability

Reverse channels that help the environment are sometimes also profitable. In rural China, for example, it's cheaper for Coke to reuse glass bottles than to rely on plastic packages or cans. Recycling has been even more important to Xerox. Customers responded well to Xerox's offer to dispose of older-model copiers with the purchase of new models. But in the first year of the program, Xerox discovered that by refurbishing parts that were still in use with new models it could save $50 million.

Reverse channels are also a way to give customers environmentally friendly choices. For example, new Ecoworx carpet tiles from Shaw Floors are manufactured using recycled carpets. Shaw also promises that when the time comes it will pick up and recycle the tiles at no cost to the customer. To make it easy for the customer to follow up, Shaw's telephone number is on the back of each tile.

Government regulations are giving some firms an extra push to think about reverse channels. For example, some "take back" laws require manufacturers to recycle or reuse hazardous materials or products at the end of their useful life—all at no cost to the customer. In Europe, auto makers must take back and recycle or reuse 85 percent of any vehicle made after 2004, and the European Community's Waste Electrical and Electronic Equipment (WEEE) Directive has firms taking back products like computers and televisions. Similar laws are cropping up in the United States.[27]

Plan for reverse channels

When marketing managers don't plan for reverse channels, the firm's customers may be left to solve "their" problem. That usually doesn't make sense. So a complete plan for Place may need to consider an efficient way to return products—with policies that different channel members agree on. It may also require specialists who were not involved in getting the product to the consumer. But if that's what it takes to satisfy customers, it should be part of marketing strategy planning.[28]

ENTERING INTERNATIONAL MARKETS

All of the strategy decisions for Place (see Exhibit 11-1) apply whether a firm is just focused on its domestic market or is also trying to reach target customers in international markets. However, intermediaries and marketing specialists who are available in one country often are not available in another. Further, the external market environment may vary from what marketing managers already know. The culture and laws, for example, are almost always different in international markets. In planning for Place, these differences pose special challenges. So, we'll briefly discuss five basic ways to enter international markets (see Exhibit 11–5).

Exporting often comes first

Some companies get into international marketing just by exporting—selling some of what the firm produces to foreign markets. Some firms start exporting just to take advantage of excess capacity—or even to get rid of surplus inventory. At the extreme, a firm may decide not to change anything about the product, the label, or even the instructions. This explains why some early efforts at exporting are not very satisfactory.

Edition

Mercedes-Benz manufactures Axor Tractor Trucks in Turkey according to European standards so that they are both powerful and economical. That combination makes Axor a leader in both domestic and export sales.

In Which We Serve.

Yet, for other firms exporting involves a more thoughtful effort to look for new growth opportunities. Exporters usually get started by working with intermediaries—and typically they're specialists in international marketing and the country where the target customers are located. They recommend marketing mix changes and handle problems such as customs, import and export taxes, shipping, exchange rates, and recruiting or working with foreign wholesalers and retailers in the foreign country.

Relationships with these international specialists and other channel partners may not be permanent. Rather, exporting often allows a firm to test an international market with a low investment of time and money. If the effort doesn't work, it's usually relatively easy to get out of a country—or to try a different approach.

Some firms tailor websites to directly sell to export customers in foreign countries. Consumer firms like Amazon.com, L.L. Bean, and Nike have used this approach.

Licensing is often an easy way

Licensing is a relatively easy way to enter a foreign market. Licensing means selling the right to use some process, trademark, patent, or other right for a fee or royalty. The licensee in the foreign market takes most of the risk, because it must make some initial investment to get started. The licensee also does most of the marketing strategy planning for the markets it is licensed to serve. If good partners are available, this can be an effective way to enter a market. Gerber entered the Japanese baby food market this way, but exports to other countries.

Exhibit 11-5   Basic Approaches for Entering International Markets

| Exporting | Licensing | Management contracting | Joint venture | Direct investment |

Generally increasing investment, risk, and control of marketing

Edition

To establish a presence more quickly in the United States, Haier of China has entered joint ventures with several American retailers, including Wal-Mart, Home Depot, Lowe's, Target, and Best Buy.

Management contracting sells know-how

Management contracting means that the seller provides only management and marketing skills—others own the production and distribution facilities. Some mines and oil refineries are operated this way—and Hilton operates hotels all over the world for local owners using this method. This is another relatively low risk approach to international marketing. The company makes no commitment to fixed facilities, which can be taken over or damaged in riots, war, or political upheaval. This can be especially important in developing nations or ones where the government is less stable.

Joint venturing increases involvement

In a joint venture, a domestic firm enters into a partnership with a foreign firm. As with any partnership, there can be honest disagreements over objectives—for example, how much profit is desired and how fast it should be paid out—as well as operating policies. When a close working relationship can be developed—perhaps based on one firm's technical and marketing know-how and the foreign partner's knowledge of the market and political connections—this approach can be very attractive to both parties. Typically the two partners must make significant investments and agree on the marketing strategy. Once a joint venture is formed, it can be difficult to end if things aren't working out.

In some situations, a joint venture is the only way a firm can enter a new market. When J.P. Morgan Chase was interested in getting a foothold in the growing market in China, stiff regulations there prohibited a foreign firm from owning a controlling share of a Chinese investment bank or money management firm. Since an entry alternative with more control was not available, J.P. Morgan entered with a minority share in a joint venture with a Chinese bank.

Direct investment involves ownership

When a foreign market looks really promising, a firm may want to take a bigger step with a direct investment. Direct investment means that a parent firm has a division (or owns a separate subsidiary firm) in a foreign market. This gives the parent firm complete control of marketing strategy planning.

Direct investment is a big commitment and usually entails greater risks. If a local market has economic or political problems, the firm cannot easily leave. On the other hand, by providing local jobs, a company builds a strong presence in a new market. This helps the firm build a good reputation with the government and customers in the host country. And the firm does not have to share profits with a partner.[29]

CONCLUSION

In this chapter we discussed the role of Place in marketing strategy. Place decisions are especially important because they may be difficult and expensive to change. So marketing managers must make Place decisions very carefully.

We discussed how product classes and the product life cycle are related to Place objectives. This helps us determine how much a firm should rely on indirect channel systems with intermediaries or direct systems.

Marketing specialists and channel systems develop to adjust discrepancies of quantity and assortment. Their regrouping activities are basic in any economic system. And adjusting discrepancies provides opportunities for creative marketers.

Channels of distribution tend to work best when there is cooperation among the members of a channel—and conflict is avoided. So we discussed the importance of planning channel systems and the role of a channel captain. We stressed that channel systems compete with each other and that vertical marketing systems seem to be winning.

Channel planning also requires firms to decide on the degree of market exposure they want. The ideal level of exposure may be intensive, selective, or exclusive. We discussed the legal issues marketing managers must consider in developing channel systems. Finally, we examined different approaches for entering international markets.

KEY TERMS

place, 291

channel of distribution, 291

direct marketing, 296

discrepancy of quantity, 297

discrepancy of assortment, 297

regrouping activities, 298

accumulating, 298

bulk-breaking, 298

sorting, 298

assorting, 298

traditional channel systems, 299

channel captain, 301

vertical marketing systems, 302

corporate channel systems, 303

vertical integration, 303

administered channel systems, 303

contractual channel systems, 304

ideal market exposure, 304

intensive distribution, 305

selective distribution, 305

exclusive distribution, 305

multichannel distribution, 307

reverse channels, 309

exporting, 309

licensing, 310

management contracting, 311

joint venture, 311

direct investment, 311

QUESTIONS AND PROBLEMS

1. Review the Dell case at the beginning of the chapter and then discuss the competitive advantages that Barnes & Noble would have over a small bookshop. What advantages does a small bookshop have?

2. Give two examples of service firms that work with other channel specialists to sell their products to final consumers. What marketing functions is the specialist providing in each case?

3. Discuss some reasons why a firm that produces installations might use direct distribution in its domestic market but use intermediaries to reach overseas customers.

4. Explain discrepancies of quantity and assortment using the clothing business as an example. How does the application of these concepts change when selling steel to the automobile industry? What impact does this have on the number and kinds of marketing specialists required?

5. Explain the four regrouping activities with an example from the building supply industry (nails, paint, flooring, plumbing fixtures, etc.). Do you think that many specialists develop in this industry, or do producers handle the job themselves? What kinds of marketing channels would you expect to find in this industry, and what functions would various channel members provide?

6. Insurance agents are intermediaries who help other members of the channel by providing information and handling the selling function. Does it make sense for an insurance agent to specialize and work exclusively with one insurance provider? Why or why not?

7. Discuss the Place objectives and distribution arrangements that are appropriate for the following products (indicate any special assumptions you have to make to obtain an answer):
   a. A postal scale for products weighing up to 2 pounds.
   b. Children's toys: (1) radio-controlled model airplanes costing $80 or more, (2) small rubber balls.
   c. Heavy-duty, rechargeable, battery-powered nut tighteners for factory production lines.
   d. Fiberglass fabric used in making roofing shingles.

8. Give an example of a producer that uses two or more different channels of distribution. Briefly discuss what problems this might cause.

9. Explain how a channel captain can help traditional independent firms compete with a corporate (integrated) channel system.

10. Find an example of vertical integration within your city. Are there any particular advantages to this vertical

Edition

integration? If so, what are they? If there are no such advantages, how do you explain the integration?

11. What would happen if retailer-organized channels (either formally integrated or administered) dominated consumer products marketing?

12. How does the nature of the product relate to the degree of market exposure desired?

13. Why would intermediaries want to be exclusive distributors for a product? Why would producers want exclusive distribution? Would intermediaries be equally anxious to get exclusive distribution for any type of product? Why or why not? Explain with reference to the following products: candy bars, batteries, golf clubs, golf balls, steak knives, televisions, and industrial woodworking machinery.

14. Explain the present legal status of exclusive distribution. Describe a situation where exclusive distribution is almost sure to be legal. Describe the nature and size of competitors and the industry, as well as the nature of the exclusive arrangement. Would this exclusive arrangement be of any value to the producer or intermediary?

15. Discuss the promotion a new grocery products producer would need in order to develop appropriate channels and move products through those channels. Would the nature of this job change for a new producer of dresses? How about for a new, small producer of installations?

16. Describe the advantages and disadvantages of the approaches to international market entry discussed in this chapter.

CREATING MARKETING PLANS

The Marketing Plan Coach software on the Student CD and the text website includes a sample marketing plan for Hillside Veterinary Clinic. Look through the "Marketing Strategy" section.

a. Why does Hillside sell its product directly instead of indirectly?

b. Hillside has a small selection of pet supplies that it sells to people who bring in their pets. What products does it resell at retail? What channel functions does it provide, and what channel functions are performed by its suppliers?

SUGGESTED CASES

13. File-It Supplies, Inc.
15. The Trujillo Group
16. Bunyan Lumber

32. Lever, Ltd.
34. Innovative Aluminum Products, Inc.

COMPUTER-AIDED PROBLEM

11. INTENSIVE VERSUS SELECTIVE DISTRIBUTION

Hydropump, Inc., produces and sells high-quality pumps to business customers. Its marketing research shows a growing market for a similar type of pump aimed at final consumers—for use with Jacuzzi-style tubs in home remodeling jobs. Hydropump will have to develop new channels of distribution to reach this target market because most consumers rely on a retailer for advice about the combination of tub, pump, heater, and related plumbing fixtures they need. Hydropump's marketing manager, Robert Black, is trying to decide between intensive and selective distribution. With intensive distribution, he would try to sell through all the plumbing supply, bathroom fixture, and hot-tub retailers who will carry the pump. He estimates that about 5,600 suitable retailers would be willing to carry a new pump. With selective distribution, he would focus on about 280 of the best hot-tub dealers (2 or 3 in the 100 largest metropolitan areas).

Intensive distribution would require Hydropump to do more mass selling—primarily advertising in home renovation magazines—to help stimulate consumer familiarity with the brand and convince retailers that Hydropump equipment will sell. The price to the retailer might have to be lower too (to permit a bigger markup) so they will be motivated to sell Hydropump rather than some other brand offering a smaller markup.

With intensive distribution, each Hydropump sales rep could probably handle about 300 retailers effectively. With selective distribution, each sales rep could handle only about 70 retailers because more merchandising help would be necessary.

Managing the smaller sales force and fewer retailers, with the selective approach, would require less manager overhead cost.

Going to all suitable and available retailers would make the pump available through about 20 times as many retailers and have the potential of reaching more customers. However, many customers shop at more than one retailer before making a final choice—so selective distribution would reach almost as many potential customers. Further, if Hydropump is using selective distribution, it would get more in-store sales attention for its pump and a larger share of pump purchases at each retailer.

Black has decided to use a spreadsheet to analyze the benefits and costs of intensive versus selective distribution.

a. Based on the initial spreadsheet, which approach seems to be the most sensible for Hydropump? Why?

b. A consultant points out that even selective distribution needs national promotion. If Black has to increase advertising and spend a total of $100,000 on mass selling to be able to recruit the retailers he wants for selective distribution, would selective or intensive distribution be more profitable?

c. With intensive distribution, how large a share (percent) of the retailers' total unit sales would Hydropump have to capture to sell enough pumps to earn $200,000 profit?

For additional questions related to this problem, see Exercise 11-3 in the *Learning Aid for Use with Basic Marketing*, 17th edition.

12

CHAPTER

Distribution Customer Service and Logistics

If you want a Coca-Cola, there's usually one close by—no matter where you might be in the world. And that's no accident. An executive for the best-known brand name in the world stated the objective simply: "Make Coca-Cola available within an arm's reach of desire." To achieve that objective, Coke works with many different channels of distribution. But that's just the start. Think about what it takes for a bottle, can, or cup of Coke to be there whenever you're thirsty. In warehouses and distribution centers, on trucks, in gyms and sports arenas, and thousands of other retail outlets, Coke handles, stores, and transports more than 400 billion servings of the soft drink a year. Getting all of that product to consumers could be a logistical nightmare, but Coke does it effectively and at a low cost. Think about it: A can of Coke at the supermarket costs about the same as what it costs you to have the Post Office deliver a letter.

Fast information about what the market needs helps keep Coke's distribution on target. Coke uses an Internet-based data system that links about one million retailers and other sellers to Coke and its bottlers. The system lets Coke bottlers and retailers exchange orders, invoices, and pricing information online. Orders are processed instantly—so sales to consumers at the end of the channel aren't lost because of stock-outs. Similarly, computer systems show Coke managers exactly what's selling in each market; they can even estimate the effects of promotions as they plan inventories and deliveries. And Coke products move efficiently through the channel. In Cincinnati, for example, Coke built the beverage industry's first fully automated distribution center. And when Coke's truck drivers get to the retail store, they knowingly stock the shelves with the correct mix of products.

Coke's strategies in international markets rely on many of the same ideas. But the stage of market development varies in different countries, so Coke's emphasis varies as well. To increase sales in France, for example, Coke installed thousands of soft-drink coolers in French supermarkets. In Great Britain, Coke emphasizes multipacks because it wants to have more inventory at the point of consumption—in consumers' homes. In Japan, by contrast, Coke has relied heavily on an army of truck drivers to constantly restock 1 million Coke vending machines, more per capita than anywhere else in the world. And, in Australia, some Coke vending machines have built-in cell phone systems; a press of a button makes a call so customers can charge the Coke to their cell phone accounts. Most U.S. firms face sanctions from doing business in Iran, but there is a loophole for foodstuffs. So, for several years Coke's Irish subsidiary has been shipping thousands of gallons of concentrate into Iran. Coke has quickly grabbed a large share of the national soft-drink market. You can imagine what conservative Muslim

315

clerics think about seeing the Coke brand everywhere they look.

Fortune magazine recently put the spotlight on Coca-Cola's commitment to sustainability, and decisions in the logistics area can have big environmental effects. For example, Coca-Cola is helping to develop vending machines that are HFC-free and 40 to 50 percent more energy efficient than conventional beverage equipment. Similarly, in the U.S. Coca-Cola is adding diesel hybrid delivery trucks that cut emissions and fuel consumption by a third; in Uruguay, Coca-Cola's Montevideo Refrescos subsidiary is using electric trucks for deliveries in congested urban areas. In spite of positive steps like these, Coca-Cola still faces some challenges concerning sustainability and logistics. For example, critics argue that in a society where there is already a safe supply of tap water it doesn't make sense to bottle water, transport it in trucks that consume fuel and contribute to pollution, and then add worry about how best to dispose of the empty bottles and bottle tops. There are also calls for a "leash" to attach the tops to the empty bottles so that they stay together for recycling—just as they stay together when they are shipped from the bottler.

In less-developed areas, the focus may be on different challenges—especially if the limitations of the Place system can make Coke products hard to find or costly. Until recently, retail stores in Afghanistan received Coke products shipped in from neighboring Pakistan—and a can of Coke sold for 40 cents. This priced many potential customers out of the market. After Coke built a local bottling plant and set up recycling systems, the price fell to about 13 cents—giving Coke a boost.

Coke is also working to increase fountain-drink sales in domestic and international markets. As part of that effort, Coke equips restaurants and food outlets with Coke dispensers. Once a Coke dispenser is installed, the retailer usually doesn't have room for a competitor's dispenser. The number of fountain outlets has grown so rapidly that one Coke account rep serves as many as 1,000 retail customers in a geographic area. That means that the little guys could get lost in the shuffle. However, to give them the service they need at a reasonable cost, Coke launched Coke.net, a password-protected Web portal where fountain customers can access account managers online, track syrup orders, request equipment repairs, or download marketing support materials.

Of course, Pepsi is a tough competitor and isn't taking all of this sitting down. It has added more non-cola products, and its edgy ads for Propel Fitness

Water and other products are helping it gain market share—which means it gets more shelf space and more Pepsi stocked at the point of purchase. Smaller players like Red Bull Energy Drink and Hansen's Natural Sodas also compete for distributors' attention and retail shelf space. Coke is pushing on new fronts as well. Who wins customers and profits in this broader competition will depend on overall marketing programs—but clearly Place has an important role to play.[1]

LEARNING OBJECTIVES

Choosing the right distribution channels is crucial in getting products to the target market's Place. But, as the Coca-Cola case shows, that alone doesn't ensure that products are placed "within an arm's reach of desire"—when, where, in the quantities that customers want them, and at a price they're willing to pay. In this chapter we discuss how marketing managers ensure that they also have physical distribution systems that meet their customers' needs—at both an acceptable service level and an affordable cost.

When you finish this chapter you should be able to:

1 understand why logistics (physical distribution) is such an important part of Place and marketing strategy planning.

2 understand why the physical distribution customer service level is a key marketing strategy variable.

3 understand the physical distribution concept and why the coordination of storing, transporting, and related activities is so important.

4 see how firms can cooperate and share logistics activities that will provide added value to their customers.

5 know about the advantages and disadvantages of various transportation methods.

6 know how inventory and storage decisions affect marketing strategy.

7 understand the distribution center concept.

8 understand important new terms (shown in red).

PHYSICAL DISTRIBUTION GETS IT TO CUSTOMERS

Whenever Product includes a physical good, Place requires logistics decisions. Logistics is the transporting, storing, and handling of goods in ways that match target customers' needs with a firm's marketing mix—both within individual firms and along a channel of distribution. Physical distribution (PD) is another common name for logistics.

There are many different combinations of logistics decisions. Each combination can result in a different level of distribution service and different costs. So, firms must determine the best way to provide the level of distribution service that customers want and are willing to pay for. We start this chapter by considering these critical logistics decisions. See Exhibit 12-1. Next, we describe the choice among different modes of transportation: Each has its own costs and benefits. We conclude with decisions about inventory and the use of distribution centers.

Logistics costs are very important to both firms and consumers. These costs vary from firm to firm and, from a macro-marketing perspective, from country to country. For some products, a firm may spend half or more of its total marketing dollars on physical distribution activities. The amounts involved are often so large that even small

Edition

Exhibit 12-1   The Role of Logistics and Physical Distribution Customer Service in Marketing Strategy

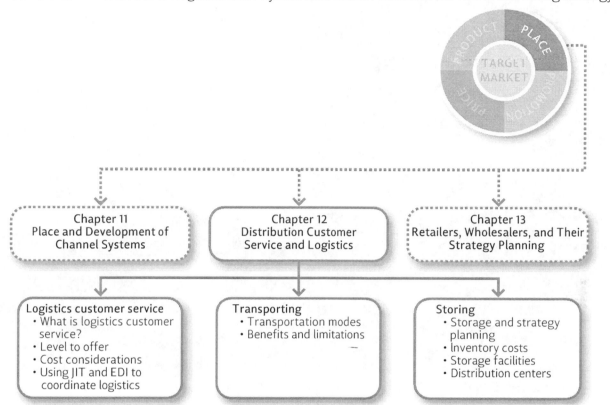

improvements in this area can have a big effect on a whole macro-marketing system and consumers' quality of life. For example, in the 1990s many supermarket chains collaborated with their suppliers and producers to create a system called Efficient Consumer Response (ECR). The basic idea of ECR involves computer links between grocers and their suppliers, which leads to continuous restocking of what actually sells each day and lower inventory costs. ECR cut grocers' costs, and prices that consumers pay, by about 11 percent. That translated to savings of almost $30 billion a year for U.S. consumers! Although it started in the United States and Canada, it's no surprise that the ECR movement spread quickly across Europe and other global regions.[2]

PHYSICAL DISTRIBUTION CUSTOMER SERVICE

From the beginning, we've emphasized that marketing strategy planning is based on meeting customers' needs. Planning for logistics and Place is no exception. So let's start by looking at logistics through a customer's eyes.

Customers want products, not excuses

Customers don't care how a product was moved or stored or what some channel member had to do to provide it. Rather, customers think in terms of the physical distribution customer service level—how rapidly and dependably a firm can deliver what they, the customers, want.

What does this really mean? It means that Toyota wants to have enough windshields delivered to make cars *that* day—not late so production stops *or* early so there are a lot of extras to move around or store. It means that business executives who rent

Edition

The physical distribution customer service level—including fast and reliable delivery of whatever assortment is needed—is critical to many business customers.

cars from Hertz want them to be ready when they get off their planes. It means that when you order a blue shirt at the Lands' End website you receive blue, not pink. It means you want your Tostitos to be whole when you buy a bag at the snack bar—not crushed into crumbs from rough handling in a warehouse.

Physical distribution is invisible to most consumers

PD is, and should be, a part of marketing that is "invisible" to most consumers. It only gets their attention when something goes wrong. At that point, it may be too late to do anything that will keep them happy.

In countries where physical distribution systems are inefficient, consumers face shortages of the products they need. By contrast, most consumers in the United States and Canada don't think much about physical distribution. This probably means that these market-directed macro-marketing systems work pretty well—that a lot of individual marketing managers have made good decisions in this area. But it doesn't mean that the decisions are always clear-cut or simple. In fact, many trade-offs may be required.

Trade-offs of costs, service, and sales

Most customers would prefer very good service at a very low price. But that combination is hard to provide because it usually costs more to provide higher levels of service. So most physical distribution decisions involve trade-offs between costs, the customer service level, and sales.

If you want a new HP computer and the Best Buy store where you would like to buy it doesn't have it on hand, you're likely to buy it elsewhere; or if that model HP is hard to get, you might just switch to some other brand. Perhaps the Best Buy store could keep your business by guaranteeing two-day delivery of your computer—by using airfreight from HP's factory. In this case, the manager is trading the cost of

Edition

Exhibit 12-2
Trade-Offs among
Physical Distribution
Costs, Customer Service
Level, and Sales

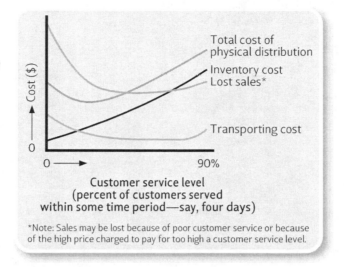

*Note: Sales may be lost because of poor customer service or because of the high price charged to pay for too high a customer service level.

319

storing inventory for the extra cost of speedy delivery—assuming that the computer is available in inventory *somewhere* in the channel. In this example, missing one sale may not seem that important, but it all adds up. A few years ago a computer company lost over $500 million in sales because its computers weren't available when and where customers were ready to buy them.

Exhibit 12-2 illustrates trade-off relationships like those highlighted in the HP example. For example, faster but more expensive transportation may reduce the need for a costly inventory of computers. If the service level is too low, customers will buy elsewhere and sales will be lost. Alternatively, the supplier may hope that a higher service level will attract more customers. But if the service level is higher than customers want or are willing to pay for, sales will be lost to competitors.

The trade-offs that must be made in the PD area can be complicated. The lowest-cost approach may not be best—if customers aren't satisfied. If different target markets want different customer service levels, several different strategies may be needed.[3]

Many firms are trying to address these complications with e-commerce. Information technology can sometimes improve service levels *and* cut costs at the same time. Better information flows make it easier to coordinate activities, improve efficiency, and add value for the customer.

PHYSICAL DISTRIBUTION CONCEPT FOCUSES ON THE WHOLE DISTRIBUTION SYSTEM

The physical
distribution concept

The physical distribution (PD) concept says that all transporting, storing, and product-handling activities of a business and a whole channel system should be coordinated as one system that seeks to minimize the cost of distribution for a given customer service level. Both lower costs and better service help to increase customer value. This seems like common sense, but until recently most companies treated physical distribution functions as separate and unrelated activities.

Within a firm, responsibility for different logistics activities was spread among various departments—production, shipping, sales, warehousing, purchasing, and others. No one person was responsible for coordinating storing and shipping decisions or customer service levels. It was even rarer for different firms in the channel to collaborate. Each just did its own thing. Unfortunately, in too many firms these old-fashioned ways persist—with a focus on individual functional activities rather than the whole physical distribution system.[4]

Edition

Exhibit 12-3
Examples of Factors
That Affect PD Service
Levels

- Advance information on product availability
- Time to enter and process orders
- Backorder procedures
- Where inventory is stored
- Accuracy in filling orders
- Damage in shipping, storing, and handling
- Online status information

- Advance information on delays
- Time needed to deliver an order
- Reliability in meeting delivery date
- Complying with customer's instructions
- Defect-free deliveries
- How needed adjustments are handled
- Procedures for handling returns

Decide what service
level to offer

With broader adoption of the physical distribution concept, this is changing. Firms work together to decide what aspects of service are most important to customers at the end of the channel. Then they focus on finding the least expensive way to achieve the target level of service.

Exhibit 12-3 shows a variety of factors that may influence the customer service level (at each level in the channel). The most important aspects of customer service depend on target market needs. Xerox might focus on how long it takes to deliver copy machine repair parts once it receives an order. When a copier breaks down, customers want the repair "yesterday." The service level might be stated as "we will deliver 90 percent of all emergency repair parts within 24 hours." This might require that commonly needed parts be available on the service truck, that order processing be very fast, and that parts not available locally be sent by airfreight. Obviously, supplying this service level will affect the total cost of the PD system. But it may also beat competitors.

Fast PD service can be critical for retailers that appeal to consumers who are eager to get a new product that is in hot demand—the latest CD or DVD release, a best-selling book, or a popular toy or video game.

Increasing service levels may also be very profitable in highly competitive situations where the firm has little else to differentiate its marketing mix. Marketing managers at Clorox, for example, must do everything they can to develop and keep strong partnerships with intermediaries. Many other firms sell products with precisely

Both Sauder and Best Software
try to help customer firms do a
better job of tracking the
status of orders and making
certain that products are
where they are needed at the
right time.

the same ingredients and are constantly trying to steal customers. Yet Clorox's high standards for customer service help it obtain a competitive advantage. For example, when the bleach buyer for a major retail chain went on vacation, the chain's central distribution center almost ran out of Clorox liquid bleach. But Clorox people identified the problem themselves—because of a computer system that allowed Clorox to access the chain's inventory records and sales data for Clorox products. Clorox rearranged production to get a shipment out fast enough to prevent the chain, and Clorox, from losing sales. In the future when another bleach supplier tells buyers for the chain that "bleach is bleach," they'll remember the distribution service Clorox provides.[5]

Find the lowest total cost for the right service level

In selecting a PD system, the total cost approach involves evaluating each possible PD system and identifying *all* of the costs of each alternative. This approach uses the tools of cost accounting and economics. Costs that otherwise might be ignored— like inventory carrying costs—are considered. The possible costs of lost sales due to a lower customer service level may also be considered. The following example clarifies why the total cost approach is important.

A cost comparison of alternative systems

The Good Earth Vegetable Company was shipping produce to distant markets by train. The cost of shipping a ton of vegetables by train averaged less than half the cost of airfreight so the company assumed that rail was the best method. But then Good Earth managers did a more complete analysis. To their surprise, they found the airfreight system was faster and cheaper.

Exhibit 12-4 compares the costs for the two distribution systems—airplane and railroad. Because shipping by train was slow, Good Earth had to keep a large inventory in a warehouse to fill orders on time. And the company was also surprised at the extra cost of carrying the inventory in transit. Good Earth's managers also found that the cost of spoiled vegetables during shipment and storage in the warehouse was much higher when they used rail shipping.

In this case, total cost analyses showed that airfreight, while more costly by itself, provided better service than the conventional means—and at a lower total distribution cost. The case also illustrates why it is important to get beyond a focus on individual functional elements of PD and instead consider the costs and service level of a whole system. This broader focus should consider how the whole channel operates, not just individual firms.

Exhibit 12-4
Comparative Costs of Airplane versus Rail and Warehouse

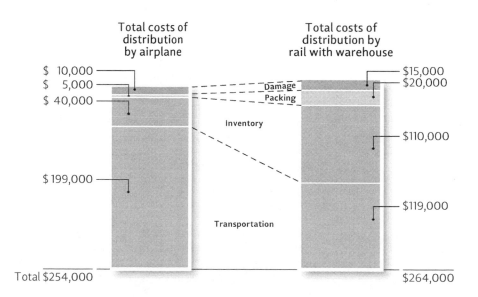

	Total costs of distribution by airplane	Total costs of distribution by rail with warehouse
Damage	$ 10,000	$15,000
Packing	$ 5,000	$20,000
Inventory	$ 40,000	$110,000
Transportation	$ 199,000	$119,000
Total	**$254,000**	**$264,000**

Edition

Many firms are now applying this type of thinking to improve value to customers and profits. For example, applying the total cost approach, National Semiconductor cut its standard delivery time in half, reduced distribution costs 2.5 percent, and increased sales by 34 percent. In the process, it shut down six warehouses around the globe and started to airfreight microchips to its worldwide customers from a new 125,000-square-foot distribution center in Singapore. In advance of these changes, no one would have said that this was an obvious thing to do. But it proved to be the smart thing.[6]

COORDINATING LOGISTICS ACTIVITIES AMONG FIRMS

Functions can be shifted and shared in the channel

As a marketing manager develops the Place part of a strategy, it is important to decide how physical distribution functions can and should be divided within the channel. Who will store, handle, and transport the goods—and who will pay for these services? Who will coordinate all of the PD activities?

There is no right sharing arrangement. Physical distribution can be varied endlessly in a marketing mix and in a channel system. And competitors may share these functions in different ways—with different costs and results.

How PD is shared affects the rest of a strategy

How the PD functions are shared affects the other three Ps—especially Price. The sharing arrangement can also make (or break) a strategy. Consider Channel Master, a firm that wanted to take advantage of the growing market for the dishlike antennas used to receive TV signals from satellites. The product looked like it could be a big success, but the small company didn't have the money to invest in a large inventory. So Channel Master decided to work only with wholesalers who were willing to buy (and pay for) several units—to be used for demonstrations and to ensure that buyers got immediate delivery.

In the first few months Channel Master earned $2 million in revenues—just by providing inventory for the channel. And the wholesalers paid the interest cost of carrying inventory—over $300,000 the first year. Here the wholesalers helped share the risk of the new venture, but it was a good decision for them, too. They won many sales from a competing channel whose customers had to wait several months for delivery. And by getting off to a strong start, Channel Master became a market leader.

A coordinated effort reduces conflict

If firms in the channel do not plan and coordinate how they will share PD activities, PD is likely to be a source of conflict rather than a basis for competitive advantage. Let's consider this point by taking a closer look at just-in-time (JIT) delivery systems (which we introduced in Chapter 7).

JIT requires a close, cooperative relationship

A key advantage of JIT for business customers is that it reduces their PD costs—especially storing and handling costs. However, if the customer doesn't have any backup inventory, there's no security blanket if a supplier's delivery truck gets stuck in traffic, there's an error in what's shipped, or there are any quality problems. Thus, a JIT system requires that a supplier have extremely high quality control in every PD activity.

A JIT system usually requires that a supplier respond to very short order lead times and the customer's production schedule. Thus, e-commerce order systems and information sharing over computer networks are often required. JIT suppliers often locate their facilities close to important customers. Trucks may make smaller and more frequent deliveries—perhaps even several times a day.

A JIT system shifts greater responsibility for PD activities backward in the channel. If the supplier can be more efficient than the customer could be in controlling PD costs—and still provide the customer with the service level required—this approach can work well for everyone in the channel. However, JIT is not always the best approach. It may

Disaster Relief Is No Logistics Picnic

Hurricanes, tsunamis, and earthquakes create immediate needs for emergency relief supplies. And the logistics involved in delivering them include many of the same activities found in the physical delivery of other goods. However, in a disaster situation, life and death often hinge upon the speed with which food, water, and medical supplies can be delivered. Yet, when bridges, roads, and airports are destroyed, local transportation can be complicated, if not impossible. And, even worse, there is no advance warning when or where aid will be needed. Imagine what it would be like for one business to be instantly ready to distribute millions of products to a target market that usually doesn't exist, moves around the world, and then without notice pops up somewhere with insatiable needs.

People in advanced societies have high expectations that help will be immediate when disaster strikes. Yet, it's nearly impossible for relief agencies to meet those expectations. Still, improved performance is on the way from both disaster relief agencies and private businesses, which have learned from recent efforts. For example, instead of stockpiling drugs, tents, and blankets, agencies are learning to rely on outsourcing. Agencies arrange open orders with suppliers who must be prepared to instantly ship supplies whenever and wherever they are needed.

Organizations with logistics expertise also lend a helping hand. As soon as Wal-Mart's emergency operation center learned that Hurricane Katrina was coming, it prestocked stores in the Gulf region with extra water, flashlights, and batteries as well as canned soup and meats. Residents survived with these crucial supplies before government aid arrived. Immediately following disasters in all parts of the world, transportation giants like FedEx, DHL, and China Southern Airlines have responded quickly with planes and trucks that facilitate delivery of needed supplies. Similarly, the Fritz Institute analyzes past relief efforts and consults with agencies to help them better prepare for future responses.

When chaos hits, coordination of relief efforts is possible only if there is good information. Agencies need to know what supplies are available, where they're located, what needs are greatest, and where and how quickly deliveries can be made. Having one central communication hub—to collect and share this type of information—and IT systems specifically dedicated to the task, are key. A new system called Suma allows relief workers to manage incoming donations, put them in the right storage places, and establish shipping priorities.

Other physical distribution solutions are decidedly low-tech, but equally important. For example, boxes need to be color coded so it's obvious which ones contain critical medical supplies and perishable food. And donated goods must be packed in cartons light enough to be carried manually in locations that have no power or equipment.[7]

be better for a supplier to produce and ship in larger, more economical quantities—if the savings offset the distribution system's total inventory and handling costs.[8]

Supply chain may involve even more firms

In our discussion, we have taken the point of view of a marketing manager. This focuses on how logistics should be coordinated to meet the needs of customers at the end of the channel of distribution. Now, however, we should broaden the picture somewhat because the relationships within the distribution channel are sometimes part of a broader network of relationships in the supply chain—the complete set of firms and facilities and logistics activities that are involved in procuring materials, transforming them into intermediate or finished products, and distributing them to customers. For example, Manitowoc is one of the world's largest manufacturers of cranes. Its huge mobile cranes are used at construction sites all around the world. Robert Ward, who is in charge of purchasing for Manitowoc, must ensure an unbroken flow of parts and materials so that Manitowoc can keep its promises to customers about when cranes will be delivered. This is difficult because each crane has component parts from many suppliers around the globe. Further, any supplier may be held up by problems with its own

Edition

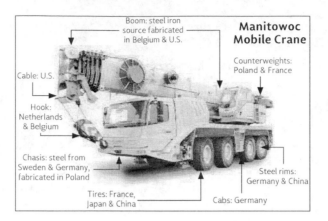

Boom: steel iron
source fabricated
in Belgium & U.S.

Manitowoc Mobile Crane

Cable: U.S.

Counterweights:
Poland & France

Hook:
Netherlands
& Belgium

Chasis: steel from
Sweden & Germany,
fabricated in Poland

Steel rims:
Germany & China

Tires: France,
Japan & China

Cabs: Germany

suppliers. In one case, Manitowoc's German factory was having trouble getting key chassis parts from two suppliers in Poland. Ward traced the problem back to a Scandinavian steel mill that was behind on shipments to the Polish firms. Manitowoc buys a lot of steel and has a lot of leverage with steel distributors, so Ward scoured Europe for distributors who had extra inventory of steel plate. The steel he found was more expensive than buying the steel directly from the mill, but the mill couldn't keep supplies flowing and the distributors could. By helping to coordinate the whole supply chain, Manitowoc was able to keep its promises and deliver cranes to its customers on schedule.[9]

Ideally, all of the firms in the supply chain should work together to meet the needs of the customer at the very end of the chain. That way, at each link along the chain the shifting and sharing of logistics functions and costs are handled to result in the most value for the final customer. This also helps all of the firms do a better job of competing against competitors who are involved in other supply chains.

It's still difficult for a manager in any one company to know what kind of logistics sharing arrangements will work best in a whole series of other companies. Because of that, many companies outsource this job to one or more firms that specialize in providing logistics services. Sometimes a logistics specialist takes over coordination of the entire logistics function for several firms in the channel. For example, UPS provides a variety of logistics services to Birkenstock, the German firm known for its sandals and shoes. UPS picks up bundles of sandals and shoes from the Birkenstock shop floor in Germany, handles the customs paperwork, and delivers the bundles directly to a UPS warehouse in the United States. From there, UPS repacks the shoes and delivers them to U.S. retailers. UPS's service has cut by three weeks the time it takes to move Birkenstock shoes from the plant to stores.[10]

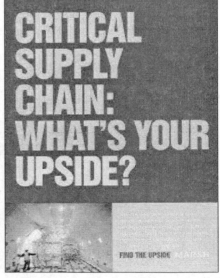

Firms often seek help from outside specialists to improve the efficiency and effectiveness of their domestic and international supply chains.

Edition

Better information helps coordinate PD

Coordinating all of the elements of PD has always been a challenge—even in a single firm. Trying to coordinate orders, inventory, and transportation throughout the whole supply chain is even tougher. But information shared over the Internet and at websites has been important in finding solutions to these challenges. Physical distribution decisions will continue to improve as more firms are able to have their computers "talk to each other" directly and as websites help managers get access to up-to-date information whenever they need it.

Internet EXERCISE

Managers who are members of the Council of Supply Chain Management Professionals usually have responsibilities in purchasing, logistics, or materials management. The website of this organization (www.cscmp.org) provides many useful resources to both members and nonmembers. Under "About CSCMP," choose "Awards" and then find the "Supply Chain Innovation Award." Choose one of the nominees of this award, and read how the nominee addressed a logistics challenge. Explain how other companies might learn from this firm's experience.

Electronic data interchange sets a standard

Until recently, differences in computer systems from one firm to another hampered the flow of information. Many firms attacked this problem by adopting electronic data interchange (EDI)—an approach that puts information in a standardized format easily shared between different computer systems. In many firms, purchase orders, shipping reports, and other paper documents were replaced with computerized EDI. With EDI, a customer transmits its order information directly to the supplier's computer. The supplier's computer immediately processes the order and schedules production, order assembly, and transportation. Inventory information is automatically updated, and status reports are available instantly. The supplier might then use EDI to send the updated information to the transportation provider's computer. In fact, most international transportation firms rely on EDI links with their customers.[11]

Improved information flow and better coordination of PD activities is a key reason for the success of Pepperidge Farm's line of premium cookies. Most of the company's delivery truck drivers use hand-held computers to record the inventory at each stop along their routes. They use a wireless Internet connection to instantly transmit the information into a computer at the bakeries, and cookies in short supply are produced. The right assortment of fresh cookies is quickly shipped to local markets, and delivery trucks are loaded with what retailers need that day. Pepperidge Farm moves cookies from its bakeries to store shelves in about three days; most cookie producers take about 10 days. That means fresher cookies for consumers and helps to support Pepperidge Farm's high-quality positioning and premium price.[12]

Ethical issues may arise

Some ethical issues that arise in the PD area concern communications about product availability. For example, some critics say that Internet sellers too often take orders for products that are not available or which they cannot deliver as quickly as customers expect. Yet a marketing manager can't always know precisely how long it will take before a product will be available. It doesn't make sense for the marketer to lose a customer if it appears that he or she can satisfy the customer's needs. But the customer may be inconvenienced or face added cost if the marketer's best guess isn't accurate. Similarly, some critics say that stores too often run out of products that they promote to attract consumers to the store. Yet it may not be possible for the marketer to predict demand, or to know when placing an ad that deliveries won't arrive. Different people have different views about how a firm should handle such situations. Some retailers just offer rain checks.

Edition

Now that you see why the coordination of physical distribution activities is so important, let's take a closer look at some of the PD decision areas.

THE TRANSPORTING FUNCTION ADDS VALUE TO A MARKETING STRATEGY

Transporting aids economic development and exchange

Transporting is the marketing function of moving goods. Transportation makes products available when and where they need to be—at a cost. But the cost is less than the value added to products by moving them or there is little reason to ship in the first place.

Transporting can help achieve economies of scale in production. If production costs can be reduced by producing larger quantities in one location, these savings may more than offset the added cost of transporting the finished products to customers. Without low-cost transportation, both within countries and internationally, there would be no mass distribution as we know it today.

Transporting can be costly

Transporting costs limit the target markets a marketing manager can serve. Shipping costs increase delivered cost—and that's what really interests customers. Transport costs add little to the cost of products that are already valuable relative to their size and weight. A case of medicine, for example, might be shipped to a drugstore at low cost. But transporting costs can be a large part of the total cost for heavy products of low value—like many minerals and raw materials. You can imagine that shipping a massive roll of aluminum to a producer of soft-drink cans is an expensive proposition. Exhibit 12-5 shows transporting costs as a percent of total sales dollars for several products.[14]

The cost of transportation adds little to the total cost of products—like pharmaceuticals—that are already valuable relative to their size and weight. But transporting costs can be a large part of the total cost for heavy products that are low in value, like sheet aluminum.

Exhibit 12–5
Transporting Costs as a
Percent of Selling Price
for Different Products

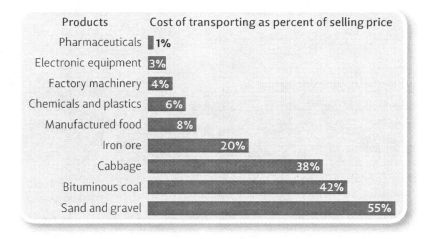

Products	Cost of transporting as percent of selling price
Pharmaceuticals	1%
Electronic equipment	3%
Factory machinery	4%
Chemicals and plastics	6%
Manufactured food	8%
Iron ore	20%
Cabbage	38%
Bituminous coal	42%
Sand and gravel	55%

**Governments
may influence
transportation**

Government often plays an important role in the development of a country's transportation system, including its roads, harbors, railroads, and airports. And different countries regulate transportation differently, although regulation has in general been decreasing.

For example, as part of their move toward unification, most European countries are reducing their transporting regulations. The construction of the tunnel under the English Channel is a dramatic example of the changes taking place. The "chunnel" allows trains to speed between England and the rest of Europe.

As regulations decreased in the United States, competition in the transportation industry increased. As a result, a marketing manager generally has many carriers in one or more modes competing for the firm's transporting business. Or a firm can do its own transporting. So knowing about the different modes is important.[15]

WHICH TRANSPORTING ALTERNATIVE IS BEST?

**Transporting function
must fit the whole
strategy**

The transporting function should fit into the whole marketing strategy. But picking the best transporting alternative depends on the product, other physical distribution decisions, and what service level the company wants to offer. The best alternative should provide the level of service (for example, speed and dependability) required at as low a cost as possible. Exhibit 12-6 shows that different modes of transportation have different strengths and weaknesses. You can find more detail at the website of the Bureau of Transportation Statistics (www.bts.gov). Low transporting cost is *not* the only criterion for selecting the best mode.[16]

Exhibit 12-6   Benefits and Limitations of Different Transport Modes

	Transporting Features					
Mode	Cost	Delivery Speed	Number of Locations Served	Ability to Handle a Variety of Goods	Frequency of Scheduled Shipments	Dependability in Meeting Schedules
Truck	High	Fast	Very extensive	High	High	High
Rail	Medium	Average	Extensive	High	Low	Medium
Water	Very low	Very slow	Limited	Very high	Very low	Medium
Air	Very high	Very fast	Extensive	Limited	High	High
Pipeline	Low	Slow	Very limited	Very limited	Medium	High

Edition

Logistics costs are often higher and service levels lower in developing economies, where highways, rail systems, distribution centers, information technology, and equipment choices are limited or inefficient.

Railroads—large loads moved at low cost

Railroads are still the workhorse of the U.S. transportation system. They carry more freight over more miles than any other mode. However, they account for less than 10 percent of transport revenues. They carry heavy and bulky goods—such as coal, steel, and chemicals—over long distances at relatively low cost. Because railroad freight usually moves more slowly than truck shipments, it is not as well suited for perishable items or those in urgent demand. Railroads are most efficient at handling full carloads of goods. Less-than-carload (LCL) shipments take a lot of handling, which means they usually move more slowly and at a higher price per pound than carload shipments.[17]

Trucks are more expensive, but flexible and essential

The flexibility and speed of trucks make them better at moving small quantities of goods for shorter distances. They can travel on almost any road. They go where the rails can't. They are also reliable in meeting delivery schedules, which is an essential requirement for logistics systems that provide rapid replenishment of inventory after a sale. In combination these factors explain why at least 75 percent of U.S. consumer products travel at least part of the way from producer to consumer by truck. And in countries with good highway systems, trucks can give extremely fast service. Trucks compete for high-value items.[18]

Ship it overseas, but slowly

Water transportation is the slowest shipping mode, but it is usually the lowest-cost way of shipping heavy freight. Water transportation is very important for international

Critics say that increased reliance on truck freight is bad for the environment, but the trade association that represents America's oil and natural gas industry says that engineers are at work on new "ultra low sulfur and advanced engines that will result in 90 percent less emissions."

shipments and often the only practical approach. This explains why port cities like Boston, New York City, Rotterdam, Osaka, and Singapore are important centers for international trade.

Inland waterways are important too

Inland waterways (such as the Mississippi River and Great Lakes in the United States and the Rhine and Danube in Europe) are also important, especially for bulky, nonperishable products such as iron ore, grain, and gravel. However, when winter ice closes freshwater harbors, alternate transportation must be used.

Internet EXERCISE

Shipping by sea can be a less costly mode of transportation. But with more than 100 carriers operating ships, it can be difficult to get a handle on all the options. OceanSchedules.com (www.oceanschedules.com) aims to change this. Go to the website and do a "port to port" search, with "Hong Kong" as the origin and "Vancouver, British Columbia" as the destination. Next select "by departure" and enter today's date and 1 week out. Finally, click "Get Schedules." How many different boats could take your shipment? Now change the longest transit time to 28 days and check what difference that makes in the number of available boats. What happens if you change the arrival date? How could this website be useful to a company shipping light fixtures from Hong Kong to Canada?

Pipelines move oil and gas

Pipelines are used primarily to move oil and natural gas. So pipelines are important both in the oil-producing and oil-consuming countries. Only a few major cities in the United States, Canada, Mexico, and Latin America are more than 200 miles from a major pipeline system. However, the majority of the pipelines in the United States are located in the Southwest, connecting oil fields and refineries.

Airfreight is expensive, but fast and growing

The most expensive cargo transporting mode is airplane—but it is fast! Airfreight rates are on average three times higher than trucking rates—but the greater speed may offset the added cost.

High-value, low-weight goods—like high-fashion clothing and parts for the electronics industry—are often shipped by air. Perishable products that previously could not be shipped are now being flown across continents and oceans. Flowers and bulbs from Holland, for example, now are jet-flown to points all over the world. And airfreight has become very important for small emergency deliveries, like repair parts, special orders, and business documents that must be somewhere the next day.

But airplanes may cut the total cost of distribution

Using planes may reduce the cost of packing, unpacking, and preparing goods for sale and may help a firm reduce inventory costs by eliminating outlying warehouses. Valuable benefits of airfreight's speed are less spoilage, theft, and damage. Although the *transporting* cost of air shipments may be higher, the *total* cost of distribution may be lower. As more firms realize this, airfreight firms—like DHL Worldwide Express, FedEx, and Emery Air Freight—have enjoyed rapid growth.[19]

These firms play an especially important role in the growth of international business. For example, Vegpro Kenya uses airfreight to ship fresh vegetables from Kenya to major European cities. The company responded to consumer demand for the convenience of ready-to-eat fresh produce. Vegpro cleans, chops, and packages vegetables in its 27,000-square-foot, air-conditioned facility at the Nairobi airport—using low-cost African labor. The next day, fresh beans, baby carrots, and other vegetables are on store shelves in Madrid, London, and Paris.[20]

Put it in a container— and move between modes easily

Products often move by several different modes and carriers during their journey. This is especially common for international shipments. Japanese firms, like Sony, ship stereos to the United States, Canada, and Europe by boat. When they arrive at the dock, they are loaded on trains and sent across the country. Then the units are delivered to a wholesaler by truck or rail.

Edition

To better coordinate the flow of products between modes, transportation companies like CSX offer customers a complete choice of different transportation modes. Then CSX, not the customer, figures out the best and lowest-cost way to shift and share transporting functions between the modes.[21]

Loading and unloading goods several times used to be a real problem. Parts of a shipment would become separated, damaged, or even stolen. And handling the goods, perhaps many times, raised costs and slowed delivery. Many of these problems are reduced with containerization—grouping individual items into an economical shipping quantity and sealing them in protective containers for transit to the final destination. This protects the products and simplifies handling during shipping. Some containers are as large as truck bodies.

Piggyback—a ride on two or more modes

Piggyback service means loading truck trailers—or flatbed trailers carrying containers—on railcars to provide both speed and flexibility. Railroads now pick up truck trailers at the producer's location, load them onto specially designed rail flatcars, and haul them as close to the customer as rail lines run. The trailers are then hooked up to a truck tractor and delivered to the buyer's door. Similar services are offered on oceangoing ships—allowing door-to-door service between cities around the world.

Transportation in developing countries can cost more

Transportation choices are usually not so good in developing countries. Roads are often poor, rail systems may be limited, and ports may be undeveloped. Local firms that specialize in logistics services may not exist at all. Even so, firms that are willing to invest the effort can reap benefits and help their customers overcome the effects of these problems.

Metro AG, a firm based in Germany that has opened wholesale facilities in Bangalore and several other major cities in India, illustrates this point. Metro focuses on selling food products and other supplies to the thousands of restaurants, hotels, and other small businesses in the markets it serves. When Metro started in India, 40 percent of the fruits and vegetables it purchased from farmers were spoiled, damaged, or lost by the time they got to Metro. These problems piled up because the produce traveled from the fields over rough roads and was handled by as many as seven intermediaries along the way. To overcome these problems, Metro gave farmers crates to protect freshly picked crops from damage and to keep them away from dirt and bacteria that would shorten their shelf life. Further, crates were loaded and unloaded only once because Metro bought its own refrigerated trucks—to pick up produce and bring it directly to its outlets. Metro used the same ideas to speed fresh seafood from fishermen's boats. Many of Metro's restaurant customers previously bought what they needed from a variety of small suppliers, many of whom would run out of stock. Now the restaurant owners save time and money with one-stop shopping at Metro. Metro is growing fast in India because it has quality products that are in stock when they're needed, and it's bringing down food costs for its customers.[22]

Transportation choices have environmental costs too

Marketing managers must be sensitive to the environmental effects of transportation decisions. Trucks, trains, airplanes, and ships contribute to air pollution and global warming; estimates suggest that on average more than half of a firm's total carbon emissions

When Metro set up its cash-and-carry wholesale operations in India, it could not rely on the same logistics systems it used in Germany. Rather, Metro had to create its own fleet of refrigerated trucks to pick up produce directly from farmers. However, this reduced stock-outs and helped Metro offer customers better-quality produce at lower prices.

come from transportation. There are other problems as well. For example, a damaged pipeline or oil tanker can spew thousands of gallons of oil before it can be repaired.

Many firms are taking steps to reduce such problems. FedEx and UPS are revamping their fleets to use more electric and alternative fuel vehicles. Rail is usually the cleanest way to move land freight a long distance, but General Electric's recently introduced Evolution locomotives have 5 percent better fuel economy and 40 percent lower emissions compared to previous models. GE is already working on a hybrid locomotive that will improve fuel economy another 10 percent. Truck manufacturers are also working to improve fuel efficiency and environmental impact. Peterbilt and International are among firms working to build diesel-hybrid 18-wheelers. The U.S. government supports these initiatives through the Environmental Protection Agency's SmartWay program. It helps freight carriers, shippers, and logistics companies improve fuel efficiency and reduce environmental impact. Both trucking and railroad firms have procedures to ensure that transporting toxic cargo is safer. Today the public *expects* companies to manufacture, transport, sell, and dispose of products in an environmentally sound manner.[23]

THE STORING FUNCTION AND MARKETING STRATEGY

Store it and smooth out sales, increase profits and consumer satisfaction

Storing is the marketing function of holding goods so they're available when they're needed. **Inventory** is the amount of goods being stored.

Maintaining the right inventory level is difficult when it's hard to forecast likely demand. Even so, a firm that is stocked out when customers are ready to buy may not only lose the sale but also damage the relationship and the possibility of future sales. Kmart ran into this problem. Many consumers decided it was no longer a convenient

Edition

Menasha, a supplier of innovative packaging, wants its client firms to realize that its package designs can help to reduce both logistics costs and environmental impacts. The Environmental Protection Agency's voluntary SmartWay Transport Partnership is another approach to achieve environmental goals by reducing fuel costs as well as air pollution.

place to shop when stores repeatedly ran out of basic staples that consumers expected to find.

Storing is necessary when production of goods doesn't match consumption. This is common with mass production. Nippon Steel, for example, might produce thousands of steel bars of one size before changing the machines to produce another size. It's often cheaper to produce large quantities of one size, and store the unsold quantity, than to have shorter production runs. Thus, storing goods allows the producer to achieve economies of scale in production.

Some buyers purchase in large quantities to get quantity discounts from the producer or transporter. Then the extra goods must be stored until there is demand. And goods are sometimes stored as a hedge against future price rises, strikes, shipping interruptions, and other disruptions.

Storing varies the channel system

Storing allows producers and intermediaries to keep stocks at convenient locations, ready to meet customers' needs. In fact, storing is one of the major activities of some intermediaries.

Most channel members provide the storing function for some length of time. Even final consumers store some things for their future needs. Which channel members store the product, and for how long, affects the behavior of all channel members. For example, the producer of Snapper lawn mowers tries to get wholesalers to inventory a wide selection of its machines. That way, retailers can carry smaller inventories since they can be sure of dependable local supplies from wholesalers. And the retailers might decide to sell Snapper—rather than Toro or some other brand that they would have to store at their own expense.

If consumers "store" the product, more of it may be used or consumed. That's why Breyer's likes customers to buy its half-gallon packages. The "inventory" is right there in the freezer—and ready to be eaten—whenever the impulse hits.

Goods are stored at a cost

Storing can increase the value of goods, but *storing always involves costs* too. Different kinds of cost are involved. See Exhibit 12-7. Car dealers, for example, must store cars on their lots—waiting for the right customer. The interest expense of money tied up in the inventory is a major cost. In addition, if a new car on the lot is dented or scratched, there is a repair cost. If a car isn't sold before the new models come out, its

Edition

Exhibit 12-7   Many Expenses Contribute to Total Inventory Cost

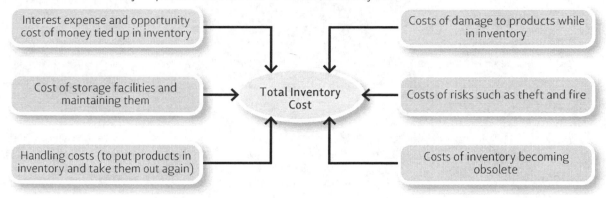

value drops. There is also a risk of fire or theft—so the retailer must carry insurance. And, of course, dealers incur the cost of leasing or owning the display lot where they store the cars.

In today's competitive markets, most firms watch their inventories closely. They try to cut unnecessary inventory because it can make the difference between a profitable strategy and a loser. On the other hand, a marketing manager must be very careful in making the distinction between unnecessary inventory and inventory needed to provide the distribution service level customers expect.[24]

Rapid response cuts inventory costs

Many firms are finding that they can cut inventory costs and still provide the desired customer service level—if they can reduce the time it takes to replace items that are sold. This is one important reason that the JIT and ECR approaches have been widely adopted. The firms involved use EDI, the Internet, and similar computerized approaches to share information and speed up the order cycle and delivery process.

SPECIALIZED STORING FACILITIES MAY BE REQUIRED

New cars can be stored outside on the dealer's lot. Fuel oil can be stored in a specially designed tank. Coal and other raw materials can be stored in open pits. But most products must be stored inside protective buildings. Often, firms can choose among different types of specialized storing facilities. The right choice may reduce costs and serve customers better.

Private warehouses are common

Private warehouses are storing facilities owned or leased by companies for their own use. Most manufacturers, wholesalers, and retailers have some storing facilities either in their main buildings or in a separate location. A sales manager often is responsible for managing a manufacturer's finished-goods warehouse, especially if regional sales branches aren't near the factory.

Firms use private warehouses when a large volume of goods must be stored regularly. Yet private warehouses can be expensive. If the need changes, the extra space may be hard, or impossible, to rent to others.

Public warehouses fill special needs

Public warehouses are independent storing facilities. They can provide all the services that a company's own warehouse can provide. A company might choose a public warehouse if it doesn't have a regular need for space. For example, Tonka Toys uses public warehouses because its business is seasonal. Tonka pays for the space only

Edition

Exhibit 12-8
A Comparison of Private
Warehouses and Public
Warehouses

Characteristics	Type of Warehouse	
	Private	Public
Fixed investment	Very high	No fixed investment
Unit cost	High if volume is low Very low if volume is very high	Low: charges are made only for space needed
Control	High	Low managerial control
Adequacy for product line	Highly adequate	May not be convenient
Flexibility	Low: fixed costs have already been committed	High: easy to end arrangement

when it is used. Public warehouses are also useful for manufacturers that must maintain stocks in many locations, including foreign countries. See Exhibit 12-8 for a comparison of private and public warehouses.[25]

Warehousing facilities cut handling costs too

The cost of physical handling is a major storing cost. Goods must be handled once when put into storage and again when removed to be sold. To reduce these costs, modern one-story buildings away from downtown traffic have replaced most old multistory warehouses. They eliminate the need for elevators and permit the use of power-operated lift trucks, battery-operated motor scooters, roller-skating order pickers,

electric hoists for heavy items, and hydraulic ramps to speed loading and unloading. Bar codes, universal product code (UPC) numbers, and electronic radio frequency identification (RFID) tags make it easy for computers to monitor inventory, order needed stock, and track storing and shipping costs. For example, a warehouse worker may wear a tiny scanner ring when removing cartons from a shelf so that information in the bar codes can be instantly read and transmitted via a Bluetooth wireless network to the firm's information system. Similarly, RFID tags may transmit detailed information about the contents of a carton as it moves along a conveyor system. Some warehouses also have computer-controlled order-picking systems or conveyor belts that speed the process of locating and assembling the assortment required to fill an order.[26]

Zappos.com says that "we are a service company that happens to sell." In practice, that means it has a warehouse that's as big as 17 football fields to support transactions from its website at the needed customer service level. Further, Zappos.com's storing, transporting, and handling must be efficient for the firm to compete with "free shipping" and "110% price protection."

CHAPTER 12

335

Distribution Customer Service and Logistics

THE DISTRIBUTION CENTER—A DIFFERENT KIND OF WAREHOUSE

Is storing really needed?

Discrepancies of assortment or quantity between one channel level and another are often adjusted at the place where goods are stored. It reduces handling costs to regroup and store at the same place—*if both functions are required.* But sometimes regrouping is required when storing isn't.

Don't store it, distribute it

A *distribution center* is a special kind of warehouse designed to speed the flow of goods and avoid unnecessary storing costs. Anchor Hocking moves over a million pounds of its housewares products through its distribution center each day. Faster inventory turnover and easier bulk-breaking reduce the cost of carrying inventory.

Today, the distribution center concept is widely used by firms at all channel levels. Many products buzz through a distribution center without ever tarrying on a shelf; workers and equipment immediately sort the products as they come in and then move them to an outgoing loading dock and the vehicle that will take them to their next stop.

Direct store delivery skips the distribution center

Some firms prefer to skip the distribution center altogether and ship products directly from where they are manufactured to retail stores. This may move products more quickly, but usually at a higher cost. Frito-Lay uses this approach. It handles more than 10,000 direct delivery routes to more than 200,000 small-store customers. The route drivers build close relationships with the many small retailers. That helps Frito-Lay better understand end consumers and adapt product mixes to particular stores. These extra services result in more shelf space and higher prices at the small stores.[27]

Managers must be innovative to provide customers with superior value

More competitive markets, improved technology, coordination among firms, and efficient new distribution centers are bringing big improvements to the PD area. Yet the biggest challenges may be more basic. As we've emphasized here, physical distribution activities transcend departmental, corporate, and even national boundaries. So taking advantage of ways to improve often requires cooperation all along the channel system. Too often, such cooperation doesn't exist—and changing ingrained ways of doing things is hard. But marketing managers who push for innovations in these areas are likely to win customers away from firms and whole channel systems that are stuck doing things in the old way.[28]

CONCLUSION

This chapter explained the major logistics activities and how they contribute to the value of products by getting them to the place that customers want or need them. If the distribution customer service level meets their needs and can be provided at a reasonable cost, customers may not even think about the logistics activities that occur behind the scenes. But if products are not available when and where they need to be, a strategy will fail. So decisions in these areas are an important part of Place and marketing strategy planning.

We emphasized the relation between customer service level, transporting, and storing. The physical distribution concept focuses on coordinating all the storing, transporting, and product-handling activities into a smoothly working system—to deliver the

desired service level and customer value at the lowest total cost.

Marketing managers often want to improve service and may select a higher-cost alternative to improve their marketing mix. The total cost approach might reveal that it is possible both to reduce costs and to improve customer service—perhaps by working closely with other members of the supply chain.

We discussed various modes of transporting and their advantages and disadvantages. We also discussed ways to reduce inventory costs. For example, distribution centers are an important way to cut storing and handling costs, and computerized information links—within firms and among firms in the channel—are increasingly important in blending all of the logistics activities into a smooth-running system.

Effective marketing managers make important strategy decisions about physical distribution. Cre-ative strategy decisions may result in lower PD costs while maintaining or improving the customer service level. And production-oriented competitors may not even understand what is happening.

KEY TERMS

336

logistics, 316
physical distribution (PD), 316
customer service level, 317
physical distribution (PD) concept, 319
total cost approach, 321

supply chain, 323
electronic data interchange (EDI), 325
transporting, 326
containerization, 330
piggyback service, 330

storing, 331
inventory, 331
private warehouses, 333
public warehouses, 333
distribution center, 335

QUESTIONS AND PROBLEMS

1. Explain how adjusting the customer service level could improve a marketing mix. Illustrate.

2. Briefly explain which aspects of customer service you think would be most important for a producer that sells fabric to a firm that manufactures furniture.

3. Briefly describe a purchase you made where the customer service level had an effect on the product you selected or where you purchased it.

4. Discuss the types of trade-offs involved in PD costs, service levels, and sales.

5. Give an example of why it is important for different firms in the supply chain to coordinate logistics activities.

6. Discuss some of the ways computers are being used to improve PD decisions.

7. Explain why a just-in-time delivery system would require a supplier to pay attention to quality control. Give an example to illustrate your points.

8. Discuss the problems a supplier might encounter in using a just-in-time delivery system with a customer in a foreign country.

9. Review the list of factors that affect PD service levels in Exhibit 12-3. Indicate which ones are most likely to be improved by EDI links between a supplier and its customers.

10. Explain the total cost approach and why it may cause conflicts in some firms. Give examples of how conflicts might occur between different departments.

11. Discuss the relative advantages and disadvantages of railroads, trucks, and airlines as transporting methods.

12. Discuss why economies of scale in transportation might encourage a producer to include a regional merchant wholesaler in the channel of distribution for its consumer product.

13. Discuss some of the ways that air transportation can change other aspects of a Place system.

14. Explain which transportation mode would probably be most suitable for shipping the following goods to a large Los Angeles department store:

   a. 300 pounds of Maine lobster.
   b. 15 pounds of screwdrivers from Ohio.
   c. Three dining room tables from High Point, North Carolina.
   d. 500 high-fashion dresses from the fashion district in Paris.
   e. A 10,000-pound shipment of exercise equipment from Germany.
   f. 600,000 pounds of various appliances from Evansville, Indiana.

15. Indicate the nearest location where you would expect to find large storage facilities. What kinds of products would be stored there? Why are they stored there instead of some other place?

16. When would a producer or intermediary find it desirable to use a public warehouse rather than a private warehouse? Illustrate, using a specific product or situation.

17. Discuss the distribution center concept. Is this likely to eliminate the storing function of conventional wholesalers? Is it applicable to all products? If not, cite several examples.

18. Clearly differentiate between a warehouse and a distribution center. Explain how a specific product would be handled differently by each.

19. If a retailer operates only from a website and ships all orders by UPS, is it freed from the logistics issues that face traditional retailers? Explain your thinking.

CREATING MARKETING PLANS

The Marketing Plan Coach software on the Student CD and the text website includes a sample marketing plan for Hillside Veterinary Clinic. Look through the "Marketing Strategy" section. To provide veterinary care to pets, Hillside needs to have a variety of medical supplies on hand. To handle that, it relies on deliveries from suppliers and its own inventory decisions. It also sells some retail pet products to customers, and that requires a separate set of decisions about how it will handle inventory.

a. What logistics issues related to medical supplies should Hillside consider? Can you think of ways in which delivery from its suppliers or its own inventory decisions will be important in its ability to help its patients?

b. With respect to the retail pet products that Hillside sells, what level of customer service should customers expect?

c. What issues are involved in storage of pet supplies?

SUGGESTED CASES

16. Bunyan Lumber   26. Best Way Canning, Inc.

COMPUTER-AIDED PROBLEM

12. TOTAL DISTRIBUTION COST

Proto Company has been producing various items made of plastic. It recently added a line of plain plastic cards that other firms (such as banks and retail stores) will imprint to produce credit cards. Proto offers its customers the plastic cards in different colors, but they all sell for $40 per box of 1,000. Tom Phillips, Proto's product manager for this line, is considering two possible physical distribution systems. He estimates that if Proto uses airfreight, transportation costs will be $7.50 a box, and its cost of carrying inventory will be 5 percent of total annual sales dollars. Alternatively, Proto could ship by rail for $2 a box. But rail transport will require renting space at four regional warehouses—at $26,000 a year each. Inventory carrying cost with this system will be 10 percent of total annual sales dollars. Phillips prepared a spreadsheet to compare the cost of the two alternative physical distribution systems.

a. If Proto Company expects to sell 20,000 boxes a year, what are the total physical distribution costs for each of the systems?

b. If Phillips can negotiate cheaper warehouse space for the rail option so that each warehouse costs only $20,000 per year, which physical distribution system has the lowest overall cost?

c. Proto's finance manager predicts that interest rates are likely to be lower during the next marketing plan year and suggests that Tom Phillips use inventory carrying costs of 4 percent for airfreight and 7.5 percent for railroads (with warehouse cost at $20,000 each). If interest rates are in fact lower, which alternative would you suggest? Why?

For additional questions related to this problem, see Exercise 12-3 in the *Learning Aid for Use with Basic Marketing*, 17th edition.

13

CHAPTER

Retailers, Wholesalers, and Their Strategy Planning

When it comes to buying consumer electronics, are you a demon or an angel? If you don't know the answer, Best Buy probably does. Best Buy is evaluating its portfolio of customers to do a better job of segmenting the angels—customers who buy high-margin items like HDTVs at full price and then add accessories, an extended service contract, and perhaps Geek Squad installation help. Best Buy is cutting free from its demons, the 20 percent of its customers who are unprofitable. Some demons are just aggressive bargain hunters. They clip competitors' ads and demand price matches or "cherry pick" and buy only deeply discounted sale products. But an unscrupulous demon might go further and buy a videocam, use it on a vacation, send in for its rebate, and then return it for a refund. Best Buy is using its customer relationship management (CRM) system to identify demons and take them off its mail promotion list. It's also charging a 15 percent restocking fee on returns, phasing out rebates, and selling returned products on the Internet (which thwarts demons from rebuying their own returns at the lower, open-box price).

On a more positive (and profitable) note, Best Buy is targeting five key segments among its angel customers: upscale suburban moms, affluent professional males, teenage entertainment/gaming enthusiasts, budget-conscious families who are practical technology adopters, and small businesses. Best Buy is analyzing each store's sales data and demographics to identify which segments are most significant. Then it is converting stores, or creating a store-within-a-store, to better focus on those segments. For example, Best Buy's research showed that female shoppers buy 55 percent of electronic items but that they didn't like the Best Buy shopping experience. Now Best Buy is focusing on the most lucrative subset of women shoppers—busy moms in suburban areas. The retailer has a nickname for a woman in this segment. She's "Jill." In the past, sales staff either didn't explain things enough or talked down to and insulted Jill. So now a store that appeals to Jill offers "personal shopping assistants." They help Jill find what she wants in less time. Rather than ask, "How many megapixels do you need?" retrained salespeople ask Jill, "What do you want to photograph?"— and then they suggest what will best suit her needs. And, rather than organize cameras by brand on the shelf, models with similar features are displayed together so that Jill can compare them more easily. Stores that target Jill have learned that she is a great candidate for small appliances when they carry a broader assortment and place them in the regular aisles on easy-to-reach shelves—not off in a corner with the stoves.

Segmented stores differ depending on the target market. Stores that target the affluent male professional ("Barry"), for instance, have a private in-store home theater demo room,

339

complete with comfy leather viewing chairs and popcorn. Barry likes the newest DVDs. So, on days when hot DVDs are released, home theater specialists roam the aisles, look for Barry, and steer him to preview DVDs in the demo room. You know you're an angel—and probably a Barry—if a $12,000 home theater setup is an impulse buy after a visit to the demo room.

Best Buy first tested the targeted stores concept in California. The test stores showed significant increases in sales, profits, and the percentage of customers who made a purchase. The reasons for these successes were measured and analyzed and then rolled out to other similar stores.

Best Buy's marketing strategy planning has not always been so sophisticated. Rather, it started in 1966 as Sound of Music, which was a conventional, limited-line retail store that sold a few select brands of hi-fi equipment. Since then, Best Buy's strategies for growth mirror some of the important trends that have emerged in retailing. Perhaps most basic, it was one of the first stores to adopt the mass-merchandising approach in selling consumer electronics; it focused on lower prices and faster turnover—rather than high markups—to draw customers and increase revenues and profits. Like other retailers who grew by creating multistore chains, it

has achieved economies of scale in areas such as buying, promotion, and management. Over time it has scrambled its product line toward innovative and profitable new products—not just stereo equipment but also categories such as digital cameras and camcorders, video systems including HDTV, and now its full line of Geek Squad in-home technical services. Similarly, Best Buy was an innovator among bricks-and-mortar retailers when it quickly took advantage of Internet retailing with a website that complements its stores' offerings. It also has developed state-of-the-art distribution centers and logistics systems, which have reduced its reliance on traditional merchant wholesalers and helped to cut costs. On the other hand, some progressive wholesalers have benefited from these changes. For example, Best Buy uses Internet-based brokers to find construction firms that can help it cut costs when it builds new stores.

Forbes magazine has named Best Buy a "company of the year" and *Fortune* has ranked it #4 on its list of most admired companies. So you know that it has been doing a lot of things right. But, it is also facing tough competition on several fronts. Further, Best Buy will soon be at a saturation level, with about 1,000 stores in North America. So it is unlikely to continue its growth by opening new outlets in the same broad product-market. It has to generate more profit from the stores that it has—with better targeting and profitable services like Geek Squad. At the same time, it is evaluating new retailing formats, like its Best Buy Mobile concept stores, which sell mobile phones and service, and its EQ-Life concept stores, which may become for health-and-wellness retailing what its current stores are for electronics.[1]

LEARNING OBJECTIVES

Retail and wholesale organizations exist as members of marketing channel systems. But they also do their own strategy planning as they compete for target customers. As the Best Buy case shows, these firms make decisions about Product, Place, Promotion, and Price. This chapter overviews the strategy planning decisions of different types of retailers and wholesalers. The chapter shows how retailing and wholesaling are evolving—to give you a sense of how things may change in the future.

When you finish this chapter you should be able to:

1 understand how retailers plan their marketing strategies.

2 know about the many kinds of retailers that work with producers and wholesalers as members of channel systems.

3 understand the differences among the conventional and nonconventional retailers—including Internet merchants and others who accept the mass-merchandising concept.

4 understand scrambled merchandising and the "wheel of retailing."

5 see why size or belonging to a chain can be important to a retailer.

6 know what progressive wholesalers are doing to modernize their operations and marketing strategies.

7 know the various kinds of merchant and agent wholesalers and the strategies they use.

8 understand why retailing and wholesaling have developed in different ways in different countries.

9 see why the Internet is impacting both retailing and wholesaling.

10 understand important new terms (shown in red).

RETAILERS AND WHOLESALERS PLAN THEIR OWN STRATEGIES

In Chapter 11, we discussed the vital role that retailers and wholesalers perform in channel systems. Now we'll look at the decisions that retailers and wholesalers make in developing their own strategies. See Exhibit 13-1. The chapter begins with a discussion of strategy planning for retailers. Retailers must create a marketing mix that provides value for a target market. We also discuss how retailing has evolved and where it stands today, including some important international differences. The chapter concludes by considering strategy planning by different types of wholesalers.

Understand how retailing and wholesaling are evolving

Understanding the how and why of past changes in retailing and wholesaling will help you know what to expect in the future. It will also make it clear that it is the whole strategy, not just one aspect of it, that ultimately is a success or failure. This may seem obvious, but it's a point that many people have ignored—at great cost.

Edition

Exhibit 13-1   Marketing Strategy Planning for Retailers and Wholesalers

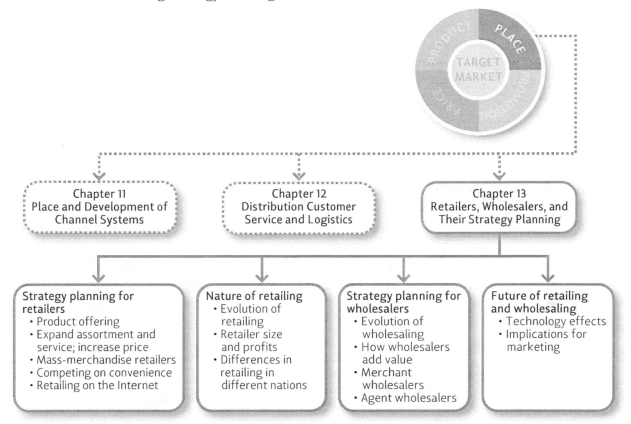

Consider the dramatic changes prompted by the Internet. A few years ago many people were proclaiming that it would quickly change everything we thought about successful retailing. Yet many creative ideas for online retailing bombed precisely because managers of dot-coms failed to understand why retailing has evolved as it has. For many consumers and many types of purchases, it won't matter that an online retailer posts low prices for an incredible assortment if there's no way to get customer service, products are not actually available, or it's a hassle to return a green shirt that looked blue on the website. *You* want to avoid the trap of this sort of incomplete thinking!

So in this chapter we'll focus on decisions that apply to all retailers and wholesalers, while highlighting how their strategies are changing.

THE NATURE OF RETAILING

Retailing covers all of the activities involved in the sale of products to final consumers. Retailers range from large chains of specialized stores, like Toys "R" Us, to individual merchants like the woman who sells baskets from an open stall in the central market in Ibadan, Nigeria. Some retailers operate from stores and others operate without a store—by selling online, on TV, with a printed catalog, from vending machines, or even in consumers' homes. Most retailers sell physical goods produced by someone else. But in the case of service retailing—like dry cleaning, fast food, tourist attractions, online bank accounts, or one-hour photo processing—the retailer is also the producer. Because they serve individual

Edition

consumers, even the largest retailers face the challenge of handling small transactions. And the total number of transactions with consumers is much greater than at other channel levels.

Retailing is crucial to consumers in every macro-marketing system. For example, consumers spend more than $4.5 *trillion* (that's $4,500,000,000,000!) a year buying goods and services from U.S. retailers.

The nature of retailing and its rate of change are generally related to the stage and speed of a country's economic development. In the United States, retailing is more varied and dynamic than in most other countries. By studying the U.S. system, you will better understand where retailing is headed in other parts of the world.

PLANNING A RETAILER'S STRATEGY

Retailers interact directly with final consumers—so strategy planning is critical to their survival. If a retailer loses a customer to a competitor, the retailer is the one who suffers. Producers and wholesalers still make *their* sale regardless of which retailer sells the product.

Consumers have reasons for buying from particular retailers

Different consumers prefer different kinds of retailers. But many retailers either don't know or don't care why. All too often, beginning retailers just rent a store and assume customers will show up. As a result, in the United States about three-fourths of new retailing ventures fail during the first year. Even an established retailer will quickly lose if its customers find a better way to meet their needs. To avoid this fate, a retailer should carefully identify possible target markets and try to understand why these people buy where they do. That helps the retailer fine-tune its marketing mix to the needs of specific target markets.[2]

Retailer's whole offering is its Product

Most retailers in developed nations sell more than one kind of product. So the brands and product assortment they carry can be critical to success. Yet it's best to take a broader view in thinking about the Product strategy decisions for a retailer's marketing mix. The retailer's *whole* offering—assortment of goods and services, advice from salesclerks, convenience, and the like—is its "Product."

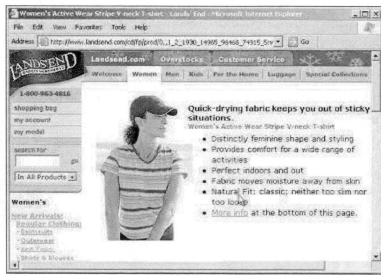

It's best to think of a retailer's Product as its whole offering—including its assortment of goods and services, advice from salespeople, the convenience of shopping, and hours it is available.

Edition

Different consumers have different needs—and needs vary from one purchase situation to another. Which retailer's Product offers the best customer value depends on the needs that a customer wants to satisfy. Whatever the effect of other consumer needs, economic needs are usually very important in shaping the choice of a retailer. Social and individual needs may also come into play. Our discussion of consumer behavior in Chapter 6 applies here.

Features of offering relate to needs

Features of a retailer's offering that relate to economic needs include

- *Convenience* (available hours, finding needed products, fast checkout, location, parking).
- *Product selection* (width and depth of assortment, brands, quality).
- *Special services* (special orders, home delivery, gift wrap, entertainment).
- *Fairness in dealings* (honesty, correcting problems, return privileges, purchase risks).
- *Helpful information* (courteous sales help, displays, demonstrations, product information).
- *Prices* (value, credit, special discounts, taxes or extra charges).

Some features that relate to social and emotional needs include

- *Social image* (status, prestige, "fitting in" with other shoppers).
- *Shopping atmosphere* (comfort, safety, excitement, relaxation, sounds, smells).

In later chapters we'll go into much more detail on the promotion and price decisions that all firms, including retailers and wholesalers, make.

Strategy requires carefully set policies

In developing a strategy a retailer should consciously make decisions that set policies on *all* of the preceding issues. Each of them can impact a customer's view of the costs and benefits of choosing that retailer. And in combination they differentiate one retailer's offering and strategy from another. If the combination doesn't provide superior value to some target market, the retailer will fail.

Consumer needs relate to segmentation and positioning

Segmentation and positioning decisions are important to retailers. And ignoring either economic or social and emotional needs in those decisions can lead to serious errors in a retailer's strategy planning.

Consider, for example, how the shopping atmosphere may have an emotional effect on a consumer's view of a retailer. How merchandise is displayed, what decorations, colors, and finishes are used, and even the temperature, sounds, and smell of a store all contribute to its store image and the shopping experience. Tiffany's, for example, offers luxury surroundings and inventive displays to attract upscale consumers—or ones who get an ego boost from Tiffany's prestige image. Of course, interesting surroundings are usually costly, and the prices that consumers pay must cover that expense. An online jewelry retailer offers a completely different shopping experience and deals with a different set of needs. So a retailer's atmosphere and image may be a plus or a minus, depending on the target market. And there's no single right answer about which target market is best. Like Tiffany's, Dollar General has been very profitable. But it has a "budget" image and atmosphere that appeals to working-class customers, many of whom just prefer to shop where they don't feel out of place.[3]

Different types of retailers emphasize different strategies

Retailers have an almost unlimited number of ways in which to alter their offerings—their marketing mixes—to appeal to a target market. Because of all the variations, it's oversimplified to classify retailers and their strategies on the basis of a single characteristic—such as merchandise, services, sales volume, or even whether they operate in cyberspace. But a good place to start is by considering basic types of retailers and some differences in their strategies.

Edition

Let's look first at conventional retailers. Then we'll see how other retailers successfully modify conventional offerings to better meet the needs of *some* consumers. Think about *why* the changes take place. That will help you identify opportunities and plan better marketing strategies.

CONVENTIONAL RETAILERS—TRY TO AVOID PRICE COMPETITION

Single-line, limited-line retailers specialize by product

About 150 years ago, general stores—which carried anything they could sell in reasonable volume—were the main retailers in the United States. But with the growing number of consumer products after the Civil War, general stores couldn't offer enough variety in all their traditional lines. So some stores began specializing in dry goods, apparel, furniture, or groceries.

Now most *conventional* retailers are single-line or limited-line stores—stores that specialize in certain lines of related products rather than a wide assortment. Many specialize not only in a single line, such as clothing, but also in a *limited line* within the broader line. Within the clothing line, a retailer might carry *only* shoes, formal wear, or even neckties but offer depth in that limited line.

Single-line, limited-line stores are being squeezed

The main advantage of limited-line retailers is that they can satisfy some target markets better. Perhaps some are just more conveniently located. But most adjust to suit specific customers. They build a relationship with their customers and earn a position as *the* place to shop for a certain type of product. But these retailers face the costly problem of having to stock some slow-moving items in order to satisfy their target markets. Many of these stores are small—with high expenses relative to sales. So they try to keep their prices up by avoiding competition on identical products.

Conventional retailers like this have been around for a long time and are still found in every community. They are a durable lot and clearly satisfy some people's needs. In fact, in most countries conventional retailers still handle the vast majority of all retailing sales. However, this situation is changing fast. Nowhere is the change clearer than in the United States. Conventional retailers are being squeezed by retailers who modify their mixes in the various ways suggested in Exhibit 13-2. Let's look closer at some of these other types of retailers.

Exhibit 13-2   Types of Retailers and the Nature of Their Offerings (*with examples*)

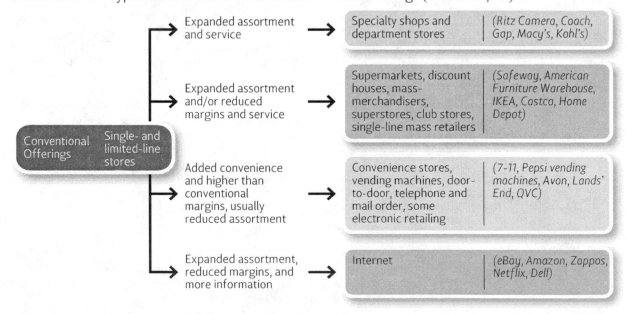

EXPAND ASSORTMENT AND SERVICE—TO COMPETE AT A HIGH PRICE

Specialty shops usually sell shopping products

A specialty shop—a type of conventional limited-line store—is usually small and has a distinct "personality." Specialty shops sell special types of shopping products, such as high-quality sporting goods, exclusive clothing, cameras, or even antiques. They aim at a carefully defined target market by offering a unique product assortment, knowledgeable salesclerks, and better service.

Catering to certain types of customers whom the management and salespeople know well simplifies buying, speeds turnover, and cuts costs due to obsolescence and style changes. Specialty shops probably will continue to be a part of the retailing scene as long as customers have varied tastes and the money to satisfy them.[4]

Department stores combine many limited-line stores and specialty shops

Department stores are larger stores that are organized into many separate departments and offer many product lines. Each department is like a separate limited-line store and handles a wide variety of a shopping product, such as men's wear or housewares. They are usually strong in customer services, including credit, merchandise return, delivery, and sales help.

Department stores are still a major force in big cities. But in the United States, the number of department stores, the average sales per store, and their share of retail business has declined continuously since the 1970s. Well-run limited-line stores compete with good service and often carry the same brands. In the United States and many other countries, mass-merchandising retailers have posed an even bigger threat.[5]

EVOLUTION OF MASS-MERCHANDISING RETAILERS

Mass-merchandising is different from conventional retailing

The conventional retailers just discussed think that demand in their area is fixed—and they have a "buy low and sell high" philosophy. Many modern retailers reject these ideas. Instead, they accept the mass-merchandising concept—which says that retailers should offer low prices to get faster turnover and greater sales volumes—by appealing to larger markets. The mass-merchandising concept applies to many types of retailers, including both those that operate stores and those that sell online. But to understand mass-merchandising better, let's look at its evolution from the development of supermarkets and discounters to modern mass-merchandisers like Wal-Mart in the United States, Tesco in the U.K., and Amazon.com on the Internet.

Supermarkets started the move to mass-merchandising

From a world view, most food stores are relatively small limited-line operations. Shopping for food is inconvenient and expensive. Many Italians, for example, still go to one shop for pasta, another for meat, and yet another for milk. This may seem outdated, but many of the world's consumers don't have access to supermarkets—large stores specializing in groceries with self-service and wide assortments.

The basic idea for supermarkets developed in the United States during the 1930s Depression. Some innovators introduced self-service to cut costs but provided a broad assortment in large bare-bones stores. Profits came from large-volume sales, not from high traditional markups.[6]

Modern supermarkets carry 45,000 product items and stores average around 47,500 square feet. To be called a supermarket, a store must have annual sales of at least $2 million, but the average supermarket sells about $20 million a year. In the United States, there are about 35,000 supermarkets, and in most areas they are at the saturation level and competition is intense. In many other countries, however, they are just becoming a force.[7]

Supermarkets are planned for maximum efficiency. Scanners at checkout make it possible to carefully analyze the sales of each item and allocate more shelf space to faster-moving and higher-profit items. *Survival* depends on efficiency. Net profits in supermarkets usually run a thin 1 percent of sales *or less!*

Although U.S. supermarkets were the first mass-merchandisers, the mass-merchandising concept is now used by many retailers. Single-line mass-merchandisers like Office Depot offer selections and prices that make it difficult for conventional retailers to compete.

Some supermarket operators have opened "super warehouse" stores. These 50,000- to 100,000-square-foot stores carry more items than supermarkets. These efficiently run, warehouse-like facilities can sell groceries at up to 25 percent less than the typical supermarket price.[8]

Discount houses upset some conventional retailers

After World War II, some retailers started to focus on discount prices. These discount houses offered "hard goods" (cameras, TVs, and appliances) at substantial price cuts to customers who would go to the discounter's low-rent store, pay cash, and take care of any service or repair problems themselves. These retailers sold at 20 to 30 percent off the list price being charged by conventional retailers.

In the early 1950s, with war shortages finally over, manufacturer brands became more available. The discount houses were able to get any brands they wanted and to offer wider assortments. At this stage, many discounters turned respectable—moving to better locations and offering more services and guarantees. It was from these origins that today's mass-merchandisers developed.

Mass-merchandisers are more than discounters

Mass-merchandisers are large, self-service stores with many departments that emphasize "soft goods" (housewares, clothing, and fabrics) and staples (like health and beauty aids) but still follow the discount house's emphasis on lower margins to get faster turnover. Mass-merchandisers, like Wal-Mart and Target, have checkout counters in the front of the store and little sales help on the floor. Today, the average mass-merchandiser has nearly 60,000 square feet of floor space, but many new stores are 100,000 square feet or more. Mass-merchandisers grew rapidly—and they've become the primary place to shop for many frequently purchased consumer products.

By itself, Wal-Mart handles 30 percent or more of the total national sales for whole categories of products. Even if you don't shop at Wal-Mart, Sam Walton (who started the company) has had a big impact on your life. He pioneered the use of high-tech systems to create electronic links with suppliers and take inefficiencies out of retailing logistics. That brought down costs *and* prices and attracted more customers, which gave Wal-Mart even

more clout in pressuring manufacturers to lower prices. Other retailers are still scrambling to catch up. It was competition from Wal-Mart on most staples such as health and beauty aids and household cleaning products that prompted firms in the supermarket supply chain to start the Efficient Consumer Response movement we discussed in Chapter 12.[9]

Supercenters meet all routine needs

Some supermarkets and mass-merchandisers have moved toward becoming supercenters (hypermarkets)—very large stores that try to carry not only food and drug items but all goods and services that the consumer purchases *routinely*. These superstores look a lot like a combination of the supermarkets, drugstores, and mass-merchandisers from which they have evolved, but the concept is different. A supercenter is trying to meet *all* the customer's routine needs at a low price. Supercenter operators include Meijer, Fred Meyer, Super Target, and Wal-Mart. In fact, Wal-Mart's supercenters have turned it into the largest food retailer in the United States.

Supercenters average more than 150,000 square feet and carry about 50,000 items. Their assortment in one place is convenient, but many time-pressured consumers think that the crowds, lines, and "wandering around" time in the store are not.[10]

New mass-merchandising formats keep coming

The warehouse club is another retailing format that quickly gained popularity. Sam's Club and Costco are two of the largest. Consumers usually pay an annual membership fee to shop in these large, no-frills facilities. Among the 3,500 items per store, they carry food, appliances, yard tools, tires, and other items that many consumers see as homogeneous shopping items and want at the lowest possible price. The growth of these clubs has also been fueled by sales to small-business customers. That's why some people refer to these outlets as wholesale clubs. However, when half or more of a firm's sales are to final consumers, it is classified as a retailer, not a wholesaler.[11]

Single-line mass-merchandisers are coming on strong

Since 1980, many retailers focusing on single product lines have adopted the mass-merchandisers' approach with great success. Toys "R" Us pioneered this trend. Similarly, IKEA (furniture), Home Depot (home improvements), Circuit City (electronics), and Office Depot (office supplies) attract large numbers of customers with their large assortment and low prices in a specific product category. These stores are called *category killers* because it's so hard for less specialized retailers to compete.[12]

Edition

Can mass-merchandisers be more convenient?

Many mass-merchandisers are so large that it's inconvenient for consumers to get in and out of the store—or to find help if they need it. But, retailers are constantly looking for low-cost ways to make shopping more convenient. Sometimes all that's needed is better in-store signs, "need help" buttons that signal for assistance, or faster checkout. The Food Lion supermarket chain uses a variation of self-checkout in its Bloom stores. Customers use a handheld scanner to record what they put in their carts; when they finish shopping, all they need to do is pay. Bloom stores are also smaller, and the arrangement of products is simpler. For example, all beverages are grouped together on the same aisle. Everyday items are located together at the front of the store for quick access. Information kiosks help consumers select and find products, print shopping lists, or review recipes.

When ideas like these prove popular, competitors quickly copy them. Still, the primary focus of most self-service mass-merchandisers is low prices, not convenience. Next we'll look at other types of retailers that target consumers who want more convenience and service, even if the price is higher.[13]

SOME RETAILERS FOCUS ON ADDED CONVENIENCE

Convenience (food) stores must have the right assortment

Convenience (food) stores are a convenience-oriented variation of the conventional limited-line food stores. Instead of expanding their assortment, however, convenience stores limit their stock to pickup or fill-in items like bread, milk, beer, and eat-on-the-go snacks. Many also sell gas. Stores such as 7-Eleven and Stop-N-Go aim to fill consumers' needs between trips to a supermarket, and many of them are competing with fast-food outlets. They offer convenience, not assortment, and often charge prices 10 to 20 percent higher than nearby supermarkets. However, as many other retailers have expanded their hours, intense competition is driving down convenience store prices and profits.[14]

Vending machines are convenient

Automatic vending is selling and delivering products through vending machines. Vending machine sales account for only about 1.5 percent of total U.S. retail sales. Yet for some target markets this retailing method can't be ignored.

While vending machines can be costly to operate, consumers like their convenience. Traditionally, soft drinks, candy bars, and snack foods have been sold by vending machines. Now some higher-margin products are beginning to use this channel. RedBox rents DVD movies from vending machines at some McDonald's restaurants.

Some retailers are trying to speed up the checkout process—and avoid the need to check IDs or confirm a customer's age—with a fingerprint reader that also replaces the need for a credit card. Systems like this may become popular in the future, but some consumers have concerns about how biometric information might be used.

In Japan, it's common to find digital cameras in vending machines, and now Zoom System is selling cameras and iPods that way in the United States.[15]

Shop at home, in a variety of ways

In-home shopping in the United States started in the pioneer days with door-to-door selling—a salesperson going directly to the consumer's home. Variations on this approach are still important for firms like Quixtar-Amway and Mary Kay. It meets some consumers' need for convenient personal attention. It is also growing in popularity in some international markets, like China, where it provides salespeople with a good income. In the United States, it now accounts for less than 1 percent of retail sales. It's getting harder to find someone at home during the day.

On the other hand, time-pressured, dual-career families are a prime target market for telephone and direct-mail retailing that allow consumers to shop at home—usually placing orders by mail or a toll-free long-distance telephone call and charging the purchase to a credit card. Typically, catalogs and ads on TV let customers see the offerings, and purchases are delivered by UPS. Some consumers really like this convenience, especially for products not available in local stores.

This approach reduces costs by using mailing lists to target specific customers and by using warehouse-type buildings and limited sales help. And shoplifting—a big expense for most retailers—isn't a problem. In recent years, many of these firms have faced increased competition, slower sales growth, and lower profits. As we will discuss, however, the Internet is opening up new growth opportunities for many of them.[16]

Put the catalog on cable TV or computer

QVC, Home Shopping Network, and others are succeeding by devoting cable TV channels to home shopping. The explosion in the number of available cable channels and new interactive cable services have helped sales from this approach grow even faster. In addition, QVC has opened a major website on the Internet. However, selling on the Internet is much more than just a variation of selling on TV or from a catalog.[17]

RETAILING ON THE INTERNET

It's in the growth stage

Internet retailing is still in the growth stage. On the one hand, Internet usage continues to rise and consumer e-commerce purchases have grown at a fast rate. In 1997, consumers spent about $2.7 billion on the Internet. To put that in perspective, it took about 3 percent of Wal-Mart's stores to rack up the same sales. By 2007 that number topped $200 billion—not including travel services. That's only about 7 percent of all

Some consumers look on the Internet for low prices on products that they need, but buying sight-unseen is sometimes a problem. For example, some U.S. consumers order low-price drugs over the Internet from Canada, but as the GlaxoSmithKline ad suggests, the customer doesn't really know where the drugs come from when they're ordered this way. On the other hand, many people have confidence in the brand name medicines that they buy for their pets at discount prices from www.1800PetMeds.com.

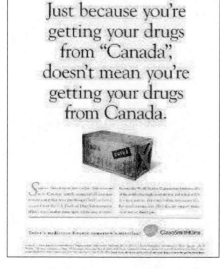

Edition

retail sales. On the other hand, retailing on the Internet continues to grow quickly—at more than 20 percent a year. So it is useful to consider what is different about it today and how it will evolve.

Moving information versus moving goods

Stripped to its essence, the Internet dramatically lowers the cost of communication and makes it faster. The Internet produces the biggest gains in businesses where better information flows result in more efficiency. That's what happens in much online B2B e-commerce. On the other hand, Place decisions for consumer markets need to deal with the challenge of getting many small purchases to the *consumer's* place. To date, much of the investment in Internet retailing systems has been directed toward moving information (like orders), not physical goods. It takes, for example, about $25 million to build a world-class website for consumer e-commerce. But it costs about $150 million to build a distribution center and systems to support a large-scale consumer web operation. There-fore, much of the attention so far has been on the "front door" of the Internet "store" and not on the back end of retailing operations where more of the big costs accumulate. The failure to understand "back door" costs has led to the downfall of many online retailers.

Convenience takes on new meanings

Traditional thinking about retail stores looked at shopping convenience from the perspective of product assortments and location. On the Internet, by contrast, a consumer can get to a very wide assortment, perhaps from different sellers, by clicking from one website to another. The assortment moves toward being unlimited.

But the Internet makes shopping inconvenient in other ways. You have to plan ahead. You can't touch a product. When you buy something, you've actually just ordered it and you don't have it to use. Someone else has to deliver it, and that involves delays and costs.

More and less information at the same time

On the Internet a consumer can't really inspect a product. Many consumers see that as a disadvantage. On the other hand, in a retail store it's often hard to get good information. At a website detailed product information is just a mouse-click away.

Better information available on the Internet makes many consumers better shoppers, even if they buy in a store rather than online. That's what many Web surfers do now. That reduces the risk of buying the wrong thing and the hassles of returning it if there's a problem.

More powerful computers and broadband Internet con-nections are also opening up many more possibilities for multimedia information—pictures, product-demo videos, and audio explanations. The Internet is also a good medium for messaging and videoconferencing. It is becoming easier for consumers to get help from a real person while at a web-site. Many failed dot-com retailers figured out too late that cutting costs by dropping human customer service support was a big mistake. They ignored the lessons learned by mass-merchandisers when they tried to do the same thing in their early days.

Internet EXERCISE

Go to the websites for Amazon (www.amazon.com), Abebooks (www.abebooks.com), and Audible (www.audible.com). Choose a popu-lar book title and search for it at each site. Is it available at each site? In what formats? New and used? How do prices compare? Are there shipping charges? What additional information is provided at each site? How are the sites simi-lar and how are they different?

The costs are sometimes misleading

The Internet makes it easy to compare products and prices from different sellers. That has put price pressure on Internet sellers who have not figured out how else to differentiate what they offer. For more expensive items, a discount price may offset delivery costs. That often isn't the case with less-expensive items. Low-cost ways of handling post-purchase deliveries need to be developed for the Internet to be really practical for everyday purchases. However, some firms are making this work. For example, Tesco in England sells groceries from a website and delivers them within 24 hours.

Another cost occurs if a product must be returned. That, of course, assumes you get what you order. The Internet is the ultimate weapon for fly-by-night operators. Fraud is already a big problem.

Where to Go to Buy an Unpopular Product

A local Borders bookstore that carries 100,000 book titles seems overwhelming. Yet, at Amazon.com online shoppers can choose from over 3 million. A local Wal-Mart stocks about 4,000 best-selling CD titles, but the iTunes "jukebox" has more than 400,000 for download. Does it really make sense for online stores to offer assortments that are so much larger?

Part of the answer to the assortment decision concerns the cost of shelf space. Retailers who have fancy facilities in high-traffic locations with ample parking have a high cost per square foot of shelf space. Even if the retailer sells products at low prices, the store will draw customers from a limited geographic area. With these limits, it makes sense for the store to carry only the products that are the most in demand (popular) with the local target market. Stocking less-popular products would be risky because most of them would just sit there running up inventory costs with little likelihood of increased sales.

The cost to store inventory is usually a lot lower for an online retailer with a warehouse somewhere off the beaten path. If the retailer can sell some of the less-popular items, the added revenue from them may offset the added inventory costs—and increase profits. When an online seller can draw customers from just about everywhere, it is likely to generate at least some sales of even the most "unpopular" products. After all, when customers who want an "unpopular" choice can't find it at a local retail store, they are likely to look for it online. So, the online retailer's ability to offer a greater assortment is often a key source of competitive advantage. Further, for some online sellers, occasional sales of a large number of unpopular products can add up to be even more than the sales of a few very popular ones. We can see this at Amazon.com where more than 30 percent of total book sales come from books that are not even among the top 100,000 most popular. Similarly, more than 25 percent of Netflix DVD rentals are titles outside the top 3,000 found at your local Blockbuster.

To get extra sales from the "unpopular" products, the trick for many online retailers is to help consumers find what they want among the endless "aisles" of choices. For example, ScannerWarehouse.com has more than 200 models of flatbed scanners, but for many customers that much choice is just confusing. To simplify the choice, the site might offer customers a simple way to "filter" the list to show only the scanners that are priced under $100 and that have a document feeder. Smart search engines are also helpful. When a customer types "George Foreman grill" into the search bar at Amazon.com, a list with more than 100 products—sorted by relevance—appears. When the searcher clicks on a specific model, the page automatically generates possible alternatives— "customers who viewed this item also viewed . . ." The page may also include links to reviews, customer ratings, an animated demo, video clips, warranty details, and many other types of information.

In the early days of the Internet many people predicted that online stores would compete primarily on price. Certainly that is true of many. However, some successful online sellers attract customers with wide product selections, tools that help figure out the best choices, and service that encourages customer loyalty.[18]

Retailers are refining their online efforts

At least four distinct approaches are used by different online retailers. Retailers that have bricks-and-mortar stores at many locations often use a website to *supplement* their stores and other promotion—and to test the online retail format. For example, when Target and Home Depot first offered products online, they used their websites primarily to promote items that had the highest profit margins and to drive traffic into their stores. For example, Target's site originally emphasized bedding and apparel rather than household supplies. Both Target and Home Depot now use their websites to offer a broad range of products.

In contrast, some retailers take a strong multichannel approach and use their websites to *complement* their stores or catalogs. This is more common among retailers who have higher profit margins on the lines they sell. For example, Williams-Sonoma sells upscale housewares. It closely coordinates its online, catalog, and store outlets so that

Edition

Many retail chains, like Best Buy, are combining "clicks and mortar" to meet consumers' needs better than would be possible with only an online website. Some Best Buy stores have a special Magnolia section to demo large-screen HDTVs and sound systems. However, specialty retailers, like Home Theater Direct, compete primarily for online customers by offering a focused product line and useful product information that is not conveniently available at stores in the customers' local market.

they focus on different benefits. At its stores customers are free to handle items and see how they look next to each other, while the website provides more detailed product information and convenient ordering.

Among online-only retailers, some try to differentiate their offering primarily by being *more efficient* than competitors. They focus on offering consumers low prices on products that are in very competitive product-markets—like books, computers, and shoes—that have lower profit margins. These online sellers, including Amazon and Zappos, need high sales volume to offset the large investments they must make in their e-commerce and logistics systems.

The essence of the fourth online approach is to differentiate by being very *focused* on the specific needs of target customers, many of whom don't have similar offerings available in their local market. Good examples include outdoor-gear seller L.L. Bean and jeweler Ross-Simons. Retailers in this category typically use the Web to supplement a catalog operation or a limited number of stores. Smaller companies who can't afford expensive brand-building advertising campaigns often use this approach also. They rely on targeted direct mail (or e-mail) promotions to acquire new customers and provide exceptional customer service to retain customers they already have.[19]

WHY RETAILERS EVOLVE AND CHANGE

The wheel of retailing keeps rolling

The wheel of retailing theory says that new types of retailers enter the market as low-status, low-margin, low-price operators and then, if successful, evolve into more conventional retailers offering more services with higher operating costs and higher prices. Then they're threatened by new low-status, low-margin, low-price retailers—and the wheel turns again. Department stores, supermarkets, and mass-merchandisers went through this cycle. Some Internet sellers are on this path.

The wheel of retailing theory, however, doesn't explain all major retailing developments. Vending machines entered as high-cost, high-margin operations. Convenience food stores are high-priced. Suburban shopping centers don't emphasize low price.

Scrambled merchandising— mixing product lines for higher profits

Conventional retailers tend to specialize by product line. But many modern retailers are moving toward scrambled merchandising—carrying any product lines they think they can sell profitably. Supermarkets and drugstores sell anything they can move in volume—panty hose, phone cards, one-hour photo processing, motor oil,

Exhibit 13-3   Retailer Life Cycles—Timing and Years to Market Maturity

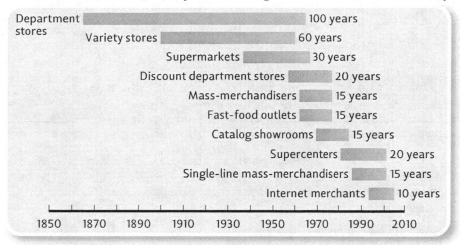

potted plants, and computer software. Mass-merchandisers don't just sell everyday items but also cell phones, computer printers, and jewelry.[20]

Product life-cycle concept applies to retailer types too

A retailer with a new idea may have big profits—for a while. But if it's a really good idea, the retailer can count on speedy imitation and a squeeze on profits. Other retailers will copy the new format or scramble their product mix to sell products that offer them higher margins or faster turnover. That puts pressure on the original firm to change or lose its market.

Some conventional retailers are in decline as these life and death cycles continue. Recent innovators, like the Internet merchants, are still in the market growth stage. See Exhibit 13-3. Some retailing formats that are mature in the United States are only now beginning to grow in other countries.

Ethical issues may arise

Most retailers face intense competitive pressure. The desperation that comes with such pressure has pushed some retailers toward questionable marketing practices.

Critics argue, for example, that retailers too often advertise special sale items to bring price-sensitive shoppers into the store or to a website but then don't stock enough to meet demand. Other retailers are criticized for pushing consumers to trade up to more expensive items. What is ethical and unethical in situations like these, however, is subject to debate. Retailers can't always anticipate demand perfectly, and deliveries may not arrive on time. Similarly, trading up may be a sensible part of a strategy—if it's done honestly.

The marketing concept should guide firms away from unethical treatment of customers. However, a retailer on the edge of going out of business may lose perspective on the need to satisfy customers in both the short and the long term.[21]

Ethics QUESTION

Farmers in poor countries get very little money for crops—such as coffee, cocoa, and bananas—that they grow for export. Some consumers in prosperous nations are willing to pay retailers higher prices for "fair trade" goods so that the farmers receive greater compensation. But critics question whether fair trade works as it should. For example, Sainsbury's is a popular British food retailer. It was charging $2.74 per pound for "fair trade" bananas versus only $.69 per pound for regular bananas. Farmers, however, only got $.16 extra from that $2.05 price premium. Critics charge that Sainsbury's makes more from the "fair trade" promotion than the farmers it is supposed to help. Many retailers have similar programs. Do you think that Sainsbury's is acting ethically? What do you think Sainsbury's and other similar retailers should do? Why?[22]

Edition

RETAILER SIZE AND PROFITS

A few big retailers do most of the business

The large number of retailers (1,119,850) might suggest that retailing is a field of small businesses. To some extent this is true. When the last census of retailers was published, over 56 percent of all the retail stores in the United States had annual sales of less than $1 million. But that's only part of the story. Those same retailers accounted for less than 8 cents of every $1 in retail sales!

The larger retail stores—those selling more than $5 million annually—do most of the business. Only about 11 percent of the retail stores are this big, yet they account for almost 70 percent of all retail sales. Many small retailers are being squeezed out of business.[23]

Big chains are building market clout

The main way for a retailer to achieve economies of scale is with a corporate chain. A corporate chain is a firm that owns and manages more than one store—and often it's many. Chains have grown rapidly and now account for about half of all retail sales. You can expect chains to continue to grow and take business from independent stores.

Many independent retail stores are finding it difficult to compete with the large retail chains that now account for the majority of all retail sales in the United States. However, some independents are working together to compete more effectively. For example, Ace Hardware is a wholesaler-sponsored voluntary chain that provides store owners with some of the advantages of a corporate chain operation—without having to give up their independence.

Large chains use central buying for different stores. They take advantage of quantity discounts and develop their own efficient distribution centers. They can use computer networks to control inventory costs and stock-outs. They may also spread promotion, information technology, and management costs to many stores. Retail chains also have their own dealer brands. Many of these chains are becoming powerful members, or channel captains, in their channel systems. In fact, the most successful of these big chains, like Home Depot and Wal-Mart, control access to so many consumers that they have the clout to dictate almost every detail of relationships with their suppliers.[24]

Independents form chains too

Competitive pressure from corporate chains encouraged the development of both cooperative chains and voluntary chains. Cooperative chains are retailer-sponsored groups—formed by independent retailers—that run their own buying organizations and conduct joint promotion efforts. Cooperative chains face a tough battle. Some, like True Value Hardware, are still adapting as they identify the weaknesses of corporate chains. For example, ads remind consumers that they don't need to waste a half-hour lost in a big store to pick up some simple item.

Voluntary chains are wholesaler-sponsored groups that work with "independent" retailers. Some are linked by contracts stating common operating procedures and requiring the use of common storefront designs, store names, and joint promotion efforts. Examples include SuperValu in groceries and Ace in hardware.

Franchisors form chains too

In a franchise operation, the franchisor develops a good marketing strategy, and the retail franchise holders carry out the strategy in their own units. Each franchise holder benefits from its relationship with the larger company and its experience, buying power, promotion, and image. In return, the franchise holder usually signs a contract to pay fees and commissions and to strictly follow franchise rules designed to continue the successful strategy.

Franchise holders' sales account for about a third of all retail sales. One reason is that franchising is especially popular with service retailers, a fast-growing sector of the economy.[25]

CHAPTER 13

355

Retailers, Wholesalers, and Their Strategy Planning

DIFFERENCES IN RETAILING IN DIFFERENT NATIONS

New ideas spread across countries

New retailing approaches that succeed in one part of the world are often quickly adapted to other countries. Self-service approaches that started with supermarkets in the United States are now found in retail operations worldwide. The supercenter concept, on the other hand, initially developed in Europe.

Mass-merchandising requires mass markets

The low prices, selections, and efficient operations offered by mass-merchandisers might be attractive to consumers everywhere. But consumers in less-developed nations often don't have the income to support mass distribution. The small shops that survive in these economies sell in very small quantities, often to a small number of consumers.

Some countries block change

The political and legal environment severely limits the evolution of retailing in some nations. Japan is a prime example. For years its Large Store Law—aimed at protecting the country's politically powerful small shopkeepers—has been a real barrier to retail change. The law restricts development of large stores by requiring special permits, which are routinely denied.

Japan is taking steps to change the Large Store Law. One such change allowed Toys "R" Us to move into the Japanese market. Even so, most experts believe that it will be years before Japan moves away from its system of small, limited-line shops. Many countries in other parts of Asia and South America impose similar restrictions. On the other hand, the European Union is prompting member countries to drop such rules.[26]

Retailers moving to international markets must adapt marketing strategies

Slow growth has prompted some large retail chains to move into international markets. They think that the competitive advantages that worked well at home can provide a similar advantage in another country. But legal and cultural differences in international markets can make success difficult. Despite success in Latin America and Canada, Wal-Mart has struggled in Germany and Japan. Similarly, French mass-merchandiser Carrefour expanded in Europe and South America, but its U.S. stores failed and it experienced legal problems in Indonesia.

Other retailers, like California-based My Dollarstore, have seen quick international growth. My Dollarstore franchises the "dollar store" concept worldwide, and it adapts its marketing strategy to the local market. In India, the price of each product is 99 rupees or about two dollars. Dollar stores in the United States target lower-income consumers, but in India the "Made in America" label attracts many higher-income consumers. Initially the merchandise in the Indian stores was the same as in U.S. stores. However, My Dollarstore quickly discovered what sold (Hershey's syrup is a hit) and what didn't (papaya and carrot juice). It also offered money-back guarantees, an unusual practice in India. Adaptations like these helped entice consumers into My Dollarstore's Indian franchises.[27]

Consumer cooperatives, like Switzerland's Migros, are important retailing institutions in some countries but have never been a major force in the U.S. market.

Edition

WHAT IS A WHOLESALER?

It's hard to define what a wholesaler is because there are so many different wholesalers doing different jobs. Some of their activities may even seem like manufacturing. As a result, some wholesalers describe themselves as "manufacturer and dealer." Some like to identify themselves with such general terms as *merchant*, *agent*, *dealer*, or *distributor*. And others just take the name commonly used in their trade—without really thinking about what it means.

To avoid a long technical discussion on the nature of wholesaling, we'll use the U.S. Bureau of the Census definition:

Wholesaling is concerned with the *activities* of those persons or establishments that sell to retailers and other merchants, or to industrial, institutional, and commercial users, but that do not sell in large amounts to final consumers.

So wholesalers are firms whose main function is providing wholesaling activities. Wholesalers sell to all of the different types of organizational customers described in Chapter 7.

Wholesaling activities are just variations of the basic marketing functions—gathering and providing information, buying and selling, grading, storing, transporting, financing, and risk taking—we discussed in Chapter 1. You can understand wholesalers' strategies better if you look at them as members of channels. They add value by doing jobs for their customers and for their suppliers.

WHOLESALING IS CHANGING WITH THE TIMES

A hundred years ago wholesalers dominated distribution channels in the United States and most other countries. The many small producers and small retailers needed their services. This situation still exists in less-developed economies. However, in the developed nations, as producers became larger many bypassed the wholesalers. Similarly, large retail chains often take control of functions that had been handled by wholesalers. Now e-commerce is making it easier for producers and consumers to "connect" without having a wholesaler in the middle of the exchange.

In light of these changes, many people have predicted a gloomy future for wholesalers. In the 1980s that seemed to be the pattern. Now, however, there are 429,500 wholesalers in the United States and they are adapting rapidly and finding new ways to add value in the channel. For example, some of the biggest B2B e-commerce sites on the Internet are wholesaler operations, and many wholesalers are enjoying significant growth.

Producing value and profits, not chasing orders

Progressive wholesalers are becoming more concerned with their customers and with channel systems. Many are using technology to offer better service. Others develop voluntary chains that bind them more closely to their customers.

Frieda's, Inc., is a good example; it is a wholesaler that each year supplies supermarkets and food-service distributors with $30 million worth of exotic fruits and vegetables. It was started by Frieda Caplan in 1962; now, her daughters Karen and Jackie run the company. It is a sign of the marketing savvy of these women that artichokes, Chinese donut peaches, alfalfa sprouts, and spaghetti squash no longer seem very exotic. All of these crops were once viewed as unusual. Few farmers grew them, supermarkets didn't handle them, and consumers didn't know about them. Caplan helped to change all of that. She realized that some supermarkets wanted to attract less price-sensitive consumers who preferred more interesting choices in the hard-to-manage produce department. So she looked for products that would help her retailer-customers meet this need. For example, the funny looking kiwi fruit with its fuzzy brown skin was popular in New Zealand but virtually unknown to U.S. consumers. Caplan worked with small farmer-producers to ensure that she could provide her retailer-customers with a steady supply. She packaged kiwi with interesting recipes and promoted it to consumers. Because of her efforts, demand has grown and most supermarkets now

carry kiwi. That has attracted competition from larger wholesalers. But that doesn't bother the Caplans. When one of their specialty items becomes a commodity with low profit margins, another novel item replaces it. In a typical year, Frieda's introduces about 40 new products—like Asian pears, kiwano melons, sun-dried yellow tomatoes, and hot Asian chiles.

Frieda's also has an advantage because of the special services it provides. It was the first wholesaler to routinely use airfreight for orders and send produce managers a weekly "hot sheet" about the best sellers. The Caplans also use seminars and press releases to inform produce buyers about how to improve sales. For example, one attention-getting story about Frieda's "El Mercado de Frieda" line helped retailers do a better job serving Hispanic customers. Similarly, Frieda's website attracts final consumers with helpful tips and recipes. And now that more consumers are eating out, Frieda's has established a separate division to serve the special needs of food-service distributors.[28]

Perhaps good-bye to some

Not all wholesalers are progressive, and less efficient ones will fail. Some wholesalers will disappear as the functions they provided in the past are shifted and shared in different ways in the channel. Cost-conscious buyers for Wal-Mart, Lowe's, and other chains are refusing to deal with some of the wholesalers who represent small producers. They want to negotiate directly with the producer. Similarly, producers see advantages in having closer direct relationships with fewer suppliers—and they're paring out weaker vendors. Efficient delivery services like UPS and Federal Express are also making it easy for many producers to ship directly to their customers, even ones in foreign markets. The Internet is putting pressure on wholesalers whose primary role is providing information to bring buyers and sellers together.[29]

Is it an ethical issue?

All of this is squeezing some wholesalers out of business. Some critics, including many of the wounded wholesalers, argue that it's unethical for powerful suppliers or customers to simply cut out wholesalers who spend money and time, perhaps decades, developing markets. Contracts between channel members and laws sometimes define what is or is not legal. But the ethical issues are often more ambiguous.

For example, Amana notified Cooper Distributing Co. that it intended to cancel their distribution agreement in 10 days. Cooper had handled Amana appliances for 30 years, and Amana products represented 85 percent of Cooper's sales. Amana's explanation to Cooper? "We just think we can do it better."

Edition

Situations like this arise often. They may be cold-hearted, but are they unethical? We argue that it isn't fair to cut off the relationship with such short notice. But most wholesalers realize that their business is *always* at risk—if they don't perform channel functions better or cheaper than their suppliers or customers can do themselves.[30]

Survivors will need effective strategies

The wholesalers who do survive will need to be efficient, but that doesn't mean they'll all have low costs. Some wholesalers' higher operating expenses result from the strategies they select, including the special services they offer to *some* customers.

WHOLESALERS ADD VALUE IN DIFFERENT WAYS

Exhibit 13-4 compares the number, sales volume, and operating expenses of some major types of wholesalers. The differences in operating expenses suggest that each of these types performs, or does not perform, certain wholesaling functions. But which ones and why? And why do manufacturers use merchant wholesalers—costing 13.1 percent of sales—when agent wholesalers cost only 3.7 percent?

To answer these questions, we must understand what these wholesalers do and don't do. Exhibit 13-5 gives a big-picture view of the major types of wholesalers we'll be discussing. There are lots more specialized types, but our discussion will give you a sense of the diversity. Note that a major difference between merchant and agent wholesalers is whether they *own* the products they sell. Before discussing these wholesalers, we'll briefly consider producers who handle their own wholesaling activities.

Manufacturers' sales branches are considered wholesalers

Manufacturers who just take over some wholesaling activities are not considered wholesalers. However, when they have manufacturers' sales branches—warehouses that producers set up at separate locations away from their factories—they're classified as wholesalers by the U.S. Census Bureau and by government agencies in many other countries.

In the United States, these manufacturer-owned branch operations account for about 4.3 percent of wholesale facilities—but they handle 28.4 percent of total wholesale sales. One reason sales per branch are so high is that the branches are usually placed in the best market areas. This also helps explain why their operating costs, as a percent of sales, are often lower. It's also easier for a manufacturer to coordinate information and logistics functions with its own branch operations than with independent wholesalers.[31]

Exhibit 13-4
U.S. Wholesale Trade by Type of Wholesale Operation

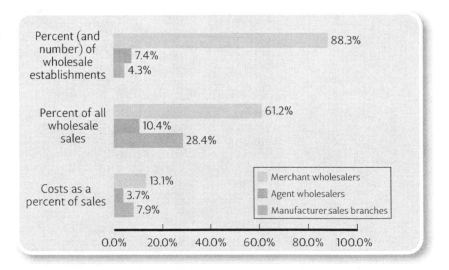

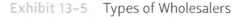

Exhibit 13–5   Types of Wholesalers

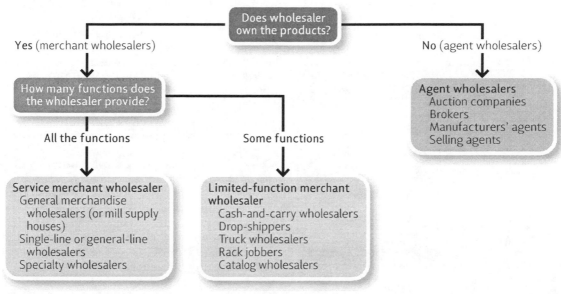

MERCHANT WHOLESALERS ARE THE MOST NUMEROUS

Merchant wholesalers own (take title to) the products they sell. They often specialize by certain types of products or customers. For example, Fastenal is a wholesaler that specializes in distributing threaded fasteners used by a variety of manufacturers. It owns (takes title to) the fasteners for some period before selling to its customers. If you think all merchant wholesalers are fading away, Fastenal is proof that they can serve a needed role. In the last decade Fastenal's profits have grown at about the same pace as Microsoft's.[32]

Exhibit 13-4 shows that almost 90 percent of the wholesaling establishments in the United States are merchant wholesalers—and they handle over 61 percent of wholesale sales. Merchant wholesalers are even more common in other countries. Japan is an extreme example. Products are often bought and sold by a series of merchant wholesalers on their way to the business user or retailer.[33]

Internet EXERCISE

Check out the different aspects of the Fastenal website (www.fastenal.com). Give examples of ways that the website is intended to help Fastenal's customers and suppliers.

Service wholesalers provide all the functions

Service wholesalers are merchant wholesalers that provide all the wholesaling functions. Within this basic group are three types: (1) general merchandise, (2) single-line, and (3) specialty.

General merchandise wholesalers are service wholesalers that carry a wide variety of nonperishable items such as hardware, electrical supplies, furniture, drugs, cosmetics, and automobile equipment. With their broad line of convenience and shopping products, they serve hardware stores, drugstores, and small department stores. *Mill supply houses* operate in a similar way, but they carry a broad variety of accessories and supplies to serve the needs of manufacturers.

Single-line (or general-line) wholesalers are service wholesalers that carry a narrower line of merchandise than general merchandise wholesalers. For example, they might carry only food, apparel, or certain types of industrial tools or supplies. In consumer products, they serve the single-and limited-line stores. In business products, they cover a wider geographic area and offer more specialized service.

Specialty wholesalers are service wholesalers that carry a very narrow range of products and offer more information and service than other service wholesalers. For

Edition

example, a firm that produces specialized lights for vehicles might rely on specialty wholesalers to help reach auto makers in different countries. A consumer products specialty wholesaler might carry only health foods instead of a full line of groceries. Some limited-line and specialty wholesalers are growing by helping independent retailer-customers compete with mass-merchandisers. But in general, many consumer-products wholesalers have been hit hard by the growth of retail chains that set up their own distribution centers and deal directly with producers.

A specialty wholesaler of business products might limit itself to fields requiring special technical knowledge or service. Richardson Electronics is an interesting example. It specializes in distributing replacement parts, such as electron tubes, for old equipment that many manufacturers still use on the factory floor. Richardson describes itself as "on the trailing edge of technology," but many of its customers operate in countries where new technologies are not yet common. Richardson gives them easy access to information from its website (www.rell.com) and makes its products available quickly by stocking them in locations around the world.[34]

Limited-function wholesalers provide some functions

Limited-function wholesalers provide only *some* wholesaling functions. In the following paragraphs, we briefly discuss the main features of these wholesalers. Although less numerous in some countries, these wholesalers are very important for some products.

Cash-and-carry wholesalers want cash

Cash-and-carry wholesalers operate like service wholesalers—except that the customer must pay cash. In the United States, big warehouse clubs have taken much of this business. But cash-and-carry operators are common in less-developed nations where very small retailers handle the bulk of retail transactions. Full-service wholesalers often refuse to grant credit to small businesses that may have trouble paying their bills.

Drop-shippers do not handle the products

Drop-shippers own (take title to) the products they sell—but they do *not* actually handle, stock, or deliver them. These wholesalers are mainly involved in selling. They get orders and pass them on to producers. Then the producer ships the order directly to the customer. Drop-shippers commonly sell bulky products (like lumber) for which additional handling would be expensive and possibly damaging. Drop-shippers in the United States are already feeling the squeeze from buyers and sellers connecting directly via the Internet. But the progressive ones are fighting back by setting up their own websites and getting fees for referrals.

3M produces about 1,600 products that are used by auto body repair shops in the United States, Europe, Japan, and other countries. To reach this target market, 3M works with hundreds of specialty wholesalers.

Edition

Truck wholesalers deliver—at a cost

Truck wholesalers specialize in delivering products that they stock in their own trucks. Their big advantage is that they promptly deliver perishable products that regular wholesalers prefer not to carry. A 7-Eleven store that runs out of potato chips on a busy Friday night doesn't want to be out of stock all weekend! They help retailers keep a tight rein on inventory, and they seem to meet a need.

Rack jobbers sell hard-to-handle assortments

Rack jobbers specialize in hard-to-handle assortments of products that a retailer doesn't want to manage—and rack jobbers usually display the products on their own wire racks. For example, a grocery store or mass-merchandiser might rely on a rack jobber to decide which paperback books or magazines it sells. The wholesaler knows which titles sell in the local area and applies that knowledge in many stores.

Catalog wholesalers reach outlying areas

Catalog wholesalers sell out of catalogs that may be distributed widely to smaller industrial customers or retailers that might not be called on by other wholesalers. Customers place orders at a website or by mail, e-mail, fax, or telephone. These wholesalers sell lines such as hardware, jewelry, sporting goods, and computers. For example, Inmac uses a catalog that is printed in six languages and a website (www.inmac.com) to sell a complete line of computer accessories. Many of its customers don't have a local wholesaler, but they can place orders from anywhere in the world. Most catalog wholesalers quickly adapted to the Internet. It fits what they were already doing and makes it easier. But they're facing more competition too; the Internet allows customers to compare prices from more sources of supply.[35]

AGENTS ARE STRONG ON SELLING

They don't own the products

Agent wholesalers are wholesalers who do *not* own the products they sell. Their main purpose is to help in buying and selling. Agent wholesalers normally specialize by customer type and by product or product line. But they usually provide even fewer functions than the limited-function wholesalers. They operate at relatively low cost—sometimes 2 to 6 percent of their selling price—or less in the case of website-based agents who simply bring buyers and sellers together. Worldwide, the role of agents is rapidly being transformed by the Internet. Those who didn't get on board this fast-moving train were left behind.

They are important in international trade

Agents are common in international trade. Many markets have only a few well-financed merchant wholesalers. The best many producers can do is get local representation through agents and then arrange financing through banks that specialize in international trade.

Agent wholesalers are usually experts on local business customs and regulations in their own countries. Sometimes a marketing manager can't work through a foreign government's red tape without the help of a local agent.

Manufacturers' agents—freewheeling sales reps

A manufacturers' agent sells similar products for several noncompeting producers—for a commission on what is actually sold. Such agents work almost as members of each company's sales force, but they're really independent wholesalers. More than half of all agent wholesalers are manufacturers' agents. Their big plus is that they already call on some customers and can add another product line at relatively low cost—and at no cost to the producer until something sells! If an area's sales potential is low, a company may use a manufacturers' agent because the agent can do the job at low cost. Small producers often use agents everywhere because their sales volume is too small to justify their own sales force.

Agents can be especially useful for introducing new products. For this service, they may earn 10 to 15 percent commission. (In contrast, their commission on large-volume established products may be quite low—perhaps only 2 percent.) A 10 to 15 percent commission rate may seem small for a new product with low sales. Once a product sells well, however, a producer may think the rate is high and begin using its own sales reps.

Edition

Export or import agents are basically manufacturers' agents who specialize in international trade. These agent wholesalers operate in every country and help international firms adjust to unfamiliar market conditions in foreign markets.

Manufacturers' reps will continue to play an important role in businesses that need an agent to perform order-getting tasks. But manufacturers' reps everywhere are feeling pressure when it comes to routine business contacts. More producers are turning to telephone selling, websites, e-mail, teleconferencing, and faxes to contact customers directly.[36]

Brokers provide information

Brokers bring buyers and sellers together. Brokers usually have a *temporary* relationship with the buyer and seller while a particular deal is negotiated. They are especially useful when buyers and sellers don't come into the market very often. The broker's product is information about what buyers need and what supplies are available. If the transaction is completed, they earn a commission from whichever party hired them. **Export and import brokers** operate like other brokers, but they specialize in bringing together buyers and sellers from different countries. Smart brokers quickly saw new opportunities to expand their reach by using the Internet. As the Internet causes consolidation, it will also provide more value. A smaller number of cyberbrokers will cut costs and dominate the business with larger databases of buyers and sellers.

Selling agents—almost marketing managers

Selling agents take over the whole marketing job of producers—not just the selling function. A selling agent may handle the entire output of one or more producers, even competing producers, with almost complete control of pricing, selling, and advertising. In effect, the agent becomes each producer's marketing manager.

Financial trouble is one of the main reasons a producer calls in a selling agent. The selling agent may provide working capital but may also take over the affairs of the business. But selling agents also work internationally. A **combination export manager** is a blend of manufacturers' agent and selling agent—handling the entire export function for several producers of similar but noncompeting lines.

Auction companies speed up the sale

Auction companies provide a place where buyers and sellers can come together and bid to complete a transaction. Traditionally they were important in certain lines—such as livestock, fur, tobacco, and used cars—where demand and supply conditions change rapidly.

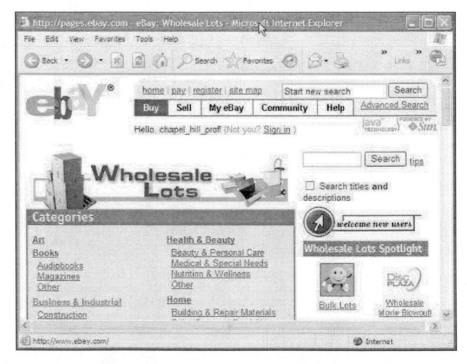

A few years ago, auctions were used for only a few specialized product categories. But now online services like eBay are making auctions a convenient and popular approach for buying and selling many different types of products.

363

Edition

Manheim is a good example of a progressive auction company. It controls at least 50 percent of the used automobile auction market. Manheim runs auctions in many states, but it offers a service called Simulcast that enables buyers and sellers to remotely participate in live auctions with real-time audio/video from virtually anywhere. It provides bidders with other helpful services as well. For example, Manheim auctions most of the Mercedes-Benz vehicles that are returned at the end of a lease. Rather than say "what you see is what you get," an expert inspector who specializes in Mercedes gives detailed ratings of each car and estimates how much any needed reconditioning will cost. The inspector's report is available to potential bidders for a modest cost so they don't need to travel to inspect cars themselves. Because the ratings add value, the whole auction process is efficient and reliable and many dealers source used cars only from Manheim. The Internet has spurred growth of all sorts of auction companies in lines of business where auctions previously were not common.[37]

WHAT WILL HAPPEN TO RETAILERS AND WHOLESALERS IN THE FUTURE?

A common theme in this chapter—and Chapters 11 and 12—is that channels of distribution are in the midst of dynamic changes. One key factor is the growth and success of large chains of retail stores. They are shifting power in channels of distribution and leading to dramatic improvements in logistics and e-commerce. But before all of this, the evolution of retailing and wholesaling was ongoing. Intermediaries that find new and better ways to add value prosper.

In time, more revolutionary change may come. Imagine, for example, what it would take for you—and everyone you know—to do most of your routine shopping on the Internet. What new marketing functions would be needed, and who would provide them?[38]

Let's admit it. You can only speculate about where retailing and wholesaling will lead. But perhaps it's good to speculate a little. The way markets work in the future will depend on creative innovations that people like you imagine, analyze, and ultimately turn into profitable marketing strategies.

CONCLUSION

Modern retailing is scrambled—and we'll probably see more changes in the future. In such a dynamic environment, a producer's marketing manager must choose very carefully among the available kinds of retailers. And retailers must plan their marketing mixes with their target customers' needs in mind—while at the same time becoming part of an effective channel system.

In this chapter we described many different types of retailers, each offering different marketing mixes that appeal to different target customers. Lower margins and faster turnover are the modern philosophy for mass-merchandisers, but this is no guarantee of success as retailers' life cycles move on.

Retailing tends to evolve in predictable patterns—and we discussed the wheel of retailing theory to help understand this. But the growth of chains and scrambled merchandising will continue as retailing evolves to meet changing consumer demands. Important breakthroughs are possible—perhaps with the Internet—and consumers probably will continue to move away from conventional retailers.

Wholesalers can provide functions for those both above and below them in a channel of distribution. These services are closely related to the basic marketing functions. There are many types of wholesalers. Some provide all the wholesaling functions—while others specialize in only a few. Eliminating wholesalers does not eliminate the need for the functions they now provide, but technology is helping firms to perform these functions in more efficient ways.

Merchant wholesalers are the most numerous and account for the majority of wholesale sales. Their distinguishing characteristic is that they take title to (own) products. Agent wholesalers, on the other hand, act more like sales representatives for sellers or buyers—and they do not take title.

Despite dire predictions, wholesalers continue to exist. The more progressive ones are adapting to a changing environment. But some less-progressive wholesalers will fail. The Internet is already taking its toll. On the other hand, new types of intermediaries are evolving. Some are creating new ways of helping producers and their customers achieve their objectives by finding new ways to add value.

KEY TERMS

QUESTIONS AND PROBLEMS

1. What sort of a "product" are specialty shops offering? What are the prospects for organizing a chain of specialty shops?

2. Distinguish among discount houses, price-cutting by conventional retailers, and mass-merchandising. Forecast the future of low-price selling in food, clothing, and appliances. How will the Internet affect that future?

3. Discuss a few changes in the marketing environment that you think help to explain why telephone, mail-order, and Internet retailing have been growing so rapidly.

4. What are some advantages and disadvantages to using the Internet for shopping?

5. Apply the wheel of retailing theory to your local community. What changes seem likely? Will established retailers see the need for change, or will entirely new firms have to develop?

6. What advantages does a retail chain have over a retailer who operates with a single store? Does a small retailer have any advantages in competing against a chain? Explain your answer.

7. Many producers are now seeking new opportunities in international markets. Are the opportunities for international expansion equally good for retailers? Explain your answer.

8. Discuss how computer systems affect wholesalers' and retailers' operations.

9. Consider the evolution of wholesaling in relation to the evolution of retailing. List several changes that are similar, and several that are fundamentally different.

10. Do wholesalers and retailers need to worry about new-product planning just as a producer needs to have an organized new-product development process? Explain your answer.

11. How do you think a retailer of Maytag washing machines would react if Maytag set up a website, sold direct to consumers, and shipped direct from its distribution center? Explain your thinking.

12. What risks do merchant wholesalers assume by taking title to goods? Is the size of this risk about constant for all merchant wholesalers?

13. Why would a manufacturer set up its own sales branches if established wholesalers were already available?

14. What is an agent wholesaler's marketing mix?

15. Why do you think that many merchant wholesalers handle competing products from different producers, while manufacturers' agents usually handle only noncompeting products from different producers?

16. What alternatives does a producer have if it is trying to expand distribution in a foreign market and finds that the best existing merchant wholesalers won't handle imported products?

Edition

17. Discuss the future growth and nature of wholesaling if chains, scrambled merchandising, and the Internet continue to become more important. How will wholesalers have to adjust their mixes? Will wholesalers be eliminated? If not, what wholesaling functions will be most important? Are there any particular lines of trade where wholesalers may have increasing difficulty?

CREATING MARKETING PLANS

The Marketing Plan Coach software on the Student CD and the text website includes a sample marketing plan for Hillside Veterinary Clinic. Look through the "Marketing Strategy" section.

a. What kind of retail operation is the vet clinic? Does it fit any of the types described in this chapter?

b. How could Hillside make use of a website?

c. The marketing plan notes future plans to offer kennel (boarding) services and pet supplies. How will this change Hillside's current strategy? Does the marketing plan provide a good sense of what needs to be done? Do you have other recommendations for Hillside?

SUGGESTED CASES

11. The Next Step
12. DrRay.com
14. Express Multimedia

15. The Trujillo Group
16. Bunyan Lumber

COMPUTER-AIDED PROBLEM

13. SELECTING CHANNEL INTERMEDIARIES

Art Glass Productions, a producer of decorative glass gift items, wants to expand into a new territory. Managers at Art Glass know that unit sales in the new territory will be affected by consumer response to the products. But sales will also be affected by which combination of wholesalers and retailers Art Glass selects. There is a choice between two wholesalers. One wholesaler, Giftware Distributing, is a merchant wholesaler that specializes in gift items; it sells to gift shops, department stores, and some mass-merchandisers. The other wholesaler, Margaret Degan & Associates, is a manufacturers' agent that calls on many of the gift shops in the territory.

Art Glass makes a variety of glass items, but the cost of making an item is usually about the same—$5.20 a unit. The items would sell to Giftware Distributing at $12.00 each—and in turn the merchant wholesaler's price to retailers would be $14.00—leaving Giftware with a $2.00 markup to cover costs and profit. Giftware Distributing is the only reputable merchant wholesaler in the territory, and it has agreed to carry the line only if Art Glass is willing to advertise in a trade magazine aimed at retail buyers for gift items. These ads will cost $8,000 a year.

As a manufacturers' agent, Margaret Degan would cover all of her own expenses and would earn 8 percent of the $14.00 price per unit charged the gift shops. Individual orders would be shipped directly to the retail gift shops by Art Glass, using United Parcel Service (UPS). Art Glass would pay the UPS charges at an average cost of $2.00 per item. In contrast, Giftware Distributing would anticipate demand and place larger orders in advance. This would reduce the shipping costs, which Art Glass would pay, to about $.60 a unit.

Art Glass' marketing manager thinks that Degan would only be able to sell about 75 percent as many items as Giftware Distributing—since she doesn't have time to call on all of the smaller shops and doesn't call on any department stores. On the other hand, the merchant wholesaler's demand for $8,000 worth of supporting advertising requires a significant outlay.

The marketing manager at Art Glass decided to use a spreadsheet to determine how large sales would have to be to make it more profitable to work with Giftware and to see how the different channel arrangements would contribute to profits at different sales levels.

a. Given the estimated unit sales and other values shown on the initial spreadsheet, which type of wholesaler would contribute the most profit to Art Glass Productions?

b. If sales in the new territory are slower than expected, so that the merchant wholesaler was able to sell only 3,000 units—or the agent 2,250 units—which wholesaler would contribute the most to Art Glass' profits? (*Note*: Assume that the merchant wholesaler only buys what it can sell; that is, it doesn't carry extra inventory beyond what is needed to meet demand.)

c. Prepare a table showing how the two wholesalers' contributions to profit compare as the quantity sold varies from 3,500 units to 4,500 units for the merchant wholesaler and 75 percent of these numbers for the manufacturers' agent. Discuss these results. (*Note*: Use the analysis feature to vary the quantity sold by the merchant wholesaler, and the program will compute 75 percent of that quantity as the estimate of what the agent will sell.)

For additional questions related to this problem, see Exercise 13-4 in the *Learning Aid for Use with Basic Marketing*, 17th edition.

14

CHAPTER

Promotion– Introduction to Integrated Marketing Communications

Back in the 1930s, in the heart of the Depression, Leo and Lillian Goodwin started the Government Employees Insurance Company—Geico. Geico kept operating costs low by only selling auto insurance to two low-risk target markets, federal employees and military officers. Geico passed the savings on in the form of lower premiums—and sales steadily grew for decades. In 1996, investor Warren Buffet's Berkshire Hathaway bought Geico.

Geico's new management was eager to accelerate earnings growth by targeting new markets. However, getting growth in the mature auto insurance market meant that Geico would need to take customers away from better-known competitors such as Allstate and State Farm. If that were not already difficult enough, many prospects didn't even know about Geico and those who did often didn't know how to pronounce the name. Ted Ward, Geico's vice president of marketing, discussed this situation with representatives of the firm's ad agency, the Martin Agency of Richmond, Virginia. Together they decided that an aggressive advertising campaign could increase awareness of Geico, bring in new customers, and result in profitable growth.

The key idea for the Geico campaign was to use an animated, talking gecko to help get attention and communicate the firm's message. In the first commercial, the charming reptile with the British accent stated, "I'm the gecko, not to be confused with Geico that can save you hundreds on car insurance. So please stop calling me." The humorous ads quickly generated awareness and interest among target customers, many of whom had never heard of Geico. The original plan was for the gecko campaign to run for a short time, but customers loved the gecko and he continues to be an important part of Geico's image and promotions.

Geico wants customers to know it offers good value—great car insurance at low prices. But to prove this, customers must get a price quote. It's quick and easy to get a quote at Geico's website, so to spur the target audience to action Geico ads remind them that "15 minutes could save you 15 percent or more on your car insurance." Many people responded to the appeal of saving money, but others didn't. Research revealed that many in the hesitant group assumed that requesting an online quote would be difficult.

To overcome this resistance, Geico came up with a clever advertising campaign to convince people that getting a quote from the website is "so easy a caveman can do it." The print and TV ads feature refined cavemen living in the modern world who are offended that the ads imply they are not intelligent. The funny spots attract attention—and a short-lived television show about the cavemen also reminded viewers of Geico's message. The caveman character generated publicity for Geico in other ways, too. He was featured on a pre-Super Bowl

TV special playing golf with NFL legend Phil Simms; on another occasion he interviewed stars on the red carpet at the Academy Awards. There's also a funny website, iheartcavemen.com, that helps people connect with the popular icon, and many people e-mail a link to the site to friends.

To communicate with many different target markets, Geico uses a variety of media and messages. Along with targeted direct-response mail, Geico's ads also appear on bumper cars at amusement parks and turnstiles at train stations. In addition, Geico sponsors NASCAR driver Mike Wallace. The gecko icon appears on the hood of Wallace's #7 car, and a website (geicogarage.com) gives NASCAR fans a behind-the-scenes peak at the driver, his family, and his crew. Geico also uses Internet search advertising. When someone types "car insurance" into the search engine at Google or Yahoo!, a sponsored link to Geico's website appears at the top of the page.

Geico's humorous ads help make Geico a familiar name, but for most people car insurance is a serious matter and they want to talk to a real person before deciding what to do. These customers can visit with a Geico salesperson at one of its local offices or call Geico's toll-free number and talk on the phone with an inside sales rep. Geico selects capable salespeople who want to be helpful—and then trains them to develop an understanding of each customer's needs and concerns so that they can then explain the benefits of Geico to the customer in a persuasive way.

Of course, Geico seeks to build an ongoing relationship with customers after they sign up for a policy. Regular contacts and updates are handled with promotional e-mails. Similarly, salespeople sometimes call customers to let them know about other Geico products, such as less-familiar umbrella insurance policies, that may benefit customers. Later, if a customer who purchases a policy has a problem, Geico's highly rated customer service team works to resolve it quickly.

While Geico is the fourth largest insurer in the United States, it is the industry's largest advertiser. Emphasizing advertising in its promotion blend has generated very good returns for Geico. In the past five years, it has acquired more new customers than any other insurance company. It has also achieved an average annual growth rate of more than 10 percent—the highest among major insurers. To catch up, competitors have increased their own promotion budgets and are trying to woo back the customers they've lost. So, to keep its growth going, Geico will need to continue to satisfy the clients who already have its policies while at the same time developing integrative marketing communications to reach new generations of car owners and offering them policies and service experiences that will convert them to customers for life.[1]

367

PROMOTION COMMUNICATES TO TARGET MARKETS

Promotion is communicating information between the seller and potential buyer or others in the channel to influence attitudes and behavior. The promotion part of the marketing mix involves telling target customers that the right Product is available at the right Place at the right Price. Just as Promotion must be fine-tuned for a specific target market, it must fit with the other variables of the marketing mix and reinforce the strategy's differentiation and positioning.

This is the first of three chapters that discuss issues important for Promotion. We begin with an overview of the major promotion methods. Marketing managers can choose from several basic types of promotion: personal selling, mass selling, and sales promotion (see Exhibit 14-1). Because these different methods have different strengths and limitations, a marketing manager typically uses them in combination to achieve specific objectives. We also discuss the specialists who are involved in managing different types of promotion and why it is important for them to work together as a team. This chapter also provides models that will help you understand how communication works. Finally, we look at some concepts that help marketing managers develop the best promotion blend.

Exhibit 14–1   Promotion and Marketing Strategy Planning

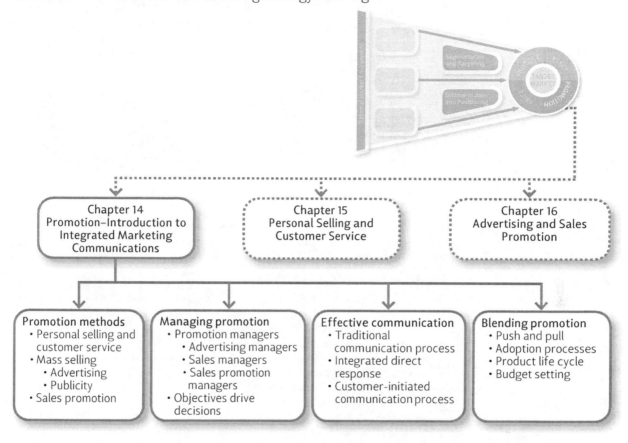

In Chapter 15, we take a closer look at the important promotion strategy decisions that marketing and sales managers make in personal selling and customer service. Chapter 16 provides a closer look at mass selling. It discusses the role of publicity and the strategy planning decisions for advertising. It shows how sales promotion complements these methods and fits with the overall promotion blend.

While we'll go into some detail about the different promotion methods, a key challenge for marketing managers is how best to blend them. So, it's helpful to begin with a brief overview of the promotion methods available.

SEVERAL PROMOTION METHODS ARE AVAILABLE

Personal selling—flexibility is its strength

Personal selling involves direct spoken communication between sellers and potential customers. Salespeople get immediate feedback, which helps them to adapt. Although some personal selling is included in most marketing mixes, it can be very expensive. So it's often desirable to combine personal selling with mass selling and sales promotion.

Mass selling involves advertising and publicity

Mass selling is communicating with large numbers of potential customers at the same time. It's less flexible than personal selling, but when the target market is large and scattered, mass selling can be less expensive.

Advertising is the main form of mass selling. **Advertising** is any *paid* form of nonpersonal presentation of ideas, goods, or services by an identified sponsor. It includes

Edition

Chick-fil-A introduced its trickster cows with this "Eat Mor Chickin" graffiti billboard in Dallas in 1995, but over the years the campaign's message has become familiar to a broader target audience as its marketing communications have expanded to include TV, radio, print, and in-store point-of-purchase materials as well as merchandise such as "cow calendars."

the use of traditional media like magazines, newspapers, radio and TV, signs, and direct mail as well as new media such as the Internet. While advertising must be paid for, another form of mass selling—publicity—is "free."

Publicity avoids media costs

Publicity is any *unpaid* form of nonpersonal presentation of ideas, goods, or services. Of course, publicity people are paid. But they try to attract attention to the firm and its offerings *without having to pay media costs*. For example, movie studios try to get celebrities on TV talk shows because this generates a lot of interest and sells tickets to new movies without the studio paying for TV time.

Many companies write press releases hoping to generate publicity in newspapers, magazines, or on television. Southwest Airlines, for example, wanted its press releases to help promote special fares and new routes. So, its public relations staff used a targeted approach to get attention from news reporters. Many reporters research story ideas on specialized search engines like Yahoo! News, so the PR staff at Southwest wanted its press releases to appear at the top of the reporters' search lists. Southwest's PR staff researched what keywords reporters used most frequently on these search engines—and then put those words in press releases. For example, PR used the phrase "cheap airfare" because it was in four times as many search requests as "cheap airline tickets." Southwest also put a hot link to its special promotion fare Web page at the very start of each press release. The link allowed Southwest PR staff to track which press release worked best; then it used that information to fine-tune other messages. These extra efforts paid off. Southwest generated $1.5 million in online ticket sales with just four press releases.[2]

If a firm has a really new message, publicity may be more effective than advertising. Trade magazines, for example, may carry articles featuring the newsworthy products of regular advertisers—in part because they *are* regular advertisers. The firm's publicity people write the basic copy and then try to convince magazine editors to print it. A consumer might carefully read a long magazine story but ignore an ad with the same information.

Some companies prepare videos designed to get free publicity for their products on TV news shows. For example, after learning that Seattle Mariner Jay Buhner loves Cheerios, a General Mills marketing manager had 162 boxes of the cereal stuffed into his spring-training locker and recorded Buhner's surprise on opening his locker. TV news programs in 12 major markets showed the video. It would have cost hundreds of thousands of dollars to get as much attention with advertising.[3]

One problem with publicity is that the media don't always say or show what the firm intends. When Segway got an order from the vice president of the United States, it seemed like a perfect opportunity for publicity. It looked even better at the White House when President Bush got on to take a ride—until he fell off the Segway with photographers snapping pictures.[4]

Exhibit 14–2
Example of Sales
Promotion Activities

Aimed at final consumers or users	Aimed at wholesalers or retailers	Aimed at company's own sales force
Contests Coupons Aisle displays Samples Trade shows Point-of-purchase materials Banners and streamers Frequent buyer programs Sponsored events	Price deals Promotion allowances Sales contests Calendars Gifts Trade shows Meetings Catalogs Merchandising aids Videos	Contests Bonuses Meetings Portfolios Displays Sales aids Training materials

Sometimes customers pass publicity on

People have always been able to tell friends about an interesting ad, story, or product, but customers can instantly spread Internet messages to many people at once, almost as if the message were a virus. Firms often try to spark this sort of viral publicity by creating a message or website that is so appealing to target customers that they'll want to pass it along. In one case, Fox Entertainment wanted its target market of youthful males to know it had released DVDs of its "American Dad!" TV show. To draw their attention, Fox developed an online fighting game that pitted animated characters from the show against characters from another show, "The Family Guy." Fox publicized its game (www.americandadvsfamilyguy.com) by sending the link to bloggers and fan sites interested in the shows. Fans quickly checked out the site, played the game, and forwarded the link to friends. Within a month, the game was played 2.8 million times, and many players bought the new DVDs right at the website.[5]

Sales promotion tries to spark immediate interest

Sales promotion refers to promotion activities—other than advertising, publicity, and personal selling—that stimulate interest, trial, or purchase by final customers or others in the channel. Sales promotion may be aimed at consumers, at intermediaries, or at a firm's own employees. Examples are listed in Exhibit 14-2. Relative to other promotion methods, sales promotion can usually be implemented quickly and get results sooner. In fact, most sales promotion efforts are designed to produce immediate results.

Less is spent on advertising than personal selling or sales promotion

Many people incorrectly think that promotion money gets spent primarily on advertising—because advertising is all around them. But all the special sales promotions—coupons, sweepstakes, trade shows, and the like—add up to even more money. Similarly, much personal selling goes on in the channels and in other business markets. In total, firms spend less money on advertising than on personal selling or sales promotion.

SOMEONE MUST PLAN, INTEGRATE, AND MANAGE THE PROMOTION BLEND

Each promotion method has its own strengths and weaknesses. In combination, they complement each other. Each method also involves its own distinct activities and requires different types of expertise. As a result, it's usually the responsibility of specialists—such as sales managers, advertising managers, and promotion managers—to develop and implement the detailed plans for the various parts of the overall promotion blend.

Edition

Sales managers manage salespeople

Sales managers are concerned with managing personal selling. Often the sales manager is responsible for building good distribution channels and implementing Place policies. In smaller companies, the sales manager may also act as the marketing manager and be responsible for advertising and sales promotion.

Advertising managers work with ads and agencies

Advertising managers manage their company's mass-selling effort—in television, newspapers, magazines, and other media. Their job is choosing the right media and developing the ads. Advertising departments within their own firms may help in these efforts—or they may use outside advertising agencies. The advertising manager may handle publicity too. Or it may be handled by an outside agency or by whoever handles public relations—communication with noncustomers, including labor, public interest groups, stockholders, and the government.

Sales promotion managers need many talents

Sales promotion managers manage their company's sales promotion effort. In some companies, a sales promotion manager has independent status and reports directly to the marketing manager. If a firm's sales promotion spending is substantial, it probably *should* have a specific sales promotion manager. Sometimes, however, the sales or advertising departments handle sales promotion efforts—or sales promotion is left as a responsibility of individual brand managers. Regardless of who the manager is, sales promotion activities vary so much that many firms use both inside and outside specialists.

Marketing manager talks to all, blends all

Although many specialists may be involved in planning for and implementing specific promotion methods, determining the blend of promotion methods is a strategy decision—and it is the responsibility of the marketing manager.

The various promotion specialists tend to focus on what they know best and their own areas of responsibility. A creative Web page designer or advertising copywriter in New York may have no idea what a salesperson does during a call on a wholesaler. In addition, because of differences in outlook and experience, the advertising, sales, and sales promotion managers often have trouble working with each other as partners. Too often they just view other promotion methods as using up budget money they want.

The marketing manager must weigh the pros and cons of the various promotion methods and then devise an effective promotion blend—fitting in the various departments and personalities and coordinating their efforts. Then the advertising, sales, and sales promotion managers should develop the details consistent with what the marketing manager wants to accomplish.

Send a consistent and complete message with integrated marketing communications

Effective blending of all of the firm's promotion efforts should produce integrated marketing communications—the intentional coordination of every communication from a firm to a target customer to convey a consistent and complete message.

The Geico case at the start of this chapter is a good example of integrated marketing communications. Different promotion methods handle different parts of the job. Yet the methods are coordinated so that the sum is greater than the parts. The separate messages are complementary, but also consistent.

An example of integrated marketing communications is Nortel Networks' Mobility Solutions group, which sells wireless communications tools to many different business customers. While personal selling plays an important role in its promotion efforts, Nortel's marketing managers also use trade shows, ads in trade magazines, weekly Web seminars, and online case studies. In addition, Nortel developed an online, virtual trade show. It helped Nortel and its partners demonstrate the complete package of solution-oriented products they provide. While Nortel relies on a variety of communication approaches to address the technical needs of its customers, it works to make the different messages consistent so they will be more effective.[6]

Internet EXERCISE

Sony produces a very wide variety of products. Does the information available on its website (www.sony.com) appear to be part of an integrated marketing communications effort? Explain your thinking.

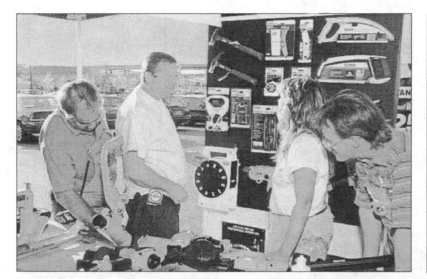

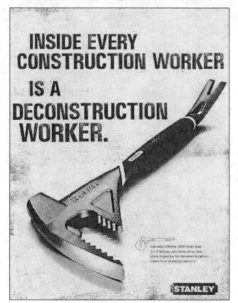

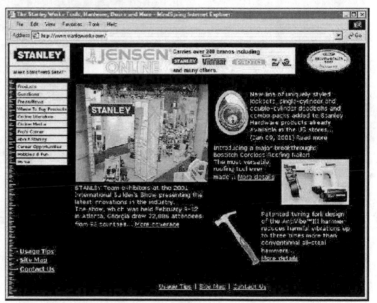

Stanley Works depends on a blend of integrated marketing communications, including sales presentations and product demonstration tours, trade ads focused on retailers, ads targeted at end users, and a website that provides information on the whole line.

It seems obvious that a firm's different communications to a target market should be consistent. However, when a number of different people are working on different promotion elements, they are likely to see the same big picture only if a marketing manager ensures that it happens. Getting consistency is harder when different firms handle different aspects of the promotion effort. For example, different firms in the channel may have conflicting objectives.

To get effective coordination, everyone involved with the promotion effort must clearly understand the plan for the overall marketing strategy. They all need to understand how each promotion method will contribute to achieve specific promotion objectives.[7]

Edition

WHICH METHODS TO USE DEPENDS ON PROMOTION OBJECTIVES

Overall objective is to affect behavior

A marketing manager usually has to set priorities for the promotion objectives. The ultimate objective is to encourage customers to choose a *specific* product. However, what promotion objectives are the current priority will depend on the market situation and target market. For example, if people in a target market have already had positive experiences with a firm's brand, then the promotion objective would probably be different from the objectives if target customers have no knowledge of a firm—or even a negative attitude toward it. So, in this section we describe some specific objectives and how different promotion methods can help achieve them.

Informing, persuading, and reminding are basic promotion objectives

Promotion objectives must be clearly defined—because the right promotion blend depends on what the firm wants to accomplish. It's helpful to think of three basic promotion objectives: *informing, persuading,* and *reminding* target customers about the company and its marketing mix. All try to affect buyer behavior by providing more information.

It's also useful to set more specific promotion objectives that state *exactly who* you want to inform, persuade, or remind, and *why*. This is unique to each company's strategy—and specific objectives vary by promotion method. We'll talk about more specific promotion objectives in Chapters 15 and 16. Here we'll focus on the three basic promotion objectives and how you can reach them.

Informing is educating

Potential customers must know something about a product if they are to buy at all. A firm with a really new product may not have to do anything but inform consumers about it. An *informing* objective can show that it meets consumer needs better than other products. Sometimes consumers try to become better educated before buying. A consumer who wants a digital camera, for example, can go to Best Buy's website to learn about digital cameras, find technical specifications, and read reviews by other customers.

Persuading usually becomes necessary

When competitors offer similar products, the firm must not only inform customers that its product is available but also persuade them to buy it. A *persuading* objective means the firm will try to develop a favorable set of attitudes so customers will buy, and keep buying, its product. A persuading objective often tries to demonstrate how one brand is better than others. To convince consumers to buy Brawny paper towels, ads show Brawny as the towel that's best for tough cleanup jobs. Spray 'n Wash convinces customers firsthand with in-store demonstrations that show how the product removes stains caused by spaghetti sauce or red wine.[8]

Reminding may be enough, sometimes

If target customers already have positive attitudes about a firm's marketing mix—or a good relationship with a firm—a *reminding* objective might be suitable. Customers who have been attracted and sold once are still targets for competitors' appeals. Reminding them of their past satisfaction may keep them from shifting to a competitor. Campbell's realizes that most people know about its soup—so much of its advertising is intended to remind.

Promotion objectives relate to adoption process

In Chapter 6, we looked at consumer buying as a problem-solving process in which buyers go through steps on the way to adopting (or rejecting) an idea or product. The three basic promotion objectives relate to these steps. See Exhibit 14-3. *Informing* and *persuading* may be needed to affect the potential customer's knowledge and attitudes about a product and then bring about its adoption. Later promotion can simply *remind* the customer about that favorable experience and confirm the adoption decision.

Exhibit 14-3
Relation of Promotion Objectives, Adoption Process, and AIDA Model

CHAPTER 14

375

Promotion—Introduction to Integrated Marketing Communications

Promotion Objectives	Adoption Process	AIDA Model
Informing	{ Awareness	Attention
	{ Interest	Interest
Persuading	Evaluation }	Desire
	Trial }	
Reminding	Decision }	Action
	Confirmation }	

The AIDA model is a practical approach

The basic promotion objectives and adoption process fit very neatly with another action-oriented model—called AIDA—that we will use in this chapter and in Chapters 15 and 16 to guide some of our discussion.

The AIDA model consists of four promotion jobs: (1) to get *Attention*, (2) to hold *Interest*, (3) to arouse *Desire*, and (4) to obtain *Action*. (As a memory aid, note that the first letters of the four key words spell AIDA, the well-known opera.)

Exhibit 14-3 shows the relationship of the adoption process to the AIDA jobs. Getting attention is necessary to make consumers aware of the company's offering. Holding interest gives the communication a chance to build the consumer's interest in the product. Arousing desire affects the evaluation process, perhaps building preference. And obtaining action includes gaining trial, which may lead to a purchase decision. Continuing promotion is needed to confirm the decision and encourage an ongoing relationship and additional purchases.

British marketers for Pampers diapers generated interest and awareness with TV ads that showed the world from a baby's perspective. To encourage desire and action, they used creative in-store and point-of-purchase advertising. For example, on the doors of restrooms with baby-changing facilities, fake door knobs were placed unreachably high, with the message: "Babies have to stretch for things. That's why they like the extra stretchiness of Pampers Active fit." They also put huge footprints on the floor in the diaper aisle. And on store shelves, in a play on babies' disobedient nature, pull-out Pampers information cards were marked "Do Not Pull."[9]

This Yahoo! ad reminds Internet advertisers that consumers indicate what they are interested in when they search for information on the Internet, so firms that sponsor search links can expect to attract more customers to their websites.

Edition

Exhibit 14-4   The Traditional Communication Process

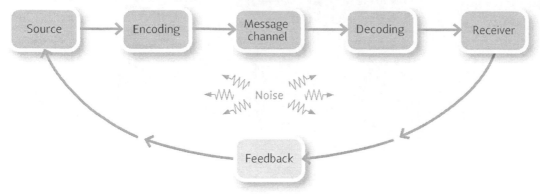

PROMOTION REQUIRES EFFECTIVE COMMUNICATION

Communication can break down

Promotion is wasted when it doesn't communicate effectively. There are many reasons why a promotion message can be misunderstood or not heard at all. To understand this, it's useful to think about a whole communication process—which means a source trying to reach a receiver with a message. Exhibit 14-4 shows the elements of the communication process. Here we see that a source—the sender of a message—is trying to deliver a message to a receiver—a potential customer. Customers evaluate both the message and the source of the message in terms of trustworthiness and credibility. For

This German ad for an innovative rolling paint ball shows how a kid might decorate a wall. The target customer's frame of reference might be important in interpreting this ad. An uptight parent might see the ad and worry about kids making a mess of their bedroom walls. A different parent might see it as a way to stimulate a kid's artistic creativity.

example, American Dental Association (ADA) studies show that Listerine mouthwash helps reduce plaque buildup on teeth. Listerine mentions the ADA endorsement in its promotion to help make the promotion message credible.

A major advantage of personal selling is that the source—the seller—can get immediate feedback from the receiver. It's easier to judge how the message is being received and to change it if necessary. Mass sellers usually must depend on marketing research or total sales figures for feedback—and that can take too long. Many marketers include toll-free telephone numbers and website addresses as ways of building direct-response feedback from consumers into their mass-selling efforts.

The noise—shown in Exhibit 14-4—is any distraction that reduces the effectiveness of the communication process. Conversations and snack-getting during TV ads are noise. The clutter of competing ads on the Internet is noise. Advertisers who plan messages must recognize that many possible distractions—noise—can interfere with communications.

Encoding and decoding depend on a common frame of reference

The basic difficulty in the communication process occurs during encoding and decoding. Encoding is the source deciding what it wants to say and translating it into words or symbols that will have the same meaning to the receiver. Decoding is the receiver translating the message. This process can be very tricky. The meanings of various words and symbols may differ depending on the attitudes and experiences of the two groups. People need a common frame of reference to communicate effectively. See Exhibit 14-5. Maidenform encountered this problem with its promotion aimed at working women. The company ran a series of ads depicting women stockbrokers and doctors wearing Maidenform lingerie. The men in the ads were fully dressed. Maidenform was trying to show women in positions of authority, but some women felt the ads presented them as sex objects. In this case, the promotion people who encoded the message didn't understand the attitudes of the target market and how they would decode the message.[10]

Exhibit 14-5
This Same Message May Be Interpreted Differently

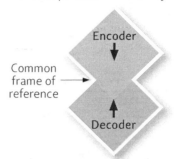

Common frame of reference

The same message may be interpreted differently

Different audiences may interpret a message differently. Such differences are common in international marketing when cultural differences or translation are problems. In Taiwan, the translation of the Pepsi slogan "Come alive with the Pepsi Generation" came out as "Pepsi will bring your ancestors back from the dead." Worse, a campaign for Schweppes Tonic Water in Italy translated the name into Schweppes Toilet Water. Many firms run into problems like this.[11]

Problems occur even when there is no translation. For example, a new children's cough syrup was advertised as extra strength. The advertising people thought they were assuring parents that the product worked well. But moms and dads avoided the product because they feared that it might be too strong for their children.

Message channel is important too

The communication process is complicated even more because the message is coming from a source through some message channel—the carrier of the message. A source can use many message channels to deliver a message. The salesperson does it in person with voice and action. Advertising must do it with media such as magazines, TV, e-mail, or Internet websites. A particular message channel may enhance or detract from a message. A TV ad, for example, can *show* that Dawn dishwashing detergent "takes the grease away"; the same claim might not be convincing if it arrived in a consumer's e-mail.

Ethical issues in marketing communications

Promotion is one of the most often criticized areas of marketing. Many criticisms focus on whether communications are honest and fair. Marketers must sometimes make ethical judgments in considering these charges and in planning their promotion.

For example, when a TV news program broadcasts a video publicity release, consumers don't know it was prepared to achieve marketing objectives. They think the news staff is the source. That may make the message more credible, but is it fair? Many say yes—as long as the publicity information is truthful. But gray areas still remain.

Critics raise similar concerns about the use of celebrities in advertisements. A person who plays the role of an honest and trustworthy person on a popular TV series may be a credible message source in an ad, but is using such a person misleading to consumers? Some critics believe it is. Others argue that consumers recognize advertising when they see it and know celebrities are paid for their endorsements.

The most common criticisms of promotion relate to exaggerated claims. If an ad or a salesperson claims that a product is the "best available," is that just a personal opinion or should every statement be backed up by proof? What type of proof should be required? Some promotions do misrepresent the benefits of a product. However, most marketing managers want relationships with, and repeat purchases from, their customers. They realize that customers won't come back if the marketing mix doesn't deliver what the promotion promises. Further, many consumers are skeptical about all the claims they hear and see. As a result, most marketing managers work to make promotion claims specific and believable.[12]

Edition

INTEGRATED DIRECT-RESPONSE PROMOTION IS VERY TARGETED

The challenge of developing promotions that reach *specific* target customers has prompted many firms to turn to direct marketing—direct communication between a seller and an individual customer using a promotion method other than face-to-face personal selling. Most direct marketing communications are designed to prompt immediate feedback—a direct response—by customers. That's why this type of communication is often called *direct-response promotion.*

Early efforts in the direct-response area focused on direct-mail advertising. A carefully selected mailing list—perhaps from the firm's customer relationship management (CRM) database—allowed advertisers to reach customers with specific interests. And direct-mail advertising proved to be very effective when the objective was to get a direct response from the customer.

Achieving a measurable, direct response from specific target customers is still the heart of direct promotion. But direct-response media now include telephone, print, e-mail, a website, broadcast, and even interactive video. The customer's response may be a purchase (or donation), a question, or a request for more information. At a website, the response may be a simple mouse-click to link to more information, put an item in a virtual shopping cart, or make a purchase.

Often the customer responds by calling a toll-free telephone number or, in the case of business markets, by sending a fax or an e-mail. Then a salesperson calls and follows up. That might involve filling an order or scheduling a personal visit with a prospect. There are many variations on this approach, and direct-response promotion is often an important component of integrated marketing communications programs. What distinguishes this general approach is that the marketer targets more of its promotion effort at specific individuals who respond directly.[13]

Now it's more than direct-mail advertising

Taco Bell created a clever, direct-response Valentine promotion. Ads invited consumers to go to the Taco Bell website. There they could fill in a form to compose an e-mail love letter. The site said that love is like Taco Bell's Beefy Melts . . . the cheesier the better. Many people who received a love letter clicked on a Taco Bell link so they could send their own letters—getting Taco Bell's cheesy message to millions of consumers.

Target customer directly with a CRM database

Direct-response promotion usually relies on a CRM database to target specific prospects. The database includes customers' names and their home and e-mail addresses—as well as past purchases and other segmenting characteristics. Marketing managers like to be in regular contact with customers to stimulate customer interest or a call for action. Greenpeace and the Cousteau Society mail newsletters to people interested in environmental issues—keeping them informed of the cause or asking for donations. To customers who request it, Circuit City sends out weekly specials via an e-mail newsletter.

CRM databases are also useful for business customers. For example, Forrester Research conducts market research on many industries and then sells its research reports. Customers register at the Forrester site and indicate specific industries and topics they want to follow. Forrester sends regular e-mails with the updates they request. Similarly, HP sends customized e-newsletters to its business customers to announce new products and to give advice on frequently asked service questions. These newsletters have increased sales of HP's new products and reduced calls to its service center. Effective e-mail programs give customers targeted information they find timely and useful.[14]

However, marketing managers should be careful they don't create ill will by bombarding customers with "spam"—e-mail messages they don't want. Growing concerns

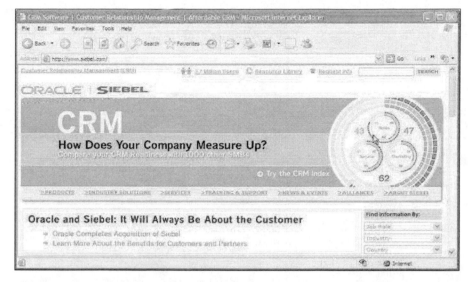

Siebel is one of the leading names in customer relationship management (CRM) software. Now that Oracle, the world's leading database firm, has acquired Siebel, the combined offering gives marketers stronger and more flexible tools for analyzing and managing marketing information.

about spam have led many businesses and individuals to use filters that screen it out. But spam filters often delete useful messages—including requested e-newsletters. So marketing managers can't rely too heavily on e-mail because they can't be sure their target customers are even getting the message.[15]

Direct-response methods raise ethical concerns

Direct-response promotion and CRM database targeting have become an important part of many marketing mixes. But critics argue that thousands of acres of trees are consumed each week just to make the paper for direct-response "junk mail" that consumers don't want. In addition, many consumers don't like getting direct-promotion telephone solicitations at any time, but especially during evening meal times when these calls are particularly frequent. Similarly, most e-mail users resent that they need to spend time dealing with the constant flow of spam that floods their e-mail boxes; there's so much spam that it slows down the whole Internet. There are many other privacy issues related to how a direct-response database might be used, especially if it includes details of a consumer's purchases.

Most firms that use direct-response promotion are very sensitive to these concerns and take steps to address them. However, many people feel that solutions to these problems require other steps and laws in these areas are changing. For example, most states have passed laws prohibiting automatic calling systems that use prerecorded messages rather than a live salesperson. Many states have their own "do not call" laws, and federal laws are under review. A host of new regulations concerning consumer privacy are also being considered by lawmakers. So marketers who do not heed warnings about consumer concerns in this area may find themselves in trouble—not only with customers but in the courts.[16]

THE CUSTOMER MAY INITIATE THE COMMUNICATION PROCESS

Traditional thinking about promotion—and for that matter about the communication process—has usually been based on the idea that it's the seller ("source") who initiates the communication. Of course, for decades consumers have been looking in the Yellow Pages for information or asking retail salespeople for help. Similarly, it's not news that organizational buyers contact potential vendors to ask questions or request bids.

In the past, a marketer usually viewed the buyer as a passive message receiver—at least until the marketer has done something to stimulate attention, interest, and

Edition

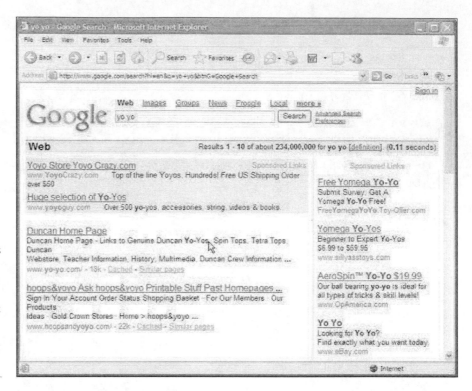

Internet search engines have reduced the time it takes for customers to search for information about products and stores. Some marketing managers have tried to understand how search engines work so that their sites show up early in the list of results. Another approach is to pay a search engine firm for a sponsored link (ad) on the first page of results. See the sponsored links on the Google results screen produced by a search for "yo yo."

desire. That's one reason that targeting is so important—so that the promotion expense isn't wasted on someone who isn't interested. Moreover, most mass-selling messages are based on the idea that you can get a customer's attention and interest for only a minute or two. Even with direct-response promotion, the marketer typically has taken the first step.

New electronic media enable interactive communication

However, this is changing. Buyers can now access a great deal of information (including pictures, video, and audio, as well as text) and place an order without the seller having been directly involved at all. The interactive technologies enabling this change take many different forms. Some of the most important are websites, e-mail list-servers, caller-controlled fax-on-demand, computerized telephone voice-messaging systems, video kiosks in malls, CD and DVD disks on personal computers, and MSN TV.

For example, England has had interactive cable TV for over a decade. Consumers can use a standard TV and remote control to get information that ranges from local weather to specials at the local supermarket. Similar systems are becoming more available in other countries as government regulations change and as cable companies upgrade their equipment.

Work is under way on interactive cable systems in which icons will appear on-screen as consumers watch a program or movie. For example, an icon might appear on a jacket worn by a talk show guest. A consumer who is interested in the product will be able to press a button on a remote control to pause the show and get more information about the product and where to buy it—or even to place an order. The same concept is already implemented on DVDs for some movies. When this type of system is available via cable (or with streaming video over the Internet), it will reshape the way many marketing communications are handled.

Internet EXERCISE
Visit the Campbell's Soup website (www.campbellsoup.com). Does the website make it easy for you to get information? Does it make you want to spend more time and get more information? Explain your answer.

CHAPTER 14

Promotion—Introduction to Integrated Marketing Communications

Exhibit 14-6
A Model of Customer-
Initiated Interactive
Communication

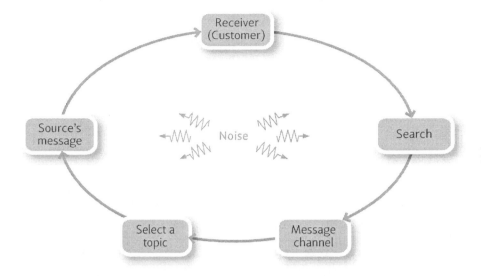

**Consumer initiates
communication with
a search process**

Consider the simple model of customer ("receiver") initiated interactive communication shown in Exhibit 14-6. At first it doesn't seem very different from the traditional communication model we considered earlier (Exhibit 14-4). However, the differences are significant.

In the model in Exhibit 14-6, a customer initiates the communication process with a decision to search for information in a particular message channel. The most far-reaching message channel to search is the Internet. The message channel is still the carrier of the message, as was the case before, but "searchable" message channels usually feature an archive of existing messages on a number of topics. There may be many available topics—even millions.

In the next step, the consumer selects one specific topic on which to receive a message. Selecting a topic might be done in one of a variety of ways, depending on the message channel. The most typical approaches involve using a mouse, remote control device, or keypad to highlight a selection from an initial list (like a table of contents or index). Of course, other approaches are common. Many dial-up telephone systems use voice-recognition.

Many consumers initiate communication when they enter search keywords into a search engine like Google or Yahoo!. What does this mean for a marketer? An online retailer that sells golf gear wants to appear near the top of the search results when someone searches for "Big Bertha golf," Callaway's popular line of golf clubs. In this case, the retailer might pay a search engine company to put a sponsored (advertising) link near the top of the list. Or, there are other technical approaches that make it more likely that a seller's website will appear near the top of the search results. Either way, the marketer wants to be sure that when customers "look" that its business is "seen"—or the firm's message won't be communicated.

**Consumer decides
how much information
to get**

Once a specific topic is selected, the message for that topic is displayed. Typically, the message is brief. But it may include a simple way to get more detailed information, select another related topic, return to the original selection process, or quit the search. Thus, after each message the consumer can decide whether to search further (say, to get more detail). This interactive approach makes it easy for the consumer to get as much information as desired. However, noise may still be a problem. For example, a consumer may waste time and still not find what is needed—because it is not available or is too hard to find. Of course, an online seller doesn't want to lose a customer who has made it to the website but then encountered some problem. So, many

Edition

online sellers have a live person who is ready to help if a customer needs it. At the Lands' End site, a customer can click a button to have a salesperson call on the phone and give help or alternatively give online help in an instant-messaging chat session.

Some messages are outside the firm's control

When customers search, they often find messages that the firm can't control. For example, a gadget lover might go to CNET.com to check the features of a product but in the process see a critical review written by an objective expert. Marketing managers can't afford to ignore websites or other places where customers post comments or get information. Complaints highlight unmet customer needs, and often the manager can do something about them. Online retailer Petco Animal Supplies, for instance, asks its suppliers to redesign products that repeatedly get poor reviews. It also makes sense for firms to encourage satisfied customers to post reviews. The owner of a California spa was horrified to learn her spa had only a two-and-a-half star rating on Yelp.com, a review site. To turn things around, she immediately sent e-mails to try to make things right with the unhappy reviewers, but she also encouraged her satisfied customers to post reviews. Soon the spa had an acceptable four-star rating at Yelp, and rather than scaring off prospects it was spurring them to action.[17]

> **Ethics QUESTION**
>
> A friend who recently took over his family's upscale Italian restaurant has complained that business has suddenly fallen off, except for the "regulars." His cook has heard that the owner of a competing restaurant has been pressuring his employees to post negative reviews on a local website about the food, service, and prices at your friend's restaurant. When you check the website, there are a number of unfavorable, anonymous reviews. You also notice that there are about 30 very upbeat reviews of the competing restaurant. Your friend wants you to help give the competitor "what he deserves" and write some negative reviews about that restaurant. Would you do what he asks? Why or why not? What else could you do?

Action, including purchase, may be immediate

The action required to make a purchase by interactive media should be fast and easy. At many Internet sites, a repeat customer can click on an item to place it in a virtual shopping cart, charge it to a credit card, and arrange for shipping.

Custom communications will be more personalized

The traditional principles of communication discussed earlier in the chapter are still important in customer-initiated interactive communication. At the same time, the interactive approach allows the marketer to customize communication to the needs and responses of the consumer. As new approaches develop in this arena, we are seeing more promotion targeted at single-person "segments." For example, many websites place "cookies" on a customer's computer so that when the customer revisits their sites the system can "remember" the customer and automatically recall past purchase activity. For example, when a customer returns to Amazon.com, the site recommends books based on that customer's purchase history.[18]

HOW TYPICAL PROMOTION PLANS ARE BLENDED AND INTEGRATED

There is no one right blend

There is no one *right* promotion blend for all situations. Each one must be developed as part of a marketing mix and should be designed to achieve the firm's promotion objectives in each marketing strategy. So let's take a closer look at typical promotion blends in different situations.

The Hanes ad (on the left) is targeted at parents and kids and designed to stimulate demand and help pull Hanes' popular products through the channel of distribution. The Hanes trade ad (on the right) is targeted at retailers and designed to inform them about the consumer promotion and encourage them to carry Hanes brand products.

Get a push in the channel with promotion to intermediaries

When a channel of distribution involves intermediaries, their cooperation can be crucial to the success of the overall marketing strategy. Pushing (a product through a channel) means using normal promotion effort—personal selling, advertising, and sales promotion—to help sell the whole marketing mix to possible channel members. This approach emphasizes the importance of securing the wholehearted cooperation of channel members to promote the product in the channel and to the final user.

Producers usually take on much of the responsibility for the pushing effort in the channel. However, wholesalers often handle at least some of the promotion to retailers. Similarly, retailers often handle promotion in their local markets. The overall effort is most likely to be effective when all of the individual messages are carefully integrated.

Promotion to intermediaries emphasizes personal selling

Salespeople handle most of the important communication with wholesalers and retailers. They don't want empty promises. They want to know what they can expect in return for their cooperation and help. A salesperson can answer questions about what promotion will be directed toward the final consumer, each channel member's part in marketing the product, and important details on pricing, markups, promotion assistance, and allowances. A salesperson can also help the firm determine when it should adjust its marketing mix from one intermediary to another.

When suppliers offer similar products and compete for attention and shelf space, intermediaries usually pay attention to the one with the best profit potential. So sales promotions targeted at intermediaries usually focus on short-term arrangements that will improve the intermediary's profits. For example, a soft-drink bottler might offer a convenience store a free case of drinks with each two cases it buys. The free case improves the store's profit margin on the whole purchase.

Firms run ads in trade magazines to recruit new intermediaries or to inform channel members about a new offering. Trade ads usually encourage intermediaries to contact the supplier for more information, and then a salesperson takes over.

Push within a firm— with promotion to employees

Some firms emphasize promotion to their own employees—especially salespeople or others in contact with customers. This type of *internal marketing* effort is basically a variation on the pushing approach. One objective of an annual sales meeting is to inform reps about important elements of the marketing strategy—so they'll work together as a team to implement it. Some firms use promotion to motivate employees to provide better customer service or achieve higher sales. This is typical in services

Edition

where the quality of the employees' efforts is a big part of the product. For example, at one time, advertising for McDonald's used the theme "We love to see you smile." The ads communicate to customers, but also remind employees that the service they provide is crucial to customer satisfaction.

Pulling policy— customer demand pulls the product through the channel

Most producers focus a significant amount of promotion on customers at the end of the channel. This helps to stimulate demand and pull the product through the channel of distribution. Pulling means getting customers to ask intermediaries for the product.

Pulling and pushing are usually used in combination. See Exhibit 14-7. However, if intermediaries won't work with a producer—perhaps because they're already carrying a competing brand—a producer may try to use a pulling approach by itself. This involves highly aggressive promotion to final consumers or users—perhaps using coupons or samples—temporarily bypassing intermediaries. If the promotion works, the intermediaries are forced to carry the product to satisfy customer requests. However, this approach is risky. Customers may lose interest before reluctant intermediaries make the product available. At minimum, intermediaries should be told about the planned pulling effort—so they can be ready if the promotion succeeds.

Who handles promotion to final customers at the end of the channel varies in different channel systems, depending on the mix of pushing and pulling. Further, the promotion blend typically varies depending on whether customers are final consumers or business users.[19]

Promotion to final consumers

The large number of consumers almost forces producers of consumer products and retailers to emphasize advertising and sales promotion. Sales promotion—such as coupons, contests, or free samples—builds consumer interest and short-term sales of a product. Effective mass selling may build enough brand familiarity so that little personal selling is needed, as in self-service and discount operations.[20]

Personal selling can be effective too. But aggressive personal selling to final consumers usually is found in channel systems for expensive products, such as those for financial services, furniture, consumer electronics, designer clothing, and automobiles.

Exhibit 14-7   Promotion May Encourage Pushing in the Channel, Pulling by Customers, or Both

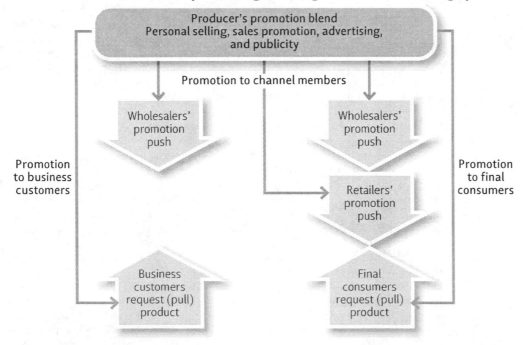

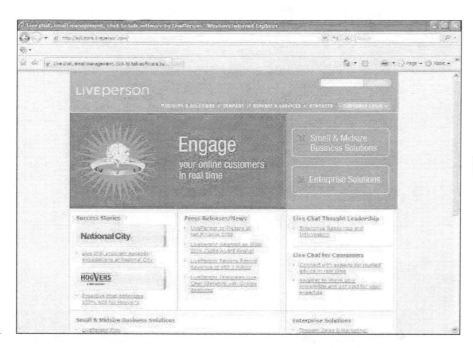

LivePerson is the leading provider of hosted solutions for managing online customer interactions. LivePerson helps firms identify the best prospects who visit the firm's website so that a salesperson can then immediately reach out and move these prospects through the sales process or provide customer support. LivePerson recently released Timpani, which combines live chat, e-mail management, and self-service/knowledge base.

Promotion to business customers

Producers and wholesalers that target business customers often emphasize personal selling. This is practical because there are fewer of these customers and their purchases are typically larger. Sales reps can be more flexible in adjusting their companies' appeals to suit each customer—and personal contact is usually required to close a sale. A salesperson is also able to call back later to follow up, resolve any problems, and nurture the relationship with the customer.

While personal selling dominates in business markets, mass selling is necessary too. A typical sales call on a business customer costs about $500.[21] That's because salespeople spend less than half their time actually selling. The rest is consumed by such tasks as traveling, paperwork, sales meetings, and strictly service calls. So it's seldom practical for salespeople to carry the whole promotion load.

Ads in trade magazines or at a B2B e-commerce website, for instance, can inform potential customers that a product is available. Most trade ads give a toll-free telephone number, fax number, or website address to stimulate direct inquiries. Domestic and international trade shows also help identify prospects. Even so, most sellers who target business customers spend only a small percentage of their promotion budget on mass selling and sales promotion.

Each market segment may need a unique blend

Knowing what type of promotion is typically emphasized with different targets is useful in planning the promotion blend. But each unique market segment may need a separate marketing mix and a different promotion blend. You should be careful not to slip into a shotgun approach when what you really need is a rifle approach—with a more careful aim.

ADOPTION PROCESSES CAN GUIDE PROMOTION PLANNING

The AIDA and adoption processes look at individuals. This emphasis on individuals helps us understand how promotion affects the way that people behave. But it's also useful to look at markets as a whole. Different segments of customers within a market may behave differently—with some taking the lead in trying new products and, in turn, influencing others.

Edition

Exhibit 14-8   The Adoption Curve

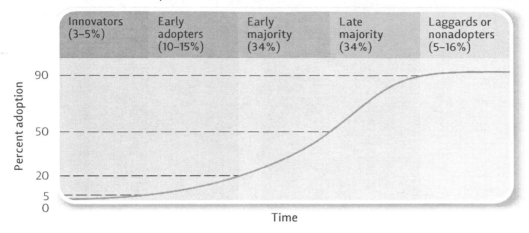

| Innovators (3–5%) | Early adopters (10–15%) | Early majority (34%) | Late majority (34%) | Laggards or nonadopters (5–16%) |

Percent adoption (y-axis: 90, 50, 20, 5, 0)

Time (x-axis)

Promotion must vary for different adopter groups

Research on how markets accept new ideas has led to the adoption curve model. The adoption curve shows when different groups accept ideas. It emphasizes the relations among groups and shows that individuals in some groups act as leaders in accepting a new idea. Promotion efforts usually need to change over time to adjust to differences among the adopter groups.

Exhibit 14-8 shows the adoption curve for a typical successful product. Some of the important characteristics of each of these customer groups are discussed next. Which one are you? Does your group change for different products?

Innovators don't mind taking some risks

The innovators are the first to adopt. They are eager to try a new idea and willing to take risks. Innovators tend to be young and well educated. They are likely to be

The website for Bathys Hawaii Watch Co. was getting about 60 hits a day until Gizmodo.com, a blog on new consumer technology that appeals to technology opinion leaders, wrote about the Bathys watch designed especially for surfers. After that, website hits jumped to 1,800 per day and sales increased by 300 percent.

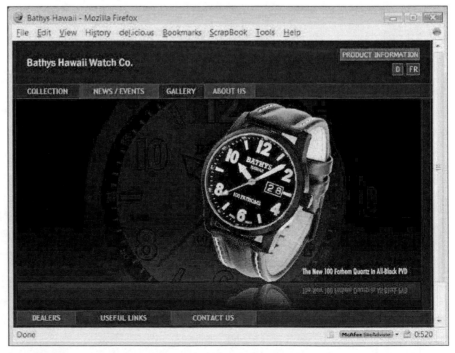

Marketers Are Wading into the Blogosphere

Many marketers are adding a new dimension to their promotion blend by using blogs. A *blog*, short for *Web log*, is a website that provides a running stream of messages, links, and comments. Blogs are usually created by an individual to express personal opinions about some topic. But many marketers like the first-person, conversational style that is typical of blogs. As with other types of personal communication, including personal selling, blogs can help make a connection with customers and enhance the relationship with them, but at a low cost.

Lego uses a blog (www.bricksonthebrain.com) to build a sense of community for its small but influential adult hobbyist segment. These Lego fanatics account for only 5 percent of sales, but their huge Lego displays often get media coverage and help to generate buzz. Lego's blog provides a way for these hobbyists to share ideas, photos, and suggestions. Similarly, yogurt maker Stonyfield Farm uses blogs to reinforce the healthy and wholesome positioning of its foods. Its "Baby Babble" blog targets new parents, and "The Bovine Bugle" tells about daily activities at a farm that supplies Stonyfield with milk.

Most blogs rely on and reflect the passions of their creators. Ed Brill is a global sales executive for IBM's Lotus Notes software. Each day about 13,000 Lotus users check what he's thinking at his blog (www.edbrill.com). One reason is that Brill provides important news

fast. For example, when the general manager of Lotus was replaced, Brill posted the news within hours and explained what it would mean for customers. But Brill's site isn't strictly business. It includes photos of Brill and his friends and comments on personal matters, like the fancy watch he received as a Valentine's gift. IBM is a big company and Lotus is a huge brand, but Brill's personal blog helps to humanize them and build relationships with customers.

Marketers for GourmetStation, a Web-based retailer of high-end food, wanted to generate a little buzz. They thought a blog "written" by the website's fictional connoisseur of fine food and wine, T. Alexander, would be just the ticket. Soon Alexander was blogging away, recommending foods and wines. However, some bloggers are very protective of "their" media—and don't like the idea of any blog that appears too commercial. Some of these critics quickly blogged their criticism of GourmetStation's blog for not being authentic—and one gave it a "Beyond Lame Award." In this case, the criticisms didn't seem to matter to customers—and instead all the attention generated more hits for the website. However, marketers need to be aware that creative promotion on the Web can draw critics. Still, firms that keep their focus on the target market are likely to win in the long run.[22]

mobile and have many contacts outside their local social group and community. Business firms in the innovator group are often specialized and willing to take the risk of doing something new.

Innovators tend to rely on impersonal and scientific information sources, or other innovators, rather than salespeople. They often search for information on the Internet, read articles in technical publications, or look for informative ads in special-interest magazines.

Early adopters are often opinion leaders

Early adopters are well respected by their peers and often are opinion leaders. They tend to be younger, more mobile, and more creative than later adopters. But unlike innovators, they have fewer contacts outside their own social group or community. Business firms in this category also tend to be specialized.

Of all the groups, this one tends to have the greatest contact with salespeople. Mass media are important information sources too. Marketers should be very concerned with attracting and selling the early adopter group. Their acceptance is crucial. The next group, the early majority, look to the early adopters for guidance. The early adopters can help the promotion effort by spreading *word-of-mouth* information and advice among other consumers.

Edition

Opinion leaders help spread the word

Marketers know the importance of personal recommendations by opinion leaders. For example, some movie fans like to be the first to see new flicks. If they like a movie, they quickly tell their friends and word-of-mouth publicity does the real selling job. When online grocer FreshDirect opened in New York City, positive word of mouth keyed its fast growth. However, consumers are even more likely to talk about a negative experience than a positive one. So, if early groups reject the product, it may never get off the ground. In a study of consumers, 64 percent said they would not shop at a store after being told about someone else's negative experience there.[23] The popularity of blogs, online review sites, and similar Web media give "word of mouse" far-reaching impact. When Hot Hot Hot, a retailer that specializes in hot sauces for food, established its website, it urged customers to click a link and e-mail its Web address to their friends. Very quickly, largely because of these referrals, 1,500 people were visiting the website each day.

When consumers are not motivated to spread the word, a company called BzzAgent helps marketing managers get conversations started. BzzAgent works with about 125,000 "agents." Agents who sign up to help with a particular campaign receive product samples and information. If they like the product, they are urged to pass the word. But BzzAgent encourages them to be ethical and disclose their status as "buzz agents." Kraft Foods, General Mills, and Dockers have run campaigns like this.[24]

While publicity stunts and word of mouth can create awareness, they aren't a substitute for a complete marketing mix that addresses a target market's needs. Consider Pontiac's giveaway of 276 of its new G6 cars to the audience of Oprah Winfrey's TV show. The giveaway generated a lot of publicity and initial word-of-mouth "buzz" was very favorable, but in the end the G6 didn't score well with consumers.[25]

Early majority group is deliberate

The early majority avoid risk and wait to consider a new idea after many early adopters have tried it—and liked it. Average-sized business firms that are less specialized often fit in this category. If successful companies in their industry adopt the new idea, they will too.

The early majority have a great deal of contact with mass media, salespeople, and early adopter opinion leaders. Members usually aren't opinion leaders themselves.

Late majority is cautious

The late majority are cautious about new ideas. Often they are older and more set in their ways, so they are less likely to follow early adopters. In fact, strong social pressure from their own peer group may be needed before they adopt a new product. Business firms in this group tend to be conservative, smaller-sized firms with little specialization.

The late majority make little use of marketing sources of information—mass media and salespeople. They tend to be oriented more toward other late adopters rather than outside sources they don't trust.

Laggards or nonadopters hang on to tradition

Laggards or nonadopters prefer to do things the way they've been done in the past and are very suspicious of new ideas. They tend to be older and less well educated. The smallest businesses with the least specialization often fit this category. They cling to the status quo and think it's the safe way.

The main source of information for laggards is other laggards. This certainly is bad news for marketers. In fact, it may not pay to bother with this group.[26]

PROMOTION BLENDS VARY OVER THE LIFE CYCLE

Stage of product in its life cycle

The adoption curve helps explain why a new product goes through the product life-cycle stages described in Chapter 10. Promotion blends usually have to change to achieve different promotion objectives at different life-cycle stages.

The ad sponsored by the American Academy of Dermatology gives reasons to see a dermatologist and focuses on building primary demand for the services of dermatologists (rather than for a particular doctor). The ad for Eucerin Plus Intensive Repair Lotion and Crème tells consumers that these products help with problems like dry skin and are dermatologist recommended, so this ad is intended to build selective demand for the Eucerin brand.

Market introduction stage—"this new idea is good"

During market introduction, the basic promotion objective is informing. If the product is a really new idea, the promotion must build primary demand—demand for the general product idea—not just for the company's own brand. Video phone service and "smart" appliances (that connect to the Internet) are good examples of product concepts where primary demand is just beginning to grow. There may be few potential innovators during the introduction stage, and personal selling can help find them. Firms also need salespeople to find good channel members and persuade them to carry the new product. Sales promotion may be targeted at salespeople or channel members to get them interested in selling the new product. And sales promotion may also encourage customers to try it.

Market growth stage—"our brand is best"

In the market growth stage, more competitors enter the market, and promotion emphasis shifts from building primary demand to stimulating selective demand—demand for a company's own brand. The main job is to persuade customers to buy, and keep buying, the company's product.

Now that there are more potential customers, mass selling becomes more economical. But salespeople and personal selling must still work in the channels, expanding the number of outlets and cementing relationships with channel members.

Banquet Homestyle Bakes illustrates this stage. When ConAgra Foods introduced Homestyle Bakes, it was the first shelf-stable meal kit with the meat already in the package. ConAgra, also the producer of Armour processed meats, had the expertise to create a tasty product that a consumer could prepare in a few minutes and then just stick in the oven. When Homestyle Bakes came out, there was no direct competition. The sales force used market research data to convince retailers to give the product shelf space, and ads used humor to highlight that the package was so heavy because it already included meat. However, over time promotion shifted to emphasize that Homestyle Bakes was adding a variety of new flavors and 10 percent more meat. Similarly, the sales force shifted its efforts to get retailers to participate in Homestyle Bakes' "Super Meals/Super Moms" contests, which offered harried moms prizes such as a visit to a spa, to keep them interested in the Homestyle brand.[27]

Market maturity stage—"our brand is better, really"

In the market maturity stage, mass selling and sales promotion may dominate the promotion blends of consumer products firms. Business products may require more aggressive personal selling—perhaps supplemented by more advertising. The total dollars allocated to promotion may rise as competition increases.

Edition

The best thing since sliced bread

Your complete source for Marketing at Retail

Displays – Temporary and Permanent
Concept and Design
Roller Programs
Assembly and Fulfillment

Special end-of-aisle displays, like this one for Wonder bread, and other point-of-purchase sales promotion materials are especially important for consumer staples in the highly competitive market maturity stage of the product life cycle.

If a firm already has high sales—relative to competitors—it may have a real advantage in promotion at this stage. For example, sales of Tylenol tablets are about four times the sales of Motrin competing tablets. If both Tylenol and Motrin spend the same percentage of sales (say 35 percent) on promotion, Tylenol will spend four times as much as its smaller competitor and will probably communicate to more people.

Firms that have differentiated their marketing mixes may favor mass selling because they have something to talk about. For instance, a firm with a strong brand may use reminder-type advertising or target frequent-buyer promotions at current customers to strengthen the relationship and keep customers loyal. This may be more effective than costly efforts to win customers away from competitors.

However, as a market drifts toward pure competition, some companies resort to price-cutting. This may temporarily increase the number of units sold, but it is also likely to reduce total revenue and the money available for promotion. The temporary sales gains disappear and prices are dragged down even lower when competitors retaliate with their own short-term sales promotions, like price-off coupons. As cash flowing into the business declines, spending may have to be cut back.[28]

Sales decline stage— "let's tell those who still want our product"

During the sales decline stage, the total amount spent on promotion usually decreases as firms try to cut costs to remain profitable. Since some people may still want the product, firms need more targeted promotion to reach these customers.

On the other hand, some firms may increase promotion to try to slow the cycle, at least temporarily. Crayola had almost all of the market for children's crayons, but sales were slowly declining as new kinds of markers came along. Crayola increased ad spending to urge parents to buy their kids a "fresh box."

SETTING THE PROMOTION BUDGET

Size of budget affects promotion efficiency and blend

There are some economies of scale in promotion. An ad on national TV might cost less *per person* reached than an ad on local TV. Similarly, citywide radio, TV, and newspapers may be cheaper than neighborhood newspapers or direct personal contact. But the *total cost* for some mass media may force small firms, or those with small promotion budgets, to use promotion alternatives that are more expensive per contact. For example, a small retailer might want to use local television but find that there is only enough money for a Web page, an ad in the Yellow Pages, and an occasional newspaper ad.

Find the task, budget for it

The most common method of budgeting for promotion expenditures is to compute a percentage of either past sales or sales expected in the future. The virtue of this method is its simplicity. However, just because this mechanical approach is common doesn't mean that it's smart. It leads to expanding marketing expenditures when business is good and cutting back when business is poor. When business is poor, this approach may just make the problem worse—if weak promotion is the reason for declining sales.

In the light of our continuing focus on planning marketing strategies to reach objectives, the most sensible approach to budgeting promotion expenditures is the task method—basing the budget on the job to be done. It helps you to set priorities

Many marketing managers view promotion on the Internet and in the Yellow Pages as "must buys" in a promotion budget.

so that the money you spend produces specific results. In fact, this approach makes sense for *any* marketing expenditure, but here we'll focus on promotion.

A practical approach is to determine which promotion objectives are most important and which promotion methods are most economical and effective for the communication tasks relevant to each objective. The costs of these tasks are then totaled—to determine how much should be budgeted for promotion (just as money is allocated for other marketing activities required by the strategy). In other words, the firm can assemble its total promotion budget directly from detailed plans rather than by simply relying on historical patterns or ratios.

This method also helps to eliminate budget fights between managers responsible for different promotion methods who see themselves as pitted against each other for limited budget dollars. The specialists may still make their own suggestions about how to perform tasks. But then the budget allocations are based on the most effective ways of getting things done, not on what the firm did last year, what some competitor does, or even on internal politics. With this approach, different promotion specialists are also more likely to recognize that they must all work together to achieve truly integrated marketing communications.[29]

CONCLUSION

Promotion is an important part of any marketing mix. Most consumers and intermediate customers can choose from among many products. To be successful, a producer must not only offer a good product at a reasonable price but also inform potential customers about the product and where they can buy it. Further, producers must tell wholesalers and retailers in the channel about their product and marketing mix. These intermediaries, in turn, must use promotion to reach their customers. And the promotion blend must fit with the rest of the marketing mix and the target market.

In this chapter, we introduced different promotion methods and we discussed the advantages and dis-

advantages of each method. We also discussed the integrated marketing communications concept and explained why most firms use a blend of different promotion methods. While the overall promotion objective is to affect buying behavior, the basic promotion objectives are informing, persuading, and reminding. These objectives help guide the marketing manager's decisions about the promotion blend.

Models from the behavioral sciences help us understand the communication process and how it can break down. These models recognize different ways to communicate. We discussed direct-response promotion for developing more targeted promotion blends. And we described an approach where customers initiate and interact with the marketer's communications. It provides new and different challenges for marketing managers.

This chapter also recognized other factors that influence decisions about promotion blends. Marketing managers must make decisions about how to split promotion that is directed at final consumers or business customers—and at channel members. Pro-motion blends are also influenced by the adoption curve and the product life-cycle stages. Finally, we described how promotion budgets are set and influence promotion decisions.

In this chapter, we considered some basic concepts that apply to all areas of promotion. In Chapters 15 and 16, we'll discuss personal selling, customer service, advertising, and sales promotion in more detail.

KEY TERMS

promotion, 368

personal selling, 369

mass selling, 369

advertising, 369

publicity, 370

sales promotion, 371

sales managers, 372

advertising managers, 372

public relations, 372

sales promotion
   managers, 372

integrated marketing
   communications, 372

AIDA model, 375

communication process, 376

source, 376

receiver, 376

noise, 376

encoding, 376

decoding, 376

message channel, 377

pushing, 383

pulling, 384

adoption curve, 386

innovators, 386

early adopters, 387

early majority, 388

late majority, 388

laggards, 388

nonadopters, 388

primary demand, 389

selective demand, 389

task method, 390

QUESTIONS AND PROBLEMS

1. Briefly explain the nature of the three basic promotion methods available to a marketing manager. What are the main strengths and limitations of each?

2. In your own words, discuss the integrated marketing communications concept. Explain what its emphasis on "consistent" and "complete" messages implies with respect to promotion blends.

3. Relate the three basic promotion objectives to the four jobs (AIDA) of promotion using a specific example.

4. Discuss the communication process in relation to a producer's promotion of an accessory product—say, a new electronic security system businesses use to limit access to areas where they store confidential records.

5. If a company wants its promotion to appeal to a new group of target customers in a foreign country, how can it protect against its communications being misinterpreted?

6. Promotion has been the target of considerable criticism. What specific types of promotion are probably the object of this criticism? Give a particular example that illustrates your thinking.

7. With direct-response promotion, customers provide feedback to marketing communications. How can a marketing manager use this feedback to improve the effectiveness of the overall promotion blend?

8. How can a promotion manager target a message to a certain target market with electronic media (like the Internet) when the customer initiates the communication? Give an example.

9. What promotion blend would be most appropriate for producers of the following established products? Assume average-to large-sized firms in each case and support your answer.

   a. Chocolate candy bar.
   b. Car batteries.
   c. Panty hose.
   d. Castings for truck engines.
   e. A special computer used by manufacturers for control of production equipment.
   f. Inexpensive plastic rainhats.
   g. A digital tape recorder that has achieved specialty-product status.

10. A small company has developed an innovative new spray-on glass cleaner that prevents the buildup of electrostatic dust on computer screens and TVs. Give examples of some low-cost ways the firm might effectively promote its product. Be certain to consider both push and pull approaches.

11. Would promotion be successful in expanding the general demand for: (a) almonds, (b) air travel, (c) golf clubs, (d) walking shoes, (e) high-octane unleaded gasoline, (f) single-serving, frozen gourmet dinners, and (g) bricks? Explain why or why not in each case.

12. Explain how an understanding of the adoption process would help you develop a promotion blend for digital tape recorders, a new consumer electronics product that produces high-quality recordings. Explain why you might change the promotion blend during the course of the adoption process.

Edition

13. Explain how opinion leaders affect a firm's promotion planning.

14. Discuss how the adoption curve should be used to plan the promotion blend(s) for a new automobile accessory—an electronic radar system that alerts a driver if he or she is about to change lanes into the path of a car that is passing through a blind spot in the driver's mirrors.

15. If a marketing manager uses the task method to budget for marketing promotions, are competitors' promotion spending levels ignored? Explain your thinking and give an example that supports your point of view.

16. Discuss the potential conflict among the various promotion managers. How could this be reduced?

CREATING MARKETING PLANS

393

The Marketing Plan Coach software on the Student CD and the text website includes a sample marketing plan for Hillside Veterinary Clinic. Look through the "Marketing Strategy" section.

a. What are Hillside's promotion objectives? How do they differ for the various goods and services the company offers?

b. Do the promotion activities recommended in the plan fit with the promotion objectives? Create a table to compare them. Label the columns: good/service, promotion objective, and promotion activities.

c. Based on the situation analysis, target market, and intended positioning, recommend other (low-cost) promotion activities for Hillside?

SUGGESTED CASES

18. Whisper Valley Volunteer Fire Department   **19.** OurPerfectWedding.com

COMPUTER-AIDED PROBLEM

14. SELECTING A COMMUNICATIONS CHANNEL

Helen Troy, owner of three Sound Haus stereo equipment stores, is deciding what message channel (advertising medium) to use to promote her newest store. Her current promotion blend includes direct-mail ads that are effective for reaching her current customers. She also has knowledgeable salespeople who work well with consumers once they're in the store. However, a key objective in opening a new store is to attract new customers. Her best prospects are professionals in the 25–44 age range with incomes over $38,000 a year. But only some of the people in this group are audiophiles who want the top-of-the-line brands she carries. Troy has decided to use local advertising to reach new customers.

Troy narrowed her choice to two advertising media: an FM radio station and a biweekly magazine that focuses on entertainment in her city. Many of the magazine's readers are out-of-town visitors interested in concerts, plays, and restaurants. They usually buy stereo equipment at home. But the magazine's audience research shows that many local professionals do subscribe to the magazine. Troy doesn't think that the objective can be achieved with a single ad. However, she believes that ads in six issues will generate good local awareness with her target market. In addition, the magazine's color format will let her present the prestige image she wants to convey in an ad. She thinks that will help convert aware prospects to buyers. Specialists at a local advertising agency will prepare a high-impact ad for $2,000, and then Troy will pay for the magazine space.

The FM radio station targets an audience similar to Troy's own target market. She knows repeated ads will be needed to be sure that most of her target audience is exposed to her ads. Troy thinks it will take daily ads for several months to create adequate awareness among her target market. The FM station will provide an announcer and prepare a tape of Troy's ad for a one-time fee of $200. All she has to do is tell the station what the message content for the ad should say.

Both the radio station and the magazine gave Troy reports summarizing recent audience research. She decides that comparing the two media in a spreadsheet will help her make a better decision.

a. Based on the data displayed on the initial spreadsheet, which message channel (advertising medium) would you recommend to Troy? Why?

b. The agency that offered to prepare Troy's magazine ad will prepare a fully produced radio ad—including a musical jingle—for $2,500. The agency claims that its musical ad will have much more impact than the ad the radio station will create. The agency says its ad should produce the same results as the station ad with 20 percent fewer insertions. If the agency claim is correct, would it be wise for Troy to pay the agency to produce the ad?

c. The agency will not guarantee that its custom-produced radio ad will reach Troy's objective—making 80 percent of the prospects aware of the new store. Troy wants to see how lower levels of awareness—between 50 percent and 70 percent—would affect the advertising cost per buyer and the cost per aware prospect. Use the analysis feature to vary the percent of prospects who become aware. Prepare a table showing the effect on the two kinds of costs. What are the implications of your analysis?

For additional questions related to this problem, see Exercise 14-3 in the *Learning Aid for Use with Basic Marketing*, 17th edition.

CHAPTER

15

Personal Selling and Customer Service

As a student in the College of Business at the University of Illinois, Pooja Gupta wanted a job that would offer interesting challenges, give opportunities for professional growth, and value her enthusiasm. She found what she wanted with Ferguson. Ferguson was actively recruiting on college campuses to find the brightest and best candidates for its sales jobs—so, in a way, the job found her.

Gupta knew that motivated young people with ability often find the best opportunities for advancement in fast-growing companies. She didn't expect, however, that her fast-growing company would be a wholesaler of plumbing supplies, pipes, valves, and fittings. To the contrary, she'd heard that many wholesalers were declining. But that didn't apply to Ferguson. For decades it has doubled in size about every five years—and now it's the largest distributor of plumbing products in the United States. And in a business that serves such a wide variety of customer types—large industrial firms, city waterworks, commercial builders and subcontractors, kitchen and bath dealers, and final consumers—you don't get that kind of growth without strong marketing strategy planning—and a very effective sales force.

It's Ferguson's sales force that gets the initial orders with new customers, builds the relationships that instill customer loyalty, and provides the exceptional customer service support that Ferguson emphasizes in its marketing strategy. What's more, salespeople at Ferguson are real experts. They understand their customers' business problems and how Ferguson's products, e-commerce, and state-of-the-art logistics systems can help solve them. An effective sales force like the one at Ferguson doesn't just happen. Someone needs to figure out the promotion jobs that require personal selling and then get the right people on the job. As the president of the company put it, "In a time when computer interfaces often replace face-to-face contact and a handshake, and quality is sacrificed for convenience, Ferguson remains committed to our long-standing philosophy. We never settle for less than the best in products, in customer service provided, and in the associates who are the Ferguson team." Ferguson's sales, which were over $9 billion in 2008, are a tribute to that philosophy.

The strength of Ferguson's parent company, Wolseley PLC, also contributes to the overall success of Ferguson's sales force. Wolseley is an international business that operates in 28 countries, has 79,000 employees, and recently had annual sales over $32 billion. Wolseley focuses on distribution of construction products, so approaches that prove successful in one of its businesses are transferred to others. Ferguson carries over a million products, provides service centers at about 1,400 locations, and has divisions that

395

specialize by different customer segments. It would be futile for sales reps to try to be expert in everything. Instead, sales managers carefully match each salesperson to particular territories, customers, and product lines. Gupta, for example, helps contractors in the Virginia market, figure out how to satisfy the needs of final consumers for whom they are building homes. She knows the current fashions in bathroom sinks for million-dollar homes, how to reduce "behind-the-wall" installation costs in big subdivisions, and the advantages and limitations of hundreds of brands from companies like Kohler, Elkay, Moen, and Jacuzzi. Other Ferguson salespeople work with cities and huge waterworks contractors on projects such as updating water purification facilities. And salespeople for Ferguson's Integrated Systems Division (ISD) are really selling a big business idea rather than "pipe." They show top executives at customer firms why they should invest millions of dollars in a full-service supply relationship where Ferguson does all of the purchasing and warehousing for entire manufacturing facilities. In stark contrast, the main sales job in one of Ferguson's new self-service Xpress outlets is to ring up sales when hurried plumbers need repair parts for a current job.

To be certain that these varied jobs are done well, Ferguson's sales managers recruit talented people using a wide variety of methods. For example, the careers section of Ferguson's website collects job applicant profiles on an ongoing basis. When a position opens up, qualified candidates are notified. And Ferguson actively recruits on college campuses, hiring about 700 graduates every year. After a pre-interview on campus, candidates go to a regional office and meet a number of managers from that area. After the best people are selected, Ferguson provides the sales training to make them even better. Of course,

the training is different for different people. For example, most new college recruits work for a short time in a Ferguson warehouse, which helps them understand the company's logistics system, its products, and its industry as well as the company's "can-do" culture. Other training methods range from self-study computer modules to role playing to working in the field with experienced managers who help them build professional problem-solving skills as well as technical knowledge. Even experienced sales reps need ongoing training on new strategies or policies (for example, ways in which the Ferguson service experience should be similar for customers regardless of what branch or division is handling the business).

To be sure that each salesperson is highly motivated,

Ferguson's sales managers must make certain that sales compensation arrangements and benefits reward salespeople for producing needed results. All of that growth isn't possible unless everyone is doing their best work and being rewarded for it. For example, the evaluation considers how well individuals work with others on a team— because part of the customer-service culture at Ferguson is based on everyone being adaptable in embracing new challenges.[1]

LEARNING OBJECTIVES

Promotion is communicating with potential customers and others in the channel. As the Ferguson case suggests, personal selling is often the best way to do it. While face to face with prospects, salespeople can adjust what they say or do to the prospect's interests, needs, questions, and feedback. If, and when, the prospect is ready to buy, the salesperson is there to ask for the order. And afterward, the salesperson works to be certain that the customer is satisfied and will buy again in the future. In this chapter, you'll learn about the key strategy decisions related to personal selling that marketing managers and the sales managers who work with them make.

When you finish this chapter you should be able to:

1. understand the importance and nature of personal selling.

2. know the three basic sales tasks—order getting, order taking, and supporting—and what the various kinds of salespeople can be expected to do.

3. understand why customer service presents different challenges than other personal selling tasks.

4. know the different ways sales managers can organize salespeople so that personal selling jobs are handled effectively.

5. know how sales technology affects the way sales tasks are performed.

6. know what the sales manager must do, including selecting, training, and organizing salespeople to carry out the personal selling job.

7. understand how the right compensation plan can help motivate and control salespeople.

8. understand when and where to use the three types of sales presentations.

9. understand important new terms (shown in red).

THE IMPORTANCE AND ROLE OF PERSONAL SELLING

Personal selling requires strategy decisions

In this chapter, we'll discuss the importance and nature of personal selling and customer service so you'll understand the strategy decisions in this area. See Exhibit 15-1.

We'll also discuss a number of frameworks and how-to approaches that guide these strategy decisions. Because these approaches apply equally to domestic and international markets, we won't emphasize that distinction in this chapter. This does not mean, however, that personal selling techniques don't vary from one country to another. To the contrary, in dealing with *any* customer, the salesperson must adjust for cultural influences and other factors that might affect communication. For example, a Japanese customer and an Arab customer might respond differently to subtle aspects of a salesperson's behavior. The Arab customer might expect to be very close to a

Exhibit 15-1   Strategy Planning and Personal Selling

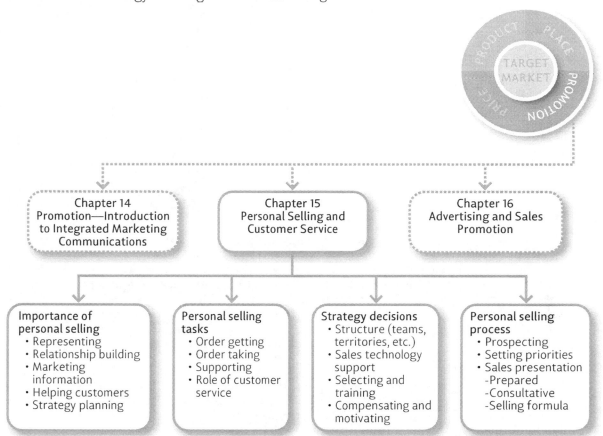

salesperson, perhaps only two feet away, while they talk. The Japanese customer might consider that distance rude. Similarly, what topics of discussion are considered sensitive, how messages are interpreted, and which negotiating styles are used vary from one country to another. A salesperson must know how to communicate effectively with each customer—wherever and whoever that customer is.[2]

Personal selling is important

Personal selling is absolutely essential in the promotion blends of some firms. Consider how you would feel if you regularly had to meet payrolls and somehow, almost miraculously, your salespeople kept coming in with orders just in time to keep the business profitable.

Personal selling is often a company's largest single operating expense. This is another reason why it is important to understand sales management decisions. Bad ones are costly in both lost sales and in actual out-of-pocket expenses.

Every economy needs and uses many salespeople. In the United States, one person out of every ten in the total labor force is involved in sales work. By comparison, that's about 20 times more people than are employed in advertising. Any activity that employs so many people and is so important to the economy deserves study. Looking at what salespeople do is a good way to start.

Helping to buy is good selling

Good salespeople don't just try to *sell* the customer. Rather, they try to *help the customer buy*—by understanding the customer's needs and presenting the advantages and disadvantages of their products. Such helpfulness results in satisfied customers and

Edition

long-term relationships. And strong relationships often form the basis for a competitive advantage, especially in business markets.

You may think in terms of an old-time stereotype of a salesperson: a bag of wind with no more to offer than a funny story, a big expense account, and an engaging grin. But that isn't true any more. Old-time salespeople are being replaced by real professionals—problem solvers—who have something definite to contribute to their employers *and* their customers.

Good salespeople try to help the customer solve problems and meet their needs. Often that requires both a trusting relationship and careful listening—to really understand the customer.

Salespeople represent the whole company—and customers too

The salesperson is often a representative of the whole company—responsible for explaining its total effort to customers rather than just pushing products. The salesperson may provide information about products, explain company policies, and even negotiate prices or diagnose technical problems.

The sales rep is often the only link between the firm and its customers, especially if customers are far away. When a number of people from the firm work with the customer organization—which is common when suppliers and customers form close relationships—it is usually the sales rep who coordinates the relationship for his or her firm. See Exhibit 7-6.

The salesperson also represents the *customer* back inside the selling firm. Recall that feedback is an essential part of both the communication process *and* the basic management process of planning, implementing, and control. For example, it's likely to be the sales rep who explains to the production manager why a customer is unhappy with product quality or to the e-commerce specialist how better order status information available on the website could cut the customer's costs.

As evidence of these changing responsibilities, some companies give their salespeople such titles as account representative, field manager, sales consultant, market specialist, or sales engineer.

Sales force aids in marketing information function as well

The sales force can aid in the marketing information function too. The sales rep may be the first to hear about a new competitor or a competitor's new strategy. And sales reps who are well attuned to customers' needs can be a key source of ideas for new products or new uses for existing products.

Material Sciences Corporation developed a product called Quiet Steel, two thin layers of steel bonded together to absorb vibration so that it doesn't rattle. A sales rep who worked with the Ford team developing the new F-150 truck probed to understand where Ford was trying to reduce noise and recommended how Quiet Steel could help. Feedback to the company about the most promising applications helps Quiet Steel reps who call on other car makers pursue similar applications. And the R&D department for Quiet Steel benefits from hearing from the sales reps about applications where the current product isn't quite right, but where there might be an opportunity for a new product.[3]

Salespeople can be strategy planners too

Some salespeople are expected to be marketing managers in their own territories. And some become marketing managers by default because top management hasn't provided detailed strategy guidelines. Either way, the salesperson may have choices about (1) what target customers to aim at, (2) which particular products to emphasize, (3) which intermediaries to rely on or help, (4) how to use promotion money, and (5) how to adjust prices. A salesperson who can put together profitable strategies and implement them well can rise very rapidly. The opportunity is there for those prepared and willing to work.[4]

WHAT KINDS OF PERSONAL SELLING ARE NEEDED?

If a firm has too few salespeople, or the wrong kind, some important personal selling tasks may not be completed. And having too many salespeople wastes money. In addition, the balance that is right may change over time with other changes in strategy or the marketing environment. That's why many firms have to restructure their sales forces.

One of the difficulties of determining the right number and kind of salespeople is that every sales job is different. While an engineer or accountant can look forward to fairly specific duties, the salesperson's job changes constantly. However, there are three basic types of sales tasks. This gives us a starting point for understanding what sales tasks need to be done and how many people are needed to do them.

Personal selling is divided into three tasks

The three basic sales tasks are order-getting, order-taking, and supporting. For convenience, we'll describe salespeople by these terms—referring to their primary task—*although one person may do all three tasks in some situations*.

ORDER GETTERS DEVELOP NEW BUSINESS RELATIONSHIPS

Order getters are concerned with establishing relationships with new customers and developing new business. Order-getting means seeking possible buyers with a well-organized sales presentation designed to sell a good, service, or idea.

Order getters must know what they're talking about, not just be personal contacts. Order-getting salespeople normally are well paid—many earn more than $100,000 a year.

Customers who are making an important purchase want relationships with salespeople whose advice they can trust.

Edition

Producers' order getters—find new opportunities

Producers of all kinds of products, especially business products, have a great need for order getters. They use order getters to locate new prospects, open new accounts, see new opportunities, and help establish and build channel relationships.

Top-level customers are more interested in ways to save or make more money than in technical details. Good order getters cater to this interest. They help the customer identify ways to solve problems; then they sell concepts and ideas, not just physical products. The goods and services they supply are merely the means of achieving the customer's end.

To be effective at this sort of "solutions selling," an order getter often needs to understand a customer's whole business as well as technical details about the product and its applications. For example, a salesperson for automated manufacturing equipment must understand a prospect's production process as well as the technical details of converting to computer-controlled equipment.

Order getters for professional services—and other products where service is a crucial element of the marketing mix—face a special challenge. The customer usually can't inspect a service before deciding to buy. The order getter's communication and relationship with the customer may be the only basis on which to evaluate the quality of the supplier.

Wholesalers' order getters—almost hand it to the customer

Salespeople for agent wholesalers are often order getters—particularly the more aggressive manufacturers' agents and brokers. They face the same tasks as producers' order getters. But, unfortunately for them, once the order-getting is done and the customers become established and loyal, producers may try to eliminate the agents and save money with their own order takers.

Retail order getters influence consumer behavior

Convincing consumers about the value of products they haven't seriously considered takes a high level of personal selling ability. Order getters for unsought consumer products must help customers see how a new product can satisfy needs now being filled by something else. Without order getters, many common products—ranging from mutual funds to air conditioners—might have died in the market introduction stage. The order getter helps bring products out of the introduction stage into the market growth stage.

Order getters are also helpful for selling *heterogeneous* shopping products. Consumers shop for many of these items on the basis of suitability and value. They welcome useful information.

ORDER TAKERS NURTURE RELATIONSHIPS TO KEEP THE BUSINESS COMING

Order takers sell to the regular or established customers, complete most sales transactions, and maintain relationships with their customers. After a customer becomes interested in a firm's products through an order getter or supporting salesperson or through advertising or sales promotion, an order taker usually answers any final questions and completes the sale. Order-taking is the routine completion of sales made regularly to target customers. It usually requires ongoing follow-up to make certain that the customer is totally satisfied.

Producers' order takers—train, explain, and collaborate

Order takers work on improving the whole relationship with their accounts, not just on completing a single sale. Even in e-commerce, where customers place routine orders with computerized order systems, order takers do a variety of important jobs that are essential to the business relationship. Someone has to explain details, make adjustments, handle complaints, explain new prices or terms, place sales promotion materials, and keep customers informed of new developments. An order taker who fails to meet a customer's expectations on any of these activities might jeopardize the relationship and future sales.

When Krispy Kreme opened a shop in Tokyo, 10,000 customers visited in the first three days. Even with well-trained order takers, the wait in line for customers was an hour or more.

Firms sometimes use order-taking jobs to train potential order getters and managers. Such jobs give them an opportunity to meet customers and better understand their needs. And frequently, they run into some order-getting opportunities.

Order takers who are alert to order-getting possibilities can make the big difference in generating new sales. Some firms lose sales just because no one ever asks for the order. Banks try to avoid this problem. For example, when a customer walks into a Bank of America branch to make a deposit, the teller's computer screen shows information about the customer's accounts. If the balance in a checking account is high but the customer does not use any of the bank's other investment services, the teller is trained to ask if the customer would be interested in learning about the bank's certificates of deposit. Some firms use more sophisticated customer relationship management (CRM) database systems that figure out which specific financial service would be best for the teller to recommend.[5]

Wholesalers' order takers—not getting orders but keeping them

While producers' order takers usually handle relatively few items, wholesalers' order takers often sell thousands of items. Sales reps who handle that many items may single out a few of the newer or more profitable items for special attention, but it's not possible to give aggressive sales effort to many. So the main job of wholesalers' order takers is to maintain close contact with customers, place orders, and check to be sure the company fills orders promptly. Order takers also handle any adjustments or complaints and generally act as liaisons between the company and its customers.

Retail order takers—often they are poor salesclerks

Order-taking may be almost mechanical at the retail level—for example, at the supermarket checkout counter. Some retail clerks perform poorly because they aren't paid much—often only the minimum wage. Even so, retail order takers play a vital role in a retailer's marketing mix. Customers expect prompt and friendly service. They will find a new place to shop, or to do their banking or have their car serviced, rather than deal with a salesclerk who is rude or acts annoyed by having to complete a sale.

SUPPORTING SALES FORCE INFORMS AND PROMOTES IN THE CHANNEL

Supporting salespeople help the order-oriented salespeople, but they don't try to get orders themselves. Their activities are aimed at enhancing the relationship with the customer and getting sales in the long run. For the short run, however, they are ambassadors of goodwill who may provide specialized services and information. There

Edition

are three types of supporting salespeople: missionary salespeople, technical specialists, and customer service reps.

Missionary salespeople can increase sales

Missionary salespeople are supporting salespeople who work for producers—calling on intermediaries and their customers. They try to develop goodwill and stimulate demand, help intermediaries train their salespeople, and often take orders for delivery by intermediaries. Missionary salespeople are sometimes called *merchandisers* or *detailers*.

Producers who rely on merchant wholesalers or e-commerce to obtain widespread distribution often use missionary salespeople. The sales rep can give a promotion boost to a product that otherwise wouldn't get much attention because it's just one of many. A missionary salesperson for Vicks' cold remedy products, for example, might visit pharmacists during the cold season and encourage them to use a special end-of-aisle display for Vicks' cough syrup—and then help set it up. The wholesaler that supplies the drugstore would benefit from any increased sales but might not take the time to urge use of the special display.

An imaginative missionary salesperson can double or triple sales for a company. Naturally, this doesn't go unnoticed. Missionary sales jobs are often a route to order-oriented jobs.

Technical specialists are experts who know product applications

Technical specialists are supporting salespeople who provide technical assistance to order-oriented salespeople. Technical specialists are often science or engineering graduates with the know-how to understand the customer's applications and explain the advantages of the company's product. They are usually more skilled in showing the technical details of their product than in trying to persuade customers to buy it. Before the specialist's visit, an order getter probably has stimulated interest. The technical specialist provides the details.

Customer service reps solve problems after a purchase

Customer service reps work with customers to resolve problems that arise with a purchase, usually after the purchase has been made. Unlike other supporting sales activities, which are needed only in certain selling situations, *every* marketing-oriented company needs good people to handle customer service. Customer service is important to both business customers and final consumers. There are times when a customer's problem simply can't be resolved without a personal touch.

When a customer firm, like a supermarket chain, buys Hobart equipment for a new store, Hobart people are there every step of the way to be certain that the customer's needs are met.

In general, all types of personal selling help to win customers, but effective customer service is especially critical in keeping them. It is often the key to building repeat business. It's useful to think of customer service reps as *the salespeople who promote a customer's next purchase—by being sure that the customer is satisfied with a previous purchase.* In this chapter, you'll see that the strategy decisions for customer service reps are the same as for others involved in personal selling. In spite of this, some firms don't view customer service as a personal selling activity—or as part of the firm's integrated marketing communications. They manage it as a production operation where output consists of responses to questions from "problem customers." That approach is one reason that customer service is often a problem area for firms. So, it's useful to take a closer look at why customer service activities are so important and why firms should manage them as part of the personal selling effort.

CUSTOMER SERVICE PROMOTES THE NEXT PURCHASE

Customer service is
not the product

People sometimes use the term *customer service* as a catch-all expression for anything that helps customers. Our focus here is on the service that is required *to solve a problem that a customer encounters with a purchase.* This highlights an important distinction in how customers look at their purchase experience. In that regard, it is useful to think about the difference between customer service and the service (or support) that is part of the product that a customer buys.

In Chapter 9, we discussed the idea that a firm's product is its need-satisfying offering, and that it may be a physical good, a service, or a combination of the two. See Exhibit 9-2. Citibank offers consumers credit card services for a fee. Wolf Camera makes prints from customers' digital images. Dell sells computer hardware and software that is supported with telephone or website technical support for some period of time after the purchase. In all of these situations, customers see service as an important aspect of what they are purchasing.

However, from a customer's perspective, that kind of service is different from the customer service that is required to fix a problem when something doesn't work as the customer hopes or expects. For example, our customer doesn't expect the Citibank ATM to eat her credit card when she's on a trip, doesn't want Wolf to charge more

Spain has one of Europe's fastest-growing immigrant populations, with more than 600,000 foreigners arriving annually. To help increase its share of this fast-growing target market, cell-phone operator Vodafone has set up customer service hotlines with representatives who can communicate in 11 languages, from Arabic to Romanian. Effective customer service is also crucial at Dell. Its DellConnect phone and online support for small business customers is available 24/7 and 365 days a year.

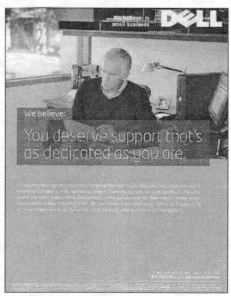

Edition

than the advertised price for her pictures, and isn't planning on Dell sending the wrong computer. These problems are breakdowns in the firms' marketing mixes. What the customer expected from the seller is not what the customer got.

When a customer service rep works to solve a customer's problem, it often involves taking steps to remedy what went wrong. But repairing a negative experience is fundamentally different from providing a positive experience in the first place. No matter how effective the customer service solution, the problem is an inconvenience or involves other types of costs to the customer. Thus, the customer value from the firm's marketing mix is lower than what the customer bargained for. Often it's also less than the value the firm *intended* to provide.

Why customer service is part of promotion

We mentioned before that customers weigh negative experiences more heavily than positive experiences when they decide whether to buy the same product (or from the same company) again. They are also more likely to tell other people about bad experiences with a company than about good ones. The practical matter is that customer service interactions arise because the customer is unhappy. So, if the firm doesn't have an effective way to provide customer service, it is, consciously or unconsciously, making a decision to kiss that customer good-bye. In today's highly competitive markets, that can be a big mistake, especially in situations where it's costly to acquire new customers or when the lifetime value of a customer is significant. Poor customer service reduces the firm's customer equity.

This is why firms should view customer service reps as a key part of personal selling. They are not just fixing the customer's problem, but rather fixing the company's problem, which is the risk of losing customers.

Customer service reps are customer advocates

A breakdown in any element of the marketing mix can result in a requirement for customer service. Ideally, a firm should deliver what it promises, but marketing is a human process and mistakes do happen. Consider, for example, a customer who decides to use Verizon cell phone service because its ad—or the salesperson at the Radio Shack who sold the phone—said that the first month of service would be free. If Verizon bills the customer for the first month, is it a pricing problem, a promotion problem, or a lack of coordination in the channel? From the customer's perspective, it really doesn't matter. What does matter is that expectations have been dashed. The customer doesn't need explanations or excuses but instead needs an advocate to make things right.

Sometimes the marketing mix is fine, but the customer makes a purchase that is a mistake. Or customers may simply change their minds. Either way, customers usually expect sellers to help fix purchasing errors. Firms need policies about how customer service reps should deal with customer errors. But, most firms simply can't afford to alienate customers, even ones who have made an error, if they expect them to come back in the future. Sometimes the toughest sales job is figuring out how to keep a customer who is unhappy.

Regardless of whether the firm or customer causes the problem, customer service reps need to be effective communicators, have good judgment, and realize that they are advocates not only for their firm but also for its customers. As that implies, the rest of the company needs to be organized to provide the support reps need to fix problems.

THE RIGHT STRUCTURE HELPS ASSIGN RESPONSIBILITY

We have described three sales tasks—order-getting, order-taking, and supporting. A sales manager must organize the sales force so that all the necessary tasks are done well. In many situations, a particular salesperson might be given two, or all three, of these tasks. For example, 10 percent of a particular job may be order-getting, 80 percent order-taking, and the additional 10 percent customer service. On the other hand,

Companies Have Customer Service Nightmares, Too

Not long ago, customers who experienced poor customer service usually had little recourse. They could scream a few curse words at the customer service rep on the other end of the line, complain to some of their friends, or simply suffer in silence and stop buying from the offending firm. Perhaps this was therapeutic for some customers, but that doesn't mean that it helped them resolve the problem. Now, frustrated customers are frequently taking matters into their own hands. In today's wired world, there are a lot of ways for angry customers who have had service nightmares to give the offending company a wake-up call.

Take Mona Shaw. She bought Comcast's Triple Play package of phone, Internet, and cable television service. However, the installer showed up two days late and then didn't even finish the job. Worse, two days later Comcast cut off all her services. Mona went to her local Manassas, Virginia, Comcast office where she waited two hours to speak to a customer service manager before being told the manager had gone home for the day. After stewing about this all weekend—hey, she couldn't watch TV—Shaw returned to Comcast's office on Monday with a hammer, which she used to smash a keyboard and a telephone, before asking, "Have I got your attention now?" Shaw was arrested, though the charges were later dropped. This incident got major play from national media, which certainly didn't help improve Comcast's already bad reputation for customer service.

Even without the benefit of coverage by news media, the Internet gives a motivated customer a way to quickly spread all of the gory details of a bad customer service experience. Michael Whitford used the Consumerist blog and YouTube to tell more than 340,000 people how he felt about Apple's customer service. Apple had refused to fix his under-warranty MacBook computer. Customer service reps said that liquid had been spilled on it, which Whitford denied. In response to this exchange, Whitford created a homemade video where he explained his problem and then used a sledgehammer to smash his MacBook. Four days after posting the video online, Apple contacted him and gave him a brand new computer—after he took down the video.

Dell Computer had a blogger of its own to contend with. Jeff Jarvis wrote about his difficulties with a new Dell laptop on his personal blog, BuzzMachine. He proclaimed to his readers that the computer was a "lemon" and that Dell wasn't doing a good job fixing it. Hundreds of other frustrated Dell customers commented on his blog about similar stories of their own. In light of this outpouring, Jarvis wrote an open letter to Michael Dell encouraging him to read blogs, write blogs, and ask for more customer input. Jarvis must have hit a nerve because Dell acted on Jarvis' suggestions and created a new Direct2Dell site where chief blogger Lionel Menchaca started giving the company a personal face. That improved communications and helped to smooth customer relations—even after some Dell laptops burst into flames because of subpar batteries from a Dell supplier.

Customers love to share their customer service nightmares. So, the best approach is for firms to make sure customers have only "sweet dream" experiences and don't need to contact customer service. But, the reality is that even the best companies sometimes make customer service mistakes. Now these firms have to make extra sure customer service responds well—or they may have their own nightmare after they see their failures documented on a blog or plastered all over the nightly news.[6]

---

organizations are often structured to have different salespeople specializing by different sales tasks and by the target markets they serve.

Sales tasks may be handled by a team

If different people handle different sales tasks, firms often rely on team selling—when different people work together on a specific account. Sometimes members of a sales team are not from the sales department at all. If improving the relationship with the customer calls for input from the quality control manager, then that person becomes a part of the team, at least temporarily. Producers of high-ticket items often use team selling. IBM uses team selling to sell information technology solutions for a

Edition

The Clorox sales team responsible for the launch of liquid bleach in the Brazilian market drew on people from R&D, marketing, and sales.

whole business. Different specialists handle different parts of the job—but the whole team coordinates its efforts to achieve the desired result.

Different target markets need different sales tasks

Sales managers often divide sales force responsibilities based on the type of customer involved. For example, Bigelow—a company that makes quality carpet for homes and office buildings—divided its sales force into groups of specialists. Some Bigelow salespeople call only on architects to help them choose the best type of carpet for new office buildings. These reps know all the technical details, such as how well a certain carpet fiber will wear or its effectiveness in reducing noise from office equipment. Often no sale is involved because the architect only suggests specifications and doesn't actually buy the carpet. Other Bigelow salespeople call on retail carpet stores. These reps encourage the store manager to keep a variety of Bigelow carpets in stock. They also introduce new products, help train the store's salespeople, and try to solve any problems that occur. Bigelow also has a group of customer service reps who are available via a toll-free number. They help final consumers who have purchased carpet but have a problem that the carpet store can't resolve.

Big accounts get special treatment

Very large customers often require special sales efforts—and relationships with them are treated differently. Moen, a maker of plumbing fixtures, has a regular sales force to call on building material wholesalers and an elite major accounts sales force that sells directly to large accounts—like Lowe's or other major retail chains that carry plumbing fixtures.

You can see why this sort of special attention is justified when you consider Procter & Gamble's relationship with Wal-Mart. Wal-Mart accounts for one-fourth or more of the total national sales in many of the product categories in which P&G competes. For instance, Wal-Mart sells about one-third of the toothpaste in the United States. If P&G wants to grow its share of the toothpaste market, it has to make certain that it stimulates an effective sales effort with Wal-Mart.

Some salespeople specialize in telephone selling

Some firms have a group of salespeople who specialize in telemarketing—using the telephone to "call" on customers or prospects. In Chapter 14, we highlighted the consumer backlash to the use of cold call telemarketing for prospecting. However, the reception to telephone selling in business markets is often quite different.

In business markets, an "inside" sales force can often build profitable relationships with small or hard-to-reach customers the firm might otherwise have to ignore. Telephone selling is also used to extend personal selling efforts to new target markets or increase the frequency of contact with current customers. The big advantage of telephone selling by an inside sales group in these situations is that it saves time and money for the seller, and it gives customers a fast and easy way to solve a purchasing problem. For example, many firms use toll-free incoming telephone lines to make it convenient for customers to call the inside sales force for assistance or to place an order. Firms also rely heavily on telephone selling to provide support a customer may need in an e-commerce situation.

Companies that produce goods and services for final consumers also rely heavily on toll-free telephone lines to give final consumers easy access to customer service reps. In most cases, there is no other practical way for the producer to be sure that retailers are taking care of customers or their problems. A customer service call center provides a way for the producer to get direct feedback from customers—and perhaps find solutions to potential problems.[7]

Sales tasks are done in sales territories

Often companies organize selling tasks on the basis of a sales territory—a geographic area that is the responsibility of one salesperson or several working together. A territory might be a region of a country, a state, or part of a city, depending on the market potential. An airplane manufacturer like Boeing might consider a whole country as *part* of a sales territory for one salesperson.

Carefully set territories can reduce travel time and the cost of sales calls. Assigning territories can also help reduce confusion about who has responsibility for a set of sales tasks. Consider the Hyatt Hotel chain. At one time, each hotel had its own salespeople to get bookings for big conferences and business meetings. That meant that people who had responsibility for selecting meeting locations might be called on by sales reps from 20 or 30 different Hyatt hotels. Now, the Hyatt central office divides up responsibility for working with specific accounts; one rep calls on an account and then tries to sell space in the Hyatt facility that best meets the customer's needs.

Sometimes simple geographic division isn't easy. A company may have different products that require very different knowledge or selling skills—even if products sell in the same territory or to the same customer. For example, Du Pont makes special films for hospital X-ray departments as well as chemicals used in laboratory blood tests.

Size of sales force depends on workload

Once the important sales tasks are specified and the responsibilities divided, the sales manager must decide how many salespeople are needed. The first step is estimating how much work can be done by one person in some time period. Then the sales manager can make an educated guess about how many people are required in total, as the following example shows.

For many years, the Parker Jewelry Company was very successful selling its silver jewelry to department and jewelry stores in the southwestern region of the United States. But top managers wanted to expand into the big urban markets in the northeastern states. They realized that most of the work for the first few years would require order getters. They felt that a salesperson would need to call on each account at least once a month to get a share of this competitive business. They estimated that a salesperson could make only five calls a day on prospective buyers and still allow time for travel, waiting, and follow-up on orders that came in. This meant that a sales rep who made calls 20 days a month could handle about 100 stores (5 a day $\times$ 20 days).

The managers used a CD-ROM database that included all of the telephone Yellow Pages listings for the country. Then they simply divided the total number of stores by 100 to estimate the number of salespeople needed. This also helped them set up territories—by defining areas that included about 100 stores for each salesperson. Obviously, managers might want to fine-tune this estimate for differences in territories—such as travel time. But the basic approach can be adapted to many different situations.[8]

Some managers forget that over time the right number of salespeople may change as sales tasks change. Then when a problem becomes obvious, they try to change

Edition

Exhibit 15-2
Examples of Possible
Personal Selling
Emphasis in Some
Different Business-
Market Selling
Situations

High — Standardized information exchanged on a recurring basis (orders, invoices, delivery status, product information, prices)

	Low	High
High	Emphasis on standardized e-commerce (with customer service)	Emphasis on both personal selling & customized e-commerce
Low	Emphasis on digital self-service	Emphasis on personal selling

Low — High

Relationship building required
(problem solving, coordination, support, cooperation)

everything in a hurry—a big mistake. Consideration of what type of salespeople and how many should be ongoing. If the sales force needs to be reduced, it doesn't make sense to let a lot of people go all at once, especially when that could be avoided with some planning.

Sometimes technology can substitute for personal selling

Some sales tasks that have traditionally been handled by a person can now be handled effectively and at lower cost by an e-commerce system or other technology. The situation that the firm faces may influence which approach makes the most sense and how many salespeople are really needed. See Exhibit 15-2.

A salesperson is required in important selling situations where there is a need to create and build relationships. Here the salesperson (or customer service rep) focuses on tasks like creative problem solving, persuading, coordinating among people who do different jobs, and finding ways to support the customer. On the other hand, information technology is cost effective for handling needs related to the recurring exchange of standardized information (such as inventory, orders, and delivery status). Similarly, details of product specifications and prices can be organized at a website. Of course, there should be some way to provide good customer service when needs arise.

Firms are always seeking new ways to help their sales reps stay in touch with customers, even when they are on the road.

In a complex relationship, using technology for standard information frees the sales rep to spend time on value-added communication.

Digital self-service is not a cure-all

When relationship building by a sales rep is not required, a firm may be able to meet customers' needs best by providing digital self-service. This is the role of ATMs for banks. If the customer needs money at an airport in the middle of the night, the ATM provides better support than the customer could get with a real person at the bank. Many firms provide self-service at websites. A computer shopper at the CompUSA website can answer a few simple questions about how she expects to use a computer, and then software at the website recommends which features are most important and what brands have those features. Similarly, a wholesaler's website might forecast the likely demand for a new product based on responses from retailers to a few questions about their local market areas.

While digital self-service works well in many situations, it has risks when it's used for customer service problems. A customer service rep can be a customer's advocate, but technology can't. The more serious the customer's problem, the less likely it is that digital self-service can resolve it; and a problem can easily escalate when the customer can't get help. For example, it may appear cost-efficient to rely on a telephone menu system that offers customers a series of choices to categorize their problem, but if the process wastes time or doesn't work, customers will be even more frustrated. Worse, the company won't know there's a problem to fix. Personal communication is expensive, but so is the cost of angry ex-customers who couldn't get help when they needed it.

We've focused on technology that substitutes for personal contact by a salesperson. But marketing managers also need to make decisions about providing sales technology support to help salespeople communicate more effectively.

INFORMATION TECHNOLOGY PROVIDES TOOLS TO DO THE JOB

Changes in how sales tasks are handled

How sales tasks and responsibilities are planned and handled is changing in many companies because of the new sales technology tools that are available. It is usually the sales manager's job—perhaps with help from specialists in technology—to decide what types of tools are needed and how they will be used.

To get a sense of what is involved, consider a day in the life of a sales rep for a large consumer packaged goods firm. Over a hasty breakfast, she plans the day's sales calls on her laptop's organizer, logs onto the company network, and sorts through a dozen e-mail messages she finds there. One is from a buyer for a supermarket chain. Sales in the chain's paper towel category are off 10 percent, and he wants to know if the rep can help. The rep downloads sales trend data for the chain and its competitors from her firm's intranet. A spreadsheet analysis of the data reveals that the sales decline is due to new competition from warehouse clubs. After a videoconference with a brand manager and a company sales promotion specialist to seek advice, she prepares a PowerPoint presentation, complete with a proposed shelf-space plan, that recommends that the buyer promote larger-size packages of both her company's and competitors' brands. Before leaving home, the rep e-mails an advance copy of the report to the buyer and her manager. In her car, she calls the buyer to schedule an appointment.[9]

Information technology is making the modern sales force more efficient and giving salespeople new ways to meet the needs of their customers while achieving the objectives of their jobs. Salesforce.com is an online solution to sales force automation.

Edition

Videoconferencing technology like the Halo system from Hewlett-Packard allows a salesperson (or sales team) to make a sales presentation to customers anywhere in the world.

New software and hardware provide a competitive advantage

The sales rep in this example relies on support from an array of software and hardware that wasn't available a decade ago. Software for CRM, spreadsheet sales analysis, digital presentations, time management, sales forecasting, customer contact, and shelf-space management is at the salesperson's fingertips. Commonplace hardware includes everything from PDAs with wireless Internet access to personal videoconferencing systems. In many situations, these technologies give sales reps new ways to meet customers' needs while achieving the objectives of their jobs.

These tools change how well the job is done. Yet this is not simply a matter that is best left to individual sales reps. Use of these tools may be necessary just to compete effectively. For example, if a customer expects a sales rep to access data on past sales and provide an updated sales forecast, a sales organization that does not have this capability will be at a real disadvantage in keeping that customer's business.

On the other hand, these tools have costs. There is an obvious expense of buying the technology. But there is also the training cost of keeping everyone up-to-date. Often that is not an easy matter. Some salespeople who have done the sales job well for a long time "the old-fashioned way" resent being told that they have to change what they are doing, even if it's what customers expect. So if a firm expects salespeople to be able to use these technologies, that requirement needs to be included in selecting and training people for the job.[10]

SOUND SELECTION AND TRAINING TO BUILD A SALES FORCE

Selecting good salespeople takes judgment, plus

It is important to hire *well-qualified* salespeople who will do a good job. But selection in many companies is done without serious thought about exactly what kind of person the firm needs. Managers may hire friends and relations, or whoever is available, because they feel that the only qualification for a sales job is a friendly personality. This approach leads to poor sales, lost customers, and costly sales force turnover.

Progressive companies are more careful. They constantly update a list of possible job candidates. They invite applications at the company's website. They schedule candidates for multiple interviews with various executives and do thorough background checks. Unfortunately, such techniques don't guarantee success. But a systematic approach based on several different inputs results in a better sales force.

One problem in selecting salespeople is that two different sales jobs with identical titles may involve very different selling or supporting tasks and require different skills. A carefully prepared job description helps avoid this problem.

Many firms turn to outside specialists, like Caliper, who can help sales managers improve the selection, training, and motivation of their sales reps.

Job descriptions should be in writing and specific

A job description is a written statement of what a salesperson is expected to do. It might list 10 to 20 specific tasks—as well as routine prospecting and sales report writing. Each company must write its own job specifications. And it should provide clear guidelines about what selling tasks the job involves. This is critical to determine the kind of salespeople who should be selected—and later it provides a basis for seeing how they should be trained, how well they are performing, and how they should be paid.

Good salespeople are trained, not born

The idea that good salespeople are born that way may have some truth—but it isn't the whole story. A salesperson needs to be taught about the company and its products, about giving effective sales presentations, and about building relationships with customers. But this isn't always done. Many salespeople do a poor job because they haven't had good training. Firms often hire new salespeople and immediately send them out on the road, or the retail selling floor, with no grounding in the basic selling steps and no information about the product or the customer. They just get a price list and a pat on the back. This isn't enough!

All salespeople need some training

It's up to sales and marketing management to be sure that salespeople know what they're supposed to do and how to do it. Hewlett-Packard Co. recently faced this problem. For years the company was organized into divisions based on different product lines—printers, network servers, and the like. However, sales reps who specialized in the products of one division often couldn't compete well against firms that could offer customers total solutions to computing problems. When a new top executive came in and reorganized the company, all sales reps needed training in their new responsibilities, how they would be organized, and what they should say to their customers about the benefits of the reorganization.

Edition

Customers who rent heavy construction equipment want to deal with a knowledgeable salesperson. So Cat selects salespeople who have experience with the applications for which the equipment will be used and gives them training on Cat products and new developments in the market.

Sales training should be modified based on the experience and skills of the group involved. But the company's sales training program should cover at least the following areas: (1) company policies and practices, (2) product information, (3) building relationships with customer firms, and (4) professional selling skills.

Selling skills can be learned

Many companies spend the bulk of their training time on product information and company policy. They neglect training in selling techniques because they think selling is something anyone can do. But training in selling skills can pay off. Estée Lauder, for example, has selling skills for the "beauty advisors" who sell its cosmetics down to a fine art—and its training manual and seminars cover every detail. Its advisors who take the training seriously immediately double their sales.[11] Training can also help salespeople learn how to be more effective in cold calls on new prospects, in listening carefully to identify a customer's real objections, in closing the sale, and in working with customers in difficult customer service situations.

Training often starts in the classroom with lectures, case studies, and videotaped trial presentations and demonstrations. But a complete training program adds on-the-job observation of effective salespeople and coaching from sales supervisors. Many companies also use Web-based training, weekly sales meetings or work sessions, annual conventions, and regular e-mail messages and newsletters, as well as ongoing training sessions, to keep salespeople up-to-date.[12]

Internet EXERCISE

Sales managers need to think about what training their salespeople need, but sales reps also need to take the initiative and stay up-to-date on what is happening in the sales profession. *Selling Power* magazine maintains a website at www.sellingpower.com. Go to the website and identify several ideas that could be used by a salesperson to enhance his or her skills.

COMPENSATING AND MOTIVATING SALESPEOPLE

To recruit, motivate, and keep good salespeople, a firm has to develop an effective compensation plan. Ideally, sales reps should be paid in such a way that what they want to do—for personal interest and gain—is in the company's interest too. Most companies focus on financial motivation—but public recognition, sales contests, and simple personal recognition for a job well done can be highly effective in encouraging greater sales effort.[13] Our main emphasis here, however, will be on financial motivation.[14]

Two basic decisions must be made in developing a compensation plan: (1) the level of compensation and (2) the method of payment.

Compensation varies with job and needed skills

To build a competitive sales force, a company must pay at least the going market wage for different kinds of salespeople. To be sure it can afford a specific type of salesperson, the company should estimate—when the job description is written—how valuable such a salesperson will be. A good order getter may be worth $100,000 to one company but only $15,000 to $25,000 to another—just because the second firm doesn't have enough to sell! In such a case, the second company should rethink its job specifications, or completely change its promotion plans, because the going rate for order getters is much higher than $15,000 a year.

If a job requires extensive travel, aggressive pioneering, or customer service contacts with troublesome customers, the pay may have to be higher. But the salesperson's compensation level should compare, at least roughly, with the pay scale of the rest of the firm. Normally, salespeople earn more than the office or production force but less than top management.

Payment methods vary

Given some competitive level of compensation, there are three basic methods of payment: (1) straight salary, (2) straight commission (incentive), or (3) a combination plan. A straight salary offers the most security for the salesperson. Commission pay, in contrast, offers the most incentive and is tied to results actually achieved. A commission is often based on a percentage of dollar sales, but it may be a financial incentive based on other outcomes—such as the number of new accounts, customer satisfaction ratings, or customer service problems resolved in some time period. Most salespeople want some security, and most companies want salespeople to have some incentive to do better work, so the most popular method is a combination plan that includes some salary and some commission. Bonuses, profit sharing, pensions, stock plans, insurance, and other fringe benefits may be included, too.

Salary gives control—if there is close supervision

A salesperson on straight salary earns the same amount regardless of how he or she spends time. So the salaried salesperson is expected to do what the sales manager asks—whether it is order-taking, supporting sales activities, solving customer service problems, or completing sales call reports. However, the sales manager maintains control *only* by close supervision. As a result, straight salary or a large salary element in the compensation plan increases the amount of sales supervision needed.

Commissions can both motivate and direct

If personal supervision would be difficult, a firm may get better control with a compensation plan that includes some commission, or even a straight commission plan, with built-in direction. One trucking company, for example, has a sales incentive plan that pays higher commissions on business needed to balance freight shipments—depending on how heavily traffic has been moving in one direction or another. Another company that wants to motivate its salespeople to devote more time to developing new accounts could pay higher commissions on shipments to a new customer. However, a salesperson on a straight commission tends to be his or her own boss. The sales manager is less likely to get help on sales activities that won't increase the salesperson's earnings.

An incentive compensation plan can help motivate salespeople, but incentives must be carefully aligned with the firm's objectives. For example, IBM at one time had a sales commission plan that resulted in IBM salespeople pushing customers to buy expensive computers that were more powerful than they needed. The sales reps got sales and increased their income, but later many customers were dissatisfied and switched to other suppliers. Now most IBM sales reps receive incentive pay that is in

Edition

Exhibit 15-3
Relation between
Personal Selling
Expenses and Sales
Volume—for Three
Basic Personal Selling
Compensation
Alternatives

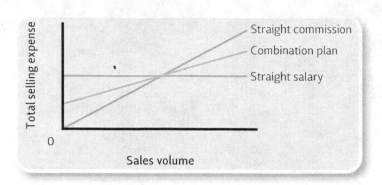

part based on satisfaction ratings they earn from their customers. Many firms use variations of this approach—because incentives that just focus on short-term sales objectives may not motivate sales reps to develop long-term, need-satisfying relationships with their customers.

Incentives should link efforts to results

The incentive portion of a sales rep's compensation should be large only if there is a direct relationship between the salesperson's efforts and results. Otherwise, a salesperson in a growing territory might have rapidly increasing earnings, while the sales rep in a poor area will have little to show for the same amount of work. Such a situation isn't fair, and it can lead to high turnover and much dissatisfaction. A sales manager can take such differences into consideration when setting a salesperson's sales quota—the specific sales or profit objective a salesperson is expected to achieve.

Commissions reduce need for working capital

Small companies that have limited working capital or uncertain markets often prefer straight commission, or combination plans with a large commission element. When sales drop off, costs do too. Such flexibility is similar to using manufacturers' agents who get paid only if they deliver sales. This advantage often dominates in selecting a sales compensation method. Exhibit 15-3 shows the general relation between personal selling expense and sales volume for each of the basic compensation alternatives.

Compensation plans should be clear

Salespeople are likely to be dissatisfied if they can't see the relationship between the results they produce and their pay. A compensation plan that includes different commissions for different products or types of customers can become quite complicated. Simplicity is best achieved with straight salary. But in practice, it's usually better to sacrifice some simplicity to gain some incentive, flexibility, and control. The best combination of these factors depends on the job description and the company's objectives.

To make it easier for a sales rep to see the relationship between effort and compensation, some firms provide the rep with that information online. For example, sales reps at Oracle, a company that sells database systems, can check a website and see how they are doing. As new sales results come in, the report at the website is updated. Sales managers can also make changes quickly—for example, by putting a higher commission on a product or more weight on customer satisfaction scores.[15]

Sales managers must plan, implement, and control

Managers must regularly evaluate each salesperson's performance and be certain that all the needed tasks are being done well. The compensation plan may have to be changed if the pay and work are out of line. And by evaluating performance, firms can also identify areas that need more attention—by the salesperson or management.[16] In Chapter 19, we'll talk more about controlling marketing activities.

Exhibit 15-4
Key Steps in the
Personal Selling Process

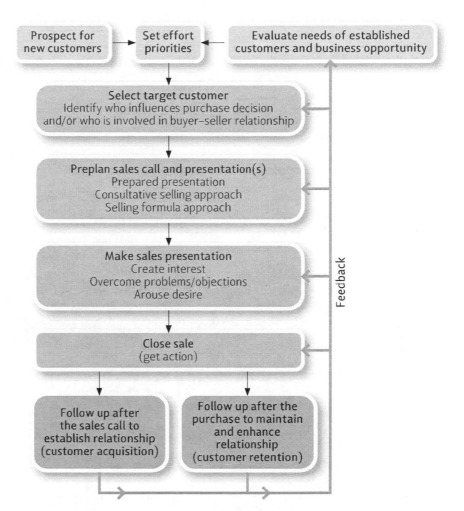

PERSONAL SELLING TECHNIQUES—PROSPECTING AND PRESENTING

We've stressed the importance of training in selling techniques. Now let's discuss these ideas in more detail so you understand the basic steps each salesperson should follow—including prospecting and selecting target customers, planning sales presentations, making sales presentations, and following up after the sale. Exhibit 15-4 shows the steps we'll consider. You can see that the salesperson is just carrying out a planned communication process, as we discussed in Chapter 14.[17]

Prospecting—
narrowing down to
the right target

Narrowing the personal selling effort down to the right target requires constant, detailed analysis of markets and much prospecting. Basically, prospecting involves following all the leads in the target market to identify potential customers.

Finding live prospects who will help make the buying decision isn't as easy as it sounds. In business markets, for example, the salesperson may need to do some hard detective work to find the real purchase decision makers.

Some companies provide prospect lists or a customer relationship management (CRM) database to make this part of the selling job easier. The CRM database may be integrated with other marketing communication tools to help salespeople spend more time working on the best prospects. ThoughtLava, a website design firm, uses its CRM database to initially contact prospects by e-mail. It uses software that tracks which prospects open the e-mail, which click through to the firm's website, and even which pages

Edition

they visit. Given this information, ThoughtLava's salespeople know in advance which of the firm's services interest each prospect, and that helps them decide which prospects to focus on.[18]

All customers are not equal

While prospecting focuses on identifying new customers, established customers require attention too. It's often time-consuming and expensive to establish a relationship with a customer, so once established it makes sense to keep the relationship healthy. That requires the rep to routinely review active accounts, rethink customers' needs, and reevaluate each customer's long-term business potential. Some small accounts may have the potential to become big accounts, and

Salespeople are constantly looking for ways to be more efficient in identifying sales leads and prospects.

some accounts that previously required a lot of costly attention may no longer warrant it. So a sales rep may need to set priorities both for new prospects and existing customers.

How long to spend with whom?

Once a set of prospects and customers who need attention have been identified, the salesperson must decide how much time to spend with each one. A sales rep must qualify customers—to see if they deserve more effort. The salesperson usually makes these decisions by weighing the potential sales volume as well as the likelihood of a sale. This requires judgment. But well-organized salespeople usually develop some system because they have too many demands on their time.[19]

Many firms provide their reps with CRM systems to help with this process also. Most of them use some grading scheme. A sales rep might estimate how much each prospect is likely to purchase and the probability of getting and keeping the business given the competition. The computer then combines this information and grades each prospect. Attractive accounts may be labeled A—and the salesperson may plan to call on them weekly until the sale is made, the relationship is in good shape, or the customer is moved into a lower category. B customers might offer somewhat lower potential and be called on monthly. C accounts might be called on only once a year—unless they happen to contact the salesperson. And D accounts might be transferred to a telemarketing group.[20]

Internet EXERCISE

Sage Software sells various software products, including ACT! personal management software that is used by many salespeople to organize information about their customers, sales calls, and tasks they need to do. Visit the ACT! website (www.act.com) for information about this product. Give a few specific examples of ways that a salesperson could use ACT! to build better relationships with customers.

Three kinds of sales presentations may be useful

Once the salesperson selects a target customer, it's necessary to make a sales presentation—a salesperson's effort to make a sale or address a customer's problem. But someone has to plan what kind of sales presentation to make. This is a strategy decision. The kind of presentation should be set before the sales rep goes calling. And in situations where the customer comes to the salesperson— in a retail store, for instance—planners have to make sure that prospects are brought together with salespeople.

A marketing manager can choose two basically different approaches to making sales presentations: the prepared approach or the consultative selling approach. Another approach, the selling formula approach, is a combination of the two. Each of these has its place.

Many firms turn to outside training specialists, like Dale Carnegie Training, for programs that can help salespeople learn how to connect with customers.

The prepared sales presentation

The prepared sales presentation approach uses a memorized presentation that is not adapted to each individual customer. This approach says that a customer faced with a particular stimulus will give the desired response—in this case, a yes answer to the salesperson's prepared statement, which includes a close, the salesperson's request for an order.

If one trial close doesn't work, the sales rep tries another prepared presentation and attempts another closing. This can go on for some time—until the salesperson runs out of material or the customer either buys or decides to leave. Exhibit 15-5 shows the relative participation of the salesperson and customer in the prepared approach. Note that the salesperson does most of the talking.

Firms may rely on this canned approach when only a short presentation is practical. It's also sensible when salespeople aren't very skilled. The company can control what they say and in what order. For example, Novartis uses missionary salespeople to tell doctors about new drugs when they're introduced. Doctors are busy, so they only give the rep a minute or two. That's just enough time to give a short, prepared pitch and leave some samples. To get the most out of the presentation, Novartis refines it based on feedback from doctors whom it pays to participate in focus groups.[21]

But a canned approach has a weakness. It treats all potential customers alike. It may work for some and not for others. A prepared approach may be suitable for simple order-taking—but it is no longer considered good selling for complicated situations.

Consultative selling—builds on the marketing concept

The consultative selling approach involves developing a good understanding of the individual customer's needs before trying to close the sale. This name is used because the salesperson is almost acting as a consultant to help identify and solve the customer's problem. With this approach, the sales rep makes some general benefit statements to get the customer's attention and interest. Then the salesperson asks questions and *listens carefully* to understand the customer's needs. Once they agree on needs, the seller tries to show the customer how the product fills those needs and to close the sale. This is a problem-solving approach—in which the customer and salesperson work together to satisfy the customer's needs. That's why it's sometimes called the need-satisfaction approach. Exhibit 15-6 shows the participation of the customer and the salesperson during such a sales presentation.

The consultative selling approach takes skill and time. The salesperson must be able to analyze what motivates a particular customer and show how the company's offering would

Edition

Edition

Exhibit 15-5
Prepared Approach to
Sales Presentation

Exhibit 15-6
Consultative Selling
Approach to Sales
Presentation

Exhibit 15-7
Selling Formula
Approach to Sales
Presentation

help the customer satisfy those needs. The sales rep may even conclude that the customer's problem is really better solved with someone else's product. That might result in one lost sale, but it also is likely to build real trust and more sales opportunities over the life of the relationship with the customer. That's why this kind of selling is typical in business markets when a salesperson already has established a close relationship with a customer.

Selling formula approach—some of both

The selling formula approach starts with a prepared presentation outline—much like the prepared approach—and leads the customer through some logical steps to a final close. The prepared steps are logical because we assume that we know something about the target customer's needs and attitudes.

Exhibit 15-7 shows the selling formula approach. The salesperson does most of the talking at the beginning of the presentation—to communicate key points early. This part of the presentation may even have been prepared as part of the marketing strategy. As the sales presentation moves along, however, the salesperson brings the customer into the discussion to help clarify just what needs this customer has. The salesperson's job is to discover the needs of a particular customer to know how to proceed. Once it is clear what kind of customer this is, the salesperson comes back to show how the product satisfies this specific customer's needs and to close the sale.

AIDA helps plan sales presentations

AIDA—Attention, Interest, Desire, Action: Most sales presentations follow this AIDA sequence. The time a sales rep spends on each of the steps varies depending on the situation and the selling approach being used. But it is still necessary to begin a presentation by getting the prospect's *attention* and, hopefully, to move the customer to *action*.[22]

Ethical issues may arise

As in every other area of marketing communications, ethical issues arise in the personal selling area. The most basic issue, plain and simple, is whether a salesperson's presentation is honest and truthful. But addressing that issue is a no-brainer. No company is served well by a salesperson who lies or manipulates customers to get their business.

Ethics QUESTION

Assume that you are a sales rep and sell costly electronic systems used in automated factories. You made a sales presentation to a customer, but he didn't place an order—and then wouldn't take your calls when you tried to inform him that your company was coming out with a more reliable model at the same price. Months later, he faxes a purchase order for immediate delivery on the model you originally discussed. You have the old model in stock, and it will be difficult to sell once the new model arrives in two weeks. Do you try to contact the customer again to tell him about the new model, or do you do what he has requested and immediately fill the order with the old model? Either way, if you make the sale, the commission will pay for your upcoming vacation to the Caribbean. Explain what you would do and why.

On the other hand, most sales reps sooner or later face a sales situation in which they must make more difficult ethical decisions about how to balance company interests, customer interests, and personal interests. Conflicts are less likely to arise if the firm's marketing mix really meets the needs of its target market. Similarly, they are less likely to occur when the firm sees the value of developing a longer-term relationship with the customer. Then the salesperson is arranging a happy marriage. By contrast, ethical conflicts are more likely when the sales rep's personal outcomes (such as commission income) or the selling firm's profits hinge on making sales to customers whose needs are only partially met by the firm's offering. A number of financial services firms, for example, have garnered bad publicity—and even legal problems—from situations like this.

Ideally, companies can avoid the whole problem by supporting their salespeople with a marketing mix that really offers target customers unique benefits. Moreover, top executives, marketing managers, and sales managers set the tone for the ethical climate in which a salesperson operates. If they set impossible goals or project a "do-what-you-need-to-do" attitude, a desperate salesperson may yield to the pressure of the moment. When a firm clearly advocates ethical selling behavior and makes it clear that manipulative selling techniques are not acceptable, the salesperson is not left trying to swim "against the flow."[23]

CONCLUSION

In this chapter, we discussed the importance and nature of personal selling. Selling is much more than just getting rid of the product. In fact, a salesperson who is not given strategy guidelines may have to become the strategy planner for the market he or she serves. Ideally, however, the sales manager and marketing manager work together to set some strategy guidelines: the kind and number of salespeople needed, what sales technology support will be provided, the kind of sales presentation desired, and selection, training, and motivation approaches.

We discussed the three basic sales tasks: (1) order-getting, (2) order-taking, and (3) supporting. Most sales jobs combine at least two of these three tasks. We also consider the role of customer service and why it is so important to a firm and its customers. Once a firm specifies the important tasks, it can decide on the structure of its sales organization and the number of salespeople it needs. The nature of the job and the level and method of compensation also depend on the blend of these tasks. Firms should develop a job description for each sales job. This, in turn, provides guidelines for selecting, training, and compensating salespeople.

Once the marketing manager agrees to the basic plan and sets the budget, the sales manager must implement the plan, including directing and controlling the sales force. This includes assigning sales territories and controlling performance. You can see that the sales manager has more to do than jet around the country sipping martinis and entertaining customers. A sales manager is deeply involved with the basic management tasks of planning and control—as well as ongoing implementation of the personal selling effort.

We also reviewed some basic selling techniques and identified three kinds of sales presentations. Each has its place—but the consultative selling approach seems best for higher-level sales jobs. In these kinds of jobs, personal selling is achieving a new, professional status because of the competence and level of personal responsibility required of the salesperson. The day of the old-time glad-hander is passing in favor of the specialist who is creative, industrious, persuasive, knowledgeable, highly trained, and therefore able to help the buyer. This type of salesperson always has been, and probably always will be, in short supply. And the demand for high-level salespeople is growing.

CHAPTER 15

419

Personal Selling and Customer Service

Edition

KEY TERMS

QUESTIONS AND PROBLEMS

1. What strategy decisions are needed in the personal selling area? Why should the marketing manager make these strategy decisions?

2. What kind of salesperson (or what blend of the basic sales tasks) is required to sell the following products? If there are several selling jobs in the channel for each product, indicate the kinds of salespeople required. Specify any assumptions necessary to give definite answers.

   a. Laundry detergent.
   b. Costume jewelry.
   c. Office furniture.
   d. Men's underwear.
   e. Mattresses.
   f. Corn.
   g. Life insurance.

3. Distinguish among the jobs of producers', wholesalers', and retailers' order-getting salespeople. If one order getter is needed, must all the salespeople in a channel be order getters? Illustrate.

4. Discuss the role of the manufacturers' agent in a marketing manager's promotion plans. What kind of salesperson is a manufacturers' agent? What type of compensation plan is used for a manufacturers' agent?

5. Discuss the future of the specialty shop if producers place greater emphasis on mass selling because of the inadequacy of retail order-taking.

6. Compare and contrast missionary salespeople and technical specialists.

7. Think about a situation when you or a friend or family member encountered a problem with a purchase and tried to get help from a firm's customer service representative. Briefly describe the problem, how the firm handled it, and what you think about the firm's response. How could it have been improved?

8. Would it make sense for your school to have a person or group whose main job is to handle "customer service" problems? Explain your thinking.

9. A firm that produces mixes for cakes, cookies, and other baked items has an incoming toll-free line for customer service calls. The manager of the customer service reps has decided to base about a third of their pay on the number of calls they handle per month and on the average amount of time on the phone with each customer. What do you think are the benefits and limitations of this incentive pay system? What would you recommend to improve it?

10. Explain how a compensation plan could be developed to provide incentives for experienced salespeople and yet make some provision for trainees who have not yet learned the job.

11. Cite an actual local example of each of the three kinds of sales presentations discussed in the chapter. Explain for each situation whether a different type of presentation would have been better.

12. Are the benefits and limitations of a canned presentation any different if it is supported with a PowerPoint presentation or DVD than if it is just a person talking? Why or why not?

13. Describe a consultative selling sales presentation that you experienced recently. How could it have been improved by fuller use of the AIDA framework?

14. How would our economy operate if personal salespeople were outlawed? Could the economy work? If so, how? If not, what is the minimum personal selling effort necessary? Could this minimum personal selling effort be controlled by law?

CREATING MARKETING PLANS

The Marketing Plan Coach software on the Student CD and the text website includes a sample marketing plan for Hillside Veterinary Clinic. Look through the "Marketing Strategy" section.

a. What personal selling tasks are performed at Hillside Veterinary Clinic and who does them?

b. If Hillside wanted to put more emphasis on "order-getting" to promote growth, what ideas do you have for how to do it?

c. Based on the situation analysis, target market, and intended positioning, recommend some ways that Hillside could actively work to improve its reputation for customer service.

421

SUGGESTED CASES

COMPUTER-AIDED PROBLEM

15. SALES COMPENSATION

Franco Welles, sales manager for Nanek, Inc., is trying to decide whether to pay a sales rep for a new territory with straight commission or a combination plan. He wants to evaluate possible plans—to compare the compensation costs and profitability of each. Welles knows that sales reps in similar jobs at other firms make about $36,000 a year.

The sales rep will sell two products. Welles is planning a higher commission for Product B—because he wants it to get extra effort. From experience with similar products, he has some rough estimates of expected sales volume under the different plans and various ideas about commission rates. The details are found in the spreadsheet. The program computes compensation and how much the sales rep will contribute to profit. "Profit contribution" is equal to the total revenue generated by the sales rep minus sales compensation costs and the costs of producing the units.

a. For the initial values shown in the spreadsheet, which plan—commission or combination—would give the rep the highest compensation, and which plan would give the greatest profit contribution to Nanek, Inc.?

b. Welles thinks a sales rep might be motivated to work harder and sell 1,100 units of Product B if the commission rate (under the commission plan) were increased to 10 percent. If Welles is right (and everything else stays the same), would the higher commission rate be a good deal for Nanek? Explain your thinking.

c. A sales rep interested in the job is worried about making payments on her new car. She asks if Welles would consider paying her with a combination plan but with more guaranteed income (an $18,000 base salary) in return for taking a 3 percent commission on Products B and A. If this arrangement results in the same unit sales as Welles originally estimated for the combination plan, would Nanek, Inc., be better off or worse off under this arrangement?

d. Do you think the rep's proposal will meet Welles' goals for Product B? Explain your thinking.

For additional questions related to this problem, see Exercise 15-3 in the *Learning Aid for Use with Basic Marketing*, 17th edition.